THE NĀRADASMṚTI

SOURCES OF ANCIENT INDIAN LAW

Series Editor
PATRICK OLIVELLE

•

DHARMASŪTRAS

The Law Codes of
Āpastamba, Gautama, Baudhāyana, and Vasiṣṭha

PATRICK OLIVELLE

•

DHARMASŪTRA PARALLELS

PATRICK OLIVELLE

•

THE NĀRADASMṚTI

Critical Edition and Translation
RICHARD W. LARIVIERE

THE NĀRADASMṚTI

Critical Edition
and
Translation

RICHARD W. LARIVIERE

MOTILAL BANARSIDASS PUBLISHERS
PRIVATE LIMITED • DELHI

First Edition : Delhi, 2003

ISBN: 81-208-1804-0

Also available at:

MOTILAL BANARSIDASS
41 U.A. Bungalow Road, Jawahar Nagar, Delhi 110 007
8 Mahalaxmi Chamber, 22 Bhulabhai Desai Road, Mumbai 400 026
236, 9th Main III Block, Jayanagar, Bangalore 560 011
120 Royapettah High Road, Mylapore, Chennai 600 004
Sanas Plaza, 1302 Baji Rao Road, Pune 411 002
8 Camac Street, Kolkata 700 017
Ashok Rajpath, Patna 800 004
Chowk, Varanasi 221 001

Printed in India
BY JAINENDRA PRAKASH JAIN AT SHRI JAINENDRA PRESS,
A-45 NARAINA, PHASE-I, NEW DELHI 110 028
AND PUBLISHED BY NARENDRA PRAKASH JAIN FOR
MOTILAL BANARSIDASS PUBLISHERS PRIVATE LIMITED,
BUNGALOW ROAD, DELHI 110 007

To
the memory
of
WILHELM HALBFASS
and
to the future of
ANNE ELIZABETH LARIVIERE
and
JOHN RICHARD LARIVIERE

FOREWORD

It gives me great pleasure to introduce this new Devanāgarī version of Richard Lariviere's award-winning critical edition and translation of the *Nārada Smṛti*. Originally published in 1988, it was the first critical edition of a metrical Smṛti, acclaimed for the vast number of manuscripts collated and for the critical acumen of the editor. It produced the first trustworthy edition of a metrical law book and reopened many questions regarding this important literary tradition, including the dating of texts as central as the *Mānava Dharmaśāstra* and the *Yājñavalkya Smṛti*.

In 1992** Lariviere's *Nāradasmṛti* was awarded the prestigious CESMEO (Centro Piemontese de Studi sul Medio ed Estremo Oriente) Prize for 1990. It has received superlative reviews in scholarly journals. As the General Editor, I feel extremely fortunate and honored to include this work in this series. Together with my own *Dharmasūtras*, published as the first volume of the series, the publication of the *Narada Smṛti* takes us substantially forward in fulfilling the goal of this series, which is to bring out fresh editions and translations of all the ancient Dharmasūtras and Dharmaśāstras, as well as those of major commentaries and Nibandhas of medieval India.

Because the original edition was published by the Department of South Asia Regional Studies of the University of Pennsylvania and because that edition was in transliterated Roman script, it did not receive the publicity or the circulation it deserved, especially within India. Many Indian scholars have continued to use Jolly's edition, when it was superseded by Lariviere's work over a decade ago. The cost of the original edition also kept it from most Indian libraries. Our hope is that this new edition will make this work, which should be on the bookshelf of every scholar of ancient India, more widely available worldwide, but especially with the Indian subcontinent.

I want to express my gratitude once again to Motilal Banarsidass and in particular to Mr. N. P. Jain, for the care and speed with which they have brought out the volumes in this series.

Cambridge, Massachusetts PATRICK OLIVELLE
November 2000

ACKNOWLEDGMENTS

This edition of the Nāradasmrti was made possible by the generous support of the National Endowment for the Humanities, the American Council of Learned Societies/Social Science Research Council Joint Committee on South Asia, the American Institute of Indian Studies, and the University Research Institute of the University of Texas.

I am fortunate and honored to have received a share of the precious resources available to these institutions, and I will always be grateful for their support. I am grateful, also, to Motilal Banarsidass for their willingness to publish this second edition of the Nāradasmrti.

I had the assistance and cooperation of the following libraries who provided me with or allowed me to make microfilm copies of manuscripts: the Nepal German Manuscript Preservation Project, Kathmandu; the Śrī Raghunāth Temple Manuscript Library (also known as the Śrī Raṇavir Siṃha SaṃskṛtānusaṃdhānaPustakālaya), Jammu; the Rajasthan Oriental Research Institute, Alwar Branch; the British Library; the Asiatic Society of Bengal, Calcutta; the Ganganātha Jhā Research Institute, Allahabad; the Harvard University Library; the National Archives, Kathmandu; the India Office Library, London; the Bayerische Staatsbibliothek, Munich; the Government Oriental Manuscripts Library, Madras; the Bodleian Library, Oxford University; the Bhandarkar Oriental Research Institute, Puṇe; the Fergusson College Library, Puṇe; the Rajasthan Oriental Research Institute, Jodhpur; and the Sarasvatī Bhavana, Saṃpūrṇānanda Saṃskṛta Viśvavidyālaya, Vārāṇasi.

This project, like so much of whatever scholarly contribution I have been able to make, grew out of discussions with Prof. Ludo Rocher, a superb teacher and friend. Prof. Rosane Rocher gave shape to most of the editorial decisions that go into a critical edition such as this. My fellow student, colleague, and good friend, Prof. Patrick Olivelle is responsible for the series in which this second edition is appearing. Without his help this work would not have seen the light of day in India and would have remained, for all practical purposes, inaccessible to one of the most valuable audiences for this text—our Indian colleagues. Prof. Olivelle also made several suggestions for improvements in the text. Dr. Kamal Adhikary of the Center for Asian Studies at UT began the work of converting the text from roman script to devanāgarī. Mr. Steven Lindquist, an especially promising student at The University of Texas, took this initial work and patiently and diligently brought the project to point where yet another former student and now colleague, Dr. Robert Fulton, integrated the changes to the text, translation, and index and produced the final camera-ready copy. To all of them, I express my gratitude.

Janis Worcester Lariviere has endured more than she ever expected when she signed on 30 years ago. I can never adequately tell her how grateful I am for her forbearance and her energy. Our daughter Anne has —for exactly 16 years today— provided the glow that sustains us. Without them, I would not know what good there can be.

Austin, Texas
June 25, 2000

Richard Lariviere

TABLE OF CONTENTS

ADDENDA

GENERAL INTRODUCTION

THE PLACE OF THE NĀRADASMṚTI IN LEGAL LITERATURE

The Nāradasmṛti is unique in the corpus of Sanskrit legal literature. It is the only original collection of legal maxims (*mūlasmṛti*) which is purely juridical in character. Unlike all the other known *mūlasmṛtis*, which contain sections dealing with righteous conduct and penance (*ācāra* and *prāyaścitta*), the Nāradasmṛti focuses solely on legal procedure (*vyavahāra*) and the substantive law that is included in this traditional category. The fact that the Nāradasmṛti is cited frequently by later writers in the Indian legal tradition testifies to its importance. There is some evidence which indicates that the Nāradasmṛti may have even influenced monarchs and their governments: when the great ruler of the Malla dynasty in Nepal, Jayasthiti, designed his legal and social reforms, he may well have consulted the Nāradasmṛti.[1]

When the text was first made available to legal scholars in Europe in the late 19th century their reaction was unanimous: here was a text the style, content, and structure of which could stand comparison with the very best of the Roman legal tradition. Auguste Barth felt that a jurisconsult would be right at home with this text, due to its method of presenting concise definitions and its well-conceived plan.[2] The legal historian Rodolphe Dareste wondered whether or not the author might have had some acquaintance with Roman law; perhaps he might even have had some texts of Ulpian or Paulus before him while composing his text.[3] Such ethnocentric hypotheses are no longer acceptable. That they could have been made at all is a testament to the juridical character of the Nāradasmṛti. Others than legal historians and Indologists recognized its importance as well: Karl Marx used Jolly's 1876 translation in preparing his Asiatic Mode of Production.[4]

Even after another century of scholarship in the field of Indian legal history, it is still the case that the Nāradasmṛti is the juridical text *par excellence*. If anything, its standing has been enhanced with time. Even K. V. Rangaswami Aiyangar—who tended to accord all virtues to Bṛhaspati to the exclusion of other texts—contended that the Nāradasmṛti is clearly a text written for practitioners.[5] The subjects, the style, and the method of presentation will be familiar to scholars

1 D. R. Regmi, *Medieval Nepal*, part I, p. 341 (see the colophon to ms K in the Introduction to the companion edition of the text).

2 *Quarante ans d'Indianisme. Oeuvres d'Auguste Barth*, vol. 3, p. 232.

3 *Etudes d'histoire du droit*, vol. 1, p. 99.

4 See Lawrence Krader, *The Asiatic Mode of Production: sources, development and critique in the writings of Karl Marx*, pp. 345-363.

5 *Bṛhaspatismṛti (Reconstructed)*, p.136.

of classical legal systems. The Nāradasmṛti is indeed the mūlasmṛti which offers the best single summary of the classical Hindu legal system.

THE NATURE OF THE TEXT

For an editor of classical Hindu legal texts, such as the Nāradasmṛti, it is impossible to provide answers to the normal questions which introductions to texts usually address: Who was the author? When and where did he live? What was there about his circumstances that contributed to the content and shape of his work? What was the history of the reception of his work? and so on. Such questions cannot be answered with any certainty for these eponymous mūlasmṛtis. For some questions there are no answers at all. For other questions the answers are mere conjecture.

According to the historian of dharmaśāstra P.V. Kane, when an author attributes his composition to Manu, Nārada, Yājñavalkya, Gautama, Viṣṇu, etc., he is obviously attempting to "invest the work with a halo of antiquity and authoritativeness."[6] If we assume that these are pseudonymous texts which were composed by an individual author, then Kane's speculation must be correct. It may be the case, however, that what we have in these *mūlasmṛtis* is not the work of a single author.[7] E. Washburn Hopkins has made some interesting suggestions with regard to the Manusmṛti which merit extensive quotation.

> I draw the conclusion that the Çāstram [i.e. the Manusmṛti] was in great part collated between the time when the bulk of the epic [i.e., the Mahābhāratà] was composed and its final completion, that previous to its collation there had existed a vast number of sententious remarks, proverbial wisdom, rules of morality etc. which were ascribed, not to this treatise of Manu at all, but to the ancient hero Manu as a type of godly wisdom. These I conceive to have floated about in the mouths of the people, not brought together but all loosely quoted as laws or sayings of Manu and these sayings were afterwards welded into one with the laws of a particular [sect] called the Mānavas—a union natural enough, as the two bodies of law would then bear the same title, although the sect had no connection with Manu except in name. I fancy this sect built up their *ācāra* ('usages') and *kuladharma* ('family law') out of their own heads, not ascribing them to Manu; then seizing this distinct mass of "Manu's sayings," they appropriated them and the two became one. According to my theory, these Manu-verses found in the Mānava treatise were simply caught up and drawn from the hearsay of the whole Brahman world, keeping

6 *History of Dharmaśāstra,* 1.310. K.P. Jayaswal, *Manu and Yājñavalkya,* pp. 74-75, refers to the author of NāSmṛ as "pseudo-Nārada."

7 Or at least *some* of these *mūlasmṛtis*, since there is no reason to assume that the nature of one particular text—its composition, evolution, etc.—is the pattern for all the other texts.

> their form after incorporation with the Mānavas' text. This was especially valuable, because every time a fraud was intended, they could invent a verse and insert it in the old text. They had so many 'Manu saids' that it was difficult to detect a new one.[8]

Except for his remark about inventing frauds,[9] I think that Hopkins was right. I doubt whether such texts as the Naradasmṛti or the Manusmṛti were composed by a single individual. It seems more likely that the verses that have been preserved in the form of what we now call *mūlasmṛtis* were part of the *Spruchweisheit* in ancient and classical India. As Hopkins suggests, these were gnomic verses known to the experts (*śiṣṭas*) of a community. The number of these verses may have been large, and they may have been attributed to any number of mythical or heroic characters in the tradition. These verses were cited in support of judgments or advice which paṇḍitas made for the members of the community, and as part of the instruction of their successors. At a certain time these verses were collected together (by an individual? a group? a school?) as compilations of "dharma verses" into dharmaśāstras. The attribution of these verses to a single mythical figure—Manu, Nārada, Bṛhaspati, and others—may have been done at the time of the compilation in order to enhance the authority of the entire text. Or, more likely, these verses may have been attributed to "Manu," or "Nārada," or "Bṛhaspati" all along while they were being cited by the above-mentioned *śiṣṭas*; the compiler(s) simply collected all of the verses attributed to Manu which were known at that time in that locality, and, in good faith, presented a collection of "Manu's verses on dharma."

This latter possibility explains how a single verse could be attributed to more than one author, as is often the case.[10] In one village the experts on dharma knew and often cited a certain verse they attributed to, say, Nārada. In another village, that same verse was known and often cited, but attributed to Kātyāyana.[11] In both cases the verse may have been handed down for generations with these

8 "On the professed quotations from Manu found in the Mahābhārata," JAOS 11 (1885), 268.

9 It makes more sense to assume that these men were honest; that they were subject to continual checks on their understanding of the tradition by their fellow *śiṣṭas*; and that the likelihood of their passing off a fraud, if ever one was intended, was thereby significantly diminished.

10 A cursory look through the notes to the verses of NāSmṛ will reveal how often this occurs. K.V. Rangaswami Aiyangar offers six possible explanations for the attribution of a single verse to two or more authors: 1) a common source, 2) accident of composition, 3) deliberate copying, 4) lost passages which would explain that the identical verse is a quotation, 5) unconscious reproduction, and 6) errors in quoting (*Bṛhaspati*, pp. 145-148).

11 The attribution would have been of little consequence to the *śiṣṭas* or to their "clients" for two reasons: (1) the fact that the verse is cited indicates that it is accepted by the community as a correct view—that it is a statement of truth, of dharma; (2) since it is true it doesn't matter which of the ancient *ṛṣis* was responsible for articulating it in just this way. Whether Bṛhaspati said it or Pitamaha, both were stating the truth; there is no difference in the veracity or reliability of these ancient authorities.

respective attributions. At the time of compilation the compiler would naturally attribute the verse to the traditional source known to him in his village or tradition. In this way a single verse could come to be included in two or more different compilations attributed to different authors. The compilation of these verses into "texts" did not establish once and for all *the* text of Nārada, Bṛhaspati, etc. Merely *compiling* Nārada verses or Bṛhaspati verses did not prevent other experts from continuing to attribute verses not found in that compilation to Nārada, Bṛhaspati, or any other ancient sage.[12]

The process of addition to these compilations must have gone on for centuries. The hearers or readers[13] of these compilations must have known other verses which their own teachers attributed to Manu, Kātyāyana, and others, and it would be natural for them to include these verses in the compilation. This type of addition may have continued until a commentary on the collection was composed. A commentary would have served to fix the text, and the expansion of the text would have been more difficult after that.[14]

12 This seems a more satisfactory explanation for the "extraneous" Nārada verses not found in NāSmṛ mss—such as those compiled by Jolly at the end of his 1889 translation—than Lingat's suggestion that there were more versions of NāSmṛ than those which have survived (*Classical Law*, p. 100).

13 K.V. Rangaswami Aiyangar argues that *nibandhakāras* quoted from manuscripts rather than from memory (*Bṛhaspati*, pp. 148-149). Jolly says that they quoted from memory (Introduction to his 1876 translation of the *Nāradasmṛti* , p. xxiii). It is likely that both techniques were used. For further thoughts on this problem, see J.D.M. Derrett, *Dharmaśāstra and Juridical Literature*, p. 24.

14 This is not to say that additions to these texts ceased once they had been commented upon. As I will demonstrate below, at least one commentator (Kalyāṇabhaṭṭa) incorporated material which he felt to be genuine into the text on which he was commenting. Let us note, in passing, that the only *mūlasmṛtis* we have from the classical period of Sanskrit literature, the Manusmṛti, the Yājñavalkyasmṛti, the Nāradasmṛti, and the Parāśarasmṛti are those for which commentaries have been preserved. The transmission of a commentary through the generations would indicate the degree of its acceptance. The existence of a commentary may have made a compiled text more accessible and lent it an air of greater authoritativeness than a text without a commentary.

The explanation which K.V. Rangaswami Aiyangar gives for the absence of even a reference to a commentary on Bṛhas is inventive: he says that it was itself a sort of commentary on Manu and hence did not need a further commentary (*Bṛhaspati*, p. 186). The absence of a commentary may be explained as easily by the hypothesis that a fixed text of Bṛhas never existed; rather there were large numbers of verses attributed to Bṛhaspati which Aiyangar collected, arranged, and made into a "reconstructed" text. The same could be true of Kane's KāSmṛ. The smṛtis in such texts as the Smṛtīnāṃ Samuccayaḥ and the Dharmaśāstrasaṃgrahaḥ are different. They are generally much later compositions. See, for example, the Devalasmṛti which explicitly states that its purpose is to explain the way in which persons residing in Sind who had been converted by the *mlecchas* (Muslims?) could be purified (*Smṛtīnāṃ Samuccayaḥ*, p. 85). See also J.D.M. Derrett, "Law and the Social Order in India Before the Muhammadan Conquests," JESHO 71 (1964), 98-99. See also Derrett's speculation on Bhāruci's role in "making his own Manu" in *Dharmaśāstra and Juridical Literature*, p. 32.

It is my view that these texts grew over time, that verses were added to them at various stages in their development, but that rarely, if ever, were verses discarded.[15] With the possible exception of some grammatical texts,[16] the trend for sāstra literature and the like is to undergo additions rather than excisions. Edgerton's observation pertaining to the Mahābhārata applies to the legal literature as well:

> ... it appears that no scribe, no redactor, ever knowingly sacrificed a single line which he found in his original. Not even if he found something which seemed to him incomprehensible, inconsistent with the context, irreligious or immoral. In that case he sometimes changed the text, doubtless feeling that a mistake had been made and that he was only doing the pious work of restoring what must have been the original intention. But there is certainly not a shred of evidence for a single deliberate omission: and I do not believe it ever took place.[17]

15 For a clear example of the conservative nature of the tradition, see the note to Mā 1.43.

16 See George Cardona, *Pāṇini: A Survey of Research*, p. 152.

17 Introduction to the Sabhāparvan, vol. 2 of Bhā, critical edition p. xxiv. For a discussion of this question as it pertains to Bhā, see V.S. Sukthankar, *Critical Studies in the Mahābhārata*, pp. 239-240, and his Prolegomena to the critical edition of the Mahābhārata, pp. LII and LXXXI. The view that texts tended to expand also guided the editing of Rām (see G.H. Bhatt's Introduction to the Bālakāṇḍa, points (3), (4), and (5) p. xxxiv). See also Śrinivāsa Ayya Śrinivāsan, *On the Composition of the Nāṭyaśāstra*, sections 8, 9.2 and 9.6. Muneo Tokunaga has demonstrated that the shorter recension of the Bṛhaddevatā is the older, against the opinion of the editor of that text, A.A. Macdonell ("On the Recensions of the Bṛhaddevatā," JAOS 101 (1981), 275-286).

The opinion that the texts expanded rather than became smaller is not held by all scholars. Georg Bühler cites the recensions of NāSmṛ as an example and claims that abridgements are as common as additions (Introduction to the Manusmṛti, p. xcv). Elsewhere Bühler states, "The larger Nārada turns out to be the older version. This discovery will perhaps help to correct the view expressed by some scholars, according to which the Indian law-books always grew in extent and never lost in bulk" (review of Jolly's TLL for 1883, *The Indian Antiquary* 14 (1885), 324). J.D.M. Derrett also claims that in the sūtra literature it was common for sūtras to be eliminated from a text if they could not be explained in an agreeable manner, yet, in his opinion, this was not so for the metrical smṛtis which, he says, "acquired almost superstitious authority" ("*Kuttā*: a Class of Land Tenures in South India," ECMHL vol. 1, p. 289).

Edgerton's view is supported by the relatively few instances in which commentators on *mūlasmṛtis* doubt the authenticity of a verse. For example, Medhātithi on Manu 9.93 states explicitly that "some" believe this is not a Manu verse (*kecid ihāhur amānavo 'yaṃ ślokaḥ*); yet he includes it in his text and comments on it. Vijñāneśvara had doubts about YāSmṛ 1.256, but explains them away. It appears that Asahāya, too, had doubts about a Nārada verse: see his commentary on Mā 2.5 where he writes, "Here, in this very place in the text, someone else's verse is found."

The Nāradasmṛti presents an instructive example of how *mūlasmṛtis* may have evolved over the centuries. There are three extant versions of the text.[18] Jolly recognized only two versions:

(1) the "shorter" or "minor" recension, referred to in his *editio princeps* as the "Vulgate";[19]

(2) the "longer" recension found in the single incomplete manuscript containing Asahāya's commentary.[20]

In addition, there is

(3) the version found in the Newārī manuscripts and the Nāradīyamanusaṃhitā (NMS).[21] These three recensions vary considerably in length and content.[22] For example, the "longer" recension contains an entire chapter, Mātṛkā 2, not found in any other manuscript;[23] the Newārī manuscripts and NMS discuss ordeals and theft in separate chapters at the end of the manuscripts; the discussion of ordeals is different in all three versions.

It is possible to trace the general pattern of development of these recensions of the Nāradasmṛti. The fact that the Newārī manuscripts and NMS agree closely is important. These represent the oldest recoverable version of the text; the other recensions are expansions of this version. The judgment that the Newārī/NMS version is the oldest surviving one is based on the following considerations.

It is a well established pattern in Indian manuscripts that there is a correlation between the script of a manuscript and the recension it records. This principle was confirmed, for example, in the editing of the Mahābhārata. V.S. Sukthankar, the original editor of that monumental project, observed,

> The reason for this concomitance between script and version appears to be that the scribes, being as a rule not conversant with any script but that of their own particular province, could copy only manuscripts written in their special provincial scripts,

18 For a detailed description of these recensions and the mss containing them see the Introduction to the companion edition.

19 Consisting of 879 verses, this recension is referred to in the companion edition by the siglum D. This is the version Jolly translated first: *Nāradīya Dharmaśāstra or The Institutes of Nārada. Translated for the First Time from the Unpublished Sanskrit Original* (1876).

20 This is the version Jolly edited, and later translated (SBE vol. 33, 1889). It consists of 1028 verses, only 550 of which are actually found in the ms containing Asahāya's commentary. It is referred to in the companion edition by the siglum P. The rest of the 1028 verses were supplied by Jolly from the "minor" recension.

21 This version consists of some 870 verses and is represented in the companion edition by the sigla X, Y, and NMS.

22 They have been compared in some detail by T. R. Chintamani ("Nārada Smṛti," *Dr. C. Kunhan Raja Presentation Volume*, pp. 153-196).

23 The translation of Mātṛkā 2 is given in the Appendix.

> exception being made in favour of the Devanāgarī, which was a sort of "vulgar" script, widely used and understood in India.[24]

Though Sukthankar admits the possibility of exceptions, he adds:

> Nevertheless, though nothing is impossible, it would be passing strange if we were to find a copy of the pure Śāradā version [of the Mahābhārata] written, say, in the Malāyālam script, or of the Grantha version in the Nepālī script. [25]

All known manuscripts of the Nāradīyamanusaṃhitā were found in the South. Though the editor of the text, K. Sāmbaśiva Śāstrī, does not describe the four manuscripts he used, he states that they were loaned to him from libraries belonging to "Namburi (sic) Brahmins of the State of Travancore" and that they were "about five centuries old."[26] Although Sāmbaśiva does not say what script his manuscripts were written in, it is likely that they were written in Malayālam script. The Nāradīyamanusaṃhitā agrees substantially with the recension recorded in the Newārī manuscripts found only in Nepal.[27] For two sets of manuscripts to be so far removed geographically and orthographically and yet to agree so closely indicates that they are derived from the same archetype.[28] The manuscripts of the other two recensions are found throughout the rest of the subcontinent, although they are hardly found in the regions of Nepal or Kerala. The version recorded by the Newārī manuscripts and the Nāradīyamanusaṃhitā is the shortest and contains the least amount of extraneous material; this further confirms that this is the oldest surviving version.[29]

The text of the Nāradasmṛti underwent "improvements" in the rest of the subcontinent, and the Newārī/NMS recension was lost there. These changes took the form of addition of verses and rearrangement of the text. The clearest example of such change is found in the chapter on Ordeals. Both Manu and Yājñavalkya discuss ordeals along with all the other modes of evidence under the heading "Non-payment of Debt" (*ṛṇādāna*). Under the heading *ṛṇādāna* in the NMS/Newārī version there is explicit mention of only two ordeals—fire and water.[30] There is, however, a separate addendum at the end of the NMS/Newārī version in which five ordeals—the balance, fire, water, poison, and holy water—are described in some detail. A separate chapter for ordeals is most unusual, as is a separate chapter on

24 Sukthankar, *Critical Studies in the Mahābhārata*, p. VII.

25 *Ibid.*

26 NMS p. 1. None of the mss used for this edition are traceable, nor are any of the mss referred to in the *New Catalogus Catalogorum*, vol. 10, with the exception of the ms with the siglum MT which is a modern transcript (made in 1923) of a ms owned by a Nambudiri brāhmaṇa.

27 There is one Newārī ms in the Asiatic Society in Calcutta (siglum C4), but it is likely that this ms was brought to Calcutta by Haraprasad Shastri since it is a very recent copy (possibly made in 1907 A.D.).

28 See V.S. Sukthankar, *Critical Studies in the Mahābhārata*, p. VII.

29 For Sukthankar's most explicit statement of this principle of critical editing as it applies to Bhā, see *ibid*., p. XLVII.

30 NāSmṛ 1.218-219. Note that these are also the only two ordeals mentioned by Manu (8.114-116): see the discussion of this point below in this Introduction.

theft in the same manuscripts. What we have here is a record of the stages of growth of these recensions. It is apparent that, originally, the Nāradasmṛti contained the mere mention of only two ordeals. For whatever reason there were more Nārada verses on ordeals in circulation among the *śiṣṭas*.[31] These were collected and appended to the "original" Nārada. This stage is represented by the NMS/Newārī recension.[32] At an even later stage, some of these verses and others were incorporated into the text at the appropriate location following the pattern of Manu, namely, under the heading "Nonpayment of Debt." This stage is represented in the "Vulgate" recension. The latest recension, that of the incomplete manuscript P (which includes the commentary of Asahāya) contains the discussion of the five ordeals found in the "Vulgate" but it adds two more ordeals—the rice and the hot gold ordeals—for a total of seven. The addition of these two ordeals was no doubt done in the interest of completeness.[33] Thus, the growth of the several recensions can be traced through the changes in the arrangement of the text as well as through the increase in the number of verses.

The chapter on Theft is probably also an attempt to expand, or to complete, the "original" text of the Nāradasmṛti. The Nāradasmṛti is organized on the principle of the traditional eighteen titles of law (*vivādapadas*, or *vyavahārapadas*). Though Manu also mentions eighteen titles of law, they do not coincide with those of Nārada.[34] They compare in the following way:

Manu		**Nāradasmṛti**	
1.	ṛṇādāna	1.	ṛṇādāna
2.	nikṣepa	2.	nikṣepa
3.	asvāmivikraya	7.	asvāmivikraya
4.	sambhūyasamutthāna	3.	sambhūyasamutthāna
5.	dattasyānapākarma	4.	dattāpradānika
6.	vetanādāna	6.	vetanasyānapākarma
7.	saṃvidvyatikrama	10.	samayasyānapākarma
8.	krayavikrayānuśaya	8. and 9.	krītānuśaya vikrīyāsaṃpradāna
9.	svāmipālavivāda		————
10.	sīmāvivāda	11.	kṣetrajavivāda

31 Perhaps ordeals came to be more accepted as modes of proof. See the Introduction to my edition of Raghunandana Bhaṭṭācārya's Divyatattva.

32 In fact, there are two versions of the Chapter on Ordeals found in the Newārī mss, one represented in the mss of recension X (which agrees closely with NMS) and another found in the mss of recension Y which also includes a truncated treatment of the hot gold ordeal.

33 In this case we can actually determine who added the last two ordeals. A refers to *five* ordeals in his commentary on NāSmṛ Mā 1.16-20 and 1.219. Yet the section on ordeals in ms P discusses seven ordeals. This must mean that Kalyāṇa added the rice and the hot gold ordeals when he "corrected and restored" the text (see the discussion of the commentaries on NāSmṛ below).

34 SmṛCa 482 notices these differences between Manu's listing of the *vivādapadas* and those followed by NāSmṛ and states explicitly that it follows the latter: *nāradīyoddeśakramānusāriṇaś ca vayam iti*.

11.	vākpāruṣya	15.	vākpāruṣya
12.	daṇḍapāruṣya	16.	daṇḍapāruṣya
13.	steya	———	
14.	sāhasa	14.	sāhasa
15.	strīsaṃgrahaṇa	———	
16.	strīpuṃdharma	12.	strīpuṃsayoga
17.	vibhāga	13.	dāyabhāga
18.	dyūtasamāhvaya	17.	dyūtasamāhvaya
		5.	abhyupetyāśuśrūṣā
		18.	prakīrṇaka

Note that the Nāradasmṛti does not have a *vivādapada steya* (theft). The chapter on Theft may have been intended to correct this lacuna. The subject matters of the other two seemingly missing titles, *strīsaṃgrahaṇa* (adultery) and *svāmipālavivāda* (disputes between master and servant), are treated under the Nāradasmṛti titles *strīpuṃsayoga* (relations between men and women), and *kṣetrajavivāda* (land disputes) and *vetanasyānapākarma* (non-payment of wages), respectively.[35]

The process of expansion of the Nāradasmṛti did not even end with the longest recension in the manuscripts. In his translation of Nārada in the Sacred Books of the East, Jolly took the longest and most inclusive text he could find, manuscript P, coupled it, since P was incomplete, with the next longest manuscript tradition available, D, and printed this hybrid text. Then, in the interest of completeness, he collected all the verses he could find attributed to Nārada in the commentaries and *nibandhas* then available and printed those which were not found in the manuscripts of the Nāradasmṛti as an appendix to his translation. In so doing, he acted like any paṇḍita who would attempt to present the most complete Nārada he could. The only difference is that the paṇḍita would have been unlikely to keep these extraneous verses separate from those found in his exemplar. Rather, he would have incorporated them into the text at what he deemed appropriate places. In doing so he would not have felt that he was engaging in any kind of distortion, since the verses he was adding were verses attributed to Nārada by learned and respected commentators and *nibandhakāras*. Nor would he have had any qualms about defying the evidence of his exemplar, since what he and other *śiṣṭas* knew outweighed anything that might be written down.[36]

The Nāradasmṛti is not the only *mūlasmṛti* to show evidence of gradual development. It has long been established that the Viṣṇusmṛti displays various strata.[37] If a proper text-critical study of the Manusmṛti were to be undertaken, it would almost certainly confirm what seems apparent when one reads that text,

35 SmṛCa 482 mentions this: *atha nāradīyābhiprāyataḥ prācīnapadaśeṣabhūtasya svāmipālavivādākhyasya padasya vidhir ucyate.*

36 A modern example of this tendency to include as much as possible is found in the collection of smṛtis, *Āryaśāstra*, edited by various paṇḍitas, Calcutta, 1962. This collection prints NāSmṛ with the section on ordeals in the chapter on debt, as Jolly's edition has it, *and* the chapter on ordeals as printed in NMS.

37 See Kane, HDh 1.112-127, especially p. 118.

namely, that it, too, was compiled over a considerable period of time by different persons with different views on certain issues. Similar assertions have been made about the Gautamadharmasūtra,[38] and, in a slightly different but related genre, it has been fairly certainly shown that there are definite stages of development in the Arthaśāstra of Kauṭilya.[39]

THE DATE OF THE NĀRADASMṚTI

P.V. Kane, the acknowledged expert and standard authority for the chronology of Sanskrit legal literature, has estimated that the Nāradasmṛti is to be dated sometime in the period 100-300 A.D.[40] Jolly determined that it must have been composed sometime around 500 A.D.[41] K.P. Jayaswal placed it around 300-400 A.D.[42] J.J. Meyer proposed the earliest date for the Nāradasmṛti: several centuries before Christ; and he attempted to prove that the Nāradasmṛti is earlier than the Yājñavalkyasmṛti, or even the Manusmṛti.[43] All these approximations are based on the relationship between the Manusmṛti and the Nāradasmṛti.

The *mūlasmṛtis* are devoid of reference to contemporaneous events, and they contain little evidence that would allow scholars to date them with any precision. There is almost no external testimony for the date of these texts. There is only one possible early reference to the Nāradasmṛti: Bāṇa's Kādambarī mentions "Nāradīya" while describing a royal palace.[44] Jolly and Bühler[45] have taken this to be a reference to the Nāradasmṛti. Kane, however, suggests that it may refer to the Nāradīya Purāṇa, as is usually the case, though he notes that the Nāradīya Purāṇa is not known to elucidate the king's duties (*rājadharma*).[46] Could this be a reference

38 Derrett, "Law and Social Order," JESHO 71 (1968), 98-99.

39 Thomas R. Trautman, *Kauṭilya and the Arthaśāstra: A Statistical Investigation of the Authorship and Evolution of the Text.*

40 HDh 1.477. Scholars have tended to accept his speculations, often with more certainty than he himself intended. While his relative chronology is one of the most complete and therefore most often cited, it must be remembered that Kane relied, for the most part, on printed editions (which are sometimes very poor) and on single mss. K.V. Rangaswami Aiyangar, particularly in the Introduction to his work on the Bṛhaspatismṛti, has attempted to cast doubt on Kane's chronologies, but his biased opinion that the text he was working on was far older, more important, and generally better than other smṛtis taints his conclusions.

41 *Hindu Law and Custom*, p. 48.

42 *Manu and Yājñavalkya*, pp. 64 and 74-75.

43 His extended and sometimes quite inventive arguments are found in *Über das Wesen der Altindischen Rechtsschriften*, pp. 82-114. He arrives at this early date for NāSmṛ by eliminating as interpolations those aspects of the text which other scholars have taken as indicators of a later time (see, e.g., pp. 81, 88, 92, 104-109, 117, 186, and 299). His reasoning often fails to be convincing, but he was the only early scholar to postulate extensive interpolation in *mūlasmṛtis*.

44 *nāradīyam ivāvarṇyamānarājadharmam*, M.R. Kale's edition, Delhi, 1968, p. 150. Bāṇa was a contemporary of King Harṣa, 7th c. A.D.

45 Jolly, Introduction to Nārada, p. xviii; Bühler, *Laws of Manu*, p. cvii, n.1.

46 HDh 1.475. The commentator Bhānucandra understands the term to mean the Nārada Purāṇa. M.R. Kale in his translation follows Kane.

to Nārada's elucidation of *rājadharma* in the Mahābhārata?[47] Bāṇa's text would then mean "where *rājadharma* is established as in the Nāradīya." In brief, the evidence of Bāṇa's passage affords little reliable evidence with which to date the Nāradasmṛti. A chronology relative to other *mūlasmṛtis* is all that can be hoped for.

The foundation of this chronological house of cards must be the Manusmṛti. It is, on stylistic grounds and on the basis of its content, the oldest of the metrical smṛtis.[48] It may be dated between the 2nd or 3rd century B.C. and the 2nd or 3rd century A.D.[49] Scholars base the chronological arrangement of subsequent smṛtis on the degree of variation from Manu's content and arrangement. The closer a text is to Manu in content and arrangement, the older it is likely to be. The chronological order that is generally accepted for the extant *mūlasmṛtis* is: Manu, Yājñavalkya, Nārada, Parāśara.[50]

One of the problems with relative chronologies of Sanskrit legal texts is that they are dependent on editions which are either defective, or which, with a few exceptions, are not based on the critical scrutiny which comes from the careful examination and comparison of all available manuscript evidence. Let us look, as an example, at one of the criteria most often used to compare the *mūlasmṛtis*: the treatment of ordeals.[51] The Manusmṛti mentions only two ordeals, fire and water (8.114-116). The Yājñavalkyasmṛti mentions five—fire, water, balance, poison, and holy water (2.95-116). Jolly's Nāradasmṛti treats seven ordeals, the previously mentioned five plus the rice and the hot gold ordeals (1.247-348 in Jolly's edition). This, it is argued by most writers who have treated the subject of relative chronologies, is evidence to support the chronology Manu, Yājñavalkya, Nārada, the reason being that the greater the detail of treatment of a particular topic in a text, the later that text must be. In the case of ordeals we have not only a greater number of ordeals but also more detail about the administration of each ordeal in each subsequent *mūlasmṛti*: Manu has three verses, Yājñavalkya has twenty-two verses, and Nārada has one hundred and two. Yet this conclusion, which is based on Jolly's edition of Nārada, is not supported by my critical edition of the text. If, as is my contention, the separate chapters on theft and on ordeals found at the end of the NMS/Newārī recension are collections of Nārada verses from extraneous sources which were, at a later stage, appended to the "original" text, then, in the "original" Nāradasmṛti there were only two ordeals, fire and water (both mentioned under the

47 Bhā 2.5.6-116; see the discussion of the personage Nārada below.

48 It is not necessary to repeat in detail here all the arguments for the dates of the various smṛtis; I will give only a brief sketch of the chronology. For details, see Kane's HDh vol. 1, and for a competent evaluation of the contentions of various scholars, see R. Lingat, *The Classical Law of India*, pp. 73-106. The most concise discussion of the problems of relative chronologies in Sanskrit legal materials is found *ibid.*, pp. 123-132.

49 *Ibid.*, p. 96.

50 *Ibid.*, pp. 92-96, 99-100, and 103. The exact position of Parāśara is somewhat problematic.

51 See, for example, Kane, HDh 1.474, and Lingat, *op. cit.*, p. 129.

rubric of "Non-payment of Debt"), and only five verses on this subject (1.218-222).[52]

Similarly, one of the arguments cited in support of the relative lateness of the Nāradasmṛti is the fact that it subdivides Manu's eighteen titles of law (*vyavahārapadas*) into 132 subdivisions (Mā 1.20-25 in Jolly's edition). These verses, again, turn out to be late additions to the P sub-recension.[53]

There are, nevertheless, cases where Nārada has expanded on Manu. Manu mentions only seven types of slaves (8.415), Nārada fifteen (5.23-42). In addition, there are certain doctrinal differences between the two texts, which indicate Nārada's distance from Manu. Among these is the fact that Nārada clearly provides for the institution of the levirate marriage (*niyoga* 12.83, 85, 87), while Manu is ambivalent (it is permitted at 9.57-63 and forbidden at 9.64-68). Widow remarriage is condemned by Manu in the strongest terms (9.65), but Nārada allows it (12. 97-102) and even seems to encourage what might be called divorce (12.16, 18).[54] Furthermore, the Nāradasmṛti contains some notions that are not found in the Manusmṛti. The enumeration of fourteen kinds of impotent males is unique to the Nāradasmṛti (12.11-13). So is the classification of remarried and wanton women (*punarbhūs* and *svairiṇīs* 12.45-52). The Nāradasmṛti does not hold the right of primogeniture to be absolute; rather, the position of head of the family is dependent on one's competence, and even the youngest son could assume that role if he were suitable (13.5). Even more remarkable is the unique claim that, in the absence of sons, daughters may inherit from their father before any other members of the family (13.47-48).

While it is fairly certain that the Nāradasmṛti is later than the Manusmṛti, the question of the relative chronology of the Nāradasmṛti and the Yājñavalkyasmṛti is less clear. If we may, for the present, use the available editions of the Yājñavalkyasmṛti as a basis for comparison, the Nāradasmṛti, which mentions only two ordeals, must be considered earlier than the Yājñavalkyasmṛti, which mentions five. The Yājñavalkyasmṛti (2.134-136) offers a more complete listing of possible heirs than the Nāradasmṛti, which makes no mention of the succession of the wife, nor does it provide rules about the succession of other relatives (*gotrajas*, or *bandhus*). On the other hand, the Nāradasmṛti is far more complete and systematic than the Yājñavalkyasmṛti in its description of legal procedure. It is therefore difficult to state with any confidence which of the two *mūlasmṛtis* is earlier. Kane believes that the two composers flourished at approximately the same time.[55] At the very least, it may be said that the state of legal development reflected in the two texts is roughly the same, and that it is therefore probable they were compiled at

52 J.J. Meyer (*Über das Wesen der Altindischen Rechtsschriften*, p. 105) was also convinced that the chapter on theft (the only one known to him, since Jolly did not print the chapter on ordeals) is not original (*unecht*).

53 See my article, "A Bogus Passage in Jolly's Nārada-Smṛti," IIJ 27 (1984), pp. 201-205.

54 This and other unorthodox views are mitigated by the interpretations of commentators.

55 HDh 1.474.

about the same time, with the distinct possibility that the Nāradasmṛti may be slightly earlier.[56] If, as K.V. Rangaswami Aiyangar and J.J. Meyer have suggested, the Nāradasmṛti is a manual for the specialist,[57] then, even in an earlier text, a greater precision of definition and enumeration might be expected. Hence, the Nāradasmṛti's lists of impotent men and slaves, and its description of twenty-one kinds of property (1.40-43), and other such elaborate treatments need not be taken as indicators of a later date.

It must be remembered, however, that the Nāradasmṛti is the only *mūlasmṛti* which has been critically edited to date. It is, therefore, even more risky to attempt to establish a relative chronology at this stage, since the comparison of an edited text with unedited versions of other texts may distort their relationships even more. Still, some estimate of the date of the Nāradasmṛti must be ventured. To continue the tradition of attempting to date this text relative to Manu, the Nāradasmṛti is closer to the time of Manu than many scholars had previously thought. If we place the Manusmṛti in the period between the 2nd or 3rd century B.C. and the 2nd or 3rd century A.D., I would date the Nāradasmṛti approximately one or two centuries later. Such a relative chronology is a shaky edifice. Even approximations of five hundred-year periods may eventually prove to be widely off the mark. Yet, this is the best we can do with the data available to us. Perhaps Lingat was right when he said that there is little likelihood of ever establishing a chronology of these texts that is sufficiently certain to satisfy the demands of critical scholarship.[58]

THE EPONYMOUS AUTHOR NĀRADA

For the reasons stated above, it is likely that there was no single "author" of this text. The text has a close connection with the Manu tradition. Recension R gives the most explicit account of the relationship between the dharmaśāstras of Manu and Nārada. There we are told that Manu Prajāpati originally composed a text in 100,000 verses and 1080 chapters, which was successively abridged by the sages Nārada, Mārkaṇḍeya, and Sumati Bhārgava, down to a text of 4,000 verses.[59] What we have in the Nāradasmṛti, according to this account, is the ninth chapter of the original Manu composition—the chapter on legal procedure. This obviously enhances the prestige of the Nāradasmṛti, since, traditionally, pronouncements by

56 NāSmṛ is explicitly organized on the basis of the *vivādapadas*, like Manu, whereas YāSmṛ is not.

57 K.V. Rangaswami Aiyangar, *Bṛhaspatismṛti (Reconstructed)*, p. 136; Meyer, *Über das Wesen der Altindischen Rechtsschriften*, pp. 87 ff.

58 *The Classical Law of India*, pp. xiv-xv and 123-132.

59 See the prose beginning of the text. The structure of this history of Manu's text on dharma is a familiar one in the Sanskrit tradition. Many purāṇas put forward the notion of an original Purāṇa that was successively abridged by various sages (see Ludo Rocher, *The Purāṇas*, pp. 41-48). See K.V. Rangaswami Aiyangar's introduction to *Bṛhaspatismṛti (Reconstructed)*, pp. 81-82 for other accounts of redactions of smṛti materials.

Manu on the subject of dharma are above challenge.[60] Even though it is clear from the critical edition that this myth of the origin of the Nāradasmṛti was added later,[61] the tradition that the Nāradasmṛti is closely related to the Manusmṛti is found in several places.[62] The Bhaviṣya Purāṇa claims that there were four versions of the "Svayambhuvaśāstra"—Svayambhuva is one of the epithets of Manu—by Bhṛgu, Nārada, Bṛhaspati, and Aṅgiras.[63] This tradition was not limited to the subcontinent. A twelfth-century inscription of Jaya Harivarman I of Champā (modern Vietnam) describes a high dignitary of his court as extremely learned, "expert in all the dharmaśāstras, following especially the *nāradīya* and the *bhārgavīya*."[64]

In a sense these myths describing the origin of the current recension of Manu or the Nāradasmṛti are admissions that the current recensions are incomplete. They are recensions of much larger works; hence, from the viewpoint of a traditional paṇḍita, verses ascribed to Manu or Nārada but not found in those texts could justifiably be added to his exemplar on the grounds that they were part of the larger, original text.

The reasons for attributing verses on dharma to Nārada were never made explicit. Nārada is an extremely well-known divine sage who appears throughout classical Sanskrit literature.[65] He is the messenger of the gods and conveys the

60 *vedārthapratibaddhatvāt prāmāṇyaṃ tu manoḥ smṛtam* |
manvarthaviparītā tu yā smṛtiḥ sā na śasyate || (Bṛhas *saṃskārakāṇḍa* 13)
"Manu's pronouncement is authoritative because of its adherence to the import of the Vedas. A text which contradicts Manu should not be taught." See also Bühler's introduction to his translation of Manu, pp. xiv-xv.

61 The tradition that NāSmṛ was part of the original Manusmṛti is found in the early commentary on Manu by Medhātithi (ca. 9th c. A.D.). On Manu 1.58 he paraphrases this account of the evolution of the text from 100,000 verses to its present form: *nāradaś ca smarati śatasāhasro 'yaṃ granthaḥ prajāpatinā kṛtas tataḥ manvādibhiḥ krameṇa saṃkṣipta iti*. Kane says that this statement proves that the "introductory words" of NāSmṛ are not "spurious or a later addition" (HDh. 3.309). In fact, all that it proves is that by the time of Medhātithi this myth was current. There is no reason to believe that Medhātithi had access to the "original" NāSmṛ. K.V. Rangaswami Aiyangar discusses an alleged similar connection between Bṛhas and Manu (Introduction to Bṛhas, pp. 184-185).

62 Not all accounts mention Nārada as one of the sages responsible for a recension (see Bhā 12.322.36-43 for an account of a 100,000-verse text attributed to Manu, Uśanas, and then Bṛhaspati).

63 CaVarCint, Dānakhaṇḍa p. 528, and SaṃMa p. 2. Much later in the tradition the divine sage Nārada comes to be recognized as an author of dharma literature in his own right. He is listed as an expounder of dharma (*dharmapravaktṛ*) by Vṛddhayājñavalkya quoted by Viśvarūpa on YāSmṛ 1.4-5 and in a list by Paiṭhīnasi quoted at ViMiPari p. 15 (although he is not mentioned in other lists of *dharmaśāstrakāras* such as those at YāSmṛ 1.4-5 and PaMā 1.12-14.) BhāgPur (II.4.25, 5.1-8; VII.1.30; XI.27.2.) states that he compiled the "*nāradīyadharma* " and told the Rāmāyaṇa to Vālmīki.

64 L. Finot, "Les inscriptions de Mi-son," BEFEO 4 (1904), 973, quoted in G. Coedès, *The Indianized States of Southeast Asia*, p. 165.

65 For a brief review of the character of the divine sage Nārada, see Jean Herbert, *Nārada: Précédé d'une étude sur les Avatārs de Vishnou*. For a more detailed survey

divine will to mortals. He is also often referred to as fond of quarrels. He comes to be closely associated with Viṣṇu-Kṛṣṇa. There are, however, no sectarian indications in the Nāradasmṛti. There is relatively little evidence that the mythical Nārada was considered a special expert on dharma, although he is occasionally depicted as being responsible for instructing mortals in law and politics. For example, it is Nārada who instructs Yudhiṣṭhira in matters of law, polity, and pleasure (dharma, artha, and kāma) by asking hundreds of questions in the Sabhāparvan of the Mahābhārata.[66]

THE COMMENTARIES ON THE NĀRADASMṚTI

Two of the three versions of the Nāradasmṛti have been commented upon. The NMS/Newārī version was commented upon by Bhavasvāmin, and the "longer" recension was commented upon by Asahāya. Unfortunately, we know very little about either of these writers.

The commentary printed in the accompanying edition is by Asahāya; it is incomplete and has been significantly altered by a certain Kalyāṇabhaṭṭa.[67] This is the only surviving work of Asahāya, yet there is evidence that he was, at one time in the tradition, a well-known commentator.[68] In addition to the commentary on the Nāradasmṛti, he probably wrote commentaries on the Manusmṛti,[69] on the Gautamadharmasūtra,[70] and on Śaṅkha-likhita.[71]

Asahāya's commentary on the Nāradasmṛti survives in one manuscript (P) and in two copies made from it (L2 and M4). Although I have made every effort to render the commentary comprehensible, many passages remain unclear. This is due to a combination of the corrupt state of the original, incomplete manuscript and to

of the events associated with Nārada in classical Sanskrit sources, see V.R. Ramachandra Dikshitar, *The Purāṇa Index*, vol. 2, pp. 225-229. The *New Catalogus Catalogorum* has nine pages of entries that are attributed to or named for Nārada.

66 This instruction goes on for 110 verses (Bhā 2.5.6-116) and Yudhiṣṭhira acknowledges Nārada's instructions as "decisions of law" (*dharmaniścaya*, Bhā 2.6.2).

67 See the introduction to the commentary which states: *dṛṣṭvāsahāyaracitaṃ nāradabhāṣyaṃ kulekhakair bhraṣṭaṃ kalyāṇena kriyate prāktanam etad viśodhya punaḥ*. "Kalyāṇa found that Asahāya's commentary on Nārada was ruined by poor scribes, and he corrected it and restored it to its original shape."

68 SaVi p. 348 says that authors (*smṛtikāras*) like Manu, Yājñavalkya, etc. and their commentators (*smṛtivyākhyātṛs*) like Asahāya, Medhātithi, Vijñāneśvara, and Aparārka all agree on the concept of *dharmavibhāga*: partition based on performing religious duties separately.

69 ViRa p. 548 quotes A's comment on Manu 9.145. Medhātithi quotes him in commenting on Manu 8.155, but the opinion mentioned there is not found in the extant commentary of A.

70 The Bālakrīḍā of Viśvarūpa on YāSmṛ 3.263-264, and the Hāralatā of Aniruddha, p. 35.

71 See V. Raghavan, "Asahāya's Commentaries on the Smṛtis of Śaṅkha and Likhita," ABORI 18 (1937), 205, where he quotes Ānandagiri in the *Nyāyaratnadīpāvalī* of Ānandānubhava (Madras Ms R4459, p.116): *śaṅkhalikhitasmṛtyoḥ vyākhyātā kaścid asahāyanāmā samasti* (sic).

the sometimes odd diction of Asahāya. There are times when one suspects that the Sanskrit found in this commentary is a sort of vernacular the vocabulary and syntax of which either borrow from or are influenced by a local dialect.[72] Since we know nothing of where Asahāya lived it is not possible at this time to identify regional influences that may have contributed to these peculiar passages. Jolly did not have much to say about the time or place of Asahāya; he only says that he must have been later than the fifth century A.D., the period when he feels the text of the Nāradasmṛti was composed.[73] K.P. Jayaswal hypothesized that Asahāya lived in Pāṭaliputra no later than the seventh century A.D. His hypothesis is based on an anecdote found in the commentary on Nāradasmṛti 1.5, which relates an incident in which a debt contracted in Pāṭaliputra was the subject of a trial. Jayaswal's view was that "Asahāya could not be later than the seventh century, for about the middle of that century Pāṭaliputra was found deserted, and Asahāya speaks of Pāṭaliputra as a living town where in the court Nārada's law was quoted and discussed."[74] Kane objected to this reasoning on the grounds that Kalyāṇabhaṭṭa had tampered with the commentary of Asahāya and therefore this evidence was unreliable.[75] Kane is correct, but he does not address Jayaswal's point. Even if this anecdote—which is even more lengthy and rambling than either Jayaswal or Kane knew since Jolly printed only portions of it—is the work of Kalyāṇabhaṭṭa, the reference to Pāṭaliputra still needs to be explained. It is very likely that Kalyāṇabhaṭṭa set the anecdote in Pāṭaliputra, not because he lived there, or even because the incident happened there, but simply because Pāṭaliputra was the city *par excellence* of Indian antiquity.[76] The anecdote is too perfect an example in support of the view of the commentator to have actually happened. Its style is too rambling and disjointed to be that of Asahāya. It is almost certainly an addition by Kalyāṇabhaṭṭa, created to support his view of the extent of the pious obligation. For this reason it has no bearing on the question of the age or location of Asahāya.

There are other references to cities in this commentary. The cities of Vaṭapadraka (Baroda?) and Saṃvāduka are mentioned in the commentary on Mā 1.24 and 25. There are references to brāhmaṇas from Bharukaccha (Broach) and Kheṭaka (Khaira) and to Narmadātīrtha at 1.124. In each of these instances, however, we have a patent interpolation by Kalyāṇabhaṭṭa, and there is no reason to think that the mention of these western Indian place names gives us any indication

72 For example, the repeated use of a word like *ākoṭana* (see Mā 1.5 and notes), and the peculiar syntax of the commentary on 1.4, 1.11, 1.15, 1.213, etc.

73 TLL for 1883, p. 5.

74 *Manu and Yājñavalkya*, p. 289. Pāṭaliputra was found deserted by Hsuan Tsang, whose pilgrimage to India lasted from 630 to 644 A.D. (see Samuel Beal, *Si-yu-ki, Buddhist Records of the Western World. Chinese Accounts of India Translated from the Chinese of Hiuen Thsiang*, vol. 3, pp. 320 ff., and D.R. Patil, *The Antiquarian Remains in Bihar*, p. 376).

75 HDh 1.549.

76 In the same way Pāṭaliputra played an important part in the life of the mythical Devadatta, the sometimes lucky, sometimes hapless kartṛ of the Mahābhāṣya (see Sukumar Sen, "The Story of Devadatta in the Mahābhāṣya," *Indian Linguistics* 12 (1947), pp. 189-196).

of the home of Asahāya. It may be that Kalyāṇabhaṭṭa was from western India, however, since the anecdotes which mention these place names are, judged on stylistic grounds, most likely his additions to the commentary of Asahāya.

There is no doubt that Asahāya is a relatively early commentator. It is not his style to cite other texts or authors in his commentary, so we do not have a point of reference after which he must have written. All that can be said is that he is earlier than Viśvarūpa and Medhātithi, both of whom quote him by name.[77] According to Kane's chronology, Viśvarūpa may be dated between 750-1000 A.D., Medhātithi between 825-900 A.D.[78]

In general, Asahāya's style is fairly terse with little ostentatious display of erudition. He does not quote from other texts or refer to other authors. This is not to say that the commentary as we have it does not include such references, but in every case these appear to be additions by Kalyāṇabhaṭṭa.

We know nothing of Kalyāṇabhaṭṭa aside from this work.[79] As indicated above, he may have been from western India, but when or exactly where he lived are likely to remain mysteries. He refers to himself often in the commentary,[80] and he seems to have been the author of a treatise on documents since he quotes from and refers to chapters of such a work.[81] He claims to have corrected and restored Asahāya's commentary on the Nāradasmṛti,[82] and to have done so at the instance of one Keśavabhaṭṭa.[83] No information about Keśavabhaṭṭa is given in the commentary, and it is impossible to determine his identity. The nature of the reference to him, however, indicates that he may have been a patron.[84]

Kalyāṇabhaṭṭa not only "corrected" the text, but he added to the commentary of Asahāya and, quite likely, to the text of Nārada itself.[85] In many instances, it is easy to identify those places where Kalyāṇabhaṭṭa has added to the commentary of Asahāya. He either mentions himself by name or he refers to a verse attributed to Kalyāṇabhaṭṭa in another part of the commentary. In other places the

77 See notes 67 and 68 above.

78 HDh 1.562 and HDh 1.583, respectively. Kane's further attempts to narrow the date of Viśvarūpa are open to question (in addition to HDh, see Kane, "The Predecessors of Vijñāneśvara," JBBRAS n.s. 1.2 (1925), 193-224).

79 There are four, perhaps five, authors with the name of Kalyāṇabhaṭṭa mentioned in the NCC, vol. 3, p. 253.

80 See the commentary on 1.102, 1.106, 1.107, 1.114, 1.145, and 2.8.

81 See the commentary on 1.102 *triṣaṣṭipatraprakaraṇe kalyāṇabhaṭṭena*; 1.106 *sāmānyagrāhapatralakṣaṇavicāraprakaraṇe kalyāṇabhaṭṭena*; 1.114 *triṣaṣṭilekhyaprakaraṇakārakakalyāṇabhaṭṭena*; *et passim*.

82 See the notes to Mā 1.1 and note 65 above.

83 See the colophon of the commentary at the end of Mā I: *ity asahāyanāradabhāṣye keśavabhaṭṭaprotsāhitakalyāṇabhaṭṭapariśodhitavyavahāramātṛkāyāṃprathamo 'dhyayaḥ*.

84 J.F. Fleet mentions a suzerain of the Western Chālukya king Someśvara IV by the name of Keśavabhaṭṭaya ("The Dynasties of the Kanarese Districts of the Bombay Presidency," *Bombay Gazetteer*, vol.1, part 2, p. 465), but the name Keśavabhaṭṭa is a common one and to make any connection would be pure speculation.

85 See my article, "A Bogus Passage in Jolly's Nārada-Smṛti," IIJ 27 (1984), pp. 201-205.

identification of Kalyāṇabhaṭṭa's hand is less clear. I have indicated in notes whenever I think—usually on stylistic grounds: Kalyāṇabhaṭṭa is prolix—that the commentary has been augmented by Kalyāṇabhaṭṭa (for example the note to 1.89).

The commentary on the Nāradīyamanusaṃhitā by Bhavasvāmin is probably later than that of Asahāya, although in his case we have even fewer data to place him geographically and chronologically than we do for Asahāya. The editor of the Nāradīyamanu-saṃhitā, K. Sāmbaśiva Śāstrī, was of the opinion that Bhavasvāmin was a Southerner because his is a common name among brāhmaṇas in Kerala where all the manuscript copies of the commentary were found.[86] This, as Kane has pointed out, is hardly conclusive.[87] Bhavasvāmin gives very little evidence for his geographical location: he mentions Kanyakubja and Mathurā in an example of transactions involving deposits;[88] he observes that in the South (*dakṣiṇasyāṃ diśi dravilaviṣayādau*) the copper *kārṣāpaṇa* is the currency, while "here" (*iha*) the *dīnāra* is current;[89] and he says that the common designation for the *kārṣāpaṇa* in Panjab also applies "here in the central region" (*iha madhyame*).[90] From all of this we may conclude that he wrote somewhere in central India. Sāmbaśiva also mentions references to Bhavasvāmin in three other texts: (1) the Bahvṛca Smārtaprāyaścitta mentions him as a commentator on kalpasūtras;[91] (2) Vāsudeva Dīkṣita in his Bālamanoramā on the Siddhāntakaumudī also mentions Bhavasvāmin (along with Dhūrtasvāmin and Rudradatta) as a commentator on the kalpasūtras;[92] and (3) Keśavasvāmin mentions Bhavasvāmin in his Baudhāyana-śrautaprayogasāra.[93] Assuming that this Keśavasvāmin is the same as the Keśavasvāmin who was the thirteenth-century author of the Nānārthārṇava-

86 NMS Introduction, p. 4.

87 HDh 1.478.

88 See the commentary on NMS 3.7 and 5.4.

89 NMS 19.116. Jolly (*Hindu Law and Custom*, p. 48) thought that the mention of the *dīnāra* indicated that NāSmṛ was definitely post-second c. A.D., but there is no compulsion to accept this reasoning, as was shown by A. B. Keith ("Denarius and the Date of the Harivaṃśa," JRAS 1907, 681-683, and "The Denarius as a Proof of Date," JRAS 1915, 504-505). See also K.V. Rangaswami Aiyangar, *Bṛhaspatismṛti (Reconstructed)*, pp. 152-156, and Kane HDh 1.477.

90 NMS 19.117. This may, however, be intended as an explanation of the verse rather than a statement of his own locality. See my article "Coins in the Nāradasmṛti's Chapter on Theft," *Journal of the Numismatic Society of India* 44 (1982), 108-113.

91 Quoted by K. Sāmbaśiva Śāstrī, op. cit. p. 3:
bodhāyanaṃ jaiminiṃ ca kauṣītakyāśvalāyanau |
vādhūlakāpastambādīn naumi śākhāpravartakān ||
tatproktakalpasūtrādivyākhyānakṛtamānasān |
ācāryān api siddhāntibhavasvāmimukhān bhaje ||

92 SiKau p. 370 under *sūtra* 496: *varṇād udāttāt* (4.1.39) *iti sūtre eteti pratīkam upādāya etaśabdaś śvetaparyāya iti kalpasūtravyākhyātāro dhūrtasvaṃi-bhavasvāmirudradattaprabhṛtayo yājñikāḥ.*

93 Quoted by K. Sāmbaśiva Śāstrī, op. cit. p. 4:
nārāyaṇādibhiḥ prayogakārair ekaikaṃ pakṣam āśritya darśapūrṇamāsādīnām prayoga uktaḥ. ācāryapādair dvedhaiva pakṣāntarāṇy uktāni. bhavasvāmimatānu-sāriṇā mayā tūbhayam aṅgīkṛtya prayogasāraḥ kriyate.

saṃkṣepa,[94] Bhavasvāmin must have lived prior to the thirteenth century. Sāmbaśiva also mentions the possibility that this Bhavasvāmin may have been the same as the Bhavasvāmin mentioned in the colophon of Rājacūḍāmaṇi Dīkṣita's Kamalinīkalahaṃsa as that author's grandfather. This would mean, according to Sāmbaśiva, that Bhavasvāmin was a mid-sixteenth-century author.[95] This seems too late for Bhavasvāmin, the commentator on the Nāradīyamanusaṃhitā. K.V. Rangaswami Aiyangar claims that Bhavasvāmin's date is the eighth century.[96] Kane, who admits that his view is conjectural, says that Bhavasvāmin must have lived sometime between 700 and 1000 A.D.[97] T. R. Chintamani seems to feel that Bhavasvāmin's date may be the eighth century.[98] To attempt to refine these estimates on the basis of the evidence available would be little more than guesswork.

The estimation of Bhavasvāmin's date is a matter of conjecture, but it is likely that he was later than Asahāya. There are at least two reasons for this: (1) Bhavasvāmin often cites variant readings of Nārada verses. This could indicate that the tradition of a Nārada corpus was more developed, but it could also simply be an indication of Bhavasvāmin's greater thoroughness or scientific spirit. (2) Unlike Asahāya, Bhavasvāmin quotes other authorities in his commentary: Pāṇini (passim), Vālmīki (NMS 2.32), Vyāsa (NMS 2.32), Vararuci (NMS 2.72), Vasiṣṭha (NMS 2.94; 16.20), and Bhṛgusaṃhitā,[99] āgama (NMS 2.192), smṛti (NMS 2.190, 220; 13.80), and śruti (NMS 2.5, 53, 97, 190). This latter point is not an indisputable argument for Asahāya's priority, yet it appears that the earlier commentators on smṛti tended to give their own explanations and to rely less on the opinions of others.

The Newārī manuscripts of the Y sub-recension, and manuscript C in particular, contain colophons which claim that these manuscripts contain a commentary (*bhāṣya*) written in the "Nepālī" language. The paṇḍitas of the Nepal German Manuscript Preservation Project identified the language as "old Newārī," but knew of no one who understands this language. Judging from the length of these passages, which are found between the Sanskrit verses, they appear to be little more than a translation or a paraphrase.

94 Published in TSS 23, 29, and 31 (1913).

95 *Loc. cit.*, p. 4.

96 Introduction to *Bṛhaspati* (p.72). He says that "Bhavasvāmin, like Mādhavasvāmin, and Skandhasvāmin, belongs to a period long anterior to Viśvarūpa (c. A.D. 800)." This claim is based on a reference to an article in the *Journal of Oriental Research* 5, 325. The reference is wrong, and I have not been able to trace the article.

97 HDh 1.481.

98 T.R. Chintamani, "Nārada Smṛti," *Kunhan Raja Presentation Volume*, p.155.

99 NMS 13.44 (a reference, not a quotation); 13.111 (a quotation of an entire verse which is very similar but not identical to Manu 10.19), and 16.20 (an exact quote from Manu 8.274).

JOLLY'S CONTRIBUTION TO THE STUDY OF THE NĀRADASMṚTI

Julius Jolly was a pioneer in Nārada studies. His translation in the Sacred Books of the East was generally sound, and his annotation helpful for its time. His edition of the text was, however, flawed by his uncritical acceptance of manuscript P as the repository of the "original" Nāradasmṛti.

Jolly had translated the "shorter" version in 1876, before he edited the Sanskrit text. Shortly before the publication of this translation, Bühler discovered the manuscript of the Nāradasmṛti with Asahāya's commentary, as he noted in his Report on Sanskrit Manuscripts 1874/75:

> The Nāradasmṛtibhāṣya of Kalyāṇabhaṭṭa is the most important acquisition of the year among the works on Dharma. It gives a full explanation of the first eight adhyāyas of the Smṛti, and helps greatly to settle the text of this interesting but difficult law book, of which very few copies are procurable. Kalyāṇa says in the introductory verses that his work is based on an older but corrupt commentary. The MS. has been written in Benares and has been procured from the library of the Rājā of Bundī through the kind offices of the Asst. Political Officer in charge of Harauti.[100]

Bühler presumably informed Jolly of this discovery after the appearance of Jolly's translation of the "shorter" version (1876). He eventually loaned Jolly his personal copy of the manuscript.[101]

Convinced that a commentary was the best way to check the accuracy of a text, Jolly proceeded to place greater reliance on this manuscript than was warranted.[102] He was thus led to adopt wrong readings, obviously spurious verses, even a spurious chapter. In addition to verses attributed to Nārada in the commentary, Jolly also occasionally accepted as Nārada verses other verses quoted in support of Asahāya's or Kalyāṇabhaṭṭa's arguments. The concordance provided in the companion edition of the text will allow easy identification of those verses in Jolly's edition which should no longer be considered part of the earliest recoverable text. Notes to the translation also refer to the location of each Nārada verse in Jolly's text.

100 Girgaum, 1875, p.10. All attempts to track down the Bundī original of this ms were unsuccessful, and there is no trace of a surviving Benares original. It is interesting that Bühler attributed the commentary to Kalyāṇabhaṭṭa.

101 Apparently Jolly used Bühler's copy of Asahāya (L2) for the edition and later acquired a copy (M4) made directly from P (see note to1.12). Bühler's copy was formerly in the Deccan College and is now in the Bhandarkar Oriental Research Institute.

102 Jolly held on to the notion that the "longer" version of ms P was older, even though he had occasional qualms such as those expressed in his Tagore Law Lectures for 1883: "Altogether, the older version of Nārada [i.e., that which is found in ms P] exhibits even more evident marks of recent composition than the current version [i.e., the "shorter" version or the "vulgate"] . . . " (p. 56). Kane, too, felt that the commentary of Asahāya provides a "valuable check for the authenticity of the text" (HDh 1.469).

The critical edition on which this translation is based benefits from the additional and crucial evidence of the Newārī manuscripts and the Nāradīyamanusaṃhitā. As his edition was nearly through the press, Jolly was shown a single Newārī manuscript which was in the possession of Cecil Bendall of the British Museum.[103] Jolly recognized that this manuscript contained important information—especially valuable, in Jolly's view, because of the great age of the manuscript: early 15th century. Though he described it extensively and listed its most important variant readings in the preface to his edition, and even though he appended its additional chapter on theft, he was not able to use these data in constituting the text.[104] The Newārī manuscripts and the Nāradīyamanusaṃhitā record the oldest recoverable version of Nārada's text; thus the translation provided here will be found to be considerably different from that which Jolly published in the Sacred Books of the East a century ago.

THE PRESENT TRANSLATION AND ANNOTATIONS

The present translation includes both the chapters on theft and on ordeals. The translation in the Appendix contains the chapter which Jolly called Mātṛkā 2, and treats the subject of the plaint. This was not part of the earliest recoverable version of the Nāradasmṛti, but it contains verses which are extensively quoted in the dharmasāstra literature, and, therefore, a translation of this spurious chapter is warranted.

I have not translated the commentary of Asahāya because much of it does not lend itself to translation (glosses, etymologies, etc.). The notes to the translation include the most important material from Asahāya's commentary—sometimes translated, sometimes paraphrased. This is the most economical way to present his ideas to readers who cannot read his sometimes abstruse prose. I have included the comments of Bhavasvāmin in the same manner. His commentary is admirable for its clarity and brevity, and it is helpful in those portions of the text for which Asahāya's commentary is lost.

TYPOGRAPHICAL CONVENTIONS

The verses of the Nāradasmṛti are printed here in bold type. The notes which follow in smaller type identify the equivalent number of the verse in the Nāradīyamanusaṃhitā and in Jolly's edition. They also contain summations or paraphrases of the comments of Asahāya, with additional glosses and comments from the commentary of Bhavasvāmin when these are of help in understanding the verse as well as my own comments. Verses given in the commentary of Asahāya are translated in these notes, and their provenance is identified in square brackets. If the provenance of a verse is unknown it is marked "[?]"

103 Referred to by Jolly as his N, it is identified as ms C in the companion edition.
104 See pp. 5-15 of the Preface to his edition.

INTRODUCTION TO THE CRITICAL EDITION

DESCRIPTION OF THE MANUSCRIPTS

The present edition is based on forty-seven mss referred to with the following sigla:

A — Rājasthan Oriental Research Institute, Alwar Branch. Ms no. 4048. Paper. Devanāgarī script. 39 folios. 29 cm by 14.5 cm. 9 lines per page. 45 *akṣaras* per line. No date, but the paper, hand, and appearance indicate that it is a very recent copy. A microfilm was used. Colophon: *iti śrīnāradīyadharmaśāstre prakīrṇakanāmavyavahārapadam aṣṭādaśaṃ samāptaṃ. samāptaṃ cedaṃ dharmaśāstraṃ.*

B — Nepal German Manuscript Preservation Project, Kathmandu. Ms no. E-3447. Reel no. E 193/7. Cf. Bernard Kölver, "Zur *Nāradasmṛti* I. Varianten zu den Büchern XIV-XVII und zum *Pariśiṣṭa*," ZDMG 123 (1973), 328-343, in which it is referred to by the following designation: Orientalische Abteilung der Stiftung Preussischer Kulturbesitz, Staatsbibliothek, Berlin. Hs.or.sim. 1112. Palmleaf. Newārī script. 119 folios numbered 1-18, 20-120, folio 19 is missing. 30 cm by 5 cm. 5 lines per page. 55-60 *akṣaras* per line. Incomplete in the end also. No date. A microfilm was used. The text breaks off after 1.145 and resumes with 1.156cd.

B2 — Nepal German Manuscript Preservation Project, Kathmandu. Ms no. 5-337. Reel no. A 51/13. Palmleaf. Newārī script. 49 folios numbered 1-7, 14-58, 60, 62-64. 31 cm by 5.5 cm. 5 lines per page. 55-60 *akṣaras* per line. Incomplete. No date. A microfilm was used. This is a carelessly written ms done by an unintelligent scribe. The text breaks off at 1.14 and resumes at 1.109. The missing folios 59 and 61 indicate that the section on ordeals is incomplete.

B3 — Nepal German Manuscript Preservation Project, Kathmandu. Ms no. 4-763. Reel no. B 32/42. Palmleaf. Newārī Script. 49 folios, numbered 4-44, 1-7, plus a final unnumbered folio. 29 cm by 5.5 cm. 7 lines per page. 45-50 *akṣaras* per line. Incomplete. No date. A microfilm was used. The text begins at Mā 1.57d. The section of the ms numbered 1-7 at the end is actually a chapter on ordeals attributed in the ms to Pitāmaha. Cf. my article "A Compilation of Pitāmaha Verses Found in Two Manuscripts from Nepal," SII 10 (1985), 103-132. At the end of folio 44b it states: *caurapratiṣedhaṃ nāma prakaraṇaṃ samāptaṃ. samāptañ ca nāradaproktañ ca dharmmamānavam iti. saṃvat āṣade (āṣāḍhe?) māse śuklatrayodaśi.*

B4 — Nepal German Manuscript Preservation Project, Kathmandu. Ms no. 5-338. Reel no. B 33/16. Palmleaf. Newārī script. 89 folios, numbered 24-112, folio 23 (?) is badly broken and contains only a few fragments of words. 22.5 cm by 4.5 cm. 5-6 lines per page. 45-50 *akṣaras* per line. Incomplete. No date. A microfilm was used. Folios 1-22 are missing: the text begins with Nāradasmṛti 1.134cd. Folio 91b contains a chapter on ordeals attributed to Pitāmaha. Cf. my article cited above under ms **B3**.

B5 — Nepal German Manuscript Preservation Project, Kathmandu. Kaiser Library ms no. 369. Reel no. C 40/2. Palmleaf. Newārī script. 80 folios numbered chaotically, missing folios 59, 64, 68, 70, 79, 80. 34.2 cm by 4.9 cm. 6-7 lines per page. 60-65 *akṣaras* per line. Incomplete. A microfilm was used. This ms is dated "631 *ratnamalladevasya vijayarājye* " (1511 A.D. Ratnamalla reigned 1482-1520 A.D. Cf. Bikrama Jit Hasrat, *History of Nepal*, p. xlvii, and D.R. Regmi, *Medieval Nepal*, vol. 1, pp. 455-467). This ms is jumbled and confused. For example, there is a gap in the text at folio 44b line 4 which is marked by half a line of *cakāras*. This gap runs from 9.16 to 11.38, but this omission is then inserted (without any special marking) after 12.51. The microfilm of this ms is photographed in incorrect order: folio 1 occurs after folio 37; folios 27-30 have no numbers; folio 10 is photographed twice; folio 36 is badly broken and photographed twice. After folio 37b what should be 38a is a blank leaf on which is written *dharmaśāstranepālibhāṣā kasmāt ko* (?). This folio is in a different hand and contains several dates. After this comes folio 1 followed by 38; folios 60 and 61 are reversed. Because of the chaotic nature of this ms it is unlikely that it played any significant role in the transmission of the text; therefore it was not fully collated.

B7 — Nepal German Manuscript Preservation Project, Kathmandu. Ms no. E-15723. Reel no. E 711/1. Paper. Devanāgarī script. 55 folios. 23 cm by 10.5 cm. 4 lines per page. 35 *akṣaras* per line. Incomplete. No date. A microfilm was used. The ms ends with 11.15.

B8 — Nepal German Manuscript Preservation Project, Kathmandu. Ms no. E-15724. Reel no. E 711/2. Paper. Newārī script. 182 folios, numbered 1-2, 4-8, 10-13, 15-185. Size unknown. 7 lines per page. 35 *akṣaras* per line. Incomplete. No date. A microfilm was used. The ms is more complete than it would appear from its numbering. The text is missing from 1.21 to 1.26. It contains a Newārī translation after each verse. Colophon:

> *idam alpadhiyā nṛṇāṃ durvijñeyaṃ yathoditaṃ* ǀ
> *nāradīyaṃ yad astīha nyāyaśāstramahārthavat* ǀǀ

nyāyaśāstraṃ samāptam.

B9 — Nepal German Manuscript Preservation Project, Kathmandu. Ms no. E-15725. Reel no. E 711/3. Newārī script. 37 folios, numbered 1-26, 28-38. 22.7 cm by 5 cm. 7 lines per page. 27 *akṣaras* per line. A microfilm was used. The short title given on the card before the first folio says, "Nāradasmṛti with Newari translation," but only the beginning and end of the ms are in Sanskrit; therefore it does not bear on the edition of this text. The ms is dated (Nepal) *saṃvat 714 kṛṣṇavadi* (?) *5 likhati vicarakocche* (?) *devajñaviṣṇusiṃhaguruṃ* (1594 A.D.). Colophon:

idam alpadhiyā nṛṇāṃ durvijñeyaṃ yathoditaṃ |
nāradīyaṃ yad astīha nyāyaśāstramahārthavat ||

nyāyaśāstram samāptaṃ.

BM — British Library, London. Ms no. Or.8. Cf. Cecil Bendall, *Catalogue of the Sanskrit Manuscripts in the British Museum*, p. 60, no. 169. Country made paper. Newārī script. 53 folios. 13.5 inches by 3 inches. 7-9 lines per page. 80 *akṣaras* per line. Complete. Dated (Nepal) *saṃvat* 820 (1699 A.D.). This ms contains the Sanskrit text with a Newārī translation after each verse. Colophon: *iti nāradaproktāyāṃ caurapratikhedhaṃ nāma prakaraṇaṃ samāptaṃ saṃvat 820 āṣāḍha kṛṣṇa 12.*

C — University Library, Cambridge University, Cambridge. Class-mark Add. 2137 (13). Palmleaf. Newārī script. 112 folios, numbered 1-4, 6-22, 24,25, 28-94, 96-117. 16.5 inches by 1.7 inches. 4-6 lines per page. 55-60 *akṣaras* per line. Incomplete. Dated (Nepal) *saṃvat 527 māghakṛṣṇaṣāṣṭhamyān tithau.* (1407 A.D.). A microfilm was used. This is the "Nepal ms" loaned to Jolly by Bendall (cf. the introduction to his edition pp. 5-8; his siglum for this ms was "N"). The text of the Nāradasmṛti begins at 5.8cd on folio 28a. The preceding text consists of a "text on *nyāya* " in Newārī. The colophon of this portion is also dated *saṃvat* 527. Folios 24b and 25 are in a different hand than the preceding and different than the text of Nārada which begins on folio 28a. The numbers on the left margin of the folios are in the *uttara licchavi* style. On the right they are written in *bhuñjimolla*, and arabic numerals have been added in the upper right corner. This ms contains a Newārī translation after each verse. The colophon reads in part:

idam alpadhiyāṃ nṛṇāṃ durvijñeyaṃ yathoditaṃ |
nāradīyaṃ yad astīha nyāyaśāstraṃ mahārthavat ||
tasyeyaṃ likhyate ṭīkā spaṣṭā nepālabhāṣayā |
imāṃ vijñāya bhūpādyāś carantu nyāyavartmanā ||

iti mānavanyāyaśāstre nāradaproktāyām saṃhitāyāṃ nyāyadharmapadāni samāptāni.

C1 — Asiatic Society of Bengal, Calcutta. Ms no. II.A.11. Cf. Kuñja Vihārī Nyāyabhūṣaṇa, *Catalogue of the Printed Books and Manuscripts Belonging to the Oriental Library of the Asiatic Society of Bengal*, p. 91. Paper. Bengali Script. 35 pages. 28 lines per page. 30 *akṣaras* per line. Complete. No date. No colophon. A microfilm was used.

C2 — Asiatic Society of Bengal, Calcutta. Ms no. II.D.82. Cf. Haraprasad Shastri, *Descriptive Catalogue of Sanskrit Manuscripts in the Government Collection under the Care of the Asiatic Society of Bengal*, vol. 3, p. 9. Paper. Devanāgarī script. 36 pages. 34 lines per page. 30 *akṣaras* per line. Complete. No date. A microfilm was used. Colophon: *iti śrīnāradīye dharmaśāstre prakīrṇakaṃ nāma vyavahārapadam aṣṭādaśaṃ samāptaṃ samāpteyaṃ nāradasmṛtiḥ.*

C3 — Asiatic Society of Bengal, Calcutta. Ms no. G-8054. Cf. Haraprasad Shastri, *op.cit.*, p. 10. Paper. Devanāgarī script. 58 folios. Size unknown. 7 lines per page. 35 *akṣaras* per line. Complete. No date. A microfilm was used. Colophon: *iti śrīnāradīye dharmaśāstre prakīrṇakaṃ nāma vyavahārapadam aṣṭādaśaṃ samāptaṃ śubhaṃ.*

C4 — Asiatic Society of Bengal, Calcutta. Ms no. G-8053. Cf. Haraprasad Shastri, *op.cit.*, p. 9. Paper. Newārī script. 41 folios, numbered 4-44. 12 inches by 4.75 inches. 7 lines per folio. 45 *akṣaras* per line. Incomplete. A microfilm was used. Very clearly written in a modern hand. The text begins with Nāradasmṛti 1.90. It is almost certainly a copy of ms **K**. For example, both mss have 19.19-26 between 19.29abc and 19.29d. In an attempt to correct the mistake of **K**, **C4** erases 19.29 abc and adds it before 19.29d, after 19.19-26. **C4** omits some verses which are present in **K**. Colophon: *iti mānavanyāyaśāstranāradaproktāyāṃ saṃhitāyāṃ nyāyadharmapadāni samāptāni. śubhasaṃvat 1027*[1] *jyeṣṭhamāsakṛṣṇapakṣadvitīyātithau pūrvabhādranakṣatre indrayoge bṛhaspativāsare mithanarāsau savitari dhanurāsigate candramasi etaddine idam poṣṭakaṃ* (sic) *sampūrṇāṃ likhitam iti śubha.* If this date is Nepal Saṃvat, it corresponds to 1907 A.D.

G — Ganganātha Jhā Research Institute, Allahabad. Ms no. *dharma* 43, S. no. 364. Paper copybook. Devanāgarī script. 43 folios. numbered 1-38, 1-5. 9 inches by 7 inches. 20 lines per page. 25 *akṣaras* per line. Complete. Dated June, 1913. A microfilm was used. This is a copy of ms **L4**. The copyist identifies himself as Śrī Prakāsa and notes that he made the copy "in two long sittings in the Trinity College Library (17th and 18th June 1913)." Colophon: *iti śrīnāradīyadharmaśāstre prakīrṇakanāmavyavahārapadam aṣṭādaśaṃ samāptaṃ. oṃ tat sat.*

H — Harvard University Library, Cambridge, Massachussetts. Ms no. Indic 56. Paper. Devanāgarī script. 24 lines per page. 22 *akṣaras* per line. Complete. Dated *saṃvat* 1879 (1822 A.D.). Colophon: *iti śrīnāradīye dharmaśāstre prakīrṇakanāmavyavahārapadam aṣṭādaśaṃ samāptaṃ. likhitaṃ lakṣmaṇaḥ vrā. sarvātmane namaḥ. saṃvat 1879.*

J — Śrī Raghunāth Temple Manuscript Library (also known as the Śrī Raṇavir Siṃha Saṃskṛtānusaṃdhāna Pustakālaya), Jammu. Ms no. 2527. Cf. M.A. Stein,

[1] Misquoted as 1887 by Haraprasad Shastri, yet correctly stated in his description of the ms (*loc.cit.*).

Catalogue of the Sanskrit Manuscripts in the Raghunātha Temple Library of His Highness the Mahārāja of Jammu and Kashmir, p. 92; also M.M. Patkar, *The Descriptive Catalogue of Sanskrit Manuscripts in the Shri Ranbir Sanskrit Research Institute*, vol. 2, pp. 402-3. Paper. Devanāgarī script. 40 folios. 9 lines per page. 42 *akṣaras* per line. Dated *saṃvat* 1912 (1855 A.D.). A microfilm was used. Colophon: *iti śrīnāradīyadharmaśāstre prakīrṇakanāmavyavahārapadam aṣṭādaśaṃ. samāptaṃ cedaṃ nāradīyaṃ dharmaśāstraṃ. śrīkṛṣṇārpaṇam astu. saṃvat 1912 mītī phālguna kṛṣṇa aṣṭamyāṃ.*

J2 — Śrī Raghunāth Temple Manuscript Library (also known as the Śrī Raṇavir Siṃha Saṃskṛtānusaṃdhāna Pustakālaya), Jammu. Ms no. 2617. Cf. M.A. Stein, *op. cit.*, p. 92; also M.M. Patkar, *op.cit.*, vol. 2, pp. 402-403. Paper. Devanāgarī script. 42 folios. 9 lines per page. 42 *akṣaras* per line. Complete. No date. A microfilm was used. Colophon: *iti śrīnāradīyadharmaśāstre prakīrṇakanāma-vyavahārapadam aṣṭādaśaṃ samāptaṃ. śubham astu.*

K — National Archives, Kathmandu. Ms no. pra 1231. Cf. Haraprasad Shastri, *A Catalogue of Palm-leaf and Selected Paper MSS. Belonging to the Durbar Library, Nepal*, vol.1 pp. 43-44; also Kaisher Bahadur, *The Judicial Customs of Nepal*, pp. 234-235. Palmleaf. Newārī script. 131 folios, numbered 11-144 (with two folios numbered 121 and two folios numbered 122), and six pages of *sūcīpattra*. 13.75 inches by 1.75 inches. 4 lines per page. 75 *akṣaras* per line. Dated Nepal *saṃvat* 500 (1380 A.D.). Incomplete. A microfilm was used. This ms contains a very brief Newārī "*ṭīkā* " after each verse. There was a folio out of order in the exemplar of this ms: 19.19-26 are found between 19.29abc and 19.29d. Colophon: *iti mānavanyāyaśāstre nāradaproktāyāṃ saṃhitāyāṃ nyāyadharma-padāni samāpnoti. nepālasthitirājamallanṛpati bhūpālacūḍāmaṇis tasyāmātya-varo 'rthikalpaddhiḍapī* (?) *sannītivārānidhiḥ. tasyārthamaṇikābhidhena kṛtinā nepālavārā kṛtā ṭīkā nyāyavikāsinī suvidinā brahmoktadharmasmṛti . . . . . svasti śrīnepālikasaṃvatsare 500 mi phālguna śukla tṛtīyāyāṃ guruvāsare śrījayasthiti-rājamalladevasya vijayarājye bhaktāpure amātyajayatavarmanaḥ pustakam idam lekhitam.* (D.R. Regmi, *Medieval Nepal*, vol. 1, p. 343 says that this corresponds to Saturday, February 9, 1380 A.D.).

K2 — National Archives, Kathmandu. Ms no. pra 1239 (? 7? 1?). Palmleaf. Newārī script. 76 folios, numbered 1-68, 76-83, plus a second 83. 32.5 cm by 4 cm. 4 lines per page. 55 *akṣaras* per line. No date. Complete, in spite of the odd numbering. A microfilm was used. This ms reverses the order of the last two chapters.

K3 — National Archives, Kathmandu. Ms no. 1249. Paper. Newārī Script. 93 folios. 12 inches by 3.5 inches. 9 lines per page. 36-42 *akṣaras* per line. Complete. Dated (Nepal) *saṃvat* 721 (1601 A.D.). A microfilm was used. This ms contains a Newārī translation after each verse. Colophon:

idam alpadhiyā nṛṇāṃ durvijñeyaṃ yathoditaṃ |

nāradīyaṃ yad astīha nyāyaśāstramahārthavān(vat?) ||
nyāyaśāstraṃ samāptaṁ.
ajñānato vadet sākṣī jñānato yadi gopyate |
ātmanaḥ sūkarī kṛtvā pitā yāsirasātalam ||
satyaṃ hanti sutaṃ hanti hanti puṇyapurākṛtaṃ |
svarge ca pitaraṃ hanti yat sākṣī anṛtaṃ vadet ||
saṃvat 721 phālgunaśuklaḥ.

K4 — Nepal German Manuscript Preservation Project, Kathmandu. Ms no. 2-69. Reel no. B 437/4. Paper. Devanāgarī script. 45 folios. 21.2 cm by 16.4 cm. 17 lines per page. 20 *akṣaras* per line. Complete. Date *saṃvat* 1883 (1826 A.D.). A microfilm was used. Nonsensical readings and peculiarities of transcription make this ms unreliable. For example, the final syllable of one verse is often written—after the double *daṇḍas* marking the end of the verse—as the first syllable of the next verse. It appears to be a poor transliteration of a Newārī ms by a scribe who was not familiar with that script.

K5 — Nepal German Manuscript Preservation Project, Kathmandu. Ms no. 1-1299. Reel no. B 415/17. Paper. Newārī script. 59 folios. 23.2 cm by 9.5 cm. 9 lines per page. 33 *akṣaras* per line. Complete. No date. A microfilm was used. Colophon: *śrīdharmaśāstraśuddhāśuddhiparaṃ samāptam iti.*

K6 — Nepal German Manuscript Preservation Project, Kathmandu. Ms no. 1-1183. Reel no. B 415/19. Paper. Newārī script. 17 folios, numbered 8, 10, 12, 15-18, 20-22, 24-27, 35, 15. Folios 35a, 35b, and 15 are sh. 23.3 cm by 8 cm. 7 lines per page. 30 *akṣaras* per line. Incomplete. No date. A microfilm was used. The first folio begins with 1.23. This ms, which is chaotic, is generally unreliable. It was not fully collated and does not bear on the constitution of this edition. Colophon: *iti mānave nyāyaśāstre śrīnāradaproktāyāṃ saṃhitāyāṃ nyāyadharmapadāni samāptāni.*

K7 — Nepal German Manuscript Preservation Project, Kathmandu. Ms no. 5-7345. Reel no. B 415/20. Paper. Newārī script. 104 folios. 26.3 cm by 8.9 cm. 7 lines per page. 40 *akṣaras* per line. Incomplete. No date. A microfilm was used. This ms contains a Newārī translation after each verse. The chapter on ordeals is missing.

L — India Office Library, London. IOL Sanskrit Ms no. 1322 (Eggeling no. 1322, I.O. no. 1300). Cf. Julius Eggeling, *Catalogue of the Sanskrit Manuscripts in the Library of the India Office, [vol.1] Part III. Saṃskṛit Literature: A. Scientific and Technical Literature. II. Rhetoric and Law*, p. 385. Paper. Devanāgarī script. 13.5 inches by 6 inches. 45 folios. 10 lines per page. 40 *akṣaras* per line. Complete. Dated *saṃvat* 1857 (1800 A.D.). This is a ms used by Jolly to which he gave the siglum "L". It is also one of the two mss he used to prepare his translation of the "short version" of the Nāradasmṛti. Colophon: *iti śrīnāradīye* *dharmaśāstre prakīrṇakaṃ nāma vyavahārapadam aṣṭādaśaṃ vivādapadaṃ samāptaṃ. śubham astu. śrīr astu. saṃvat. 1857. miti śrāvaṇakṛṣṇā- - -.*

L2 — India Office Library, London. IOL Sanskrit Ms no. 5372 (Keith no. 5372, Bühler no. 178). Cf. Arthur Berriedale Keith, *Catalogue of the Sanskrit Manuscripts in the Library of the India Office, vol. 2, part I. Vedic, Scientific, and Techn. Lit., Poetical Literature*, pp. 390-391. Paper. Devanāgarī script. 11.4 inches by 5.4 inches. 113 folios. 9 lines per page. 40 *akṣaras* per line. Incomplete. This is a copy of ms **P** dated on folio 113, *saṃvat* 1936 (1879 A.D.). It was Bīhler's personal copy and was used by Jolly for the preparation of his edition (see note to 1.12 in the companion Translation).

L3 — India Office Library, London. IOL Sanskrit Ms no. 5371 (Keith no. 5371, Bühler no. 176). Cf. Keith, *op. cit.*, p. 390. European paper, watermarked W. Revell. Devanāgarī script. 8 inches by 12.75 inches. 107 folios. 17 lines per page. 25 *akṣaras* per line. Complete. No date, but the catalogue states that the ms was copied about 1872 A.D. Colophon: *iti śrīnāradīye dharmaśāstre prakīrṇakaṃ nāma vyavahārapadaṃ saptadaśaṃ* (marginal correction fh to *aṣṭādaśaṃ*) *samāptam. samāpteyaṃ nāradasmṛtiḥ.*

L4 — India Office Library, London. IOL Sanskrit Ms no. 5370 (Keith no. 5370, Bühler no. 177). Cf. Keith, *ibid.*, p. 390. European paper, watermarked T.H. Saunders, 1863. The ms is dated *san* 1272. Since the catalogue says that this is a copy of a ms from Bengal, this is probably the Bengali era; thus the date would correspond to 1866 A.D. Devanāgarī script. 12.5 inches by 8 inches. 19 folios. 28 lines per page. 35 *akṣaras* per line. Complete. Jolly used this ms and gave it the siglum "y" or sometimes "Y". Colophon: *iti śrīnāradīye dharmaśāstre prakīrṇakaṃ nāma vyavahārapadam aṣṭādaśaṃ samāptam. iti tārik 13 phalguna san 1272 sāla. oṃ tat sat.*

M — Bayerische Staatsbibliothek, Munich. Cod. sanscr. 301. Paper. Devanāgarī script. 70 folios. 10.5 cm by 23 cm. 7 lines per page. 35 *akṣaras* per line. Complete. No date. Colophon: *iti śrīnāradīye dharmaśāstre prakīrṇakaṃ nāma vyavahārapadaṃ saptadaśaṃ samāptam. 17. dohā. rāmacandratho rāt ko jhāṃsī grāmasudhām. tat sutane lekhanakiyo mahāṃ 'devaśubhanām.*

M2 — Bayerische Staatsbibliothek, Munich. Cod. sanscr. 302. Paper. Devanāgarī script. 43 folios. 11.5 cm by 33 cm. 7 lines per page. 56 *akṣaras* per line. Complete. No date. The last folio has "copied from a m.s. belonging to Pandita Bāla Śāstrī of the Government Sanskrit College no date given." This is a ms which was used by Jolly, with the siglum s. Colophon: *iti śrīnāradīye dharmaśāstre prakīrṇakaṃ nāma vyavahārapadaṃ saptadaśam. samāptaṃ cedaṃ nāradīyaṃ dharmaśāstraṃ śrīmatsaṃkaṣṭanāśinī vijayatetarām.*

M3 — Bayerische Staatsbibliothek, Munich. Cod. sanscr. 302. Paper. Devanāgarī script. 43 folios. 11.5 cm by 33 cm. 7 lines per page. 56 *akṣaras* per line. Complete. Dated *saṃvat* 1260 (1203 A.D.). This ms has many Roman script notations and corrections, probably by Jolly who used it with the siglum C. Colophon: *iti śrīnāradīye dharmaśāstre prakīrṇakaṃ nāma vyavahārapadam aṣṭādaśam samāptaṃ oṃ namo gaṇeśāya. śrī pūrṇacandraguptena. vaiśākha san 1260 sāl.*

M4 — Bayerische Staatsbibliothek, Munich. Cod. sanscr. 304. Paper. Devanāgarī script. 114 folios. 16 cm by 23.5 cm. 11 lines per page. 40 *akṣaras* per line. Incomplete. No date. This is Jolly's copy of ms **P** (see note to 1.12 in the companion Translation). At the top of the first folio is written "*Abschrift von Deccan College Ms in S.R. Bhandarkars letztem Report (1904?).*" Cf. Julius Jolly, *Catalogus Codicum Manuscriptorum Bibliothecae Regiae Monacensis, tomi I pars VI: Die Sanksrit-Handschriften Nr. 287-413 der Königlich Hof- und Staatsbibliothek in München*, pp. 11-12. Colophon: *iti nāradīye dharmaśāstre kalyāṇabhaṭṭakṛtabhāṣye antevāsiprakaraṇaṃ samāptam. śubham astu.*

MT — Government Oriental Manuscripts Library, Madras. Ms no. R. no. 4325 (T-3-103/10 3/4 x 9 5/8). Paper copybook. Devanāgarī script. 241 pages. 20 lines per page. 30-35 *akṣaras* per line. Incomplete. Dated 1923-24. After the last page is written: "transcribed in 1923-24 from a ms. of Nārāyaṇa Nambudiri pada Purumallimana (?) Chadusseri (?) fort." This is the only ms I could obtain that includes Bhavasvāmin's commentary. It agrees very closely with K. Sāmbaśiva Śāstrī's edition of the text. The text breaks off before NMS 43.

Ox — Bodleian Library, Oxford University, Oxford. Shelf mark: Ms. Chandra Shum Shere C.263(3). Paper. Devanāgarī script. 56 folios, numbered 1-45, 1-10, and 9. Folios 1-45 are 18 inches by 10 inches; the remaining folios are 14.5 inches by 7.75 inches. A microfilm was used. This is a collection of folios from two different mss. Folios 1-45 have 9 lines per page and 35 *akṣaras* per line; the remaining folios have 8 lines per page and 43 *akṣaras* per line. Incomplete. No date. The first part, written with very poor ink which has faded to illegibility in places, ends at 15-16.9c. The second part, in a different hand, begins mid-word at 12.38a and ends mid-word at 15-16.23d; starts again mid-word at 17.2a and ends at 18.3d.

P — Bhandarkar Oriental Research Institute, Pune. Ms no. 27/1874-75. Paper. Devanāgarī script. 90 folios. 10 lines per page. 50 *akṣaras* per line. Incomplete. Dated *saṃvat* 1926 (1869 A.D.). A microfilm was used. The first folio, in a different hand, was copied either from **L2** or **M4** or from Jolly's edition after Kane consulted it for his *History of Dharmaśāstra* (first published in 1930; repeated in the second edition vol. 1 p. 547). The exemplar of this ms had a folio out of place, and this affected the commentary on 1.124-126. An antecedent of this ms must have marked vowels in the Bengali manner, for example तयोः would have been written as तयाः. This was not always clear to subsequent scribes, and nonsensical readings such as तायाः resulted. This ms was copied for Georg Bühler on the occasion of his search for mss in 1874-75. (Cf. Bühler, *Report on Sanskrit Manuscripts 1874/75*, p. 10). The date which it bears must be that of its exemplar. This ms contains Asahāya's commentary. The text breaks off at 5.19. It is the exemplar for **L2** and **M4**. Unless otherwise indicated, the mention of **P** includes its copies.

P2 — Fergusson College Library, Pune. No ms number. Paper. Devanāgarī script. 48 folios. 5.5 inches by 11.3 inches. 8 lines per page. 45 *akṣaras* per line. Complete. Dated *śaka* 1802 (1880 A.D.). A microfilm was used. A sheet accompanying the ms says "Copied from a ms in Poona by Joshi in śake 1802." Colophon: *iti śrīnāradīye dharmaśāstre prakīrṇakaṃ nāma vyavahārapadam aṣṭādaśaṃ samāptaṃ cedaṃ nāradīyaṃ dharmaśāstraṃ. śrīr astu. śubhaṃ bhavatu.*

R — Rajasthan Oriental Research Institute, Jodhpur. Ms no. 8410. 57 folios. 8.5 inches by 5.5 inches. 15 lines per page. 25 *akṣaras* per line. Complete. Dated *saṃvat* 1930 (1873 A.D.). A photocopy was used. Colophon: *iti śrīnāradīye dharṃaśāstre prakīrṇakaṃ nāma vyavahārapadaṃ saptadaśaṃ m 17. samāptaṃ cedaṃ dharmaśāstram. māghakṛṣṇāṣṭamyāṃ 8 ravivāsare saṃvat 1930. likhitam idan nandarāmaśarmaṇā śrīmaddhanumatsaiṃhavarmaṇoḥ śrīgovarddhano jayati śrīhariḥ.*

V — Sarasvatī Bhavana, Sampūrṇānanda Saṃskṛta Viśvavidyālaya, Varanasi. Ms no. 13358. Paper. Devanāgarī script. 26 folios. 12.7 cm by 5 cm. 11 lines per page. 52 *akṣaras* per line. Complete. No date. A photocopy was used. This is a carelessly copied ms. Folio 1a begins: *oṃ nā. 30 atha nāradīyasmṛtiḥ patre 26 pustakaṃ śrīkṛṣṇajośī rāmanaravāla*. Colophon: *iti śrīnāradīye dharmaśāstre prakīrnakanāmavyavahārapadam aṣṭādaśaṃ. samāptaṃ. śrīprasanna. patre 26.*

V2 — Sarasvatī Bhavana, Saṃpūrṇānanda Saṃskṛta Viśvavidyālaya, Varanasi. Ms no. 12168. Paper. Devanāgarī script. 6 folios, numbered 41-46. 3.5 inches by 8 inches. 8 lines per page. 25 *akṣaras* per line. Incomplete. No date. The text begins at 5.41 and breaks off at 11.6.

V3 — Sarasvatī Bhavana, Saṃpūrṇānanda Saṃskṛta Viśvavidyālaya, Varanasi. Ms no. 11872. Paper. Devanāgarī script. 42 folios, numbered 1-30 (with two folios numbered 8), 42-52, 54. 11.7 inches by 4.8 inches. 8-9 lines per page. 30 *akṣaras* per line. Dated *saṃvat* 1932 (1875 A.D.). A photocopy was used. The ms contains many minor corrections by a second hand. Text missing between 6.15ab and 12.93d. There is no folio 53, but no text is missing. Colophon: *iti śrīnāradīye dharmaśāstre prakīrṇakaṃ nāma vyavahārapadaṃ saptadaśaṃ. samāptaṃ cedaṃ nāradīyaṃ dharmaśāstraṃ. śrīmatsaṃkaṣṭanāśinī vijayate tagame* (sic). *granthaḥ samāptaḥ. śrī saṃvat 1932 mīti māghasudī 5 vārasomavāraḥ. granthasaṃkhyā 980.*

V4 — Sarasvatī Bhavana, Saṃpūrṇānanda Saṃskṛta Viśvavidyālaya, Varanasi. Ms no. 13520. Paper. Devanāgarī script. 24 folios. 7.5 inches by 3.5 inches. 16 lines per page. 37 *akṣaras* per line. Complete. Dated *saṃvat* 1868 (1811 A.D.). A photocopy was used. Folio 1a has: *idaṃ pustakaṃ bhaṭṭopanāmakadivākaraṃ. bhaṭṭānām iti sarvair vibhāvanīyam.* Colophon: *śrīḥ iti śrīnāradīye dharmaśāstre prakīrṇakaṃ nāma vyavahārapadam aṣṭādaśaṃ. samāpto 'yaṃ granthaḥ. saṃvat 18* ॥ *68* ॥ . . .

V5 — Sarasvatī Bhavana, Saṃpūrṇānanda Saṃskṛta Viśvavidyālaya, Varanasi. Ms no. 69590. Paper. Bengali script. 7 folios. 10.8 inches by 3.8 inches. 12 lines per page. 56 *akṣaras* per line. Incomplete. No date. A photocopy was used. The text breaks off at 1.117c.

V6 — Sarasvatī Bhavana, Saṃpūrṇānanda Saṃskṛta Viśvavidyālaya, Varanasi. Ms no. 68416. Paper. Devanāgarī script. 42 folios. 10.25 inches by 4.25 inches. 11-12 lines per page. 45 *akṣaras* per line. Complete. No date. A photocopy was used. Colophon: *iti śrīnāradīye dharmaśāstre prakīrṇakaṃ nāma vyavahārapadaṃ saptadaśam samāptaṃ cedaṃ nāradīyaṃ dharmaśāstraṃ śrīmatsakaṣṭanāśinī vijayate taṃ sam* (?).

V7 — Sarasvatī Bhavana, Saṃpūrṇānanda Saṃskṛta Viśvavidyālaya, Varanasi. Ms no. 67545. Paper. Devanāgarī script. 73 folios. 7.75 inches by 4 inches. 7-8 lines per page. 30 *akṣaras* per line. Complete. Dated *saṃvat* 1926 (1869 A.D.). Colophon: *iti śrīnāradīye dharmaśāstre prakīrṇakaṃ nāma vyavahārapadaṃ saptadaśam. samāptaṃ cedaṃ nāradīyaṃ dharmaśāstraṃ. saṃvat 1926.*

V8 — Sarasvatī Bhavana, Saṃpūrṇānanda Saṃskṛta Viśvavidyālaya, Varanasi. Ms no. 13210. Paper. Devanāgarī script. 55 folios, numbered 1-31, 1-13, 1-12a. 10.25 inches by 3.75 inches. 9 lines per page. 28-38 *akṣaras* per line. Incomplete. Dated *saṃvat* 1932 (1875 A.D.). Carelessly written. It is a collection of parts of three different mss. Folios 1-32 (numbered 1-31) are in a single hand, ending mid-word at 5.40d. The second part (numbered 1-13) is in a second hand and begins with the last *akṣara* of 6.15b, ending mid-word at 12.81a. The third part begins mid-word at 12.112b. Colophon: *iti śrīnāradīye dharmaśāstre prakīrṇakaṃ nāma vyavahārapadaṃ saptadaśaṃ. samāptaṃ cedaṃ nāradīyaṃ dharmaśāstraṃ. śrīmatsaṃkaṣṭanāśinī vijayate tāsam. granthaḥ samāptaḥ. śrī saṃvat 1932 mā vaiś ca.*—— Compare with the colophon of **V3**.

The following mss could not be used:
— Oriental Research Institute, University of Mysore, Mysore. Film no. N-2347. Ms no. P-3624. Palmleaf. Grantha script. 18 folios. 39 cm by 4 cm. 700 *granthas*. Worm-eaten and damaged. The microfilm was illegible, and a transcript could not be obtained.

— Oriental Institute, Baroda. Ms no.10041. Palmleaf. Grantha Script. 18 folios. 7 lines per page. 55-65 *akṣaras* per line. The microfilm was virtually illegible; it was not possible to obtain a transcript.

— H.R. Rangaswami Iyengar and T.T. Srinivasagopalachar, *A Descriptive Catalogue of the Sanskrit Manuscripts in the Government Oriental Library, Mysore*, vol. 2, Dharmaśāstra (smṛtis), pp. 40-43, no. 38 Nārada Smṛtiḥ. Palmleaf. 15.75 inches by 1 5/8 inches. Grantha script. 18 folios. 11 lines per page. 56 *akṣaras* per line. Complete. A copy could not be obtained.

— *List of Manuscripts Collected by the Curator for the Publication of Sanskrit Manuscripts, Trivandrum*. Published as appendixes to the Annual Administration Reports of the Travancore State (relating to the years 1100-1114 Kollam Era [1924-1938 A.D.]). Ms nos. 1100.6 (incomplete) and 1102.6 (incomplete, with Bhavasvāmin's commentary). Probably identical with T. Gaṇapati Śāstrī, *A Catalogue of Manuscripts Collected by the Curator for the Publication of Sanskrit Manuscripts, Trivandrum*; vol. 5, mss nos. 29 and 30. Copies of these mss could not be obtained.

— A. Cabaton, *Bibliothèque Nationale Département des Manuscrits. Catalogue Sommaire des Manuscrits Sanscrits et Pālis*, p. 139, "no. 842—Smṛti. Note de la main de Burnouf: Collection de smritis ou de recueils de lois Vichnu, Bharadvāja, Brihaspati, Dakcha, Yama, Likhita, Añgira, Nārada, Yadjñavalkya, en sanscrit et en caractères telingas . . . XVIIIe siècle. Ecriture telinga. 77 olles de 420 x 30 mm. 7 lignes. 40 à 45 akṣ (Sanscrit Telinga 38. — Burnouf, 66.)." According to the photoduplication section of the Bibliothèque Nationale, this ms could only be photographed by a special process.

— Amarendra Mohan Tarkatīrtha, *A Brief Catalogue of Sanskrit Manuscripts in the Post-Graduate Department of Sanskrit*, (Calcutta University). Ms no. 986. Paper. Bengali script. 52 folios, numbered 2-53. 13 inches by 5 inches. This ms was in such a state of deterioration that it was impossible even to examine it carefully without destroying it.

— Albrecht Weber, *Die Handschriften-Verzeichnisse der Königlichen Bibliothek zu Berlin. Fünfter Band. Verzeichniss der Sanskrit- und Prakrit-Handschriften*. vol. 2. p. 326-328. 2 mss. Copies of these mss could not be obtained.

— *Catalogue of Sanskrit Manuscripts in the Punjab University Library* (Lahore), vol. 1, p. 91, ms no. 318, Nāradasmṛti, 11-13 leaves(?), the last chapter (*antimādhyāya*). Vol. 2, app. p. 40, ms no. 656, Nāradasmṛti, 11 leaves, 350 *granthas*, palm leaf, *draviḍalipi*, third *adhyāya*. I did not have access to these mss.

— Hṛishīkeśa Śāstrī and Śiva Chandra Gui, *A Descriptive Catalogue of Sanskrit Manuscripts in the Library of the Calcutta Sanskrit College. Volume II Smṛti and Nīti*, pp. 15-16, no. 21 Nāradasaṃhitā—foolscap paper 16 inches by 4 inches (?). 19 folios. 8 lines. Bengali script. Complete. Colophon: *iti śrīnāradīye dharmaśāstre prakīrṇakaṃ nāma vyavahārapadam aṣṭādaśaṃ samāptaṃ oṃ namo gaṇeśāya oṃ*. This ms could not be located.

The following mansucripts could not be traced:
— Rajendralala Mitra, *Notices of Sanskrit MSS*, vol. 3, Calcutta, 1876, pp. 168-169. no. 1195. Country paper. 22 inches by 4 inches. 30 folios. 7 lines per page. 997 *ślokas*. Bengali script. Place of deposit: Calcutta, Bharatacandra Śiromaṇi.
— "Four parts of the diary of Pandit R.A. Śastri's tour in search of Sanskrit Manuscripts handed over to the Catalogus Catalogorum work," part 1, p. 107 and part 2 p. 211.
— Gustav Oppert, *Lists of Sanskrit Manuscripts in Private Libraries in Southern India*, vol. 1, mss nos. 1002, 5072, 6597, vol. 2, mss nos. 6313, 8496, 9600, 9823, 10317.
— Archibald Edward Gough, ed., *Papers relating to the Collection and Preservation of the Records of Ancient Sanskrit Literature in India.* From a classified catalogue of Sanskrit works in the library of the Mahāraja of Mysore dated 1869: "number 62, number in the old catalogue 540, grantha script, listed with 12 other 'minor' smṛtis," this volume comprises also a totally distinct work called *Sandhyābhāṣya by Nārāyaṇa.*
—*A Catalogue of Sanskrit Manuscripts in the North-Western Provinces.* Part V, Allahabad 1880. Appendix — "A Classified List of Mss. Purchased for the Library of Sanskrit College, Benares, from January, 1870, to April, 1880." pp.158-159 "No. 3 —Nāradasmṛti — 44 leaves—9 lines — original incomplete, rather recent, and incorrect."
—*A Catalogue of Sanskrit Manuscripts in Private Libraries of the North-West Provinces.* Compiled by Order of the Government, N.-W.P. part 1, Benares, 1874, p. 162-163: "No. 262—Nāradasmṛti—20 leaves—11 lines—paper—nāgarī. In the possession of Pūrṇānanda, Benares," and this tantalizing entry: "No. 265—Nāradasmṛtiṭippaṇa by Rāmanātha—29 leaves—5 lineṣ—paper—nāgarī. In the possession of Veṇi Datta, Benares."
— Four mss in the possession of private individuals used by K. Sāmbaśiva Śāstrī for his edition of the NMS.

The following mss proved to be of different texts:
— Oriental Research Institute, University of Mysore, Mysore. Ms no. P-3154/7. Palmleaf. Grantha script. 11 folios, numbered 38-50, numbers 48 and 49 are actually one folio. 36.5 cm by 4 cm. 7 lines per page. 55-65 *akṣaras* per line. Complete. No date. This is not the same Nāradasmṛti as the text edited here. Judging from the folio numbers, it is likely to be a part of some *smṛtisaṃgraha.*
— Oriental Research Institute and Manuscripts Library, University of Kerala, Trivandrum. Ms no. 5571. The Nāradasmṛti of this ms is a Vaiṣṇava text.
— H.R. Rangaswami Iyengar and T.T. Srinivasagopalachar, *A Descriptive Catalogue of the Sanskrit Manuscripts in the Government Oriental Library, Mysore*, vol. 2, pp. 40-43, no. 39. The same Vaiṣṇava text.
— *A Catalogue of the Sanskrit Manuscripts in the Adyar Library*. Part 1 By the Paṇḍitas of the Library, p. 101 "Nāradasmṛti — 9J 36 — devanāgarī — 76 leaves." The same Vaiṣṇava text.

GENEALOGICAL RELATION OF THE MANUSCRIPTS

The genealogy of the mss can be summarized in a *stemma codicum* as follows:

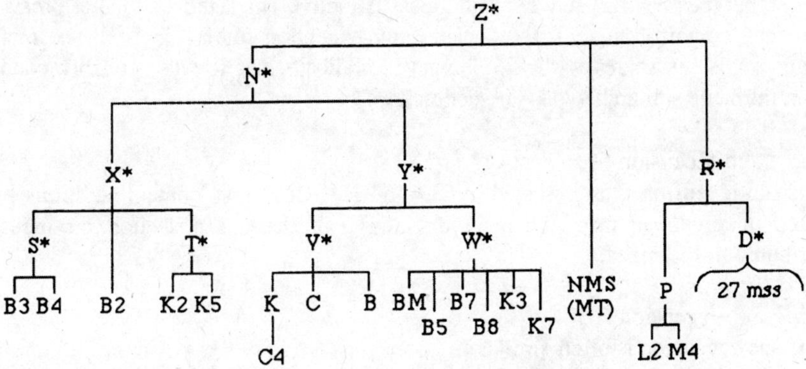

Note about the sigla: The mss represented by the sigla fall into three categories:

(1) The siglum NMS represents K. Sāmbaśiva Śāstrī's edition of the Nāradīyamanusaṃhitā.

(2) All other sigla without an asterisk represent mss which have been used for this edition.

(3) Those sigla with asterisks represent postulated archetypes and sub-archetypes.

This stemma is based on a close and systematic comparison of all of the mss described above. A few examples will illustrate the genealogical relation.

a Recension N*

The mss of sub-recensions **X*** and **Y*** (**B3**, **B4**, **B2**, **K2**, **K3**, **K**, **C4**, **C**, **B**, **BM**, **B5**, **B7**, **B8**, **K5**, and **K7**) have readings in common which are different than those of all other mss. All, except **B7**, are in Newārī script. Their most distinct trait is that they contain the separate final chapters on theft and ordeals. The only exception to this is **BM**, which omits the chapter on ordeals, but has the chapter on theft.[2] **N*** apparently added a corrupt summary of the prose introduction to Mātṛkā 1.[3] The full introduction is found only in **P**, but apparently came to be well-

2 **B7** and **K7** are incomplete in the end. Their other characteristics, however, clearly place them in recension **Y***. **NMS** incorporates the chapter on theft with the chapter on *prakīrṇaka*.

3 *āsīd idaṃ tamobhūtaṃ na prājñāyata kiṃcana* | [Manu 1.5ab]
tataḥ svayaṃbhūr bhagavān prādurāsīc caturmukhaḥ || [Manu 1.6ad]
ity evam ārabhya karmaprakāravyākhyātavyam tatra navamaṃ prakaraṇaṃ vyavahāro nāma yatremām ādau devarṣināradaḥ sūtrīyāṃ mātṛkāṃ cakāra asyā mukhaḥ.

known in the tradition fairly early.[4] The summary in **X*** and **Y*** of this introduction is so elliptical that it looks like a later addition to the text.[5]

aa Sub-recension **X*.**

This recension is comprised of three groups of mss derived from the postulated sub-archetypes **S*, B2,** and **T***. The most distinctive characteristic of these mss is that they contain Mātṛkā 1 and 2. The only exception to this is **K2.** The many features this ms shares with **K5**, however, indicate that it was probably copied from the same sub-archetype (see section **aac**).[6]

aaa Sub-recension **S*.**

This sub-recension is represented by **B3** and **B4**. Both mss contain additions not found in any other mss; the most distinctive of these is a section on ordeals attributed to Pitāmaha.[7]

aab Sub-recension **B2.**

This sub-recension is often similar to recensions **S*** and **T***, but it is different in several respects. For example, at 1.205 it agrees with **S*** and **T***, yet at 1.206 it omits an addition in **S*** and **T***; at 20.43 it omits an addition in **S*** and **T*** and adds a different, corrupt verse. There is occasional conflation between **B2** and **Y***; thus, at 20.10 **B2** agrees with **Y*** in adding two verses. There are occasions when **B2** has unique readings, such as four additional verses at 18.52, and the omission of 18.12. On rarer occasions **B2** agrees with **D*** (see the variants at 18.11). In addition to being a conflation of recensions and sub-recensions, **B2** is a ms carelessly written by an unintelligent scribe. Its value is thereby diminished.

aac Sub-recension **T*.**

This sub-recension is represented by mss **K2** and **K5**. In addition to readings that are unique but as viable as other readings (see, e.g., 1.110, 1.122, 1.148, 19.27, 19.61), this sub-recension is characterized by the omission of 1.53 and by the reversal of the order of the chapters on theft and ordeals.

ab Sub-recension **Y*.**

This recension is represented by sub-recensions **V*** and **W***. The most distinctive feature of these mss is that they do not contain Mātṛkā 1 or 2, except that they have

4 See the Introduction to the companion Translation.

5 This impression is reinforced by the absence of such a summary in NMS.

6 **B4** lacks the beginning of the text, yet the ratio of verses per folio indicates that the missing folios contained the two mātṛkas. **B**, **BM**, and **B5** have only the first verse of Mātṛka 1. Their other characteristics, however, clearly place them in recension **X***.

7 The Pitāmaha text is not included in this edition. It was edited, translated and annotated in my article,
"A Compilation of Pitāmaha Verses Found in Two Manuscripts from Nepal," SII 10 (1985), 103-132.

the crude summary common to the **N*** recension.[8] In addition to this **BM**, **B7**, **B8**, **K2**, **K3**, and **K7**, together with **K2** in sub-recension **T***, have:

asyāyam ādyaḥ ślokaḥ
dharmaikatānāḥ puruṣā yadāsan satyavādināḥ ।
tadā na vyavahāro abhūn na dveṣo nāpi matsaraḥ ॥

after which Chapter One begins. The only exception to this is **B**, which has only the verse "*āsīd idaṃ . . .* ",[9] and then proceeds to Chapter One (*ṛṇādānam*). All of these mss have other characteristics which clearly place them in sub-recension **Y***.[10]

aba Sub-recension **V***.

This sub-recension is represented by **K**, **C4**, **C**, and **B**. **C4** is a copy of **K**: both mss begin at 1.90, and have a folio out of order in the chapter on theft. **C4** contains additional scribal errors (such as carelessly written *repha* and *emātrā*: misplaced, or often left out), misreadings (see 19.2,17, 21, 24, 30, and 64), and corrections of **K** (see the description of **C4** above). Unique readings distinguish these mss from those representing sub-recension **W*** (e.g. 19.24 and 19.38).

abb Sub-recension **W***.

This sub-recension is represented by **BM**, **B5**, **B7**, **B8**, **K3**, and **K7**. It is characterized by unique omissions such as Mā 1.25, 1.113, 1.114, 1.133, 1.146; the reverse order of verses 1.18 and 1.19; as well as unique readings such as those found at 1.2, 1.10, 1.19, and 1.81.

b Recension **NMS**.

This recension is represented by the text of the edition of NMS. None of the mss used for that edition were traceable, and only one other ms belonging to this recension was discovered, **MT**. It is extremely close to **NMS**. Mss of this recension are from the extreme south of India. While the editor of NMS does not tell us much about the mss he used for his edition, it is almost certain that they were written in a southern script (see the Introduction to the companion Translation). The separate chapter on theft found in the mss of recension **N*** is not separate in **NMS**. It is incorporated in the "miscellaneous" chapter (*prakīrṇakam*). **NMS** is further characterized by omissions at 19.36, 19.66, Mā 3.8, 10; and 15-16.12-13; as well as unique readings at 12.9, 10, 13, 14, 17, 21, 22, 49, and 50.

c Recension **R***.

This recension consists of two branches, one represented by ms **P** and its copies, the other by sub-recension **D***. This recension is characterized by the incorporation of the treatment of ordeals in the chapter on debt. **D*** and **P** are distinguished from one another by (a) the fact that **P** is considerably longer—in those chapters that

8 Given above under footnote 3.
9 *Ibid*.
10 Due to the loss of its first few folios, **K** and its copy, **C4**, begin at 1.90. **C** begins at 5.8cd.

survive; (b) **P**'s inclusion of the unique Mātṛkā 2; and (c) numerous unique readings, *e.g.*, an additional verse after 1.22 in **D***.

ca Sub-recension **P**

This ms and its direct copies **M4** and **L2** include the commentary of Asahāya.

cb Sub-recension **D***

The mss of this sub-recension are the most numerous. They include most of the mss in devanāgarī script and the two mss in Bengali script (**C1** and **V5**). Variations in their readings are for the most part insignificant. This is the version to which Jolly referred as the "Vulgate."

CONSTITUTION OF THE TEXTS

THE NĀRADASMṚTI

This edition is an attempt to reconstruct the earliest possible recension of the Nāradasmṛti.

In those instances where the readings of the various recensions are equally viable I have followed the principle that the reading of the recensions represented by the mss of **X***, **Y***, and **NMS** are to be preferred. In those cases where there is disagreement among **X*** and **Y***, those readings which are common to **NMS** and one of these two recensions is preferred. The reason for this is that the wide separation geographically and orthographically between **NMS** (South India and *grantha* script) and **X*** and **Y*** (Nepal and Newārī script) makes it unlikely for shared readings to be the result of common innovations. These recensions are also the shortest, and since there is a pattern in *dharmaśāstra* whereby texts tend to increase in length over time, this is a further argument for accepting the readings attested in these recensions as the earliest surviving ones.[11]

I have not relied upon extrinsic testimonia in establishing the text. Not only was the evidence of the 47 mss enough to establish the text; if my view of the nature of the evolution of *mūlasmṛtis* is correct, the inclusion of extrinsic testimonia would distort the edition, and diminish its fidelity to the earliest possible recension.

The chapter divisions and titles are found in the mss. There are only two significant variations. (1) Mātṛkā 2 is found only in ms **P** and its copies. It is clearly an innovation. (2) Separate chapters on theft and on ordeals are found only in **X***, **Y***, and **NMS**, and are therefore included as part of the "original" text, Chapter 20. There are four different treatments of ordeals attributed to Nārada. The treatments of ordeals in **D*** and **P** represent later expansions on the chapter found

[11] For a fuller discussion of the growth of these texts and of the importance of geographical and orthographical separation of mss, see the Introduction to the companion Translation.

in **X***,**Y***, and **NMS**.[12] The treatment found in **NMS** is printed as a separate Appendix A rather than as variants to the more coherent version in **X*** and **Y***, in order to facilitate comparison with the other treatments.

THE COMMENTARY OF ASAHĀYA

The entire surviving fragment of the commentary of Asahāya is published here for the first time. Jolly included only extracts in his edition of the Nāradasmṛti, and often failed to indicate omissions. It should be noted that the text of Nārada on which Asahāya commented was very different from the "original" Nāradasmṛti. These variations are noted in the text and discussed in the notes to the translation. The edition of the commentary is based on the testimony of three mss— **P**, **L2**, and **M4**—, the latter two of which are direct copies of the corrupt, incomplete **P**. Emendations have been made in a number of places, and are duly noted.

CRITICAL APPARATUS

Sub-recensions and postulated archetypes are indicated in the stemma codicum above by an asterisk.[13] These sub-recensions include all of the mss listed below the sub-recension. Sub-recension **D*** includes 27 mss, i.e., most of the devanāgari and Bengali mss. Variations in the readings of these mss are, for the most part, insignificant. For this reason, I chose not to complicate further an already complex critical apparatus with these insignificant variants, except in those few cases in which particular readings had special noteworthy features.

There are two types of variant readings: (1) errors that are presumed not to have occurred in the earliest recension, i.e. errors introduced by scribes in the process of transmission of the text; and (2) readings which are not necessarily wrong and that could easily have occurred in the earliest recension. In general, the critical apparatus contains the latter type of reading. Except for a few troublesome places (e.g. 19. 31-32), clearly wrong or nonsensical readings, as well as mechanical errors such as the omission of *anusvāra* or *repha*, have not been noted, nor have the characteristic Newārī confusion between *ṣ* and *kh*, or the Bengali confusion of sibilants.

None of the mss follows the rules of *saṃdhi* with any consistency. *Saṃdhi* has been regularized in this edition with the exception of the ends of the first and third *pādas* of *ślokas*, where the *saṃdhi* is often irregular, and where the majority of mss retain these irregularities. Variations in *saṃdhi* are not noted in the critical apparatus, with the exception of the addition or omission of *avagraha*, which may have a bearing on the interpretation of the text.

12 For a discussion of the importance of the treatment of ordeals in tracing the evolution of the Nāradasmṛti, see the Introduction to the companion Translation.

13 The asterisk is not used in the critical apparatus to the text.

TYPOGRAPHICAL CONVENTIONS

The text of the Nāradasmṛti is printed in boldface. In the commentary, proper names are underlined. *Lemmata* are printed in boldface. Those portions of the commentary which are italicized are those which Asahāya took to be part of the text of the Nāradasmṛti. The *lemmata* for these portions are printed in italics as well. Passages which are hopelessly corrupt are marked with [?—>] at the beginning and [<—?] at the end. [?] indicates that the provenance of a verse is unknown. (?) indicates an uncertain reading. Emendations are marked in brackets < >. An asterisk (*) after a *lemma* indicates that the commentary is glossing a reading found in **P**, and that this reading has been rejected and is to be found in the variant readings. [*****] indicates a suspected omission.

ABBREVIATIONS

A	Asahāya.
add	adds, addition, added.
ABORI	*Annals of the Bhandarkar Oriental Research Institute*, Pune.
add	adds, addition, added.
ĀDha	*Āpastambadharmasūtra*, edited by Umeśa Candra Pāṇḍeya, KSS 93, ^{2}1969 ·
AgPur	*Agni Purāṇa*, edited by Jīvānanda Vidyāsāgara, Calcutta, 1882.
ALB	*Adyar Library Bulletin: Brahmavidyā*, Adyar.
All.	*Indian Law Reports, Allahabad Series.*
ALS	Adyar Library Series, Adyar.
Āna	*Ācāranavanīta*, by Appayadīkṣita, ms in the Sarasvatī Mahal Library, Tanjore, as cited in Dhko.
Apa	*Aparārka*, by Aparāditya (commentary on YāSmṛ) ĀSS 46, 1903.
ĀSS	Ānandāśrama Sanskrit Series, Pune.
AV	*Atharvaveda (Śaunaka)*, edited by Viśva Bandhu, Vishveshvarānanda Institute Series 13-17, 1960-64.
Bāla	*Bālambhaṭṭī*, by Bālambhaṭṭapāyaguṇḍe (commentary on Mitā), edited by S.S. Setlur, Madras, 1912.
Balakrīḍa	*Bālakrīḍā*, by Viśvarūpa (commentary on YāSmṛ), edited by T. Gaṇapati Śāstrī, TSS 74 and 81, 1922, 1924.
Bau	Baudhāyana.
BauDha	*Baudhāyanadharmasūtra*, edited by Umeśa Candra Pāṇḍeya, KSS 104, 1972.
BauVi	*Baudhāyanavivaraṇa*, by Govindasvāmi (commentary on BauDha), edited by L. Śrīnivāsācārya, BS 34, 1907.
BEFEO	*Bulletin de l'Ecole Française d'Extrême-Orient*, Hanoi, Paris.
Bhā	*Mahābhārata*, edited by V.S. Sukthankar, et al., Pune, 1933-1972.
BhāCa	*Manubhāvārthacandrikā*, by Rāmacandra (commentary on Manu), edited by V.N. Mandlik, Bombay, 1886.
BhāgPur	*The Śrīmad Bhāgavata Purāṇa*, edited by C.L. Goswami, Gorakhpur, 1971.
Bhava	Bhavasvāmin's commentary on NMS.
BHSD	*Buddhist Hybrid Sanskrit Grammar and Dictionary*, 2 volumes, by Franklin Edgerton, reprint Delhi, 1972.
BI	Bibliotheca Indica, Calcutta.
Bom.	*Indian Law Reports, Bombay Series.*
Bom. H.C.R.	*Bombay High Court Reports*, 1862-1875.
Bom.L.R.(J)	*Bombay Law Reporter* (Journal).

BORI	Bhandarkar Oriental Research Institute, Pune.
Brahma	*Brahmapurāṇa*, ĀSS 28, 1895.
Brahmāṇḍa	*Brahmāṇḍa Purāṇa*, edited by J.L. Shastri, Delhi, 1973.
Bṛhas	*Bṛhaspatismṛti (reconstructed)*, edited by K.V. Rangaswami Aiyangar, GOS 85, 1941.
BS	Bibliotheca Sanskrita, Mysore.
BSOAS	*Bulletin of the School of Oriental and African Studies*, University of London.
BSS	Bombay Sanskrit Series, Bombay.
CaDā	*Caturvargacintāmaṇi Dānakhaṇḍa*, see CaVarCint.
CaKā	*Caturvargacintāmaṇi Kālakhaṇḍa*, see CaVarCint.
CaMa	*Caturviṃśatimatasaṃgraha*, by Bhaṭṭojīdīkṣita, edited by Devīdatta Parājuli, Benares Sanskrit Series 33, 1907-8.
Candra	*Vivādacandra*, by Misaru Miśra, edited by Jayanandana Śarmā, Patna, 1931.
CaŚrā	*Caturvargacintāmaṇi Śrāddhakhaṇḍa*, see CaVarCint.
CaVarCint	*Caturvargacintāmaṇi*, by Hemādri, edited by Bharatacandra Śiromaṇi, Yogeśvara Bhaṭṭācārya, Kāmākhyānātha Tarkaratna, Yajñeśvara Smṛtiratna, and Pramathanātha Tarkabhūṣaṇa, BI 72, 1873-1911.
CC	*Catalogus Catalogorum*, by Theodor Aufrecht, reprint Wiesbaden, 1962.
CHLT	*Collection of Hindu Law Texts*, series editor, J.R.Gharpure, Bombay.
ChSS	Chowkhamba Sanskrit Series.
comm	comment, commentary.
D	the recension of the *Nāradasmṛti* found in most of the *devanāgarī* mss, Jolly's "vulgate".
Dā	*Dāyabhāga*, by Jīmūtavāhana, edited by Jīvānanda Vidyāsāgara, Calcutta, [2]1893.
DaCa	*Dattakacandrikā*, by Kubera, edited by Yajñeśvara Bhaṭṭācārya, Calcutta, [2]1885.
DāNi	*Dāyabhāganirṇaya*, by Bhaṭṭojīdīkṣita, microfilm of BORI ms 84 of1895-98.
DaNī	*Daṇḍanītiprakaraṇa*, by Keśava Paṇḍita, edited by V.S. Bendrey, Pune, 1959.
DāTa	*Dāyatattva*, by Raghunandana Bhaṭṭācārya, edited by Jīvānanda Vidyāsāgara, Calcutta, 1895.
DaVi	*Daṇḍaviveka*, by Vardhamāna, edited by Kamalakṛṣṇa Smṛtitīrtha, GOS 52, 1931.
DeSmṛ	*Devalasmṛti*, as printed in *Smṛtīnām Samuccayaḥ*, edited by Vināyaka Gaṇeśa Āpaṭe, ĀSS 48, 1929.
deva	devanāgarī.
DhāPā	*The Dhātupātha* in *Pāṇini's Grammatik*, edited by Otto Böhtlingk, reprint Hildesheim, 1971.

Dhko	*Dharmakośa*, Volume One (unless otherwise specified) in 3 parts, edited by Laxman Śāstrī Joshi, Wai, 1937-1941.
DīKa	*Dīpakalikā*, by Śūlapāṇi, edited by J.R. Gharpure, CHLT 26, 1939.
DiTa	*The Divyatattva of Raghunandana Bhaṭṭācārya: Ordeals in Classical Hindu Law*, edited by Richard W. Lariviere, Delhi, 1981.
ECMHL	*Essays in Classical and Modern Hindu Law*, 4 volumes, by J.D.M. Derrett, Leiden, 1976-1978.
F.B.	Full Bench.
fh	first hand.
GaBhā	*Gadādharabhāṣya*, by Gadādhara (commentary on Pāraskaragṛhyasūtra), edited by Mahādeva Gaṅgādhāra Bākre, Bombay ,1917.
GauDha	*Gautamadharmasūtra*, edited by Narahara Taḷekar, ĀSS 61, 1966.
GauMi	*Gautamadharmasūtramitākṣarāṭīkā*, by Haradatta, edited by Narahara Taḷekar, ĀSS 61, 1966.
GoRā	*Govindarājīya*, by Govindarāja (commentary on Manu), edited by V.N. Mandlik, Bombay, 1886.
GOS	Gaekwad's Oriental Series, Baroda.
GṛhaKa	*Gṛhasthakalpataru*, by Lakṣmīdhara, edited by K.V. Rangaswaṁi Aiyangar, GOS 101, 1944.
GṛhaRa	*Gṛhastharatnākara*, by Caṇḍeśvara Ṭhākkura, edited by Kamalakṛṣṇa Smṛtitīrtha, BI 249, 1928.
GṛSaṃPa	*Gṛhyasaṃgrahapariśiṣṭa* by Gobhilaputra, edited by Maurice Bloomfield, ZDMG 35 (1881) 533-587.
Hāra	*Hāralatā*, by Aniruddha Bhaṭṭa, edited by Kamalakṛṣṇa Smṛtitīrtha, BI 176, 1909.
HDh	*History of Dharmaśāstra*, 5 volumes, by P.V. Kane, Pune, [2]1968 - [2]1975.
I.A.	*Indian Appeals*.
IIJ	*Indo-Iranian Journal*, Dordrecht.
IOL	India Office Library, London.
J	Jolly, Jolly's verse number in his edition of the Nāradasmṛti.
JBBRAS	*Journal of the Bombay Branch of the Royal Asiatic Society*.
JESHO	*Journal of the Economic and Social History of the Orient*, Leiden.
JILI	*Journal of the Indian Law Institute*, Delhi.
JOIB	*Journal of the Oriental Institute*, Baroda.
JRAS	*Journal of the Royal Asiatic Society*, London.
KāNī	*The Nītisāra, or the Elements of Polity by Kāmandaki*, edited by Rājendralāla Mitra, BI 4, 1861.
KāSmṛ	*Kātyāyanasmṛti (reconstructed)*, by P.V. Kane, Pune, n.d.

Kau	the author Kauṭilya, or *Kauṭilīya Arthaśāstra*, 3 volumes, edited by R.P. Kangle, Bombay, [2]1969 , [2]1971 , 1965.
KLT(J)	*Kerala Law Times* (Journal).
KSS	Kashi Sanskrit Series, Benares.
L2	a ms copy of Asahāya's commentary. See the Introduction to the companion Edition.
L.R.I.A.	*Law Reports, Indian Appeals* (Privy Council).
M4	a ms copy of Asahāya's commentary. See the Introduction to the companion Edition.
Mā	Mātṛkā.
MaBhā	*Maskaribhāṣya on Gautamadharmasūtra*, edited by L. Śrinivasacharya, BS 50, 1917.
MaCa	*Manvarthacandrikā*, by Rāghavānanda (commentary on Manu), edited by V.N. Mandlik, Bombay, 1886.
Mad.	*Indian Law Reports, Madras Series*.
MaMu	*Manvarthamuktāvalī*, by Kullūkabhaṭṭa (commentary on Manu), edited by V.N. Mandlik, Bombay, 1886.
Manu	the author Manu, or *Manusmṛti*, edited by Vāsudeva Paṇaśīkara Śarmā, Bombay, [5]1915.
MaPā	*Madanapārijāta*, by Viśveśvarabhaṭṭa, edited by P.K. Malla, Lucknow, 1886.
MaPu	*Matsyapurāṇa*, edited by Jīvānada Vidyāsāgara, 1876.
MaRa	*Madanaratna*, by Madanasiṃhadeva, as cited in Dhko volume 3.
MāSo	*Mānasollāsa*, by Bhūlokamalla Someśvara, edited by G.K. Shrigondekar, GOS 28, 84,138, 1967,1939,1961.
MaVi	*Manvarthavivaraṇa*, by Sarvajñanārāyaṇa (commentary on Manu), edited by V.N. Mandlik, Bombay, 1886.
Maya	*Mayamata*, by Mayamuni, edited by T. Ganapati Shastri, TSS 65, 1919.
mc	marginal correction.
Medhā	*Manusmṛtibhāṣya* by Medhātithi (commentary on Manu), edited by V.N. Mandlik, Bombay, 1886.
Mitā	*The Mitākṣarā commentary on the Yājñavalkyasmṛti*, edited by Narayan Ram Acharya, Bombay, [5]1949 .
mn	marginal note.
ms(s)	manuscript(s).
MU	*Muṇḍaka Upaniṣad*, in *Eighteen Principal Upaniṣads*, volume 1, edited by V.P. Limaye and R.D. Vadekar, Pune, 1958.
Muktā	*Smṛtimuktāphala*, by Vaidyanātha Dīkṣita, edited by J.R. Gharpure, CHLT 25, Bombay, 1937-1940.
NāBhā	see NMS.
NāMā	the Mātṛkā in Jolly's edition of the Nāradasmṛti.
Nanda	*Nandinī*, by Nandanācārya, (commentary on Manu), edited by V.N. Mandlik, Bombay, 1886.
NāSmṛ	the present translation and companion Edition of the Nāradasmṛti.

NCC	*New Catalogorus Catalogorum: An Alphabetical Register of Sanskrit and Allied Works and Authors*, vols 1-5 (1949-1969) edited by V. Raghavan, vols 6-10 (1971-1978) edited by K. Kunjunni Raja, Madras.
NīTī	Nīlakaṇṭha's commentary on Bhā, Bombay, 1878-1888.
NMS	*The Nāradīyamanusaṃhitā with the Bhāṣya of Bhavasvāmin*, edited by K. Sāmbaśiva Śāstrī, TSS 97, 1929.
NṛPra	*Nṛsiṃhaprasādaḥ: Vyavahārasāraḥ*, by Śrī Dalapatirāja, edited by Vināyaka Śāstrī Tillū, Princess of Wales Sarasvatī Bhavana Series 53, Benares, 1934.
n.s.	new series
no(s).	number(s).
om	omits, omitted.
P	a ms copy of Asahāya's commentary on the Nāradasmṛti. See the Introduction to the companion Edition.
PaMā	*Parāśaradharmasaṃhitā with the commentary of Sāyaṇa Mādhavācārya*, edited by Vāman Śāstrī Islāmpurkār and R.G. Bhandarkar, BSS 47,48,59,64,67, 1983-1919.
Paṇha	*Praśnavyākaraṇasūtra*, by Sudharmasvāmin, Bombay, 1916.
PiSmṛ	*Die Fragmente des Pitāmaha*, by Karl Scriba, Leipzig, 1902.
Pitā	Pitāmaha.
PraKā	*Vyavahāraprakāśa*, by Śarabhojī, as cited in Dhko.
PraPā	*Prayogapārijāta*, by Nṛsiṃha, edited by Vāsudeva Śarmā, Bombay 1916.
PraRa	*Prayogaratna*, by Nārāyaṇabhaṭṭa, edited by Vāsudeva Śarmā, Bombay, 1915.
PSM	*Pāia Sadda Mahaṇṇavo*, by Hargovind Das Sheth, Prakrit Text Society Series 7, Benares, 1963.
PuMa	*Puruṣārthacintāmaṇi*, by Viṣṇubhaṭṭa, edited by Vāsudeva Śarmā, Bombay, 1906.
R	a family of largely devanāgarī mss. See the Introduction to the companion Edition.
Raghuvaṃśa	*The Raghuvaṃśa*, by Kālidāsa, edited by Jīvānanda Vidyāsāgara, Calcutta, 1902.
RāKau	*Rājadharmakaustubha*, by Anantadeva, edited by Kamalakṛṣṇa Smṛtitīrtha, GOS 72, 1935.
Rām	*The Vālmīkirāmāyaṇa*, 7 volumes, edited by G.H. Bhatt, U.P. Shah, et al., Baroda, 1960-1975.
RāRa	*Rājanītiratnākara*, by Caṇḍeśvara, edited by K.P. Jayaswal, Patna, 1936.
RāTar	*Rājataraṅgiṇī*, by Kalhaṇa, 2 volumes, edited by Vishva Bandhu, Woolner Indological Series 5, Hoshiarpur,1963,1965.
Ratna	*Madanaratna*, by Madanasiṃhadeva, as cited in Dhko.
RLS	*Religion, Law and the State*, by J.D.M. Derrett, New York, 1968.

RV	*Ṛgvedasaṃhitā*, 5 volumes, Pune, Vaidika Saṃśodhana Maṇḍala, 1936-1972.
ŚaLi	*Śaṅkhalikhitau*, as printed in *Smṛtīnāṃ Samuccayaḥ*, edited by Vināyaka Gaṇeśa Āpaṭe, ĀSS 48, 1929.
SaṃGa	*Saṃskāragaṇapati*, by Rāmakṛṣṇabhaṭṭa (commentary on the Pāraskaragṛhyasūtra), edited by Richard Simon, Kiel, 1889.
SaṃKau	*Saṃskārakaustubha*, by Anantadeva, Bombay, 1913.
SaṃMa	*Saṃskāramayūkha*, by Nīlakaṇṭha, edited by Narahari Śāstrī Śeṇḍe, Bombay, 1913.
SaṃPra	*Saṃskāraprakāśa*, by Mitramiśra, edited by Viṣṇu Prasāda Śarmā, ChSS 30.1, 1906-32.
SaṃRa	*Saṃskāraratnamālā*, by Gopināthabhaṭṭa, edited by K.S. Āgāśe, B.S. Phaḍake, and H.N. Āpaṭe, ĀSS 39, 1899.
SaṃTa	*Saṃskāratattva*, by Raghunandana Bhaṭṭācārya, edited by Jīvānanda Vidyāsāgara, Calcutta, 1985.
Samu	*Vyavahārārthasamuccaya*, by Śarabhojī, as cited in Dhko.
SaṃVa	*Saṃskāravatsa*, by Keśavadāsa, as cited in Dhko.
SāPra	*Sāpiṇḍyapradīpa*, by Nāgojībhaṭṭa, as cited in Dhko.
SaVi	*Sarasvatīvilāsa*, by Pratāparudra, edited by R. Shama Sastry, Oriental Library Sanskrit Series 71, Mysore, 1927.
SBE	*Sacred Books of the East*, Delhi (reprints).
SBE 33	*The Minor Law Books*, translated by Julius Jolly, reprint Delhi, 1969.
S.C.	*All India Reporter, Supreme Court.*
Setu	*Vivādārṇavasetu*, as cited in Dhko.
sh	second hand.
SII	*Studien zur Indologie und Iranistik*, Reinbek.
SiKau	*Siddhānta Kaumudī of Śrī Bhattojī Deekshita, with the Commentary Śrī Bālamanoramā of Śrī Vasudeva Deekshita. Pūrvārdham*, edited by S. Chandrasekhara Sastrigal, Trichinopoly, 1910.
Śilpa	*Śilparatna*, by Śrīkumāra, edited by T.Ganapati Śāstrī, TSS 75, 98, 1922-29.
Sindhu	*Nirṇayasindhu*, by Kamalākarabhaṭṭa, edited by Gopāla Śāstrī Neṇe, ChSS 52, 1919-1930.
SmṛCa	*Smṛticandrikā*, by Devaṇṇabhaṭṭa, edited by L. Srinivasacharya, BS 43-45, 48, 52, 56, 1914-1921.
SmṛCi	*Smṛticintāmaṇi*, by Gaṅgāditya, edited by Ludo Rocher, GOS 161, 1976.
SmṛSā	*Smṛtisāra*, by Haranātha, IOL Sanskrit ms no. 1489, as cited in Dhko.
ŚrīMū	*Śrīmūla*, by T. Gaṇapatiśāstrī (modern commentary on Kau), TSS 78, 80,82, 1924-25.
sub	substitute, substituted.

Subo	*Subodhinī*, by Viśveśvarabhaṭṭa (commentary on Mitā), edited by J.R. Gharpure, CHLT 4, 1930.
ŚuNī	*Śukranītisāra*, edited by Gustav Oppert, Madras, 1882.
Śuśruta	*Śuśrutasaṃhitā*, edited by Bhaskar Govind Ganekar, Delhi, ^{2}1952.
TaiSaṃ	*Kṛṣṇayajurvedīyataittirīyasaṃhitā*, ĀSS 42, ^{3}1959- ^{3}1978 .
TLL	Tagore Law Lectures.
TSS	Trivandrum Sanskrit Series.
typo	typographical error.
U	*Ujjvalā*, by Haradatta Miśra (commentary on ĀDha), edited by Umeśa Candra Pāṇḍeya, KSS 93, ^{2}1969.
Uta	*Udvāhatattva*, by Raghunandana Bhaṭṭācārya, edited by Jīvānanda Vidyāsāgara, Calcutta, 1895.
Vai	*Vaijayantī*, by Nandapaṇḍita (commentary on ViSmṛ), edited by V. Krishnamacharya, ALS 93, 1964.
Vaikhā	*Vaikhānasasmārtasūtra*, edited by W. Caland, BI 242, 1927; translation by Caland, BI 251, 1929.
VāRā	*Vālmīkīyarāmāyaṇa*, see Rām.
VaSmṛ	*Vāsiṣṭhasmṛti*, edited by Alois Anton Führer, BSS 23, ^{2}1916 .
Vedavyā	*Vedavyāsasmṛti*, as printed in *Smṛtīnāṃ Samuccayaḥ*, edited by Vināyaka Gaṇeśa Āpaṭe, ĀSS 48, 1929.
ViBha	*Vivādabhaṅgārṇava*, by Jagannātha, as cited in Dhko.
ViBhā	Viśvanātha's commentary on Pāraskaragṛhyasūtra, edited by Mahādeva.Gaṅgādhara Bākre, Bombay, 1917.
ViCa	*Vivādacandrikā*, by Anantarāma, microfilm of ms in the Prajñā Pāṭhaśālā Maṇḍala, Wai, Maharashtra. (This is a transcript of IOL Sanskrit ms no 1278b.)
ViCi	*Vivādacintāmaṇi*, by Vācaspati Miśra, edited by Lakṣmīkānta Jhā, Patna, 1937.
ViDhPu	*Viṣṇudharmottarapurāṇa*, Bombay, Veṅkaṭeśvara Press, n.d.
VīMi	*Vīramitrodaya*, by Mitra Miśra (commentary on the YāSmṛ), edited by N.S. Khiste, ChSS 62, 1930.
VīMiPari	*The Vīramitrodaya Paribhāṣāprakāśa*, by Mitra Miśra, edited by Parvatīya Nityānanda Śarmā, ChSS 30.1, 1906.
ViPā	*Vidhānapārijāta*, by Anantabhaṭṭa, edited by Tāraprasanna Vidyāratna (vols. 1 and 2) and Īśvaracandra Śāstrī (vol. 3), BI 156 (vols. 1 and 2) and 273 (vol. 3), 1903-1911 and 1951.
ViPu	*Viṣṇupurāṇa*, Bombay, Veṅkaṭeśvara Press, 1910.
ViRa	*Vivādaratnākara*, by Caṇḍeśvara, edited by Kamala Kṛṣṇa Smṛtitīrtha, BI 103, 1931.
ViSau	*Vivāhasaukhya*, by Ṭodaramalla, as cited in Dhko.
ViSmṛ	*Viṣṇusmṛti*, edited by V. Krishnamacharya, ALS 93, 1964.
Viśvarūpa	*Yājñavalkyasmṛti with Ṛjumitākṣarā*, by Vijñāneśvara, *Bālakrīḍā*, by Viśvarūpa, *Bālambhaṭṭī*, by Vaidyanātha

	Pāyaguṇḍe, and *Subodhinī*, by Viśveśvara Bhaṭṭa, edited by S.S. Setlur, Madras, 1912.
ViTā	*Vivādatāṇḍava*, by Kamalākarabhaṭṭa, edited by Maṇilāl Nabhubhai Dvivedi, Baroda, 1901.
ViVya	*Vivādavyavahāra*, by Gopālasiddhāntavāgīśa, microfilm of BORI ms no. 356 of 1887-91.
VVRI	Vishveshvarananda Vedic Research Institute, Hoshiarpur.
VyaCi	*Vyavahāracintāmaṇi*, by Vācaspati Miśra, edited by Ludo Rocher, Gentse Orientalistische Bijdragen 1, Gent, 1956.
VyaKa	*Kṛtyakalpataru*, by Bhaṭṭa Lakṣmīdhara, volume XII, *Vyavahārakāṇḍa*, edited by K.V. Rangaswami Aiyangar, GOS 119, 1953.
VyaMa	*Vyavahāramayūkha*, by Bhaṭṭa Nīlakaṇṭha, edited by P.V. Kane, BSS 80, 1926.
VyaMā	*Vyavahāramātṛkā*, by Jīmūtavāhana, edited by Asutosh Mukherjee, Memoirs of the Asiatic Society of Bengal, volume III, no. 5, Calcutta, 1912.
VyaNi	*Vyavahāranirṇaya*, by Varadarāja, edited by K.V. Rangaswami Aiyangar and A.N. Krishna Aiyangar, ALS 29, 1942.
VyaNir	*Vyavahāranirṇaya*, by Mayārāma, microfilm of BORI ms 140 of 1892-95.
VyaPra	*Vīramitrodaya*, *Vyavahāraprakāśa*, by Mitra Miśra, edited by Viṣṇu Prasāda Bhāṇḍārī, ChSS 30.7, 1929-30.
Vyāsa	*Vyāsasmṛti*, edited by Batakrishna Ghosh, Calcutta, 1944.
VyaSau	*Vyavahārasaukhya*, by Ṭoḍaramalla, as cited in Dhko.
VyaTa	*Vyavahāratattva*, by Raghunandana Bhaṭṭācārya, edited by Jīvānanda Vidyāsāgara, Calcutta, 1895.
VyaU	*Vyavahāroddyota* or *Vyavahārakāṇḍa* of the *Dinakaroddyota*, by Dinakarabhaṭṭa, microfilm of ms in the Prajñā Pāṭhaśālā Maṇḍala, Wai, Maharashtra.
W	the sub-recension of the NāSmṛ represented by mss BM B5 B7 B8 K3 K7
X	a family of Newārī mss. See the Introduction to the companion Edition.
Y	a family of Newārī mss. See the Introduction to the companion Edition.
Yājña	Yājñavalkya.
YāSmṛ	*Yājñavalkyasmṛti*, edited by Narayan Ram Acharya, Bombay, ^{5}1949.
WIS	Woolner Indological Series, VVRI, Hoshiarpur.
Z*	the postulated original archetype of the NāSmṛ.
ZDMG	*Zeitschrift der Deutschen Morgenländischen Gesellschaft*, Wiesbaden.
ZVR	*Zeitschrift für vergleichende Rechtswissenschaft*, Leipzig, Stuttgart.

मातृका

१ व्यवहारः

[श्रीगणेशाय नमः ।
ॐ नमो विनायकाय ।
नमः सकलकल्याणहेतवे वृषकेतवे ।
अमोघासारदुष्पारसंसाराम्भोधिसेतवे ।।
सर्वप्रकरणारम्भसिद्धिबुद्धिविधायिने ।
सगिरिगणनाथाय नमः कल्याणदायिने ।।

यः संख्याव्यवहारविस्तरगतौ योऽष्टादशाख्यैः पदैर्द्वात्रिंशाख्यैः पदैर्[1] द्वात्रिंशच्छतभेदभिन्नपदकैरुक्तश्च तन्निर्णयः । सोऽस्मिन्नेव महर्षिनारदकृते शास्त्रे परं नापरे कल्याणोऽवददेतदत्र भुवनेऽपयर्धां विधायङ्गुलिम् । दृष्ट्वासहायरचितं नारदभाष्यं कुलेखकैर्भ्रष्टं कल्याणेन क्रियते प्राक्तनमेतद्विशोध्य पुनः ।] इह ह[2] स्माह[3] भगवान्मनुः प्रजापतिः[4] सर्वभूतानुग्रहार्थमाचारस्थितिहेतुभूतं शास्त्रं चकार । यत्रादौ[5] **लोकसृष्टिर्भूतप्रविभागः सद्देशप्रमाणं**[6] परिषल्लक्षणं[7] वेदवेदाङ्गयज्ञविधानमाचारो **व्यवहारः** कण्टकशोधनं राजवृत्तं **वर्णधर्माश्रमप्रविभागो**[8] विवाहन्यायस्त्रीपुंसविकल्पो दायादनुक्रमः[9] श्राद्धविधानं[10] शौचविकल्पो[11] भक्ष्याभक्ष्यलक्षणं विक्रयाविक्रेयमीमांसा पातकभेदाः स्वर्गनरकानुदर्शनं प्रायश्चित्तान्युपनिषदो रहस्यानीत्येवं चतुर्विंशति प्रकरणानि । तदेतत् श्लोकशतसहस्रमासीत्तेनाध्यायसहस्रेण मनुः प्रजापतिरुपनिबध्य[12] देवर्षये नारदाय प्रायच्छत्[13] स च तस्मादधीत्य महत्वान्नायं ग्रन्थः सुकरो मनुष्याणां शक्यो[14] धारयितुमिति द्वादशभिः सहस्रैः संचिक्षेप[15] । तच्च[16] सुमतये[17] भार्गवाय प्रायच्छत्स[18] चतस्मादधीत्य तथैवायुर्ह्रासादल्पीयसी[19] मनुष्याणां शक्तिरिति ज्ञात्वा[20] चतुर्भिः सहस्रैः संचिक्षेप । तदेतत्पितृमनुष्या ह्यधीयन्ते[21] विस्तरेण शतसहस्रं देवगन्धर्वादयो यत्रायमाद्यः श्लोको भवति ।

आसीदिदं[22] तमोभूतं न प्राज्ञायत किंचन । **[Manu 1.5ab]**
ततः स्वयंभूर्भगवान्प्रादरासीच्चतुर्मुखः[23] ।। **[Manu 1.6ad]**

इत्येवमधिकृत्य क्रमात्प्रकरणात्[24] प्रकरणमनुक्रान्तम् । तत्र तु नवमं प्रकरणं व्यवहारो नाम यस्येमामादौ[25] देवर्षिर्नारदः सूत्रस्थानीयां[26] मातृकां चकारेत्यस्या मुखं[27] । तस्मिञ्छतसहस्रोपनिबद्धे ग्रन्थराशावाद्यः श्लोको ऽयं व्याख्यायते । आसीदिदं तमोभूतमित्यादि । तत्रासीदिति भूतकालप्रत्ययेन प्रागवस्था जगतो

निर्दिश्यते । तमोभूतमिति । अलक्षरूपत्वात्तम एवेदमिति जगदभिसंबध्यते । अमुमेवार्थं स्फुटं चिकीर्षुराह न प्राज्ञायत किंचनेति । तस्मिंस्तमोभूते जगति स्वयंभूर्भगवान्प्रादुरासीच्चतुर्मख इति । स च स्वयंभूरतो यतस्तस्योत्पत्तेः कर्ता कश्चिदन्यो न वर्तते । भगवानिति पूजापदम् । प्रादुः शब्दः प्रकाशार्थः । आसीदिति भूतकालपर्यायः । प्रादुरासीत्प्रकाश आसीदिति । चतुर्मुख इति रूपनिर्देशः । स च स्वयंभूः प्रजापतिर्ब्रह्मा । स चास्याज्ञाततमसान्धस्य जगतस्तत्स्वयमशीतिशतसहस्रं धर्मव्यवस्थास्थितिज्ञापकं शास्त्रं कृत्वा सहाचारसंव्यवहारप्रकाशकमुद्योतकमकरोत् । तस्माच्छास्त्राद्व्यवहाराद्यय एवायमिति सुप्रपञ्चितो! ऽभिहितः सर्वलोकोपकारित्वात् नारदमहर्षिणा[28] ।

धर्मैकतानाः पुरुषा यदासन्सत्यवादिनः ।
तदा न व्यवहारोऽभून्न द्वेषो नापि मत्सरः ॥१॥

अस्यायमाद्यश्लोकः । तत्र धर्मः श्रुतिस्मृत्युदितः शिष्टाचारलक्षणश्च । धर्म एकतानो येषां ते **धर्मैकतानाः** । तानशब्दो बलवाची प्रधानवाची च । तेन धर्मैकबला धर्मैकप्रधानाश्च **पुरुषा यदासन्** इति यदाभवन्

तदा न व्यवहारोऽभून्न द्वेषो नापि मत्सरः ।

तस्मिन्काल एषां त्रयाणामप्यसंभवहेतुरयमेव प्रथमः । धर्मस्य व्यवहारद्वेषमत्सरैः सह छायातपविरोधः । यत्रातपस्तत्र न छाया यत्र छाया तत्र नातपः । यदा धर्मस्तदा न व्यवहारद्वेषमत्सराः । यदा पुनरिमे तदा न धर्म इत्येतदर्थमेवेदमभिहितंभगवता नारदेन

धर्मैकतानाः पुरुषा यदासन्सत्यवादिनस् ।
तदा न व्यवहारोऽभून्न द्वेषो नापि मत्सरः ॥

नष्टे धर्मे मनुष्येषु व्यवहारः प्रवर्तते ।
द्रष्टा च व्यवहाराणां राजा दण्डधरः कृतः ॥२॥

अद्ययुगसामर्थ्यात् । नष्टे धर्मे मनुष्याणां* धर्मस्य प्रतिपक्षे प्रबलीभूतो रविचन्द्रानलोद्द्योताभावे बहलतमोराशिरिव[29] व्यवहारः प्रवृत्तः । द्वेषमत्सरावपि तथैवेति प्रकटार्थमिदमेकं व्याख्यानं । पूर्वपक्षप्रायं चैतत् । यतो मुनिमतान्तर्गतभावार्थसिद्धान्तव्याख्यानं द्वितीयमिदम् । **नष्टे धर्मे मनुष्याणां** तस्यैव धर्मस्याभ्युद्धरणार्थं **व्यवहारः** प्रवर्तितः प्रजापतिना । न धर्मप्रतिपक्षभूतः । तथा

१ B B5 om this verse; b — BM K2 K7 यदा स्युः; cd — NMS om.

२ B8 om this verse and the remainder of Mā 1; a — P मनुष्याणां; b — Y T B2 प्रकीर्तितः; NMS प्रकल्पितः; d — P स्मृतः.

हि कामक्रोधलोभान्धयोर्वादिप्रतिवादिनोरितरेतरं प्राणिनि संभवावसरप्राप्तसाक्षिलिखितदिव्यैः प्रमाणैर्धनरूपं बुध्यतोर् [?-->]... यदा राज्ञा धर्माधिकरणसहितेन...सायमग्रतः...[<--?] समुपवेशितविनीतवेषयोस्तयोरेकः[30] परिमिताक्षरां सामर्थ्यमात्रामष्टभाषादोषविहितामादेयभाषां कार्यते । द्वितीयोऽपि परिमिताक्षरमेव पूर्वं पत्रार्थसंबद्धमनाकुलमसंकीर्णं चोत्तरं दाप्यते । तदनन्तरं च द्वितीयपादे यथानिजपरीक्षापरिशुद्धैर्यः सत्यं प्रतिपद्यते स जयपत्रं लभते । यः पुनरस्य कुटः शठः स दद्याद् द्विगुणं दण्डं पणं धनमुपक्षयं चेति । एवमेतन्मुनिमतान्तर्गतभावार्थसिद्धान्तव्याख्यानमिदं द्वितीयमुक्तं । एवमनेनार्थेन नष्टे धर्मे मनुष्याणांधर्मस्यैवाभ्युद्धरणार्थं व्यवहारः प्रवर्तितो न तु प्रतिपक्षभूत इति प्रतिपादितमिद्रं । यथोक्तं **राजा दण्डधरः स्मृतस्** तदाप्येतदर्थमेव । उक्तं च

दुर्बलानामनाथानां बालवृद्धतपस्विनाम् ।
अनार्यैः परिभूतानाम्सर्वेषां पार्थिवो गतिः ।। [ŚaLi 25]

दण्डधरश्चैतदर्थम् । यतो

यदि नैताः प्रजा राजा दण्डेनातोद्य पालयेत् ।
ततोऽन्योन्यमभिघ्नन्त्यो विनश्येयुः परस्परम् । [?Dhko1969]
सर्वो दण्डजितो लोको दुर्लभो हि शुचिर्नरः ।
दण्डस्य हि भयात्सर्वं जगद्भोगाय कल्पते ।। [Manu 7.22]
अपि भ्राता सुतो वापि श्वशुरो मातुलोऽपि वा ।
नादण्ड्यो नाम राज्ञोऽस्ति धर्माद्धि चलितः स्वकात् ।। [YāSmṛ 2.356]

इति ।

लिखितं साक्षिणश्चात्र द्वौ विधी संप्रकीर्तितौ ।
संदिग्धार्थविशुद्ध्यर्थं द्वयोर्विवदमानयोः ॥३॥

अत्र वादिप्रतिवादिनोः परस्परं **विवदमानयोर्**एकतरस्यापि दोषेण योऽर्थः संदिग्धो भूतः तस्य **संदिग्धार्थस्य विशुद्ध्यर्थं** स्फुटीकरणार्थं **लिखितं साक्षिणश्**चैव द्वावेव **विधी** मुनिनात्र प्रकीर्तितौ न तु सत्याधिकगुणमपि तृतीयं दिव्यम् । तथातोयगतिसंततनित्यप्रवृत्तस्याष्टादशपादोपलक्षितलोकसंव्यवहारस्य या शीघ्रसुखोपायसाधनभूता मानुषी क्रियैवैषा साक्षिलिखितपूर्वा तावन्नित्योपयोगिनी । या

३ BM om this verse and the remainder of Mā 1; b — P परिकीर्तितौ; d — B7 K2 K3 K7 add

न्यायेनोपार्जितो येन सुखं गच्छति नान्यथा ।
नान्यथा सुगतिश्चैव ये भवन्ति न लुब्दकाः ।। [?]

B2 K5 add

संप्रतिज्ञो प्रतिज्ञश्च स पुनर्द्विविधः स्मृतः ।
स प्रतिज्ञोऽधिको यत्र विलेखापूर्वको भृत्यः ।। [?]

K add इत्येवमारभ्य कर्मप्रकारव्याख्यातव्यं तत्रैनं नवमप्रकरणं व्यवहारो नाम यसयेमां देवर्षिनारदः सूत्रस्थानीयात्मातृका चेत्यस्यामुखं.

पुनर्दैविकी क्रिया सातिमहत्स्वेव प्रयोजनेषु महतैव प्रारम्भेण परिक्षीणोपक्षय-महादण्डस्वरूपा भवतीत्येतदर्थं साक्षिलिखितावेवात्र श्लोके गृहीताविति ।

सोत्तरोऽनुत्तरश्चैव स विज्ञेयो द्विलक्षणः ।
सोत्तरोऽभ्यधिको यत्र विलेखापूर्वकः पणः ॥४॥

अस्य भाष्यम् । व्यवहार इत्यनुवर्तते । व्यवहार एकः **सोत्तरो**ऽपरो**ऽनुत्तर** इति **द्विलक्षणो** ज्ञेयः । सोत्तरलक्षणं चास्यैव श्लोकस्योत्तराधेन व्याख्यातं

सोत्तरोऽभ्यधिको यत्र विलेखापूर्वकः पण ॥

इति । अत्र च व्यवहारस्य सोत्तरत्वे पणाधिक्यं केचिदपरिज्ञानादेव ब्रुवते । यत्किल लभ्यद्रव्यादधिकः **पणो** यत्र भवति स एव **सोत्तर** उच्यते । यत्पुनर्लभ्यद्रव्यादधिकः पणो न भवति सो**ऽनुत्तर** इति । तदिदमसमञ्जसं वचनं। मनागपि न घटते । यतः येन व्यवहारिकेण परिपूर्णविभवतया कस्यचित्सा <...............> रिणस्योपरि पञ्चारूढपत्रलिखितपूर्वाणि द्रम्माणां दशसहस्राणि प्रयुक्तानि तस्मिंश्च व्यवहारके स्वर्गते तदीयपुत्रोऽपि विधिविलसितवशाद्दरिद्रो जातः । तत्पत्रमादाय द्रव्योद्धरणायर्णिकपार्श्वमागतः । ऋणिकेणापि साध्याद्धर्माधिकरणाग्रे मिथ्यावादितया निराकृतः । तदा यस्यैकदिनभोजनोपायो नास्ति तस्य द्विगुणीभूतद्रव्यं विंशतिसहस्राणामधिकपणकरणसामर्थ्यं कुत सम्भवतु । ततश्चाधिकपणकरणेन विना व्यवहारस्य सोत्तरत्वगौरवं कथमापाद्यताम् । अतोऽर्थापत्त्यैव ज्ञायते । न हि मुनिमतानीदृशानि भवन्ति येष्वशक्यसाधनोपायम् उपन्यस्य सदर्थसाधने भाषा एव तावदनुष्ठानसम्भवः सम्पद्यते । किं तर्ह्यत्र मुनिनारदान्तर्गतभावार्थोऽयमेवैष्वेवाक्षरेषु लक्ष्यते । यदेकं तावद्बल्लभ्य द्रव्यं व्यवहारसंदेह एव स्थितं तिष्ठत्येव द्वितीयं पुनरिदं यदमर्षितो वादी प्रतिवादी वैवंविधप्रभूतद्रव्यव्यवहारेऽपि शतद्वयमात्रं शतैकमात्रं वार्धशतमात्रमपि यावन्निजविभवानुसारेणद्रव्यमुपन्यस्यति स एवाभ्यधिकः पणो दरिद्रस्य । अतः पणाधिक्यमेतद् द्वितीयद्रव्योपन्यास एव द्रष्टव्यम् । न पुनरनवस्थाप्रसङ्गो द्रव्याधिक्यविषय इति । तथा चोक्तमेवान्यैरपि च

वादी वा प्रतिवादी वा यः समर्थः स्वतारणे ।
द्रव्यं वित्तानुसारेण करोति सपणः स्मृतः ॥ [?]

अथवा किमन्येनायमभ्यधिकः पणशब्दः प्रशंसायामेव संबध्यते । यथा समस्त-युक्तव्यवहाराणां मध्ये स एव**ाभ्यधिको** व्यवहारो **यत्र विलेखापूर्वकः पण** इति यथोक्तं सोऽपि पणो यदि विलेखापूर्वको भवति तदा सोत्तरो व्यवहार उच्यते । अन्यथा पुनरनुत्तर एव । अस्य निगमः । लेखा लेखनम् । विशेषेण लेखा **विलेखा**तत्पूर्वकः **पणः** कर्तव्य इति । अत्रापि मुनिभावार्थो ऽयम् । यदि

४ cd — C3 K4 om.

विलेखालिखिताक्षरनिबन्धपूर्वः पणो भवति तदा सोत्तरो व्यवहारोऽसौ । यदि पुनर्वाङ्मात्र एवानिबद्धाक्षरो मुक्तवचनैर्जल्पित एव न त्वक्षरैर्निर्बद्धस्तदा सपणः कृतोऽपि अकृतवद द्रष्टव्यः । यतोऽनक्षरैर्निबद्धः पणो निर्णयकाले व्यभिचरत्येवेति ।

विवादे सोत्तरपणे द्वयोर्यस्तत्र हीयते ।
स पणं स्वकृतं दाप्यो विनयं च पराजये ॥५॥

इदानीं सोत्तरनिर्णय उच्यते । अत्र तावत्पणोपन्यास एव निरूप्यते । येन धनिकेनर्णिकपार्श्वे द्रव्यं लभ्यं तेन द्रव्यप्रार्थनमात्रैव भाषा करणीया । तं चोपन्यस्यति वादी । तदा भाषायामधिकप्रार्थनदोषः । अतो यदा प्रतिवादी सत्यार्थेऽपि तस्य मिथ्योत्तरं ददाति तदा धनी स्वसत्यावष्टम्भखरीकरणार्थम् ऋणिकस्यामर्षादधिकद्रव्यवाहनार्थं च तृतीयपादे स्थितः पणमुपन्यस्य क्रियोपन्यासमपि करोति तदैष वादिनः क्रियोपन्यासकालः । प्रतिवाद्यपि यदासन्तमेवाभियोगं दत्तमात्मनो जानाति तदा भाषान्तरमेव मिथ्योत्तरं दत्त्वा तस्यैवोत्तरस्यावष्टम्भनिश्चयार्थं वादिनः स्वामर्षादेव ब्रूते । यत्किल लभ्य-द्रव्यादधिकः पणो यत्र भवति ससाकोटनद्रव्यवाहनार्थं पणोपन्यासं करोति । एष प्रतिवादिनः पणोपन्यासकालः । अत्र च यः पणो वादिप्रतिवादिनोरेकतरेणापि रोषामर्षादुपन्यस्तः स सोत्तरशब्देनोच्यते । तेन सह यो वादः स सोत्तरपणः तस्मिन् **विवादे सोत्तरपणे** य एव कश्चिद् **धीयते** अवसायं प्राप्नोति स एव हि पराजयेन मिथ्यावादित्वाद्द्विगुणं दण्डं च राज्ञात्मने दाप्य इति । अत्र श्लोके केचित्पाठान्तरं पठन्ति । यथा **स पणं स्वकृतं दाप्यत** इति । एवमप्यत्र न किंचिद्दुष्यत इति । यतो द्यूतेन द्यूतकारयोर्द्वयोरपि परस्परं दीव्यतोर्य एव पणजयं प्राप्नोति स एव पणं ददातीत्येव न किंचिद्भ्रान्तम् ।

सारस्तु व्यवहाराणां प्रतिज्ञा समुदाहृता ।
तद्धानौ हीयते वादी तरंस्तामुत्तरो भवेत् ॥६॥

अत्र सर्वेषां अपि **व्यवहाराणां** सारभूता **प्रतिज्ञा समुदाहृता** । सा च प्रतिज्ञा विचार्या । पण एव तावत्प्रतिज्ञा न भवति तस्य श्लोकद्वयेन निर्लोडितत्वात्[31] पुनरुक्तदोषसम्भवाच्च । ततः प्रतिज्ञां केचिच्छरीरनिग्रहो यथा[32] संवदन्ति । यस्य किल धनपणो न संभवति स व्यवहारे दोषान्धत्वादेवमपि वदति । यथा यद्यहं

५ c — P स एव हि पणं; D सुकृतं.

हारयामि तदा मम हस्तोऽपगच्छति पादो वा मम प्रतिज्ञेयम् । तदिदमपि वचनं प्रतिज्ञा[33] यतोऽत्र श्लोक एतदुक्तम् ।

तद्धानौ हीयते वादी तरंस्तामुत्तरो भवेत् ॥

तद्यदि हस्तखण्डनं न करोति हस्तखण्डनप्रतिज्ञामुद्दिश्य न करोति । न खण्डयति । तत्किंतत्प्रतिज्ञातं **हानौ हीयते वादी** लभ्यद्रव्यं न लभते । किं वा हस्तखण्डने कृते **तरंस्तामुत्तरो भवेद्** इति[34] । अस्मादर्थात्प्रमाणक्रियाभिः खरीकृतं[35] द्रव्यमसौ लभते । यत एतदुभयथाप्यनर्थकं तत एवेयमपि प्रतिज्ञा न भवति । प्रतिज्ञा चात्रेयम् । यद्धनिकस्य क्वचिदनागतमेव द्रव्यप्रार्थनां[36] कुर्वत ऋणिकेण स्वल्पद्रव्यभूक्तिरपि कृता । अथवा कस्मिंश्चित्प्रदेशे स्थितेन वाचैव क्वचिदीदृशं प्रतिपन्नमासीत् । यथा प्रयच्छामि तच्च[37] द्रव्यमहम्यदि पालयित्वा[38] गृह्णासीत्यादि [?-->] द्रव्यसंप्रतिपत्यं[39] चलं दर्शयित्वापि यदा खरं गृहीतेन धर्माधिकरणाग्रे मिथ्याक्षता भवति धनिकोऽपि तदेव प्रदेशोद्देशपूर्वकं संप्रतिपत्यं चलं द्रव्यसिद्धेः प्रतिज्ञाय दिव्येनाधिष्ठितो भवति । तदास्यैव[40] संप्रतिपत्यं चलत्वसिद्धिप्रतिज्ञा दिव्येनावान्तरसाध्यमानवादिनो मूलिकलभ्यद्रव्यसाधका भवतीति । [<--?] इयमीदृशोदाहरणा प्रतिज्ञा सर्वव्यवहारणामपि सारभूता भवतीति ।

तद्धानौ हीयते वादी तरंस्तामुत्तरो भवेद् ॥

इत्यादिषु सार्विकमिदमिति । तथा चोक्तं

यत्र वादी क्रियाकाले सर्वसिद्धिमुदीरयेत् ।
दिव्येन तां खरीकुर्वन्सा प्रतिज्ञा प्रकीर्तिता ॥ [?]

कुलानि श्रेणयश्चैव गणाश्चाधिकृतो नृपः ।
प्रतिष्ठा व्यवहाराणां गुर्वेभ्यस्तूत्तरोत्तरम् ॥७॥

यदा **व्यवहारप्रतिष्ठा**र्थमर्थिप्रत्यर्थिनोः परस्परं सुचिरमपि विवदतोर्न निर्णयो भवति तदा कुलादयस्त्रयः[41] पदार्था व्यवहारप्रतिष्ठाहेतवः । **उत्तरोत्तर**गरीयसस्त्वेते[42] समुद्दिष्टाः । तत्र **कुलानि** कतिचित्पुरुषगृहीतानि । **श्रेणयः** प्रधानवणिक्प्रतिबद्धाः प्रकृतयः । **गणा** ब्राह्मणस्थानादिसमूहाः । **अधिकृतो** धर्माधिकारणे नियुक्तः प्राड्विवाकः । **नृपः** सवयमेव प्रजापालः । एतेषु स्थानेषु व्यवहारणां निष्पत्तिः प्रतिष्ठामुखेनैव भवतीति **गुर्वेभ्यस्तूत्तरोत्तरम्** इति । एभ्यः स्थानेभ्य उत्तरोत्तरं व्यवहारनिष्पत्तिस्थानं गुरु प्रधानमित्यर्थः ।

स चतुष्पाच्चतुःस्थानश्चतुःसाधन एव च ।
चतुर्हितश्चतुर्व्यापी चतुष्कारी च कीर्त्यते ॥८॥

७ b — NMS नृपैः.

अष्टाङ्गोऽष्टादशपदः शतशाखस्तथैव च ।
त्रियोनिर्द्व्यभियोगश्च द्विद्वारो द्विगतिस्तथा ॥९॥

अत्रानेन श्लोकद्वयेनापि व्यवहारस्य संख्यापूर्वकः संज्ञासूत्रोपन्यास एव कृतः । सविस्तरार्थप्रतिपत्तिविवरणं वक्ष्यमाणमुपरितनश्लोकैः श्लोककार एव करिष्यति ।

धर्मश्च व्यवहारश्च चरित्रं राजशासनम् ।
चतुष्पाद्व्यवहारोऽयमुत्तरः पूर्वबाधकः ॥१०॥

एवं चतुष्पादोऽयमभिहितो व्यवहार अस्य चैवं निर्दिष्टचतुष्पादस्य चतुर्णामपि पादानां विवरणश्लोकोऽयमनुगत एव भवति ।

तत्र सत्ये स्थितो धर्मो व्यवहारस्तु साक्षिषु ।
चरित्रं पुस्तकरणे राजाज्ञायां तु शासनम् ॥११॥

तत्र सत्ये स्थितो धर्म इति । यदा धनिकर्णिकयोरेकान्तव्यवहारेऽपि परस्परं सत्याच्चलनं नास्ति तदासौ सत्यव्यवहार उच्यते । तस्मिन्सत्यसंव्यवहारे साक्षाद्धर्म एव स्थितः । स च व्यवहारचरित्रराजशासनानामदत्तावकाशस्वरूपत्वेन स्वतो वर्तमानधर्म एवोच्यते । **व्यवहारस्तु साक्षिष्व्** इति यदुक्तं तत्र धनि-कर्णिकयोरेकतरदोषादपि सत्यधर्मचलनशङ्कोत्पत्तौ संजातायां साक्षिप्रत्ययो यः संव्यवहारः प्रवर्तते स व्यवहार इत्युच्यते । स चोत्तरपूर्वस्य बधयोत्पन्नस्तेन **पूर्वबाधक** इति । यच्च **चरित्रं पुस्तकरण** इत्युक्तं तच्चरित्रमिति पत्रक-भूर्जचीरकसंपुटिकादिषु साक्षिस्वहस्तसुनिबद्धं कृत्वा यो व्यवहारः प्रवर्तते स चरित्रमित्युच्यते । स च पूर्ववाख्यादुत्तरः पूर्वबाधक इति । यस्तु राज्ञा समावेदितो व्यवहारः स राजशासनायत्तः सर्वेषामप्येतेषामधिकः सर्वोत्तरश्च । यत इत्युक्तम् ।

ग्रामे दृष्टः पुरे याति पुरे दृष्टस्तु राजनि ।
राज्ञा दृष्टः कुदृष्टो वा नास्ति पौनर्भवो विधिः ॥

तदेवायं चतुर्विभागरूपत्वाच्चतुष्पादो व्यवहारः तथा तदत्र लोकसंव्यवहारः संव्यवहार इत्युच्यते । स च द्विविधः प्रयोजनापेक्षया प्रवर्तितोऽपि देशका-लवशात् ।

८ d — NMS चतुष्कारीति.
२ P om this verse.

सामाद्युपायसाद्यत्वाच्चतुःसाधन उच्यते ।
चतुर्णामाश्रमाणां च रक्षणात्स चतुर्हितः ॥१२॥

सामभेदोपप्रदानदण्डैश्चतुर्भिरपि साधनोपायैर्यथावसरप्रयुक्तैः साध्यते तेन **चतुःसाधन** उक्त । एवं चायमस्कलितप्रवर्तमानो[43] व्यवहारः परमसमृद्ध्या **चतुर्णाम्** अपि वर्णानाम**आश्रमाणां च रक्षणात्** परिपालनाच्**चतुर्हितो** भवतीति ।

कर्तृनथो साक्षिणश्च सभ्यान्राजानमेव च ।
व्याप्नोति पादशो यस्माच्चतुर्व्यापी ततः स्मृतः ॥१३॥

स च यदि सुदृष्टो भवति ततश्चतुरोऽप्येतान्**पादशो** धर्मरूपेण **व्याप्नोति** । अथ कुदृष्टो भवति ततस्तानेव पापरूपेण व्याप्नोतीति **व्यापी**ति ।

धर्मस्यार्थस्य यशसो लोकपक्तेस्तथैव च ।
चतुर्णां करणादेषां चतुष्कारी प्रकीर्तितः ॥१४॥

लोकपक्तिर्जनानुरागः । शेषं प्रसिद्धम् । एतेषां **चतुणम**पि **करणाच्चतुःकारी**ति ।

राजा सपुरुषः सभ्याः शास्त्रं गणकलेखकौ ।
हिरण्यमग्निरुदकमष्टाङ्गः स उदाहृतः ॥१५॥

तत्र **राजा सपुरुषो** दुष्टावकोटनार्थं तस्यानवसरे राजकीयचक्षुर्भूतो राजनियुक्तः[44] प्राड्विवाकः पुरुषः स उभयात्मकः सत्यश्च राजपुरुषश्च । तथा **सभ्या** उपरिवक्ष्यमाणलक्षणाः । तथा **शास्त्रं** मनुनारदविश्वरूपात्मकं । सत्यासनं भेदव्यवहारदण्डनियमसंदेहविच्छेकारकं । तथा **गणकः** वणिग्वारिकः स्थानप्रतिबद्धः । भाषोत्तरक्रियाजयपत्त्रादिलिखनोपयोगी । **हिरण्यमग्निरुदकम्** इति । एतान्यपि त्रीणि प्रत्यक्षदेवतास्वरूपाणीत्येतान्यष्टावप्यङ्गानि यदा सभायां संनिहितानि भवन्ति तदा दिव्यादिष्वपि धर्मः साक्षादवतीर्य सत्यासत्ययोर्विभक्तिं परिस्फुटीकरोति ।

१२ a — Jolly सामाध्युपाय-
१३ a — D नलं.
१४ b — P -पङ्क्तिस्; d — P -कारीति चोच्यते.
१५ a — P स्तपुरुषः; D सभ्यः; d — P समुदाहृतः.

ऋणादानं ह्युपनिधिः संभूयोत्थानमेव च ।
दत्तस्य पुनरादानमशुश्रूषाभ्युपेत्य च ॥१६॥
वेतनस्यानपाकर्म तथैवास्वामिविक्रयः ।
विक्रीयासंप्रदानं च क्रीत्वानुशय एव च ॥१७॥
समयस्यानपाकर्म विवादः क्षेत्रजस्तथा ।
स्त्रीपुंसयोश्च संबन्धो दायभागोऽथ साहसम् ॥१८॥
वाक्पारुष्यं तथैवोक्तं दण्डपारुष्यमेव च ।
द्यूतं प्राकीर्णकं चैवेत्यष्टादशपदः स्मृतः ॥१९॥
एषामेव प्रभेदोऽन्यः शतमष्टोत्तरं स्मृतम् ।
क्रियाभेदान्मनुष्याणां शतशाखो निगद्यते ॥२०॥

अथाष्टादशपदमुच्यते तस्य सूत्रम् । एवं चैषामष्टादशव्यवहारपदानां मध्ये यस्य यस्य पदस्य ये ये निरूपार्था व्यवहारभेदा मुनिना दृष्टास्तस्य तस्यैव ते ते संख्यापूर्वकाः संयोज्यसंततप्रकरणस्थिता एव द्वात्रिंशन्मात्रा अपिसविस्तरमभिहिताः । एष सकलशास्त्रार्थसंग्रहः । तेषां च यथाक्रमस्थितिभेदसहितानामष्टादशव्यवहारपदानामनुलग्ना एव निर्णया भविष्यन्ति । तेन व्यवहारभेदा अपि द्वात्रिंशदधिकशतप्रमाणाः शाखोपशाखावस्थिताः संक्षेपविस्तरसंख्योपलक्षिता इहाभिलिख्यन्ते । तत्र तावत्संक्षेपसंख्येयम् ।

ऋणादानं पञ्चविंशति षडौपनिधिके स्मृताः ।
संभूयोत्थे त्रयो भेदाश्चतुर्दत्ताप्रदानके ॥ [J Mā 1.21]
नवभेदा अशुश्रूषा वेतनं स्याच्चतुर्विधम् ।
अस्वामिविक्रये तु द्वौ विक्रीयादानमेकधा ॥ [J Mā 1.22]
कृत्वा मुक्तं चतुर्भेदं समयाकार्यमेकधा ।
क्षेत्रवादो द्वादशधा स्त्रीपुंसोर्भेदविंशति ॥ [J Mā 1.23]
दायभागे तु एकोना भेदा द्वादश साहसे ।
वाग्दण्डपारुष्ययोस्तु द्वयोर्भेदास्त्रयः स्मृताः ॥ [J Mā 1.24]
द्यूताह्वयं चैकभेदं षड्भेदं तु प्रकीर्णकम् ।
एवमेषां प्रभेदानां द्वात्रिंशच्छतमेव वै ॥ [J Mā 1.25]

इदानीमियमेव भेदसंख्या प्रत्येकतामुद्दिष्टव्यवहारपदशाखाभेदैः सविस्तरादभिलिख्यते । तत्र **ऋणादाने** [1-2] देयादेयादिभेदाः कृता [3] ऋणभेदो [4] धनभेद [5] आपद्ब्राह्मणवृत्तिर् [6] प्रमाणभेदः [7-8] कुसीदवार्धुषिकभेदौ [9] प्रतिभूभेद [10] आधिभेदो [11] लेख्यभेदो [12]ऽसाक्षिभेदः [13-14]

१६ a — D ऋणाद्यानं.
१७ c — D विक्रेय-; d — D क्रीत्वानुशयम्.
२० a — D तेषां; b — द्वात्रिंशदधिकं शतम्.

पूर्वोत्तरसाक्षिनियमः [15] षड्विवादपदकसाक्षिनिन्दा [16] साक्षिप्रत्युद्धारः [17] कूटसाक्षिकं [18] साक्ष्यधिश्रावणा [19] साक्षिबलाबलं [20] लेख्यसाक्ष्यभावविधिर् [21] धटविधिर् [22] अग्निविधिर् [23] उदकविधिर् [24] विषविधिः [25] कोशविधिरिति पञ्चविंशतिभेदमृणादानं भवेत् । तथा **औपनिधिके** [1] न्यास [2] औपनिधिकं [3] याचितकम् [4] अन्वाहितकं [5] शिल्पिहस्तगतमिति भेदाः षट् । **संभूयसमुत्थाने** [1] सामवायिकम् [2] ऋत्विग्याज्यं [3] शौल्किकं चेति भेदत्रयम् । **दत्ताप्रदानिके** [1] देयम् [2] अदेयं [3] दत्तम् [4] अदत्तं चेति भेदचतुष्टयम् । **अशुश्रूषाभ्युपगमे** [1] शुश्रूषभेदो [2] ऽशुभकर्मभेदः [3] शिष्यवृत्तम् [4] अन्तेवासिवृत्तम् [5] अधिकर्मकृद्वृत्तम्[45] [? 6-8 ?] [9] स्वामिप्रसादाद्दास्यविमोक्षश्चेति भेदा नव । **वेतनस्यानपाकर्मणि** [1] भृतकवेतनं [2] गोपालादिकं [3] पण्यस्त्रीशुल्कविधानं [4] भाटकविकल्पश्चेति भेदचतुष्टयम् । **अस्वामिविक्रये** [1] ऽस्वामिविक्रयो [2] निधिलाभाश्चेति भेदद्वयम् । विक्रीयासंप्रदानमेकभेदनम् । **क्रीत्वानुशये** [1] कालभेदः [2] परिभुक्तवासोनियमो [3] धातुक्षयभेदस् [4] तान्तवसंस्कारश्चेति भेदचतुष्टयम् । समस्यानपाकर्मैकभेदम् । तथा **क्षेत्रजे** [1] क्षेत्रवादो [2] गृहवाद [3] उद्यानवादो [4] निपानवाद [5] आयतनवादो [6] ग्रामवादश् [7] चतुष्पथादिभूषणप्रतिषेधः [8] सेतुविधानं [9] खिलविषयः [10] सस्यरक्षा [11] सस्यवृद्धिर् [12] हेतुविधानं **स्त्रीपुंसयोः संबन्धे** [1] पुंस्त्वपरीक्षा [2] कन्यादाननियम [3] ऋत्विग्व्यतिक्रमदोषः [4] कन्यादानकालः [5-6] कन्यावरयोरदुष्टदूषणापराधो [7] विवाहविधिः [8] स्वैरिण्यादिविधानम् [9] अपत्यताविवेकः [10] संग्रहणविधानं [11] स्त्रीव्यतिक्रमदण्डौ [12] गुरुतल्पलक्षणं [13] पश्वादिगमनविधिर् [14] पत्न्यभावेऽपत्यविधिः [15] जारजातविधानं [16] नियुक्तानियुक्तापरगमनविधिः [17-18] दुष्टस्त्रीपुरुषविधानं [19] प्रोषितभर्तृकानिर्णयः [20] संकेतलक्षणं चेत्येवं विंशति भेदाः । **दायभागे** [1] रिक्थभागविवेकस् [2-3] तद्भागनिरूपणाविभाज्यनियमः [4] स्त्रीधननिरूपणा [5] स्त्रीया अभावे स्त्रीधननिरूपणा [6] भ्रातृद्रव्यविधिर् [7] मातापितृपुत्रविभागो [8]ऽक्षातपितृपुत्रिकादिविधिर् [9] अनियुक्तपितृविधानं [10] दीर्घतीव्रामयादिपुत्रांशविधिः [11] संसृष्टिपुत्रविभागः [12] प्रेतादिभ्रातृ-द्रव्यलब्धविधिः [13] कुटुम्बार्थे युक्तायासादिविधिर् [14] विभागसंदेहनिर्णयः [15] पुत्रसंख्यानियमश्चेति भेदानामेकोनविंशति [?] । **साहसे** [1] साहसलक्षणं [2] साहसदण्डविधानम् [3] आधिच्छलस्तेयं [4] क्षुद्रद्रव्यमध्यमोत्तमविधानं [6] द्विविधतस्करलक्षणं [7] तस्करस्य व्यवकर्षणं [8] भक्तावकाशदानादि [9] चौरविधिः [10] साहसस्तेयदण्डः [11] पदेन चौरान्वेषणविधिश् [12] चौराभावे चौरादिद्रव्यापनयनं चेति द्वादशभेदाः । **वाक्पारुष्ये** [1] तद्भेद [2-3] उभयोर्दण्डलक्षणं चेति भेदत्रयम् । **द्यूतसमाह्वयमे**कभेदम् । **प्रकीर्णके** [1] राज्ञा स्वयं वर्णाश्रपालनं [2] राजोपवर्णनं [3] राजब्राह्मणवृत्तिः [4] स्वद्रव्यदाने

राज्ञोऽभ्यनुज्ञा [5] ब्राह्मणकर्मवृत्तिनिरूपणं [6] अष्टमङ्गलकविधानामिति षड्भेदाः । एवमेतेष्वष्टादशप्रधानव्यवहारपदेष्वन्तर्गतव्यवहारपदभेदा द्वात्रिंशदधिकशतम् ।

कामात्क्रोधाच्च लोभाच्च त्रिभ्यो यस्मात्प्रवर्तते ।
त्रियोनिः कीर्त्यते तेन त्रयमेतद्विवादकृत् ॥२१॥

इदानीं त्रियोन्यादिकमुच्यते । **कामा**दयस्त्रयोऽपि **यस्मात्प्रवर्तते** तस्मात्त्रियोनिर् एव व्यवहार उच्यते ।

द्व्यभियोगस्तु विज्ञेयः शङ्कातत्त्वाभियोगतः ।
शङ्कासतां तु संसर्गात्तत्त्वं होढादिदर्शनात् ॥२२॥

तत्र द्विप्रकार एवाभियोगो भवति । एकः **शङ्काभियोगो**द्वितीय**स्तत्त्वाभियोग**श्च । एतयोश्च द्वयोरपि लक्षणमेकस्यैव श्लोकस्यार्धेनाभिहितम् । शङ्का सदासत्संसर्गादिति । असन्तो ये प्रसिधाश्चौरकर्मवृत्तयः । तथा वेश्याद्यूतव्यसनं चासत् । एतेषु यस्य सदात्यासक्तिर्दृश्यते तस्य गृहभेदज्ञस्योपरि नाष्टिकस्य पुरुषस्य महती शङ्का समुत्पद्यते । तेनार्थचलनं तस्यासत्सङ्गिनो नाष्टिकोऽभियोगं यं ददाति स **शङ्काभियोग** उच्यते । यस्तु तत्त्वाभियोगः स **होढादिदर्शनाद** भवति । स्वकीयं द्रव्यं यन्नष्टं तद्धोढमुच्यते । चोरितं च तद् दृष्ट्वा योऽभियोगः परस्य दीयते स **सत्त्वाभियोग**[46] उच्यते । तत्र शङ्काभियोगस्य देवकुलं निर्णयस्थानम् । तत्त्वाभियोगस्य राजकुलमिति ।

पक्षद्वयाभिसंबन्धाद् द्विद्वारः समुदाहृतः ।
पूर्ववादस्तयोः पक्षः प्रतिपक्षस्तदुत्तरम् ॥२३॥

<..............> तेन द्वारेण व्यवहारः प्रविशति । द्वितीयं द्वारं प्रतिपक्षस्थित उत्तरवादी यानि वदति तेन द्वारेण प्रविशतीति ।

२१ b — D यः संप्रवर्तते; c — K5 कथ्यते.
२२ b — D -तत्त्वाभिदर्शनात्; d — होढाभिदर्शनात्.
२३ c — D पूवपादस्; d — D add
सुनिश्चतवलाधाभनस्त्वर्थी स्वार्थप्रचोदितः ।
लेखयेत्पूर्वकार्यं तु कृतकार्यविनिर्णयः ॥ [J Mā 2.1]

भूतच्छलानुसारित्वाद् द्विगतिः स उदाहृतः ।
भूतं तत्त्वार्थसंयुक्तं प्रमादाभिहितं छलम् ॥२४॥

व्यवहारो[47] यथा प्रवेशकाले द्विर्द्वारः तथा निर्गमनकालेऽपि द्विर्गतिः । तत्र व्यवहारस्यैका गतिर्धर्मन्यायतत्त्वभूतार्थनिर्णयेन भवति । द्वितीया **प्रमादाभिहित-**निर्णयेन यथाकथानकमस्ति । अस्मिन्स्थाने वटपद्रके[48] संव्यवहारो वृत्तः । तद् ग्रामनाम विस्मृत्य प्रमादाद्वादीति वदति । यथा संवादुकाग्रामस्थितस्य[49] मम पार्श्वादनेनदेवदत्तेन गृहीतद्रम्म ५०० शतवृद्ध्या तदद्य बहोः कालाद् द्विगुणीभूतं द्रव्यमहं प्रार्थयामि । तच्छ्रुत्वा देवदत्तेनोत्तरं दत्तं । यथाहम्संवादुग्रामस्थितस्य[50] पार्श्वात्तिष्ठन्तु तावत्पञ्चशतानि । एकद्रम्ममपि न गृह्णामि । एतत्प्रादेशमिथ्योत्तरं दत्त्वा तेनान्यग्रामनामच्छलकत्वाद्द्रव्यं गृहीतम् । शुद्धश्चासौ देवदत्तः । इयं **प्रमादाभिहितच्**छलनिर्णयगतिर्द्वितीया । तथा चास्त्येवैतत् ।

दिव्यान्यप्यप्रमाणानि नीयन्ते वाक्यवञ्चकैः ।
देशकालप्रमाणादावप्रमादी भवेदतः ।। [J Mā 1.30]

यत्र चेयमीदृशी छलगतिर्वादिन एव प्रमाददोषात्संपद्यते तत्र तस्य स्वचर्यावसितस्य वादिनः किं करोतु राजा किं सभ्याः । यत्र पुनर्धनी साक्ष्योपन्यासकाले स्वकीयं साक्षिणं नवकम्बलम्प्रावृतं दृष्ट्वा राजाधिष्ठित-करणस्याग्रे वदति । यथायं नवकम्बलो देवदत्तो मम तस्मिन्काले कार्ये च साक्षी । एतच्छ्रुत्वा शठः प्रतिवादी यदि चाकुलं गृहीत्वैवं वदति । यथा कुतोऽस्य नवकम्बलाः यदि नवकम्बला अस्य विद्यन्ते ततो वदतु साक्ष्यमन्यथा न प्रमाणं ममेत्यादिकं छलग्राहिणं प्रति तत्रेत्यत्र मुनिमतमिदम् ।

तत्र शिष्टं छलं राजा मर्षयेद्धर्मसाधनः ।
भूतमेव प्रपद्येत धर्ममूला यतः श्रियः ॥२५॥

शिष्टो विशिष्टः तस्य छलग्राहिणा प्रतिवादिना चाकुलमारोप्यते । तद् **राजा मर्षयेत्** । न गृह्णीयादित्यर्थः । तथा यावद्व्यवहारस्य निर्णयो न भवति तावद्यदि वादी स्वकीयं प्रमादाभिहितं वचनं ज्ञात्वा वटपद्रक ग्रामं च सम्यक् स्मृत्वा तमेव वटपद्रक ग्रामस्थितसंव्यवहारं कीर्तयति, तदा वादिना तत्स्वकीयं प्रमादाभिहितं छलं शिष्टं कथितमित्यर्थः । तं वादिशिष्टच्छलं **राजा मर्षयेद्धर्मसाधनः** । क्षमयेदित्यर्थः । उत्तराक्रान्तभाषाच्छलेन भूतार्थनाशं न[51] कुर्यात् । धर्मन्यायमेव प्रतिपद्यते । **यतः** कारणादेवं व्यवहारातो राज्ञो **धर्ममूलाश्च श्रियस्**तस्य यतः कारणादिति वक्ष्यमाणम्[52] ।

धर्मेणोधरतो राज्ञो व्यवहारान्कृतात्मनः ।
संभवन्ति गुणाः सप्त सप्त वह्नेरिवार्चिषः ॥२६॥

धर्मेण व्यवहारान्पश्यतो राज्ञः । यथा[53] वह्नेः प्रतापिनः **सप्तार्चिषः** तथा तस्यापि प्रतापाङ्गभूताः **सप्त गुणाः** सम्भवन्ति ।

धर्मश्चार्थश्च कीर्तिश्च लोकपक्तिरुपग्रहः ।
प्रजाभ्यो बहुमानश्च स्वर्गे स्थानं च शाश्वतम् ॥२७॥

अथ के के तदुच्यते । तत्र **लोकपक्ति**र्जनानुरागः । **उपग्रह** आश्रायणीयत्वम् । अन्यत्सर्वं प्रतीतम् । एते च वह्नेर्गुणा ह्यस्य सम्भवन्ति ।

तस्माद्धर्मासनं प्राप्य राजा विगतमत्सरः ।
समः स्यात्सर्वभूतेषु बिभ्रद्वैवस्वतं व्रतम् ॥२८॥

तस्मादेवंविधमहार्थलाभाद् **राजा विगतमत्सरो** रागद्वेषविवर्जितो **वैवस्वतो** यमो धर्मराजस्तस्य **व्रतं** लोकानां स्वकृतशुभाशुभफलदत्वं । त**द्बिभ्रद्धा**रयन्[54] । **धर्मासनं** धर्माधिकरणं प्राप्य **सर्वभुतेषु समः स्याद्** इति[55] ।

धर्मशास्त्रं पुरस्कृत्य प्राड्विवाकमते स्थितः ।
समाहितमतिः पश्येद्व्यवहाराननुक्रमात् ॥२९॥

धर्मशास्त्रं पुरस्कृत्य यत्किमपि सभ्यैः प्राड्विवाकसहितैरवधारितं तदेव **प्राड्विवाकमते स्थितः** प्रमाणीकृत्य **समाहितमति**रेकचित्तः । तत्र स्थितः परिहृतगीतनृत्यक्रियाक्रीडासक्तिः राजा व्यवहारान्**पश्येत्** । **अनुक्रमाद्** इति भाषोत्तरक्रियानिर्णयचतुष्पादानुक्रमादित्यर्थः ।

आगमः प्रथमं कार्यो व्यवहारपदं ततः ।
विवित्सा निर्णयश्चैव दर्शनं स्याच्चतुर्विधम् ॥३०॥

२७ b — D अपग्रहः; c — P NMS बहुमानं.

३० c — P चिकित्सा; D चैतद्; NMS चेति.

आगमः सम्बन्धः । तत्तद्दृणादानाद्यष्टादशपदानां मध्ये कतमदिदं **व्यवहारपदम्** । तस्यापि मध्ये कतमोऽयं तदीयशाखाभेद इति व्यवहारस्य नाम करणीयम् । ततस्तस्य चतुष्पादक्रियानिर्वाहादिका व्याधेरिव **चिकित्सा*** करणीया । ततः प्रमाणपरीक्षानुसारेण तस्य व्यवहारस्य **निर्णयः कार्य** इति व्यवहार**दर्शनं स्याच्चतुर्विधम्** इति ।

धर्मशास्त्रार्थशास्त्राभ्यामविरोधेन मार्गतः ।
समीक्षमाणो निपुणं व्यवहारगतिं नयेत् ॥३१॥
यथा मृगस्य विद्धस्य व्याधो मृगपदं नयेत् ।
कक्षे शोणितलेशेन तथा धर्मपदं नयेत् ॥३२॥

किंचिद्धर्मशास्त्रोक्तमर्थशास्त्रविरुद्धं भवति । किंचित्पुनरर्थशास्त्रोक्तं धर्मशास्त्रविरुद्धं भवति । तयोरितरेतरतारतम्यालोचनेन यथा लोकाचारविरुद्धं न भवति तथा ससभ्योऽपि राजा **व्यवहारगतिं नयेत्** । अनया रीत्या । **कक्षं** वनगहनम् । यथा तस्मिन्वनगहने स्थितो मृगः संग्रहं दुरानेयो भवत्येवं परमार्थधर्मोऽपि संग्रहं दुरानेयः । तस्य **विद्धस्य व्याधो** मृगलुब्धकः प्रचुरतृणच्छन्नभूम्यां दुर्लभमपि तन्मार्जप्रहारनिर्गमस्थानं संततशोणितपातेनपदं तावन्नयेत् । यावदग्रतः पतितः स एव मृगो दृष्टस्तेन । एवं राजापि ससभ्यः क्रियामार्गानुसारेण ताव**द्धर्मपदं नयेत्** । यावत्परमार्थधर्म एव दृष्ट इति ।

यत्र विप्रतिपत्तिः स्याद्धर्मशास्त्रार्थशास्त्रयोः ।
अर्थशास्त्रोक्तमुत्सृज्य धर्मशास्त्रोक्तमाचारेत् ॥३३॥

यदा व्यवहारस्य निर्णयदानकाले तथा दण्डनिगमनावसारे सर्वशास्त्रोक्ता महती लघ्वी वाकोटना दृश्यते धर्मशास्त्रोक्ता चान्यादृशाकारा दृश्यते तदा तयोः शास्त्रयोः परस्परं विप्रतिपत्तौ विसंवादेऽ**र्थशास्त्रोक्तमुत्सृज्य धर्मशास्त्रोक्तमेवाचरेद्** इति ।

धर्मशास्त्रविरोधे तु युक्तियुक्तोऽपि धर्मतः ।
व्यवहारो हि बलवान्धर्मस्तेनावहीयते ॥३४॥

३१ b — P यन्नतः; NMS पार्थिवः; c — P संपश्यमानो; D समीक्ष्यमाणो; D नियुतं; d — NMS व्यवहारगतीर्घनाः.
३२ c — P शोनितपादेन.
३४ b — P विधिः स्मृतः; d — NMS अपचीयते; D अभिहीयते.

यत्र पुनरर्थापत्त्या विप्रतिपत्तिः स्याद्धर्मशास्त्रोक्तलोकव्यवहारयोस्तत्र धर्मशास्त्रोक्तम् उत्सृज्य लोकव्यवहारस्थमाचरेत् । यथा स एव बलवान् । तथा च धर्मशास्त्रोक्तम्

अपुत्रां गुर्वनुज्ञातो देवरः पुत्रकाम्यया ।
सपिण्डो वा सगोत्रो वा घृताभ्यक्त ऋतावियात् ।। [YāSmṛ 1.68]

यथा च

नष्टे मृते प्रव्रजिते क्लीबे च पतिते पतौ ।
पञ्चस्वापत्सु नारीणां पतिरन्यो विधीयते ।। [NāSmṛ 12.97]

इत्यादिकधर्मशास्त्रोक्तमपि लोकाचारव्यवहारे परित्यक्तम् । मातुलसंबन्धस्तु धर्मशास्त्रपरिवृतोऽपि दाक्षिणात्यकृतोऽपि परिहार्य एव सर्वत्र न वर्तते । स्थानपानभोजनादिना सर्वलोकेऽप्याहृतः । अतोऽत्र **युक्तियुक्तो** विधिः स्मृतः । सर्वथैवमेव वक्ष्यमाणम् ।

देशे देशे य आचारः पारम्पर्यक्रमागतः ।
स शास्त्रार्थबलान्नैव लङ्घनीयः कदाचन ॥[?]॥

इति सोऽप्यनुवर्तनीय एवेति ।

सूक्ष्मो हि भगवान्धर्मः परोक्षो दुर्विचारणः ।
अतः प्रत्यक्षमार्गेण व्यवहारगतिं नयेत् ॥३५॥

सौक्ष्म्यं कथं महतो धर्मस्य यस्मात्परोक्षो दुर्विचारणः कथं यस्मादागमानुमानप्रमाणपरिछेद्यस्तथा बहुधागमपरस्परविरोधात्संदेहः । तेन **दुर्विचारणो** यत आगमेनापि परिछेत्तुं न शक्यते । अतः **प्रत्यक्षमार्गेण** तस्य **गतिं नयेत्** । प्रत्यक्षोऽसय मर्गो लैङ्गिकमनुमानम् । शुभाशुभात्मकं सुखदुःखमुपभूज्यत इति । समस्तागमसमर्थितमिदम् । अथवा प्रत्यक्षमार्गो विवेकिसाधुविशिष्टपूर्वप्राचां मार्गः । तेन धर्मगमिं नयेदिति ।

यात्यचौरोऽपि चौरत्वं चौरश्चायात्यचौरताम् ।
अचौरश्चौरतां प्राप्तो माण्डव्यो व्यवहारतः ॥३६॥

३५ a — NMS बलवान्; b — C1 C2 K4 V5 L L3 द्रष्टव्यः सुप्रयत्नतः; cd — C1 C2 K4 V5 L L3 om.

एवं भगवान्धर्मो दुर्विचारणः । येन चौरक्षिप्तरिक्थमात्रदर्शनादविज्ञातधर्मपरमार्थनृपतिपार्श्वाद**चौरोऽपि** महर्षिर्माण्डव्यो मौनव्रततपःस्थितोऽदत्तोत्तरत्वाच्**चौरतां प्राप्तः** । अतः कारणात्पात्रपात्रपर्यालोचनापि निपुणतया कर्तव्येति ।

स्त्रीषु रात्रौ बहिर्ग्रामादन्तर्वेश्मन्यरातिषु ।
व्यवहारः कृतोऽप्येषु पुनः कर्तव्यतामियात् ॥३७॥

स्त्रीष्व् इति पत्नीदुहितृस्त्रीकृतः । अथवा स्त्रीभिरेव व्यवहारो दृष्टो । **रात्राविति** रात्रिः शयनाय न तु व्यवहाराय । तस्यां साक्षादेव प्रमाणव्यवहारासंभवः । **बहिर्ग्रामाद**रण्य इति । **अन्तर्वेश्मनि** गृहमध्ये । **अरात्रिषु** शत्रुषु । एतेषु प्रदेशेषु व्यवहारः कृतोऽपि न प्रतिष्ठितः । तेन **पुनः कर्तव्यतां** प्राप्नोतीत्यर्थः ।

गहनत्वाद्विवादानामसामर्थ्यात्स्मृतेरपि ।
ऋणादिषु हरेत्कालं कामं तत्त्वबुभुत्सया ॥३८॥

विवादानां गहनत्वाद् लोकानां च व्यग्रतया चिरवृत्तप्रयोजनस्मरणस्या**सामर्थ्यादृणादिषु** व्यवहारेषूत्तरवादिन उत्तरकालं दद्यात् । **कामम**ेवमपि भवति । **तत्त्वबुभुत्सया** सद्भावबोधार्थं बोद्धुमिच्छा बुभुत्सा ।

गोभूहिरण्यस्त्रीस्तेयपारुष्यात्ययिकेषु च ।
साहसेष्वभिशापे च सद्य एव विवादयेत् ॥३९॥

ऋणादिषु मध्यपतितत्वादेष्वपि कालहरणे प्राप्ते तदपवादः क्रियते । एतेषु पुनर्व्यवहारविशेषेषु सद्य एवोत्तरं दापयेदिति ।

अनावेद्य तु यो राज्ञे संदिग्धेऽर्थे प्रवर्तते ।
प्रसह्य स विनेयः स्यात्स चास्यार्थो न सिध्यति ॥४०॥

३८ d — D add
अभियुक्तो न चेद् ब्रूयात्वध्यो दण्ड्यश्च धर्मतः ।
न चेद्विपक्षात्प्रब्रूयाद्धनं प्रतिपराजितः ॥ [Manu 8.58]
३९ b — P -वाग्दण्डात्ययकेषु; c — D अभिशापेषु;
d — D add
सद्यो वैकाहपञ्चाहौ त्र्यहं वा गुरुलाघवात् ।
लभेन्मासं त्रिपक्षं वा सप्ताहं वा ऋणादिषु ॥ [Dhko 161, 170]
४० a — NMS D अनिवेद्य.

राजसाधारणसंदिग्धेऽर्थे **यो राज्ञेऽनावेद्यैव प्रवर्तते** स विनयप्राप्तो भवति । तदर्थसिद्धिरपि नास्त्येवेति । कर्तव्येऽर्थे सिद्धिरपि नास्त्येवेति ।

वक्तव्येऽर्थे न तिष्ठन्तमुत्क्रामन्तं च तद्वचः ।
आसेधयेद्विवादार्थी यावदाह्वानदर्शनम् ॥४१॥
स्थानासेधः कालकृतः प्रवासात्कर्मणस्तथा ।
चतुर्विधः स्यादासेधो नासिद्धस्तं विलङ्घयेत् ॥४२॥

अस्मात्स्थानाद्यदि त्वमद्य गच्छसि ततस्तव राजकीयाज्ञायं **स्थानासेध** उच्यते । अस्मात्पत्तनादियन्तं कालं यावद्यदि गच्छसीत्ययं **कालकृत** आसेधः । यत उच्चलितस्तत्र यदि यास्यसीति **प्रवासाद**ासेधोऽयम् । अस्मिन्कर्मणि यदि लगिष्यसीति **कर्मण** आसेधोऽयम् । एवमयमासेध**श्चतुर्विधो** भवति । एतेषां एकेनापि प्रकारेणारम्भक आरब्धो य आसिद्धो न व्यतिक्रमेत्तमासेधम् । अन्यथा राजापराधपतितः संभवेदिति ।

नदीसंतारकान्तारदुर्देशोपप्लवादिषु ।
आसिद्धस्तं परासेधमुत्क्रामन्नापराध्नुयात् ॥४३॥

नादीसंतारः पारगमनम् । **कान्तारं** भयानकं वनम् । **दुर्देशः** कुप्रदेशः । **उपप्लवो** देशभङ्गः शोकाद्युपप्लवो वा । ईदृशेषु प्रदेशेष्ववसरेषु चासिद्ध आसेधं व्युत्क्रामन्नृपस्यापराधप्राप्तो न भवतीति ।

राजप्रत्यक्षदृष्टानि[56] सुहृत्संबन्धिबान्धवैः ।
प्राप्तद्विगुणदण्डानि कार्याणि पुनरुद्धरेत् ।। [J Mā 1.50]

अयं श्लोकोऽत्राप्रस्तुतोऽपि मूलग्रन्थं दृष्ट्वा लिखितः । यानि कार्याणि राज्ञा स्वयं प्रत्यक्षदृष्टानि कृतानि यानि च सुहृत्संबन्धिबान्धवैर्दृष्टानि परं यानि द्विगुणदण्डप्राप्तानि द्विगुणपणेन द्वितीयवारं दृष्टानि तानि पुनरुद्धरेत् । न पुनः पुनरपि तान्येवापदिशेदिति ।

आसेधकाल आसिद्ध आसेधम्यो व्यतिक्रमेत् ।
स विनेयोऽन्यथा कुर्वन्नासेद्धा दण्डभाग्भवेत् ॥४४॥

ये शास्त्रे निषिद्धा **आसेधकालास्**तैर्विना सुस्थकालस्थितो य **आसिद्धः** यथाप्रयोजनं संबध्यमानार्थे य आसिद्धो यस्तमासेधं न गणयति क्रामत्येव स राज्ञा स्वकीय-

४३ d — D नापराध्यति.

प्रतापस्याखण्डनार्थं **विनेयः** विनयं ग्राह्यः । अथ कदाचिदासेधदातापि च शास्त्रनिषिद्धकाले वा प्रयोजनसंबन्धरहितोऽपि वैवमेव राजाज्ञया कस्याप्यसेधं करोति । तत एवमन्यथा कुर्वन्स एवासेद्धा दण्डमर्हति ।

निर्वेष्टुकामो रोगार्तो यियक्षुर्व्यसने स्थितः ।
अभियुक्तस्तथान्येन राजकार्योद्यतस्तथा ॥४५॥
गवां प्रचारे गोपालाः सस्यबन्धे कृषीवलाः ।
शिल्पिनः चापि तत्कालमायुधीयाश्च विग्रहे ॥४६॥
अप्राप्तव्यवहारश्च दूतो दानोन्मुखो व्रती ।
विषमस्थश्च नासेध्यो न चैनानाह्वयेन्नृपः ॥४७॥

निर्वेष्टुकामः परिणेतुमुद्यतः । तथा **रोगार्तः** । **यियक्षुः** यज्ञार्थामुद्यतः । व्यसनाभिभूतश्च यो भवति । तथान्येन य आक्षिप्तस्तथा गोषु गोप्रचारस्थिता **गोपालाः** । सस्यारम्भकाले **कृषीवलाः** । **शिल्पिनश्च** प्रतिष्टाकाले । आयुद्धधारिणो **विग्रहकाले** । **अप्राप्तव्यवहारः** पोगण्डः । **दूतः** राजकार्योद्यतोऽन्यत्रेरितकार्यो दूतो वा । **दानोन्मुखः** पर्वनिमित्तकाले । **व्रती** निमित्तगृहीतव्रतस्थः । **विषमस्थश्च** तत्काले राजदैविकाभिभूतः । एते सर्वेऽपि एवं स्थिताः कार्यकर्त्री बलेनापि नासेधनीयाः । न च राजच्छलपतिता भवन्तीति । अथवोक्ता बलेनावेदिता भवन्ति तत एवम्भूतान्राजापि ज्ञात्वा **नाह्वयेदि**ति ।

नाभियुक्तोऽभियुञ्जीत तमतीर्त्वार्थमन्यतः ।
न चाभियुक्तमन्येन न विद्धं वेद्धुमर्हति ॥४८॥

वादिना प्रतिवादी यो**ऽभियुक्तः** स तं वाद्यभियोगमन्तेऽनीत्वा[57] परिसमाप्तिमनीत्वा तमेव वादिनं न प्रत्य**भियुञ्जीत** । द्वयोर्वादिनोरेककालमनिर्णयगमकत्वात् । तं च स्वकीयाभियोगं निर्वाह्य यदि सत्यमेव किमपि तस्य स्वकीयमभियोगकारणमप्यस्ति । ततः स एव प्रतिवादी तस्य वादिनस्तत्क्षणमेवाभियोगं दत्त्वा स्वयं वादी भवति । यश्चान्येनाभियुक्तः प्रारब्धव्यवहारस्तिष्ठति तमपि **नाभियुञ्जीता** । यतो **न विद्धं वेद्धुमर्हति** । येन व्याधेन मृगः प्रथमं विद्धः तं यदि द्वितीयोऽपि विध्यति तस्य वृथाश्रमः । प्रथमस्यैव तत्राधिकारो न द्वितीयस्येति ।

४५ d — P राजकार्याद्यतस्.
४६ b — P सस्यारम्भे.
४७ d — P चैतान्.
४८ b — NMS अन्तरा; NMS व्यद्धुम्.

यमर्थमभियुञ्जीत न तं विप्रकृतिं नयेत् ।
नान्यत्पक्षान्तरं गच्छेद्गच्छन्पूर्वात्स हीयते ॥४९॥

अत्र प्रथमं भाषाकृतास्य पार्श्वे मयोपलभ्यसुवर्णगद्याणकदश । द्वितीयवेलायां विंशतिद्रम्माणकावतारं परिकल्प्य स्वहृदय आवेदयति मयास्य पार्श्वे लभ्यद्रव्य-शतद्वयमिति । अथवा प्रथमं लभ्यद्रव्यं जनं प्रार्थयित्वा द्वितीयवेलायामधिकं प्रार्थयते । अधिकं वा प्रथममुक्त्वा जनं वदति । इमां सर्वथापि अर्थविप्रकृतिं विनाशतां न नयेत् । तथा**न्यत्पक्षान्तरं गच्छेद्** इति । प्रथमं स्वकीयसुवर्णस्य विंशतिगद्याणकप्रार्थनां कृत्वा द्वितीयवेलायां वदति मदीयपुत्रस्यानेन दातव्यमस्ति द्रम्मपञ्चाशदिति । एतदन्यत्**पक्षान्तरमु**च्यते । तं न गच्छेत् । यतो द्वितीय-पक्षान्तरं गच्छन्पूर्वपक्षाद्वादी हीयत इति ।

न च मिथ्याभियुञ्जीत दोषो मिथ्याभियोगिनः ।
यस्तत्र विनयः प्रोक्तः सोऽभियोक्तारमाव्रजेत् ॥५०॥

न चार्थसंबन्धं विनैव कामक्रोधलोभान्धतया मिथ्याभियोगः केनापि[58] कार्यः[59] कर्तव्यः कदापि । यतो मिथ्याभियोगदातुर्महान्दोषः । यस्तत्र विनयः प्रोक्तः स मिथ्याभियोगदातारमा**व्रजेत्** । आगच्छेदित्यर्थः ।

सापदेशं हरन्कालमब्रुवंश्चापि संसदि ।
उक्त्वा वचो विब्रुवंश्च हीयमानस्य लक्षणम् ॥५१॥

तत्र**आपदेशो** व्याजः । सव्याजं कालहरणं कुर्वन्तावदपटुरहं तावदशुचिरहं नोत्तरं प्रयच्छामीति । तथा च यश्च सभ्यैः पृष्टो न ब्रवीतीति । यश्च प्रथमं वचनमुक्त्वा पश्चाद् ब्रवीतीति । न मया तदुक्तमिति । एतैश्चिह्नैस्तस्य **हीयमानस्य लक्षणं** ज्ञेयमिति ।

पलायते य आहूतः प्राप्तश्च विवदेन्न यः ।
विनेयः स भवेद्राज्ञा हीन एव स वादतः ॥५२॥

५० b — B2 K5 D -योगतः.
५१ a — D हरेत्; c — P उक्ता वाचो.
५२ c — D राज्ञां; d — D विवादतः; B2 K5 add
अर्थिना लेखितो सर्वं व्यवहारे यथाक्षरम् ।
प्रत्यर्थिनोत्तरं देयं दीयते पदतोऽन्यथा ॥ [?]

यश्च **राज्ञा चाहूतः** सन्**पलायते** । तथा पलायमानोऽपि पुरुषैर्यत्नादानीतः । तत्र प्राप्तः प्रचोद्यमानोऽपि किंचिन्न वदेत्स विनेयो राज्ञा भवति । यतो **हीन एव स** तस्मा**द्वादत** इति ।

सम्यक्प्रणिहितं चार्थं[60] पृष्टः सन्नाभिनन्दति[61] ।
अपदिश्य च यो देश्यं पुनस्तमनुधावति ।। [J Mā 1.60]

सम्यक्करणेन करणाग्रे प्रथममावेदितमपि यावत्सभ्यैः पृष्टस्तावत्तमेव नाभिनन्दति न समर्थयतीत्यर्थः तथापदिश्यार्थमलपित्वा पुनस्तमेवानुधावति । अस्यायमर्थः सभ्यैः पृष्टः किं तव साक्षिणो लिखितं च किंचिदस्ति (इति)। एवं पृष्टः प्रथमं वदति न किंचिदस्ति (इति)। एवमपदिश्य पुनस्तमेव वदत्यनुधावति । यथा विद्यते मम लिखितं साक्षिण एवेति । सोऽपि हीयमानः ।

सन्ति ज्ञातार इत्युक्त्वा दिशेत्युक्तो दिशेन्न यः ।
एतैस्तु कारणैः सर्वैर्धर्महीनान्विनिर्दिशेत् ।। [J Mā 1.61]

यश्चैवम्वदति यथा लिखितं मम विद्यते साक्षिणो वा । तच्छ्रुत्वा सभ्यैरुक्तम्यदि ज्ञातारः सन्ति ततो दिश आवेदयेत्यर्थः । तावता न दिशति न तत्रानयति । एतान्सर्वानप्येतैर्लक्षणैर्धर्महीनान्विनिर्दिशेत् ।

निर्णिक्तव्यवहारेषु प्रमाणमफलं भवेत् ।
लिखितं साक्षिणो वापि पूर्वमावेदितं न चेत् ॥५३॥
यथा पक्वेषु धान्येषु निष्फलाः प्रावृषो गुणाः ।
निर्णिक्तव्यवहाराणां प्रमाणमफलं तथा ॥५४॥

इह सर्वव्यवहारेष्वपि वादिना विद्यमानप्रमाणोपन्यासो नियमेन तृतीयपादे कर्तव्यः । यदि पुनस्तेन स न कृतस्तत उभयपक्षप्रतिभूग्रहणपूर्वेऽनिर्णिक्तव्यवहार एनम्[62] उपन्यस्तमपि विफलं भवेत् । व्यर्थमित्यर्थः । **पूर्वमावेदितं न चेदि**त्यस्य तु दुष्टर्णिकोपालम्भावसरे[63] साधूदासीनलोकानां[64] पुरतः पूर्वमेवैवमावेदितं न भवेत् । अनेन दुष्टर्णिकेन मम द्रव्यं दातव्यमस्ति तच्च साक्षिप्रमाणसहितं तथापि न प्रयच्छति । अतोऽयं मया राजकुले समर्पणीय इत्यादिपूर्वजल्पावसरे यदि साक्षिप्रमाणं क्वचिदपि **नावेदितं** न कीर्तितं भवेत् । ततो निर्णिक्तव्यवहारे तत्पश्चादुपन्यस्तमापि न प्रमाणं भवति । यदि पुनरेवं तत्पूर्वमावेदितो यद्यपि दैवयोगाद्वा करणराजसभाक्षोभाद्वा मतिविभ्रमाद्वा वादिना तृतीयपादे तन्नोपन्यस्तं तथापि प्रतिभूपर्यन्तनिर्णिक्तव्यवहारेऽपि यावदद्यापि करणं तत्रैव तिष्ठति तावत्तेन तत्प्रमाणमुपन्यस्तं सभ्यैः परीक्ष्य प्रामाणीकरणीयमेव । न पुनस्तत्र छलमवतारणीयम् । तथा हि पूर्वमेव सूक्तं कृतमिदं

तत्र संप्रतिपत्त्रैका सापदेपो परास्मृता ।
विपूर्वा तु तृतीया स्यात्प्रतिवादी विनिर्णयेत् ।। [?]

तत्र शिष्टं छलं राजा मर्षयेद्धर्मसाधनः ।
भूतमेव प्रपद्येत धर्ममूला यतः श्रियः ।। [NāSmṛ 25]

इत्यादिभिर्वचनैः । अयं च प्रमाणावकाशः पूर्वावेदितविस्मृतस्यैवोक्तः । यत्पुनः प्रमाणं न पूर्वावेदितं न वापि क्रियाकाले सूपन्यस्तं तद्विद्यमानमपि निर्णिक्तव्यवहाराणां यथात्यन्ताभावेनाप्रमाणं तदायं सोदाहरणश्लोकोऽभिहितो महर्षिणा । यथा पक्वेष्विति । यथा पक्वेषु धान्येषु वृष्टेर्गुणाः पुनः प्रकरणप्रारम्भादिका निष्फलाः । एवं निर्णिक्तव्यवहाराणामपि वादिप्रतिवादिसभ्यानां पुनर्वादप्रारम्भविचारादिका गुणा निष्फला अतिक्रान्तावसरत्वादिति ।

अभूतमप्यभिहितं प्राप्ताकालं परीक्ष्यते ।
यत्तु प्रमादान्नोच्येत तद् भूतमपि हीयते ॥५५॥

प्राप्तावसरं यदुपन्यस्तं भवति तत्प्रदुष्टसाक्षिकं परीक्ष्य परिहरेत् । यत्पुनरतिक्रान्तस्वकीयावसरं **तद् भूतमप्य्** उपन्यस्तं वादिप्रमादात्तस्य ग्रन्थिछुटितद्रव्यमिव तदेवापुण्यैरेव तद् भूतं प्रणष्टमिति । अतो वितर्क्यते । ननु प्रथममुक्तं

तत्र शिष्टं छलं राजा मर्षयेत् । [NāSmṛ 25ab]

यथाभूतमेवार्थं प्रतिपद्येतेत्यादिकमुक्त्वा सांप्रतमेतदुक्तम् । अतिक्रान्तकालोपन्यासच्छलाद् भूतमपि हीयते तदयं स्ववचनविरोधः । कथम् । अत्रोच्यते । प्रवृत्तव्यवहारमध्ये वादिप्रतिवादिनोः स्वकीयस्वकीयावसरेषु वदतोर्यानि वाकुलानि भवन्ति तानि राज्ञा ग्रहीतव्यानि । तान्येव

छलं निरस्य भूतेन व्यवहारान्नयेत्तु यः । [YāSmṛ 2.19ab]

यत्पुनर्निर्णिक्तव्यवहाराणां प्रमाणं तद्यदि गृह्यते [?-->] यथा निष्पन्नप्रासादस्य हि सूत्रस्थित एकपक्षेष्वकाशात्सर्वध्वसं कृत्वा मूलादारभ्य पुनः प्रारम्भो दुष्करो भवति । [<--?] तथा व्यवहारस्यापि तेन यत्तु प्रमादादवसरप्राप्तं नोच्यते तस्यैव ग्रन्थिछुटितमिव नष्टं नात्र धर्माधिकरणस्य स दोषः । अत एवैतद्वक्ष्यति । सनिश्चितबलाधानेन भवितव्यम् । अर्थिना साधनेनेत्यर्थः ।

तीरितं चानुशिष्टं च यो मन्येत विधर्मतः ।
द्विगुणं दण्डमास्थाय तत्कार्यं पुनरुद्धरेत् ॥५६॥

अत्र **तीरितानुशिष्ट**शब्दौ द्वावप्येतौ स्मृतितन्त्रसामयिकौ । उपदेशात्प्रक्रमाच्च तयोः सार्थकत्वमिदम् । **यत्तीरितम्** इत्युक्तं तद्व्यवहारस्य चतुर्थपादनिर्णयावसरे वादिप्रतिवादिनोः सभ्यैरेकवाक्यतयोच्चरितजयपराजयशब्दमात्रप्रकटीकृतनिर्णयं ।

५५ b — P परीक्षयेत्.

एतत्तीरितमित्युक्तम् । **अनुशिष्टं** पुनरुच्यते । यत्सभ्यैरेव तदनन्तरमपराधसारासारपर्यालोचनया निष्टङ्कितं निगदितदण्डं तदनुशिष्टं । तथा हि

उद्दिष्टजयशब्दं यत्तत्तीरितमिहोच्यते ।
उद्दिष्टाद्दत्तदण्डं च अनुशिष्टं कुदृष्टके ।।[?]

एतन्निर्णयस्य स्वारूपमास्थानद्वयम् । अस्मिन्निगदस्थानद्वयम् । अस्मिन्निगदस्थानद्वय एकतमप्रदेशेऽपि स्थित्वा य एवात्मानं विधर्मणा कुन्यायेन पराजितं मन्येत स एव तत्र स्थित एव । राजकुले **द्विगुणं दण्डं** स्वमा**स्था**योत्तरकरणं चोद्दिश्य तत्पुरतः **तत्कार्यं पुनरुद्धरेद्** इति ।

दुर्दृष्टे व्यवहारे तु सभ्यास्तं दण्डमाप्नुयुः ।
न हि जातु विना दण्डं कश्चिन्मार्गेऽवतिष्ठते ॥५७॥

दुर्दृष्टे व्यवहारेऽन्तःकरणेन पनुर्विचारिते कृते वादिप्रतिवादिनोर्यस्यैवावसायो भवति स एव द्विगुणं दण्डं प्राप्नुयादिति । तद्दण्डहेतुश्चात्रैवायमुक्तः

न हि जातु विना दण्डं कश्चिन्मार्गेऽवतिष्ठति [*sic*] ॥

रागादज्ञानतो वापि लोभाद्वा योऽन्यथा वदेत् ।
सभ्योऽसभ्यः स विज्ञेयस्तं राजा विनयेद्भृशम् ॥५८॥

रागात्पूर्वसंभूतक्रोधात् । **अज्ञानतो** मूर्खत्वात् । **लोभादु**पचारात् । यतस्ततो वा हेतो**र्योऽन्यथा वदेत्** । न्यायविपरीतमित्यर्थः । स **सभ्योऽसभ्यो विज्ञेयः** । सभ्यायोग्यो न भवातीत्यर्थः । **तं** पापं **विनयेन्नृ**प इति । अयं च बहुमध्यादेक एवोक्तः । एकवचनं कथमुक्तं । उच्यते समाधिः । यदि बहूनां मध्य एक एवाहंकारीभूत्वा शेषसभ्यान्स्वावष्टम्भेन निष्प्रभान्कृत्वा रागादिवशादन्यायवादिन एव पक्षपाताज्जयं ददाति ततस्तमेकैकमात्मशुद्धिपरैः सभ्यैः सूचितं राजा विनयेत् । अथा सर्वेऽपि कृतकोषपानादिसमयस्था एकवाक्यतयान्यायजयप्रदा भवन्ति ततः सर्वेऽपि राज्ञा विनेया दण्डं ग्राह्याः । एकवचनमपि जात्याख्यायां बहुवचनवाचकमेव भवति । यथा संपन्नो यव इति । यथा पक्वो व्रीहिरित्युक्ते पक्वा व्रीहय इति संबध्यते ।

किंतु राज्ञा विशेषेण स्वधर्ममनुरक्षता ।
मनुष्यचित्तवैचित्र्यात्परीक्ष्या साध्वसाधुता ॥५९॥

५७ a — D वा; c — D यातु; d — D दुर्गे.
५८ d — P NMS D पापं; P नृपः.
५९ b — D परिरक्षता; c — D नराणां चित्त-.

अस्मिन्श्लोके महर्षिणा महती मतिः संपदः संपत् शुभाशुभनिमित्तभूता सर्वसाधारणत्वेन **विशेषेण** चोपन्यस्ता । यतः काररणात्सर्वोऽपि लोको दुर्जनकथितमात्रश्रुतग्राह्यविचारकश्च । निर्दोषानपि साधुबन्धुकलत्रपुत्रमित्रान् दुर्जनभिन्नचित्तः सहसा परित्यजन्संपदा शुभेन च परित्यज्यते । असंपदाशुभेन च परिगृह्यते । यः पुनः प्रजापालो बहुपरिवार एव सृष्टः प्रजापालो बहुपरिग्रहपरिवार एव सृष्टः प्रजापतिना तेन स्वपरिग्रहपालनधर्मम**नुरक्षता** विशेषेण **साध्वसाधुता परीक्ष्या** । इयमेव **साध्वसाधु**परीक्षा सम्यगनुष्ठिता तस्य महतोः श्रीशुभयोर्हेतुभूता भवति । सा च **मनुष्यचित्तवैचित्र्यात्**परीक्ष्या। अथवा परीक्ष्यमप्येतदेव यन्मनुष्यचित्तवैचित्रयं चित्रविचित्रता वैचित्र्यमनेकप्रपञ्चरूपतेत्यर्थः । तत्र तावत्प्रस्तुतार्थ उच्यते । महर्षिणा सभ्याकोटनमुक्त्वानन्तरमेव **किंतु**शब्दं विकल्पवाचकमादौ प्रयुज्यायं परीक्षादरश्लोकोऽभिहितः । तेनायमर्थः समर्थ्यते । यदि कश्चिद् दुष्टदुर्जनस्वभावतया चिरन्तनस्वकीयामर्षपूरितो राज्ञः कर्णे स्थित्वा निर्दोषाणामपि सभासदां दुष्टत्वं कथयितं ततस्तस्यैव राजार्थविध्वंसकरणेन स्वार्थैकनिष्ठस्याननुकूलशास्त्रचित्तस्य साध्वसाधुता परीक्ष्या । [?-->] पश्चात्सभ्यानां यतः सभ्याः राजाङ्गभूतास्तेषां यस्य तस्यैव वचनाच्छायामङ्गे कृते धर्माधिकरणलाघवाद्राज्ञ एव प्रतापलाघवं भवति । [<--?] न केवलमत्रैव सर्वपरिग्रहस्याप्युपरि राज्ञा श्रुतमात्रग्राहेणा न भवितव्यम् । श्रुतविचारकेण गम्भीरमतिना च भवितव्यम् । अन्यथा बन्धुरपि भवति शत्रुर्दुर्जनकृतगुढचक्रकाभिन्नः[65] । निजचित्तशङ्कयापि च कल्पितया निरपराधोऽपि । इत्यपधार्य न कार्यं कदाचिदविचार्य कार्यसद्भावं बन्धुसुहृद्भृत्यकलत्रपुत्रनिर्घातनं सहसा तेषां शङ्कादोषे संजातेऽपि शुभतः स्ववित्ताद्वा सपरिचरः कर्तव्यः प्रयत्नतत्त्वनिर्वाद इति ।

पुरुषाः सन्ति ये लोभात्प्रब्रूयुः साक्ष्यमन्यथा ।
सन्ति चान्ये दुरात्मानः कूटलेख्यकृतो जनाः ॥६०॥
अतः परीक्ष्यमुभयमेतद्राज्ञा विशेषतः ।
लेख्याचारेण लिखितं साक्ष्याचारेण साक्षिणः ॥६१॥

इदानीं मनुष्यचित्तवैचित्र्यस्य व्याख्यामाह । **पुरुषाः** सन्तीति । अनेन श्लोकद्वयेन पुरुषचित्तवैचित्र्यं दर्शयित्वा साक्षिप्रमाणयोरपि परीक्षादरो दर्शितः । यथोक्तम्

लेख्याचारेण लिखितं साक्ष्याचारेण साक्षिणः ॥

६० b — D ये ब्रूयुः; c — D दुराचारः; d — D नराः.

६१ d — D add

लेख्यमालेख्यवत्केचिल्लिखन्ति कुशला नराः ।
अतो न लेखसामर्थ्यात्सिद्धिरैकान्तिकी मता ॥ [Dhko 96, 377]

इत्य् । तदग्रतो लेख्याचारपरीक्षा साक्ष्याचारपरीक्षा च सविस्तरा भविष्यति । तेनोभयाकारप्रकरण उभयमध्ये तत्परीक्ष्यमित्युक्तम् । तत्रैव वक्ष्याम इति ।

असत्याः सत्यसंकाशाः सत्याश्चासत्यदर्शनाः ।
दृश्यन्ते विविधा भावास्तस्माद्युक्तं परीक्षणं ॥६२॥
तलवद् दृश्यते व्योम खद्योतो हव्यवाडिव ।
न तलं विद्यते व्योम्नि न खद्योते हुताशनः ॥६३॥
तस्मात्प्रत्यक्षदृष्टोऽपि युक्तमर्थः परीक्षितुम् ।
परीक्ष्य ज्ञापयनर्थान्न धर्मात्परिहीयते ॥६४॥

अत्र यथाकाशो भूतलवद् दृश्यते । परं दृश्यमानोऽपि तत्र भूतलं नास्ति । यथा च **खद्योते** वह्निस्फूलिङ्गसदृशेऽपि दृश्यमाने तत्र वह्निर्नास्ति तथा क्वचित् पुरुषवचनेऽपि सत्याभासे दृश्यमानेऽपि सत्यं न भवति । तस्मात्**प्रत्यक्षदृष्टो**ऽप्यर्थस्तात्पर्यतः **परीक्षितुं** युक्तः । यत एव **दृश्यन्ते विविधा भावा**स्तत एव परीक्ष्य **ज्ञापयनर्थान्धर्मान्न परिहीयते** ।

एवं पश्यन्सदा राजा व्यवहारान्समाहितः ।
वितत्येह यशो दीप्तं ब्रध्नस्याप्नोति विष्टपम् ॥६५॥

एवं अनेन प्रोक्तक्रमेण **सह*** नित्यमेव यथार्थाधिकरणेन तात्पर्यतोऽर्थान् । तथा धर्माधिकरणेऽधिकतरतात्पर्यत एकचित्तो **राजा व्यवहारान्**पश्येत् । **इह** लोके **यशो दीप्तम्** इति भुवनप्रकाशं विस्तार्य । अनेन महता पुण्यसंचरयेनोपार्जितं परलोकत्रि**विष्टपं** स्वर्गे स्थानं शाश्वतं प्राप्नोति । इत्यसहायनारदभाष्ये केशवभट्टप्रोत्साहितकल्याणभट्टपरिशोधितव्यवहारमातृकायां प्रथमोऽध्यायः ।

६२ b — P D -संनिभाः.

६४ a — B2 B3 -दृष्टे; b — Jolly typo परोक्षितुम्; c — D यत्नान्.

६५ a — P सह; d — P प्रेत्याप्नोति त्रिविष्टपम्; B2 K5 add मानवधर्मशास्त्रे नारदप्रोक्तायां संहितायां व्यवहारमातृका समाप्ता; D add इति श्रीनारदीयधर्मशास्त्रीये व्यवहारमातृकायां प्रथमोऽध्यायः

मातृका

२ भाषा[66]

सुनिश्चितबलाधानस्त्वर्थी स्वार्थप्रचोदितः ।
लेखयेत्पूर्वपक्षं[67] तु कृतकार्यविनिश्चयः[68] ।। [J Mā 2.1]

अर्थी पूर्वपक्षं लेख्ययेत । भाषमित्यर्थः । स्वार्थप्रचोदितो न राज्ञा प्रचोदितो न वैरिणा । स्वकीयेनैवार्थेन प्रचोदितः । तथा कृतकार्यविनिश्चयः । यावदिदं प्रारब्धप्रयोजनं मयान्तं न नीतं तावदन्यन्न करोमीति कृतनिश्चयः । एतदर्थिकर्तव्यमुक्तम् । अतः प्रत्यर्थिकर्तव्यमुच्यते ।

पूर्वपक्षश्रुतार्थस्तु प्रत्यर्थी[69] तदनन्तरम् ।
पूर्वपक्षार्थसंबन्धं प्रतिपक्षं निवेशयेत् ।। [J Mā 2.2]

तथा धन्यर्थीत्युक्तः । ऋणी प्रत्यर्थीयभिहितः । तथा भाषायाः पूर्वपक्षसंज्ञा । तदुत्तरस्य प्रतिपक्षसंज्ञा । अर्थिना लिखिते
पूर्वपक्षश्रुतार्थस्तु प्रत्यर्थी तदनन्तरम् ।
पूर्वपक्षार्थसंबन्धं प्रतिपक्षं निवेशयेत् ।।
उत्तरं दद्यादित्यर्थः ।

श्वो लेखनं वा स लभेत् त्र्यहं सप्ताहमेव वा ।
अर्थी तृतीयपादे तु युक्तं सद्यो ध्रुवं जयी ।। [J Mā 2.3]

अत्र श्लोकेन पूर्वार्धेनोत्तरवादिनः कार्यमुक्तम् । उत्तरार्धेन पूर्ववादिनः । तद्यथा । अनन्तरोक्तः प्रत्यर्थी यद्युत्तुरकालं प्रार्थयति तदागामिदिवस उच्यते । ततः श्वो लेखनमागामिदिवसे लेखनं वा स लभेत् । अथवा त्र्यहं सप्ताहं वोत्तरकालस्तस्य दातव्यः । अर्थी तृतीयपादे तूत्तरकालं न लभते । सद्यो ध्रुवे जयं लभते । तत्पूर्ववादिलिखितार्थस्य क्रियाद्वारेण खरीकरणसहितमिति ।

मिथ्या संप्रतिपत्तिर्वा प्रत्यवस्कन्दमेव वा ।
प्राङ्न्यायाविधिसाध्यं वा उत्तरं स्याच्चतुर्विधम् ।। [J Mā 2.4]

तत्र मिथ्यार्थिलिखितभाषार्थस्यापह्नवः । इयं च मिथ्यापि चतुर्विधा दृष्टा

मिथ्यैतन्नाभिजानामि तदा तत्र न संनिधिः ।
अजातश्चास्मि तत्काल एवं मिथ्या चतुर्विधा ।। [J Mā 2.5]

संप्रतिपत्तिस्तु भाषार्थस्य कल्पसमर्थना । प्रत्यवस्कन्दनं वादिन[70] एव सकारणं प्रत्यभियोगवादिनः । प्राङ्न्यायविधिसिद्धिर्ममायं पूर्वमेवास्मिन्नर्थेऽमुकामुककुलजस्याग्रे पराजित इति प्रतिवादिवचनम् । एवं चतुर्विधोत्तरलक्षणं दर्शितमिति । अथ परकीयश्लोकोऽत्रैव मूलग्रन्थे लिखितो दृष्टः । सोऽपि चतुर्विधोत्तरवादी कष्टव्याख्यानश्च भविष्यति भावः । तथापि लिख्यत इति ।

मिथ्या च विपरीतं च पुनः शब्दसमागमम् ।
पूर्वपक्षार्थसंबन्धमुत्तरं स्याच्चतुर्विधम् ।। [J Mā 2.6]

तत्र मिथ्या सूक्ता कृतैव । विपरीतमिति मिथ्याया विपरीतं संप्रतिपत्त्युत्तरं भवति । पुनरिति पुनरपि विपरीतं वादिन एव प्रत्यवस्कन्दनोत्तरमित्यर्थः । चतुर्थं चोत्तरं शब्दसमागममुक्तम् । तत्र वलिताभिप्रायेणाप्तोपदेशः शब्दसमागम उक्तः । तेन पुनराप्तोपदेशशब्दसमागमः प्राङ्न्यायोत्तरमुक्तम् । एतेषां चतुर्णां यदि पूर्वपक्षार्थसंबद्धत्वं भवति तत्तदुत्तरं प्रतिवादिना दातव्यमिति ।

भाषाया उत्तरं यावत्प्रत्यर्थी न निवेशयेत्[71] ।
अर्थी तु लेखयेत्तावद्यावद्वस्तु विवक्षितम् । [J Mā 2.7]

अर्थी भाषायां स्वकीयं विवक्षितं वस्तु तावदेव लेखयेत्यावत्प्रत्यर्थ्युत्तरं न निवेशयेत् । उत्तराक्रान्तभाषायां तु तस्य विवक्षितवस्तुनोऽन्यस्यापि भूयो लेखनाधिकारो नास्ति ।

अन्यार्थमर्थहीनं च प्रमाणागमवर्जितम् ।
लेख्यं हीनाधिकं भ्रष्टं भाषादोषास्तूदाहृताः ।। [J Mā 2.8]

अत्रान्यार्थादयो भाषादोषाः प्रोक्ताः । ते च प्रत्येकं प्रकाशार्थाः क्रियन्ते ।

लब्धव्यं येन यद्यस्मात्स तत्तस्मादवाप्नुयात् ।
न त्वन्योऽन्यद्[72] अथान्यस्मादित्यन्यार्थमिदं त्रिधा ।। [J Mā 2.9]
इत्यन्यार्थदोषस्वरूपं प्रथमम् । अथार्थहीनम् ।
मनसाहमपि ध्यातस्त्वन्मित्रेणेह शत्रुवत् ।
अतोऽन्यथा महाक्षान्त्या[73] त्वमिहावेदितो मया ।। [J Mā 2.10]
इत्यर्थहीनदोषो द्वितीयः । प्रमाणवर्जितमुच्यते[74] ।

द्रव्यप्रमाणहीनं यत्फलोपाश्रयवर्जितम्[75] ।
प्रमाणवर्जितं नाम[76] लेख्यदोषं तदुत्सृजेत् ।। [J Mā 2.11]

इति तृतीयम् । आगमवर्जितमुच्यते ।

आगमवर्जितं[77] दोषं पूर्वपादे[78] विवर्जयेत् ।
एकस्य बहुभिः सार्धं पुरराष्ट्रविरोधकम् ।। [J Mā 2.12]

इति चतुर्थः । हीनाधिकमुच्यते ।

बिन्दुमात्रापदवर्णेष्वेकाविधिष्टया (?)[79]।
हीनाधिका भवेद्व्यर्था तां यत्नेन विवर्जयेत् ।। [J Mā 2.13]

अत्र दोषद्वयमुक्तम् ।

भ्रष्टं तु दुःस्थितं यत्स्याज्जलतैलादिभिर्हतम् ।
भाषायां तदपि स्पष्टं विस्पष्टार्थं विवर्जयेत् ।। [J Mā 2.14]

इत्येते सप्त भाषादोषाः । अष्टम उच्यते ।

सत्या भाषा न भवति यद्यपि स्यात्प्रतिष्ठिता ।
बहिश्चेद्भ्रस्यते धर्मान्नियताद्व्यवहारिकात् । [J Mā 2.15, Manu 8.164]

विवरणोदाहरणमिदम् ।

गन्धमादनसंस्थस्य मयास्यासीत्तदर्पितम् ।
व्यवहारिकधर्मस्य बाह्यमेतन्न सिध्यति ।। [J Mā 2.16]

इत्यष्टमोऽयं भाषादोषः । एवमेतैरष्टभिरपि दोषैर्विवर्जिता भाषादेया भवतीति ।

अन्याक्षरनिवेशेन अन्यार्थगमनेन च ।
आकुलं च क्रियादानं क्रिया चैवाकुला भवेत् ।। [J Mā 2.17]

यदा वाद्यन्यादृशार्थस्याक्षरनिवेशं कृत्वा व्यवहारकाल अन्यादृशमेव प्रभूततरार्थोत्पादकमर्थमुपन्यस्यति तदा क्रियादानमाकुलं भवति । किं तावत्प्रथमनिवेशिताक्षरप्रधानव्यवहारस्य क्रियाः संचारयन्तु सभ्याः किं वा प्रभूततरार्थोत्पादकप्रधानस्येत्येवं क्रियाया आदानमाकुलं भवति । यदा च प्रथमवादी द्वितीयेन द्वितीयश्च प्रथमेन सभ्याश्च द्वाभ्यामपि व्याकुलास्तदार्थापत्त्या क्रियापि व्याकुला भवतीति ।

रागादीनां यदेकेन कोपितः करणे वदेत् ।
तदादौ तु लिखेत्सर्वं वादिनः फलकादिषु ।। [J Mā 2.18]

रागादीनां कामक्रोधलोभानां मध्ये येनैव भावेन कोपेन वादी करणमागत्य वदेत्तदेव फलकादिष्विति फलकपत्रभूर्जसंपुटिकाकुड्येष्वपि यथासंभवं तत्क्षणमेव लेखको लिखेद् झटित्यक्षरनिबद्धं कुर्यात् ।

निराकुलावबोधाय[80] धर्मस्थैः सुविचारितम् ।
तस्मादन्यद्व्यपोह्यं स्याद्वादिनः फलकादिषु ।। [J Mā 2.19]

तेषु फलकादिषु यत्किमपि वादिनः सक्तं प्रथममेव लिखितं तस्माद्यदन्यदभ्यधिकं किंमपि तद्धर्मज्ञैः सुविचारितं व्यपोह्यमपनेतव्यमित्यर्थः । तच्च किमर्थं राजकुलावबोधार्थं वादिनश्चेति ।

वादिभ्यामभ्यनुज्ञातं शेषं च फलके स्थितम् ।
ससाक्षिकं लिखेयुस्ते प्रतिपत्तिं च वादिनोः ।। [J Mā 2.20]

अयं श्लोको वादस्थानकप्रस्थानेन विवरणाय वादिभ्यामभ्यनुज्ञातम् । अयं श्लोको महर्षिणा कृतः स्पष्टान्धकं नाम । दुर्घटान्वयः सान्वयः । तत्र तावद् दुर्घटान्वय उच्यते । अस्मिञ्छ्लोके वाक्यचतुष्टयम् । तत्र वादिभ्यामभ्यनुज्ञातमित्येकं वाक्यम् । शेषं च फलके स्थितमिति द्वितीयम् । ससाक्षिकम्लिखेयुस्त इति तृतीयम् । प्रतिपत्तिं च वादिनोरिति चतुर्थम् । एतत्पादचतुष्टयमप्यर्थतो दुरन्वयम् । वादिभ्यामभ्यनुज्ञातमिति यदुक्तम् । अत्र वादिनोः परस्परं विप्रतिपत्तिबद्धामर्षचित्तयोः खलकप्रविष्टयोरिव न्यायस्थानोपस्थितयोः । कुत आकाशन्निपत्य स्नेहः समागच्छतु येन सस्नेहैकवाक्यतया ताभ्यां द्वाभ्यां वादिभ्यामभ्यनुज्ञातं किंचिद्वस्तु भविष्यति तदवस्थायोर्न तादृश्री भाषा संभाव्यते । नाप्युत्तरम् । तदभावे च किमन्यद्वस्तु तादृषं यल्लिखेयुः कारणिकाः । एवं तावदिदं प्रथममेव वाक्यमिति दुर्घटान्वयम् । ततश्च शेषं च फलके स्थितमिति यदुक्तं तत्रापि यत्कस्यापि वस्तुनः किंचिदुच्चरितं[81] भवति तच्छेषमुच्यते । अत्र चानिर्दिष्टस्वरूपवस्तुनः कस्य शेषमुच्चरितं भवतु कीदृशं तावद्भवतु यल्लिखेयुः । एवमनिर्दिष्टाङ्कितमूलरहितशेषस्यासंभवे शेषं च फलके स्थितं लिखेयुरिति । द्वितीयमपीदं वाक्यं दुर्घटान्वयमेव । यच्चोक्तं ससाक्षिकं ततस्तस्यार्थस्योत्तरत्राव्यभिचारार्थं श्रोतारः साक्षिणो ये तत्रानेतव्याः ते किं तावत्कारणिकैरुत वादिनाथवा प्रतिवादिना । एवं च साक्ष्यानयकस्याप्यसंभवे दृश्यमाने ससाक्षिकं लिखेयुरिति तृतीयमपीदं वाक्यं दुर्घटान्वयमेव । यच्च प्रतिपत्तिं च वादिनोर्लिखेयुरिति चतुर्थं वाक्यं तदेतेषामपि वाक्यानामर्थस्य लेखनक्रियार्थप्रसिद्धम् । तेषु त्रिष्वपि वाक्येषु निरर्थकेषु गतेषु सत्स्विदमपि चतुर्थं नैव सार्थेन सह याति । तत्प्रतिबद्धत्वात् । तत्प्रतिबद्धं हि यत्तन्निवृत्तौ तस्यापि निवृत्तिरिति । एवमयं चतुष्पादश्लोकोऽपि दुर्घटान्वयः । किंतु स्मृतितन्त्रसांकेतिकशब्दार्थां मुनिश्लोका दुर्बोधा एव भवन्ति । न पुनर्निरर्थकाः । तद्यदि पक्षेण वा मासेन वा सुचिरमपि विचिन्त्यास्य मुनिकृतस्पष्टान्धकश्लोकस्य सार्थकत्वकरणस्यापि वाञ्छास्ति । ततस्तद्वचनात्पालयामस्तावत् । अथ तदापि वयमेव

प्रष्टव्याः । ततोऽभिमानग्रस्ततामुत्सृज्य[82] पृच्छत येन कथयामः । अथवा किमस्माभिरप्यवश्यमेवोद्धतता त्याजनीया । [?-->] भवन्तस्तद् ब्रुयतामियम् । या प्रत्याकलितपादाभ्याम्[83] अनुज्ञावर्तिना मुनिना अत्र श्लोके किं लिखेयुरिति । [<--?] क्रियाः के लिखेयुः कारणिकाः । किं लिखेयुः । यत्किमपि वादी भाषाप्रथमपादे स्थितो वदति ते फलकस्थितं लिखेयुः । यच्चोक्तं शेषं च लिखेयुरिति तदिह भाषा यावत्फलकेऽभिलिख्यते यावच्च सोत्तरेणावष्टभ्यते तावत्सर्वोऽपि भाषावादिनामेव स्वकीयपादे स्थितो वादी यदि किमपि विस्मृत्य कुलेखितं प्रसाधयति । सुस्मृतं च सत्यं च लेखयति । तत इदं तस्य प्रत्याकलितमुच्यते पश्चादाकलितमित्यर्थः । तच्च कालप्रदेशधनिकर्णिकवित्तसंख्याफलोपाश्रयाणां षण्णामपि प्रधानवस्तूनां मध्ये यदभिप्रेतं तमच्छलग्राहिणो भूत्वा कारणिका लिखेयुरिति । तथा च प्रत्याकलितलक्षणम्

> वादिभ्यां लिखिताच्छेषं यत्पुनर्वादिना स्मृतम् ।
> तत्प्रत्याकलितं नाम स्वपादे तस्य लिख्यते ।। [J Mā 2.21]

तत्र वादिभ्यामिति द्विवचननिर्देशः कृतस्तद्द्वितीयस्योत्तरवादिनोऽपि प्रत्याकलितस्यायमेव विधिर्द्रष्टः । यच्च ससाक्षिकमुक्तं तच्च साक्षिनिर्देशकाले तृतीयपादेऽप्ययमेव विधिर्दृष्टव्यः । यच्चानुज्ञातमित्युक्तं तद् द्वाभ्यामपि वादिभ्यां श्रुतधारिभ्यां द्वयोरपि यथासंभवं लिख्यत इति ।

> अर्थिना संनियुक्तो वा प्रत्यर्थिप्रहितोऽपि वा ।
> यो यस्यार्थे विवदते तयोर्जयपराजयौ ।। [J Mā 2.22]

यदि कदाचिच्छरीरापाटवाद्वा स्वयं वक्तुं निष्प्रभुत्वाद्वार्थिना प्रत्यर्थिना वापटुशरीरेण करणाग्रे स्वयमेव नियुक्तो भवति । एवमुक्त्वा यथास्य जयेन मम जयः पराजयेन पराजयः । अथवा पटुशरीरेण गृहस्थितेनैव तस्यापि प्रधानपुरुस्य हस्ते संदिश्य यः कोऽपि प्रहितो भवेत् । एवं तयोरर्थिप्रतिहस्तकयोः करणाग्रे प्रतिष्ठतोर्यस्यार्थे विवदते तस्य जयपराजयाविति ।

> यो न भ्राता न च पिता न पुत्रो न नियोगकृत् ।
> परार्थवादी दण्ड्यः स्याद्व्यवहारेऽपि विब्रुवन् ।। [J Mā 2.23]

अनेके पुरुषाः कामक्रोधलोभग्रस्ताः परकीयार्थ एव संबध्यमाना अनियुक्ता अपि धनिकत्वं कृत्वा परान्विद्वेषन्ति । तन्निवारणार्थं श्लोक इति ।

पूर्ववादं परित्यज्य योऽन्यमालम्बते पुनः ।
वादसंक्रमणाज्ज्ञेयो हीनवादी स वै नरः ।। [J Mā 2.24]

यो वादी पूर्वपादलिखितस्वप्रज्ञार्थं क्रियया निर्वाहयितुमसमर्थोऽन्यपादाश्रितमभियोगमवतारयति स तस्मात्संक्रमणाद्धीनवादीति ज्ञेयः । वक्तव्य इत्यर्थः ।

सर्वेष्वपि विवादेषु वाक्छले नापहीयते ।
पशुस्त्रीभूम्यृणादाने शास्योऽप्यर्थान्न हीयते ।। [J Mā 2.25]

अन्येषु सर्वेषु विवादेषु वाक्छले नापहीयते नावसायं प्राप्नोति । यत्र पुनर्गोमहिष्यादिपशु वादः । यश्च स्त्रीविषयसंबध्यमानो वादः । तथा गृहक्षेत्रादिको वादः । यो भूमि वादः । यश्च पञ्चविंशतिभेदभिन्नर्णादान वादः । एतेषु सर्वेष्वपि प्रधानवादेषु केनापि द्विरुक्तवाक्छलमात्रेणावसायं न प्राप्नोति । शास्योऽपि विनयं प्राप्तोऽपि । तस्मात्प्रक्रान्तकीयार्थान्नावहीयते न परिच्यवत इति ।

अभियुक्तोऽभियोगस्य यदि कुर्यादपह्नवम् ।
अभियोक्ता दिशेद्देश्यं प्रत्यवस्कन्दितो न चेत् ।। [J Mā 2.26]

अभियुक्तः प्रतिवादी यद्यभियोगस्यापह्नवं मिथ्या करोति तदाभियोक्ता वादी देश्यं दिशेदिति । क्रियामानयेदित्यर्थः । यदि स एव वादी प्रतिवादिना प्रत्यवस्कन्दनोत्तरेण नाभियुक्तो भवति । तत्र च प्रत्यवस्कन्दनोत्तरे प्रतिवाद्येव नयेद्देश्यमिति ।

पूर्वपादे हि लिखितं यथाक्षरमशेषतः ।
अर्थी तृतीयपादे तु क्रियया प्रतिपादयेत् ।। [J Mā 2.27]

यदर्थिना पूर्वभाषायां लिखितं तत्तेन तृतीयपादेन क्रियया खरीकरणीयमित्यर्थः ।

क्रियापि द्विविधा प्रोक्ता मानुषी दैविकी तथा ।
मानुषी लेख्यसाक्षिभ्यां धटादिर्दैविकी स्मृता । [J Mā 2.28]

मिथ्या कुर्वतः प्रतिवादिनः साधनार्थं क्रिया द्विप्रकारा दृष्टा मानुषी दैविकी च । तत्र मानुषी लेख्यसाक्षिरूपा । दैविकी

धटोऽग्निरुदकं चैव विषं कोषश्च पञ्चमः । [NāSmṛ 20.6ab]
इत्येवमादिकेति ।

दिवा कृते कार्यविधौ ग्रामेषु नगरेषु वा ।
संभावे साक्षिणां चैव दिव्या न भवति क्रिया ।। [J Mā 2.29]

यानि दिवा कृतानि कार्याणि भवन्ति तेषु श्रोतारो द्रष्टारश्च संभवन्ति । लिखितमपि संभवति । तेनैतेषु प्रदेशेषु मानुष्येव क्रिया प्रमाणं न दैविकी । तथा संभवे साक्षिणामिति यच्च ससाक्षिकमेव प्रयोजनं वृत्तं तत्र साक्षिसंभव एव विद्यमाने दिव्या क्रिया न भवति ।

अरण्ये निर्जने रात्रावन्तर्वेश्मनि साहसे ।
न्यासस्यापह्नवे चैव दिव्या संभवति क्रिया ।। [J Mā 2.30]

अरण्ये वनमध्ये पट्टने वा निर्जन प्रदेशे रात्रौ च मानुषासंभव एकान्ते गृहमध्ये वा । तथा साहसे व्यवहारे तथा न्यासस्यापह्नव एतेषु प्रदेशेष्वर्थेषु च मानुषीक्रियाभावे दिव्या संभवति क्रियेति ।

कारणप्रतिपत्त्या च पूर्वपक्षे विरोधिते ।
अभियुक्तेन वै भाव्यं विज्ञेयं पूर्वपक्षवत् ।। [J Mā 2.31]

अत्र कारणप्रतिपत्तिरिति संस्कारेण सह संप्रतिपत्तिः । प्रत्यवस्कन्दनोत्तरमित्यर्थः । सर्वत्र कारणोत्तरे प्रतिवादी संप्रतिपत्तिं कृत्वा कारणं ब्रवीति । अतस्तेन कारणप्रत्युत्तरेण पूर्वपक्षे विरोधिते भाषार्थे निरर्थकीकृतेऽभियुक्तेन प्रतिवादिना भाव्यं भावनीयम् । तत्स्वकीयं कारणमुपन्यस्तं खरीकरणीयमित्यर्थः । एतत्तेन विज्ञेयं पूर्वपक्षवत् । पूर्वपक्षं वादित्वं प्रति प्राप्तेन तत्स्वकीयं कारणं क्रियया खरीकरणीयमित्यर्थः । एतत्तेनाभियुक्तेन ज्ञेयमिति ।

पलायते य आहूतो मौनी साक्षिपराजितः ।
स्वयमभ्युपपन्नश्च अवसन्नश्चतुर्विधः ।। [J Mā 2.32]

य आहूत आकारितोऽपि राजपुरुषैः प्रस्तुतव्यवहारखेटनार्थं पालायते सोऽवसन्नः प्राप्तावसाय उच्यते । मौनीति यः प्रस्तुतव्यवहारे स्वकीयं प्राप्तावसरं प्रोत्साह्य-मानोऽपि न वदति मौनी तूष्णीं स्थितः तिष्ठति । अयमप्यवसायं प्राप्तो द्वितीयः ।

तथा च साक्षिभिर्यः पराजयं प्रापितः । अयमप्यवसायं प्राप्तो तृतीयः । तथा व्यवहारार्थमागतः स्वकीयमन्यायं यः स्वयमेव प्रतिपद्यते स स्वयमभ्युपपन्नश् चतुर्थोऽवसायं प्राप्तः । इत्ययमवसन्नश्चतुर्विध इति ।

अन्यवादी क्रियाद्वेषी नोपस्थाता निरुत्तरः ।
आहूतप्रपलायी च हीनः पञ्चविधः स्मृतः ।। [J Mā 2.33]

अत्र ये समनन्तरपूर्वश्लोके दर्शिताश्चत्वारः प्राप्तावसाया[84] उक्ताः पुनरस्मिन्श्लोके मौन्याहूतप्रपलायी[85] च हीनवादित्वविनयमात्रेणानुगृह्य पुनरपि वादयोग्यत्वमापादितौ । ततस्तेषां चतुर्णां मध्ये निश्चितौ द्वावेवावसन्नौ प्राप्तावसायौ प्रतिष्ठितान्तावेको यः साक्षिभिः पराजितो । द्वितीयो यः स्वयमभ्युपपन्नः स्वकीयमन्यायवादित्वं प्रतिपन्नः । अतो ये हीनवादशब्देन प्राप्ता विनयमात्राकोटनाः । न तु प्राप्तावसायाः पुनरपि वादयोग्या भवन्तीति । ते पञ्चाप्यत्रोच्यन्ते । तत्रान्यवादी यो मतिभ्रंशात्किंचिदन्यद्वदति । यश्च क्रियाद्वेषीति <.....>[86] दूषणं प्रयच्छति । यश्च राजदैविकादिना नोपस्थानकर्ता जातः । यश्च तत्क्षणं एवोत्तरमदत्वोत्तरकालं प्रार्थयति । यश्च स्वकीयवैरिणं दानग्रहणिकं वा दृष्ट्वा तद्भयात्प्रपलायनः । एते पञ्चाप्येतैरेव छलैश्च प्राप्तवसाया न भवन्ति । तत्क्षणमात्रवादहीनाः पुनरपि वादयोग्या भवन्तीत्यर्थः ।

मणयः पद्मरागाद्या दीनारादि हिरण्मयम् ।
मुक्ताविद्रुमशङ्खाद्याः प्रदुष्टाः स्वामिगामिनः ।। [J Mā 2.34]

यदेतेषां[87] वस्तूनां स्वाम्येतानि जातिशुद्धानि निर्दोषाणि भणित्वा विक्रीणाति ग्राहकोऽपि तत्प्रत्ययादेव मूल्यं दत्त्वा गृह्णाटि । यावदन्यत्र सुदूरमपि गत्वा परीक्षापयति तावत्कृत्रिमाणि कूटाणि यदि भवन्ति । ततस्तानि स्वामिगानि भवन्ति । तेन तेषां स्वामिना तानि गृहीत्वान्यानि वा गुणप्रयुक्तानि दत्त्वा परितोषणीयो ग्राहकः । मूल्यं वा समर्पणीयमस्येत्यर्थः ।

गन्धमाल्यमदत्तमदत्तं तु भूषणं वास एव वा ।
पादुकेति राजोक्तं तदाक्रामन्वधमर्हति[88] ।। [J Mā 2.35]

एतानि वस्तूनि राजकीयानि यो दर्पात्स्वयमाक्रामति[89] स राज्ञः सकाशकाद् वधमर्हतीति ।

पण्यमूल्यं भृतिर्न्यासो दण्डो यच्चावहारकम् ।
वृथादानाक्षिकपणा वर्धन्ते नाविवक्षिताः ।। [J Mā 2.36]

पण्यमूल्यं वक्रीतक्रयाणकमूल्यम्[90] । भृतिः कर्मकरवृत्तिः । न्यासः[91] स्थापनिकमुक्तं द्रव्यम् । दण्डो दोषविनयो राजकुले । अवहारकमुच्छिन्नकं गृहीतम् । वृथादानं यच्चारणादीनां[92] प्रतिपन्नम् । आक्षिकपणा द्युतहारितद्रव्यम् । एते पणाः सुचिरकालागतेनापि धनिना सामकाः स्वरूपस्थिता ग्रहीतव्याः । एत अविचारिता अविवक्षिता न वर्धन्त इत्यर्थः ।

मिथ्याभियोगिनो ये स्युर्द्विजानां शूद्रयोनयः ।
तेषां जिह्वां समुत्कृत्य राजा शूले विधापयेत् ।। [J Mā 2.37]

द्विजानां शूद्रयोनयः प्रेषणाकारिण एव विहिताः । यदा पुनस्त एव शूद्रा द्विजानामेव मिथ्याभियोगिनो ये स्युर्भवन्ति दर्पाद्वा निजदुर्वचनाविक्षेपकारिणो भवन्ति तदा तान्शूद्रान्राजा खण्डितजिह्वान्कृत्वा शूले निधापयेत् [*sic*] । ततस्तेन पापेन न गृह्यते । अन्यथा शिष्टपालनार्थं दुष्टनिग्रहार्थं करग्राहिणो निर्मितस्य राज्ञ एव स दोष इति ।

आज्ञा लेखः पट्टकः शासनं वा
आधिः पत्त्रं विक्रयो वा क्रयो वा ।
राज्ञे कुर्यात्पूर्वमावेदनं यस्
तस्य ज्ञेयः पूर्वपक्षः विधिज्ञैः ।। [J Mā 2.38]

यो राज्ञे पूर्वमावेदयति तस्य पूर्वपक्षो ज्ञेयः । आज्ञा[93] । एतेन राजाज्ञा न गणिता । लेखः । प्रभुसक्तलेखेनायं प्रारब्धः । पट्टकः । अनेन दासी मदीया-वष्टब्धा पट्टकलिखितम् । शासनम् । अयं मदीयं शासनग्राममवष्टभ्य भुङ्क्ते । ममेदं । शासनाम्तिष्ठति । आधिः । अयमाधिः प्रथमं ममर्णिकेन कृतः । तत्केन भोक्तव्यः । पत्त्रम् । एष मम लिखितगृहीतमपि द्रव्यं न प्रयच्छति । क्रयोऽस्य हस्ताद्भाण्डं मया क्रीतं मूल्यद्रव्यं च दत्तम् । भाण्डं मम नार्पयति । इत्यादिकानि पूर्वपक्षस्य भाषावादिनो वेदनोदाहरणान्युक्तानीति ।

साक्षिकदूषणे कार्यं पूर्वसाक्षिविशोधनम् ।
शुद्धेषु साक्षिषु ततः पश्चात्साक्ष्यं विशोधयेत् ।। [J Mā 2.39]

यदा प्रतिवादी साक्षिकदूषणं[94] प्रयच्छति तदा पूर्वं साक्षिविशोधनमं साक्षिप्र-करणोक्तन्यायेन कर्तव्यम् । यदि चादुष्टदूषणं करोति ततः क्रियाद्वेषि-हीनवादिविनयं ग्राह्यः । ततः शुद्धेषु साक्षिषु साक्षिवचमं विशोध्यम् । व्याजं निर्व्याजं चेति ।

साक्षिसभ्यावसन्नानां दूषणे दर्शनं पुनः ।
स्वचर्यावसितानां तु नास्ति पौनर्भवो विधिः ।। [J Mā 2.40]

ये साक्षिभिर्वा स्वसाक्ष्येणावसायं प्राप्ताः ये च सभ्यैश्चावसायं प्रापिताः विधर्मिणो मन्यन्ते तेषां तीर्तानुशिष्टन्यायेन राजोत्तरकरणस्यावधिष्ठितो भूत्वा पुनर् व्यवहारदर्शनं कुर्यादिति । ये पुनश्च चर्यावसिता भवन्ति कूटसाक्षिप्रपञ्चकरणेन वा कूटीभूताः स्वयमेव स्वकीयसंबद्धाः प्रपश्यन्ते तेषां नास्ति पौनर्भवो विधिः । पुनर्व्यवहारदर्शनं च नास्तीति ।

स्वयमभ्युपपन्नोऽपि स्वचर्यावसितोऽपि सन् ।
क्रियावसन्नोऽप्यर्हेत परं सभ्यावधारणम् ।। [J Mā 2.41]

अत्रावसन्नास्त्रयोऽभिहिताः । एकः स्वयमभ्युपपन्नः । स्वमुखेन प्राप्तावसायः । द्वितीयः स्वचर्यावसन्नः । कूटलिखितसाक्षिप्रपञ्चेन प्रपञ्चकरणेन स्वकीयदुष्टचर्यया दुश्चरित्रेणावसन्नः । तृतीय उद्दिष्टसाक्षिभिरेवावसायं प्रापितः । अयं त्रिविधोऽप्यवसन्नो राज्ञा स्वेच्छया विधूत्य [?] दण्डनीयः । किं तर्हि परं सभ्यावधारणमं सोऽप्यर्हेत । किमुक्तं भवति । यावत्सभ्यैर्दण्डावधारणं निगदितम्तावन्न धारणीयोऽसाविति ।

पक्षानुत्सार्य कार्यस्तु सभ्यैः कार्यविनिश्चयः[95] ।
अनुत्सारितनिर्णिक्ते विरोधः प्रेत्य चेह[96] च ।। [J Mā 2.42]

यदा निर्णयकालो भवति लग्नस्तदा वादिप्रतिवादिनोः पक्षैः सर्वैस्तत्क्षणसंबध्यमानकैः सह द्वावप्युत्सार्य सभ्यैर्निर्णयः कर्तव्यः । यदा पुनरनुत्सातिपक्षयोर्त्र्यत्यक्षयोरेव सभ्या निर्णयं पर्यालोचयित्वा प्रयच्छन्ति तदा तयोर्य एवैकः प्राप्तावसन्नः । [?-->] तैः कर्तुमभिप्रेत एवाकृतप्रतिभूरनिबद्ध एव किंचिदन्तरम्[97] उत्पादयति [<--?] राज्ञः कारिणकानां च तेनैव विघ्नेनार्थनाशादैहिकविरोधो दुष्टनिग्रहशिष्टप्रातिपाल्याच्च पारत्रिकविरोधः प्रपद्यत इति ।

सभैरेव जितः[98] पश्चाद्राज्ञा शास्यः स्वशास्त्रतः ।
जयिने चापि देयं स्याद्यथावज्जयपत्रकम् [99]।। [J Mā 2.43]

तत्र व्यवहारे यः कश्चित्प्राप्तावसायो भवति स सभ्यैः प्रकटितदण्डो[100] निगदितदण्ड इत्यर्थः । राज्ञा शास्त्रानुसारवच्छास्यः । यश्च प्राप्तजयो भवति तस्मै जयपत्रं दातव्यमिति ।

व्यवहारमुखं चैतत्पूर्वमुक्तं स्वयंभुवा ।
मुखशुद्धौ हि शुद्धिः स्याद्व्यवहारस्य नान्यथा ।। [J Mā 2.44]

योऽयं व्यवहारमातृकानामाध्यायोपलक्षितः । एतत्सर्वं व्यवहारानां मुखम् । सर्वव्यवहारार्थव्यापित्वात् । स्वयंभुवा ब्रह्मणाभिहितमनया प्रत्यङ्गीकृतव्यवहारमुखशुद्धिः स्यात् । मुखशुद्धौ तु शुद्धिव्यवहारस्य स्वयंभुवा कीर्तितेति । इति नारदीयमातृकायां द्वितीयोऽध्यायः । इति नारदव्यवहारसंहितायां कल्याणभट्टपरिशोधितासहायभाष्यव्यवहारमातृका समाप्ता ।

मातृका

३ सभा

इदानीं व्यवहारविधिरुच्यते ।

नानियुक्तेन वक्तव्यं व्यवहारे कथंचन ।
नियुक्तेन तु वक्तव्यमपक्षपतितं वचः ॥१॥

अत्र राजसभाव्यवहारकाले लोकाचारस्वाजन्यपक्षपक्षाश्रयस्थिता भहवो लोका वादिप्रतवादिभ्यां सह धर्माधिकरणमागच्छन्ति । तत्र केचिज्ज्ञानिनः केचिदज्ञानिनः केचिज्ज्ञानाभिमानिनः । यदि साकोटनं निषिद्धा न भवन्ति ततस्ते सभ्यानेवानेकप्रमादवाक्यैर्विक्षोभ्य द्रावयन्ति । परस्परं च वादकलहकारिणो भवन्ति । ततोऽर्थनिगदमुच्यते । ये सभ्याः सभायां व्यवहारदर्शननियुक्तास्तानेव केवलान्मुक्त्वा यः कश्चिदनियुक्तस्तटस्थितः कोऽपि किमपि वदति स राज्ञा विनयं ग्राह्यः । **नानियुक्तेन वक्तव्यमि**त्यागमबालादिति । श्लोकपूर्वार्धेनानियुक्त-वक्तव्याकोटनाभिहिता । उत्तरार्धेन नियुक्तानामपि सैव दर्शिता । यथा **नियुक्तेनैव वक्तव्यमपक्षपतितं वचः** । **नियुक्तेन तु** सभ्येन धर्मासनस्येन केवलं धर्म-मूर्तिमेवावस्थापयता किमपि धर्मशास्त्रोक्तव्यवहारनिर्णयवचनं तदेव वक्तव्यम् । न पुनर्वादिनोरेकतमस्यापि पक्षपाताश्रितं[101] वक्तव्यमिति ।

अनियुक्तो[102] नियुक्तो वा शास्त्रज्ञो[103] वक्तुमर्हति ।
दैवीं वाचं स वदति यः शास्त्रमुपजीवति[104] ॥ [J Mā 3.2]

अस्यायमर्थः । यदि कथमपि सर्वेऽपि सभासदो बुद्धिक्षोभाच्छास्त्रार्थं[105] विस्मृत्याथवा लोभादिना कारणेन शास्त्रोक्तं न्यायमार्गमुत्सृज्य व्यवहारस्यान्या-ययुक्तं निर्णयं दातुं प्रवृत्ता भवन्ति तत्र च प्रसङ्गागतः कश्चित्स्मृतितन्त्र-व्यवहारमार्गज्ञो ब्राह्मणः प्रत्यक्षस्तिष्ठति । तेन शास्त्रोक्तवचनपाठपूर्वकं प्रतिषेभधनीयाः सभासदः एवं प्रबोधयतो वदतस्तस्य छलं नास्ति । अनियुक्तोऽपि शास्त्रज्ञो वक्तुमर्हति । यतः शास्त्रं नाम देव नाम देवभाषा । अतः
दैवीं वाचं स वदति यः शास्त्रमुपजीवति ।

१ Y om this verse; d — D add
व्यवहारेषु सर्वेषु नियोक्तव्या बहुश्रुताः ।
गुणवत्यपि नैकस्मिन्विश्वसेद्धि विचक्षणः ॥ [?]

युक्तरूपं ब्रुवन्सभ्यो नाप्नुयाद् द्वेषकिल्बिषे ।
ब्रुवाणस्त्वन्यथा सभ्यस्तदेवोभयमाप्नुयात् ॥२॥

शास्त्राचाराविरुधं यत्तद्**युक्तरूपमु**च्यते । एवंविधं वाक्यं **ब्रुवन्सभ्यो नाप्नुयाद् देवषकिल्बिषे** । ऐहिकामुष्मिकबाध इत्यर्थः । युक्तवादी सभ्य इहलोकबाधाकरं लोकद्वेषं परलोकबाधाकरं च किल्बिषं नाप्नुयात् । **अन्यथा तु ब्रुवाणः सद्यस्*** तत्क्षणात् **तदेवोभयमाप्नुयाद्** इति ।

राजा तु धार्मिकान्सभ्यान्नियुञ्ज्यात्सुपरीक्षितान् ।
व्यवहारधुरं वोढुं ये शक्ताः सद्गवा इव ॥३॥

अत्र योऽयं व्यवहारभारः स दुर्विज्ञेयः । विषमपदधर्ममार्ग अजाताकृतस्कन्धैर्बालवृषभकैरिव बालकुडबुद्धिभिः निर्वाहयितुं न पार्यते । अतो[106] **व्यवहारधुरं वोढुं ये शक्ताः सद्गवा** इव शास्त्राचारलोकाचारदृष्टपरम्पराः प्रौढमतयो ये तान्**धार्मिकान्राजा नियुञ्ज्यात्सुपरीक्षितान्**कृत्वेति ।

धर्मशास्त्रार्थकुशलाः कुलीनाः सत्यवादिनः ।
समाः शत्रौ च मित्रे च नृपतेः स्युः सभासदः ॥४॥

अत्र सभासल्लक्षणं अभिहितम् । इह धर्मशास्त्रेषु स्मृतितन्त्रसांकेतिकशब्दगूढार्थदुःखबोधानि मुनिवचनानि बाहुल्येन भवन्ति । तेषु सूक्तप्रतिषिद्धपुनःसंभावितसापेक्षनिरपेक्षवचनार्थेष्वप्राप्तगुरुपारम्पर्यार्थविचारक्षोदकौशला मन्दमतयः न सम्यग्न्यायदण्डप्रमाणनिर्णयविदः **सभासदः** सभायोग्या न भवन्तीत्येतदर्थं सविशेषमिदमभिहितं **धर्मशास्त्रार्थकुशला** इति । **कुलीनाः** कुलमाहात्म्यात्पक्षपातविकृतिं न भजन्ते । **सत्यवादिनः** स्वभावादेवानृतादुद्विजन्ते । **समाः शत्रौ च मित्रे च** तस्मिन्काले परित्यक्तद्वेषस्नेहभाव एवंविधा **नृपतेः सभासदः स्युर्** इति ।

तत्प्रतिष्ठः स्मृतो धर्मो धर्ममूलश्च पार्थिवः ।

२ a — Jolly वदन्; c — P sh सद्यस्.
३ b — D नियुञ्जीत परीक्षितान्; d — D add
दश वा वेदशास्त्रज्ञास्त्रयो वा वेदपारगाः ।
यद् ब्रूयुः कार्यमुत्पन्नं स धर्मो धर्मसाधनं ।। [Dhko 44]
४ c — D समा मित्रे च शत्रौ; d — D add
धर्माणां संशयच्छेत्ता राजा च सुधराधिपः ।
तस्मान्न वाच्यमेकेन वचनं तु ससंशयम् ।। [Dhko 44]

सह सद्भिरतो राजा व्यवहारान्विशोधयेत् ॥५॥

तत्प्रतिष्ठ इति । एवंलक्षणोक्तसभ्यप्रतिष्ठितो **धर्मो** भवति । **पार्थिवश्च धर्ममूलः** । अतः कारणात्सह सद्भिः सभासद्भिर्व्यवहारविशोधनं कुर्यात् । यथा राज्ञः प्रत्यक्षस्य प्रमाणधर्ममार्गस्थिता व्यवहारा विशुध्यन्ति तथा न परोक्षस्य । अतोऽत्यादरेणेदमुक्तं

सह सद्भिरतो राजा व्यवहारान्विशोधयेत् ॥

इति ।

शुद्धेषु व्यवहारेषु शुद्धिं यान्ति सभासदः ।
शुद्धिश्च तेषां धर्माद्धि धर्ममेव वदेत्ततः ॥६॥

यदा राजा व्यवहारान्विशोधयेत्तदा **शुद्धेषु व्यवहारेषु सभासदः शुद्धिं** प्राप्नुवन्ति । दुराराधोऽपि लोक एवं ब्रवीति । यत्र राज्ञा प्रत्यक्षेणायं व्यवहारो दृष्टः तत्रावश्यं सभासदां कश्चिद्दोषो नास्तीति । इत्येवं **शुद्धिं यान्ति सभासद** इति ।

यत्र धर्मो ह्यधर्मेण सत्यं यत्रानृतेन च ।
हन्यते प्रेक्षमाणानां हतास्तत्र सभासदः ॥७॥

अत्र धर्मन्यायाचारस्य मूलं सभासद एव । प्रधानेऽप्रधाने[107] च गुणदोषाः सज्यन्ते । तेन तान्प्रति पुनरिदमुक्तम् **। यत्र धर्मोऽधर्मेण सत्यमनृतेन च प्रेक्षमाणानां सर्वेषां** एव **हन्यते** तदा **हतास्तत्र सभासद** एव ये व्यवहार-नियुक्तवादिनः । ये पुनरनियुक्तवादिनो निषिद्धवक्तव्यास्तेषां धर्मे सत्यघातकमपि दूरवर्तीति ।

विद्धो धर्मो ह्यधर्मेण सभां यत्रोपतिष्ठते ।
न चेद्विशल्यः क्रियते विद्धास्तत्र सभासदः ॥८॥

५ a — X सत्प्रतिष्ठः; d — D add

वृषो हि भगवान्धर्मस्तस्य यः कुरुते ह्यलम् ।
वृषलं तं विदुर्देवास्तस्माद्धर्मं न लोपयेत् ॥ [Manu 8.16]
एक एव सुहृद्धर्मो निधनेऽप्यनुयाति यः ।
शरीरेण समं नाशं सर्वमन्यद्धि गच्छति ॥ [Manu 8.17]

६ d — D add

रौति धर्मः सभामध्ये भिद्यमानोऽनृतेपुभिः ।
अधर्ममग्रतः कृत्वा वध्योऽप्येप दुरात्मभिः ॥ [Dhko 46]

८ NMS om this verse; c — X चास्य; X P विशल्यं; P कृन्तन्ति.

तत्र यथा लोकः शस्त्राभिघातपीडितो वैद्यपार्श्वमागच्छति । तत्र च ते सभासदस्तस्य तदवस्थधर्मस्याधर्मस्योद्धरणव्यापारनियुक्ताधिकारिणोऽपि यदा तत्पाप**शल्यं*** **न कृन्तन्ति*** नापनयन्ति तदा संक्रमणतन्त्रप्रयोगसंक्रामितवृश्चिकविषेणेवोपेक्षितपापशल्येन त एव **सभासदो विद्धा** भवन्ति । अतः कारणाद् इत्युक्तम् ।

सभा वा न प्रवेष्टव्या वक्तव्यं वा समञ्जसम् ।
अब्रुवन्विब्रुवन्वापि नरो भवति किल्बिषी ॥९॥

अत्र सभ्यैः **सभायाम्*** एककालमेव **न प्रवेष्टव्यम्*** । न पुनरधर्मन्याययुक्तमित्यर्थः । तथा तस्यां प्रविष्टः सभ्योऽ**ब्रुवन्**निर्णयप्राप्तावसरश्च **विब्रुवन्**धर्मन्यायविपरीतं **किल्विषी** भवति महापातकीत्यर्थः ।

ये तु सभ्याः सभां गत्वा तूष्णीं ध्यायन्त आसते ।
यथाप्राप्तं न ब्रुवते सर्वे तेऽनृतवादिनः ॥१०॥

ये सभ्या अधर्मविच्छेदस्थानभूतां **सभां प्राप्य*** वादिप्रतिवादिनोः संदेहविच्छेदार्थिनोरपि अन्यकार्यव्यासक्ता इव किंचिदन्यदेव कार्यान्तरं **ध्यायन्त** इव **तूष्णीं** तथा **आसते** तिष्ठन्ति । एकस्य जयं द्वितीयस्य पराजयमवसरप्राप्तमपि न ब्रुवते । ततस्ते सर्वेऽपि अनृतवादिसमाना राज्ञा द्रष्टव्याः । अनृतवादिविनययोग्या इत्यर्थः ।

पादोऽधर्मस्य कर्तारं पादः साक्षिणमृच्छति ।
पादः सभासदः सर्वान्पादो राजानमृच्छति ॥११॥
राजा भवत्यनेनास्तु मुच्यन्ते च सभासदः ।
एनो गच्छति कर्तारं निन्दार्हो यत्र निन्द्यते ॥१२॥

एतच्छ्लोकद्वयमपि संततार्थनिगमप्रतिबद्धत्वादेकत्रैवोक्तम् । यदत्र यौ वादिप्रतिवादिनौ व्यवहारमत्सरारूढौ धर्माधिकरणमुपस्थितौ । न तौ द्वावपि सत्यौ न

९ a — P सभायां; P प्रवेष्टव्यं.
१० NMS om this verse; a — P प्राप्य.
११ X add
तस्माद्धर्मो न हन्तव्यो मा नो धर्मो हतो वधीत् । [Manu 8.15cd]
वृषो हि भगवान्धर्मस्तस्य यः कुरुते ह्यलम् ।
वृषलं तं विदुर्देवास्तस्माद्धर्मं न लोपयेत् ॥ [Manu 8.16]
१२ a — D has 12-13 after 14.

चापि द्वावप्यसत्यौ । तयोरवश्यमेकेन सत्येन भवितव्यम् । अपरेणासत्येन । तत्र यदासत्यस्यैव सभासदो जयं प्रयच्छन्ति पराजयं तु सत्यस्यैव तदा तस्य कुदृष्टव्यवहारस्य यत्पापमेनःशब्देनोक्तं ततश्चतुर्भागविभक्तं भवति । तस्य पापस्य **पादो** गच्छति **कर्तारं पादः साक्षिणः पादः सभासदः सर्वान्पादो राजानमृच्छति** राजानं गच्छतीत्यर्थः । यदा पुनर्**निन्दार्ह** एव निन्द्यत असत्यस्य पराजयः क्रियत इत्यर्थस्तदा **राजा भवत्यनेना** अपापः । **सभासदो**ऽपि तस्मात्पापाद्विमुच्यन्ते । तत्सर्वमेवै**नः कर्तारमे**वैकं प्रतिपद्यते । अन्याय-कर्तारमित्यर्थः ।

अन्धो मत्स्यानिवाश्नाति निरपेक्षः सकण्टकान् ।
परोक्षमर्थवैकल्याद्भाषते यः सभां गतः ॥१३॥

अत्र व्यवहारशास्त्राध्ययनस्यानध्ययनस्य माहात्म्यमुपवर्णितं किल । यस्य चक्षुरिन्द्रियं भवति निर्मलं च स वक्त्रजिह्वातालुभेदिनो मत्स्यकण्टकानपनीय मत्स्यानेवाश्नाति । यः पुनर**न्धः** स कण्टकातिव्याप्तान्तदपनयनासमर्थो **निरपेक्षः सकण्टकानेव मत्स्यानश्नाति** । एवं शास्त्रचक्षुः **परोक्षमर्थवैकल्याद**र्थासामर्थ्याद् **भाषते यः सभां गत** इति ।

तस्मात्सभ्यः सभां प्राप्य रागद्वेषविवर्जितः ।
वचस्तथाविधं ब्रुयाद्यथा न नरकं पतेत् ॥१४॥

तस्मादेतत्सर्वमवधार्य **सभ्यः** सभास्थानं **प्राप्य रागद्वेषविवर्जितो** भूत्वा तादृश-मपक्षपतितं **वचो ब्रुयात्**यथा नरके न गच्छेत्परकीयदोषसमर्थनपातकादिति ।

यथा शल्यं भिषग्विद्वानुद्धरेद्यन्त्रयुक्तितः ।
प्राड्विवाकस्तथा शल्यमुद्धरेद् व्यवहारतः ॥१५॥

यथा नष्टशल्यमदृष्टमपि दुःखोद्धरणीयमपि **भिषग्**वैद्यः स च **विद्वान्**शल्योद्धरण-प्रयोगकुशलो बहुप्रकारं यन्त्रतन्त्रप्रयोगयुक्तिभिः **शल्यमुद्धरेत्** । एवमेव प्राड्विवाकः पापाशल्यं व्यवहारान्तर्गतमनुपलक्ष्यमपि व्यवहारयुक्तिभिर् **उद्धरेद्** इति ।

१३ d — NMS सभा-.
१४ d — P व्रजेत्.
१५ b — NMS -युक्तिभिः; P -शक्तितः; c — D शल्यान्.

यत्र सभ्यो जनः सर्वः साध्वेतदिति मन्यते ।
स निःशल्यो विवादः स्यात्सशल्यः स्यादतोऽन्यथा ॥१६॥

इत्यत्र व्यवहारदर्शनागतोऽपि लोकः **सभ्यजनो** जनशब्दादवगम्यते । अत्र व्यवहारे निष्पन्ने सर्वे सभ्याः तथा सर्वोऽपि सभ्यजनः साधु तदस्य लोकोऽपि **साध्वेतदिति मन्यते** जानाति स एव व्यवहारो **निःशल्यो** ज्ञेयः । **अतोऽन्यथा** विपरीतस्वरूपः **सशल्य** एवावमन्तव्यः ।

न सा सभा यत्र न सन्ति वृद्धा
वृद्धा न ते ये न वदन्ति धर्मम् ।
नासौ धर्मो यत्र न सत्यमस्ति
न तत्सत्यं यच्छलेनानुविद्धम् ॥१७॥

एवमत्र क्रमाक्रमं तारतम्येन छलरहितस्य सत्यस्यैव प्रतिष्ठा दर्शिता इति । एतत्सभालक्षणमभिहितम् ।

१६ d — D वदतो.
१७ c — P नो.

व्यवहारपदानि

१ ऋणादानम्

ऋणं देयमदेयं च येन यत्र यथा च यत् ।
दानग्रहणधर्माच्च ऋणादानमिति स्मृतम् ॥१॥

अत्रायम् **ऋण**शब्दः स्मृतितन्त्रसमयसांकेतिकः। यस्य पार्श्वाद्येन किमपि गृहीतं तस्य संबध्यमानपुरुषसहितस्य तेन संबध्यमानपुरुषसहितेन तत्सव्याजमपि यत्र पुनः प्रदेयं प्रत्यर्पणीयं तत्रैवायमृणशब्दो रूढिमुपागतो नान्यत्र । स च पुनरपि सांकेतिकशब्दद्वयोपलक्षितो विषयव्यापकत्वेन स्थितः । तथैकमधमर्णमुक्तं द्वितीयमुत्तमर्णमुक्तं चेति । तत्र तावदधमर्णं यथा

हिरण्यधान्यवस्त्राणां वृद्धिर्द्विस्त्रिचतुर्गुणा ।
रसस्याष्टगुणा वृद्धिः स्त्रीपशूनां च संततिः ।। [NāSmṛ 1.92]

इत्यादिकमधमर्णमुक्तम्। उत्तमर्णं पुनः पितृपितामहप्रपितामहेष्टजनबन्धुवर्गेभ्यो नित्यजलाञ्जलिप्रदानतिलोदकपितृतर्पणपूर्वकं नित्यनैमित्तिकैकोद्दिष्टपार्वणकालस्य वृद्धिश्राद्धेषु पिण्डप्रदानोपलक्षितमुत्तमर्णमिदमिति। अत्र केचिच्चोदयन्ति । हिरण्य-धान्यवस्त्राणां [NāSmṛ 1.92a] इत्यादिकमधमर्णगृहीतं भुक्तं च युज्यते संतत्या देयम् । उत्तमर्णमपि पितृपैतामहसंक्रान्तं हिरण्यधान्यं संतत्यानृनीकर्तुं युक्तमेव दातुम् । या पुनरसंक्रान्तपूर्वजस्य वराटकमात्रधनापि संततिः सा कथमधम-र्णोत्तमर्णप्रदानाधिकारिणी भवत्विति । अत्रोच्यते न संयक् । आक्षोद्यमिदम् । यतः येन शरीरेण धर्मार्थकाममोक्षपुरुषार्थानामुपभोगसाधनक्षमः[108] पुरुषो भवति तदेव शरीरं हिरण्यधान्यादिकपदार्थसर्वाभ्यधिकं पूर्वजप्रसादसंक्रान्तं संततेः । अतः साधूत्तमर्णाधमर्णप्रदानाधिकारिणी पूर्वा संततिरिति । यथा च संतत्या कियद्दूरं यावदिदमृणद्वयमपि दातव्यमित्येतत्पुरत एव पुरुषोत्तमविचारप्राप्तावसरं वक्ष्यामः । एवमृणशब्दमात्रस्य निगम उक्तः । इदानीं येन यत्र यथा च यच्च तद् **देयमदेयं** चेत्यादिकं सविस्तर वक्ष्यमाणपदार्थं दानधर्मग्रहणधर्माभ्यामुपलक्षितं यदृणादानव्यवहारपदं तत्पञ्चविंशतिव्यवहारभेदभिन्नमभिधीयते ।

पितर्युपरते पुत्रा ऋणं दद्युर्यथांशतः ।

१ a — B2 B3 यस्य; b — V V3 V4 V6 V7 V8 Ox धनग्रहण-; B5 L V V3-8 Ox -धर्मांश; M4 -धर्माभ्यां; c — B B2 B3 K2 K5 यस्मिन्नेतानि दृश्यन्ते; d — B3 K2 K5 तदुच्यते.

विभक्ता ह्यविभक्ता वा यस्तामुद्वहते धुरम् ॥२॥

अत्र येषां पित्रा कृतम् **ऋणं** स यावज्जीवति तावत्स्वयमेव दद्यात् । तस्मिंस्तु **पितर्युपरते** मृते तदृणं तत्**पुत्रा** एव **दद्युः** । यदि **विभक्तास्**ततः स्वांशतो दद्युः । अथा**विभक्तास्**ततः सामान्यमेव दद्युः । यो वा **तामुद्धरेद्*** **धुरम्** इति । अत्रैतदुक्तं भवति । यदि ज्येष्ठः सुचिरदूरप्रवसितो भवति कुष्ठक्षयपातकादिभिरयोग्यो भवति तदा यः कोऽपि पितृधनभारस्य धुरमुद्धरेत्स कनिष्ठोऽपि पितृकृतमृणं दद्यादित्यर्थः ।

पितृव्येणाविभक्तेन भ्रात्रा वा यदृणं कृतम् ।
मात्रा वा यत्कुटुम्बार्थे दद्युस्तद्रिक्थिनोऽखिलम् ॥३॥

इत्यत्र पितृभ्राता पितृव्यशब्देनोच्यते । तेन **पितृव्येणा**विभक्तेन **यदृणं कृतम्** । अथवा **मात्रा भ्रात्रा वा कुटुम्बार्थे** यदृणं कृतं भवति । ये केचित्तद्रिक्थभाजस्ते सर्वे तत्सर्वमिति । यदि विभक्तास्ततः स्वांशतो दद्युः । अथवाविभक्तास्ततः सामान्यमेव दद्युरिति ।

क्रमादव्याहतं प्राप्तं पुत्रैर्यन्नर्णमुद्धृतम् ।
दद्युः पैतामहं पौत्रास्तच्चतुर्थान्निवर्तते ॥४॥

इत्यस्मिञ्छ्लोके तथाग्रतो द्वितीयश्लोकेऽपि चतुर्थपुरुषो ऋणदायकः कृती स्फुटोऽपि कैश्चिन्मन्दमतिभिर्मुनिकृतवचनभावार्थमबुद्ध्वासव [?] ऋणदानवाक्यं तत ईदृशं च युक्तिविरुद्धमज्ञानतः प्रवर्तितम् । संजल्पतामुपेक्षमाणानामपि[109] पापानुबन्धजंननमेव भवतीत्येतदुच्यते । ननु[110] येन स्वयमेव कृतमृणं सोऽवश्यं तद्दद्यात्येव । न तु चर्वितचर्वणं कोऽपि करोति । तन्न कोऽपि **गणयति** । ये पुनस्तदीयपुत्रतः संततिपुरुषाः स्वयमकृतमप्यृणं संततिसंबन्धेन दाप्यन्ते लक्ताः [?-->] त एव पितामहाः पौत्रिका ग्राह्यन्ते[111] [<--?] तेनैतदुक्तं । स्वयमकृतर्णैरपि संततिगुणदाप्यैः पुत्रैर्यन्नर्णमुद्धृतं तत्तेषामेव ये पौत्राः स्वयंस्वयमकृतधनदायकाः । तेषामेव स्वकीयपितामहानां स्वयमकृतर्णदायकानां सक्तं तदृणम् । तस्मादेव **क्रमादव्याहतं प्राप्तम्** एव दद्युरिति । **तच्छतुर्थाद्** इति च ।

२ a — BM B B2 B5 B8 K3 K7 ऊर्ध्वं गते; B3 K2 K5 ऊर्ध्वं मृते; a — BM पुत्रां; B5 पुत्राद्; d — BM B B5 B7 K2 K3 K5 K7 तम्; BM B B7 उधरते; B5 K2 K3 K5 K7 उधरणे; P ये वा तामुद्धरेद्.

३ b — B K2 भ्राता; c — B5 माता; BM B B2 B3 B5 B7 K5 K7 स्व-

४ b — BM B B8 K3 K7 V7 यत्रर्णं उदधृतम्; K2 यदृणमुद्धरेद्; c — B7 B8 K3 K7 पौत्रा.

तेभ्यः संततिगुणदायकेभ्यः पुत्रेभ्यो यश्चतुर्थः तस्माद्दृणसंबन्धो निवर्तते । मूलिकस्य पञ्चमत्वात् । यः पुनर्मूलिकचतुर्थः स पितृपितामहप्रपितामहानामुत्तमर्णाधमर्णदाता सर्वमुनिभिरपि समर्थितः । तथा चायमपि द्वितीयश्लोकेनैतं निःसंदिग्धं कर्तुकामः प्राह ।

इच्छन्ति पितरः पुत्रान्स्वार्थहेतोर्यतस्ततः ।
उत्तमर्णाधमर्णेभ्यो मामयं मोचयिष्यति ॥५॥

इत्यस्मिन्द्वितीयश्लोक उत्तमर्णाधमर्णयोरेकयोगनिर्देशोऽयमेतदर्थं कृतः । येनैकयोगनिर्दिष्टानामर्थानां[112] सह वा प्रवृत्तिः सह वा निवृत्तिर्भवति । यथा मूलिकचतुर्थ <:> पितृपितामहप्रपितामहानां त्रयाणामपि पुरुषाणामुत्तमर्णं पितृपिण्डोदकादिकं ददाति तथा हिरण्यधान्यादिकमधमर्णमेतेषां त्रयाणामपि ददात्येवेत्यर्थः । तथा च वृद्धप्रपितामहोऽप्येतदाह

पूजनीयास्त्रयोऽतीता उपजीव्यास्त्रयोऽग्रतः ।
एतत्पुरुषसंतानमृणयोः स्याच्चतुर्थके ॥ [J 1.6]

पूजनीयास्त्रयोऽतीता इति । अतीताः पितृपितामहप्रपितामहास्त्रयोऽपि चतुर्थकेनोत्तमर्णाधमर्णयोर्द्वयोरपि[113] निर्ऋणीकर्तव्याः । त्रयोऽग्रत इति । तेनैव चतुर्थकेन पुत्रपौत्रप्रपौत्रास्त्रयोऽप्युत्तमर्णाधमर्णयोर्निर्ऋणीकरणार्थमेवोपजीव्या इति ।

एतत् पुरुषसंतानमृणयोः स्याच्चतुर्थके । [J 1.6cd]

एकपुरुषसंततिक्रमोद्दिष्टचतुर्थपुरुषस्येति । तथा च याज्ञवल्क्येनापि यदुक्तम्

ऋणं लेख्यकृतं देयं पुरुषैस्त्रिभिरेव तु ।
आधिस्तु भुज्यते तावद्यावत्तन्न प्रदीयते ॥ [YāSmṛ 2.90]

इत्यत्रापि येन स्वकीयं नामकमारोप्य लेख्ये स्वयमेव कृतमृणं भवति तेन तदवश्यमेव दातव्यमित्यत्र को विचारः । विचारस्त्वयम् । यत्स्वयमकृतर्णेऽपि[114] संततिपूर्वपुरुषसंबन्धगुणदाप्यैः कियन्मात्रैस्तद्दृणं दातव्यमित्यस्मिन्नर्थ इदमभिहितं मुनिना पुरुषैस्त्रिभिरेव तु [YāSmṛ 2.90b] । ते च पुरुषास्तदीयसंततिपूर्व <पुरुष> ान्तरोत्पन्नाः पुत्रादयः संबध्यन्ते । न सोऽपि । पुत्रपौत्रप्रपौत्रैः[115] स्वीयसंतत्युत्पन्नैः पुरुषैस्त्रिभिर्दातव्यमित्यर्थः । येन पुनः स्वयंकृतमृणं सोऽस्वयंकृतर्णदायकपुरुषाणामसमानधर्मित्वाद्बाह्यः । यदपि मुनिभिरभिहितम् । यत्तु किल चतुर्थाद्वा पञ्चमाद्वा ऋणदानमेव सर्वं निवर्तते तदपि विच्छिन्नभुक्तिचिह्नैरिति दानस्य दूरपुरुषान्तरे मा क्वचिदसमर्थकूटपत्राणामपि संभवो भविष्यतीत्यप्यमन्दमुनिभावार्थः[116] । एतत्कारणनिराकरणमात्रमेवैतदभिहितम् । न पुनः परमार्थतः सिद्धादेशेन चतुर्थात्पुरुषात्परत ऋणदानसंबन्धनिवृत्त्यर्थं । परमार्थतस्त्वयं मुनिहृदयभावार्थो यतो यावद्व्यवहारस्य धनं न प्रवेशितं तावत्तदीयसं-

ततिपूर्वपुरुषान्तरशतस्यापि मध्ये कोऽपि निर्ऋणी न भवति । अस्य चार्थस्य च परीक्षाकरणार्थमनेनैव मुनिनास्य श्लोकोत्तरार्धं[117] इदमभिहितम् ।

आधिस्तु भुज्यते तावद्यावत्तन्न प्रदीयते । [YāSmṛ 2.90cd]

अत्र यदि सत्यमेव परमार्थात्पुरुषतश्चतुर्थात्परत ऋणदानसंबन्धो[118] निवर्तते ततस्तच्चतुर्थान्निवर्तत [NāSmṛ 1.4d] इत्यस्मादेव मुनिवचनबलाच्चतुर्थेन पुरुषेण स्वयमेव निर्ऋणीभूतेन द्रव्यमदत्त्वैव व्यवहारकपार्श्वाद्गृहं क्षेत्रं चाधिरुद्दालनीयो भवति । तेनापि निर्विकल्पमेव भोक्तव्यो भवति । न चैतत्कोऽपि कर्तुं लभते शक्नोति वा । सोऽतः स्वकीयपूर्वजकृतमृणं व्यवहारकस्य दत्त्वा स्वकीयमाधिं लभते । नान्यथा । अतः सत्यमिदमुच्यते सद्भिः

उक्तानि प्रतिषिद्धानि पुनःसंभावितानि च ।
सापेक्षनिरपेक्षाणि स्मृतिवाक्यानि के विदुः ।। [?]

इति । तथा च

धर्मशास्त्रार्थकुशलाः कुलीना [NāSmṛ Mā 3.4ab]

इत्यस्य विवरणे सविशेषतरमिदमुक्तम् । इह धर्मशास्त्रे तु केचित् स्मृतितन्त्रसमयसांकेतिकशब्दगूढार्थदुरवबोधाः[119] श्लोका भवन्ति । केचिन्मुनिहृदयान्तर्गतभावगूढार्थदुरवबोधा भवन्ति । तेषु चोक्तप्रतिषिद्धपुनः संभावितसापेक्षनिरपेक्षदशविधवाक्यार्थप्रकरणसंबन्धे सति वाक्येष्वसंप्राप्तगुरुपारंपर्योपदेशार्थविचारक्षोदकौशला[120] मन्दमतयो न सारासारापराधानुसारदण्डप्रमाणनिर्णयविदः सभासदः सभायोग्या न भवन्तीति । अत एतदुक्तं धर्मशास्त्रार्थकुशलाः कुलीनाः [NāSmṛ Mā 3.4] कुलपौरुषाः स्वभावादेवाधर्मरुचयो न भवन्ति । सत्यवादिनः स्वभावादेव नानृतं ब्रुवते । समाः शत्रौ च मित्रे चेति [NāSmṛ Mā 3.4c]. तस्मिन्व्यवहारावसरे धर्माधिकरणस्थिता धर्ममेव केवलमनुसृत्य कस्याप्युपरि मत्सरस्नेहभावाश्रयानुवर्तनात्पक्षवादिनो न भवन्ति ये ते नृपतेः स्युः सभासद इति ।

अन्धो मत्स्यानिवाश्नाति निरपेक्षः सकण्टकान् ।
पारोक्षमर्थवैकल्याद्भाषते यः सभां गतः ।। [NāSmṛ Mā 3.13]

इत्य । एवं संततिपुरुषशतेऽप्यप्रवेशितधनस्यासिद्धिर्निर्ऋणत्वे । चतुर्थे पुरुषे सर्वस्मृतिषूत्तमर्णाधमर्णदायक<त्वं> सुप्रतिष्ठितमपि येऽधमर्णदानं बाह्यं कुर्वन्ति ते मन्दमतयो बाह्या निरपेक्षाः सकण्टकमत्स्याशनपापभाजो भवन्तीति कः संदेहः । अत एव मन्दमतिस्मार्तनिराकरणमिदं धर्मसार्थकं कल्याणभट्टस्य । तथा ह्युक्तमेवैतत्कपिलाचार्येण षष्टितन्त्रे

अपारसंसारमहार्णवस्य प्राप्तं परं पारमिदं सुपात्रम् ।
मत्पक्षपातेन विनार्थयुक्तिः प्रणीयते यावदुपैति शान्तम् ।।[?]

यच्चास्मिन्नेवार्थे पाटलिपुत्रवृत्तमुपाख्यानमभिलिख्यते । श्रीपाटलिपुत्रनगरे ब्राह्मणः श्रीधरो नाम व्यवहारकः । तेन स्वसंततिसहितस्यात्मनो वर्तनार्थमतिक्लेशार्जितं धनं वणिग्देवधरनाम्नः पुत्रपौत्रप्रपौत्रसंततिमहाधनं संपन्नस्योपरिद्विकशतमास-

कलान्तरलाभवृद्ध्या प्रयुक्तं द्रम्माणां दश सहस्राणी । ततस्तस्यैकमासे गते देवधरेण[121] कलान्तरे द्रम्मशतद्वयं दत्तम् । यावद् द्वितीयमासः प्रविष्टस्तावद्देवधरः संनिपातदोषान्मृतः । देवधरस्य पुत्रो विषूचिकामृतः । देवधरस्य प्रपौत्रो महिधरो बालस्तिष्ठति । स द्यूतमद्यवेश्याव्यसनी । सूनुभिर्मातुलैः प्रतिग्राहितः । तेऽपि स्मार्तदुर्धरनाम्ना ब्राह्मणेनागत्याभिहिताः । यथा व्यवहारकश्रीधरस्य रूपकोऽपि न दातव्यः । अहं वः स्मृत्याचारेण स्थानमध्येऽपि रक्षयिष्यामि । तैश्चोक्तम् । यद्येवं ततो द्रम्मसहस्रमेकं लञ्चपातं[122] दास्यामः । वयं भवद्भिर्[123] एव संतुष्टाः । एवं तेषां परस्परं निष्पन्ने द्वितीयमासे च परिपूर्णे संजाते व्यवहारकश्रीधरेण ते महिधरकुटुम्बधुरंधरा मातुलाः कलान्तरेण द्रम्मशतद्वयं प्रार्थिताः । तैश्चोक्तं । तव मूलमपि नास्ति । कुतः कलान्तरम् । ब्राह्मणस्मार्तदुर्धरेण कथितं तच्चतुर्थान्निवर्तते [NāSmṛ 1.4d] इति । तच्छ्रुत्वा श्रीधरोऽदृष्टमुद्गरपाताभिघात इव मूर्छामधिगम्य लब्धचेतनः सकुटुम्बपरिवारस्वजनपरिवृतो महता न्यायकलकलप्रघोषेण शालामधि गत्वा श्रीधरस्य[124] अदृष्टमुद्गरपाताभिघात-वृत्तान्तेन देवधरप्रपौत्रं महिधरं समातुलमाहूयोभयपक्षेऽपि न्यायाविचलप्रतिभुवौ गृहीत्वा महिधरमातुला उक्ताः । श्रीधरस्य कलान्तरं कस्मान्न प्रयच्छत[125] । तैश्चोक्तदानाग स्वकीयजयपराजयदत्तनियोगो ब्राह्मणदुर्धरो नियुक्तः । तेन चोक्तमेते वणिजोऽस्माकं पूर्वजपारंपर्येण मित्रस्थाने । तेनाहं ब्रवीमि । किं न श्रुतं भवद्भिरिति नारदवचनम्

दद्युः पैतामहं पौत्रास्तच्चतुर्थान्निवर्तते । [NāSmṛ 1.4cd]

तेन देवधरप्रपौत्रो महिधरश्चतुर्थो न ददाति । तथा च याज्ञवल्क्येनाप्युक्तम्

ऋणं लेख्यकृतं देयं पुरुषैस्त्रिभिरेव तु । [YāSmṛ 2.90ab]

अत्रापि त्रय एव पुरुषा ऋणं प्रयच्छन्ति । एतत्स्मार्तदुर्धरवचनमुपहस्य महाजनेन स्मृतिवाक्यविषयविभागबाह्यं स्मार्तदुर्धरस्य प्रतिबोधार्थं च त्रिकालावधारितं दत्तसमस्तमहाजनानुमतिपरिणीतसकलशास्त्रपरमार्थो भट्टः स्मार्तशेखरो नाम प्राह । हे दुर्धर भवान्स्मृतिशास्त्रवाक्यार्थविभागेषु न क्षुण्णः । न चापि शब्दार्थ-व्याख्याने । तदुभयमपि प्रतिपाद्यमेव । इह समस्तस्मृतिशास्त्रेष्वपि षट्त्रिंशति-प्रकारो वाक्यार्थो भवति । तद्यथा

[१] विधिश्च [२] नियमश्चैव [३] परिसंख्या तथापरा ।
[४] उत्सर्गश् [५] चापवादश्च [६] निषेधः [७] प्रसवस्तथा ॥
[८] समुच्चयो [९] विकल्पश्च यद् [१०] अङ्गाङ्गित्वमेव च ।
[११] अर्थवादो [१२]ऽनुवादश्च [१३] व्यवस्था [१४] लिङ्गदर्शनम् ॥
[१५] अर्थः [१६] प्रकरणं [१७] लिङ्गं शब्दस्यान्यस्य [१८] संनिधिः[126] ।
[१९] अन्यथानुपपत्तिश्च [२०] तथार्थापत्तिरेव च ॥
[२१] भूतार्थवाद [२२] औपम्यं[127] [२३] गौणमुख्यार्थदर्शनम् ।
[२४] पुनरुक्तं [२५] निरासश्च [२६] न निर्बीजार्थवादता ॥
एवमाद्यास्तु वाक्यार्थाः स्मृतितन्त्रे प्रकीर्तिताः ।

जिज्ञासमानैः स्मृत्यर्थं वेदितव्याः प्रयत्नतः ।।
विस्तरान्[128] स्मृतिवाक्यार्थानेतानज्ञाय तत्त्वतः ।
यस्मात्तत्त्वाभिमानी स्यात्साम्भसीवोन्मुखः प्लवेत् ।।[?]

तद्दुर्धर त्वमेतेषां स्मृतिवाक्यानामक्षुण्णत्वाद्ग्राह्यः । यथा शब्दार्थव्याख्यानेऽप्यक्षुण्णस्त्वं[129] तथोच्यते । यदेतन्नारदोक्तम् ।

क्रमादव्याहतं प्राप्तं पुत्रैर्यन्नर्णमुद्धृतम् ।
दद्युः पैतामहं पौत्राः [NāSmṛ 1.4abc]

इत्येतद्विधिवाक्यार्थस्य चाप्रवृत्तौ प्रवर्तनः सार्थको विषयविभागः प्रवृत्तौ तु प्रवर्तनो[130] अविषयश्चर्वितचर्वणदोषात् । तदिह येन स्वयंकृतमृणं स स्वकृतकर्मनिस्तारणार्थमृणादानेऽपि स्वयंवृत्त एव । नास्य विधिवाक्यस्य विषयोऽसौ । तेनात्र पुरुषगणनायां न संबध्यते सिद्धस्य साधनं व्यर्थम् [?] इति । ये पुनः स्वयमकृतर्णं दाप्यन्ते लक्तास्ते पुत्रपौत्रप्रपौत्राः त्रयः पुरुषाः । एतेष्वेवाप्रवृत्तिप्रवर्त्तनविषयो यो विधिवचनस्मृतिवाक्यार्थो न सिद्धसाधनविषयः । अतस्तदस्वयंकृतमपि संततिसंबन्धपूर्वक्रमागतम् । पुत्रैर्यन्नर्णमुद्धृतं तत्तेषामेव पुत्राणां । ये पौत्राः समानधर्मिणस्ते स्वपैतामहमृणं दद्युरिति । शब्दार्थव्याख्यानेऽप्यक्षुण्णस्त्वम् [131]। यथोक्तं

तच्चतुर्थान्निवर्तते [NāSmṛ 1.4d]

तत्तस्मात्प्रपौत्रात्[132] संततिक्रमायातविशोधितर्णसंबन्धात्परतो निवर्तते । पञ्चमो न ददातीत्यर्थः । एवमर्थः[133] चतुर्थपुरुषर्णदानस्यैकं साधनमिदम् । यच्च याज्ञवल्क्येनोक्तम्

ऋणं लेख्यकृतं देयं पुरुषैस्त्रिभिरेव तु ।।[YāSmṛ 2.90ab]

अयमपि विधिवचनवाक्यार्थः । अप्रवृत्तिप्रवर्तनविषय एव । अतो येन कृतमृणं तदीयैः संततिपुरुषैरकृतमपि त्रिभिरेव दातव्यमिति । द्वितीयोऽयं प्रकारः । तथा **चेच्छन्ति पितरः पुत्रान्** इति । अत्रोत्तमर्ण<आधमर्ण>योरेकयोगनिर्देशात्तृतीयः प्रकारः । तथा च वृद्धप्रपितामहोऽप्येतदाह । यदुक्तम्

पूजनीयास्त्रयोऽतीता उपजीव्यास्त्रयोऽग्रतः ।
एतत्पुरुषसंतानमृणयोः स्याच्चतुर्थके ।। [J 1.6]

अयमुत्तम् <आधमर्ण> र्णयोश्चतुर्थपुरुषदापने चतुर्थः प्रकारः । यत्पुनस्तच्चतुर्थान्निवर्तत [NāSmṛ 1.4] इत्येके चतुर्थपुरुषादयः । पुरुषशतमपि यावद्व्यवहारकस्य द्रव्यमदत्त्वा कश्चिदाधिं न लभते । न निर्ऋणी कोऽपि भवति । तत्र चतुर्थस्य व्यवहार इत्ययं चतुर्थपुरुषर्णदापने पञ्चमः प्रकारः । अतो जड स्मार्तदुर्धर स्मृत्यर्था न व्याख्यायन्ते । अन्यथार्थकरणाद्[134] अज्ञानजनितपापं तत्तेषां उपतिष्ठते । अन्यच्च कुस्मार्तदुर्धर किमिदमपि त्वया न श्रुतम्

ऋक्थग्राही ऋणं दद्याद्योषिद्ग्राहस्तथैव च । [YāSmṛ 2.51ab]

तथा

यत ऋक्थमृणं ततः [NāSmṛ 1.14d]

तथा च

धनस्त्रीहारिपुत्राणां ऋणभाग्यो धनं हरेत् । [NāSmṛ 1.20ab]
एष सामान्यपैतृकधनस्य विधिरुक्तः । यत्पुनरिदं श्रीधरसक्तमेव धनं दशसहस्रमात्रं स्वरूपस्थितमेव तिष्ठति । तद्धि मासकलान्तरितमेव । लञ्चोपचारलोभच्छ्रीधरस्योद्दालितुमिच्छसि न लज्जसीत्युक्त्वा दुःस्मार्तदुर्धरस्यावसायो <...> योगसुखम् <...>

अतः पुत्रेण जातेन स्वार्थमुत्सृज्य यत्नतः ।
पिता मोक्षितव्य ऋणाद्यथा न नरकं पतेत् ॥६॥
तपस्वी चाक्तिहोत्री च ऋणवान्म्रियते यदि ।
तपश्चैवाग्निहोत्रं च सर्वं तद्धनिनां धनम् ॥७॥

अत्राजन्माक्तिहोत्रपालनमखण्डिततपःसमाचरणं चातिकष्टेन निर्वाह्यते । द्वयमप्येतदपि महाफलम् । तच्च प्रभूतमपि पय इवर्णिकैकचुलुकप्रवेशेन विनाशितम् । परिपाकफलस्याक्षमत्वं भवति । सर्वं च तद्धनिकस्यैव भवति नर्णिकस्येति ।

न पुत्रर्णं पिता दद्याद्दद्यात्पुत्रस्तु पैतृकम् ।
कामक्रोधसुराद्यूतप्रातिभाव्यकृतं विना ॥८॥

अत्र पितुः पुत्रस्य परस्परमेकत्वसंबन्धः समान एव । कः केन कृतमृणं दद्यात[135] इति विशेष्यते । पुत्रकृतमृणं पिता न दद्यात । अत्र तावन्निषेधः । **दद्यात्पुत्रस्तु पैतृकम्** इत्यत्र विधिः । किं त्वेतदपि विकल्पितम् । यत्**कामा**न्धेन दाशीसंबन्धे कृतम् । यत्पुत्रस्यैवोपरि **क्रोधा**न्धेन कृतम् । तथा यत्सुरापानव्यसनान्धेन कृतम् । तथा यद्**द्यूत**व्यसनान्धेन कृतम् । तथा यत्परस्य प्रतिभुवा स्थितेन कृतम् । एतावन्न दद्यात् ।

पितुरेव नियोगाद्यत्कुटुम्बभरणाय च ।
कृतं वा यदृणं कृच्छ्रे दद्यात्पुत्रस्य तत्पिता ॥९॥

६ P om this verse; c — NMS ऋणात्पिता समुद्धार्यो; D पिता ऋणान्मोचनीयो; d — D व्रजेत्; D add
तस्मादधिकमादाय स्वामिने न ददाति यः ।
स तस्य दासो भृत्यः स्त्री पशुर्वा जायते गृहे ॥ [Dhko 692)
याच्यमानं न दीयेत ऋणं वापि प्रतिग्रहम् ।
तद्धनं वर्धते तावद्यावत्कोटिशतं भवेत् ॥ [J 1.7]
कोटिशते तु संपूर्णे जायते तस्य वेश्मनि ।
ऋणसंशोधनार्थाय दासो जन्मनि जन्मनि ॥ [J 1.8]
७ a — D वाक्तिर्होत्री वा; d — V6 तत्सर्वं धनिनां; B2 B3 K3 K5 भवेत्.
९ P om this verse; a — D यः; b — D वा.

अथवा कुटुम्बभरणार्थं कृतम् । अथवा क्वचिदपि प्राणान्तिककृच्छ्रे यत्कृतं तत्पुत्रकृमपि पिता दद्यादियुक्तं ।

शिष्यान्तेवासिदासस्त्रीवैयावृत्त्यकरैश्च यत् ।
कुटुम्बहेतोरुत्क्षिप्तं वोढव्यं तत्कुटुम्बिना ॥१०॥

इत्यत्र न केवलमीदृशं पुत्रकृतमेव पिता दद्यात् । **कुटुम्बहेतोरुच्छिन्नं***[136] उद्यामकं[137] गृहीत्वा व्ययितं[138] तच्छिष्यादिभिरपि कृतं **कुटुम्बिना दातव्यम्*** । तत्र **शिष्यो** विद्यार्थी । **अन्तेवासी** जल्पितकालावधिवासी शिष्यः । **दासो** गृहजातः क्रीतो वा । **स्त्री** पत्नी माता वा । **वैयावृत्त्यकरः**[139] व्यावृत्तस्य भावो वैयावृत्त्यम । तत्कर्तुं शीलमस्येति वैयावृत्त्यकरः । व्यापारकारीत्यर्थः । एतैरपि कुटुम्बार्थे कृतमृणं कुटुम्बिना दातव्यमित्युक्तम्

ग्रहीता यदि नष्टः स्यात्कुटुम्बार्थे कृतो व्ययः ।
दातव्यं ज्ञातिभिस्तस्य विभक्तैरपि तदृणम् ।। [J 1.13]

अत्रैषां नामोद्दिष्टानां मध्ये येन केनापि कुटुम्बार्थे कृतमृणं कुटुम्बप्रतीतं स यदि देशान्तरं गतो रोगादिना नष्टवान् । ततो व्यवहारकस्य तदृणं ज्ञात्याद्यैर्विभक्तैरपि दातव्यमित्युक्तम् ।

नार्वाग्विंशतिमाद्वर्षात्पितरि प्रोषिते सुतः ।
ऋणं दद्यात्पितृव्ये वा ज्येष्ठे भ्रातर्यथापि वा ॥११॥

इत्यत्र यानि कुटुम्बव्ययकृच्छ्रकृतादीन्यृणानि शेषादिभिरपि कृतानि विभक्तदायादैरपि व्यवहारकाणां निर्विकल्पं दातव्यान्येवेति । तत्कथमपि तेषु कालहरणं नास्ति । यदा पुनर्व्यवहारकश्च सपादिकसार्धकद्विगुणादिलाभं प्रतिपद्यते । तद्गृहीतद्रव्येण भाण्डायोगस्थिताः[140] । पिता वा पितृव्यो वा ज्येष्ठो भ्राता वा

१० b — P -वैयापृत्यकरश्; BM B B5 B7 B8 K3 K7 -व्यावृत्तकरणश्; B2 -व्यावृत्तकरैश्; L K4 V V3-8 Jolly -प्रेष्यकृत्यकरश्; c — P उच्छिन्नं; d — P दातव्यं; X add
ग्रहीता यदि नष्टः स्यात्कुटुम्बार्थे कृतो व्ययः ।
दातव्यं बान्धवैस्तत्स्यात्प्रविभक्तैरपि स्वतः ।। [J 1.13]
मिथो दायः कृतो येन गृहीतो मिथ एव वा ।
मिथ एव प्रदातव्यो यथा दायस्तथा ग्रहः ।। [Manu 8.195]

११ a — N विंशतिमावर्शात्; NMS D संवत्सराद्विंशात्; P has the reading above, but as a sh mc, the original is like D; d — D add
व्याधितोन्मत्तवृद्धानां तथा दीर्घप्रवासिनां ।
ऋणमेवंविधं पुत्रो जीवतामपि दापयेत् ।। [Dhko 697, 712]

जलवर्त्मना स्थलवर्त्मना वा दूरे देशान्तरगतो भवति । न चागच्छति जीवमानश्च श्रूयते । अस्मिन्विषये

नार्वाग्विंशतिमाद्वर्षात्पितरि प्रोषिते सुतः ।

इत्यादिकं सार्थकम् । [?-->] इत्यादिकं यदा पुनः कुटुम्बेऽपि द्रव्यं समर्प्य शतं यः कश्चिद्दूरगतस्तिष्ठति तदा व्यवहारकस्येयमाकोटनाधर्ममपीडाकारिणी (-कारिणो?) भवति । दशविधवाक्यार्थप्रतिपादनाय योऽयं विषयविभागो दृष्टः पञ्चविंशतिप्रकारस्मृतिवाक्यार्थविषयविभागसामर्थ्यादिति । [<--?]

दाप्यः परर्णं एकोऽपि जीवत्स्वधिकृतैः कृतम् ।
प्रेतेषु तु न तत्पुत्रः परर्णं दातुमर्हति ॥१२॥

अत्रायं श्लोको मुनिहृदयान्तर्गतगूढभावार्थदुरवबोधः । स्फूटान्धक एव इव वा । आध्याहार्यं विषयविभागमुद्दिश्य स्फूटीक्रियते । अयं श्लोकः सामान्यग्राहकप्रतिभूविषये द्रष्टव्यः । बहुभिरेककालकृतैः सामान्यग्राहकैः भूत्वा यदृणं कृतं भवति तेषु बहुष्वप्यक्षमेषु **जीवत्सु** यो द्रव्यदानक्षमः स धनिकेन शोध्यो **दाप्यः** । **परर्णम**प्यसाविति । तथा चोक्तमेव नवविधप्रतिभूप्रकरणे सामान्यग्राहकपत्रे वचनमिदम्

ये जीवन्ति मृतानां हि ये श्रेष्ठा जीविनामपि ।
धनी तान्स्वेच्छयादत्ते जीवच्छ्रेष्ठानुगामिनः ॥ [?]

इति । दाप्यः **परर्णमेकोऽपी**त्यस्य श्लोकस्य यथार्थं व्याख्यानं विधिवचनविषयं चेति । उत्तरार्धं तु निषेधविषयं व्याख्यायते । **प्रेतेषु** तेषु सामान्यग्राहकेषु लोकान्तरीभूतेषु यथा पिता तथा **तत्पुत्रो**ऽपि **न परर्णं दातुमर्हति** । स्वकीयांशमात्रमेव ददद्विशुध्यतीयुक्तम् ।

न स्त्री पतिकृतं दद्यादृणं पुत्रकृतं तथा ।
अभ्युपेतादृते यद्वा सह पत्या कृतं भवेत् ॥१३॥

अत्र **स्त्री अभ्युपेतादृत** इति । स्वयं प्रतिपन्नं विना **पुत्रकृतमृणं न दद्यात्**[14] । प्रतिपन्नं तु दद्यादित्यर्थः । तथा **सह पत्या कृतं** विना पतिकृतं अपि न दद्यात् । स्त्रीसहकृतं तु दद्यादित्यर्थ इत्युक्तम् ।

दद्यादपुत्रा विधवा नियुक्ता या मुमूर्षुणा ।
यो वा तद्रिक्थमादद्याद्यतो रिक्थमृणं ततः ॥१४॥

१२ L2 om this verse; b — D अवियुतैः.

१३ c — L K4 V V3-8 Ox यद्युपेताद; d — L4 K4 V V3-8 Ox ताभ्यां.

अत्र या स्त्री विधवीभूता**पुत्रा** च । तत्र[142] यदि पत्या म्रियमाणेन निरूपिता ततः प्रतिकृतमृणं दद्यात् । अथवा सैव रिक्थग्राहिणीर्णं दद्यात् । अथवा तस्या[143] अयोग्यत्वात्दायादा रिक्थं गृह्णन्ति । ततो य एव रिक्थं गृह्णाति स एवर्णं ददाति । **यतो रिक्थं** संचरति **तत ऋणम**पीत्युक्तम् ।

न च भार्याकृतमृणं कथंचित्पत्युराभवेत् ।
आपत्कृतादृते पुंसां कुटुम्बार्थो हि विस्तरः ॥१५॥

अत्र **भार्याकृतमृणं पत्युर्** न संबध्यते । **आपत्कृतादृत** इति । पतिपुत्रदुहित्रादिकुटुम्बस्यापदुद्धरणार्थं तु पत्नीकृतमप्यृणं कुटुम्बपतिर्दद्यात् । यतः **कुटुम्बार्थो हि दुस्तरः*** । [?-->] आपत्काले तु संप्राप्ते दूरव्यवहितस्य भर्तुस्तात्क्षणिकं तस्मान्नेध्य तमह्यं प्राप्यमिति । [<--?]

अन्यत्र रजकव्याधगोपशौण्डिकयोषिताम् ।
तेषां तत्प्रत्यया वृत्तिः कुटुम्बं च तदाश्रयम् ॥१६॥

अत्र **रजकः** प्रसिद्धः । **शौण्डिको** वरटः । एतेषां रजकादीनां स्त्रीप्रत्ययमेव लोकसंव्यवहारो वर्तनं जीवनं च । **कुटुम्बम** येतदीयस्त्रीसमाश्रयमेव । एतेषां स्त्रीभिः कृतमृणं कुटुम्बार्थे[144] कृतमापत्कृतं विना नित्यमेव रजकादयः पतयो निर्विकल्पं दद्युरिति ।

पुत्रिणी तु समुत्सृज्य पुत्रं स्त्री यान्यमाश्रयेत् ।
ऋक्थं तस्या हरेत्सर्वं निःस्वायाः पुत्र एव तु ॥१७॥

अत्र या स्त्री विधवा पुत्रवती च क्रमागतस्त्रीधनवती च कामान्धा पुत्रमुत्सृज्य त्यक्त्वान्यं **भर्तारमाश्रयेत्** । स्त्रीधनस्वकीयसहितापि । तस्या यत्स्त्रीधनं तत्सोऽन्य एव भर्ता गृह्णीयान्न पुत्राः । या पुनर्निःस्वा स्त्रीधनरहिता भर्तृधनसहितान्यं याति । तद्धनमन्यो भर्ता न लभते । तस्य पितृधनस्य पुत्रः स्वामीति ।

१४ b — P आदत्ते.

१५ b — P पत्युर्वापि कथं भवेत्; D कथंचिद्यत्पुरा भवेत्; B3 B5 B8 K2 K3 K5 K7 कथं यद्यत्पुरा भवेत्; c — BM B B3-5 B8 K3 -कृतम्; d — BM B कुटुम्बार्थे; P दुष्टरः.

१६ D om this verse; b — B -योषितः; P पतिर्दद्यातजाव्याध-; d — BM B5 B7 B8 K3 K7 -आश्रितम्.

१७ c — D धनं; P द्रव्यं; P सोऽन्यो.

या तु सप्रधनैव स्त्री सापत्या चान्यमाश्रयेत् ।
सोऽसया दद्यादृणं भर्तुरुत्सृजेद्वा तथैव ताम् ॥१८॥

अत्र **या तु स्त्री** विधवा बालपुत्रवती च भर्तृसक्तधनसहिता[145] **चान्यं भर्तारमाश्रयेत्** । **सो**ऽन्य एव भर्ता तदीयपूर्वभर्तृकृतम् **ऋणं दद्यात्** । प्रधनकादितदीयपरिग्रहप्रतिग्राहित्वात् । अथर्णिकस्य[146] बहुत्वात्पुष्यमाणं न पश्यत्यन्यो भर्ता । ततस्तां तथैवाविनाशितप्रधनकमुत्सृजन्विशुध्यति । धनिक एव तत्प्रतिगृह्णाति ।

अधनस्य ह्यपुत्रस्य मृतस्योपैति यः स्त्रियम् ।
ऋणं वोढुः स भजते तदेवास्य धनं स्मृतम् ॥१९॥

यो[147] यस्य तु पुरुषस्यर्णयुक्तस्य चापुत्रस्य च स्त्रियमुपैति गृह्णाति स तत्पत्नी-परिग्रहमात्रसंग्रहादपि प्रथमपतिकृतमृणं दद्यात् । यतस्तदेव तस्य रिक्थं यतो रिक्थमृणं ततः [NāSmṛ 1.14] इति न्यायात् ।

धनस्त्रीहारिपुत्राणामृणभाग्यो धनं हरेत् ।
पुत्रोऽसतोः स्त्रीधनिनोः स्त्रीहारी धनिपुत्रयोः ॥२०॥

अत्र यस्य पुरुषस्यर्णयुक्तस्य मृतस्य धनं दायादैराक्रम्य[148] गृहीतम् । पत्नी च निर्धना पुत्रमप्युत्सृज्यान्यस्य गृहे प्रविष्टा । पुत्रोऽपि धनमातृविहीनः केवलस् तिष्ठति । तदा व्यवहारकारस्त्रयाणां मध्ये विधृत्य कः[149] धनं गृह्णातु । केन च तद्दातव्यमिति । अस्यार्थस्य निगमार्थमेतदुक्तम् । एतेषां मध्येऽप्य् **ऋणभाग्यो धनं हरेत्** । धनस्य प्राधान्यात् । धनग्राह्यृणं दद्यात् । तस्मिन्विद्यमाने नान्यः कश्चिदिति । यस्य तु सर्णमृतस्य पुरुषस्य धनस्याभावान्न धनहारी कश्चिज्जातः । स्त्रिया[150] अप्यभावान्न स्त्रीहारी कश्चिदस्ति । पितृमातृधनवर्जितः पुत्रः

१८ a —BM B B5 B7 B8 K3 K7 invert 18 and 19; B3 K2 K5 च; N L V V4 V5 V6 V8 संप्रधनैव; K4 समधनैव; P सधनैंव; b — B7 B8 K7 साप्रत्या; BM साप्रीत्या; L K4 V5 add
तस्या ऋणं हरेत्सर्वं निःस्वायाः पुत्र एव तु ।
d — D add
भार्या स्नुपा प्रस्नुपा च भार्यायाश्च प्रतिग्रहः ।
एतान्हरन्नृणं दाप्यो भूमिं यश्चोपजीवति ॥ [cf. J 1.25]
दारमूलाः क्रियाः सर्वा वर्णानामनुपूर्वशः ।
यो यस्य हरते दारान्स तस्य हरते धनम् ॥ [?]

१९ d — P स आभजेद्धनम्वोढुः सैव तस्य धनं यतः; Jolly स आभजेदृणं वोढुः सैव तस्य धनं यतः; B3 K2 K5 वोढव्यं तदृणं तेन तदेवास्य धनं स्मृतम्.

२० Y B2 om this verse; b —K2 ऋणभागो.

केवलस्तिष्ठति । तदासतोः[151] स्त्रीहरिधनहारिणोः **पुत्र** एव बीजसंभवसंबन्धात् पितॄणं[152] प्रयच्छतीति । यस्य तु धनस्य हारी न कश्चिदस्ति । न पुत्रो विद्यते । पत्न्येव धनपुत्रोविहीनान्यस्य गृहे प्रविष्टा । तदा धनहारिपुत्रयोरसतोरविद्यमानयोः **स्त्रीहार्य्** ऋणं दद्यादिति । त्रयाणामपि **धनस्त्रीहारिपुत्राणां** समुदितानामपि मध्ये येनर्णं देयं तद्दर्शितम् । तथा द्वयोरभावे एकैकेन येनर्णं देयं तदपि सग्रन्थपाठं दर्शितम् । यस्य पुनर्धनस्त्रीहारिविद्यमानत्वमस्ति[153] । तत्राक्षरैरनुक्तोऽपि निगमोऽर्थापत्तितारतम्यादवगन्तव्यः । तथा हि यस्य पुत्रो धनहारी[154] च विद्यते स्त्रीहारी नास्ति तत्रापि धनहारिपुत्रयोर्द्वयोरपि विद्यमानयोर्धनप्राधान्याद्धनग्राह्यृणं दद्यात् । यथात्र धनहारिस्त्रीहारिणोरपि द्वयोर्विद्यमानयोर्धनहार्य्[155] एवर्णं दद्यादित्युक्तम् । यस्य पुनर्निर्धनत्वाद्धनं नास्ति । पुत्रश्च[156] विद्यते । तदा तयोः स्त्रीहारिपुत्रयोर्द्वयोर्मध्ये केनर्णं देयमित्यत्राप्यर्थापत्तितारतम्यापेक्षया । यदि रूपयौवनसंपन्ना काममदोद्धता प्रधानाभिमता च स्त्री तदा तस्य[157] स्त्रीहारी ऋणं[158] दद्यात् । यतस्तदेव तस्य धनम् [NāSmṛ 1.19d] इत्युक्तमेव । अथवा सापि स्त्री निर्भाग्या कर्मकारित्वग्रासमात्रभोजना ततः **पुत्रोऽसतोः स्त्रीधनिनोर्** इति न्यायात्पुत्र एवर्णं दद्यात् । इति विस्फुटीकृतमिदम् ।

उत्तमा स्वैरिणी या स्यादुत्तमा च पुनर्भुवाम् ।
ऋणं तयोः पतिकृतं दद्याद्यस्तामुपाश्नुते ॥२१॥

अयं ग्रन्थकारश्चतस्रः[159] स्वैरिण्यो वक्ष्यति तिस्रः पुनर्भुवः । तासां चतसृणां स्वैरिणीनां **यान्तिमा*** स्वैरिणी ।

देशधर्मानवेक्ष्यय स्त्री गुरुभिर्या[160] प्रदीयते ।
उत्पन्नसाहसान्यस्मै सान्तिमा स्वैरिणी स्मृता[161] ॥ [NāSmṛ 12.52]

अस्मिञ्श्लोके यैवंलक्षणान्तिमा **स्वैरिणी** निर्दिष्टा[162] सोत्तमा । या **पनर्भुवाम**प्यन्तिमात्वादेवोत्तमा तृतीया ।

असत्सु देवरेषु स्त्री बान्धवैर्या प्रदीयते ।
सवर्णायासपिण्डाय पुनर्भू सा तृतीयका ॥ ॥ [NāSmṛ 12.48]

अस्मिञ्श्लोके या पुनर्भू निर्दिष्टा सोत्तमा । एतयोरन्तिमोत्तमयोः स्वैरिणीपुनर्भुवोः स्त्रियोर्यः संग्रहीता स एव तत्पूर्वपतिकृतमृणं दद्यादिति समुदायार्थः । विशेषार्थश्चायम् । अत्र उत्तमशब्दः सर्वसाधारणः । एतासां सप्तानामपि मध्ये यैव काचिद्भाग्यसौभाग्यगुणैरुत्तमा तस्यैव ग्रहीता तत्पतिकृतमृणं दद्यान्न पुत्र इति विशेषनियमात् ।

२१ a — B B5 D P अन्तिमा; D NMS स्वैरिणीनां या; BM K2 K3 B स्वैरिणी यास्या; b — B B8 K3 K4 K5 K7 V V4 पुनर्भुवा; d — P B3 ते; L त; V V3-8 Ox तु; P समस्नुते; Jolly add
भार्या स्नुषा च भृत्या च भार्यायाश्च परिग्रहः ।
एतावद्भिर्ऋणं देयं भूमिं यश्चोपजीवति ॥ [J 1.25]

भार्या स्नुषा च भृत्या <च भार्याया>श्च परिग्रहः ।
एतावद्भिर्ऋणं देयं भूमिं यश्चोपजीवति ।। [J 1.25]

अत्र भार्यास्नुषादिनामेतेषां नामोद्दिष्टानां मध्ये येनैव तत्कुटुम्बार्थे कृतमृणं तेनैव देयम् । अत्रास्वतन्त्र्यदोषस्य संभवो नास्ति । अयं प्रथमः पक्षः द्वितीयः पुनस्त्वयं यदि तेषां मध्ये येनैव कुटुम्बार्थे यदुद्धरणार्थे[163] कृतमृणं तद्गृहपरिनादाया-दैर्वादातव्यमिति । अथवैतेषां मध्ये य एव कश्चित्तत्कुटुम्बभूमिमुपजीवति । स एव कृतमृणं प्रयच्छत्येष तृतीयः पक्ष इति ।

विभक्ता भ्रातरो ये स्युः पृथग्दारक्रियाधनाः ।
यो ह्यपुत्रो मृतस्तेषां तत्पत्नी तत्समश्नुते ।। ।। [J 1.25*]

इत्यृणादाने देयादिभेदः ।

स्त्रीकृतान्यप्रमाणानि कार्याण्याहुरनापदि ।
विशेषतो गृहक्षेत्रदानाधमनविक्रयाः ॥२२॥

पत्नीदुहितृवधूप्रभृतिसर्वस्त्रीकृतानि सर्वाण्यपि कार्याण्य**प्रमाणानि** । अतस्ताभिः कृतान्यप्यकृतानीव द्रष्टव्यानि । **विशेषतो गृहक्षेत्रदान<आधमन्>अविक्रयाः** । [?-->] प्रमाणकृताऽपि बलवतीत्य् [<--?] अर्थः ।

एतान्यपि प्रमाणानी भर्ता यद्यनुमन्यते ।
पुत्रः पत्युरभावे वा राजा वा पतिपुत्रयोः ॥२३॥

अत्र या स्त्री गृहनायिका[164] कुटुम्बभरणपालनक्षमा प्रौढा[165] पतिर्मन्द-प्रभावोऽप्रौढोऽनुमतिमात्रदानयोग्यः । स च **यद्यनुमन्यते** ततः कृतान्यपि सर्व-कार्यानी प्रमाणानि । **प्रत्युरभावे राजा वा** यद्यनुमन्यते ।

भर्त्रा प्रीतेन यद्दत्तं स्त्रियै तस्मिन्मृतेऽपि तत् ।
सा यथाकाममश्नीयाद्दद्याद्वा स्थावरादृते ॥२४॥

२२ b — P मनीपिणः; d — B BM B -दानायतन-; B5 K2 K3 K5 K7 -दानापनन-; V V3 V4 V7 V8 -दानाधामन-; B3 -दानाध्यपल-; D add
नाधिकारो भवेत्स्त्रीनां दानविक्रयकर्मसु ।
यावत्संजीवमाना स्यात्तावद्भोगस्य सा प्रभुः ।। [?]

२३ a — BM B B3 B5 K3 K7 NMS एव; P अभावे च राजा च; B3 प्रतिपुत्रयोः.

२४ D om this verse; d — D add तथा हितमविज्ञेयं क्षेत्रादिकमनाहितम् । V5 further adds तयोर्हितमविज्ञेयं क्षत्राधिं च मनोहितम् ।

अत्र यत्किमपि **भर्त्रा** परितुष्टेन **दत्तम्** । तच्च द्रव्यं **यथाकाममश्नीयाद्दद्याद्** वा[166] गृहक्षेत्रादिस्थावरवर्जितमिति ।

तथा दासकृतं कार्यमकृतं परिचक्षते ।
अन्यत्र स्वामिसंदेशान्न दासः प्रभुरात्मनः ॥२५॥

यथा स्त्रीकृतं तथा **दासकृतम**पि **कार्यमकृतम्** एव **परिचक्षते** ब्रुवते गुरवः । यदि पुनः स एव स्वामिसमादेशात्करोति । ततः सर्वं तत्कृतमपि प्रमाणमेवेति ।

पुत्रेण च कृतं कार्यं यत्स्यात्पितुरनिच्छतः ।
तदप्यकृतमेवाहुर्दासः पुत्रश्च तौ समौ ॥२६॥

पितुरसंमतात्**पुत्रेणापि** यत्**कृतं कार्यं** तदप्य**कृतमेव** द्रष्टव्यम् । यतो यथा दासोऽस्वतन्त्रस्तथा पुत्रोऽपि पितरि जीवत्यविभक्तभाग अस्वतन्त्र एवेति ।

अप्राप्तव्यवहारश्चेत्स्वतन्त्रोऽपि हि नर्णभाक् ।
स्वातन्त्र्यं तु स्मृतं ज्येष्ठे ज्यैष्ठ्यं गुणवयःकृतम् ॥२७॥

अत्र किल पितरि मृते पुत्रः **स्वतन्त्रः** स्यात् । स च **ऋणभाग**पि संभवति । तन्निषेधार्थमाह । **अप्राप्तव्यवहारो**[167] यावत्पोगण्ड इत्यर्थः । तावत्स्वतन्त्रोऽप्यक्षमत्वादृणभाक्त संभवति । स्वतन्त्रत्वं **ज्येष्ठे** भवति । ज्येष्ठत्वं गुणैर्वयसा च कृतं भवतीति ।

त्रयः स्वतन्त्रा लोकेऽस्मिन्राजाचार्यस्तथैव च ।
प्रति प्रति च वर्णानां सर्वेषां स्वगृहे गृही ॥२८॥

अस्मि**न्लोके** एते यथोक्तास्**त्रायो**ऽपि **स्वतन्त्रा** उत्तराधरविशेषापेक्षया । तद्यथा राजा स्वतन्त्र उत्तरगुरुनिरपेक्षत्वात्प्रजा<ध्>अरत्वापेक्षया । **आचार्यो**ऽपि शिष्याधरत्वापेक्षया । तथा सर्ववर्णानामपि स्वकीये स्वकीये गृह अधरपरिवारापेक्षया[168]

२५ B7 om this verse; b — परिपक्षते; c — V6 अन्यत्र.
२६ b — P NMS D अच्छन्दतः पितुः; c — V3 V4 V7 V8 अस्याकृतम्; d — P तत्.
२७ a — NMS तु; c — P हि.
२८ a — B5 यत्र; c — P D प्रतिवर्णं.

अस्वतन्त्राः प्रजाः सर्वाः स्वतन्त्रः पृथिवीपतिः ।
अस्वतन्त्रः स्मृतः शिष्य आचार्ये तु स्वतन्त्रता ॥२९॥
अस्वतन्त्राः स्त्रियः पुत्रा दासाश्च सपरिग्रहाः ।
स्वतन्त्रस्तत्र तु गृही यस्य यत्स्यात्क्रमागतम् ॥३०॥

अत्र श्लोकद्वयेऽपी इतरेतरापेक्षया स्वतन्त्रत्वमस्वतन्त्रत्वं च प्रदर्शितमिति ।

गर्भस्थैः सदृशो ज्ञेय आ वर्षादष्टमाच्छिषुः ।
बाल आ षोडशाज्ज्ञेयः पोगण्डश्चापि शब्यते ॥३१॥
परतो व्यवहारज्ञः स्वतन्त्रः पितरौ विना ।
जीवतोरस्वतन्त्रः स्वाज्जरयापि समन्वितः ॥३२॥

तत्वात्पुत्रोऽपि[169] वृद्धत्वमपि प्राप्तोऽविभक्तभागस्वतन्त्र एवेति । कार्यकारणयोग्य-त्वापेक्षयैतदुच्यते । **अष्टमाद्वत्सरादर्वाग्गर्भस्थसदृशः*** शौचाद्यक्षमः । अष्टभ्यः[170] **परतः** शौचाध्ययनक्षमो बाल इत्युच्यते पोगण्डश्च । व्यवहारे त्वक्षम[171] आ षोडशाद्वत्सरादिति

तयोरपि पिता श्रेयान्बीजप्राधान्यदर्शनात् ।
अभावे बीजिनो माता तदभावे तु पूर्वजः ॥३३॥

अत्र मातापित्रोः समानं गौरवमुक्त्वा विशेषं दर्शयति । तयोरपि मातापित्रोः **पिता श्रेयान्** । बीजप्राधान्यात् । **बीजिनस्त्व**भावे **माता** । मातुरभावे तत्**पूर्वजः** श्रेयान् । उत्तरोत्तरापेक्षया चाधरस्यास्वतन्त्रत्वं[172] तदनुदर्शितम् ।

२९ a — B5 अस्वतन्त्रः; c — B3 अस्वतन्त्र्यः; d — BM B8 K5 K7 आचार्यस्; V8 साचार्ये

३० b — P दासादिस्; P D सपरिग्रहः; cd — Y K4 om; d — V V3 V5-8 गृहीतस्य; B3 ते स्युः क्रमागतः; K2 K5 B3 add
द्वौ गुरू पुरुपस्येह पिता माता च धर्मतः ।
स्वतन्त्रः सर्वकार्येपु धर्माद्विचलितो न चेत् ॥(?)

३१ a — V3 V5 V7 P NMS गर्भस्थ-; BM B5 B7 ज्ञेया; B8 B3 ज्ञेयो; V ज्ञेयः; b — BM B7 K3 K7 वर्पादा अप्टमाच् B B5 P NMS D अप्टमाद्वत्सराच्.; c — B3 K2 K3 ज्ञेयाः; d — L K4 V6-8 पौगण्डश्; D पांगण्ड इति; P शस्यते

३२ ab — Y om; a — V8 व्यवहारतः; b — B3 K2 K5 पितरम्; c — BM B3 B5 B8 K2 K5 K7 जीवतोऽप्य्.

३३ a — Y तेपां; D श्रीमान्; cd — B7 om; c — BM B B5 K3 K5 जीवितो; d — V तदाभावे

स्वतन्त्राः सर्व एवैते परतन्त्रेषु सर्वदा ।
अनुशिष्टौ विसर्गे च विक्रये चेश्वरा मताः ॥३४॥

एते पश्चादुक्ताः **स्वतन्त्रा** राजाचार्यगृहपतयस्ते सर्वेऽपि स्वकीयपरतन्त्रेष्वेव **सर्वदा** । तद्यथा राजा स्वतन्त्रः प्रजासु । **परतन्त्रेष्वे**तेषु स्वतन्त्रता[173] । **अनुशिष्टा**वाकोटने ताडने[174] **विसर्गे** परित्यागे **विक्रय** अपि यावदीश्वराः प्रभव इत्यर्थः ।

यद्बालः कुरुते कार्यमस्वतन्त्रस्तथैव च ।
अकृतं तदिति प्राहुः शास्त्रे शास्त्रविदो जनाः ॥३५॥

अत्र स्वतन्त्रोऽपि **बालः** शिशुर्यत्**कार्यम्कुरुते** । तथा प्रौढोऽपि दासादिरस्वतन्त्रो यत्कुरुते तत्कृतमप्यकृतमाहुर्धर्मशास्त्रज्ञा इति ।

स्वतन्त्रोऽपि हि यत्कार्यं कुर्यादप्रकृतिं गतः ।
तदप्यकृतमेवाहुरस्वतन्त्रः स हेतुतः ॥३६॥

अत्र किल पितुः परोक्ष्ये ज्येष्ठपुत्रः कार्यकरणे प्रमाणं । यवतात्राप्ययं हेतुरप्रमाणो दृष्टः । यद्यसाव**प्रकृतिं गतः कुर्यात्त**त्कृतमप्य**कृतमा**हुः । अप्रकृतिं गत इति । भूतग्रहगृहीतो वा द्यूतादिव्यसनगृहीतो वा स्वभावप्रकृतिपरित्यक्तः । अनेन हेतुना **स्वतन्त्रोऽप्यस्**वतन्त्रः सहेतुकः । तेनापि दानाधमनविक्रयादिकार्यं कृतमप्यकृतमेव द्रष्टव्यमिति ।

कामक्रोधाभियुक्तार्तभयव्यसनपीडिताः ।
रागद्वेषपरीताश्च ज्ञेयास्त्वप्रकृतिं गताः ॥३७॥

अप्रकृतिगतलक्षणमिदमुक्तं सप्ताकारमिति ।

कुले ज्येष्ठस्तथा श्रेष्ठः प्रकृतिस्थश्च यो भवेत् ।
तत्कृतं स्यात्कृतं कार्यं नास्वतन्त्रकृतं कृतम् ॥३८॥

३४ B7 om this verse; a — K2 स्वतन्त्रः; b — X D नित्यशः; c — NMS निसर्गं; d — B3 विक्रिये.
३५ a — B5 V5 वारः; d — P धर्म-
३६ a — V4 तत्; b — B गतिः; cd — V4 om; c — P अकृतं तदपि प्राहुर्; d — P अस्वतन्त्रस्य; J अस्वातन्त्र्यस्य; P हेतुकः.
३७ B7 V4 om this verse; b — P -क्रोधाभिभूतार्त-; c — K5 B3 - परीक्षाश्; d — V7 ज्ञेयस्.
३८ b — P NMS तु; c — P प्राहुर्.

अत्र श्लोके समस्तकृताकृतोपसंहार[175] उक्तः । यः **कुले ज्येष्ठो** वयसा गुणैश्च । तथा श्रेष्ठः संव्यवहारप्रतिष्ठायुक्तः । **प्रकृतिस्थश्**चाविप्लुतचित्तः पुरुषो **यो भवेत्** । **तत्कृतं** तु ज्ञेयम्तेन **कृतं** कृतमिति प्रतितिष्ठति । **यत्पुनरस्वतन्त्रकृतं कार्यं** तन् **न कृतम्** इति द्रष्टव्यम् । पाद्वलतीत्यर्थ । इत्यृणादाने कृताकृतभेदो द्वितीयः ।

धनमूलाः क्रियाः सर्वा यत्नस्तत्साधने मतः ।
रक्षणं वर्धनं भोग इति तस्य विधिः क्रमात् ॥३९॥

धर्मार्थकामक्रियाः सर्वा अपि **धनमूला** यतस्तस्**तत्साधन** उद्यमः कर्तव्यः । तत्साधनोपायश्च त्रिविध उक्तः । प्रथमं **रक्षणं** द्विपदचतुष्पदादिभ्यस्ततश्च **वर्धनं** कृषिकलान्तरवाणिज्यादिभिः । तदनन्तरं **भोगः** । ऐहिकामुष्मिकसुखार्थेनेति धन-भेदाधिकारः श्लोकसंबन्धः ।

तत्पुनस्त्रिविधं ज्ञेयं शुक्लं शबलमेव च ।
कृष्णं च तस्य विज्ञेयः प्रभेदः सप्तधा पृथक् ॥४०॥

तच्च धनमेकं **शुक्लम्** उच्यते । द्वितीयं **शबलं** । तृतीयं **कृष्णम्** इत्येवं तावत्**त्रिविधम्** इदम् । पुनश्च **पृथग्** इत्येकैकं सप्तसप्तभेदभिन्नं भवतीति ।

श्रुतशौर्यतपःकन्याशिष्ययाज्यान्वयागतम् ।
धनं सप्तविधं शुक्लमुदयोऽप्यस्य तद्विधः ॥४१॥

तत्र **श्रुता**गतं विद्वत्ताप्राप्तम् । **शौर्या**गतं पुरुषकारप्राप्तं । **तपसा**गतं यमनियमकाम्याकाम्यकर्मयथोक्तविध्यनुष्ठानपात्रताप्राप्तम् । कन्यागतं **कन्या** विवाहनिमित्तप्राप्तम् । तथा **याज्य**प्राप्तम् । तथा**न्वयागतं** पूर्वजकुलक्रमप्राप्तम् । एवं सप्तस्थानागतं धनं **शुक्लम्** इत्युच्यते । **उदयोऽप्यस्य तद्विध** इति । विनियोग-फलप्राप्तिरपि तस्य श्रेयस्कारिणी शुद्धैव द्रष्टव्या ।

कुसीदकृषिवाणिज्यशुल्कशिल्पानुवृत्तिभिः ।
कृतोपकारादाप्तं च शबलं समुदाहृतम् ॥४२॥

३९ Y om verses 39-63; b — B3 K5 यतस्; X तत्साधयेद्धनम्

४० b — D शुद्धं; d — D विभागः; D पुनः

४१ c — K4 समविधं; D शुद्धम्; d — Jolly उद्योगस्तस्य.

४२ b — V7 -वाणिज्या-

तत्र **कुसीदं** वृद्धिप्रायः । **कृषिः** कर्षणम् । **वाणिज्यं** भाण्डकविक्रयः । **शुल्कं** कन्यासंप्रदाने धर्म्यं चाधर्म्यं च । **शिल्पमा**लेख्यादिविज्ञानम् । **अनुवृत्तिः** सेवाराधनम् । **कृतोपकारः** प्रत्युपकारः । तैः सप्तभिः प्रकारैर्ब्राह्मणस्य धनं यद्भवति । तच्छ**बलम्** इत्युच्यते । मध्यममित्यर्थः ।

पार्श्विकद्यूतदौत्यार्तिप्रतिरूपकसाहसैः ।
व्याजेनोपार्जितं यच्च तत्कृष्णं समुदाहृतम् ॥४३॥

तत्रोत्**कोचो*** लञ्चोपचारः । **द्यूतम**क्षादिक्रीडा । **दौत्यं** दूतकर्म । **आर्तः** कश्चिद्रोगार्तो व्यसनी । तथा **प्रतिरूपकं** सुवर्णरजतादीनां कूटप्रतिकृतिकरणं । **साहसं** चौर्यादि । **व्याजं** छलम् । एतैः सप्तभिः प्रकारैर्धनं यदुपार्जितं भवति तत्**कृष्णम्** इत्युच्यते । अधममित्यर्थः । एवं शुक्लशबलकृष्णसंज्ञाभिस्त्रिविधं धनमेकैकशश्च सप्तप्रकारमप्यभिहितम् ।

तेन क्रयो विक्रयश्च दानं ग्रहणमेव च ।
विविधाश्च प्रवर्तन्ते क्रियाः संभोग एव च ॥४४॥

अत्र जगत्यपि क्वचित्कीदृशेनापि तेन त्रिविधेनैकविंशतिभेदभिन्न **क्रयो विक्रयश्च दानं ग्रहणं** च **विविधाश्च** कर्म**क्रियाः** प्रवर्तन्ते विविध**संभोगाश्चे**ति ।

यथाविधेन द्रव्येण यत्किंचित्कुरुते नरः ।
तथाविधमवाप्नोति स फलं प्रेत्य चेह च ॥४५॥

एते शुक्लशबलकृष्णा भेदा धनस्यैतदर्थं दर्शिताः । येनैतेषां विनियोग इहलोक-परलोकफलानां त्रयाणामपि वर्णानां यच्छुभं तत्सर्ववर्णसाधारणं त्रिविधं भवति ।

तत्पुनर्द्वादशविधं प्रतिवर्णाश्रयात्स्मृतम् ।
साधारणं स्यात्त्रिविधं शेषं नवविधं स्मृतम् ॥४६॥

४३ b — NMS पार्श्वक-; P उत्कोच; D -चौर्य- for -दौत्य-; P -आर्त- for -आर्ति-; d — P हि; P तदुदाहृतम्
४४ c — NMS प्रयुज्यन्ते
४५ a — K2 om; b — V V3-8 लभते; d — D परत्र.
४६ b — X कृतम्; c — Jolly स्वात्; d — D विदुः.

वर्णे वर्णे विशेषशुभत्रिविधधनत्वाच्च शेषं **नवविधं** भवति । एवमेव **द्वादशविधम्** अपि शुद्धधनं निगमव्याख्यातैः श्लोकैरिदानीमुच्यते ।

क्रमागतं प्रीतिदायः प्राप्तं च सह भार्यया ।
अविशेषेण वर्णानां सर्वेषां त्रिविधं धनम् ॥४७॥

एतत्सर्ववर्णसामान्यं त्रिविधं शुद्धधनम् ।

वैशेषिकं धनं ज्ञेयं ब्राह्मणस्य त्रिलक्षणम् ।
प्रतिग्रहेण यल्लब्धं याज्यतः शिष्यतस्तथा ॥४८॥
त्रिविधं क्षत्रियस्यापि प्राहुर्वैशेषिकं धनं ।
युद्धोपलब्धं कारश्च दण्डश्च व्यवहारतः ॥४९॥
वैशेषिकं धनं ज्ञेयं वैश्यस्यापि त्रिलक्षणम् ।
कृषिगोरक्षवाणिज्यैः शूद्रस्यैभ्यस्त्वनुग्रहात् ॥५०॥

एवं ब्रह्मणादीनां त्रयाणामपि वर्णानां त्रिविधं धनं दर्शितम् । शूद्रस्तु सर्वाशी सर्वविक्रयी । तस्यापि शुभमेकप्रकारमेव दर्शितम् । एषां ब्राह्मणादीनां प्रेषणपरितोषणसंप्राप्तानुग्रहादिभिः ।

सर्वेषामेव वर्णानामेष धर्म्यो धनागमः ।
विपर्ययादधर्म्यः स्यान्न चेदापद्गरीयसी ॥५१॥

निजनिजवर्णवृत्तिविहितो **धनागमो धर्म्यो** भवति । **विपर्ययात्त्व**न्योन्यवर्णवृत्तिसमाचरणाद**धर्म्यः** स्यात् । इत्यृणादाने बहुप्रकारधनभेदस्तृतीयः । इदानीमापद्ब्राह्मणवृत्तिरुच्यते ।

आपत्स्वनन्तरा वृत्तिर्ब्राह्मणस्य विधीयते ।
वैश्यवृत्तिस्ततश्चोक्ता न जघन्या कथंचन ॥५२॥

४७ d — P शुभम्.
४८ b — P शुभं त्रिधा; d — K2 राज्यतः.
४९ b — P शुद्धं; c — P कराद्युद्धोपलव्धं; d — P दण्डाच्.
५० b — Jolly वैशस्यापि; P त्रिधा शुखम्.
५१ b — K2 K5 V5 धर्मो; c — K2 K5 V5 अधर्मः.

ब्राह्मणस्यापत्सु स्वकीयवृत्त्या कुटुम्बावर्तनपीडास्वनन्तरवृत्तिरविरुद्धा । क्षत्रियवृत्तिरित्यर्थः । तथावृष्ट्या कुटुम्बावर्तनपीडासु वृत्त्यसंभवे ततो वैश्यवृत्तिरुक्ता । न **जघन्या** कथमपि शूद्रवृत्तिर्न तस्येति ।

न कथंचन कुर्वीत ब्राह्मणः कर्म वार्षलम् ।
वृषलः कर्म न ब्राह्मं पतनीये हि ते तयोः ॥५३॥

वृशलशब्देन शूद्र उच्यते । तस्य कर्म सर्वाशितं सर्वविक्रयत्वं च । एतद्वर्षलं कर्म ब्राह्मणः कथमपि आपद्गतोऽपि न कुर्यात् । तथा ब्राह्मणस्य यत्कर्म तच्छूद्रः सन्यज्ञोपवीतवेदाध्ययनव्याहृतिहोमादिकं न कथंचन कुर्वीत **। पतनीये हि ते तयोः** । इतरेतरविरुद्धकर्मणा । तयोर्ब्राह्मणवृषलयोः । पतनीये भवत इत्यर्थः ।

उत्कृष्टं चापकृष्टं च तयोः कर्म न विद्यते ।
मध्यमे कर्मणी हित्वा सर्वसाधारणे हि ते ॥५४॥

शूद्रस्य ब्राह्ममुत्**कृष्टं** ब्राह्मणस्य शूद्रकर्मा**पिकृष्टम्** । तत एव तयोस्ते कर्मणी निषिद्धे । ये तु **मध्यमे** द्वे **कर्मणी** क्षत्रवृत्तिर्वैश्यवृत्तिश्चैते ब्राह्मणस्यापि क्वचिदापत्काले विहिते । शूद्रस्यापि क्वचिदधिकापत्काले[176] विहित इति ।

आपदं ब्राह्मणस्तीर्त्वा क्षत्रवृत्त्या हृतैर्धनैः ।
उत्सृजेत्क्षत्रवृत्तिं तां कृत्वा पावनमात्मनः ॥५५॥

यदापदा ब्राह्मणः क्षत्रियवृत्तिं कारितस्ताम**आपदं तीर्त्वा** तां **क्षत्रियवृत्तिमुत्सृजेत्** । **कृत्वा पावनमात्मनः** । ब्राह्मणेषु प्रसह्य प्रायश्चित्तं भवतीत्यर्थः ।

तस्यामेव तु यो वृत्तौ ब्राह्मणो रमते रसात् ।
काण्डपृष्ठश्च्युतो मार्गात्सोऽपाङ्क्तेयः प्रकीर्तितः ॥५६॥

५३ b — D कुर्वीत ब्राह्मणः कर्म वार्पलं न कदाचन; c — D वा ब्राह्मं; K2 K5 ब्राह्मं च; d — NMS पतनीयौ; NMS तौ.

५४ a — D वापकृष्टं वा; b — B3 K2 K5 कर्मदोपो य कल्प्यते; d — K2 K5 सर्वसाधारणी.

५५ b — D क्षत्रवृत्त्यर्जितैर्धनैः; P क्षत्रवृत्त्याश्रिते जने; NMS क्षत्रवृत्त्या भृते जने.

५६ a — D मोहाद्; b — D सदा; c — P काण्डस्पृष्ठश्; d — P मार्गादपाङ्क्तेयः; K4 om.

यः पुनस्तत्रैव रतिं बध्नाति स ब्राह्मणः **काण्डपृष्ठ**[177] इति । पतितः क्षत्रिकः पतितसावित्रीक[178] । स्वर्गाच्च्यवतेऽसौ[179] पितृश्राद्धकर्मादिष्व**पाङ्क्तेयः प्रकीर्तितः** ।

वैश्यवृत्तावविक्रेयं ब्राह्मणस्य पयो दधि ।
घृतं मधु मधूच्छिष्टं लाक्षाक्षाररसासवाः ॥५७॥
मांसौदनतिलक्षौमसोमपुष्पफलपलाः ।
मनुष्यविषशस्त्राम्बुलवणापूपवीरुधः ॥५८॥
नीलीकौषेयचर्मास्थिकुतपैकशफा मृदः ।
उदश्वित्केशपिण्याकशाकाद्यौषधयस्तथा ॥५९॥

अत्र प्रसिद्धानि प्रतीतानि । **मधूच्छिष्टं** तुच्छकमदनं[180] च तदुच्यते । **क्षारा** गुडाद्याः । **रसा** घृततैलाद्याः । **आसवः**[181] सुरा । **ओदनः** कूरः । **क्षौमं** तसरः । **सोमो** यज्ञद्रव्यम् । **उपलाः** पाषाणाः । **मनुष्यः** पुरुषः । **अम्बु** पानीयम् । **अपूपाः** पक्वान्नम् । **वीरुधो** गुल्मलतादयः । **कौशेयं** पट्टसूत्रम् । **कुतपमू**र्णासंभूतम् । **एकशफा** एकसंतततखुरा अश्वसमाः[182] । **उदश्वित्त**क्रम् । केशश्चमराद्याः । **पिण्याकः** खलः । **शाकान्यार्द्रौषधय** एतद् ब्राह्मणस्याविक्रेयं श्लोकत्रयोद्दिष्टम् इति ।

ब्राह्मणस्य तु विक्रेयं शुष्कं दारु तृणानि च ।
गन्धद्रव्यैरकावेत्रतूलमूलतुशादृते ॥६०॥

ब्राह्मणस्य वैश्यवृत्तावपि वर्तमानस्य **शुष्कदारूणि तृणानि** च शुष्काणि विक्रेयाणि तत्र गन्धद्रव्यमुशीरवालकमुस्ताद्यम् । एरका पर्णिपुष्पग्रन्थीनि । **वेत्रतूलमूल-कुशश्च*** प्रसिद्धाः । एतान्विना**र्ते** ।

स्वयं शीर्णं च विदलं फलानां बदरेङ्गुदे ।
रज्जुः कार्पासिकं सूत्रं तच्चेदविकृतं भवेत् ॥६१॥

५७ b — P D -वृत्त्या चाविक्रेयं.

५९ b — NMS नील; P L2 D चेल-; M4 चैल-; K4 V5 -कुतुपै-; V4 -कुतुथै-; V3 कुन्तपै; d — L V4 V7 उदस्वित्-; V8 उपस्वित्-; L V8 -शकमौपधयस्; K4 V V3-7 -शाकान्यौपधयस्; X -शाकाद्या औपधीस्; P -शाकार्द्रौशधयस्.

६० a — V V3 V4 V7 V8 त्वविक्रेयं; d — K2 -द्रव्यरसाचैत्रतूलमूलतुपाद्; K5 -द्रव्यरसावैत्रतूलमूलतुपाद्; D -द्रव्यैलका; P -कुशाद्.

६१ a — B3 K2 शीर्पं च; NMS विशीर्णं; b — P वदिरेङ्गुदे; d — K2 अविकृतिं.

अत्र **स्वयं शीर्णं च** यदन्यदपि फलं किंचित्पतितं भवति । तथा **विदलं** मुद्गमाषाढकीवल्ल्याद्यम् । फलाद्यं **फलानां** मध्ये वैराणीङ्**गुदानि** च **रज्जुर्** वलिवसुवादिकम् । तथा यच्च **कार्पासोद्भवं सूत्रं** तद्यद्य**विकृतं** रक्तं न भवेत् । एतानि ब्राह्मणस्य विक्रेयाणीति ।

अशक्तौ भेषजस्यार्थे यज्ञहेतोस्तथैव च ।
यद्यवश्यं तु विक्रेयास्तिला धान्येन तत्समाः ॥६२॥

अत्र तिला यथा अन्यद्धान्यं विक्रेयं । तथा तेऽपि तिला धान्यसमा एव यज्ञार्थमभ्यनुज्ञाताः । अथवा**शक्तावप**पाटवे भेषजार्थं चेति ।

अविक्रेयाणि विक्रीणन्ब्राह्मणः प्रच्युतः पथः ।
मार्गे पुनरवस्थाप्य राज्ञा दण्डेन भूयसा ॥६३॥

अत्र यान्य**विक्रेयाणि** निर्दिष्टानि तानि **विक्रीनन्ब्राह्मणो** मार्गच्युतो भवति । स च **राज्ञा पुनरपि मार्गे** संस्थापनीयः । महता **दण्डेने**ति । इति ऋणादान आपद्ब्राह्मणवृत्तिश्चतुर्थः । अतः प्रमाणभेदो भवति ।

प्रमाणानि प्रमाणस्थैः परिपाल्यानि यत्नतः ।
सीदन्ति हि प्रमाणानि प्रमाणैरव्यवस्थितैः ॥६४॥

अत्र यत्किमपि प्रमेयं वस्तु प्रकर्षेण मेयं प्रमेयं तत्त्वतो ज्ञेयमित्यर्थः । तत्सर्वं प्रमाणैः परिच्छिन्नं स्फुटीभवति यथा गणितं संख्यया तुलितं तुलया मेयं मापनेन[183] । तर्कादयः प्रमेयाः प्रत्यक्षादिभिः प्रमाणैः । तथात्रापि द्वात्रिंशच्छत-भेदोपलक्षितो[184]ऽष्टादशपदव्यवहारः प्रमेयभूतः लिखितसाक्षिभुक्तिदिव्यप्रमाणैः परिच्छिन्नः[185] स्फुटीभवति । अतो मतानि **प्रमाणानि प्रमाणस्थैः** पुरुषैः साधुनृपतिसभ्यादिभिर् **यत्नतः परिकल्प्यानि*** । किमुक्तं भवति । रूढि-प्रतिष्ठितान्यपि तानि पूर्वदग्धलोकानां हेतुवादशतैर्दूषितानि न दातव्यानि यतः प्रमाणैः व्यवस्थापरिब्रष्टैः सद्भिर्यानि प्रमेयाणि निसंदिग्धीकर्तुम्[186] अभिप्रेतानि तानि सीदन्ति सिद्धिं न प्राप्नुवन्तीत्यतः प्रमाणरक्षणे यत्न उपन्यस्त इति ।

६२ b — D यज्ञार्थेऽपि

६३ a — D विक्रीणानस्त्वविक्रेयं; d — D add इति श्रीनारदीये धर्मशास्त्रे ऋणादानस्तृतीयोऽध्ययः.

६४ a — L प्रमाणज्ञैः; b — P परिकल्प्यानि; V7 यतः; c — D च; P प्रमेयानि; d — D पुरुषस्यापराधतः.

लिखितं साक्षिणो भुक्तिः प्रमाणं त्रिविधं स्मृतं ।
धनस्वीकरणे येन धनी धनमुपाश्नुते ॥६५॥

तत्र तावल्**लिखित**प्रशंसा

नाकरिष्यद्यदि स्रष्टा लिखितं चक्षुरुत्तमम् ।
तत्रेयमस्य[187] लोकस्य नाभविष्यच्छुभा गतिः ॥ [J 1.70]
देशकालफलद्रव्यप्रमाणावधिनिश्चये ।
सर्वसंदेहविच्छेदि लिखितं चक्षुरुत्तमम् ॥ [J 1.71]

अथ **साक्षि**प्रशंसा[188]

गृहीत्वापि मार्गे[189] द्रव्यं योऽपह्नवितुमिच्छति ।
स्थापितः साक्षिभिर्मार्गे स दुःसाध्योऽपि साध्यते ॥ [J 1.72]

अथ **भुक्ति**प्रशंसा

लिखितं स्याद्बहुच्छिद्रं साक्षिणो नाजरामराः ।
भुक्तिस्त्वनर्थसंबद्धा संततैवार्थसाधकी ॥ [J 1.73]
तदेतत्त्रिविधं ज्ञेयं प्रमाणाय न साधितम् ।
संदेहमागतमपि धनी धनमवाप्नुयात् ॥ [J 1.74]

लिखितं बलवन्नित्यं जीवन्तस्त्वेव साक्षिणः ।
कालातिहरणाद् भुक्तिरिति शास्त्रेषु निश्चयः ॥६६॥

अत्र बलाबलप्रमाणं निरूपणेनोक्तं । यदेतल्**लिखितं** नाम तत्प्रयत्नरक्षितं सन्मृतेष्वपि धनिकसाक्षिषु पुत्रपौत्रप्रपौत्रसंततिसंबध्यमानद्रव्यस्योभयपक्षसंभावितसंव्यवहारस्य प्रतिष्ठाप्रविष्टं द्रव्यप्रमाणसंदेहविच्छेदकारकं भवति । **साक्षिणस्तु जीवन्त एव** प्रमाणमिति जीवतां चैतदपेक्षया **लिखितं बलवन्नित्यम्** इत्युक्तम् । यदा पुनः **कालातिहरणं** भवति तदा चतुर्थपञ्चमपुरुषोपरिष्टादप्यपरिमितकालादपि संतत-भुक्त्यैव धनी धनमवाप्नुयादिति शास्त्रस्य **निश्चयः** । एतत्प्रमाणबलाबलमुक्तम् ।

त्रिविधस्यास्य दृष्टस्य प्रमाणस्य यथाक्रमम् ।
पूर्वं पूर्वं गुरु ज्ञेयं भुक्तिरेभ्यो गरीयसी ॥६७॥

६५ a — Y लिखितान्; K2 साक्षिणं भुक्तिं; b — Y NMS विदुः; c — B5 D -स्वीकरणं; BM X नैव; d — P D अवाप्नुते; Jolly अवाप्नुयात्.

६६ a — B5 लिखिता; b — X जीवत्स्वपि हि साक्षिपु; Y जीवन्तस्तेऽपि साक्षिणः; P जीवन्तश्चैव साक्षिणः; d — X शास्त्रस्य निश्चयः; P शास्त्रविनिश्चयः; Ox शास्त्रेपु निर्णयः.

६७ c — V7 V8 Ox M गुरुर्, d — P तेभ्यो; D त्वाभ्यां; NMS वैपां.

तत्र पूर्वस्य गुरुत्वे निर्दिष्टे लिखितप्रमाणस्यैवाधिक्यमुपपद्यते । उत्तरोत्तरं भुक्तेर्मान्द्यगौरवव्याख्यानमागच्छति । पुनश्चास्मिन्नेव श्लोकचतुर्थपादेऽभिहितं **भुक्तिस्तेभ्यो* गरीयसी**ति भुक्तेरेवातिगौरवमापादितम् । तत्कथमेतद्योजनीयम् । अत्रोच्यते । स्थावरविषये निरागमाया दुर्बलत्वं दृष्टं । यथोक्तमत्रैव

संभोगो दृश्येते यत्र न दृष्येतागमः क्वचित् ।
आगमः कारणं तत्र न भोगस्तत्र कारणम् ।। [NāSmṛ 1.76]

एवमनागमाया भुक्तेः दुर्बलत्वमात्रं प्रतिष्ठते । तस्याः पूर्वं प्रमाणं साक्षिण उक्ताः । ते च यदि स्थावरस्यागमप्रतिष्ठाकारिणो भवन्ति ततो भुक्तिः प्रतिष्ठते नान्यथा । एवं भुक्तेः पूर्वस्य साक्षिणः प्रमाणस्य गुरुत्वमापन्नम् । ततश्चागमद्वारेणैव साक्षिभ्यो लिखितं श्रेय इति । एवं चागमप्रतिष्ठिता सती भुक्तिस्तेभ्यः साक्षिलिखित-दिव्येभ्यो गरीयसीति योजितमिदम् ।

विद्यमानेऽपि लिखिते जीवत्स्वपि हि साक्षिषु ।
विशेषतः स्थावराणां यन्न भुक्तं न तत्स्थिरम् ॥६८॥

अत्र तु साक्षिलिखितयोरपि प्रमाणयोर्भुक्तिप्रमाणं विना दुर्बलत्वमुपदर्शितम् । अतोऽर्थाद्गम्यते । आगमभुक्तयोरितरेतरमाधानाधेयसंबन्धः[190] । एकैकं प्रमाणमप्य-प्रमाणम् । यदुभयप्रमाणसंपन्नं वस्तु तदविचलं प्रमाणमिति । **विशेषतः स्थावराणाम्** अपि युक्तोऽपि यत्रोपजीव्यते[191] तदपि भुक्तिं विना न[192] **स्थिरं** भवति न तत्प्रतिष्ठितं भवतीत्यर्थः ।

भुज्यमानान्परैरर्थान्यः स्वान्मौर्ख्यादुपेक्षते ।
समक्षं जीवतोऽप्यस्य तान्भुक्तिः कुरुते वशे ॥६९॥

स्वकीया**नर्थान्**द्विपदचतुष्पदस्थावरादिकान्प्रीतिसमर्पितबलात्कारगृहीतशून्याक्रान्तादि प्रपञ्चैः परैः **भुज्यमानान्यो मौर्ख्यादुपेक्षते** तस्य **जीवतोऽपि** चिरकालातिक्रान्ता भुक्तिस्तान्पराणामेव वशीकुरुते । प्रत्यक्षं प्रापयति । किं पुनर्मृतस्येति ।

६८ b — K2 om.

६९ a — Y B3 भुज्यमानं; K2 K5 भुज्यमान्य; K5 fh mc भुज्यमानान्; Y अर्थं; b — Y यत्स्यान्मोहाद्, D यस्तान्मोहाद्; NMS यः स्वमौढ्याद्; K5 fh mc स्यान्; c — D प्रत्यक्षं; K5 fh mc पश्यतो; d — NMS स्वकान्.

यत्किंचिद्दश वर्षाणि संनिधौ प्रेक्षते धनी ।
भुज्यमानं परैस्तूष्णीं न स तल्लब्धुमर्हति ॥७०॥

एत**द्दश** वर्षकालप्रमाणमुपन्यस्तं न तच्छलार्थं किं तर्हि संव्यवहारस्थितिरक्षणार्थं किल । द्रव्यसंबन्धं विनापि कः स्वकीयमर्थं **भुज्यमानम्** इयन्तं कालमुपेक्षते । **तूष्णीं** यत्पनरुपेक्षितं तदर्थात्प्रतिष्ठितद्रव्यसंबन्धं भवति । अतस् तदुपरिष्टात्मुधिकया प्रार्थयन्नपि न स तल्लब्धुमर्हति । यत्[193] पुनर्देश-कालबलापेक्षया तं स्वार्थमुद्धर्तुं[194]न क्षमः । प्रतिवचः प्रतिदिनं प्रतिमासं[195] प्रतिवर्षं च करोति । ततः कालान्तरेऽपि तत्तस्य न प्रणश्यति व्यवहार उत्तरं लभत इत्यर्थः ।

उपेक्षां कुर्वतस्तस्य तूष्णीं भूतस्य तिष्ठतः ।
कालेऽतिपन्ने पूर्वोक्ते व्यवहारो न सिध्यति ॥७१॥
अजडश्चेदपोगण्डो विषये चास्य भुज्यते ।
भुक्तं तद्व्यवहारेण भोक्ता तद्धनमर्हति ॥७२॥

यदि जडो न भवति । दीर्घतीव्रामयग्रस्तामूकान्धबधिरोऽपि वा । यदि **चापो-गण्डोऽ**बालः[196] प्रत्यक्षतोऽसय सक्तं स्थावरादिकमनुपरवंश्यापरेण तु **भुज्यते**[197] । ततोऽर्थप्रतिष्ठितं द्रव्यं **व्यवहारेण** तद् भुक्तं । यो **भोक्ता** स एव **तद्धनमर्हति** ।

आधिः सीमा बालधनं निक्षेपोपनिधी स्त्रियः ।
राजस्वं श्रोत्रियस्वं च नोपभोगेन जीर्यते ॥७३॥

यत्किंचिदाधिकृतं वस्तु तत्सुचिरकालादपि तेन द्रव्येण लभते । न भोगेन प्रणश्यति । तथा परसीमा चिराक्रान्तापि स्वस्थीभूते देशे पुनर्लभ्यते[198] न

७० a — D वर्पान्तः; b — H प्रेक्ष्यते.
७१ Y P om this verse; c — D K2 ऽभिपन्ने; D पूर्वोक्तो; NMS पूर्वोक्तो and variant पूर्वोक्ते; d — NMS B3 विद्यते.
७२ a — H M अपौगण्डो; b — V V3 V6 V8 M वास्य; c — P D Y भग्नं.
७३ b — L V V7 H निःक्षेपो-; d — P श्रोत्रियद्रव्यं न भोगेन प्रणश्यति; B3 B5 श्रोत्रियस्वं नोपभोगेन प्रणश्यति.

नश्यति । तथा मातापित्रोः परोक्षे येन सधनो बलपरिग्रहीतद् **बालधनं** चिरभोगेनापि न प्रणश्यति । तथा निक्षेपो न्यास[199] उपनिधिः निक्षेपमध्ये[200]ऽन्तर्हितसारद्रव्यम् । तथा स्त्री निक्षेपभूता या भुक्ता । तथा **राजस्व**शब्देन भूमिरुक्ता । **श्रोत्रियद्रव्य***शब्देन गावोऽभिहिताः । एतेषु सविशेणन्यासाश्चिरकालातिक्रमेऽपि न नश्यन्तीति ।

प्रत्यक्षपरिभोगाच्च स्वामिनो द्विदशाः समाः ।
आध्यादीन्यपि जीर्यन्ते स्त्रीनरेन्द्रधनादृते ॥७४॥

आध्यादीनां यः स्वामी तस्य प्रत्यक्षं अनुपरतवंश्या[201] **द्विदशाः समाः** विंशतिवर्षाणि येन भुक्तानि तस्यैव तानि जीर्येरन्परिणतिं यान्तीत्यर्थः । **स्त्रीधनं** सुप्रतीतम् । **नरेन्द्रधन**शब्देन पर्यायेण तु भूमिरुक्ता किल । नरेन्द्राणां भूमिरेव धनमित्यतः । स्त्रीनरेन्द्रधने तु विंशतिवर्षैरपि न नश्यत इति ।

स्त्रीधनं च नरेन्द्राणां न कदाचन जीर्यते ।
अनागमं भुज्यमाणं वत्सराणां शतैरपि ॥७५॥

एवं[202] निरन्तरभोगेन न प्रणश्यति मुनिवचनसिद्धादेशादिति ।

निर्भोगो यत्र दृश्येत न दृश्येतागमः क्वचित् ।
आगमः कारणं तत्र न भोगस्तत्र कारणं ॥७६॥

एवं तु पनरत्रागमस्यैव माहात्म्यं दर्शितमिति ।

७४ a — B K2 K5 प्रत्यक्षपरिभोगश्; c — V3 V6 V8 R M आध्यादीन्
७५ a — Y तु; b — Y कदाचित्र; D कथंचन.
७६ a — P D संभोगो; Y K5 न भोगो; X Jolly दृश्यते यत्र; b — V V4 V6 V8 R Ox M दृश्येतागमं; d — D न संभोग इति स्थितिः, D add
आगमेन विशुद्धेन भोगो याति प्रमाणताम् ।
अविशुद्धागमो भोगः प्रामाण्यं नैव गच्छति ।। [J 1.85]
भोगं केवलतो यस्तु कीर्तयेन्नागमं क्वचित् ।
भोगच्छलापदेशेन स विज्ञेयस्तु तस्करः ।। [J 1.86]
अनागमं तु यो भुङ्क्ते बहून्यब्दशतान्यपि ।
चौरदण्डेन तं पापं दण्डयेत्पृथिवीपतिः ।। [J 1.87]

अनागमं भुज्यते यन्न तद्भोगोऽतिवर्तते ।
प्रेते तु भोक्तरि धनं याति तद्वंश्यभोग्यताम् ॥७७॥

अत्र यावदद्भोक्ता जीवति तावद**नागमं** भुज्यमानं परकीयं भवति यथा तथास्योद्धरणसंभवो भवति । यदा पुनरनागमभोक्ताप्यप्रार्थित एव मृतस्तदा तद्वस्तु तदीय**वंश्यभोग्यतां याति** । अतो नोपेक्षणीयमित्यर्थः ।

आहर्तैवाभियुक्तः सन्नर्थानामुद्धरेत्पदम् ।
भुक्तिरेव विशुद्धिः स्यात्प्राप्तानां पितृतः क्रमात् ॥७८॥

कश्चित्परकीयार्थानाम**आहर्ता** स एवार्थो धनिना स्वार्थसंचितार्थमारम्भणीयः । स चाहर्तैव तेनाभियुक्तः **सन्**तमर्थं प्रतिष्ठापदं नयेत् । तस्मिन्पुनर्थाहर्तरि मृते तदीयसंततेरुपरतपितृक्रमागता **भुक्तिरेव** प्रतिष्ठातिशुद्धिकारिणी भवति[203] ।

अन्यायेनापि यद् भुक्तं पित्रा पूर्वतरैस्त्रिभिः ।
न तच्छक्यमपाकर्तुं[204] क्रमात्त्रिपुरुषागतम् ॥ [J 1.91]

यत्किमपि वस्तु वृद्धप्रपितामहेनाहृतम्[205] अन्येनापि विनागममपि ततश्च प्रपितामहेनापि भुक्तं तदनन्तरं पितामहेनापि । एवमनेन पुरुषपारम्पर्येण पितुः पूर्वतरैस्त्रिभिर्यद् भुक्तं तत्पितुः क्रमात्त्रिपुरुषागतं चलस्थिरादिकं वस्तु तत्केनाप्यपहर्तुं न शक्यम् । अत्र भाषाया एवमुत्थानमित्यर्थः ।

अन्वाहितं हृतं न्यस्तं बलावष्टब्धं याचितम् ।
अप्रत्यक्षं च यद् भुक्तं षडेतान्यागमं विना ॥७९॥

अत्र**अन्वाहितम्** इति यत्किमप्यसारं[206] प्रति वस्तुसमर्थपरपार्श्वात्सारं वस्तु कार्यार्थं गृहीतं । तथा **हृतं** यत्तस्करन्यायेन । तथा यत्कार्यार्थं **याचितम्** । तथा यद्देशान्तरगतस्य परोक्षे **भुक्तं** । एतैः षड्भिः प्रकारैः प्राप्तं यद् भुक्तं तद्**विनागमं** भुक्तमित्युच्यते । तेषु भुक्तिरप्रमाणमित्यर्थः[207] ।

तथारूढविवादस्य प्रेतस्य व्यवहारिणः ।

७७ a — P NMS भुज्यतेऽनागमं यत्तु; b — B3 यत्नतं भोगो; B5 यद्यत्नं भोगो; D यन्न तद्भुक्तं; P पदं नयेत्, D X पर नयेत्; Y ऽतिवर्द्धयेत्; d — DY -वंश-; D add
स्मार्ते काले क्रिया भुमेः सागमा भुक्तिरिष्यते ।
अस्मार्ते लिखिताभावे क्रमात्त्रिपुरुषागता ॥ [J 1.89]

७८ b — Jolly V3 V4 स्यात्नार्थानाम्; NMS अर्थतस्तद्धरेत्; d — P D प्राप्ता या.

७९ a — D अन्वाहितहृत-; All देवनागरी mss -न्यस्त-.; b — All mss -प्टब्ध-; d — BM B5 एतान्; B एतेन्-; NMS आगमाद्; BM B5 विदुः.

पुत्रेण सोऽर्थः संशोध्यो न तं भोगोऽतिवर्तते ॥८०॥

एवमेतेषां प्रकारणामेकेनाप्यन्यायेन परकीयमर्थं भुञ्जन्यः कश्चिदर्थो धनिना न्यायार्थं प्रारब्धोऽनिष्पन्नव्यवहार एव प्रेतीभूतः । तस्य सक्तः स तदवस्थ एव व्यवहारः **पुत्रेण संशोध्यः** । **सोऽर्थः** पितृकामभुक्त्या ततो न भवतीत्यर्थः ।

यद्विनागममप्यूर्ध्वं भुक्तं पूर्वैस्त्रिभिर्भवेत् ।
न तच्छक्यमपाकर्तुं क्रमात्त्रिपुरुषागतम् ॥८१॥
सन्तोऽपि न प्रमाणं स्युर्मृते धनिनि साक्षिणः ।
अन्यत्र श्रावितं यत्स्यात्स्वयमासन्नमृत्युना ॥८२॥

मृते धनिनि यदि कश्चिद्वदति मम धनिनामुकामुकगौर्महिषी बलीवर्दो वामुकाकेदरो वामुकप्रयोजने पर्वणि वा प्रतिपादितः । तथा चामुकाः साधवः साक्षिणो नाम विद्यन्ते । अन्योऽपि यदि कश्चिद्वदति तव पित्रा मम द्रम्मशतं दातव्यम् । अमुकामुकसाक्षिण इति[208] । ततो **मृते धनिनि** मृतान्तरे **सन्तोऽपि** साधवः साक्षिणो **न प्रमाणं स्युः** । **अन्यत्र स्वयं श्रावितादिति*** यदा पुनः तेनैव धनिना समासन्नमृत्युना कथंचित्साक्षिणां अत्रैव स्वमुखेनैव कोऽप्यर्थः श्रावितः स्यात् । अथवासौ मुमूर्षुः केनापि धनिना जल्पयितः तेनापि सम**ासन्नमृत्युना** सोऽर्थः स्वमुखेन प्रतिपन्नः । ततस्तस्मिन्मृतेऽपि **साक्षिणः प्रमाणम्** इति ।

न हि प्रत्यर्थिनि प्रेते प्रमाणं साक्षिणां वचः ।
साक्षिमत्करणं तत्र प्रमाणं स्याद्विनिश्चये ॥८३॥

अत्रार्थी धनी उच्यते । प्रत्यर्थ्यृणी । तस्मिन्**प्रत्यर्थिन्**यृणिके प्रेतीभूते **साक्षिणां वचो** वचनं **न हि प्रमाणं** यतः **साक्षिमत्कारणं*** तस्य जीवत एव च न मृतस्येति ।

श्रावितस्त्वातुरेणापि यस्त्वर्थो धर्मसंहितः ।
मृतेऽपि तत्र साक्षी स्यात्षट्सु चान्वाहितादिषु ॥८४॥

८० c — D ऽशः; d — X P भोगपदं नयेत्; D भोगो निवर्त्तयेत्.

८१ P om this verse; a — All देवनागरी mss अत्यन्तं; W अप्यर्था; NMS आगमेन विना पूर्वं; b — W स्युः.

८२ b — V3 V8 साक्षिनाः; c — P श्रावितात्यस्मात्.

८३ b — Z साक्षिनो; c — V6 V8 M साक्षिसत्-, Ox साक्षितत्-; P V6 V8 M कारणं; d — P तस्य जीवितः; Y V4 स्याद्विनिश्चयः.

अत्र**ातुरेण** पित्रा पुत्रपरोक्षेऽपि योऽर्थो धर्मदत्तादिः[209] साक्षिणां पुरतः श्रावितः स प्रमाणं[210] । तथा **षट्सु चान्वाहितादिषु** । तस्मिन्नातुरत्वे समुपस्थिते संजातपश्चात्तापो यद्वदति साक्षिपुरतः । यथा मयामुकपार्श्वात्सारममुकं वस्वसारप्रतिवस्तुनान्वाहितं तदर्पणीयम् । तथामुकेनामुकं वसु मम निक्षिप्तं तदर्पणीयम् । तथामुकं मया बलादवष्टब्धं तन्मोक्तव्यम् । तथामुकं याचितं तदर्पणीयममुकं परोक्षं भुक्तं तन्मोक्तव्यमिति । एतेषु षट्स्वन्वाहितादिषु मृतेऽपि तस्मिन्साक्षिणः प्रमाणानीति ।

क्रियर्णादिषु सर्वेषु बलवत्युत्तरोत्तरा ।
प्रतिग्रहाधिक्रीतेषु पूर्वा पूर्वा गरीयसी ॥८५॥

ऋणादिषु व्यवहारपदेषु **सर्वेष्व**पि या या **उत्तरा**न्तिमा **क्रिया** द्रव्यवृद्धिपरिच्छेदविषये भवति । तया तया पश्चिमा बाध्येत । सोत्तरोत्तरा प्रमाणं । प्रतिग्रहे पुनर्येन प्रथमं ग्रामो लब्धस्तस्य प्रमाणम् । येन पश्चाल्लब्धस्तस्य न प्रमाणम् । आधिरपि यस्य पूर्वाधिस्तस्य प्रमाणम् । पश्चात्कृताधिरप्रमाणं । क्रीतमपि येन पूर्वं क्रीतं तस्य प्रमाणं । पश्चात्क्रीतमप्रमाणम् । एवमेतेषु **प्रतिग्रहाधिक्रीतेषु** व्यवहारपदेषु पूर्वा क्रिया बलवतीति । इत्यृणादाने प्रमाणभेदः पञ्चमः । अतः कुसीद*वार्द्धुषिकभेदौ भवतः ।

स्थानलाभनिमित्तं हि दानग्रहणमिष्यते ।
तत्कुसीदमिति प्रोक्तं तेन वृत्तिः कुसीदिनाम् ॥८६॥

अत्र **स्थान**शब्दो[211] द्रव्याश्रितः स्वस्थानाश्रितः परदेशाश्रितश्च द्रष्टव्यः । तद्यथा । स्थानस्थितस्याविनष्टद्रव्यपिण्डस्य यो वृद्धिलाभः । तथा स्वस्थाने स्वस्यैव व्यवहारकस्य यो लाभः । तथा स्थाने स्थाने देशे यो वृद्धिक्रमाचारेण लाभस्तस्य स्थानलाभस्य निमित्तं दानं प्रयोग्यं ग्रहणं सवृद्धिकस्य तस्येति **दानग्रहणमिष्यते** । एतच्च प्रयोग्यदानग्रहणं स्मृतिसमयशब्देन **कुसीदम्**[212] इति नाम प्रोक्तम् । तेन कुसीदेन[213] प्रयोग्येन **कुसीदिनां**[214] प्रयोजकानां **वृत्तिर्** इति ।

वसिष्ठविहितां वृधिं सृजेद्वित्तविवर्धिनीम् ।
अशीतिभागं गृह्णीयाच्छते मासस्य वार्धुषी ॥ [J 1.99]

८४ a — D श्रावितेनान्तरेणापि; c — P D साक्ष्यं.

८५ a — P यदृणादिषु; D क्रियार्थादिषु; b — Jolly उत्तरा क्रिया; Y उत्तरोत्तरं; c — D -ग्रहादि-; d — P वलीयसी.

८६ c — P H Ox कुशूदम्; d — L V5 H नान्याद; V7 V8 R Ox कुसीदिना; P H Ox कुशीदिनाम्.

एकस्य प्रयुक्तस्य मासे भुक्तेऽशीतिभागवृद्ध्या सपादो द्रम्मो भवति । इयं वसिष्ठविहितातिधर्मवती वृद्धिः । एनां वृद्धिं वित्तविवर्धिनीं प्रयोजकः सृजेत्प्रवर्तयेदिति ।

द्विकं त्रिकं चतुष्कं च पञ्चकं च समं स्मृतम् ।
मासस्य वृद्धिं गृह्णीयाद्वर्णानामनुपूर्वशः ।। [J 1.100]

अत्र ब्राह्मणेषु प्रयोगवृद्धौ द्विकं शतं धर्म्यम् । क्षत्रियेषु त्रिकं वैश्येषु चतुस्कं शूद्रेषु पञ्चकम् । इयं शते मासवृद्धिर्वर्णानामनुक्रमेणेति ।

द्विकं शतं वा[215] गृह्णीत सतां वृत्तमनुस्मरन् ।
द्विकं शतं हि गृह्णाणो न भवत्यर्थकिल्बिषी ।। [J 1.101]

अथवा सर्ववर्णेष्वपि साधुपुरुषेभ्यः सकाशाद् द्विकमेव शतं गृह्णीयात् । एतत्सतां वृत्तमित्येवं स्मरन् । एवमनया वृद्ध्या प्रयोजकोऽर्थकिल्बिषी न भवति ।

कायिका कालिका चैव कारिता च तथा स्मृता ।
चक्रवृद्धिश्च शास्त्रेषु तस्य वृद्धिश्चतुर्विधा ॥८७॥

इत्यत्र श्लोके चतुर्विधवृद्धिनामचतुष्टयमिदमुक्तम् । लक्षणंत्विदमुच्यते ।

कायाविरोधिनी शश्वत्पणपाद्या तु कायिका ।
प्रतिमासं स्रवति या वृद्धिः सा कालिका स्मृता ॥८८
वृद्धिः सा कारिता नाम यर्णिकेन स्वयंकृता ।
वृद्धेरपि पुनर्वृद्धिश्चक्रवृद्धिरुदाहृता ॥८९

अनेन श्लोकद्वयेन चतुर्विधापि वृद्धिर्व्याख्याता । किं यदिदं[216] मुनिमतं[217] संक्षिप्तव्याख्यानं तदपि विस्तरव्याख्यानं विनापि नातिपरिस्फुटं भवतीत्यत एतदुच्यते । अतीतकाला वृद्धिः फलं यस्यां प्राप्यते । सा **कालिका** वृद्धिरुच्यते । **प्रतिमास**वृद्धिः स्रावणी वृद्धिः फलदेत्यर्थः । सा च शास्त्रोक्ता वर्णानुक्रमेण पञ्चकशतमवधिभूता दृष्टा या पुनर्ऋणिकेनैवापात्रभूतेनाथवा पात्रभूतेनैव सविशेषार्तिवशात्स्वमुखेनैव दशैकादधिका करवृद्धिर्वा[218] कृता । वृद्धिः सा **कारिता नाम यर्णिकेन स्वयंकृते**ति । अथ **कायो**च्यते । सा च कायाविरोधिनी । धरणविधारणादिना न प्रार्थयति । इयं दूरादेव न घटते । अत्र **काय**शब्दो

८७ a — D कालिका; P कायिता; b — P कायिका; NMS कारिका; P परा; d — P शास्त्रेऽस्मिन्वृद्धिर्दृष्टा चतुर्विधा.
८८ ab — P om; b — D NMS पणपादादि; c — P NMS Ox V V3 V6 V8 R H स्रवन्ती; d — NMS L V5 Y सा वृद्धिः; D मता.
८९ b — V-V8 R H Ox M धार्मिकेन; BM B5 K2 K5 यार्णिकेन; B3 धार्णिकेन; B धर्णिकेन; B5 स्वकृता; ab — P कायाविरोधिनी स्वस्वपरपादादिका क्रमात्; D add भिन्देदर्थपरीमाणं कालेनेहर्णिकस्य यत् ।

द्रव्यपिण्डप्रतिबन्ध एव द्रष्टव्यः । द्रव्यपिण्डो द्रव्यकायः । तस्याविरोधिनी मूलद्रव्यकायस्याविनाशिनी । सा च स्वस्वपरिमाणपादादिका[219] । किमुक्तं भवति । ऋणिकस्योपरि यो द्रव्यपिण्डकायो दिवसभाटकवृद्ध्याचारेण स्वः स्वः दिनप्रतिदिनं पणः[220] पणो देयः । पादः[221] पादो वा देयः । इत्यनेन क्रमेण तं पणं पादं वा प्रतिदिनं गृह्णतो धनिकस्य सुचिरकालेनापि मूलद्रव्यकायमध्यात्किंचिन्न पतति । अपरिमितद्रव्यप्रवेश इति । यदा तदा स द्रव्यपिण्डकायर्णिकेनाखण्डित एव संपूर्णो देयः । इत्येषा कायाविरोधिनी वृद्धिः **कायिके**ति नामोच्यते । अथ **चक्रवृद्धिर्** उच्यते यस्यां पनर्वृद्धावेको द्रम्मः पञ्चशतेन दत्तः । तत्र विंशतिभिर्मासैर्जातं द्र [म्मयोः] २. एतद् द्रव्यमन्यैर्विंशतिभिर्मासैर्जातं द्र [म्मानां] ४. एतेऽप्यन्यैर्विंशतिभिर्भूता द्र । ८. पश्चादन्यैर्विंशतिभिर्जाता द्र । १६. पुनरन्यैर्द्र । ३२. इयं वृद्धिरपि पुनर्वृद्धिरुच्यते । अनया वृद्ध्या यावदेक एव मूलिकद्रम्मः[222] कस्यापि राज्ञ उपरि स्थितो वर्षः <द्र> । ३३ मास ४ तावत्कालेन द्र[223] । ४०. अत्र विंशतिमात्रिकाः परिवर्ता भवन्ति[224] । स चैकद्रम्मः पञ्चशतपञ्चकवृद्ध्या यावद्विंशतिवारगुणितः तवात्तेन राज्ञा तस्य मूलिकैकद्रम्मं धनिकस्य दातव्यं जातं । एवं चतुर्विधापि वृद्धिरियं सविस्तरा व्याख्याता ।

ऋणानां सार्वभौमोऽयं विधिर्वृद्धिकरः स्मृतः ।
देशाचारविधिस्त्वन्यो यत्रर्णमवतिष्ठति ॥९०॥

अर्थानां वृद्धिकरविधिः सर्वभूमिसामान्यो दृष्टः । अन्या तु **देशावस्थितिर्*** या यत्र प्रसिद्धा सा तत्रैव **यत्रर्णमप्यवतिष्ठते*** । व्यवहारतः प्रतिष्ठते ।

द्विगुणं त्रिगुणं चैव तथान्यस्मिंश्चतुर्गुणम् ।
तथाष्टगुणमन्यस्मिन्देशे देशेऽवतिष्ठते ॥९१॥

कस्मिंश्चिद्देशे द्विगुणावधिवृधिरेव । केष्वपि पुनस्त्रि**गुणचतुर्गुणाष्टगुणा**प्यन्यदेशेषु वृद्धिर**वतिष्ठते** ।

हिरण्यधान्यवस्त्राणां वृद्धिर्द्वित्रिचतुर्गुणा ।
घृतस्याष्टगुणा वृद्धिः स्त्रीपशूनां च संततिः ॥९२॥

९० a — P अर्थानां; V V3-5 V7-8 M सर्वभौम्ये; b — Y एष वृद्धिरुदाहृतः; c — D देशाचारविधेस्त्वन्यो; P या देशावस्थितिस्त्वन्यो; Y देशाचरस्थितिस्तवन्या; d — D यतायं; Y D P अवतिष्ठते.

९१ D om this verse; b — P वापि तथान्यत्र; d — P Y देयं.

९२ c — P Y D रसस्याष्टगुणा.

हिरण्यं यथा कयापि वृद्ध्या गृहीतं तथा तावद्वर्धते[225] यावद् द्विगुणीभूतम् । **धान्यं** जल्पितवृद्ध्या[226] च दीयमानं प्रतिग्राह्यं तावद्वर्धते यावत्त्रिगुणम् । **वस्त्रं** तावद्वर्धते यावच्चतुर्गुणम् । रसस्तावद्यावदष्टगुणो भूतः । **स्त्रीपशुनां** च समाधत्तानं या **संततिरु**त्पद्यते सा द्रम्मधनिकस्य भवतीति ।

सूत्रकर्पासकिण्वानां त्रपुषः सीसकस्य च ।
आयुधानां च सर्वेषां चर्मणस्ताम्रलोहयोः ॥९३॥
अन्येषां चैव सर्वेषामिष्टकानां तथैव च ।
अक्षय्या वृद्धिरेतेषां मनुराह प्रजापतिः ॥९४॥
तैलानां चैव सर्वेषां मद्यानां मधुसर्पिषां ।
वृद्धिरष्टगुणा ज्ञेया गुडस्य लवणस्य च ॥९५॥
न वृद्धिः प्रीतिदत्तानां स्यादनाकारिता क्वचित् ।
अनाकारितमप्यूर्ध्वं वत्सरार्धाद्विवर्धते ॥९६॥

एषामनन्तरोक्तानां वस्तूनां प्रीतिसंव्यवहारेण दत्तानामविचारिता वृद्धिर्नास्ति तावद्यावत्षण्मासं । ततः परं त्व <ना> कारितापि वृद्धिः षण्मासादुपरि भवतीति ।

प्रीतिदत्तं तु यत्किंचिन्न तद्वर्धत्ययाचितम् ।
याच्यमानमदत्तं चेद्वर्धते पञ्चकं शतम् ।। [J 1.109]

प्रीतिदत्तं यत्किमपि भवति तत्तावन्न वर्धते यावन्न याचितम् । यदा पुनर्याच्यमानमपि न दीयते तदा षण्मासादर्वागपि तद्दिवसादारभ्य पञ्चकशतवृद्ध्या वर्धते ।

एष वृद्धिविधिः प्रोक्तः प्रतिवृद्धस्य धर्मतः ।
वृद्धिस्तु योक्ता धान्यानां वार्धुष्यं तदुदाहृतम ॥९७॥

एष **विधिः प्रतिवृद्धस्य**[227] **कर्मण*** उद्दिष्टः । कर्मशब्दः क्वचिद्धिरण्यपर्यायवाचको दृष्टः। या पुनर्धान्यस्य* वृद्धिर्भवति ततो वार्धुषिकं नाम वर्तमानमुच्यते किल ।

९३ a — X -कर्पासकोर्णानां; P NMS Y om verse 93-95; b — All mss त्रपुणः; c — X अनेकानां; d — B3 K2 चर्मणां चर्मणां तथा.

९४ a — X उरस्त्राणां विचित्राणाम्; d — B3 प्रजापतेः.

९५ d — X लवणापूपवीरुधाम्.

९६ d — P प्रवर्धते.

९७ b — Y प्रवृत्तिस्तु; NMS प्रवृद्धस्येह; Jolly प्रीतिदत्तस्य; P कर्मणः; Y स्वधर्मतः; c — P धान्यस्य; d — Y वार्धुपस्; X वार्धुपं; Y उदाहृतः.

आपदं निस्तरेद्वैश्यः कामं वार्धुषकर्मणा ।
आपत्स्वपि हि कष्टासु ब्राह्मणस्य न वार्धुषम् ॥९८॥

कृषिगोरक्षादिवृत्तिर्वैश्यस्य शास्त्रविहिता शास्त्रोत्पादकैव[228] । तत्पुनर्धान्यवृद्धि-प्रयोजनं[229] तस्यापि निषिद्धम् । तेनैतदुक्तम् । यदि काचिदापद्भवति ततस्ताम**आपदं** कामम् इच्छया **वार्धुषिकर्मणा*** **निस्तरेत्** । **ब्राह्मणस्य** पुनरिदं वार्धुषिकं च कष्टास्वप्यापत्सु न विहितमतिनिषिद्धत्वादिति ।

ब्राह्मणस्य तु यद्देयं सान्वयस्य न चास्ति सः ।
स्वकुल्यस्यास्य निवपेत्तदभावेऽस्य बन्धुषु ॥९९॥

अत्र **ब्राह्मणस्य यत्**किमपि येन दातव्यं विद्यते । तस्य ब्राह्मणस्यापि यदाभावः तदा तदीयस्वकुल्येषु निक्षिपेत् । कुल्यन्यस्थीन्युच्यन्ते । तान्येकानि समानि येषां ते सकुल्याः पितृपितृव्यतत्सुतादयः । तेषु स्वकुल्येषु निक्षिपेत् । **तदभावेऽस्य बन्धुषु** मातृभगिनीभागिनेयादिष्विति ।

यदा तु न स्वकुल्याः स्युर्न च संबन्धिबान्धवाः ।
तदा दद्यात्स्वजातिभ्यस्तेष्वसत्स्वप्सु निक्षिपेत् ॥१००॥

स्पष्टार्थः श्लोकः । ईदृशं च ब्राह्मणस्योग्रत्वं दृष्टं । येन कथमप्यात्मार्थे न धारणीयमित्युक्तं यच्चापि तत्पुण्योद्देशेन तडागखननेन तथा व्ययेदिति ।

गृहीत्वोपगतं दद्यादृणिकायोदयं धनी ।
अददद्याच्यमानस्तु शेषहानिमवाप्नुयात् ॥१०१॥

९८ a — B5 पापदं; b — L वार्धुप्य-; P वार्धुपि; d — D ब्राह्मणः स्यात्र वार्धुपी.

९९ b — P अन्वयश्चास्य नास्ति चेत्; Y सान्वयं यस्य नास्ति चेत्; X सान्वयस्तु न चास्ति सः; c — P निक्षिपेत स्वकुल्येभस्; Jolly निक्षिपेत्तत्स्वकुल्येपु; BM स्वकुलेऽस्य निवपेत्; B5 स्वकुलस्य निवपेत्; B स्वकुलस्य निवततस्, L V3-5 V7 V8 M स्वकुलेभ्योऽस्य निर्वपेत्; V स निर्वपेत्तत्सकुल्येपु; V6 संकुलो निर्वपेत्तस्य कुल्येपु; Ox संकुले निर्वपेतस्य कुल्येपु; H सकुल्यस्यास्य निर्वपेत्; NMS सपिण्डेभ्योऽस्य निवपेत्.

१०० a — D सकुल्यः; P सकुल्याः; D स्यान्; c — P द्विजातिभ्यस्.

१०१ Y om this verse. b — D ऋणिकस्योदयं, d — K5 fh mc शोकहानिम्.

ऋणिकाद्वृद्धिस्कन्धकं वानुदयभूतं **गृहीत्वा धन्युपगतं दद्यात्** । ऋणिकस्य तां तु प्रविश्योपगतमुपरिपृष्टं वा याच्यमानोऽप्यप्रयच्छन्**शेषहानिमवाप्नुयात्** । ऋणी वदति प्रवेशितधनमिदं पत्र इति ।

लेख्यं दद्यादृणे शुद्धे तदभावे प्रतिश्रवम् ।
धनिकर्णिकयोरेवं विशुद्धिः स्यात्परस्परम् ॥१०२॥

यत्किंचित्पत्रलिखितमृणं तन्निःशेषं धनिकस्य ऋणी दद्यात् । तदभावे **प्रतिश्रयं*** इति । हृतप्रणष्टाद्यपायबाहुल्यात्तदभावे लेख्याभावे धनी ऋणिकस्य **प्रतिश्रयं*** विशुद्धिपत्रं दद्यात् । एवं **धनिकर्णिकयोः परस्परं विशुद्धिर्** भवति । तथा चोक्तं त्रिषष्टिपत्रप्रकरणे कल्याणभट्टेन ।

पाटनं वा विशुद्धिर्वा सर्वदत्तधने[230] भवेत् ।
पृष्ठं वोपगतं वा स्यात्सशेषधनचीरके ॥[?]

इति कुषिदवार्धुषिकभेदः षष्ठः[231] । अतः प्रतिभूभेदो भवति ।

विश्रम्भहेतू द्वावत्र प्रतिभूराधिरेव च ।
लिखितं साक्षिणश्च द्वे प्रमाणे व्यक्तिकारके ॥१०३॥

वृद्धिलाभार्थप्रयोगस्य क्रियमाणस्य विश्वासमूलहेतू[232] **द्वावेव** प्रतिभुवो द्वितीयमाधिः । तेषां च द्रव्यवृद्धिप्रमाणप्रतिभ्वाधीनां चतुर्णामप्यङ्गानां **व्यक्तिकारके** संदेहप्रणाशने[233] द्वयमेव **प्रमाणम्*** । **लिखितं साक्षिणाश्**चेति ।

उपस्थानाय दानाय प्रत्ययाय तथैव च ।
त्रिविधः प्रतिभूर्दृष्टस्त्रिष्वेवार्थेषु सूरिभिः ॥१०४॥

अत्र यदा धनिकेन ऋणिको विधृत एवं ब्रूते । यथा मया तव किंचिन्न दातव्यम् । धनिकस्तु ब्रूते यद्याचारेण प्रतिष्ठापयामि । ततोऽहं गृह्णामि । न्यायकरणस्यैवो**पस्थान**प्रतिभुवं[234] देहि । एवमुक्त्वा ऋणी धनिकस्य यं प्रतिभुवं प्रयच्छति । एवमुक्त्वा यथामुकं हि ते मया न्यायोपस्थानं करणीयम् । अस्मिन्नर्थे

१०२ a — P विशुद्धर्णे; b — P D प्रतिश्रयम्.

१०३ a — Y -हेतोर्, b — B3 प्रतिभूताधिर्; BM प्रतिभुस्ताभिर्; c — D चेति; d — X V4-7 Ox M प्रमाणं; Y -कारणे.

१०४ a — V8 उपस्थानदानाय; d — D add
निक्षेपः प्रातिभाव्यं च ऋणशेपश्च यो भवेत् ।
याच्यमानं न दत्तं चेद् वृद्धिं तत्र विनिर्दिशेत् ॥ [?]

त्वं मयास्योपस्थानप्रतिभूर्दत्तः । एवमुक्तः स पुरुषो यथा स्थितो धनिकेन च गृहीतः । तदासवुपस्थानप्रतिभूरित्युच्यते । इदानीं **दान**प्रतिभूरुच्यते । स च यदा धनिकपार्श्वाद् द्रव्यमृणिको ग्रहीतुमुद्यतः द्वितीयं तृतीयं वा पुरुषं सामान्यग्राहकं स्वांशदायकं वा पाठयित्वा प्रतिमुखं प्रयच्छति । तदासौ द्रव्यदानप्रतिभूः स्थित इत्युच्यते । अयं च द्वितीयः । तथा यदा धनिकेन ऋणिको विधृत एवं ब्रूते । यथा मया तव किंचिन्न दातव्यमासीत्ततदा काल एव सर्वं मया प्रवेशितमिति कारणोत्तरं प्रयच्छति मिथ्योत्तरं वा ददाति । ततश्च धनिको वदति । यद्येवं तर्हि अमुकादित्यभुवने समनन्तरागामि षष्ठ्यां तण्डुलभक्षणप्रत्ययार्थमेव मम कंचित्प्रतिभुवं प्रयच्छ । एवमुक्त ऋण्यस्मिन्नर्थे यं पुरुषं प्रत्ययकरणाय तस्य प्रयच्छतिं स प्रत्ययप्रतिभूरित्युच्यते । इति त्रिविधोऽप्युक्त इति ।

ऋणिष्वप्रतिकुर्वत्सु प्रत्यये वा विवादिते ।
प्रतिभूस्तदृणं दद्यादनुपस्थापयंस्तथा ॥१०५॥

अत्रातिव्याप्त्यर्णिकभयत्रासजननार्थमेव मुनिना प्रत्ययोपस्थानप्रतिभुवोरप्यृणदानविधिरुक्तः । युक्तिभिस्तु पुनरनेनैव बाधितः । यत एकं तावदिदमस्ति ।

उक्तानि प्रतिषिद्धानि पुनः संभावितानि च ।
सापेक्षनिरपेक्षाणि मुनिवाक्यानि के विदुः ॥[?]

अन्यथानेनैव मुनिनैतदुक्तम् ।

यत्र विप्रतिपत्तिः स्याद्धर्मशास्त्रार्थशास्त्रयोः ।
अर्थशास्त्रोक्तमुत्सृज्य धर्मशास्त्रोक्तमाचरेत् ॥[NāSmṛ Mā1.33]

अन्यच्च

धर्मशास्त्रविरोधे तु परस्परमुपस्थिते ।
लोकाचाराविरुद्धार्थो युक्तियुक्तो विधिः स्मृतः ॥[cf. NāSmṛ Mā1.34]

अतोऽस्मिन्लोकाचाराविरुद्धार्थयुक्तियुक्तविशेषः । उक्तं च वसिष्ठेन तदभिलिख्यते ।

नव[235] प्रतिभुवो लोके पृथगर्थसमाश्रिताः ।
अन्योन्यार्थस्य पूरस्था स्वस्वनामार्थनिर्गमाः ॥ [Dhko 676]
सामान्यग्राहकोऽत्रैको द्वितीयः स्वांशदायकः ।
दर्शनेऽथ उपस्थाने प्रत्यये धर्मजल्पिते ॥[Dhko 677]
पालने च[236] सातौ[237] शीले नव प्रतिभुवो ह्यमी[238] ।
सुता अपि तयोर्दद्युर्यौ स्थितौ द्रव्यदायकौ ॥[Dhko 677]

१०५ b — L V5 H प्रसवे; X वापि भाविते; B5 वादिपातिते; BM वा विपादिते; D वापि याचिते;
d — B -स्थापयंत्; B5 -स्थापय; D add
दर्शनप्रतिभूर्यत्र मृतः प्रात्ययिकोऽपि वा ।
न तत्पुत्रा ऋणं दद्युर्दद्युर्दानाय ये स्थिताः ॥ [YāSmṛ 2.54]

शेषाः प्रतिभुवः सप्त न दाप्यन्ते न तत्सुताः ।।[Dhko 677]

अत्र सामान्यग्राहकांशावेव दायिनौ । शेषसप्तप्रतिभुवां द्रव्यदाननिषेधो विहितः । स्वस्वनामार्थकारित्वमेव तेषां । एतदपि न तत्सुतानामिति । पुनश्चोक्तं तेनैव मुनिना विशिष्टतरम् ।

धनिन ऋणिकानां हि ये स्युः प्रतिभुवः स्थिताः ।
ते गवामिव गोपाला रक्षपालास्तपोवने ।।[Dhko 677]
समर्पयन्ति धनिके जीवसन्तकाम्[239] (?) ।
राजदैविकहान्या तु रक्षपालो न गृह्यते ।।[Dhko 677]
प्रतिभूः प्राणरक्षां यः[240] करोति धनिकर्णिनोः ।
अनेन किं न पर्याप्तं प्रतिभूः प्रकृतस्तयोः ।।[Dhko 677]
ऋणिद्रव्यं दद्धनिन ऋणिकस्य धनिद्रव्यम् ।
प्रतिभूर्व्यवहाराङ्गं न पीड्यमुभयोरपि ।।[Dhko 677]

एवमिमं लोकाचाराविरुद्धार्थं युक्तियुक्तं धर्ममनुसरता वृद्धवसिष्ठेन दर्शनादिसप्तप्रतिभुवां संव्यवहारभङ्गरक्षाप्रतिष्ठमनेनेति ।

बहवश्चेत्प्रतिभुवो दद्युस्तेऽर्थं यथाकृतम् ।
अर्थेऽविशेषिते ह्येषु धनिनश्छन्दतः क्रिया ॥१०६॥

बहवश्चेत्प्रतिभुवः स्थिताः स्वकीयस्वकीयांशमुपस्थितं द्रव्यं गृह्णन्ति[241] । ततस्ते **यथाकृतम्** ऋणं तथैव स्वांशस्थितं **दद्युः** । अथ सामान्यग्राहकत्वेन यदृच्छादापनीयत्वेन समुपस्थापकत्वेनाजीवतः[242] श्रेष्ठगामित्वेनार्थोऽविशेषितो भवति । ततो **धनिनश्[243]छन्दतः क्रिया** तेषां मध्ये यत्र सुलभं धनं धनी पश्यति तमेव विधृत्य गृह्णाति । तथा चोक्तमेव सामान्यग्राहपत्रलक्षणविचारप्रकरणे कल्याणभट्टेन ।

ये जीवन्ति मृतानां हि ये श्रेष्ठा जीविनामपि ।
धनी तान्स्वेच्छयादत्ते जीवच्छ्रेष्ठानुगामिनः ।।[?]

तथा चायमेव महर्षिनारदः पुरस्ताद्विशेषमिदं[244] वक्षयति ।

दाप्यः परर्णमेकोऽपि जीवत्स्वधिकृतैः कृतम् ।
प्रेतेषु तु न तत्पुत्रः परर्णं दातुमर्हति ।।[NāSmṛ 1.12]

अस्यायमर्थः । सामान्यग्राहकत्वाधिकृतैर्बहुभिः कृतमृणं यत् । तत्रेषु जीवत्स्वेकोऽपि परकीयमृणं दापयितव्यः मृतेषु तेषु न तदीयपुत्रः परर्णं दातुमर्हति । स्वकीयांशमात्रं तु दद्यादयमत्र विशेषो दर्शित इति ।

यं चार्थं प्रतिभूर्दद्याद्धनिकेनोपपीडितः ।

१०६ a — NMS स्युः; b — X र्णं; NMS ऽर्थे; c — All mss विशेपिते; NMS त्व.

ऋणिकस्तं प्रतिभुवे द्विगुणं प्रतिपादयेत् ॥१०७॥

यदा धनिकेनोपपीड्य प्रतिभूरेव धनं ग्राह्यते तद **ऋणिकः** परोक्षत्वादिकं स्वकीयं क्रूरमाभाव्य तस्मै **प्रतिभुवे द्विगुणं प्रतिदापयेत्** । यच्च न कालान्तरेण द्विगुणं[245] प्रतिभूवहिनमहादोषस्य प्रायश्चित्तमिदं सद्यो द्विगुणद्रव्यदापनम् । तथा चोक्तं प्रकरणकारकल्याणेन

ऋणिद्वयं तद्धनिन ऋणिनस्तद्धनिद्वयम् ।
प्रतिभूर्व्यवहाराङ्गं न पीड्यमुभयोरपि ।।[?]

अथर्णिनः प्रत्यक्षस्याप्यविदितमप्यपीडितोऽपि प्रतिभूरेव साध्याद्द्विगुणलोभात् सवयमेव धनं ददाति तत ऋणी कृतस्य तत्सममेव दद्यान्न द्विगुणम् । ऋणिकदोषपीडापीडितलोकः प्रमाणमिति ।

धर्मेन व्यवहारेण छलेनाचरितेन[246] च ।
प्रयुक्तं साधयेदर्थं पञ्चमेन[247] बलेन[248] च ।। [Manu 8.49, J 1.122]

अत्र चाणक्ये सामभेदोपप्रदानदण्डाश्चत्वार एव कार्यसाधनोपाया दृष्टाः । अत्रापि त एव चत्वारः केवलमन्यनामभिर्धर्मव्यवहारेऽस्य न बल संज्ञा निरुक्ताः । अधिकमत्राचरितं । अभोजनम् । तच्चर्णोग्राहणविषयमेव सोपयोगं न सार्वत्रिकम । तदुक्तम्धर्मेण । तत्साक्ता प्रियधर्मस्मरणाय प्रथममर्थं साधयेत् । तेनासिध्यमानं भेदेन राजकीयसभाभयदर्शनव्यवहारेण । तथा चोपप्रधानलोभं[249] दर्शयित्वा छलेन । तथा दण्डेन स्वकीयबलेनैव पादबन्धनाचारीप्रक्षेपादिना । एवमेतैः सामादिभिर्धर्मादिभिरुपायैः स्वकीयमर्थं साधयेत् । यथैतदाचरितमुक्तम् तच्चरिगतिभक्षणयोरित्यस्य धातोर्भक्षणार्थरूपमिदम् । चरितं भक्षितम् । न चरितमभक्षितम् । अभोजनमित्यर्थः । तद्वाभोजनं तस्यैव साधनार्थं यः परकीयधनं गृहीत्वा न प्रयच्छति । यः पुनर्धनी स्वकीयमर्थमुद्राहयति तस्याभोजने प्रायश्चित्तं नास्ति । केवलं राज्ञो वा गुरुस्थानमितस्य बालस्याप्युपरोधनार्थं वाचरणात्प्राणान्तिकभयदर्शनार्थं वा । धनी स्वकीयभृत्य-पुत्रेणाभोजनं कारयति स्वयं वा करोति । अयमेवैको विषयो धनिनः स्वयं भोजने न सर्वत्रेति ।

यः स्वकं साधयेदर्थमुत्तमर्णोऽधमर्णकात् ।
न स राज्ञा निषेद्धव्य ऐहिकामुष्मिकार्थतः ।।[Manu 8.50, J 1.123]

ये शठा दुष्ठाः परकीयं धनं गृहीत्वा भक्षयित्वा युध्यमाना राजाश्रिता भूत्वात्मानं रक्षयितुमिच्छन्तो निषेधं कारयन्ति । स्वच्छन्देन व्यवहारेण राज्ञा धनी स्वमर्थं साधयन्न निषेद्धव्यः । ऐहिकामुष्मिकार्थत इति ऐहिकार्थसंव्यवहारभङ्गभयात् । आमुष्मिकार्थं साधुवर्तनभङ्गपातकभयात् । इति प्रतिभूभेदः समाप्तः ।

१०७ a — P यथार्थं; D यमर्थं.

अधिक्रियत इत्याधिः स विज्ञेयो द्विलक्षणः ।
कृतकालोपनेयश्च यावद्देयोद्यतस्तथा ॥१०८॥

अत आधिभेदो भवति । **अधिक्रियत** अप्यधनिना संबन्धाधिकारमानीयत **इत्याधिः** । स च द्विविधः । चलाधिः स्थिराधिश्च । सोऽपि द्विलक्षणो ज्ञेयः । एकः **कृतकालोपनेयः** । द्वितीयो **यावद्देयोद्यतः** । तत्र **कृतकालोपनेयो** यः स द्विप्रकारः । एको दीयमाने धने प्राप्तकालावधावाधिपालैः समर्पणीयः । द्वितीयस्त्वतिपुष्यमाणो धनिनैवं विचार्य गृह्यते । यथा पञ्च वर्षाणि दश वेयन्तं कालं क्षणकं[250] यावन्न मोचनीयः । तत्परतो ऋणिके । अयमपि **कृतकालोपनेय** उच्यते । अस्मिन्दिवसे गृहीतं द्रव्यं तस्मिन्नेव वृद्धिफलभोग्यन्यायेन समर्पितः । यावद्देयं धनं जातं तावदेव तत्क्षणं समर्पितः । यथा यावद्देयं धनं तिष्ठति तावदपरिमितकालमपि भोक्तव्यः । अनेन क्रमेण य उद्यतः समर्पितः । यथा क्रमेण य उद्यतः समर्पितः स याव**द्देयोद्यता**धिरुच्यते । एवं कृतकालोपनेयो यावद्देयोद्यतश्चाधिर्द्विविधोऽपि सविस्तरं व्याख्यात इति ।

स पुनर्द्विविधः प्रोक्तो गोप्यो भोग्यस्तथैव च ।
प्रतिदानं तथैवास्य लाभहानिर्विपर्यये ॥१०९॥

स पुनराधिरन्यप्रकारेण **द्विविधः** । एको **गोप्यो** घटितसुवर्णरौप्यादिः । भोग्यः मञ्जुषागवादिभ्यः न गोप्यः गुपी रक्षणे धातुः [DhāPā 1.422] । तेन रक्षणीय इत्यर्थः । द्वितीयो **भोग्यः** प्रकाश एव गृहक्षेत्रादिः । उपचारस्**तथैवास्येति** । अस्य द्विविधस्यापि आधेर्गुप्तस्य कालान्तरोपाश्रयोपचारः । भोग्यस्य फलोपाश्रयोपचारः । **विपर्यये** फलहानिरिति । विपरीतार्थो **विपर्यय** उच्यते । यतो गोप्यस्य[251] भोगः क्रियते ततस्तस्य कालान्तरे फलहानिर्भवति । अथ प्रकाशस्याभोगः क्रियते । ततस्तस्य सस्यनिवासादिफलहानिर्भवति । इत्ययं **विपर्यय** इति ।

प्रमादाद्धनिनस्तद्वदाधौ विकृतिमागते ।
विनष्टे मूलनाशः स्याद्दैवराजकृतादृते ॥११०॥

१०८ b — NMS तु ज्ञेयो; c — L H -कालापनेयश्; d — Y X V3 V5 H -देयोऽन्यतस्; V4 V8 R -देयो ततस्.
१०९ a — X ज्ञेयो; c — P D Y उपचारस्; d — Jolly विपर्यते; X add
यः स्वामिनाननुज्ञातमाधिं भुङ्क्तेऽविचक्षणः ।
तेन वृद्धिः प्रमोक्तव्या तस्य भोगस्य निष्क्रयः ॥ [cf. Manu 8.150]
११० Y om verses 110-112; c — K2 K5 मूलहानिः.

अत्र यथा लाभहानिर्विपर्यये भवति **तद्वद्धनिनः प्रमादा**दाधिनाशे **मूलनाशो**ऽपि भवति । तत्र प्रमादः । चलादिवृषभादिकस्याकालवाहनमतिवाहनं चेत्यादि । गोप्याधेश्च धनिकप्रमादः प्रकाशमोचनमित्यादिना धनिप्रमादेनाधिनाशे संजाते **विकृतिं** वा प्राप्ते काणकूटभक्तादौ मूलनाशे भवति । यदा पुनः प्रकाशं राजदैविकादाधिनाशो भवति तदा धनिनो मूलनाशो नास्ति । राजिकं यथास्वल्पेऽपराधे राजगृहीतसर्वस्वेन सह तन्मध्यस्थाधेर्नष्टस्य तथैव चौरापहृतस्याप्याधेर्मूलनाशो नास्तीयेवोक्तम् ।

न भोक्तव्यो बलादाधिर्भुञ्जानो वृद्धिमुत्सृजेत् ।
मूल्येन तोषयेच्चैनमाधिस्तेनोऽन्यथा भवेत् ॥[Manu 8.144, J 1.127]

कृतकालोपनेयो य आधिः स पूर्व एवावधौ बलावष्टम्भेन न भोक्तव्यः । अथ कथमपि कृतम् । ततः कालान्तरवृधिं परित्यजेत् । यच्च मूल्यमाधिर्लभते तेन मूल्येनाधिधनिनं परितोषयेत् । अन्यथाधिस्तेनदोषं प्राप्नुयादिति ।

यः स्वामिनाभ्यनुज्ञातमाधिं भुङ्क्तेऽविचक्षणः ।
तेनार्धवृद्धिर्मोक्तव्या तस्य भोगस्य निष्क्रयः ॥[Manu 8.150, J 1.128]

वर्धमानकालान्तरेणाधिं समर्पितमाधिस्वामिनः पार्श्वादसंप्राप्ताभ्यनुज्ञात एव । य आधिं भुङ्क्ते सोऽविचक्षणो मूर्खः । तेन[252] धनिना यथारूढवृद्धेरर्धं परित्यजनीयम् । एष स्थलभोगस्य निष्क्रयः ।

न त्वेवाधौ सोपकारे कौसीदीं वृद्धिमाप्नुयात् ।
न चाधेः कालसंरोधान्निसर्गोऽस्ति न विक्रयः ॥[Manu 8.143, J 1.129]

अस्य भाष्यम् । अत्र यः सोपकार आधिः स वृद्धिफलभोग्य एव । तस्मिन्सोपकार आधौ कौसीदीं वृधिं न कश्चिदाप्नुयात् । यावच्च विचारितकालावधिसंरोधो[253] न चालनीयः । तावदवान्तर एवाधेर्न तस्य क्वचिद्दानमस्ति न विक्रय इति ।

रक्ष्यमाणोऽपि यत्राधिः कालेनेयादसारताम् ।
आधिरन्योऽधिकर्तव्यो देयं वा धनिने धनम् ॥१११॥

यत्र धनिना प्रयत्नरक्ष्यमाणाधिः **कालेन** शीर्णतामसारतामाप्नोति । तत्र्णिकेन धनिकस्याधिर**न्योऽधिकर्तव्यः** । अथवा **धनमे**व दातव्यमिति ।

अथ शक्तिविहीनः स्यादृणी कालविपर्ययात् ।
शक्यप्रेक्षमृणं दाप्यः काले काले यथोदयम् ॥११२॥

१११ c — P तत्राधिरन्यो कर्तव्यां; D आधिरन्योऽथवा कार्यो; D add
बलाद्दत्तं वलाद्भुक्तं वलाद्यच्चावलेखितं ।
सर्वान्वलकृतानर्थानकृतान्मनुरब्रवीत् ॥ [Manu 8.168]
११२ a — Jolly अत्र; c — D प्रेक्ष्यशक्तिम्.

अथ कदाचि**दृण्यन्य**मथाधिं कर्तुमशक्तः । धनमपि दातुमशक्तस्ततो यथाशक्त्यनुसारेण स्कन्धकस्थित्या **काले काले यथोदयं** यथालाभं धनं **दाप्य** इति ।

शक्तो वा यदि दौरात्म्यान्न दद्याद्धनिने धनम् ।
राज्ञा दापयितव्यः स्याद् गृहीत्वांशं तु विंशकम् ॥११३॥

स्वयमुद्रहणे निष्क्रये पञ्चकं शतं गृहीत्वेति ।

स्ववाक्षंप्रतिपत्तौ तु ऋणिकं दशकं शतम् ।
विनयं दापयेद्राजा द्विगुणं तु पराजितम् ।। [J 1.133]

धनिना धारणिक आवेदितः सन्यदि स्ववाचैव संप्रतिपत्त्युत्तरेण प्रतिपद्यते । यथा सत्यमिदमस्ति । मयास्यैतद्दातव्यमिति । ततः स्ववाक्प्रतिपन्नगुणात्स्वयमेव धनिकस्याप्रतिपादने दोषाच्च राजर्णिनं[254] विनयाद्दापयेद्दशकमेव शतम् । अथासौ मिथ्या कस्याप्रतिपादयति[255] धनी च यथासंभवं क्रियाभिः स्वधनं लभ्यं खरीकरोति । तदा तदृणिकं पराजितं राजा तमेव दशकशतविनयं द्विगुणं प्रतिपादयेत् । विंशतिद्रम्मेणैकशतमित्यर्थः ।

नश्येदृणपरीमाणं कालेनेहर्णिकस्य चेत् ।
जातिसंज्ञाधिवासानामागमो लेख्यतः स्मृतः ॥११४॥

अत्र पराजितस्यर्णिकस्य यदि समस्तद्रव्यपूरणपरिमाणं न स्यात् । ततो देशकालानुसारेण स्कन्धकपत्रे लिखापनीय ऋणिकः । एवमपि संज्ञयैव[256] साधितं द्रव्यं भवति । **जातिसंज्ञाधिवासानां लेख्यत आगम** इति यदुक्तं तत्पञ्चारूढपत्रम् । नवाङ्गसंपूर्णमागमशब्देन सूचितम् । यथोक्तं त्रिषष्टिलेख्यप्रकरणकारककल्याणभट्टेन । तत्कालिकराजधनिकर्णिकसाक्षिलेखकैरङ्गैः पञ्चभिरेतैः पत्रं पञ्चारूढं भवति । तथा च कालप्रदेशधनिकर्णिकवित्तसंख्यासोपाश्रयर्णिकमतसाक्षिसलेखकान्तैरङ्गैरेभिरप्यचलक्रमस्थैः कल्याणभट्टगदितं भवतीह पत्रम् । इति ऋणादान आधिभेदोऽष्टमः ।

लेख्यं तु द्विविधं ज्ञेयं स्वहस्तान्यकृतं तथा ।

११३ W om this verse; b — D P NMS ऋणिकः सधनो यस्तु दौरात्म्यान्न प्रयच्छति; d — P गृहीत्वा पञ्चकं शतं; D गृहीत्वा विंशकं शते.

११४ a — Jolly न स्याद्; X पश्येद्; D अर्थपरीमानं; Jolly NMS द्रव्यपरीमाणं; b — L कालेन धनिकस्य; ab — W om.

असाक्षिमत्साक्षिमच्च सिद्धिर्देशस्थितेस्तयोः ॥११५॥

अथ लेख्यभेदो भवति । अत्रैकं **स्वहस्तकृतं** द्वितीयम**न्यहस्त**लिखितम् । एवं तावद्द्विविधमेवोक्तं । एतयोस्तु यत्स्वहस्तलिखितं तत्साक्षिभिर्विनापि प्रमाणम् । यत्त्वन्यहस्तलिखितं तत्साक्षिसहितं प्रमाणम् । स्वहस्तलिखितस्यैतन्माहात्म्यं यद्विनापि साक्षिभिस्तत्प्रमाणमेवेति । यथोक्तं **सिधिर्देशस्थितेस्तयोः** तद्देशाचार-माहात्म्यं दर्शितम् । यस्मिन्देशे या देशस्थितिरालेख्यसिद्धिरिति ।

देशाचाराविरुद्धं यद्व्यक्ताधिकृतलक्षणम् ।
तत्प्रमाणं स्मृतं लेख्यमविलुप्तक्रमाक्षरम् ॥११६॥

अत्र लेख्यप्रामाण्यमुक्तं । तदिह यल्लेख्यमदेयदानलेखनेनास्वतन्त्रोपरिलिखितादिना च देशाचारविरोधेन वर्जितं यत्त**देशाचाराविरुधम्** । यत्र लेख्ये **व्यक्तमा**धिप्रति-भूसुस्थलक्षणं यत्र च पत्रलिखितक्रमोऽ**विलुप्तः** । अविनष्टः । यत्राक्षराण्यप्य-विलुप्तानि लेख्यं प्रमाणमिति । तथा चाह कल्याणोऽपि

लिखितं लक्षणज्ञेन युक्तिन्यायैकवर्त्मना ।
अर्थतो ग्रन्थतश्चैवमत्र न व्यभिचारवत् ॥

मत्ताभियुक्तस्त्रीबालबलात्कारकृतं च यत् ।
तदप्रमाणकरणं भीतोपधिकृतं तथा ॥११७॥

अत्र **मत्तेन** लिखितं तथा ब्रह्मनहत्याद्यभिशस्तेन यत् । **स्त्रिया** यत् । **बालेन** च कृतं यत् । तथार्थसंबन्धेन विनैव **बलात्**कारेण कारितं यत् । तथैव **भीतोपधिकृतं**[257] यत्करणमिति । अपर्यायात्तत्करणम**प्रमाणम्** इति ।

मृताः स्युः साक्षिणो यत्र धनिकर्णिकलेखकाः ।
तदप्यपार्थं लिखितमृते त्वाधेः स्थिराश्रयात् ॥११८॥

११५ b — Y स्वहस्ताद्व्याकृतं, c — NMS असाक्षिकं; d — NMS देशस्थितिस्.
११६ b — Jolly व्यक्तावधिविलक्षणम्; D व्यक्ताविकृतिलक्षणम्; c — K2 om from स्मृतं through अप्रमाण- in verse 117; Y कृतं.
११७ P om this verse; d — V5 ends with भीतो-.
११८ d — P न चेदाधिः स्थिराश्रयः; D add
यदि लब्धं भवेत्किंचित्प्रज्ञाप्तिर्वा कृता भवेत् ।
प्रमाणमेव लिखितं मृता यद्यपि साक्षिनः ॥ [Dhko 358]

यत्र पत्रे **धनिकर्णिकसाक्षिलेखकाश्च**सर्वेऽपि **मृताः तदप्य**प्रमाणं किलान्यथा तादृशैः पत्रैः जनस्य कूटप्रपञ्चकृतैर्विश्वासः[258] संभवति । एतदर्थमुक्तम् । यत्र तु लेख्य आधिर्भुक्तिसहितः स्थिरीकरणचिह्नभूतस्तिष्ठति । तत्तेषु सर्वेषु मृतेष्वपि प्रमाणमेवेति ।

आधिर्यो द्विविधः प्रोक्तो जङ्गमः स्थावरस्तथा ।
सिद्धिरत्रोभयस्यास्य भोगो यद्यस्ति नान्यथा ॥११९॥

यस्मिन्नत्र **जङ्गमः स्थावरो** वा प्रकारद्वयमध्य आरूढ एवाधिर्न तु भुक्तः । ततो भोगेन विना तयोर्लिखितमात्राधिचिह्नयोरपि सिद्धिर्नास्तीति ।

दर्शितं प्रतिकालं यच्छ्रावितं श्रावितं च यत् ।
लेख्यं सिध्यति सर्वत्र मृतेष्वपि हि साक्षिषु ॥१२०॥

अत्र धनिकसंतत्यर्णिकसंततेर्यत्**प्रतिकालं दर्शितम्** । यदा यदा किंचित्फलं प्रार्थ्यते तत्प्रार्थितम् । तथा यत्प्रतिकालं **श्रावितं** कालान्तरे स्कन्धकं वा गृहीतम् । अथवा श्रावितमेव भूयो भूयः कथितम् । तदेवमृणिकसंततेः[259] । संतानारूढप्रत्ययमेव **मृतेष्वपि हि** साक्ष्यादिषु सर्वेष्वपि प्रमाणमेवेति[260] ।

अश्रुतार्थमदृष्टार्थं व्यवहारार्थमेव च ।
न लेख्यं सिद्धिमाप्नोति जीवत्स्वपि हि साक्षिषु ॥१२१॥

यत्पुन**र्लेख्यमृ**णिकसंततेः स्वयम**दृष्टार्थं** स्वकीयपूर्वजेभ्यः सकाशाद**श्रुतार्थम्** । केवलमाचारव्यवहारार्थमेवागतं दृष्टम् । एवंविधं
न लेख्यं सिद्धिमाप्नोति जीवत्स्वपि हि साक्षिषु ॥
तथापि कृतकत्वाशङ्कयेति ।

लेख्ये देशान्तरन्यस्ते दग्धे दुर्लिखिते हृते ।
सतस्तत्कालकरणमसतो दृष्टदर्शनम् ॥१२२॥

११९ d — B2 B3 K5 भोगान्भवति; P भोगो यत्रास्ति.
१२० b — P प्रार्थितं; NMS स्नावितं; P तथा.
१२१ a — D अविज्ञातं; b — P D आगतम्
१२२ a — K2 K5 देशान्तरं न्यस्ते; b — BM दग्धेऽभिलिखिते; B5 दग्ध अलिखिते; c — P L V8 H Ox -हरणं; d — P द्रष्टृदर्शनम्; NMS ऽदृष्टदर्शनम्; B2 B3 K5 दृष्टदर्शनात्.

अस्य श्लोकस्यार्थो द्वयोरपि वादिप्रतिवादिनोः सोपयोगः । वादिनस्तावत्यदा वादिना प्रतिवादी लिखितद्रव्यसंबन्धे[261] पृष्टः[262] । न च तत्पत्रं तस्य हस्ते । ऋणी च वदति दर्शयतु ममायं पत्रम् । यदि विद्यमानं[263] स्यात्तदानपेक्षया[264] तदानयनाय धर्माधिकरणेन विशिष्टैर्वा **कालहरणं*** देयम् । अथवा यदीदं[265] पत्रं दग्धं हृतं वा तदासतोऽविद्यमानस्य तद् **द्रष्टृदर्शनम्*** अपि[266] साधुजनसाक्ष्यपेक्षया प्रमाणम् । ते च ते द्रष्टारः साक्षिलेखकाः साधवो यदि जीवन्ति । अथवा केचिदुदासीनाः प्रश्नकाल आगता[267] यैस्तल्लिख्यमानं दृष्टम् । अविद्यमानं पत्रमानीतं च । वादिना किंतु यावद्वाच्यते तावदङ्कनष्टत्वादक्षरभ्रष्टत्वाद्वासत्पत्रं संदेहमागतं तदा तस्यासतो[268] अशोभनस्य ये तत्काललिख्यमानस्य साक्षिलेखकोदासीनादयो[269] द्रष्टारः[270] केचित्तेऽङ्कभ्रान्त्यपनोदे नामवर्ण भ्रान्त्यपनोदे वा प्रमाणं भवन्ति । एवमयं वादिसंबध्यमानः श्लोकोऽभिहितः । इदानीं प्रतिवादिसंबध्यमानोऽयमेवोच्यते । यदागृहीतधनपत्रेण वा प्रवेशितधनपत्रेण[271] वा सहायागतेन धनपत्रेण वा पत्रारूढपितृनामजातिद्रव्यप्रमाणर्णिमतसाक्षिलेखाद्यङ्क-परिपूर्णलिखितबलात्कश्चिदृणी धर्माधिकरणमानीतः । तेन चोत्तरकालेऽभिहितं । यथा सत्यमिदमस्ति । मया तत्पत्रं लिखितमासीत् । किंतु किल कार्यार्थं द्वितीयदिने द्रव्यमभिग्रहीष्यामि । तावत्कार्यं वोढनीयम् । मया द्रव्यं न गृहीतम् । पत्रं च प्रमादात्पार्श्वे स्थित्वा मया न पाटितम् । तावत्कतिपयदिवसागमेनैतास्य पित्रोक्तोऽहं यथा त्वदीयमगृहीतार्थं पत्रं मया तस्मिन्नेव दिनेऽनादरेण बहिरेव मुक्तं किल निरर्थकत्वात् । त्वन्निरोधाच्च[272] पाटयिष्यामि । तावत्तद्देयं नष्टं येनातिप्रयत्नेनान्वेषयतापि मया तत् क्वचिन्न दृष्टम् । तन्मा कश्चिद्दैवयोगात्कालान्तरेऽपि[273] तव यश्चाकरीभवति । अतोऽहमेव प्रणष्टिविशुद्धिपत्रं[274] प्रयच्छामि । एवमुक्त्वा तेनास्य पित्रा तत्काल एव मम प्रणष्टिविशुद्धिपत्रं दत्तम् । तच्च मयातिप्रयत्नेन तत्कालेऽमुकायतने[275] वसता[276] तत्रैवामुकपार्श्वे धवलगृहमञ्जूषायां स्थापितम् । इत्येवं प्रतिवादिनोत्तरे दत्ते तदानयनापेक्षया तद्दानार्थं तस्य सतस्तत्**कालहरणं*** देयम् । **असतस्तद् द्रष्टृदर्शनं** प्रमाणमित्यादिकं प्रतिवादिनोऽपि सोपयोगार्थमिति ।

यस्मिन्स्यात्संशयो लेख्ये भूताभूतकृते क्वचित् ।
तत्स्वहस्तक्रियाचिह्नप्राप्तियुक्तिभिरुद्धरेत् ॥१२३॥

यत्र **लेख्ये भूताभूतकृते**ऽर्थे विप्रत्ययो भ्रान्तिर्भवेदिति तत्परीक्ष्यं **स्वहस्तक्रियाचिह्नयुक्तिप्राप्तिभिर्** इति । **स्वहस्त**प्रतिविश्वासकेन । **क्रियया** तदारूढसाक्षिभिः । चिह्नेन लेखकलिपि**चिह्न**निरूपनेण । युक्त्या चानया युज्यमानार्हता[277] **युक्ति**रयुक्तिस्तद्विपर्यये । पुरुषत्रयदारिद्र्ये द्रम्मलक्षधनिकत्वात् ।

१२३ a — P यत्र; d — Y -चिह्नं प्राप्ति; P D -युक्तिप्राप्ति-.

प्राप्तिर्द्विविधा । एका कथमनेन[278] पत्रमिदं प्राप्तम् । द्वितीया जल्पतः सक्षोभ अक्षोभ वा । कीदृश्यस्य[279] **प्राप्तिरित्यादि** भूताभूतलेख्यसंशयम् **उद्धरेदिति** ।

लेख्यं यच्चान्यनामाङ्कं हेत्वन्तरकृतं भवेत् ।
विप्रत्यये परीक्ष्यं तत्संबन्धागमहेतुभिः ॥१२४॥

अत्रान्यनामरूपोऽङ्को यस्य लेख्यस्य तद**न्यनामाङ्कम्** उच्यते । तच्च द्विविधं भवति । एकं यस्य सक्तं द्रव्यं तस्यैव नाम्ना लिखितं किंतु तस्य पार्श्वाद्येन किमपि क्रीतं लब्धं वा । तस्य तद् द्रव्यं प्रार्थयतः । तत्पत्रमन्यनामाङ्कं भवति । तयोश्च द्वयोरपि यथासंख्येन विप्रत्ययसंभवरूपमुच्यते[280] । तत्र प्रथमेऽन्यनामाङ्के यस्य सक्तं द्रव्यं तस्मिन्नामारूढं[281] स आगत्य पत्रं व्यासेधयति । तं धनिकं सुतं च वदत्यस्यर्णिकस्योपरि यत्पत्रं तन्मदीयम् । मन्नामाङ्कितं त्वदीयपितुः पार्श्वस्थापनिकभूतं मया मुक्तम् । तदर्प्यतामिति । धर्माधिकरणस्याग्र ईदृशे विप्रत्ययोपन्यासे कृते तेन सद्रव्यपत्रध्वनिनोत्तरं दत्तं यथायमस्मदीयपितु-रष्टप्रहरिकः कर्मकर आसीत् । तदा काले च स दायादभयादस्यैव नाम्ना पत्रमिदमभिलिखितवान्[282] । ऋणिनापि स्वहस्तेनास्मदीयपितुः समर्प्य तत्पार्श्वात् स्वहस्तेन द्रम्मा अपि गृहीताः । यदि किंचिदिदमन्यथा ततो ममावसायः पृच्छ्यतामेतदसावृणिकः कस्तव धनीति । ततो धर्माधिकरणसभ्यैरस्य विप्रत्ययस्य परीक्षार्थे पठितोऽयं श्लोकः

लेख्यं यच्चान्यनामाङ्कं हेत्वन्तरकृतं भवेत् ।
विप्रत्यये परीक्ष्यं तत्संबन्धागमहेतुभिः ॥

इति । अत्र च संबन्धागमहेतूनां त्रयाणामपि परीक्ष्यावेदकानां[283] कल्याणकृतं श्लोकत्रयमिदमस्ति । तत्र **संबन्धः**

अन्वयज्ञातिवैवाह्या[284] मैत्र्येकव्यवहारतः ।
युज्यते द्रव्यसंबन्धे निःसंबन्धे नियुज्यते [285]।।[?]

अथ**ागमः**

अन्वयक्रीतमाधत्तं लब्धप्रीत्याप्तलक्षणैः ।
सागमं षड्भिरेतैः स्याद्विना त्वेतैर्निरागमम् ।।[?]

अथ **हेतुः**

वितर्के च निमित्ते च हेतुशब्दः प्रयुज्यते ।
प्रमाणं संशयोत्तीर्णं सन्निमित्तं च नान्यथा ।।[?]

१२४ a — Jolly typo चान्यमामाङ्कं; c — X V3 V8 R परीक्षं.

इति सभ्यैः श्लोकत्रयमिदमेवं व्याख्यातमृणिकेनापि[286] धर्माधिकरणपृष्टेन तस्मिन्नेव धनिके समर्पितेऽन्यनामाङ्कस्यापि पत्रस्य यस्यार्थसंबन्धस्तस्य प्रामाण्यम् । न पुनरर्थसंबन्धवर्जितस्य नाममात्रस्येति । निर्णयं दत्त्वोत्तरवादिनोः जयो प्रदत्त इति । एवं प्रथमस्यान्यनामाङ्के लेख्यस्वरूपं निर्णयस्वरूपं च परिस्फुटीकृतम् । इदानीं द्वितीयस्योच्यते केनापि भारुकच्छीयब्राह्मणेनादित्यभट्टनाम्ना खेटकीयब्राह्मणसोमभट्टनाम्ना उपर्युक्तं मूलिकं द्रम्मसहस्रद्वयं तेनापि संततिर्हितेनोपस्थितमृत्युकालेन वात्मनः श्रेयोऽर्थिना दीक्षितमङ्गलभट्टनाम्ना [287]नर्मदातीर्थस्थितेन प्रधानब्राह्मणाय साक्षिचतुष्टयप्रत्यक्षं तत्पत्रमुदकचुलुकपूर्वेण प्रतिपादितम् । तेन चागत्य पत्रहस्तेन द्रव्यार्थं सोमभट्टः प्रारब्धः तावदादित्यभट्टभ्रात्रा बुद्धभट्टेनागत्य व्यासेधः कृतः । धर्माधिकरणस्याग्रे चैवमभिहितं यथा तेनास्मदीयपत्रेण सह मङ्गलदीक्षितभट्टनाम्नः पार्श्वे भ्रातृद्रव्यं मया बहु लब्धव्यमतस्तदभावेऽन्यैर्वा प्रत्यक्षीकृतसाक्षिभिर्निर्हरेत् । अथवा तत्रापि पूर्वसाक्षिणामप्रत्यक्षत्वेन तत्रापि विशुद्धिलिखितमेव श्रेयः कालकालान्तरेष्वपि साक्षिभ्यो लिखितं श्रेय [NāSmṛ 1.125c] इति वचनात् । यत्र पुनः लिखितपूर्वः प्रथमव्यवहारः तत्रर्णिप्रवेशोऽपि लिखितपाटनं वा विशुद्धिलिखितं वा सविशेषमेतदेव श्रेयः । न पुनस्तत्र साक्षिणः कृता अपि श्रेयांसो भवन्ति । विनाशितत्वपरवशत्वादिदोषात्[288] । तथा लिखितान्न तु साक्षिणोऽभ्यधिका भवन्तीति[289] । असमुत्पन्ने दीक्षितेन धर्मलब्धस्य प्रधानसाक्षिचतुष्टयमुपन्यस्तं तेषामपि बुद्धभट्टेन मृतान्तरदूषणं दत्तम् । तच्च सभ्यैः परिहृतमनेन नारदश्लोकेन

श्रावितस्त्वातुरेणापि यस्त्वर्थो धर्मसंहितः ।
मृतेऽपि तत्र साक्ष्यं स्यात्षट्सु चान्वाहितादिषु ।।[NāSmṛ 1.84]

इत्युक्तोभयशम्बलव्ययेन साधुब्राह्मणद्वयं साक्षिणां प्रतिपृच्छकं भारुकच्छस्थितं प्राहितं तेनागत्य दीक्षितपक्षसमर्पितं दीक्षितव्यावस्थितं[290] एवमीदृशे महति विप्रत्यये तस्य जयपत्रं सभ्यैः प्रसादीकृतमिति । एतद् द्वितीयमप्यन्यनामाङ्कलेख्यस्योदाहरणं विस्फुटीकृतमिति ।

लिखितं लिखितेनैव साक्षिमत्साक्षिभिर्हरेत् ।
साक्षिभ्यो लिखितं श्रेयो लिखितेन तु साक्षिणः ॥१२५॥

अत्र **हरेदि**ति[291] क्रियापदेन[292] **लिखितं** कृत्वर्णिकेन धनिकस्यापि तं तद्धनिकस्य प्रवेषिते धने तेनैव हस्तीकृतेनर्णी तमृणसंबन्धं निर्हतेत् । यदि पुनर्धनी तस्य लिखितस्य हृतनष्टदग्धादि[293] कारणमुपन्यस्यति[294] । ततस्तदीयं प्रणष्टविशुद्धिपत्रं ग्राह्यम् । अत इदमुक्तं **लिखितं लिखितेनैव** निर्हरेदिति । यत्र पुनः प्रथम-

१२५ a — Y लिखितालिखितेनैव; b — P तेन हस्तीकृतेन च; d — D P लिखितान्न.

संव्यवहारकरणं **साक्षिमत्**संजातम् । तत्रर्णे विशोध्यमाने तैरेव साक्षिभिः प्रत्यक्षीकृतैस्तदृणं निर्हरेत्[295] ।

छिन्नभिन्नहृतोन्मृष्टनष्टदुर्लिखितेषु च ।
कर्तव्यमन्यल्लेख्यं स्यादेष लेख्यविधिः स्मृतः ॥१२६॥

अत्र लिखितमाहात्म्यं प्रथमोक्तमपि पुनरत्र प्रस्तावागतमुच्यते

देशकालफलद्रव्यप्रमाणावधिनिश्चये ।
सर्वसंदेहविच्छेदि लिखितं चक्षुरुत्तमम् ॥ [J 1.71]

एतदर्थं धनिना लिखितं कारितमपि यदि कथमपि प्रमादा**द्दग्धं*** वा **छिन्नं** वा भवति अथवोदकतैलादिद्रववस्तुना **भिन्नं** भवति अथवान्यद्रव्यम् चौरगृहीतं भवति अथवा प्रधाननामाक्षराङ्कप्रदेशेषु कुत्सितलिखिताद्धंशितमथवा[296] उ**न्मृष्टं*** भवति अथवा पतितत्वा**न्नष्टं** भवति । अथवा **दुर्लिखितम्** इति प्रधानाङ्कस्थाने संजातन्यूनाधिकाङ्कदोषम् । सहस्रे प्रयुक्त एकाङ्कस्योपरि कुलेखको द्विबिन्दुरूपम्[297] यदा ददाति तदा तत् शतमेव भवति । नवशतानां मूलनाशः संभवति[298] । अथवा[299] शते प्रयुक्त एकाङ्कोपरि शून्यत्रयं ददाति तदा धनिकदोषादृणिककृतसहस्रमिथ्याप्रयुक्तशतस्यापि प्रणाशः । अथवा न्यूनाधिकप्रधाननामाक्षरं[300] ग्राहको गोसम इति लिखनीये गलितैकाक्षरं लिखितागमोऽयं नाक्षरदोषः । अथवा ग्राहको गोसम एवं लेखनीये लिखितं समः । एवमूनाधिकाङ्काक्षरप्रधानस्थानभ्रान्तिकारिदुर्लिखितमुच्यते । एवं च तेषु दग्धभिन्नकृतछिन्ननष्टदुर्लिखितदोषैः । अवसन्नभूतेषु[301] पुनरपि कालान्तरे कालदायकग्राहक द्रव्यफलप्रमाणादीनामविस्मरणार्थं **कर्तव्यमन्यल्लेख्यं** स्याद् इत्युक्तं महर्षिणा । तच्च तेन निश्चितं **कर्तव्यम्** इति धनिकर्णिकयोर्विशेषनामोच्चारणं न कृतं[302] । यथा संभवकृते लेख्यप्रमाणार्थं यद्यृणी प्रत्यक्ष एव तिष्ठति तदासौ धनिनान्यलेख्यकरणाय विधारणीयः । तेनाप्यवश्यमेव करणीयमन्यल्लेख्यं स्यादिति । अथवा कदाचिद्ग्राहको मृतः । दूरदेशान्तरव्यवहितो वा वर्तते । यत्रास्य वायमेकतमः[303] प्रमादः संपन्नः तदा धनिनैवात्मना नित्यानित्यतालोचस्थितेन स्वसंततेरनष्टद्रव्यसंबन्धकरणार्थिनाल्पं भूर्जचीरकं वा समानीयान्यं लेखकमाहूय तथैव तदवस्थितनवाङ्कक्रमपरिपूर्णं तनैव धनिना कर्तव्यमन्यल्लेख्यं स्यादेवं **लेख्यविधिः स्मृतः**[304] । यद्यसावृणी समागतस्तत्सुतो वा वदति न मयैतत्कृतं लेख्यं कूतं अन्येन कारितं तदास्यैव श्लोकस्योत्तरार्धमाश्रयेत् ।

अधरीकृत्य तत्पत्रमर्थे दिव्येन निर्णयः ।
न हि भूर्जछलादार्यैरर्थनाशः समर्थ्यते ॥ [?]

१२६ b — P दग्धविन्नहृतछिन्नमृष्ट-; D -हृतमृष्टनष्टेष्वलिखितेपु; c — NMS लेख्यमन्यद्धि कर्तव्यम्; d — D add इति श्रीनारदीये धर्मशास्त्रे लेख्यविधिश्चतुर्थोऽध्यायः.

अर्था बहिश्चराः प्राणा भूर्जं पादकपर्दकम् ।
तथा वृत्तार्थस्मरणाल्लिखितं यत्तदिष्यते ॥ [?]
खरीकरणार्थस्य (?) न भूर्जस्योपयुज्यते ॥ [?]

इति जीर्णपत्रार्थोद्धरणश्लोकस्य कल्याणभट्टकृतविवरणमिदम् । इत्यृणादाने लेख्यभेदो नवमः[305] । इदानीं साक्षिभेदो भवति ।

संदिग्धेषु तु कार्येषु द्वयोर्विवदमानयोः ।
दृष्टश्रुतानुभूतत्वात्साक्षिभ्यो व्यक्तिदर्शनम् ॥१२७॥

यानि कानिचित्संदिग्धानि कार्याणि तेषु **द्वयोर्** वादिप्रतिवादिनोरपि विवदतोरिति । अन्यान्यार्थबद्धाग्रहयोर्विवादं कुर्वतोः **साक्षिभ्यः** कार्य**व्यक्तिदर्शनं** स्फुटीभवति । यतस्त उदासीनाः । श्रुतार्थत्वादनुभूतार्थत्वाद्वा यत्साक्षिकाले किमपि ब्रुवते तस्माद्व्यक्तिदर्शनं कार्यनिर्णयो भवतीत्यर्थः ।

समक्षदर्शनात्साक्षी विज्ञेयः श्रोत्रचक्षुषोः ।
श्रोत्रस्य यत्परो ब्रूते चक्षुषः कायकर्म गत् ॥१२८॥

प्रत्यक्षदर्शनात्**साक्षी**त्युच्यते । तत्राक्षीणि यत्तेषां प्रतिपत्तिसानुभवं प्रयोजनं तत्प्रत्यक्षग् । तषां च **श्रोत्रस्य** यच्छब्दश्रवणं तत्परतोऽर्थसानुभवम् । यत्तु चक्षुःसानुभवं तत्**स्वयम्*** वार्थ**दर्शन**सानुभवमिति ।

एकादशविधः साक्षी स तु दृष्टो मनीषिभिः ।
कृतः पञ्चविधस्तेषां षक्तिधोऽकृत उच्यते ॥१२९॥

अत्रैकादशविधाः साक्षिणो दृष्टाः । तेषां च पञ्च साक्षिणः कृता भवन्ति । ते च प्रत्येकमुच्यन्ते ।

लिखितः स्मारितश्चैव यदृच्छाभिज्ञ एव च ।
गूढश्चोत्तरसाक्षी च साक्षी पञ्चविधः स्मृतः ॥१३०॥

१२७ a — BM B B5 P च; c — P श्रुतदृष्टानु-.
१२८ d — BM B चक्षुपा; P चक्षुपोर्; P दर्शनं स्वयम्; X L H कार्यकर्मकृत्; V V3-4 V6-8 R Ox कार्यकर्मवत्.
१२९ b — D शास्त्रें; P शास्त्र-.
१३० a — NMS लेखितः; d — D कृतः.

लिखितः पत्रारूढः । **स्मारितः** कर्णकथितः । **यदृच्छाभिज्ञो**ऽनुपरोधेनागतः कृतः । **गूढः** कुड्यान्तरितश्रोता । **उत्तरसाक्षी** साक्षिजल्पितश्रोता । एवं **पञ्चविधः साक्षी** कृतो भवति ।

अकृतः षड्विधश्चापि सूरिभिः परिकीर्तितः ।
ग्रामश्च प्राड्विवाकश्च राजा च व्यवहारिणाम् ॥१३१॥
कार्येष्वभ्यन्तरो यः स्यादर्थिना प्रहितश्च यः ।
कुलं कुलविवादेषु भवेयुस्तेऽपि साक्षिणः ॥१३२॥

षडेते पुनरकृता अपि साक्षिणो भवन्ति । तद्यथा ग्राममध्ये वृत्तप्रयोजनस्य **ग्राम** एव साक्षी । धर्माधिकरणवृत्तस्य **प्राड्विवाक** आस्थानस्थः । राज्ञः पुरतो वृत्तस्य **राजा** । तथा यः कार्यस्या**भ्यन्तरः** । तथा कार्यार्थमर्थिना यः **प्रहितः** तथा **कुलविवादेषु** कुलहरकमेव साक्षी । एते षडपि साक्षिणोऽकृता अपि भवन्ति । एवं कृताकृतभेदेनैकादशविधिः साक्ष्युक्तः ।

कुलीना ऋजवः शुद्धा जन्मतः कर्मतोऽर्थतः ।
त्र्यवराः साक्षिणोऽनिन्द्याः शुचयः स्युः सुबुद्धयः ॥१३३॥

कुलिनाः कुलोत्पन्नाः । **ऋजव** आर्जवस्वभावाः । तथा **जन्मतः कर्मतोऽर्थतश्च** शुद्धा ये भवन्ति । **शुचयो** ये त्वलुब्धाः । **शुद्धबुद्धयः*** प्रतिष्ठितशास्त्रबुद्धयः । **अनिन्द्या** लोकप्रसिद्धाः । एवंविधाः साक्षिणो भवन्ति । त्रयाणामधो द्वावेको वोभ्यानुसारेण ।

ब्राह्मणाः क्षत्रिया वैश्याः शूद्रा ये चाप्यनिन्दिताः ।
प्रतिवर्णं भवेयुस्ते सर्वे सर्वेषु वा पुनः ॥१३४॥

एते चात्वारोऽपि वर्णाः स्वकीयस्वकीयवर्णसाक्षिणो भवन्ति । अथवा **सर्वेषु** वर्णेषु **सर्वे** वर्णा भवन्ति ।

श्रेणीषु श्रेणिपुरुषाः स्वेषु वर्गेषु वर्गिणः ।

१३१ a — X षड् वै पुनरनिर्दिष्टाः; P षडेते पुनरुद्दिष्टास्; D अकृतः षड्विधस्त्वेषां; b — B3 K5 साक्षिणः; P त्वकृताः स्वयम्, X समुदाहृताः; D add त्रयः पुनरनिर्दिष्टाः साक्षिणः समुदाहृताः.
१३२ a — NMS अधिकृतो; Y यस्माद्; b — X तथा; c — P कुल्याः; D कुल्य-; cd — B om.
१३३ d — P शुद्धबुद्धयः; W स्युः सुशुद्धयः.
१३४ c — B4 begins here; d — X तेषु; B2 V3 V8 om; P स्मृताः;

बहिर्वासिषु बाह्याश्च स्त्रियः स्त्रिषु च साक्षिणः ॥१३५॥

श्रेणीष्वष्टादशप्रकृतिनिबद्धासु ये **श्रेणिपुरुषास्ते** तन्मद्यपतितत्वात्तादृशा एव साक्षिणः प्रमाणम् । **स्वेषु वर्गेषु** भाटवर्गेषु भाटिका इत्यादयः । **बहिर्वासिष्व**न्त्यजातिषु **बाह्या** एव । स्त्रीषु च व्यवहारोत्पत्तौ **स्त्रिय** एव साक्षित्वमर्हन्ति । एतेषु साक्षिपरीक्षा नास्ति ।

श्रेण्यादिषु तु वर्गेषु कश्चिच्चेद्द्वेष्यतामियात् ।
तेभ्य एव न साक्षी स्याद्द्वेष्टारः सर्व एव ते ॥१३६॥

अत्र **श्रेण्यादिषु वर्गेषु** यदि **कश्चिद्रा**जगामित्वाद्वाक्पारुष्यदण्डपारुष्यदोषाद्वा **द्वेष्यतां** गच्छेत् । ते भहवोऽपि द्वेष्टृत्वात्तस्य साक्षित्वं नार्हन्ति । यतो **द्वेष्टारः सर्व एव ते** तस्येति । इत्यृणादाने साक्षिभेदो दशमः । अतोऽसाक्षिभेदो भवति ।

असाक्ष्यपि हि शास्त्रेषु दृष्टः पञ्चविधो बुधैः ।
वचनाद्दोषतो भेदात्स्वयमुक्तेर्मृतान्तरः ॥१३७॥

यश्च साक्षी न भवति सोऽ**पि** पञ्चप्रकारवचनदोषभेद**स्वयमुक्तेर्**[306] **मृतान्तर** इत्यादि । ते प्रत्येकं व्याख्यास्यन्ते ।

श्रोत्रियाद्या वचनतः स्तेनाद्या दोषदर्शनात् ।
भेदाद्विप्रतिपत्तिः स्याद्विवादे यत्र साक्षिणः ॥१३८॥
स्वयमुक्तेरनिर्दिष्टः स्वयमेवैत्य यो वदेत् ।
मृतान्तरोऽर्थिनि प्रेते मुमूर्षुश्राविताहृते ॥१३९॥
श्रोत्रियास्तापसा वृद्धा ये च प्रव्रजिता नराः ।
असाक्षिणस्ते वचनान्नात्र हेतुरुदाहृतः ॥१४०॥
स्तेनाः साहसिकाश्चण्डाः कितवा वधकास्तथा ।
असाक्षिणस्ते दुष्टत्वात्तेषु सत्यं न विद्यये ॥१४१॥
राज्ञा परिगृहीतेषु साक्षिष्वेकार्थनिश्चये ।

१३५ a — K5 L V V3 V6-7 NMS श्रेणिपु; c — P D स्युः.
१३६ a — D P NMS सर्वेपु; c — P साक्ष्यं.
१३७ a — P शास्त्रेऽस्मिन्; d — P L2 -उक्ति-; M4 -उक्तिर्; Jolly typo नृतान्तरः.
१३८ P om this verse; b — BM B स्तेयाद्यः; d — D साक्षीणां यतः.
१३९ P om this verse.
१४१ P L2 om from here through 143c; b — D M4 च ये.

वचनं यत्र भिद्यते ते स्युर्भेदादसाक्षिणः ॥१४२॥
अनिर्दिष्टस्तु साक्षित्वे स्वयमेवैत्य यो वदेत् ।
सूचीत्युक्तः स शास्त्रेषु न स साक्षित्वमर्हति ॥१४३॥
योऽर्थः श्रावयितव्यः स्यात्तस्मिन्नसति चार्थिनि ।
क्व तद्वदतु साक्षित्वमित्यसाक्षी मृतान्तरः ॥१४४॥

इत्यत्र व्याख्यानं कुर्वता मुनिनैव परिस्फुटं व्याख्या कृता । केवलं **मृतान्तर**साक्ष्येव विस्फुटीकरणार्थमुदाहरणमापेक्षते । यः कश्चिद्वाणिज्यधनं[307] संव्यवहारशतं प्रतिपाद्य साक्षिद्वयं कृत्वा प्रारम्भयति । एवमुक्त्वा यथामुकमासदिवसे त्रिकशतवृद्ध्या मम पार्श्वात्त्वदीय [*****] पित्रा गृहीतद्रम्माणां पञ्चशतानि तानि मे दीयतामिति । यदैवैकः प्रायं [*****] त्वपस्थिते [*****] यदर्थेऽपि पितृसक्त ऋणी प्रारब्ध एवं भणित्वा यथा यथामुकदिनपञ्चकशतवृद्ध्या मदीयपितुः सकाशाद्गृहीतद्रम्माणां शतपञ्चकं तन्मे प्रदीयतामिति । एवं श्रुत ऋणिनि तत्पितुर्मृतस्य कूटसाक्षिणां राजकुलदण्डापनादिकं भयमपश्यता ज्ञातसङ्केतं [*****] साक्षिद्वयमनाकृत्वैवमभिहितं भवति । तदा तत्कालमेव त्वदीयपितुर्जीवत एतयोः केशववासुदेवयोस्त्वदीयसाक्षिणोः केनापि प्रयोजनेन क्वच्चिद्ग्रामान्तरं तयोः [*****] अन्यदिदं स्वकीयं श्रीधरदेवधरनामानं साक्षिद्वयं कृत्वा सकलान्तरा अपि द्रम्माः प्रवेशिताश् । एवं तस्य धनिकमुत्तमस्यापि यदा द्वितीयश्च पापिष्ठ ऋणं भुक्तमुपस्थितो भवति । तदायं श्लोकोऽवतरति ।

योऽर्थः श्रावयितव्यः स्यात्तस्मिन्नसति चार्थिनि ।
क्व तद्वदतु साक्षित्वमित्यसाक्षी मृतान्तरः ॥

इति । अस्यार्थः । योऽर्थोऽ**र्थं** [*****] **श्रावयितव्यः** साक्षिणो भवति । एवं यथा त्वया प्रत्यक्षेण मम प्रत्यक्षमेते द्रम्मा गृहीताः । एतदीदृशम्[308] **साक्षित्वम**सौ साक्षी **तस्मिन्नसति चार्थिनि** मृत इति । कस्याग्रे **वदतु** । तदा तस्मिन्न**सती**दं तं कूटसाक्षिदातारं को दण्डापयतु । अस्मादनवस्थाभयान्मृतान्तरसाक्षी अप्रमाण उक्तो मुनिना । यत्र पुनः सत्यमेव द्रव्यं लभ्यं भवति । सत्यं वा द्रव्यं प्रवेशितं भवति । तदनुनष्टं हस्तचिह्नाङ्कितं लिखितमेव प्रमाणमुपन्यस्तं यथा

लिखितं बलवन्नित्यं जीवन्तश्चैव साक्षिणः । [NāSmṛ 1.66ab]
साक्षिभ्यो लिखितं श्रेयो लिखितान्न तु साक्षिणः ।। [NāSmṛ 1.125cd]

यश्चात्रापि प्रथममभिहितम्

१४२ c — B4 K2 K5 भिद्येतस्.
१४३ a — NMS स्वयमुक्तेरनिर्दिष्टः; d — P L2 ते साक्षित्वमर्हन्ति.

मुमूर्षुश्रावणादृते [NāSmṛ 1.139d]
तन्मृतान्तरोऽप्येतेषु प्रदेशेषु साक्षिणः प्रमाणमुक्ताः । यथा
श्रावितश्चातुरेणापि यस्त्वर्थो धर्मसंहितः ।
मृतेऽपि तत्र साक्ष्यं स्यात षट्सु चान्वाहितादिषु ।। [NāSmṛ 1.84]
इति मृततान्तरसाक्षिविवरणप्रकरणं इदं कल्याणीयमिति । इति साक्षिभेद एकादशः[309] । इदानीं पूर्वोक्तसाक्षिनियमो भवति ।

द्वयोर्विवदतोरर्थे द्वयोः सत्सु च साक्षिषु ।
पूर्वपक्षो भवेद्यस्य भवेयुस्तस्य साक्षिणः ॥१४५॥

अयं श्लोकोऽनुक्तविषयविभागत्वात्स्पष्टार्थक[310] एव भाति । तदस्य विषयविभागः । अस्वामिविक्रय ऋणादाने च[311] व्यवहारोपदेशार्थोऽस्य च स्पुटीकरणार्थः । यदा कश्चित्समागत्य किंचिदेवं वदति । यथा यो यं वृषभः त्वत्पार्श्वे तिष्ठति स मदीयो वर्तते[312] । मत्सकाशाच्चौरैर्हृतस्यानेन सह सप्त गोरूपाणी गतानि । तानि यदि तव पार्श्वे लभ्यानि । तथा च रक्तवर्णपुण्डुकचमरपुच्छशुक्लपादाद्यभिज्ञानस्पाष्टीकृतं चतुर्भिः साक्षिभिरात्मीयमिभमहं संभावयामीति । तच्छ्रुत्वा द्वितीयेनाभिहितम् । इह प्रजापतेः सृष्टिं कुर्वतोऽनेकानि द्विपदचतुष्पदानि समानाभिज्ञानानि भवन्ति । यदि सदृशाभिज्ञानमात्रेण लभ्यते । ततः स्वकीयपत्नी योद्वलित्वा गता तस्या यान्यनुज्ञानानि भ्रूकर्णनासिकाक्षिदन्तजिह्वाहस्तपादादिकानि तानि परस्त्रियोऽपि दृक्ता कस्मात्स्वगृहे न प्रवेशयसि । तदेष वृषभो गृहजातो वर्धितो यस्मिन्ग्रामे स्थितस्तस्मद्ग्रामादहमपि साक्षिचतुष्टयमानीय स्वकीयं संभावयामीति । अस्मिन्नर्थेऽयं श्लोकोऽवतरति **द्वयोर्** इति । अत्र पूर्वकालः पक्षो यस्य भवति तस्य साक्षिणः प्रमाणानि भवन्ति । न पुनरल्पावान्तरकालवादिन इति । एतत्कल्याणीयं विवरणमिति विस्पष्टोदाहरणसहितमिति ।

आधर्यं पूर्वपक्षस्य यस्मिन्नर्थे वशाद्भवेत् ।
प्रष्टव्याः साक्षिणस्तत्र विवादे प्रतिवादिनः ॥१४६॥

अत्राधरभावो लाघवम् । असाध्यमानत्वात्पूर्वपक्षस्य । **यस्मिन्**भवति विवादे । उत्तरपक्षो गरीयान्साध्यस्तत्सिद्धौ निषिक्तः[313] । तदा **साक्षिणः प्रतिवादिन**[314] ये

१४५ a — Y विवदयोर्; d — Y तेऽपि.

१४६ W om this verse; a — B3 K5 आधार्यं; L V3 V6-8 R Ox अधर्म्यं; d — P D विवादे साक्षिणस्तत्र प्रष्टव्याः; D add
अर्थ्युक्तं हि यदा वाक्यं प्रत्यर्थी प्रतिपद्यते ।
अनृतस्यापदेशेन तदादर्यं प्रचक्षते ।। [Dhko 220]

प्रष्टव्याः । प्रतिवादिनोद्दिष्टा इति । एवं च ते प्रतिवादिन उद्दिष्टा भवन्तीति । शास्त्रान्तरे चाह

सापदेशप्रतिज्ञानादाधर्यमुपजायते ।
पूर्वपक्षस्य साध्यस्तु विशेषः प्रतिवादिनः ।। [?]

तद्यथा कश्चिदाह यत्तेनैव पञ्चकशतवृद्ध्या पणशतं गृहीतं कस्माद् द्वैगुण्यं प्राप्तं न ददाति तस्य सिद्धौ साचिव्यं कर्तुमिच्छामीति । स आह यथा प्रतिज्ञातमस्य पणशतं सत्यं मया गृहीतं[315] ततः तस्मै दत्तमित्यत्र[316] पूर्वपक्षप्रतिज्ञातपणशतग्रहणसंप्रतिपत्तिरेव । न वादिनः साध्यं किंचिदस्ति । यत्तु विशेषतः संप्रदानं तत्साध्यं प्रतिवादिनेति । यथा दत्तमित्येवं **प्रतिवादिनः साक्षिन** आभवन्तीति ।

न परेण समुद्दिष्टं उपेयात्साक्षिणं रहः ।
भेदयेत्तं न चान्येन हीयेतैवं समाचरन् ॥१४७॥

तत्र यः परोद्दिष्टं **साक्षिणं** रहसि संभाषेतासौ हीयेत भेदयंश्च तर्जनभर्त्सनादिना लौकिकभेदेन चार्थसंप्रदानेनेति ।

साक्ष्युद्दिष्टो यदि प्रेयाद्गच्छेद्वापि दिगन्तरम् ।
तच्छ्रोतारः प्रमाणं स्युः प्रमाणं ह्युत्तरक्रिया ॥१४८॥

तत्र यदि **साक्ष्युद्दिष्टो** म्रियते देशान्तरं वा **गच्छेत्तस्य** मुमूर्षोर्यियासोर्वा तदर्थं पृष्टस्यर्थिनोद्देशश्रुतार्थस्य वा स्वयं विश्रावयतो वचनं श्रुतं यैस्त उत्तरसाक्षिणः प्रष्टव्या इत्ययं चासौ प्राक्सूत्रस्थानोक्तोत्तरसाक्षी प्रष्टव्यः ।

सुदीर्घेणापि कालेन लिखितं सिद्धिमाप्नुयात् ।
जानता चात्मना लेख्यं अजानानस्तु लेखयेत् ॥१४९॥

तत्र योऽसौ पञ्चविधः प्रयुक्तः साक्षी तस्य भेदफलविवक्षयेदमुच्यते । **सुदीर्घेणापि कालेन** लिखितस्य साक्षित्वम् । तेन च लिपिसमयज्ञेन**ात्मनैव** स्वनाम **लेख्यम्** । यथा कश्चिद्देशे साक्षिणश्च स्वहस्तेन मतमारोपयिष्यन्तीति ।

१४७ b — B2 X साक्षिणो; c — V V3 V6 V7 R वान्येन; d — D समाचरेत्; N add
यस्यानर्थकृतात्पीडा शारीरादधिकं भवेत् ।
पूर्वपक्षो भवेत्तस्य न तु पूर्वं निवेदनात् ।। [KāSmṛ 122]

१४८ a — B B2 उद्दृष्टा; b — K2 K5 व्रजेद्; d — D उत्तरा क्रिया; P उत्तराः क्रियाः.

१४९ a — D सुचिरेणापि; b — NMS BM Jolly लिखितः; c — Y स्वजानन्नात्मना लेख्यं; P D आत्मनैव लिखेज्जानन्न; d — P न चेदन्येन.

लेखकेन विलिखित आत्मनैव लिखेदत्राहं साक्षी देवदत्त इति । न चेल्लिपिज्ञस्तदान्येन **लेखयेत्** । तस्य कालान्तरे निरूपयतश्चिह्नाय भवतीति । एवं च लेखकविधिरुद्दिष्टः ।

सिद्धिरुक्ताष्टमाद्वर्षात्स्मारितस्येह साक्षिणः ।
आ पञ्चमात्तथा सिद्धिर्यदृच्छोपगतस्य तु ॥१५०॥
आ तृतीयात्तथा वर्षात्सिद्धिर्गूढस्य साक्षिणः ।
आ वै संवत्सरात्सिधिं वदन्त्युत्तरसाक्षिणः ॥१५१॥

इति कालो नियम्यते ।

अथवा कालनियमो न दृष्टः साक्षिणं प्रति ।
स्मृत्यपेक्षं हि साक्षित्वमाहुः शास्त्रविदो जनाः ॥१५२॥
यस्य नोपहता पुंसः स्मृतिः श्रोत्रं च नित्यशः ।
सुदीर्घेणापि कालेन स साक्षी साक्ष्यमर्हति ॥१५३॥

आभ्यामपि काले नियमप्रतिषेधः साक्षित्वस्यानुस्मरणबलेन क्रियते । तदयुक्तमविशेषेण कृयतां मा[317] कार्षीदिति[318] चैकविषयमनुमत्तवदिति । अत्रोच्यते । आचार्यमतदर्शनेन प्राक्कालनियमनं स्वमतेन वा न स्मरणोपपत्तिमता पुनरन्यथावचनमेव । मा भूदन्यशास्त्रदर्शनेन कालनियम आगममात्राद्विनैव पार्हतः स्वमतेन विकल्प इति । अनुस्मरणे **श्रोत्रं** वानुपहतं चेतश्च इति हेतुत्वेनोपादाय स्वतां प्रश्नार्थमन्यथावचनं लिखितसाक्ष्यत्कर्षार्थं नेति ।

असाक्षिप्रत्ययास्त्वन्ये षड्विवादाः प्रकीर्तिताः ।
लक्षणान्येव साक्षित्वं एषामाहुर्मनीषिणः ॥१५४॥

अत्र विनैव साक्षिभिः लिङ्गादिभिर्वक्ष्यमाणेषु षट्सु विवादेषु विनयो भवति ।

उल्काहस्तोऽग्निदो ज्ञेयः शस्त्रपाणिस्तु घातकः ।

१५० B om this verse; a — BM B5 आ अप्टमाद्वत्सरात्; P D NMS अष्टमाद्वत्सरात्सिद्धिः; c — P has a gap from here through संवत्सरात् in verse 151; d — D च.

१५१ B om this verse; ab — V4 om; d — D आ संवत्सरतः सिद्धिर्वदन्त्य्; BM B5 आ संवत्सरसिद्धिस्तु वदत्य्; NMS आ वत्सरात्तथा सिद्धिं वदन्त्य्.

१५२ a — B5 अथ कालेन नियमो; P एतावदवधेः प्रश्नकालनियमो; b — D दृधः.

१५३ B om this verse; a — BM नोपहताः; B5 नोपहतः; D बुद्धिः; b — P मतिः; P साक्षिणः.

१५४ ab — B om; c — D P साक्षित्वे; d — D P Y येपाम्; NMS तेपाम्.

केशाकेशिगृहीतश्च युगपत्पारदारिकः ॥१५५॥
कुद्दालपाणिर्विज्ञेयः सेतुभेत्ता समीपगः ।
तथा कुठारपाणिश्च वनछेत्ता प्रकीर्तितः ॥१५६॥
अभ्यग्रचिह्नो विज्ञेयो दण्डपारुष्यकृन्नरः ।
असाक्षिप्रत्यया ह्येते पारुष्ये तु परीक्षणम् ॥१५७॥

तत्रागते सत्य**क्तिदघातकसेतुभेदकानां** विषयः । **छेत्तुर्वनस्य**[319] निषेधातिक्रमे । **केशाकेशिग्रहणं** च **युगपत्पारदारिके** । **दण्डपारुष्यं** घातकविषयम् । वाक्यसंबन्धे चैव हि षड्विवादा इति । प्रत्यक्षचिह्नत्वाच्च विनैव साक्षिभिः प्रत्ययेऽत्र दोष इति । अप्रत्यक्षे त्वत्र चिह्नेऽपि पारुष्यपरीक्षणमेव न्याय्यं ततः ।

कश्चित्कृत्वात्मनश्चिह्नं द्वेषात्परमुपद्रवेत् ।
हेत्वर्थगतिसामर्थ्यैस्तत्र युक्तं परीक्षणम् ॥१५८॥

निगदव्याख्यानश्लोकः । **हेतुः** कारणं तत्सामर्थ्येन परीक्षा कर्तव्या ।

नार्थसंबन्धिनो नाप्ता न सहाया न वैरिणः ।
न दृष्टदोषाः प्रष्टव्याश्च व्याध्यार्ता न दूषिताः ॥१५९॥

तत्र परीक्षा साक्षीप्रमाणच्छेद्या । न च वाक्पारुष्यविषयैव केवलमियं साक्षिणां साधुता विवक्षिता । किंतु यत्र यत्र साक्षिप्रमाणावतारः तत्रापि यथोच्यमाना अर्थिसंबन्धिप्रभृतयः साक्षिणो न भवन्ति । तत्रा**र्थसंबन्धी** यः स्याद् द्वेष्टि विवक्षितार्थसंसिद्धा चार्थसिद्धिः । **आप्त**त्विष्टः स्वकुल्यश्चोच्यते । तथा **सहाया** इत्येकार्थसंभूयकारिणः । **वैरी** शत्रुः । **दृष्टदोष**स्त्वन्यकार्येषु कूटसाक्षित्वादिनापि ज्ञायते । अन्यशास्त्रमतेन वाग्दण्डादिसामीप्याच्च । यदा चामी प्रतिवादिना **प्रतिदूषिता*** भवन्ति प्रश्नकाले तदा न **प्रष्टव्याः** । इत्येवं वक्ष्यमाणेष्विति ।

दासनैकृतिकाश्रद्धवृद्धस्त्रीबालचाक्रिकाः ।
मत्तोन्मत्तप्रमत्तार्तकितवग्रामयाजकाः ॥१६०॥

१५५ a — V3 V7-8 R उच्छाहस्तो; d — D पारजायिकः.
१५६ B K2 om this verse; b — P B5 समीपतः; c — Y अथ; B3 K5 कुठारहस्तश्.
१५७ a — D अत्युग्रचिह्नो; K5 अभ्युग्रचिह्नो; Jolly प्रत्यक्षचिह्नो.
१५९ b — D साक्षिणः; c — D कर्तव्यो; d — X हार्द्यार्ता; P साक्षिण प्रतिदुपिताः;
D add न साक्षी नृपतिः कार्यो न कारुककुशीलावौ ।
१६० b — P -कृतिकास्राद्ध-; Y B3 B5 -कृतिकश्राद्ध-; X -कृतिकश्रन्त-; X -वक्रिणः; B -चाक्रियाः; B2 -चक्रियतः.

तत्र **दासो** गृहजातः । **नैकृतिकश्**छलव्यवहारी । **अश्राद्धो*** न श्राद्धमर्हतीति । दुर्बलादि**वृद्धः** संव्यवहारायोग्यः । लुप्तस्मृत्यादिकरणत्वात् । **उन्मत्तो** वायुदोषात् । **प्रमत्तः** प्रमादशीलः **आर्तो** व्यसनार्तः । **कितवो** द्यूतकारः । **ग्रामयाजकः** ग्रामर्त्विक् ।

महापथिकसामुद्रवणिक्प्रव्रजितातुराः ।
लुब्धकश्रोत्रियाचारहीनक्लीबकुशीलवाः ॥१६१॥

महापथिको दीर्घाध्वगः । **सामुद्रो वणिक्**समुद्रयात्रानिरतः । **प्रव्रजितो** भिक्षुः । **आतुरो** रोगी । **व्यङ्गो***ऽङ्गहीनः । एक एक एव । **श्रोत्रियः** छान्दसः । **आचारहीनः** प्रच्युतः स्वधर्मात् । **क्लीबः** षण्ढः प्रजननासमर्थः । **कुशीलवश्**चारण इति ।

नास्तिकव्रात्यदाराग्नित्यागिनोऽयाज्ययाजकाः ।
एकस्थालीसहायारिचरज्ञातिसनाभयः ॥१६२॥

तत्र **नास्तिको** मिथ्यादृष्टिः । **व्रात्यो**ऽकृतसंस्कारः **दाराग्नित्यागिनो** धर्मभार्यावैतानाक्तित्यागिनः । **अयाज्ययाजका** निन्दितयाजकाः । **एकस्थाली** सहभोजनः । **सहायारी** मित्रशत्रू । **चरो** राजनियुक्तः । **ज्ञातिर्**बन्धुः । **सनाभिः** सोदर्य इति ।

प्राग्दृष्टदोषशैलूषविषजीव्यहितुण्डिकाः ।
गरदाग्निदकीनाशशूद्रापुत्रोपपातिकाः ॥१६३॥

तत्र प्राग्दृष्टो दोषो यस्य स **प्राग्दृष्टदोषः** । प्राग्जन्माशुभदोषकर्मपरिणामप्राप्तारोगचिह्नः तत्कर्मा वा तदात्रासीद् हत्यास्तेनादिदृष्टदोषोऽपीति । शैलूषो नतः । **विषजीवी** विषविक्रेता[320] वा । **अहितुण्डिकः** सर्पादिदन्दशूकग्राही । **गरदो** द्वेषसंबन्धाद्विषस्य दाता । **अग्निंदो** गृहादिदाहकः । **कीनाशः** क्षुद्रः कदर्यो वा । **शूद्र्याः** पुत्रः शूद्रीपुत्रः । **औपपातिका** उपपातकसंयोगात् ।

क्लान्तसाहसिकश्रान्तनिर्धनान्त्यावसायिनः ।
भिन्नवृत्तासमावृत्तजडतैलिकमूलिकाः ॥१६४॥

१६१ b — V6-8 R H Ox -जितान्तगः; L -जिताङ्गतः; d — P D व्यङ्गैक-.
१६२ d — B3 K2 K5 एकस्थान-.
१६३ d — D -पुत्रोपनायिनः; X -पुत्रानपाश्रिताः; B -पुत्रोपजातिकाः; B2 -पूजानयाश्रिताः.
१६४ b — NMS B5 K2 -साहसिकशान्त-; NMS -निर्धूतान्ता-; d — NMS भिन्नवृत्त्यसम्-; Y B3 विन्नवृत्तसम्-; K2 भिन्नवृत्तिसम्-; D -तैलिकसौनिकाः.

तत्र **क्लान्तः** खिन्नः । **साहसिकः** प्रसह्यायुक्तकारी । **श्रान्तो** निःसङ्गः । **निर्धनो** द्युतादिव्यसनदोषाद् हृतसर्वस्वः । **अन्त्यावसायी** चण्डालः । **भिन्नवृत्तो** मिथ्या-दृष्टिः । **असमावृत्तो** ब्रह्मचारी प्राक्स्नानात् । **जडो** निरिन्द्रियः । **तैलिकश्**चक्रादि-तैलिकचाक्रिकः । **मूलिको** मूलद्रव्यविक्रयजीवन इति ।

भूताविष्टनृपद्विष्टवर्षनक्षत्रसूचकाः ।
अघशंस्यात्मविक्रेतृहीनाङ्गभगवृत्तयः ॥१६५॥

तत्र **भूताविष्टः** सग्रहः । **नृपद्विष्टो** राजद्विषः । **वर्षनक्षत्रसूचकः** सांवत्सरसूचकः । **अघशंसी** पापस्तेनो हिंस्रो वा । **आत्मविक्रेता** धनेन दासत्वमुपगतः । **हीनाङ्गो** बाहुपादहीनः । **भगवृत्तिस्**स्त्रीजीवनो मुखभगो वा ।

कुनखी श्यावदन्श्वित्रिमित्रध्रुक्शठशौण्डिकाः ।
ऐन्द्रजालिकलुब्धोग्रश्रेणीगणविरोधिनः ॥१६६॥

उग्रः क्रूरः । क्षत्रियाद्वा शूद्रायां जातः ।

वधकृच्चित्रकृन्मङ्खः पतितः कूटकारकः ।
कुहकः प्रत्यवसितस्तस्करो राजपूरुषः ॥१६७॥

वधकः* सौनिकः । **चित्रकृल्** लेख्यक्रियोपजीवी । **मङ्खः** कपटजीवी । **पतितः** पातकी । **कूटकारकः** कूटलेख्यककार्षापणादिकर्ता । **कुहकः** मन्त्रौषध्याद्युपाया-श्रयाद्वशीकरणादिकर्ता । **प्रत्यवसितः** प्रव्रज्यापतितवृत्तः । **तस्करश्**चौरः । **राजपुरुषः*** सेवक इति ।

मनुष्यविषशस्त्राम्बुलवणापूपवीरुधाम् ।
विक्रेता ब्राह्मणश्चैव द्विजो वार्धुषिकश्च यः ॥१६८॥
च्युतः स्वधर्मात्कुलिकः स्तावको हीनसेवकः ।
पित्रा विवदमानश्च भेदकृध्येत्यसाक्षिणः ॥१६९॥

१६५ d — D वकवृत्तयः.
१६६ b — P स्यामदन्तश्च मित्र-; NMS श्वित्री-.
१६७ P has this verse in a sh m; a — P D वधकश्चर्मकृत्पङ्गुः.
१६८ b — X D P मनुष्यपशुमांसास्थिमधुक्षीराम्बुसर्पिपाम्.
१६९ b — Y स्तवको; NMS हीनसेविता; Y हीनसेवकाः.

निगदव्याख्यातौ श्लोकौ । **स्तावकस्तु** नक्ताचार्यजातीयः । **भेदकृत्**सस्नेहयोर् अद्रव्यैर्योजकः । एते साक्षित्वेऽनिर्दिष्टा न प्रश्नार्हाः ।

असाक्षिणो ये निर्दिष्टा दासनैकृतिकादयः ।
कार्यगौरवमासद्य भवेयुस्तेऽपि साक्षिणः ॥१७०॥

येऽम्यनन्तरोक्ता दासाद्यः । साक्षित्वेनेष्टाः । एत एव यदि कार्याद्गुणी <.....>।

साहसेषु च सर्वेषु स्तेयसंग्रहणेषु च ।
पारुष्ययोश्चाप्युभयोर्न परीक्षेत साक्षिणः ॥१७१॥

एषु तु विवादपदेषु परीक्षा च न कर्तव्या[321] । उद्देशमात्रादेव द्रष्टव्या इति ।

तेषामपि न बालः स्यान्नैको न स्त्री न कूटकृत् ।
न बन्धवो न चारातिर्ब्रूयुस्ते साक्ष्यमन्यथा ॥१७२॥
बालोऽज्ञानादसत्यात्स्त्री पापाभ्यासाच्च कूटकृत् ।
विब्रुयाद्बान्धवः स्नेहाद्वैरनिर्यातनादरिः ॥१७३॥

श्लोकावेतौ निगदव्याख्यातौ । दासनैकृतिकादिषु प्रतिषेधोत्सर्गस्य गौरवाद्यपेक्षया विवक्षितार्थाविति ।

अथवानुमतो यः स्याद् द्वयोर्विवदमानयोः ।
असाक्ष्येकोऽपि साक्षित्वे प्रष्टव्यः स्यात्स संसदि ॥१७४॥

अत्रैकस्योभयानुमतस्य विशिष्टविषयसंसदि जनताप्रत्यक्षं प्रष्टव्यत्वमनुज्ञातम् ।

यस्त्वात्मदोषभिन्नत्वादस्वस्थ इव लक्ष्यते ।
स्थानात्स्थानान्तरं गच्छेदेकैकं चोपधावति ॥१७५॥

१६९ b — Y स्तवको; NMS हीनसेविता; Y हीनसेवकाः.
१७० D has verses 170-171 after 178; a — X उद्दिष्टा.
१७१ b — B5 स्तेये ग्रहणेपु; d — W असाक्षी नोपपद्यते.
१७२ a — NMS न तत्रापि च; b — P D Y न स्त्री नैको; H न स्त्र्यभ्यासी; d — B5 साक्षिणोऽन्यथा.
१७४ a — Jolly उभयानुमतो; c — P L2 असाक्षिको; d — NMS D तु
१७५ a — D NMS -दोपदुष्टत्वाद्; b — is sh; cd — P om; d — D चानुधावति.

कासतेऽनिभृतोऽकस्मादभीक्ष्णं निश्वसत्यपि ।
भूमिं लिखति पादाभ्यां बाहु वासो धुनोति च ॥१७६॥
भिद्यते मुखवर्णोऽस्य ललाटं स्विद्यते तथा ।
शोषमागच्छतश्चोष्ठावूर्ध्वं तिर्यक्च वीक्षते ॥१७७॥
त्वरमाण इवाबद्धमपृष्टो बहु भाषते ।
कूटसाक्षी स विज्ञेयस्तं पापं विनयेन्नृपः ॥१७८॥

अत्र प्राड्विवाकस्य व्यवहारदर्शनमुपदिश्यते । साक्षिप्रश्नकाल उपस्थित इङ्गिताकारादि परीक्षेत । न केवलमुक्तदोषदूषित एव न प्रश्नार्हः । एवंक्रियोऽपि न प्रष्टव्यः । **कूटसाक्षी** स इति विनयेच्च । दण्डं दण्डयन्न दोषः ।

श्रावयित्वा च योऽन्येभ्यः साक्षित्वं तद्विनिह्नुते ।
स विनेयो भृशतरं कूटसाक्ष्यधिको हि सः ॥१७९॥

यश्**चान्येभ्यो**ऽपि[322] तत्साक्ष्यं **श्रावयित्वा** प्रपद्य च । पुनः साक्ष्यप्रदानकाल अन्यथा ब्रुयात्तस्य महादण्डः कर्तव्यः । कूटसाक्ष्यं कूटं साक्षित्वं कूटसाक्षिभ्योऽधिकं यस्मादिति ।

आहूय साक्षिणः पृच्छेन्नियम्य शपथैर्भृशम् ।
समस्तान्विदिताचारान्विज्ञातार्थान्पृथक्पृथक् ॥१८०॥

साद**रमाहूय साक्षिणः समस्तान्पृच्छेत्** । पूर्वश्रुतार्थानेकैकशः । विज्ञाताचाराणामेषाम्[323] । अथवा समस्ता**न्विदिताचारान्पृच्छेद**विज्ञाताचारांस्त्वेकैकशः । अप्रतिदूषिता ह्यविज्ञाताचारा अपि[324] प्रष्टव्या एवेति । प्रश्नश्चोभयथापि युक्तः । **नियम्य शपथैर्भृशं** सुतरामिति ।

१७६ a — P D क्रामत्यनिभृतो; B B2 B5 कासत्यनिभृतो.

१७७ b — Y ललाटे भिद्यते; c — Y चोष्ठाम्.

१७८ a — Y इवावृद्धं; D इवाकस्माद्; NMS इवापृष्टो; P वदेत्तत्र; M4 वरमाणो वदेत्तत्र; bc — P M4 om; b — NMS वह्लवद्धं च; d — NMS भृशं.

१७९ a — P D BM B2 तथा; b — P D BM B2 यो विनिह्नुते; NMS योऽपि निह्नुते; d — D add
अज्ञानाद्बालभावाच्च साक्षि यद्यनृतं वदेत् । [Manu 8.118cd]
लोभात्सहस्रं दण्डस्तु मोहात्पूर्वं तु साहसम् ।। [Manu 8.120ab]
भयाद्वै मध्यमो दण्डो मैत्र्यात्पूर्वं चतुर्गुणं । [Manu 8.120cd]
कामाद्दशगुणं प्रोक्तं क्रोधात्तु त्रिगुणं परम् । [Manu 8.121ab]
X add
यस्मिन्यस्मिन्कृते कार्ये कूटसाक्ष्यं कृतं भवेत् [Manu 8.117ab]

१८० a — N NMS साक्षिणं.

सत्येन शापयेद्विप्रं क्षत्रियं वाहनायुधैः ।
गोबीजकाञ्चनैर्वैश्यं शूद्रं सर्वैस्तु पातकैः ॥१८१॥

शपथनिर्देशार्थं श्लोकः ।

पुराणैर्धर्मवचनैः सत्यमाहत्म्यकीर्तनैः ।
अनृतस्यापवादैश्च भृशमुत्त्रास्य साक्षिणः ॥१८२॥

प्रश्ने विध्युपन्यासार्थं श्लोकः ।

नग्नो मुण्डः कपालेन भिक्षार्थी क्षुत्पिपासितः ।
दीनः शत्रुगृहं गच्छेद्यः साक्ष्यमनृतं वदेत् ॥१८३॥
नगरे प्रतिरुद्धः सन्बहिर्द्वारे बुभुक्षितः ।
अमित्रान्भूयशः पश्येद्यः साक्ष्यमनृतं वदेत् ॥१८४॥
यां रात्रिमधिविन्ना स्त्री यां चैवाक्षपराजितः ।
यां च भाराभितप्ताङ्गो दुर्विवक्ता स तां वसेत् ॥१८५॥
साक्षी साक्ष्यसमुद्देशे गोकर्णशिथिलं चरन् ।
सहस्रं वारुणान्पाशानात्मनि प्रतिमुञ्चति ॥१८६॥
तस्य वर्षशते पूर्णे पाशमेकं प्रमुच्यते ।
एवं स बन्धनात्तस्मान्मुच्यते नियुताः समाः ॥१८७॥

१८१ b — Y विप्रः क्षत्रियो; d — Y वैश्यः शूद्रः.
१८२ d — D उत्त्रासयेदिमान्; P उद्वासयेदिमान्; D add
स्वभावशीलादन्यत्र दुस्त्यजा प्रकृतिर्नृणाम् । [?]
सत्य साक्षी ब्रुवन्साक्ष्ये लोकानाप्नोति पुष्कलान् ।
इह त्वाददते कीर्तिं वाग्चैषा ब्रह्मपूजिता ॥ [Manu 8.81]
X B2 add
ब्रह्मघ्नो ये स्मृता लोका ये च स्त्रीवालघातिनः ।
मित्रद्रुहः कृतघ्नस्य ते ते स्युर्ब्रुवतो मृषा ॥ [Manu 8.89]
१८३ a — D B कपाली च; c — D P अन्धः; NMS क्रुद्धः.; d — Jolly typo अमृतं; D add
साक्ष्येऽनृतं वदन्पाशैर्वध्यते वारुनैर्भृशं ।
विवशः शतमाजातीस्पापयोनिपु जायते ॥ [cf. Manu 8.82]
ब्रह्मघ्नो ये स्मृता लोका ये च स्त्रीवालघातिनः ।
मित्रद्रुहः कृतघ्नस्य ते ते स्युर्ब्रुवतो मृषा ॥ [Manu 8.89]
१८४ D BM B om this verse; b — NMS वहिर्दारो; ab — P नक्तो मुण्डः कपालेन परद्वारे बुभुक्षितः.
१८५ a — B K2 अधिभित्रा; B2 अपि विना; b — X च द्युतपराजितः; d — K2 R Ox दुर्विभक्ता
१८६ a — P साक्ष्ये; D साक्षि-; b — P वचः; c — B BM वरुणं पाशम्.
१८७ b — P पाश एवं; NMS पाश एकः; P add तदा पाशाद्विनिर्मुक्तः स्त्री संभवति मानवः । [J 1.205cd]; D add
स यदा पापनिर्मक्तस्तदा स्त्रीत्वं तु गच्छति । [?]; c — P सं-; d — P नियताच्; N नियतं; P च सः; B5
सदा; P add पशुगोऽश्वपुरुपाणां हिर्ण्यं भूर्यथाक्रमम् । [J 1.206cd]; X B2 add
पृप्टो हि साक्ष्यं यः साक्षी जानानोऽप्यन्यथा वदेत् ।
स पूर्वानात्मनः सप्त कूले हन्यात्तथावरान् ॥ [?]

यावतो बान्धवांस्यस्मिन्हन्ति साक्ष्येऽनृतं वदन् ।
तावतः संख्यया तस्मिन्शृणु सौम्यानुपूर्वशः ॥१८८॥
पञ्च पश्वनृते हन्ति दश हन्ति गवानृते ।
शतमश्वानृते हन्ति सहस्रं पुरुषानृते ॥१८९॥
हन्ति जातानजातांश्च हिरण्यार्थेऽनृतं वदन् ।
सर्वं भूम्यनृते हन्ति मा स्म भूम्यनृतं वदीः ॥१९०॥
एकमेवाद्वितीयं तत्प्राहुः पावनमात्मनः ।
सत्यं स्वर्गस्य सोपानं पारावारस्य नौरिव ॥१९१॥
अश्वमेधसहस्रं च सत्यं च तुलया धृतम् ।
अश्वमेधसहस्राद्धि सत्यमेव विशिष्यते ॥१९२॥
वरं कूपशताद्वापि वरं वापीशतात्क्रतुः ।
वरं क्रतुशतात्पुत्रः सत्यं पुत्रशताद्वरम् ॥१९३॥
भूर्धारयति सत्येन सत्येनोदेति भास्करः ।
सत्येन वायुः पवते सत्येनापः स्रवन्ति च ॥१९४॥
सत्यमेव परं दानं सत्यमेव परं तपः ।
सत्यमेव परो धर्मो लोकानामिति नः श्रुतम् ॥१९५॥
सत्यं देवाः समासेन मनुष्यस्त्वनृतं स्मृतम् ।
इहैव तस्य देवत्वं यस्य सत्ये स्थिता मतिः ॥१९६॥
सत्यं ब्रूह्यनृतं त्यक्त्वा सत्येन स्वर्गमेष्यसि ।
उक्त्वानृतं महाघोरं नरकं प्रतिपत्स्यते ॥१९७॥
निरयेषु च ते शश्वज्जिह्वामुत्कृत्य दारुणाः ।
असिभिः शातयिष्यन्ति बलिनो यमकिंकराः ॥१९८॥

१८८ a — Y वान्धवान्; P X तस्मिन्; B2 D अस्मिन्; b — L V4 V6 Ox B B5 वदेत्; X वचः; c — X B2 P संप्रवक्ष्यामि; D संख्यया तस्य; d — D प्रवक्ष्याम्यनुपूर्वशः; X B2 यथावदनुपूर्वशः; D add
अन्नानृते जन्म हन्ति द्वे वा सस्यानृते तथा ।
त्रीणि यानानृते हन्याच्चतुर्थं वाहनानृते ॥ [Dhko 316]
१८९ c — X B2 कन्यानृते; d — B2 दश हन्ति गवानृते.
१९० b — B B5 वदेत्; d — V6-8 R भूयोऽनृतं; P वदः; B B5 V V3-8 वदेत्.
१९१ B4 om verses 191-194ab.
१९२ L om from here through सत्यं in verse 193.; c — P NMS तु.
१९३ a — NMS परं; c — NMS परं; d — NMS परं.
१९४ b — L NMS सत्येनोदयते रविः; L V6 add सत्यं ब्रूह्यनृतं त्यक्त्वा सत्येन स्वर्गमेष्यसि । [NāSmṛ 1.197ab]; H add
इहैव तस्य देवत्वं यस्य सत्ये स्थिा मतिः ।
सत्यं ब्रूह्यनृतं त्यक्त्वा सत्येन स्वर्गमेष्यसि । [NāSmṛ 1.196cd-197ab]
c — BM B B5 D प्लवते.
१९५ d — NMS वै; BM NMS श्रुतिः.
१९६ b — NMS स्मृताः; c — B इति देवस्य.
१९७ b — V V4 V7 R Ox एप्यति; c — D त्यक्त्वानृतं; d — X प्रतिपत्स्यसि.

शूलैर्भेत्स्यन्ति चाक्रुद्धाः क्रोशन्तमपरायणम् ।
अवाक्शिरसमुत्क्षिप्य क्षेप्स्यन्त्यग्निहृदेषु च ॥१९९॥
अनुभूय च दुःखास्ताश्चिरं नरकवेदनाः ।
इह यास्यस्यभव्यासु गृध्रकाकादियोनिषु ॥२००॥
ज्ञात्वैताननृते दोषाञ्ज्ञात्वा सत्ये च सद्गुणान् ।
सत्यं वदोद्धरात्मानं मात्मानं पातयिष्यसि ॥२०१॥
न बान्धवा न सुहृदो न धनानि महान्त्यपि ।
अलं तारयितुं शक्तास्तमस्युग्रे निमज्जतः ॥२०२॥
पितरस्त्ववलम्बन्ते त्वयि साक्षित्वमागते ।
तारयिष्यति किंवास्मानात्मानं पातयिष्यति ॥२०३॥
सत्यमात्मा मनुष्यस्य सत्ये सर्वं प्रतिष्ठितम् ।
सर्वथैवात्मनात्मानं श्रेयसा योजयिष्यसि ॥२०४॥
यां च रात्रिमजनिष्ठा यां रात्रिं च मरिष्यसि ।
वृथा तदन्तरं ते स्यात्कुर्याश्चेत्सत्यमन्यथा ॥२०५॥
नास्ति सत्यात्परो धर्मो नानृतात्पातकं परम् ।
साक्षिधर्मे विशेषेण सत्यमेव वदेत्ततः ॥२०६॥

१९८ a — X D P नरकेपु.

१९९ a — P शूलो; NMS शूले; BM B5 चाक्षिप्य; B च शीघ्रं; NMS मत्स्यानिवाक्षिप्य; b — Y क्षेप्स्यन्त्यम्हिृदेपु च; c — L अवास्थितं सम्-; V6-8 R H Ox अवांछितं सम्-; P अवस्थितं सम्-; NMS अवाक्छिरसम्; P उत्कृत्य; d — P उग्रहृदेपु च; D त्वां हुताशने; X add कुम्भीपाके वैतरण्यां पूयासृग्मेदसां हृदे ॥

२०० a — P तास्तीव्राश्; b — X नरकायतनाः; c — Jolly P mc यास्यसि पापासु.

२०१ b — D तान्गुणान्; d — P आत्मानं; Jolly नात्मानं; NMS पीपतश्चिरं; D प्रातयेत् स्वयं; Jolly पातय स्वयम्.

२०२ c— P D NMS धारयितुम्; D हस्तं.

२०३ d—Y चात्मानं किमस्मान्; NMS किन्त्वस्मानात्मानं; X किंवास्मान्किंवास्मात्; P किं त्वस्मान्किञ्चायं; D किं त्वस्मानुताहो; BM B L H पातयिष्यसि.

२०४ c — X सर्वात्मना त्वमात्मनं; D Jolly सत्यमुक्त्वात्मनात्मानं; cd — P om; d — D Jolly संनियोजय.

२०५ b — NMS यां रात्रिमजनिष्ठास्त्वं यां च रात्रिं मरिष्यसि; D यां रात्रिमजनिष्ठास्त्वं यां रात्रिं च मरिष्यति; X अजायथाश्च यां रात्रिं यां च रात्रिं मरिष्यसि; P यस्यां रात्रावयायिष्ट यस्यां रात्रौ मरिष्यति; Y याञ्च रात्रिमजायिष्ठा यां च रात्रिं मरिष्यसि; c —NMS तदन्तरं corrected by the editor to तदन्तरा; P तदन्यं तत्तुभ्यं; Jolly तदन्तरं तुभ्यं.; d — X मिथ्या चेद्व्याहरिष्यसि; Y कुर्याच्चेत्सत्यमन्यथा; D साक्ष्यं चेदन्यथा कृतं; P साक्ष्यं चेदन्यथाकृथाः; NMS साक्ष्यं चेदन्यथा वदेः; X add

यच्चात्र सुकृतं किंचिदमुत्रार्थमुपार्जितम् ।
तत्ते सर्वं गुणो गच्छेत्कुर्याच्च साक्ष्यमन्यथा ॥ [?]

P add

ब्रह्मघ्नस्य तु ये लोका ये च स्त्रीबालघातिनाम् ।
ये च लोकाः कृतघ्नस्य ते ते स्युर्ब्रुवतो वृथा ॥ [J 1.225]

२०६ d — NMS वदेर्; Jolly typo तदेत्; NMS अतः; B2 X Y add पुराणोक्तौ द्वौ श्लोकौ; D add पुराणोक्तौ (द्वौ) श्लोकौ शुभौ; P add पुराणोक्तौ कौ भवतः, but mc पुराणोक्तौ तथैवात्र श्लोकौ द्वौ भवतः शुभौ ।

यः परार्थे प्रहरति स्वां वाचं पुरुषाधमः ।
आत्मार्थे किं न कुर्यात्स पापो नरकनिर्भयः ॥२०७॥
अर्था वै वाचि नियता वाङ्मूला वाग्विनिःसृताः ।
यो ह्येतां स्तेनयेद्वाचं स सर्वस्तेयकृन्नरः ॥२०८॥

अमी श्लोकाः शपथसत्यमाहात्म्यानृतनिन्दाया निगदसुबोधा इति न व्याख्यांताः ।

साक्षिविप्रतिपत्तौ तु प्रमाणं बहवो यतः ।
तत्साम्ये शूचयो ग्राह्यास्तत्साम्ये स्मृतिमत्तराः ॥२०९॥
स्मृतिमत्साक्षिसाम्यं तु विवादे यत्र दृश्यते ।
सूक्ष्मत्वात्साक्षिधर्मस्य साक्ष्यं व्यावर्तते पुनः । २१०॥

तस्मात्स्मृतिमत्साक्षिसाम्याद् **व्यावर्तते** । **साक्ष्यम**नुस्मरणं[325] सक्तं न भवति । समक्षदर्शनानुपलब्धेरेकविषयमेवैक[326] आहुः । उद्दिष्टाः साक्षिण[327] इत्यन्य आहुः । न वयमित्युभयेषां च सतां[328] **साम्यं** किंपुनर्विवक्षया समक्षदर्शनमिति विनिश्चय एव नोपपद्यते । ततश्च तन्निमित्तोत्पन्नस्य साक्ष्यस्याभाव एवेति **साक्ष्यं व्यावर्तते** साक्षिण एव ते[329] न भवन्तीति । एवं च कृत्वा प्राक्प्रतिज्ञातभेदादसाक्षिण इति समर्थितं भवतीति ।

निर्दिष्टेष्वर्थजातेषु साक्षी चेत्साक्ष्यमागतः ।
न ब्रूयादक्षरसमं न तन्निगदितं भवेत् ॥२११॥
देशकालवयोद्रव्यप्रमाणाकृतिजातिषु ।
यत्र विप्रतिपत्तिः स्यात्साक्ष्यं तदसदुच्यते ॥२१२॥

२०७ a — P प्रहिणुयत्; BM B प्रहरते; V7 V8 R H Ox and NMS घचोररेचतेद बय तहे दतिोर फरोम प्रहरतिघ ऽपहरति; d — D NMS पापं; D निरयनिर्भयः.

२०८ a — P अर्थ चैवाचि; M4 अर्थं वै चैव; L2 अर्थे वै चैव; Jolly वाच्यर्था नियताः सर्वे; b — P वाग्विनिश्चिताः; NMS वाचि मिश्रिताः; c — L2 D हीनां; P M4 हीतां; ट वैषां; NMS वैतां; Jolly हितां; NMS स्तेययेद्; D — B4 K2 -स्तेनकृन्.

२०९ cd — L V4 H om; d — X स्मृतिरुत्तराः; Y स्मृतिमुत्तमाः; D सुचिमुत्तराः.

२१० a — D शुद्धिमत्साक्षिसाम्यं; W स्मृतिमत्साक्षिसाम्यं; c — Y B2 NMS तीक्ष्णत्वात्; d — P D NMS ततः; D add

स्वसाक्षिवर्जितो यस्तु दैवाद्वादी कथंचन ।
उद्धारं तस्य नेच्छन्ति दिव्येनापि मानीषिणः ।। [J 1.231]

२११ b — P D साक्ष्य; Y B2-5 NMS P आगते; c — P अक्षरं सम्यक्.

२१२ P om this verse; d — B BM साक्षी; P D NMS अपि चान्यथा; Y अपि विश्रसा.

यदि च साक्षी यथाप्रश्नं निविष्टाक्षरसममेवमेतदहं[330] जाने इति नापि विवादे देशकालादीनां साक्षिवचनादसाम्यं तदपि साक्ष्यं [?-->] विश्रेसेद्(?)[331]इत्यपरः पाठः । विश्रांस(?)[332]विश्रमाते (?)[333]। [<--?] असाक्ष्यमेव तदिति ।

ऊनमभ्यधिकं चार्थं प्रब्रूयुर्यत्र साक्षिणः ।
तदप्यनुक्तं विज्ञेयमेष साक्ष्यविधिः स्मृतः ॥२१३॥

सुबोधपाठार्थश्लोकः पौनरुक्त्याक्षरसमत्वादेव प्रागुक्त इति यम् **उनमधिकं*** वा यथा प्रसूतादर्थात्साक्षिनां वचनं **तत्राक्षरसमम्** इत्येव[334] [1.211] वचनं **निगदितम्** इति [I.211] । को[335] विशेष उच्यते ह्यर्थजातमिति प्रागुक्त इदं त्वमनुकूलमिति । को विशेषो बहूनामर्थानामुनाधिकेनैवाक्षरसममेकस्यापि[336] तद्वप्[337](?)इत्युउच्यते । एकेषामर्थानामक्षरसाम्यमानो[338] येषामानुगुण्येन वचनं तेषां सिद्धिः । वैगुण्यं वापि । पराजीयत[339] इति [?-->] तदेतदुभयमपि मा भूदिति प्रागुक्तं **तन्निगदितं**[340] **भवेद्** इत्य् [1.211] एकस्य निर्द्विधासिद्ध्यसिद्धि-पक्षाभ्यां न्याय्यं कर्तुमर्थस्येति । न्यूनाधिकं चोच्यमानमुक्तमेवेति । न्यूनपक्षे तु वादः । अधिको वा प्रसूतमेव सिध्येदिति वातिसिध्यति । [<--?]

प्रमादाद्धनिनो यत्र न स्याल्लेख्यं न साक्षिणः ।
अर्थं चापह्नुयाद्वादी तत्रोक्तस्त्रिविधो विधिः ॥२१४॥
चोदना प्रतिकालं च युक्तिलेशस्तथैव च ।
तृतीयः शपथश्चोक्तस्तैरेवं साधयेत्क्रमात् ॥२१५॥

तत्र **चोदना** साक्षिप्रयुक्ते प्रयोजने साक्षिणां ऋणिकस्य च[341] **प्रतिकालं** संस्मरणम । **युक्तिलेशः** पूर्वदत्तस्य द्रव्यस्य पूर्वसंप्रतिपत्तिर्यस्य वा युत्युद्देशः । तृतीयः **शपथः** । दत्तशुद्धकृतनाशतण्डुलकोशादिकैरुपायैरेनमर्थापह्नविनं **साधयेद्** इति ।

अभीक्ष्णं चोद्यमानो यः प्रतिहन्यान्न तद्वचः ।
त्रिचतुःपञ्चकृत्वो वा परतोऽर्थं तमावहेत् ॥२१६॥

२१३ a — BM अप्यधिकं; B अव्यधिकं; P वाप्यधिकं; P L2 D NMS वार्थं; V6 स्वार्थं; c — B2 B4 B3 D अयुक्तं; d — B3 B4 साक्षीविधिः; X B2 add
यस्य दृश्यते सप्ताहादुक्तवाक्यस्य (B4 -वाक्यश्च; K2 B2 -वाक्य-) साक्षिणः ।
रोगोऽग्निर्ज्ञातिमरणं सा वै तस्य विभावना ॥ [cf. Manu 8.108 and Dhko 323]

२१४ c — P D NMS चापह्नुते.

२१५ a — X प्रतिघातश्; c — NMS P प्रोक्तस्; d — D Jolly एनं; P इमं; NMS ऋणं; Y चोदयेत्; NMS शोधयेत्.

अभीक्ष्णं वचनं बहुशः पृच्छ्यमानोऽप्यृणी यदा तदीयं वचः कथमपि न प्रतिपद्यते[342] तदा चोदनायाः **परत** अन्यमुपाचरेत् । युक्तिलेशादिकं तथा च वक्ष्यति ।

चोदनाप्रतिघाते तु युक्तिलेशैस्तमन्वियात् ।
देशकालार्थसंबन्धपरिमाणक्रियादिभिः ॥२१७॥

अत्र **चोदनाप्रतिघाते** सामान्यवचनपृच्छाया असंप्रतिपत्तौ **युक्तिलेशैस्**तथान्वियात् । अथ कैस्तैर् **देशकालार्थसंबन्धपरिमाणक्रियाभिर्** यथाक्रमं स्वयं स्मृतैस्तस्य स्मारितैरिति ।

युक्तिष्वप्यसमर्थासु शपथैरेनमर्दयेत् ।
अर्थकालबलापेक्षं अग्न्यम्बुसुकृतादिभिः ॥२१८॥

यदा युक्तिभिरभियुक्ताभिर्न संप्रतिपत्तिमागच्छतीति ऋणी तदा तम**ग्न्यम्बुसुकृतादिभिः शपथैर्दयेत्**पीडयेदिति । एतच्च **देशकालबलापेक्षं*** कुर्यात् । यादृशं देशकालयोर्बलं विभाव्यते तद्बलापेक्षं[343] साधनं कार्यमिति ।

सत्यादित्यभियुक्तस्य शपथो न यथा मया ।
ग्राहीतो ग्राहीतो वापि न च जातेन कस्यचित् ।। [Dhko 440]
यदहं पापकारीति शङ्कादोषवंशं गतः ।
तद्यथा सर्वमथ तं स याम्येष तथाधुना ।। [Dhko 440]
सत्येन येन मां देवा मे मातापितरस्तथा ।
रक्षन्तु शपथादस्मात्तन्वौदीन्यम्(?)अन्यथा ।। [Dhko 440]

अनेन श्लोकत्रयेणापि शपथकरणमार्गोऽसौ दर्शितः । स च सामान्यप्रयोजनशङ्कः । स महानियोगेषु पुनः ।

दीप्ताग्निर्यं न दहति यमन्तर्धारयन्त्यापः ।
स तरत्यभिशापं तं किल्बिषी स्याद्विपर्यये ॥२१९॥

२१६ b — B BM B5 NMS ऽपि; c — D P त्रिश्चतुः-; NMS त्रिश्चतुप्-; B2 B5 -कृतो; d — Y समारभेत्; P NMS समाचरेत्; D स दापयेत्.

२१७ b — P तथान्वियात्; B2 B5 समान्वियात्; X समन्वीयात्; B तमन्ययात्.

२१८ c — P B4 NMS देशकाल-

२१९ b — Y B4 K2 K5 अपि; B2 B3 अपः; ab — D दीप्तोऽयं न दहत्यग्निरापो नो मज्जयन्ति च; P यमन्तर्धारयन्त्यापो दीप्तोऽग्निर्न दहेच्च माम्; M4 यमं तद्धारयन्त्यापो दीप्तोऽम्निर्न दहेच्च यम्; Jolly यमन्तर्धारयन्त्यापो दिप्तो ऽग्निर्न दहत्येव; NMS दीप्तो यं न दहत्यग्निरापोऽन्तर्धारयन्ति यम्; D add न चार्तिमिच्छति क्षिप्रं स ज्ञेयः शपथे शुचिः ।। [Manu 8.115cd]; c — P शापयत्य्; Jolly typo शाययत्य्;

यं[344] पुरुषं उदकदिव्यविधिनिक्षिप्तम**ाप** **अन्तर्धारयन्ति** मग्नमेव धारयन्ति पञ्चदिव्याधिश्रावणाय । हस्तगृहीतो **दीप्तोऽग्निर्*** न दहेत् । शमयत्यभिशापं[345] तमन्यथा **किल्बिषी** पापी भवति ।

स्त्रीणां शीलाभियोगेषु स्तेयसाहसयोरपि ।
एष एव विधिर्दृष्टः सर्वार्थापह्नवेषु च ॥२२०॥

यदा **स्त्रीणां शील**चारित्रखण्डनाभियोगो[346] भवति । तथास्**तेयसाहसा**भियोगो भवति । तथा ये केचिदर्थास्तेषाम**पह्नवेषु** मिथ्यासु । एवंविधेषु महाभियोगेषु **एष** महा दिव्य**विधिर्दृष्टः** शपथादिरिति ।

शपथा ह्यपि देवानामृषीणामपि च स्मृताः ।
वसिष्ठः शपथं शेपे यातुधाने तु शङ्कितः ॥२२१॥

अत्र **शपथा** अपि न सामान्या भवन्ति । सत्यश्रावणाय तेऽप्यमोघा एव भवन्तीत्यृषिदेवाचीर्णमार्गदर्शनं माहात्म्यार्थमभिहितम् । तथा हि **यातुधानेन*** रक्षसाभिशङ्कितो महर्षि**र्वसिष्ठः शपथं** कृत्वा विशुद्ध इति ।

सप्तर्षयस्तथेन्द्राय पुष्करार्थे समागताः ।
शेपुः शपथमव्यग्राः परस्परविशुद्धये ॥२२२॥

महदिदं पुराणोपाख्यानं । किं तेन । अत्रायं समुदायार्थः । यद्येवं महर्षीणामपीदृशानि शङ्काप्रयोजनानि शपथप्रत्ययशुद्धिप्रयोजनानि वृत्तपूर्वाणि किं पुनर्मनुष्याणामिति ।

अयुक्तं साहसं कृत्वा प्रत्यापत्तिं भजेत यः ।
ब्रूयात्स्वयं वा सदसि तस्यार्धविनयः स्मृतः ॥२२३॥

D अभिशापान्तं; d — P अतोऽन्यथा; D add
अरण्ये निर्जने रात्रावन्तर्वेश्मनि साहसे ।
न्यासस्यापह्नवे चैव दिव्या संभवति क्रिया ।। [J 1.241]

२२० a — NMS शीलाभियोगे च; c — D प्रोक्तः; d — X सर्वथाप-; NMS यः; D add
उपरिष्टात्तु वक्ष्यामि दव्यिानां तु यथाविधि ।
चतुर्णां तु विशेपेण मनुना परिकीर्तितम् ।। [Dhko 449]

२२१ a — NMS ऋपि-; b — D च यथा; NMS पुरा सृष्टाः स्वयम्भुवा; d — D NMS यातुधानेति; B2 यातुधानेपु; P यातुधानेन; D कीर्तिताः; NMS शब्दितः.

२२२ a — P तथेन्द्रेण; NMS तथा सेन्द्राः; b — D NMS तपोधनाः; P पुष्करार्थेन शङ्किताः.

अत्रा**युक्तं**[347] वियुक्तं विरुद्धं किमपि कस्यापि **कृत्वा**थवा चौर्यादिकं **साहसम्** अपि कस्यापि कृत्वा तेनावेदितः सन्धर्माधिकरणस्याग्रे यः **प्रत्यापत्तिं** करोति मिथ्या न करोति तस्याधममध्यमोत्तमानुसरेण यः शास्त्रे विहितो दण्डस्तस्य विनयस्यार्धमेव विनयोऽस्य भवतीति । अनावेदितोऽपि यः **स्वयम्** एव प्रतिपत्तिं करोति तस्यायमेव क्रम इति ।

गूहमानस्तु दौरात्म्याद्यदि पापं स जीयते ।
सभ्याश्चात्र न तुष्यन्ति तीव्रो दण्डश्च पात्यते ॥२२४॥

यदि पुनरयुक्तसाहसादिकं कृत्वा करणावेदितोऽपि मिथ्यां करोति पश्चात्स दिव्यादिक्रियाभिः पराजीयते च तदा[348] तस्य सभ्याः कुपितो भवन्ति **तीव्रो दण्डश्च** तस्य द्विगुणादिक इति । इति ऋणादाने लेख्यसाक्ष्यभावविधिभेदः ।

२२३ D om this verse; b — X भजेत्तु; c — P B सदिति; d — B तस्यार्थम् विनयः.

२२४ D om this verse; a — B2 गूह्यमानस्य; b — P Y पापः; B5 जीर्यते; NMS हीयते; c — Y तस्य; NMS चास्य; NMS दुष्यन्ति; d — NMS पार्थिवात्; X add ऋणादनं विंशतिप्रभेदः । यत्र ऋणगतिः स्वतन्त्रास्वतन्त्रकरणं धनविकल्पः । धनागमो वृत्तिनियमः । प्रमाणकरणदानग्रहनविधिः प्रतिभूकरणमाधिविधिः साक्षिप्रश्नश्चेति दशप्रभेदाः; NMS add इति ऋणाडानं प्रथमं विवादपदम्.

व्यवहारपदानि

२ निक्षेपः

स्वद्रव्यं यत्र विश्रम्भान्निक्षिपत्यविशङ्कितः ।
निक्षेपो नाम तत्प्रोक्तं व्यवहारपदं बुधैः ॥१॥

अथ उपनिधिः षड्भेदो भवति । **स्वम्*** इति स्वकीयं द्रव्यं यो **निक्षिपति** तस्य निक्षेपः संबध्यते । [?-->] यः पुनः परकीयं परादेशात्परनाम्ना च समर्पयत्यपरादेशकारित्वात्तस्य[349] निक्षेपस्य स्वयमर्पितस्यापि प्रतियाचमानं निराकरोति[350] । [<--?] **स्वं* द्रव्यम्** इति । अस्य पदस्यायमर्थः । तदिह स्वं द्रव्यं यो **निक्षिपति** यच्च पति**विश्रम्भादविशङ्कितो** निक्षिपति । अनेनोक्तेन तदुक्तं भवति । किल यत्राविश्वासाच्छङ्का भवति तत्र साक्षिलिखितग्रहणविरहितं कोऽपि वराटकमपि न ददाति । यत्र पुनर्विश्वासान्निःशङ्कः पुरुषो भवति तत्र साक्षिलिखितग्रहणवर्जितमेव सुवर्णसहस्रादिकमपि निक्षिपति । यत्र चायमीदृशो विश्वासनिःशङ्कः पुरुषो भवति परं प्रव्रजते तत्रैव निक्षेपो नाम तत्प्रोक्तं **व्यवहारपदं बुधैर्** इति निक्षेपलक्षणमभिहितमिति ।

कुलजे वृत्तसंपन्ने धर्मज्ञे सत्यवादिनि ।
महापक्षे च धनिनि[351] निक्षेपं निक्षिपेद्बुधः ॥ [Manu 8.179, J 2.2]

एभिः सप्तभिर[?]पि गुणैः संपन्ने पुरुषे निक्षेपं निक्षिपेद्बुधः ।
स कालान्तरेष्वपि विप्रतिपत्तिं न गच्छतीति ।

यो यथा...[352]

यः पुरुषो यस्य हस्ते यमर्थं येन प्रकारेण निक्षिपेत्तेनैव पुरुषेण तस्यैव हस्तात्स एवार्थः तेनैव प्रकारेण ग्रहीतव्यः । यथा दायस्तथा ग्रह इति वचनात् ।

न चेद्दद्यात्तु निक्षेप्तुस्तद् द्रव्यं तु यथाविधि ।
उपसंगृह्य दाप्योऽसौ दिव्यादिभिर्व्यवस्थितः ॥ [J 2.2]

अथ निक्षेपग्राही लोभं गच्छति निक्षेप्तुस्तद् द्रव्यं न प्रयच्छिति तदावेदितो राज्ञोपसंगृह्य दिव्यादिप्रमाणसाधितो द्विगुणदण्डाकोटितः कृतः[353] दाप्यः ।

१ a -- D P स्वं द्रव्यं; NMS विस्रम्भान्.

अन्यद्रव्यव्यवहितं द्रव्यमव्याकृतं च यत् ।
निक्षिप्यते परगृहे तदौपनिधिकं स्मृतम् ॥२॥

निक्षेपलक्षणमभिहितम् । इदानीमौपनिधिकलक्षणमुच्यते । **अन्यद्रव्यव्यवहितम्** इति मञ्जिष्ठापोटलमध्ये विंशतिगद्याणका ग्रन्थिबद्धाः । अथवा ग्रन्थिमुद्रितं[354] यथा वस्त्रमध्ये मौक्तिकहारः। तद्बाभ्यन्तरसारद्रव्यं तदवस्थं तस्यापि न कथितम्। तथा हस्ते निक्षिप्तमेवं स्थितं द्रव्यं यन्निक्षिप्यते **तदौपनिधिकम्** इत्युच्यते । तदपि यथास्थितं[355] ग्रन्थिमुद्रितमेव प्रदेयम् । ग्रन्थिभेदे ग्रहीतुर्दोषो भवतीति ।

स पुनर्द्विविधः प्रोक्तः साक्षिमानितरस्तथा ।
प्रतिदानं तथैवास्य प्रत्ययः स्याद्विपर्यये ॥३॥

यो निक्षेपः साक्षिप्रत्यक्षो मुक्तः । असावश्यं साक्षिप्रत्यक्षमेव समर्पणीयः । यः पुनरसाक्षिमान्स विनैव साक्षिभिरर्पणीयः । इत्यस्य **द्विविधो**[356] निर्गमः । अथ विपर्ययो निक्षेपस्योपनिधेर्वा हानिर्मिथ्या भवति । तदानीं तदनुसारेण **प्रत्ययो** दिव्यशपथादिको भवतीति ।

याच्यमानस्तु यो दात्रा निक्षेपं न प्रयच्छति ।
दण्ड्यः स राज्ञा दाप्यश्च नष्टे दाप्यश्च तत्समम् ॥४॥

प्रकटार्थ एव श्लोकः । विशेषोऽयं याचितेऽनर्पिते राजदैविकं ग्रहीतुर्न निक्षेप्तुरिति ।

यश्चार्थं साधयेत्तेन निक्षेप्तुरननुज्ञया ।
तत्रापि दण्ड्यः स भवेत्तच्च सोदयमावहेत् ॥५॥

यदि ग्राहको निक्षेपद्रव्येण तेन कंचित्स्वार्थं स्वेच्छया साधयति । **निक्षेप्तुरननुज्ञया**संमतेन[357]---[358]तदा **दण्ड्यः स भवेत्** । तं च साधितमर्थं **सोदयं** सोपाश्रयं दाप्य इति ।

२ b — P अव्यवहृतं; d — P L2 रतं; M4 मृतं; N add
असंख्यातमविज्ञातं समुद्रं यन्निधीयते ।
तं जानीयादुपनिधिं निक्षेपं गणितं विदुः ॥ [Dhko 747]
४ c — P दुष्टात्मा.
५ a — P म्तं (?); L2 त्वं; M4 यं; d — P दाप्यस्तच्चापि सोदयम्.

ग्रहीतुः सह योऽर्थेन नष्टो नष्टः स दायिनः ।
दैवराजकृते तद्वन्न चेत्तज्जिह्मकारितम् ॥६॥

यस्तु निक्षेपो युक्तश्चलो वा ग्रहीतुः सक्तधनेन तादृशेनैवसह नष्टः स निक्षेपदायिनो नष्टः । राजदैविकमपि तथैव योज्यम् । किन्तु **तज्जिह्मकारितम्** इति । तेनैव यदि कृतप्रपञ्चरक्षितं[359] न भवति । जिह्मकारिते निश्चितज्ञाने शिरोपस्थानेन सह साधनमर्थस्येति ।

स्वयमेव तु यो दद्यान्मृतस्य प्रत्यनन्तरे ।
न स राज्ञाभियोक्तव्यो न निक्षेप्तुश्च बन्धुभिः ॥ [Manu 8.186, J 2.10]

निक्षेपदातुर्मृतस्य यः प्रत्यनन्तरस्तदीयद्रव्याधिकारी[360] तस्य स्वयमेव गत्वा ग्राहकोऽयाचित एवाज्ञातो[361] वा साधुत्वान्यासं समर्पयति । स तेन साधनेन तदीयबन्धुभिः शेषोपनिधिस्तस्योपरि जल्पयिवा नाभियोक्तव्यो न राज्ञेति ।

अच्छलेनैव चान्विच्छेत्तमर्थं प्रीतिपूर्वकम् ।
विचार्य तस्य वा वृत्तं साम्नैव परिशोधयेत् ॥ [Manu 8.187, J 2.11]

तत्र निश्चितार्थप्रमाणपरिच्छेदपरिज्ञातमेवापह्नुत एवं शिरोपस्थानं दृष्टं नोपालब्ध-मेतदर्थमच्छलमेवापच्यस्य(?)प्रीतिपूर्वकगेव साम्नैव शेषशङ्कामपि विशोधयेदिति ।

चौरैर्हृतं जले मग्नमग्निना दग्धमेव च ।
न दद्याद्यदि तस्मात्स न संहरति किंचन ॥ [Manu 8.189, J 2.12]

यदि तस्मात्पुनर्निक्षेपात्किंचिद् गृहीत्वा कोऽपि नियोगः कृतः सप्रत्ययः स भाव्यते । तदा भाविनि चौरजलाग्न्युपद्रवे तद्दद्यादसाविति ।

यो निक्षेपं नार्पयति यश्चानिक्षिप्य याचते ।
तावुभौ चौरवच्छास्यौ दण्डं दाप्यौ च तत्समम् ॥ [Manu 8.191, J 2.13]

यो निक्षिप्तं द्रव्यं मिथ्याशया शाठ्याद्वा कालहरणादिना नार्पयति स चौरः । यश्चानिक्षिप्तमेव निक्षिप्तमुक्त्वा प्रार्थयति दिव्यावसन्नो भवति स राज्ञा चौरवच्छास्यः । द्रव्यसमं च दण्डं दाप्य इति ।

६ b — P L2 प्रयिनः; d — D N add

अनेकार्थाभियुक्तेन सर्वार्थव्यपलापिना ।
विभावितैकदेशेन देयं यदभियुज्यते ॥ [Dhko 542]

X add

निक्षेपस्यापहर्तारं तत्समं दापयेद्दमं ।
तथोपनिधिहर्तारमविशेषेण दापयेत् ॥ [cf. Manu 8.192]
यः कृतो येन यत्रैव यावांश्च कुलसंनिधौ ।
तावानेव स विज्ञेयो विब्रुवन्दण्डमर्हति ॥ [cf. Manu 8.194]
उपधाभिश्च यः कश्चित्परद्रव्यं हरेन्नरः ।
ससहायः स हन्तव्यः प्रक्षाशं विविदैर्वधैः ॥ [cf. Manu 8.193]

एष एव विधिर्दृष्टो याचितान्वाहितादिषु ।
शिल्पिषूपनिधौ न्यासे प्रतिन्यासे तथैव च ॥७॥

अत्र योऽयं **विधिर्न्या**सोपनिधिव्यवहारपदकयोरपि सविस्तरोऽभिहितः । **एष एव** याचितान्वाहितशिल्पोपनिधिरिति । अत्र **याचितं** कार्यार्थं प्रार्थित्वा यदानीतमिति । अन्वाहितं पौलवृषभमन्वाहितसारं कार्यमात्रं सारकं समर्प्य सारभूतो गुरुभरकरणार्थं च धुर्यकवृषभो यः[362] समानीतो भवति स[363] एतदीयद्रव्यम**न्वाहितमु**च्यते । अनु आहितमन्वाहितमिति । शिल्पे **शिल्पि**हस्तसंस्करणमुक्तो **न्यासोपनिधी** व्याचक्षते[364] [?] । **प्रतिन्यासस्**तु कस्यापि हस्ते निक्षिप्तं द्रव्यं सोऽपि कार्यकालापेक्षया यदन्यस्य हस्ते निक्षिपति स प्रतिन्यासः । एतेषु सर्वेष्वयमेव विधिरिति ।

प्रतिगृह्णाति पोगण्डं यश्च सप्रधनं नरः ।
तस्याप्येष भवेद्धर्मः षडेते विधयः समाः ॥८॥

योऽनाथं[365] बालं सप्रधनं नाथाबुद्ध्या प्रतिगृह्णाति तदीयधनस्याप्ययमेव विधिर्द्रष्टव्यः । **सडेते विधयः समा** इति । याचितविधिरन्वाहितविधिः[366] शिल्पहस्तविधिर्न्यासविधिः प्रतिन्यासविधिः[367] पौगण्डविधिश्चेति । **षडेते विध्यस्**तुल्या द्रष्टव्याः ।

इति नारदीयकल्याणभाष्ये षड्व्यवहारपदे भेदसहितमुपनिधिर्नाम द्वितीयं व्यवहारपदं समाप्तम् ।

७ c — P L2 शिल्पां चापनिधौ न्यासो.

८ d — D N add इति श्रीनारदीये धर्मशास्त्रे निक्षेपांपनिधिनामद्वितीयविवादपदं समाप्तम्. NMS add औपनिधिकं द्वितीयं विवादपदं.

व्यवहारपदानि

३ संभूयसमुत्थानम्

वणिक्प्रभृतयो यत्र कर्म संभूय कुर्वते ।
तत्संभूयसमुत्थानं व्यवहारपदं स्मृतम् ॥१॥

संभूय एकत्र मिलित्वा संव्यवहारं प्रति यत्तदुत्थानं नाम व्यवहारपदमुच्यते।

फलहेतोरुपायेन कर्म संभूय कुर्वताम् ।
आधारभूतः प्रक्षेपस्तेनोत्तिष्ठेयुरंशतः ॥२॥

यद्वणिग्भिर्मिलित्वा[108] द्रम्मसहस्रपिण्डेन वाणिज्यं प्रारब्धम्। तत्रैकेनार्धे पञ्च शतानि निक्षिप्तानि। अन्येन पञ्चमांशे शतद्वयम्। अन्येनापि शतद्वयमेव। अपरेण दशमांशे शतमेकम्। एतेषां स्वांशप्रक्षेपो लाभव्यययोराधारभूतः।

समोऽतिरिक्तो हीनो वा यत्रांशो यस्य यादृशः ।
क्षयव्ययौ तथा वृद्धिस्तस्य तत्र तथाविधाः ॥३॥

तत्रायव्ययौ स्वकीयस्वकीयांशावतारेण संबध्येते।

भाण्डपिण्डव्ययोद्धारभारसारान्ववेक्षणम् ।
कुर्युस्तेऽव्यभिचारेण समये स्वे व्यवस्थिताः ॥४॥

यः प्रथमारम्भे समयः कृतस्तत्र**ाव्यभिचारेण**ाविलोपनेन भाण्डपिण्डव्ययोद्धार् सारान्ववेक्षणानि स्वांशानुसारेण कर्तव्यानीति।

१ d — Y विदुः.
२ K2 om all but the last word of this verse.
३ b — P तत्रांशो; c — P क्षेपययौ.
४ c — NMS व्यवहारेण; d — Y समयेन.

प्रमादान्नाशितं दाप्यः प्रतिषिद्धकृतं च यत् ।
असंदिष्टश्च यत्कुर्यात्सर्वैः संभूयकारिभिः ॥५॥

एतैश्च सर्वैरपि सामुदायिकैः समर्पितं **प्रमादाद्** यो नाशयति स तन्**नाशितं दाप्यः** प्रतिषिद्धं चासंमतकृतं च यत्किमपिहानिकारि भवति तदपि दाप्य एवेति।

दैवतस्कर राजोत्थे व्यसने समुपस्थिते ।
यस्तत्स्वशक्त्या संरक्षेत्तस्यांशो दशमः स्मृतः ॥६॥

दैवात्प्रदीपने दह्यमानं यः कश्चिदेक एव[369] रक्षति। तथा **तस्कर**वृन्दात्। तथोन्मार्गीभूतग्रहणोद्यतराज्ञः पार्श्वाद्यः स्वकीयेन प्राणव्यायामेन तत्सामान्यभाण्डं रक्षति तस्य दशमांशः क्लेशफले भवति।

एकस्य चेत्स्याद्व्यसनं दायादोऽस्यतदाप्नुयात् ।
अन्यो वासति दायादे शक्ताश्चेत्सर्व एव वा ॥७॥

तेषां संभूयकारिणो मध्ये यद्य**ेकस्य** कस्यापि मृत्युः स्यात्तदा तदीयांशं पुत्रादि**दायादा** अधिकारिणस्त आप्नुयुः। **असति दायादे** तेषां एकतमो वा यस्तन्निर्हर्तुं शक्तः। अथवा यदि शक्तास्तदा तदीयांशं **सर्व एव** ते गृह्णीयुरिति। इति संभूयसमुत्थाने सामवायिकभेदः प्रथमः।

ऋत्विजां व्यसनेऽप्येवमन्यस्तत्कर्म निस्तरेत् ।
लभेत दक्षिणाभागं स तस्मात्संप्रकल्पितम् ॥८॥

ऋत्विजां अपि एकयज्ञे संश्रये प्रचरतां यद्येकस्य कस्यापि व्यसनं भवति तदा तदीयकर्मधुरम**न्यः** कश्चिन्निर्वाहयेत्। **दक्षिणाभागम**पि तत्प्रकल्पितं निर्वाहक एव लभेत्।

ऋत्विग्याज्यमदुष्टं यस्त्यजेदनपकारिणम् ।
अदुष्टं वर्त्विजं याज्यो विनेयौ तावुभावपि ॥९॥

६ a — P दैवतस्कररराजन्य; D Jolly दैवतस्कररराजभ्यो; c — P रक्षेत.

७ a — NMS तद्.

८ c — B5 K2 K3 तद्दक्षिणा-.

९ c — NMS अदुष्टमृत्विजं.

अदुष्टमप्यनपकारिणमपि **याज्यं** यद्यृत्विक्कर्मारूढोऽपि क्रोधलोभादिनावान्तर एव त्यजति। अथवा एवम**ृत्विजं याज्य** एव त्यजति। ततः प्राप्तव्यवहारयोर्द्वयोरपि तयोर्दोषवान्स एव राज्ञा विनयं ग्राह्यः।

ऋत्विक्तु त्रिविधो दृष्टः पूर्वजुष्टः स्वयंकृतः ।
यदृच्छया च यः कुर्यादार्त्विज्यं प्रीतिपूर्वकम् ॥१०॥

एतच्च त्रिविधत्वमेतदर्थं दर्शितं यत्**क्रमागतेश्व्** इति।

क्रमागतेष्वेष धर्मो वृतेष्वृत्विक्षु च स्वयम् ।
यादृच्छिके तु संयाज्ये तत्त्यागे नास्ति किल्बिषम् ॥११॥

य ऋत्विजः पूर्वसेविताः क्रमागताः। तथा ये **स्वयं** वृता भवन्ति तेषां **त्यागे**ऽयं युक्तपरित्यागविनयविचारो दृष्टः। यस्तु न **पूर्वजुष्टो** न च स्वयंवृतो **यदृच्छया**गतः **प्रीतिपूर्वकमार्त्विज्यं** करोति तस्य तत्कुर्वत एवान्यः कश्चिद् गुणातिरिक्तः स्नेहातिरिक्तो वा समागतो भवति। तदा तं यदृच्छयागतं पतित्यजतस्तं स्नेहातिरिक्तं तदीयकर्माधिकारयतो दक्षिणाभागं च तस्य प्रयच्छतो याज्यस्य छद्मावकाशो नास्तीति। इति संभूयसमुत्थान ऋत्विग्याज्यव्यवहारभेदो द्वितीयः।

शुल्कस्थानं वणिक्प्राप्तः शुल्कं दद्याद्यथोपगम् ।
न तद् व्यतिहरेद्राज्ञां बलिरेष प्रकल्पितः ॥१२॥

अथ शौल्किकभेदो भवति **शुल्कस्थानम्** इति। यच्छुल्**कं** नाम एष राज्ञो **बलिः** प्रवर्तितभागः तं व्यतिक्रम्य **वणिङ्** न **व्यतिहरेत्**।

शुल्कस्थानं पतिहरन्न काले क्रयविक्रयी ।
मिथ्योक्त्वा च परीमाणं दाप्योऽष्टगुणमत्ययम् ॥१३॥

अत्राष्टगुणशुल्कविनयस्य स्थानत्रयमुद्दिष्टम्। एकं **शुल्कस्थानं** परिहृत्यादत्तशुल्कस्यैव वणिजो गच्छतः। द्वितीयमदत्तशुल्कभाण्डस्याकाले क्रयविक्रये कुर्वतः।

१० a — NMS प्रोक्तः; b — Y पूर्वदृष्टः; NMS पूर्वैर्जुष्टः; NMS स्वयंवृतः.
११ c — P यदृच्छिकेषु; Jolly यादृच्छिकेषु; P याज्यस्य.
१२ b — Jolly यथोदितम्; c — P D राज्ञो; d — P D प्रकीर्तितः.

तृतीयं भाण्ड**परिमाणं मिथ्या** जनस्य कथयतः। एतेष्वपराधेषु पतितो वणिक्शुल्का**ष्टगुणमत्ययं** दण्डं दद्यादिति।

सदा श्रोत्रियवर्ज्याणि शुल्कान्याहुः प्रजानता ।
गृहोपयोगि यच्चैषां न तु वाणिज्यकर्मणि ।। [J 3.14]

अत्र श्रोत्रियशब्देन ब्राह्मणः परिगृहीतः। ब्राह्मणस्य यत्किमपि गृहोपयोगि द्रव्यं भवति तद्वर्जं राज्ञां शुल्कं। अथ सोऽपि वाणिज्यं कुर्वन्किंचिन्नयत्यानयति वा ततः शुल्कं ददाति।

प्रतिग्रहो द्विजातीनां धनं रङ्गोपजीविनाम् ।
स्कन्धवाह्यं च यद् द्रव्यं न तद्युक्तं प्रदापयेत् ।। [J 3.15]

ब्राह्मणस्य प्रभूतमपि यत्प्रतिग्रहधनं तथा रङ्गोपजीविनामपि नटगायनादीनाम्। तथा च सर्वजनसामान्यमपि स्कन्धवाह्यं यत्किमपि वाहनरूढमेतत्त्रिविधमपि द्रव्यं राजा शुल्कं न दापयेत्।

कश्चिच्चेत्संचरन्देशात्प्रेयादभ्यागतो वणिक् ।
राजास्य भाण्डं तद्रक्षेत्यावद्दायाददर्शनम् ॥१४॥
दायादेऽसति बन्धुभ्यो ज्ञातिभ्यो वा तदर्पयेत् ।
तदभावे सुगुप्तं तद्धारयेद्दशतीः समाः ॥१५॥
अस्वामिकमदायादं दशवर्षस्थितं ततः ।
राजा तदात्मसात्कुर्यादेवं धर्मो न हीयते ॥१६॥

इति संभूयसमुत्थाने शौल्किकभेदस्तृतीयः। समाप्तं चैतत्संभूयसमुत्थानं नाम तृतीयव्यवहारपदम्।

१४ a — Jolly देशान्; b — Jolly आभ्यागतां.

१५ b — P NMS समर्पयेत्.

१६ b — NMS दशवर्षोपितं; d — P च; NMS add इति सम्भूयसमुत्थानं तृतीयं विवादपदम्; N add इति सम्भूयसमुत्थानं विवादपदं समाप्तम्; D add इति श्रीनारदीये धर्मशास्त्रे संभूयसमुत्थानं तृतीयविवादपदम्।

व्यवहारपदानि

४ दत्ताप्रदानिकम्

इदानीं चतुर्भेदं दत्तस्यादानं नाम चतुर्थं व्यवहारपदं भविष्यति ।

दत्त्वा द्रव्यमसम्यग्यः पुनरादातुमिच्छति ।
दत्ताप्रदानिकं नाम तद्विवादपदं स्मृतम् ॥१॥

सुबोधाधिकारः श्लोकोऽयम ।

अदेयमथ देयं च दत्तं चादत्तमेव च ।
व्यवहारेष विज्ञेयो दानमार्गश्चतुर्विधः ॥२॥

देयं ज्ञेयं दानपिषय **अदेयं** च **दत्तं** ज्ञेयं कीदुशम**दत्तं** चेत्ययं **दानमार्गश्चतुर्विधो**ऽपि व्यवहारे **विज्ञेयः**

तत्र ह्यष्टावदेयानि देयमेकविधं स्मृतम् ।
दत्तं सप्तविधं विद्याददत्तं षोडशात्मकम् ॥३॥

तत्रांष्टप्रकारम**देयम** । **देयमे**कप्रकरमेव । सप्तप्रकारं **दत्तम्** । अदत्तं षोडश-प्रकारम् । एतानि प्रतिपदमुच्यन्ते ।

अन्वाहितं याचितकमाधिः साधारणं च यत् ।
निक्षेपः पुत्रदारं च सर्वस्वं चान्वये सति ॥४॥

अत्र परस्य सामान्यकार्यकरणमात्रं किंचिद्वस्तु समर्प्यातिसविशेषकार्य-करणक्षमवस्तु ततः समानीयते । अनु पश्चात् । **अन्वाहितमे**तदादौ कृत्वा । अन्यत्सुबोधं सर्वम् । एतान्यष्टावदेयानि दत्तान्यपि चलन्ति ।

१ a — D दानम्; d — Y व्यवहारपदं.

३ a — P D तत्रेहप्टाव्.

आपत्स्वपि हि कष्टासु वर्तमानेन देहिना ।
अदेयान्याहुराचार्या यच्चान्यस्मै प्रतिश्रुतम् ॥५॥

एतेषाम् <...> अमिति ।

कुटुम्बभरणाद् द्रव्यं यत्किंचिदतिरिच्यते ।
तद्देयमुपहृत्यान्यद्ददद्दोषमवाप्नुयात् ॥६॥

कुटुम्बे कुटुम्बिनावश्यमेव भरणीयं तस्माद् व्ययाद्य**त्किंचिदतिरिच्यते** तदेव दातव्यम्[370] । एकविधमेव दृष्टम् । यत्पुनर्दीयमानं कुटुम्बपीडाकारि त**द्ददद्दोषम् आप्नुयान्** न पुण्यमिति ।

यस्य त्रैवार्षिकं वित्तं पर्याप्तं भृत्यवृत्तये ।
अधिकं वापि विद्येत स सोमं पातुमर्हति ।। [J 4.7]

एतत्कुटुम्वं च भरणावित्तप्रमाणमुक्तम् । अतो यस्याधिकमस्ति स सोमपानं यज्ञत्वं स्वयं कर्तुमर्हति विप्र इति ।

पण्यमूल्यं भृतिस्तुष्ट्या स्नेहात्प्रत्युपकारतः ।
स्त्रीशुल्कानुग्रहार्थं च दत्तं दानविदो विदुः ॥७॥

एतेषु सप्तस्वप्यविरुद्धस्थानेषु यद्दत्तं तदेव **दत्तमि**त्युच्यते । शेषं पुनः षोडशविधमदत्तं विज्ञेयम्[371]।

अदत्तं तु भयक्रोधशोकवेगरुजान्वितैः ।
तथोक्तोचपरीहासव्यत्यासच्छलयोगतः ॥८॥
बालमूढास्वतन्त्रार्तमत्तोन्मत्तापवर्जितम् ।
कर्ता ममायं कर्मेति प्रतिलाभेच्छया च यत् ॥९॥
अपात्रे पात्रमित्युक्ते कार्ये चाधर्मसंहिते ।
यद्दत्तं स्यादविज्ञानाददत्तं तदपि स्मृतम् ॥१०॥

५ a — B5 K2 अप्टासु.
६ d — P तद्देयं सुहृदन्यस्माद् कुटुम्वी आप्नुयात्; D देयमविहिंस्यान्यान्यथान्याय समाप्नुयात्.
७ b — NMS प्रतुपकारितः; c — Jolly स्त्रीभुत्त्यनु-; d — P सप्तविधं स्मृतम्.
८ b — D -शांकावेग-; Jolly D रुगन्वितैः; d — Jolly -परिहास-.
९ b — D -स्वतन्त्रान्ध-; P -स्वतन्त्रत्व-.
१० bcd — P om; D -संज्ञिते.

दुष्टेन साधुरटव्यां प्राप्तोऽभिहितः । द्रम्माणां शतं ददासि ततो जीवस्यन्यथा म्रियसे । सोऽपि भयाद्ददाति । दास्यामीत्येवं **भय**प्रतिश्रुतमदत्तमिति विज्ञेयम् । एतदेकम् । तथा गृहस्थो दूरदेशागतः सहसैव पत्न्यासने प्रतिपादिते क्रोधाद् गृहोपरि द्वेषे च समुत्पन्ने वदति । ब्राह्मण यन्मदीयगृहे किंचिदासनशयनीयादिकं च पश्यसि तत्सर्वं मया तव दत्तम् । इत्युक्तेऽपि **क्रोधद्वे**षदत्तमदत्तमिति विज्ञेयम् । एतद् द्वितीयम् । अत्यन्तेष्टमरणाच्**छोका**र्तो वदति । अहं वनं यास्याम्यद्यैव स्वगृहं तु मया ब्राह्मणेभ्यो दत्तमिति । एतत्तृतीयं ज्ञेयं । तथा **रुजान्वितः** संनिपातितो वदति । ब्राह्मण मया तव सुवर्णशतं दत्तम् । एतद्रुजान्वितदत्तमदत्तं चतुर्थम् । तथा व्यवहारको यः सभ्यं वदति । यदि मम जयं ददासि[10] ततोऽहं तव लञ्चया शतं दास्यामीत्येतदु**त्कोच**प्रतिश्रुतं दत्तमप्यदत्तं पञ्चमम् । तथा हास्येन यद्दत्तं तत्**परिहास**दत्तमप्यदत्तं षष्टम् । तथा यस्य कामुकस्य चूतमञ्जरी नाम वेश्या प्राणप्रियतरा । [?-->] कूदियतरा कुदिन्याग्रतः कटुप्त्वात् ृ [<--?] त्रिंशद्योजनस्तिथठक्कुरस्य समर्पिता । तं च विरहाग्निदीप्तं [?] ददासि । स च वदति । अवश्यं प्रयच्छामि । अयं च तव प्रतिभूरिति लब्धसुष्ठके प्रच्छन्ना प्रकटीकृत्य चूतवृक्षसक्ता मञ्जरी दर्शिता । इति **व्यत्यासछलयोगतो** दत्तमदत्तमं सप्तमम् । व्यत्यासो व्यपदेशः । तत्सहितं[11] छलं व्यत्यासछलमिति । तथा **बालेन** दत्तमदत्तम् । तथा **मूढेन** दत्तमदत्तम् नवमम् । तथा**स्वतन्त्रेण** दत्तं दशममदत्तम् । तथा देशको नदीपूरणीयमानोऽर्तो यद्ददति यो मां म्रियमाणं रक्षयति तस्याहं सवर्णशतं दास्यामीति प्रतिश्रुतेऽपि तेन**आर्तेन** दत्तमवत्तगेकादशमम् । सुरा**मत्तेना**पवर्जितं दत्तं परित्यक्तमदत्तं द्वादशम् । **उन्मत्तेन** सग्रहेणापवर्जितं दत्तमदत्तं त्रयोदशम् । तथा कर्ता मामायं कर्मेति किंचिदनागतमेव समर्पितं पुनरसौ विज्ञानी तस्यानाहितः संजातः संजातः [?] एतदपि **प्रतिलाभेच्छया** दत्तं चतुर्दशमम् । तथा सूद्रस्य यज्ञोपवीतं दृष्ट्वाज्ञानाद् ब्राह्माणबुद्धया दानं दत्तमेतद**पात्रमि**त्युक्ते दत्तमदत्तम्पञ्चदशमम् । तथा देवार्चकस्य सुवर्णमुखकोशदेशोपशोभार्थं द्रव्यं यद्दत्तं यावता द्यूतवेश्याद्यधर्मेण तद्विनाशितुमुध्यतः । ईदृशेऽकार्ये **वाधर्मसंहिते** दत्तमदत्तं षोडशम् । एवमेतद् सोदाहरणं षोडशप्रकारमपि दत्तमुपवर्णितमिति ।

गृह्णात्यदत्तं यो लोभाद्यश्चादेयं प्रयच्छति ।
अदत्तादायको दण्ड्यस्तथादेयस्य दायकः ॥११॥

१० bcd — P om; D -संज्ञिते.

११ a — P add यां; N मोहाद्; d— P अदेयदायको दण्ड्यस्तथा दण्डप्रतीछकः.
D add इति श्री ना । धर्म । दत्ताप्रदानिक नाम चतुर्विवादपदं प्रतीप्सक; N add तथादत्तप्रतीच्छकः । दत्ताप्रदानिकं नाम विवादपदं समाप्तम्; Jolly add तथादत्तप्रतीच्छकः; NMS add इति दत्ताप्रदानिकं विवादपदम् ।

अत्रैवमेतत्षोडशप्रकारमपि दत्तमदत्तमुक्तम् । तद्यो लोभात्प्रतिगृह्णाति । यश्चाष्टप्रकारमप्यदेयं प्रयच्छत्येतौ द्वावप्य**देयदायको*ऽदत्तप्रतीच्छको*** राज्ञा दण्ड्ययौ इति नारदीयसंहितायाः कल्याणविवरणे दत्ताप्रदानिकं नाम व्यवहारपदं चतुर्थं चतुर्भेदम् ।

व्यवहारपदानि

५ अभ्युपेत्याशुश्रूषा

इदानीं शुश्रूषाभ्युपगमो नवभेद उच्यते ।

अभ्युपेत्य तु शुश्रूषां यस्तां न प्रतिपद्यते ।
अशुश्रूषाभ्युपेत्यैतद्विवादपदमुच्यते ॥१॥

अत्र**अशुश्रूषाभ्युपेत्य** व्यवहारपदस्य नाम लक्षणमात्रमिदमुद्दिष्टमधिकारश्लोके-ऽस्मिन्निति ।

शुश्रूषकः पञ्चविधः शास्त्रे दृष्टो मनीषिभिः ।
चतुर्विधः कर्मकरस्तेषां दासास्त्रिपञ्चकाः ॥२॥

अत्र **शुश्रूषकः** पञ्चप्रकारो दृष्टः । चतुःप्रकारः **कर्मकरः** । पञ्चदशप्रकारो **दास** इति ।

शिष्यान्तेवासिभृतकाश्चतुर्थस्त्वधिकर्मकृत् ।
एते कर्मकराः प्रोक्ता दासास्तु गृहजादयः ॥३॥

अत्र **शिष्यश्चान्तेवासी** च **भृतकश्चाधिकर्मकृच्चैते** चत्वारोऽपि **कर्मकरा** उक्ताः । ये पुनः पञ्चदश दासास्ते गृहदासीजातमादावुक्त्वाग्रतः[108] सविस्तरं वक्ष्यति ।

सामान्यमस्वतन्त्रत्वमेषामाहुर्मनीषिणः ।
जातिकर्मकृतस्तूक्तो विशेषो वृत्तिरेव च ॥४॥

येषां च शुश्रूषककर्मकरदासानां सर्वेषामप्य**स्वतन्त्रत्वं** सामान्यं यस्तु **विशेषः** स जातिवशादेषां **वृत्तिश्च** कर्मानुसारिणी । इति शुश्रूषकभेदः ।

२ a—R om this verse. d — NMS शेषा.
३ c — P D ज्ञेया; d — N गृहजातयः.

कर्मापि द्विविधं ज्ञेयमशुभं शुभमेव च ।
अशुभं दासकर्मोक्तं शुभं कर्मकृतां स्मृतम् ॥५॥

कर्म शुभाशुभतया **द्विविधं** दृष्टम् । तत्र **शुभं** कर्मकराणाम**शुभं** दासानामिति ।

गृहद्वाराशुचिस्थानरथ्यावस्करशोधनम् ।
गुह्याङ्गस्पर्शनोच्छिष्टविण्मूत्रग्रहणोज्झनम् ॥६॥
इष्टतः स्वामिनश्चाङ्गैरुपस्थानमथान्ततः ।
अशुभं कर्म विज्ञेयं शुभमन्यदतः परम् ॥७॥

निगदव्याख्यातौ श्लोकौ । अशुभकर्मभेदः ।

आ विद्याग्रहणाच्छिष्यः शुश्रूषेत्प्रयतो गुरुम् ।
तद्वृत्तिर्गुरुदारेषु गुरुपुत्रे तथैव च ॥८॥

यावद्विद्याग्रहणसमाप्तिस्तावच्छि**ष्यो गुरुं** शुश्रूशयेत् । गुरुपत्नीं गुरुपुत्रं च तद्वदेवेति ।

ब्रह्मचारी चरेद्भैक्षमधःशाय्यनलङ्कृतः ।
जघन्यशायी सर्वेषां पूर्वोत्थायी गुरोर्गृहे ॥९॥

जघन्यश्शायी पश्चाच्छायी । शेषं प्रसिद्धम् ।

नासंदिष्टः प्रतिष्ठेत तिष्ठेद्वापि गुरुं क्वचित् ।
संदिष्टः कर्म कुर्वीत शक्तश्चेदविचारयन् ॥१०॥

अनादिष्टो न गच्छेन्न **तिष्ठेत्** । यच्छादिष्टस्तद**विचारयन्**यदि **शक्तः** । नो चेत्स्वरूपं निवेदयेत् ।

५ d — D शिप्यकृतं.

७ a — P D इच्छतः; b — P अथोऽन्ततः.

८ b — NMS शुश्रूपन्.

९ b — D अनहंकृतः.

१० a — D नासंदिग्धः; b — P D वा गुरुणा; c — P D प्रतिकुर्वीत.

यथाकालमधीयीत यावन्न विमना गुरुः ।
आसीनोऽधो गुरोः कूर्चे फलके वा समाहितः ॥११॥

स्पष्टार्थोऽध्ययनविधिः ।

स्रोतोवहेव सर्वत्र विद्या निम्नानुसारिणी ।
निम्नवर्ती भवेत्तस्मात्तदर्थी सर्वदा गुरोः ॥ [J 5.12]

स्रोतोवहा नदी यथा सा निम्नानुसारिणी तथा विद्यापि । तस्माद्यो विद्यार्थी तेन सर्वदा गुरोः प्रणतेन भवितव्यमिति ।

अनुशास्यश्च गुरुणा न चेदनुविधीयते ।
अवधेनाथवा हन्यात्रज्ज्वा वेणुदलेन वा ॥१२॥

यदि गुरोरादेशकारी न भवति ततो **गुरुणानुशास्यः** शिक्षणीयः । बुद्ध्वा **रज्ज्वा** वांशावयवेन वास्फालनीयः[375] । **अविधि**नेति* निष्ठुरमित्यर्थः ।

भृशं न ताडयेदेनं नोत्तमाङ्गे न वक्षसि ।
अनुशास्याथ विश्वास्यः शास्यो राज्ञान्यथा गुरुः ॥१३॥

कुपितेनापि गुरुणा न **भृशं** ताड्यः शिष्यः । **उत्तमाङ्गे** न ताड्यो न **वक्षसि** । ताडितोऽप्यनन्तरमाश्वास्यः । यदि पुनरतिक्रोधादधिकं ताडनं गुरुः करोति तदा स गुरुरेव शिष्येण वेदितो **राज्ञा शास्यो** दण्डनीय इत्यर्थः ।

समावृत्तश्च गुरवे प्रदाय गुरुदक्षिणाम् ।
प्रतीयात्स्वगृहानेषा शिष्यवृत्तिरुदाहृता ॥१४॥

यदा च शिष्यः **समावृत्तो** भवति समाप्तविद्यः तदा **गुरवे दक्षिणां** दत्त्वा गृहं प्रतिगच्छेदिति ।

स्वशिल्पमिच्छन्नाहर्तुं बान्धवानामनुज्ञया ।
आचार्यस्य वसेदन्ते कालं कृत्वा सुनिश्चितम् ॥१५॥

११ c — P पार्श्वे.
१२ a — NMS अनुशिष्यश्; c — P अविधिनाथवा बुद्ध्वा; D अवदेनाथ शास्यः स्याद्; NMS शिष्यान्.
१३ c — NMS अनुशिष्य च; d — NMS दण्ड्यो.
१४ c — D स्वगृं ह्य; X स्वां गृहान्, P एषां.

यश्च शिल्पादिविज्ञानविद्यार्थी भवति स **कालं निश्चितम**वधिं कृत्वा गुरुगृहे **वसेद्** इति ।

आचार्यः शिक्षयेदेनं स्वगृहाद्दत्तभोजनम् ।
न चान्यत्कारयेत्कर्म पुत्रवच्चैनमाचरेत् ॥१६॥

आचार्यश्च तेनान्तेवासिना तदेव शिल्पकर्म **कारयेन्नान्यत्स्वगृहे* दत्तभोजनं शिक्षयेत्पुत्रवत्**पश्येन्न कर्मकरवत् ।

शिक्षयन्तमदुष्टं च यस्त्वाचार्यं परित्यजेत् ।
बलाद्वासयितव्यः स्याद्वधबन्धौ च सोऽर्हति ॥१७॥

यस्तु शिष्यः । अथानध्याप्यानाह ।

अनध्याप्याः क्षत्रियेण ब्राह्मणक्षत्रियविशः ।[376]
असंभवे ब्राह्मणस्य अध्याप्या वृत्तिवर्जिताः ।।[a]
सति विप्रेऽध्यापयिता गृहीता गुरुनिष्कृते ।[377]
चतुःसौवर्णिको दण्डस्तस्य दाप्यो विजानता ।।[b]
वैश्यस्य द्विगुणः कार्यो राज्ञा धर्मं विजानता ।[378]
शूद्रश्चतुर्थो वर्णः स्यादेकजातिरसौ स्मृतः ।।[c]
नास्याधिकारो धर्मेऽस्ति न धर्मात्प्रतिषेधनम् ।
श्रौते धर्मे नाधिकारो न स्मार्तात्प्रतिषेधनम् ।।[d][379]
स्मार्तं धर्मं स शृणुयात्कृत्वा ब्राह्मणमग्रतः ।
क्षत्राद्या दण्डनीयास्ते प्रायश्चित्तपराङ्मुखाः ।।[e]
अनध्यायाध्यापने तु क्षत्रियस्य विजानता ।
अष्टौ चान्द्रायणा देया वैश्यस्य द्विगुणाः स्मृताः ।।[f]
त्रिगुणानि तु शूद्रस्य उक्तानि क्रमकारिणः ।
श्रौतशब्दोच्चरणेऽस्य जिह्वाच्छेदोऽभिधीयते ।।[g]
उष्णेन त्रपुणा श्रोत्रपूरणं श्रवणात्तथा ।
धारणे देहभेदस्तु शीघ्रं कार्यो महीभृता ।।[h]

एतदपि प्रायश्चित्तपराङ्मुखस्य । श्रौतशब्दोच्चरणे तु अष्टचान्द्रायणा मताः ।[380]

श्रवणेऽधारणार्थं च द्विगुणानि (?) विनिर्दिशेत् ।
आधारणार्थश्रवणे कार्यं विप्रप्रसादनम् ।।[i]
श्रवणाद्द्विगुणा कार्या धारणेनेव तानि तु (?) ।[381]

१६ b — P स्वगृहे.

विस्मरणे च कर्तव्यमनभ्यासे च तस्य च ।।[j]

महापातकाद्यदुष्टं गुरुं **शिक्षयन्तं** च **परित्यजेतन्**तेवासी[116] च गुरुणा **बलाद्वासयितव्यः वधबन्धौ च सोऽर्हति** । वधशब्देन पितृनेवावधिकृतम् (?)।

शिक्षितोऽपि कृतं कालमन्तेवासी समाप्नुयात् ।
तत्र कर्म च यत्कुर्यादाचार्यस्यैव तत्फलम् ॥१८॥

यः शिष्यः विनयवृत्तिकालः प्रथमं गुरोः शुश्रूषेत शिल्पतः[117] **कृतं**[118] **कालम**सौ **शिक्षितो**ऽपि निष्पन्नोऽपि समाप्तिं नयेत् । तत्कालमध्ये यदन्ते**वासि कर्म कुर्या**त्तस्य कर्मणः **फलं** गुरोरेव भवति निःशेषं न शिष्यस्य किंचित् ।

गृहीतशिल्पः समये कृत्वाचार्यं प्रदक्षिणम् ।
शक्तितश्चानुमान्यैनमन्तेवासि निवर्तयेत् ॥१९॥

शिक्षितश्च शिष्यः संपूरितशिल्पकालसमयस्तं गुरुमनुज्ञां वाच्य प्रदक्षिणीकृत्य च गुरुगृहा**न्निवर्तते*** स्वग्रहं प्रयादिति[119] ।

वेतनं वा यदि कृतं ज्ञात्वा शिष्यस्य कौशलम् ।
अन्तेवासि समादद्यान्न चान्यस्य गृह वसेत् ।। [J 5.21]

अथ शिष्यस्य विज्ञानकौशलं दृष्ट्वा गुरुणा तस्य किंचिद्वेतनं जल्पितं भवति ततः शिष्यस्तदादद्यात् । न चाचार्यगृहे वसेदिति । इत्यन्तेवासिवृत्तम् । इति नारदीयधर्मशास्त्रे कल्याणभट्टकृतभाष्य अन्तेवासिप्रकरणं समाप्तम्[120] ।

भृतकस्त्रिविधो ज्ञेय उत्तमो मध्यमोऽधमः ।
शक्तिभक्त्यनुरूपा स्यादेषां कर्माश्रया भृतिः ॥२०॥
उत्तमस्त्वायुधीयोऽत्र मध्यमस्तु कृषीवलः ।
अधमो भारवाहः स्यादित्येवं त्रिविधो भृतः ॥२१॥
अर्थेष्वधिकृतो यः स्यात्कुटुम्बस्य तथोपरि ।
सोऽधिकर्मकरो ज्ञेयः स च कौटुम्बिकः स्मृतः ॥२२॥
शुभकर्मकरास्त्वेते चत्वारः समुदाहृताः ।
जघन्यकर्मभाजस्तु शेषा दासास्त्रिपञ्चकाः ॥२३॥

१८ a — B5 शिष्यतो; c — D यः.
१९ b — Jolly प्रदक्षिणाम्; X प्रदक्षिनः; d — P D निवर्तते.
२० a — N दृष्ट; d — M2 L एषा; M2 L4 कर्मश्रिया.
२१ d — D एष.
२२ c — D ऽपि कर्मकरो.

गृहजातस्तथा क्रीतो लब्धो दायादुपागतः ।
अनाकालभृतस्तद्वदाधत्तः स्वामिना च यः ॥२४॥
मोक्षितो महतश्चर्णात्प्राप्तो युद्धात्पणे जितः ।
तवाहमित्युपगतः प्रव्रज्यावसितः कृतः ॥२५॥
भक्तदासश्च विज्ञेयस्तथैव वडवाभृतः ।
विक्रेता चात्मनः शास्त्रे दासाः पञ्चदशा स्मृताः ॥२६॥
तत्र पूर्वश्चतुर्वर्गो दासत्वान्न विमुच्यते ।
प्रसादाद् स्वामिनोऽन्यत्र दास्यमेषां क्रमागतम् ॥२७॥
यश्चैषां स्वामिनं कश्चिन्मोक्षयेत्प्राणसंशयात् ।
दासत्वात्स विमुच्यते पुत्रभागं लभेत च ॥२८॥
अनाकालभृतो दास्यान्मुच्यते गोयुगं ददत् ।
संभक्षितं यद्दुर्भिक्षे न तच्छुध्येत कर्मणा ॥२९॥
आधत्तोऽपि धनं दत्त्वा स्वामि यद्येनमुद्धरेत् ।
अथोपगमयेदेनं स विक्रीतादनन्तरः ॥३०॥
दत्त्वा तु सोदयमृणं ऋणी दास्यात्प्रमुच्यते ।
कृतकालाभ्युपगमात्कृतकोऽपि विमुच्यते ॥३१॥
तवाहमित्युपगतो युद्धप्राप्तः पणे जितः ।
प्रतिशीर्षप्रदानेन मुच्यते तुल्यकर्मणा ॥३२॥
राज्ञ एव तु दासः स्यात्प्रव्रज्यावसितो नरः ।
न तस्य प्रतिमोक्षोऽस्ति न विशुद्धिः कथंचन ॥३३॥
भक्तस्योपेक्षणात्सद्यो भक्तदासः प्रमुच्यते ।
निग्रहाद्वडवायाश्च मुच्यते वडवाभृतः ॥३४॥
विक्रीणीते य आत्मानं स्वतन्त्रः सन्नराधमः ।
स जघन्यतरस्तेषां नैव दास्यात्प्रमुच्यते ॥३५॥

२३ c — Y कर्मणा भाजस्; d — D शेप.
२४ a — D गृहे जातस्; c — NMS अशनादिभृतस्; d — D अनाकालभृतो; D लोके आहितः.
२५ a — R मांहितो; b — NMS ऋणाच्च मोक्षितोऽनल्पाद्युद्धप्राप्तः; D पणार्जितो.
२६ b — N वडवाहृतः; NMS वडवाभृतः; M3 L4 च उदाहृतः
२७ c — D प्रमादाद्; D धनिनो; d — D दासम्.
२८ a — B4 C D यो वैषां.
२९ c — N संवर्द्धितश्च; D भक्षेन्; M2 M3 L4 तु यद्वैक्षं.
३० a — D आहितो; c — L M3 M4 यदोपगमयेद्; d — D विक्रेताद्.
३१ a — D ऋणं तु सोदयं दत्त्वा; c — D कृतकालव्यपगमात्.
३२ b — D ध्वजप्राप्तः; D पणार्जितः; L4 पणाज्जितः; c — NMS प्रतिपुरुपदानेन.
३३ a — D राज्ञाम्; c — Y नरस्य; D विप्रमोक्षो; d — N कदाचन.
३४ c — D वडवानां; d — N वडवाहृतः; NMS वडवाभृतः.
३५ d — NMS
विक्रीनाति स्वतन्त्रः सन्य आत्मानं नराधमः ।

चौरापहृतविक्रीता ये च दासीकृता बलात् ।
राज्ञा मोक्षयितव्यास्ते दासत्वं तेषु नेष्यते ॥३६॥
वर्णानां प्रातिलोम्येन दासत्वं न विधीयते ।
स्वधर्मत्यागिनोऽन्यत्र दारवद्दासता मता ॥३७॥
तवाहमिति चात्मानं योऽस्वतन्त्रः प्रयच्छति ।
न स तं प्राप्नुयात्कामं पूर्वस्वामी लभेत तम् ॥३८॥
अधनास्त्रय एवोक्ता भार्या दासस्तथा सुतः ।
यत्ते समधिगच्छन्ति यस्य ते तस्य तद्धनम् ॥३९॥
स्वदासमिच्छेद्यः कर्तुमदासं प्रीतमानसः ।
स्कन्धादादाय तस्यापि भिन्द्यात्कुम्भं सहाम्भसा ॥४०॥
अक्षताभिः सपुष्पाभिर्मूर्धन्येनमवाकिरेत् ।
अदास इति चोक्त्वा त्रिः प्राङ्मुखं तमथोत्सृजेत् ॥४१॥
ततःप्रभृति वक्तव्यः स्वाम्यनुग्रहपालितः ।
भोज्यान्नः प्रतिगृह्यश्च भवत्यभिमतश्च सः ॥४२॥

सुजघन्यतमस्तेषां सोऽपि दास्यान्न मुच्यते ॥

३६ b — Y दासत्कृता.

३७ d — Y सताम्; B सत्यम्.

३८ b —NMS तवास्मीति य आत्मानमस्वतन्त्रः.

३९ ab —M2 M3 L L4 तेषां यत्किंचन द्रव्यं तत्स्वद्रव्यं प्रकीर्तितम्.

४० a — NMS यं; c — D तस्यासौ; NMS तस्याथ.

४१ a — L L4 M2 M3 साक्षताभिः; b — L L4 M2 M3 अद्भिर्.

४२ Jolly om this verse. D add इति श्रीनारदीये धर्मशास्त्रे शुश्रूषाभ्युपेत्यैतद्दानादानविधिः पञ्चमः; NMS add इत्यभ्युपेत्याशुश्रूषा पञ्चमं विवादपदम्.

व्यवहारपदानि

६ वेतनस्यानपाकर्म

भृतानां वेतनस्योक्तो दानादानविधिक्रमः ।
वेतनस्यानपाकर्म तद्विवादपदं स्मृतम् ॥१॥
भृताय वेतनं दद्यात्कर्मस्वामी यथाक्रमम् ।
आदौ मध्येऽवसाने वा कर्मणो यद्विनिश्चितम् ॥२॥
भृतावनिश्चितायां तु दशभागं समाप्नुयुः ।
लाभगोबीजसस्यानां वणिग्गोपकृशीबलाः ॥३॥
कर्मोपकरणं चैषां क्रियां प्रति यदाहृतम् ।
आप्तभावेन कुर्वीत न जिह्मेन समाचरेत् ॥४॥
कर्माकुर्वन्प्रतिश्रुत्य कार्यो दत्त्वा भृतिं बलात् ।
भृतिं गृहीत्वाकुर्वाणो द्विगुणां भृतिमावहेत् ॥५॥
कालेऽपूर्णे त्यजेत्कर्म भृतिनाशोऽस्य चार्हति ।
स्वामिदोषादपाक्रामन्यावत्कृतमवाप्नुयात् ॥६॥
भृतिषड्भागमाभाष्य पथि युग्यकृतं त्यजन् ।
अददत्कारयित्वा तु कर्मैवं सोदयां भृतिम् ॥७॥
अनयन्भाटयित्वा तु भाण्डवान्यानवाहने ।
दाप्यो भृतिचतुर्भागं सममर्धपथे त्यजन् ॥८॥
अनयन्वाहकोऽप्येवं भृतिहानिमवाप्नुयात् ।
द्विगुणां तु भृतिं दाप्यः प्रस्थाने विघ्नमाचरन् ॥९॥
भाण्डं व्यसनमागच्छेद्यदि वाहकदोषतः ।
दाप्यो यत्तत्र नष्टं स्याद्दैवराजकृतादृते ॥१०॥

२ d — Y विनिश्चयम्.

३ d — D वणिभोगकृपी-; Y -वालात्.

४ a — D क्रियोपकरणं-; b — NMS प्रति यदर्पितम्-; D यत्प्रत्युदाहृतम्; c — D तत्स्वभावेन.

५ a — Y कर्मकुर्वन्-; c — M3 गृहीत्वाकर्माणो; d — Y द्विगुणं.

६ D om this verse. a — NMS त्यजन्; b — NMS भृतिनाशमवाप्नुयात्; c — NMS अपाक्रमेद्.

७ b — D आदद्यात्पण्यं; c — X तथैव d — Jolly सोदयां भृतिमावहेत्; cd — D अनयंश्चापि तद्देशं भृतिहानिमवाप्नुयात्.

८ Y om this verse. NMS has it after 5. b — NMS नादयित्वा तु भाण्डं वा; ab — D अददन्कारयित्वा तु दण्डधान्याधिकं धनं; d — NMS सर्वां.

९ d — Y आचरेत्.

१० c — NMS नश्येत्तु; c — D स दाप्यो यत्प्रणष्टं स्याद्.

गवां शताद्वत्सतरी धेनुः स्याद् द्विशताद्भृतिः ।
प्रति सम्वत्सरं गोपे सदोहश्चाष्टमेऽहनि ॥११॥
उपानयेत् गा गोपाय प्रत्यहं रजनीक्षये ।
चीर्णाः पीताश्च ता गोपाः सायाह्ने प्रत्युपानयेत् ॥१२॥
स्याच्चेद्गोव्यसनं गोपो व्यायच्छेत्तत्र शक्तितः ।
अशक्तस्तूर्णमागम्य स्वामिने तन्निवेदयेत् ॥१३॥
अव्यायच्छन्नविक्रोशन्स्वामिने चानिवेदयन् ।
वोढुमर्हति गोपस्तां विनयं चापि राजनि ॥१४॥
नष्टविनष्टं कृमिभिः श्वहतं विषमे मृतम् ।
हीनं पुरुषकारेण गोपायैव निपातयेत् ॥१५॥
अजाविके तथारुद्धे वृकैः पाले त्वनायति ।
यत्प्रसह्य वृको हन्यात्पाले तत्किल्बिषम्भवेत् ॥१६॥
तासां चैवानिरुद्धानां चरन्तीनां मिथो वने ।
यामुत्पत्य वृको हन्यान्न पालस्तत्र किल्बिषी ॥१७॥
विघुष्य तु हृतं चौरैर्न पालो दातुमर्हति ।
यदि देशे च काले च स्वामिनः स्वस्य शंसति ॥१८॥
एतेन सर्वपालानां विवादः समुदाहृतः ।
मृतेषु च विशुद्धिः स्यात्पालस्याङ्कादिदर्शनात् ॥१९॥
शुल्कं गृहीत्वा पण्यस्त्री नेच्छन्ती द्विस्तदावहेत् ।
अप्रयच्छंस्तदा शुल्कमनुभूय पुमान्स्त्रियम् ॥२०॥
अयोनौ क्रमते यस्तु बहुभिर्वापि वासयेत् ।
शुल्कमष्टगुणं दाप्यो विनयस्तावदेव च ॥२१॥
पराजिरे गृहं कृत्वा स्तोमं दत्त्वा वसेत्तु यः ।
स तद् गृहीत्वा निर्गच्छेत्तृणकाष्ठेष्टकादिकम् ॥२२॥

११ b — D विशता (?विंशता) c — M2 संवत्सरे-; d — NMS सदोहो वाप्टमेऽहनि.
१२ a — D उपानयति या गोपः.
१३ a — D सा चेद्गौर्व्यसनं गच्छेद्-; c — NMS अशक्तावभिपत्यारं; D अशक्तं प्रतिपन्नां तु.
१४ d — NMS चैव राजतः cd — N गोपस्तत्रापराध्नोति स च तद्वोढुमर्हति.
१५ d — D पालयैव-; d — N add

वालाश्चर्मापरे सक्थी वस्तिस्नायूनि रोचनम् ।
दद्यात्पशुमते सर्वं मृतेष्वङ्कांश्च दर्शयेत् ॥ [?]

१६ c — D यां-; d — D हन्यान्न पालस्तत्र किल्विपी.
१७ D om this verse. a — NMS अनवरुद्धानां; N NMS याः; c — NMS प्रसह्य
१८ a — D विघुष्यापहृतं; d — D चापि.
१९ a — D अनेन-; d — D पालस्य स्वामिदर्शनात्; Jolly वालशृङ्गादिदर्शनात्.
२० b — D आप्नुयात्.
२१ a — D वा समाक्रामेद्; c — D सोऽप्टगुणं; D विनयं; d — D तु.
२२ d — N M2 त्यक्त्वा सर्वमथोपितः; N M2 त्यक्त्वा सर्वं मुधोपितः; D add

स्तोमवाहीनि भाण्डानि पूर्णकालान्युपानयेत् ।
ग्रहीतुराभवेद्भग्नं नष्टं चान्यत्र संप्लवात् ॥२३॥

स्तोमं विना वसित्वा तु परभूमावनिच्छतः ।
निर्गच्छंस्तृणकाष्ठानि न गृह्णीयात्कदाचन ।। [J 6.21]

२३ c — L l4 M3 गृहीतुना भवेद्; M2 गृहीतुर्न भवेद्; d — D add इति श्रीनारदीये धर्मशास्त्रे वेतनस्यानपाकर्मेति षष्ठम्; NMS add इति वेतनस्यानपाकर्म षष्ठमं विवादपदम्; N add इति वेतनस्यानपाकर्म नाम विवादपदमं समाप्तम्.

व्यवहारपदानि

७ अस्वामिविक्रयः

निक्षिप्तं वा परद्रव्यं नष्टं लब्ध्वापहृत्य वा ।
विक्रीयतेऽसमक्षं यद्विज्ञेयोऽस्वामिविक्रयः ॥१॥
द्रव्यमस्वामिविक्रीतं प्राप्य स्वामी समाप्नुयात् ।
प्रकाशं क्रयतः शुद्धिः क्रेतुः स्तेयं रहः क्रयात् ॥२॥
अस्वाम्यनुमताद्दासादसतश्च जनाद्रहः ।
हीनमूल्यं अवेलायां क्रीणंस्तद्दोषभाग्भवेत् ॥३॥
न गूहेतागमं क्रेता शुद्धिस्तस्य तदागमात् ।
विपर्यये तुल्यदोषः स्तेयदण्डं च सोऽर्हति ॥४॥
विक्रेता स्वामिनेऽर्थं च क्रेतुर्मूल्यं च तत्कृतम् ।
दद्याद्दण्डं तथा राज्ञे विधिरस्वामिविक्रये ॥५॥
परेण निहितं लब्ध्वा राजन्युपहरेन्निधिम् ।
राजगामी निधिः सर्वः सर्वेषां ब्राह्मणादृते ॥६॥
ब्राह्मणोऽपि निधिं लब्ध्वा क्षिप्रं राज्ञे निवेदयेत् ।
तेन दत्तं च भूञ्जीत स्तेनः स्यादनिवेदयन् ॥७॥
स्वमप्यर्थं तथा नष्टं लब्ध्वा राज्ञे निवेदयेत् ।
गृह्णीयात्तत्र तं शुद्धमशुद्धं स्यात्ततोऽन्यथा ॥८॥

१ c — L L4 M3 विक्रीयेता; NMS परोक्षं; Y यः;. d — NMS स ज्ञयो.
२ b — NMS तदप्नुयात्-; c — D प्रकाशविक्रये-; d — D क्रमात्.
३ a — Y तु गताद्-; b — L4 M3 तलाद्; L वलाद्.
४ a —NMS न गुहेदागमं; M3 न गृहेतागमं; Y कथयच्चागमं-; c — Y अन्यथा तुल्यदोपः स्यात्-; d — N add
अतोऽस्वामिकृतो यस्तु दायो स क्रिय एव वा ।
अकृतः स तु विज्ञेयो व्यवहारेप्वयं स्थितिः ॥ [Dhko 762]
५ a —M2 L4 स्वामिनो-; b — D स्वं क्रेत्रे; D तत्समम्-; d — Y अस्वामि विक्रयेत्(?).
६ a —L L4 निहतं-; Y दृष्ट्वा.
७ a — Y inverts 7 and 8-; c — Y दत्तश्च; Y अप्यतोऽन्यथा.
८ c — Y तत्तथा; d — N शुद्धिरशुद्धिर्; N add अस्वामिविक्रयो नाम द्विप्रभेदः सप्तमव्यवहारपदं सपाप्तम्; D add इति श्रीनारदीये धर्मशास्त्रेऽस्वामिविक्रयो नाम सप्तमं विवादपदं; NMS add इति अस्वामिविक्रयः सप्तमं विवादपदं.

व्यवहारपदानि

८ क्रीतानुशयः

विक्रीय पण्यं मूल्येन क्रेतुर्यन्न प्रदीयते ।
विक्रीयासंप्रदानं तद्विवादपदमुच्यते ॥१॥
लोकेऽस्मिन्द्विविधं द्रव्यं जङ्गमं स्थावरं तथा ।
क्रयविक्रयधर्मेषु सर्वं तत्पण्यमुच्यते ॥२॥
षड्विधस्तस्य तु बुधैर्दानादानविधिः स्मृतः ।
गणिमं तुलिमं मेयं क्रियया रूपतः श्रिया ॥३॥
विक्रीय पण्यं मूल्येन क्रेतुर्यो न प्रयच्छति ।
स्थावरस्य क्षयं दाप्यो जङ्गमस्य क्रियाफलम् ॥४॥
अर्घश्चेदपहीयेत सोदयं पण्यमावहेत् ।
स्थायिनामेष नियमो दिग्लाभो दिग्विचारिणाम् ॥५॥
उपहन्येत वा पण्यं दह्येतापह्रियेत वा ।
विक्रेतुरेव सोऽनार्थो विक्रीयासम्प्रयच्छतः ॥६॥
निर्दोषं दर्शयित्वा तु सदोषं यः प्रयच्छति ।
मूल्यं तद्द्विगुणं दाप्यो विनयं तावदेव च ॥७॥
तथान्यहस्ते विक्रीय योऽन्यस्मै संप्रयच्छति ।
सोऽपि तद्द्विगुणं दाप्यो विनेयस्तावदेव च ॥८॥
दीयमानं न गृह्णाति क्रीतं पण्यं च यः क्रयी ।
विक्रीणानस्तदन्यत्र विक्रेता नापराध्नुयात् ॥९॥
दत्तमूल्यस्य पण्यस्य विधिरेष प्रकीर्तितः ।
अदत्तेऽन्यत्र समयान्न विक्रेतुरतिक्रमः ॥१०॥
लाभार्थे वणिजां सर्वपण्येषु क्रयविक्रयः ।

१ a — M3 L4 विक्रेय; b — D क्रेत्रे; NMS प्रयच्छति.
२ b — L स्थावरे-; ab — Y द्रव्यं तु द्विविधं ज्ञेयं स्थावरं जङ्गमं तथा.
३ a — BM विधिर्; N विधि-; b — NMS -विधिक्रमः; c — D गणितं तुलितं; Y ज्ञेयं-; d — B C B5 श्रियाः.
४ b — D क्रेत्रे; c — D उदयं; L4 M3 देयं.
५ a — L M2 युक्तश्; D Y L M2 अपचीयेत; b — NMS आभवेत्; c — NMS M2 L4 M3 B5 स्थानिनाम्.
६ a — V V2 V4 V6 V7 R उपहार्येण; Jolly द्रव्यं.
७ c — NMS स; D तु-; d — Y चिरे यस् (?).
८ a — D तथान्यहस्तविक्रीतं; b — M2 न प्रयच्छति; d — D MNS विनयं; D चैव राजनि.
९ b — Y क्रीत्वा; NMS यत्; cd — Y स एवास्य भवेद्दोषो विक्रेतुं न प्रयच्छति.
१० b — D एवं; c — NMS अदत्तमूल्ये; M2 समये; MNS विक्रीते; d — Y विक्रेतुर्नास्त्यतिक्रमः.

स च लाभोऽर्धमासाद्य महान्भवति वा न वा ॥११॥
तस्माद्देशे च काले च वणिगर्घं पराक्रमेत् ।
न जिह्मेन प्रवर्तेत श्रेयानेवं वणिक्पथः ॥१२॥

११ a — NMS लाभार्थो; b — NMS C सर्वः पण्येषु; Y -विक्रयं; c — D सदा लाभार्घमासाद्य.
१२ b — L L4 M3 अर्थं; D समाश्रयेत्; c — D जिह्मं च; L L4 M3 जिह्मे च; d — NMS एष; D add इति श्री नारदीये धर्मशास्त्रे विक्रीयासंप्रदानं नामाष्टमं विवादपदम्; N add विक्रीयासम्प्रदानमष्टमव्यवहारपदं समाप्तम्; NMS add इति विक्रीयासम्प्रदानमष्टमं विवादपदम्.

व्यवहारपदानि

१ विक्रीयासंप्रदानम्

क्रीत्वा मूल्येन यः पण्यं क्रेता न बहु मन्यते ।
क्रीत्वानुशय इत्येतद्विवादपदमुच्यते ॥१॥
क्रीत्वा मूल्येन यत्पण्यं दुष्क्रीतं मन्यते क्रयी ।
विक्रेतुः प्रतिदेयं तत्तस्मिन्नेवाह्न्यविक्षतम् ॥२॥
द्वितीयेऽह्नि ददत्क्रेता मूल्यात्त्रिंशांशमावहेत् ।
द्विगुणं तत्तृतीयेऽह्नि परतः क्रेतुरेव तत् ॥३॥
क्रेता पण्यं परीक्षेत प्राक्स्वयं गुणदोषतः ।
परीक्ष्याभिमतं क्रीतं विक्रेतुर्न भवेत्पुनः ॥४॥
त्र्यहाद्दोह्यं परीक्षेत पञ्चाहाद्वाह्यमेव तु ।
मुक्तावज्रप्रवालानां सप्ताहं स्यात्परीक्षणम् ॥५॥
द्विपदामर्धमासं स्यात्पुंसां तद्द्विगुणं स्त्रियाः ।
दशाहं सर्वबीजानामेकाहं लोहवाससाम् ॥६॥
परिभुक्तं च यद्वासः क्लिष्टरूपं मलीमसम् ।
सदोषमपि विक्रीतं विक्रेतुर्न भवेत्पुनः ॥७॥
मूल्याष्टभागो हीयेत सकृद्धौतस्य वाससः ।
द्विः पादस्त्रिस्त्रिभागस्तु चतुःकृत्वोऽर्धमेव च ॥८॥
अर्धक्षयात्तु परतः पादांशापचयः क्रमात् ।
यावत्क्षीणदशं जीर्णं जीर्णस्यानियमः क्षये ॥९॥
लोहानामपि सर्वेषां हेतुरग्निक्रियाविधौ ।
क्षयः संस्क्रियमाणानां तेषां दृष्टोऽग्निसंगमात् ॥१०॥

१ a — NMS यत्; c — D C क्रीता-; Y एवं.
२ a — N यः; d — NMS तत्रैवाहन्य.
३ b — D आहरेत्; c — D तु.
४ d — NMS नाभवेत्.
५ d — D मणिमुक्ताप्रवालानां सप्ताहः.
६ a — D अर्धमासः; c — Jolly दशाहः; D दशाहात्; d — Jolly एकाहो; D एकाहात्.
७ B om this verse. b — NMS क्लिन्नरूपं; c — Y D तत्क्रीतं; d — NMS नाभवेत्.
८ a — L हीयते; c — Y त्रिभागस्य; d — NMS चतुर्धौते.
९ a — D अर्धक्रयात्; b — L L4 M3 पादशो यः क्रमात्ह्रसेत्; d — Y ततो न स्यात्परिक्षयेत्.
१० b — Y भाण्डानां पुनरावर्तनं स्मृतम्.

सुवर्णस्य क्षयो नास्ति रजते द्विपलं शतम् ।
शतमष्टपलं ज्ञेयं क्षयस्स्यात्त्रपुसीसयोः ॥११॥
ताम्रे पञ्चपलं विद्याद्विकारा ये च तन्मयाः ।
तद्धातूनामनेकत्वादयसोऽनियमः क्षये ॥१२॥
तान्तवस्य च संस्कारे क्षयवृद्धी उदाहृते ।
सूत्रकार्पासिकोर्णानां वृद्धिर्दशपलं शतम् ॥१३॥
स्थूलसूत्रवतां तेषां मध्यानां पञ्चकं शतम् ।
त्रिपलं तु सुसूक्ष्माणामन्तःक्षय उदाहृतः ॥१४॥
त्रिंशांशो रोमविद्धस्य क्षयः कर्मकृतस्य तु ।
कौषेयवल्कलानां तु नैव वृद्धिर्न च क्षयः ॥१५॥
क्रीत्वा नानुशयं कुर्याद्वणिक्पण्यविचक्षणः ।
वृद्धिक्षयौ तु जानीयात्पण्यानामागमं तथा ॥१६॥

११ b — D राजते; d — D तु.
१३ a — Y तुवत्तस्य; b — Y वृद्धिक्षयमुदाहृता; d — NMS शते; Y स्मृतम्.
१४ a — Y -सूत्रसतां; c — Y द्विपलं; d — D एपा वृद्धिरुदाहृता.
१५ a — D रोमवद्धस्य; b — NMS च; d — D सैव.
१६ a — Y अनुशयं; d — Y यस्य पणस्य यादृशौ; D add इति श्री नारदीये धर्मशास्त्रे क्रीतानुशयं नाम विवादपदम्; X Y add इति क्रीत्वानुशय नाम व्यवहारपदं समाप्तम्; NMS add इति क्रीत्वानुशयो नवमं विवादपदम्.

व्यवहारपदानि

१० समयस्यानपाकर्म

पाषण्डनैगमादीनां स्थितिः समय उच्यते ।
समयस्यानपाकर्म तद्विवादपदं स्मृतम् ॥१॥
पाषण्डनैगमश्रेणीपूगव्रातगणादिषु ।
संरक्षेत्समयं राजा दुर्गे जनपदे तथा ॥२॥
यो धर्मः कर्म यच्चैषामुपस्थानविधिश्च यः ।
यच्चैषां वृत्त्युपादानमनुमन्येत तत्तथा ॥३॥
प्रतिकूलं च यद्राज्ञः प्रकृत्यवमतं च यत् ।
बाधकं च यदर्थानां तत्तेभ्यो विनिवर्तयेत् ॥४॥
मिथः संघातकरणमहितं शस्त्रधारणम् ।
परस्परोपघातं च तेषां राजा न मर्षयेत् ॥५॥
पृथग्गणांश्च ये भिन्द्युस्ते विनेया विशेषतः ।
आवहेयुर्भयं घोरं व्याधिवत्ते ह्युपेक्षिताः ॥६॥
दोषवत्करणं यत्स्यादनाम्नायप्रकल्पितम् ।
प्रवृत्तमपि तद्राजा श्रेयस्कामो निवर्तयेत् ॥ ७

१ a — D पापण्डि-; M2 पाखण्डि-.

२ b — D पापण्डि-; b — L4 M3 -पुग-; d — B2 पुरे ।

३ c — Y यश्-; d — Y तं ।

४ a — D नानुकूलं; D राजा; b — Y प्रकृत्यभिमतश् ।

५ b — Y अमिथः; NMS अहिते; c — NMS परस्परोपतापं ।

६ a — NMS om. NMS विभिन्द्युस्ते; d — L L4 M3 व्याधिं ये ते ह्युपेक्षिताः-; M2 व्याधिं यत्ते ह्युपेक्षिताः ।

७ d — D add इति श्री नारदीये धर्मशास्त्रे समयस्यानपाकर्म दशमं विवादपदम्; N add इति समयस्यानपाकर्म नाम व्यवहारपदं समाप्तम्; NMS add इति समयस्यानपाकर्म दशमं विवादपदम् ।

व्यवहारपदानि

११ क्षेत्रजविवादः

सेतुकेदारमर्यादाविकृष्टाकृष्टनिश्चयाः ।
क्षेत्राधिकारा यत्र स्युर्विवादः क्षेत्रजस्तु सः ॥१॥
क्षेत्रसीमाविरोधेषु सामन्तेभ्यो विनिश्चयः ।
नगरग्रामगणिनो ये च वृद्धतमा नराः ॥२॥
ग्रामसीमासु च बहिर्ये स्युस्तत्कृषिजीविनः ।
गोपशाकुनिकव्याधा ये चान्ये वनगोचराः ॥३॥
समुन्नयेयुस्ते सीमां लक्षणैरुपलक्षिताम् ।
तुषाङ्गारकपालैश्च कुम्भैरायतनैर्द्रुमैः ॥४॥
अभिज्ञातैश्च वल्मीकस्थलनिम्नोन्नतादिभिः ।
केदारारामार्गैश्च पुराणैः सेतुभिस्तथा ॥५॥
निम्नगापहृतोत्सृष्टनष्टचिह्नासु भूमिषु ।
तत्प्रदेशानुमानाच्च प्रमाणैर्भोगदर्शनैः ॥६॥
अथ चेदनृतं ब्रूयुः सामन्तास्तद्विनिश्चये ।
सर्वे पृथक्पृथग्दण्ड्या राज्ञा मध्यमसाहसम् ॥७॥
गणवृद्धादयस्त्वन्ये दण्डं दाप्याः पृथक्पृथक् ।
विनेयाः प्रथमेन स्युः साहसेनानृते स्थिताः ॥८॥
नैकः समुन्नयेत्सीमां नरः प्रत्ययवानपि ।
गुरुत्वादस्य धर्मस्य क्रियैषा बहुषु स्थिता ॥९॥
एकश्चेदुन्नयेत्सीमां सोपवासः समाहितः ।
रक्तमाल्याम्बरधरः क्षितिमारोप्य मूर्धनि ॥१०॥
यदा च न स्युर्ज्ञातारः सीमाया न च लक्षणम् ।

१ b — D -निश्चये; c — D क्षेत्राधिकारो यस्तु स्याद्.
२ a — NMS -विरोधे तु; D -विवादेषु; d — Y मुख्यतमा जनाः.
३ c — Y गोपाः शाकुनि-; d — D वनजीविनः.
४ c — NMS -पालानां; Y -पालास्थि; d — D कूपैर्.
५ a — NMS अभिज्ञानैश्च; c — Y केदाराधारमर्गैश्च.
६ b — L4 M3 निम्नगापहृतैर्दृष्टनष्ट-; d — N प्रमाणा-; D पुराणैर्.
७ b — NMS -विनिर्णये; B2 विनिश्चयेत्; d — BM C -साहसात्.
८ a — NMS गणि-; b — Y दण्ड्या हन्याः; c — NMS दण्डगत्या; d — L साहसं नानृत-.
९ M3 om this verse. c — D कार्यस्य.
१० b — D सोपवासाः; NMS Y समुन्नयेत्.

तदा राजा द्वयोः सीमामुद्धरेदिष्टतः स्वयम् ॥११॥
एतेनैव गृहोद्यानानिपानायतनादिषु ।
विवादविधिराख्यातस्तथा ग्रामान्तरेषु च ॥१२॥
अवस्करस्थलश्वभ्रभ्रमस्यन्दनिकादिभिः ।
चतुष्पथसुरस्थानरथ्यामार्गान्निरोधयेत् ॥१३॥
परक्षेत्रस्य मध्ये तु सेतुर्न प्रतिषिध्यते ।
महागुणोऽल्पबाधश्च वृद्धिरिष्टा क्षये सति ॥१४॥
सेतुस्तु द्विविधो ज्ञेयः खेयो बन्ध्यस्तथैव च ।
तोयप्रवर्तनात्खेयो बन्ध्यः स्यात्तन्निवर्तनात् ॥१५॥
नान्तरेणोदकं सस्यं नश्येदभ्युदकेन तु ।
य एवानुदके दोषः स एवाभ्युदके स्मृतः ॥१६॥
पूर्वप्रवृत्तमुत्सन्नमपृष्ट्वा स्वामिनं तु यः ।
सेतुं प्रवर्तयेत्कश्चिन्न स तत्फलभाग्भवेत् ॥१७॥
मृते तु स्वामिनि पुनस्तद्वंश्ये वापि मानवे ।
राजानमामन्त्र्य ततः प्रकुर्यात्सेतुकर्म तत् ॥१८॥
अतोऽन्यथा क्लेशभाक्स्यान्मृगव्याधानुदर्शनात् ।
इषवस्तस्य नश्यन्ति यो विद्धमनुविध्यति ॥१९॥
अशक्तप्रेतनष्टेषु क्षेत्रिकेष्वनिवारितः ।
क्षेत्रं चेद्विकृषेत्कश्चिदश्नुवीत स तत्फलम् ॥२०॥
विकृष्यमाणे क्षेत्रे चेत्क्षेत्रिकः पुनराव्रजेत् ।

११ a — D यदि; b — M2 सीमायां; c — Y स्वयं; d — D उन्नयेद्.

१२ c — Y एप एव; NMS अनेनैव; d — D add
सीमामध्ये तु जातानां वृक्षानां क्षेत्रयोर्द्वयोः ।
फलपुष्पं च सामान्यं क्षेत्रस्वामिपु निर्दिशेत् ॥ [J 11.13]
अन्यक्षेत्रोपजातानां शाखास्त्वन्यत्र संस्थिताः ।
स्वामिनस्ता विजानीयादन्यक्षविनिर्गताः ॥ [J 11.14]

१३ b — NMS -स्वभ्रमार्ग-; Y स्यन्दनिकादयः; M2 M3 -स्यन्दनकादयः. d — NMS दूपयेत्; D add
शोधयन्ति तु ये मोहाद् वलाद्वापि कथंचन ।
दण्डयेत्तादृशान्राजा साहसेनोत्तमेन च ॥ [J 11.16]

१४ a — N न; b — N प्रतिहन्यते; c — NMS ऽल्पदोपश्च; N यांऽल्पवाधां वहुगुणां.

१५ a — X D प्रोक्तः; b — NMS खन्यो; c — NMS -प्रवर्तने; X -प्रवर्तमानात्; NMS खन्यो; Y खेयं; d — L L4 M3 वन्धः; Y तन्निवरणात्; NMS विनिवर्तने.

१६ a — Y सस्या; b — NMS नाशोऽप्यत्युदकेन तुः; Y न चैवाभ्युदके सति; c — NMS यावाननुदके; L4 M3 यत्रैवानुदके; d — NMS तावानत्युदके.

१७ a — D -प्रवर्त्तम्; d — BM C तस्य फलभाग्.

१८ a — Y सुतो; b — Jolly -दांश्ये वावि; d — Y कृत्.

१९ b — NMS -निदर्शनात्; N मृगव्याधस्य दर्शनात्; d — B2 C add
पृथोरपीमां पृथिवीं भार्यां पूर्वविदो विदुः ।
स्थाणुच्छेदस्य केदारमाहुः शल्यवतो मृगम् ॥ [Manu 9.44]

२० c — Y यद्.

खिलोपचारं तत्सर्वं दत्त्वा स्वक्षेत्रमाप्नुयात् ॥२१॥
तदष्टभागापचयाद्यावत्सप्त गताः समाः ।
संप्राप्ते त्वष्टमे वर्षे भुक्तं क्षेत्रं लभेत सः ॥२२॥
संवत्सरेणार्धखिलं खिलं तद्वत्सरैस्त्रिभिः ।
पञ्चवर्षावसन्नं तु स्यात्क्षेत्रमटवीसमम् ॥२३॥
क्षेत्रं त्रिपुरुषं यत्स्याद्गृहं वा स्यात्क्रमागतम् ।
राजप्रसादादन्यत्र न तद्भोगः परं नयेत् ॥२४॥
उत्क्रम्य तु वृतिं यत्र सस्यघातो गवादिभिः ।
पालः शास्यो भवेत्तत्र न चेच्छक्त्या निवारयेत् ॥२५॥
समूलसस्यनाशे तु तत्स्वामी सममाप्नुयात् ।
वधेन पालो मुच्येत दण्डं स्वामिनि पातयेत् ॥२६॥
गौः प्रसूता दशाहाच्च महोक्षाजाविकुञ्जराः ।
निवार्यास्तु प्रयत्नेन तेषां स्वामी न दण्डभाक् ॥२७॥
माषं गां दापयेद्दण्डं द्वौ माषौ महिषीं तथा ।
अजाविके सवत्से तु दण्डः स्यादर्धमाषकः ॥२८॥
अदण्ड्या हस्तिनोऽश्वाश्च प्रजापाला हि ते स्मृताः ।
अदण्ड्या गर्भिणी गौश्च सूतिका चाभिसारिणी ॥२९॥
प्रोक्तस्तु द्विर्निषण्णानां वसन्त्यां तु चतुर्गुणम् ।
प्रत्यक्षचारकाणां तु चौरदण्डः स्मृतस्तथा ॥३०॥
या नष्टाः पालदोषेण गावः क्षेत्रं समाश्रिताः ।
न तत्र गोमिनो दण्डः पालस्तं दण्डमर्हति ॥३१॥
राजग्राहगृहीतो वा वज्राशनिहतोऽपि वा ।
अथ सर्पेण दष्टो वा गिर्यग्रात्पतितोऽपि वा ॥३२॥
सिंहव्याघ्रहतो वापि व्याधिभिः चैव पातितः ।

२१ d — M3 L4 स क्षेत्रम्.

२२ a — NMS -भागोपचयाद्; b — N समाः.

२३ b — NMS स्याद्; d — Y तत्.

२४ a — N यस्य; b — N वास्य; c — N राज्ञः प्रसादाद्; d — X निवर्तयेत्; Y विवर्तयेत्.

२५ a — Y यस्या; X यः स्यात्; b — NMS दण्ड्यो; d — NMS स चेच्छक्तो न वारयेत्.

२६ a — D -घाते; b — NMS ध्यान्यम्; X स तम्; Y om this verse.

२७ b — D दशाहं तु महोक्षो वाजिकुञ्जरौ; c — DY स्युः.

२८ ab — N गावः पादं प्रदण्ड्यादि महिपीद्विगुणमं ततः; c — Y ऽथ वत्से तु; NMS च वत्से च.

२९ a — Y हृस्वास्; b — D मताः; c — D गन्तुकी; d — D वाभिसारिणी; NMS चातिसारिणी; D add नप्टा भम्ना च लम्ना च वृपभः कृतलक्षणः ।

३० a — D प्रोक्तं तु छिन्ननासायां; NMS प्रोक्तः स द्विगुणः सत्रे; b — D add सन्नानां द्विगुणः प्रोक्तो वसतां तु चतुर्गुणः [J 1.34ab]; c — D नृणाम्.

३१ a — D यदाप्नुयुः; c — D गोमिनां; d — Y तद्.

३२ a — Y -ग्रह-; d — D वृक्षाद्वा पतितो भवेत्.

न तत्र दोषः पालस्य न च दोषोऽस्ति गोमिनाम् ॥३३॥
गोभिस्तु भक्षितं धान्यं यो नरः प्रतिमार्गति ।
सामन्तस्य शदो देयो धान्यं यत्तत्र वापितम् ।
गवत्रं गोमिने देयं धान्यं तत्कर्षिकस्य तु ॥३४॥
ग्रामोपान्ते च यत्क्षेत्रं विवीतान्ते महापथे ।
अनावृते चेत्तन्नाशे न पालस्य व्यतिक्रमः ॥३५॥
पथि क्षेत्रे वृतिः कार्या यामुष्ट्रो नावलोकयेत् ।
न लङ्घयेत्पशुर्नाश्वो न भिद्याद्यां च सूकरः ॥३६॥
गृहं क्षेत्रं च विज्ञेयं वासहेतुः कुटुम्बिनाम् ।
तस्मात्तन्नाक्षिपेद्राजा तद्धि मूलं कुटुम्बिनाम् ॥३७॥
वृद्धे जनपदे राज्ञो धर्मः कोशश्च वर्धते ।
हीयते हीयमाने च वृद्धिहेतुमतः श्रयेत् ॥३८॥

३३ a — D व्याघ्रादिभिर्हतो; ab — NMS om; b — D वाप्युपद्रुतः; c — B 2 पालानां; d —D add सस्यं
विनाशयेद् गौश्चेत्र दण्डः कल्पितो यतः ।
३४ b — D प्रतियाचते; c — M3 L4 सदृशस्तस्य समो देयं; cd— D सामन्तानुमते देयं धान्यं यत्तत्र भक्षितम्; e —
M2 M3 L4 गावस्तु; L गवलं; f— NMS तत्कृपकस्य तु; Y add
स्थाणुछेदस्य केदारमाहुः साल्यवतो मृगम् । [Manu 9.44cd]
इपवस्तस्य नाश्यन्ति यो विद्धमनुविध्यति । [NāSmṛ 11.19cd]
अशक्तप्रेतनष्टेपु क्षेत्रिकेष्वनिवारितः । [NāSmṛ 11.19cd]
विकृष्यमाणे क्षेत्रे चेत्क्षेत्रिकः पुनराव्रजेत् । [NāSmṛ 11.20ab]
D add
एवं हि विनयः प्रोक्तो गोपैः सस्यावपातनात् । [J 11.39ab]
b— Y विवीकान्ते; c— NMS अनावृतं; BM नश्येत; Y वश्येत; d— NMS गोपस्य.
३६ a— Y कुर्यात्; c— D वाश्वो; d— NMS add
खाटखाटंस्य केदारमाहुः शल्यवतो मृगम् । [cf. Manu 9.44cd]
इपवस्तस्य नश्यन्ति यो विधमनुविध्यति । [NāSmṛ 11.19cd]
अशक्तप्रतनष्टेपु क्षेत्रिकेष्वनिवारितः । [NāSmṛ 11.20ab]
विकृष्यमाणे क्षेत्रे चेत्क्षेत्रिकः पुनराव्रजेत् ।
वीजापचारं तत्सर्वं दत्त्वा स्वं क्षेत्रमाप्नुयात् । [NāSmṛ 11.21]
३७ a— D गृहक्षेत्रे; b— D दृष्टे द्वे वासहेतू; c— D ते नोत्क्षिपेद्.
३८ a— L4 वितिः; M2 वृत्तिः M3 रितिः; d— D add इति श्री नारदीये धर्मशास्त्रे क्षेत्रसीमा नाम एकादशमं
विवादपदं समाप्तम्; N add इति क्षेत्रसीमाविवादपदं समाप्तम्; NMS add इति क्षेत्रविवाद एकादशमं
विवादपदम्.

व्यवहारपदानि

१२ स्त्रीपुंसयोगः

विवाहादिविधिः स्त्रीणां यत्र पुंसां च कीर्त्यते ।
स्त्रीपुंसयोगनामैतद्विवादपदमुच्यते ॥१॥
स्त्रीपुंसयोस्तु संबन्धाद्वरणं प्राग्विधीयते ।
वरणाद्ग्रहणं पाणेः संस्कारोऽथ द्विलक्षणः ॥२॥
तयोरनियतं प्रोक्तं वरणं दोषदर्शनात् ।
पाणिग्रहणमन्त्राभ्यां नियतं दारलक्षणम् ॥३॥
ब्राह्मणक्षत्रियविशां शूद्राणां च परिग्रहे ।
स्वजात्या श्रेयसी भार्या स्वजात्यश्च पतिः स्त्रियाः ॥४॥
ब्राह्मणस्यानुलोम्येन स्त्रियोऽन्यास्तिस्र एव तु ।
शूद्रायाः प्रातिलोम्येन तथान्ये पतयस्त्रयः ॥५॥
द्वे भार्ये क्षत्रियस्यान्ये वैश्यस्यैका प्रकीर्तिता ।
वैश्याया द्वौ पती ज्ञेयावेकोऽन्यः क्षत्रियापतिः ॥६॥
आ सप्तमात्पञ्चमाद्वा बन्धुभ्यः पितृमातृतः ।
अविवाह्याः सगोत्राः स्युः समानप्रवरास्तथा ॥७॥
परीक्ष्यः पुरुषः पुंस्त्वे निजैरेवाङ्गलक्षणैः ।
पुमांश्चेदविकल्पेन स कन्यां लब्धुमर्हति ॥८॥
सुबद्धजत्रुजान्वस्थिः सुबद्धांसशिरोधरः ।
स्थूलघाटस्तनूरुत्वगविलग्नगतिस्वरः ॥९॥
विट् चास्य प्लवते नाप्सु ह्लादि मूत्रं च फेनिलम् ।
पुमान्स्यांल्लक्षणैरेतैर्विपरीतैस्तु पण्डकः ॥१०॥

१ b — Y यच्च; D यथा; Y प्रकल्प्यते; X च कल्प्यते; c — X स्त्रीपुंसयोगसंज्ञं तद्.

२ b — D संवन्धे; d — M2 ऽयं.

३ c — D -मन्त्रश्च.

४ c — D सजातिः; d — D सजातिश्च; Y स्त्रियः.

५ b — Y तिस्रः; BM C B5 पत्न्योऽपराः स्मृताः B2 भार्म्यावराः स्मृताः; c — M2 प्रतिलोमेन; M3 L4 प्रतिलोम्येन; d — Y तथा स्युः.

६ a — Y भार्या-; d — Y ज्ञेय; BM ज्ञेया.

८ a — Y NMS परीक्ष पुरुषं; Y पुंसो.

९ a — NMS -जान्वास्थि-; D सुवद्धजघनजान्वस्थि-; b — D N सुवद्धांशशिरोरुहः; c — Y स्थूलघाटान्तनुजिह्वां; NMS स्थूलघाटातानूजत्वग्; M3 L4 स्थूलघाटोतानूयश्च; d— Y विलग्नगतिसुस्वरः (ऽविलग्न- ?).

१० a — D रेतोऽस्यांत्प्लवते; b — NMS रावि; d — NMS M3 विपरीतस्तु; D -पण्ढकः.

चतुर्दशविधः शास्त्रे स तु दृष्टो मनीषिभिः ।
चिकित्स्यश्चाचिकित्स्यश्च तेषामुक्तो विधिः क्रमात् ॥११॥
निसर्गपण्डो वध्रिश्च पक्षपण्डस्तथैव च ।
अभिशापाद्गुरो रोगाद्देवक्रोधात्तथैव च ॥१२॥
ईर्ष्यापण्डश्च सेव्यश्च वातरेता मुखेभगः ।
आक्षिप्तो मोघबीजश्च शालीनोऽन्यपतिस्तथा ॥१३॥
तत्राद्यावप्रतीकारौ पक्षाख्यो मासमाचरेत् ।
अनुक्रमात्त्रयस्यास्य कालः संवत्सरः स्मृतः ॥१४॥
ईर्ष्यापण्डादयो येऽन्ये चत्वारः समुदाहृताः ।
संत्यक्तव्याः पतितवत्क्षतयोन्या अपि स्त्रियाः ॥१५॥
आक्षिप्तमोघबीजाभ्याम्पत्यावप्रतिकर्मणि ।
पतिरन्यः स्मृतो नार्या वत्सरं संप्रतीक्ष्य तु ॥१६
शालीनस्यापि धृष्टस्त्रीसंयोगाद्भज्यते ध्वजः ।
तं हीनवेगमन्यस्त्रीबालाद्याभिरुपक्रमेत् ॥१७॥
अन्यस्याम्यो मनुष्यः स्यादमनुष्यः स्वयोषिति ।
लभेत सान्यं भर्तारमेतत्कार्यं प्रजापतेः ॥१८॥
अपत्यार्थं स्त्रियः सृष्टाः स्त्री क्षेत्रं बीजिनः प्रजाः ।
क्षेत्रं बीजवते देयं नाबीजी क्षेत्रमर्हति ॥१९॥
पिता दद्यात्स्वयं कन्याम्भ्राता वानुमते पितुः ।
मातामहो मातुलश्च सकुल्या बान्धवास्तथा ॥२०॥
माताभावे तु सर्वेषां प्रकृतौ यदि वर्तते ।
तस्यामप्रकृतिस्थायां दद्युः कन्यां स्वजातयः ॥२१॥
यदा तु नैव कश्चित्स्यात्कन्या राजानमाव्रजेत् ।

११ b — X D पण्ढो.

१२ a — D -पण्ढो; NMS Y M2 वधश्च; L L4 वभ्रश्च; M3 वद्रश्च; b — D -पण्ढस्.

१३ a — D -पण्ढश्च; M3 L4 ईर्ष्यापण्ढश्च; NMS आक्षिप्त-; Y मोघवीजीव; d — X ऽन्यापतिस्.

१४ b — Y पक्षाख्ये; NMS पक्षाख्यं; Y तु समाचरेत्; c — D अनुक्रमात्तु यस्यास्य; NMS अनुक्रमत्रयस्यास्य.

१५ a — D ईर्ष्यापण्ढादयो; M2 L4 ईर्षापण्डादयो; M2 L4 ऽन्ये ये; c — D त्यक्तव्यास्ते; d — Jolly स्त्रिया; X स्त्रियः.

१६ a — NMS आक्षिप्तमोघवीजौ च; Y आक्षिप्तमोघवीजीव; b — D कृतेऽपि पतिकर्मणि; Y पत्यपप्रतिकर्मणि; c — M भार्या; d — D वत्सरार्धं; B5 वत्सल्यं; D प्रतीक्ष्य तु; M3 L4 संप्रतीक्षतु; M2 संप्रतीक्षेत.

१७ b — X D दुष्टस्त्रीसंयोगाद्; D भ्रश्यते; d — D तं हीनवेगमन्यस्त्रीवालाद्याभिरुपाचरेत्; X तं हीनवेगवत्स्त्रीभिर्वालाद्याभिरुपक्रमेत्; Y तं हीनवेगमत्वा स्त्री न लाभश्च उपक्रमेत्; NMS तं हीनवेपमत्तस्त्रीवालान्धाभिरुप्रक्रमेत्.

१८ b — Y त्वयांपिति; d — Y प्रजापतिः.

१९ b — D नराः; d — M3 L4 स वीजि-; L सवीजो.

२० c — D पितामहो; M3 L4 मातुलाश्च; d — Y स्वकुल्या.

२१ a — D माता त्वभावे; d — D सनामयः; NMS सजातयः.

अनुज्ञया तस्य वरं प्रतीत्य वरयेत्स्वयम् ॥२२॥
सवर्णमनुरूपं च कुलरूपवयःश्रुतैः ।
सह धर्मं चरेत्तेन पुत्रांश्चोत्पादयेत्ततः ॥२३॥
प्रतिगृह्य च यः कन्यां नरो देशान्तरं व्रजेत् ।
त्रीनृतून्समतिक्रम्य कन्यान्यं वरयेद्वरम् ॥२४॥
कन्या नर्तुमुपेक्षेत बान्धवेभ्यो निवेदयेत् ।
ते चेन्न दद्युस्तां भर्त्रे ते स्युर्भ्रूणहभिः समाः ॥२५॥
यावन्तश्चर्तवस्तस्याः समतीता पतिं विना ।
तावत्यो भ्रूणहत्याः स्युस्तस्य यो न ददाति ताम् ॥२६॥
अतोऽप्रवृत्ते रजसि कन्यां दद्यात्पिता सकृत् ।
महदेनः स्पृशेदेनमन्यथैष विधिः सताम् ॥२७॥
सकृदंशो निपतति सकृत्कन्या प्रदीयते ।
सकृदाह ददानीति त्रीण्येतानि सकृत्सकृत् ॥२८॥
ब्राह्मादिषु विवाहेषु पञ्चस्वेषु विधिः स्मृतः ।
गुणापेक्षं भवेद्दानमासुरादिषु च त्रिषु ॥२९॥
कन्यायामप्राप्तशुल्कायां ज्यायांश्चेद्वर आव्रजेत् ।
धर्मार्थकामसंयुक्तं वाच्यं तत्रानृतं भवेत् ॥३०॥
नादुष्टां दूषयेत्कन्यां नादुष्टं दूषयेद्वरम् ।
दोषे तु सति नागः स्यादन्योन्यं त्यजतोस्तयोः ॥३१॥
दत्त्वा न्यायेन यः कन्यां वराय न ददाति ताम् ।
अदुष्टश्चेद्वरो राज्ञा स दण्ड्यस्तत्र चोरवत् ॥३२॥
यस्तु दोषवतीं कन्यामनाख्याय प्रयच्छति ।
तस्य कुर्यान्नृपो दण्डं पूर्वसाहसचोदितम् ॥३३॥

२२ a — Y चैव; b — D आश्रयेत्; c — NMS वरं तस्य.
२३ b — D कुलशिलवयःश्रुतै; d — D प्रजां.
२४ b — X D वरो.
२५ a — D अपेक्षेत; d — N सर्वभ्रूणहनः.
२६ b — N D समातीयुः; NMS विना पतिम्.
२७ a — D अतः प्रवृत्ते; L अथो प्रकृते; d — D अन्यथैवं; Y अन्यथैपां; Y स्मृतः; X सदा.
२८ c — BM B5 C ददामीति; d — D Y सताम्; N add
व्यञ्जनैस्तु समुत्पन्नैः सोमो भुञ्जेत योपितः ।
पयोधरैस्तु गान्धर्वो रजस्यग्निः प्रकीर्तितः ॥ [GṛSaṃPa 2.19]
Y add
तस्मादव्यञ्जनोपेतामरजामपयोधराम् ।
अभुक्तपूर्वां सोमाद्यैर्दद्याद् दुहितरं पिता ॥ [GṛSaṃPa 2.20]
२९ b — Jolly एप.
३० a — D दत्तशुल्कायां; c — L L4 M2 M3 -संयुक्ते; Jolly -कामासंयुक्तो; d — Jolly वाक्यं.
३१ c — D गागः.
३२ d — D चौरवत्.

अकन्येति तु यः कन्यां ब्रूयाद् द्वेषेण मानवः ।
स शतं प्राप्नुयाद्दण्डं तस्या दोषमदर्शयन् ॥३४॥
प्रतिगृह्य तु यः कन्यामदुष्टामुत्सृजेद्वरः ।
विनेयः सोऽप्यकामोऽपि कन्यां तामेव चोद्वहेत् ॥३५॥
दीर्घकुत्सितरोगार्ता व्यङ्गा संसृष्टमैथुना ।
धृष्टान्यगतभावा च कन्यादोषाः प्रकीर्तिताः ॥३६॥
उन्मत्तः पतितः क्लीबो दुर्भगस्त्यक्तबान्धवः ।
कन्यादोषौ च यौ पूर्वौ एष दोषगणो वरे ॥३७॥
अष्टौ विवाहा वर्णानां संस्कारार्थं प्रकीर्तिताः ।
ब्राह्मस्तु प्रथमस्तेषां प्राजापत्यस्तथैव च ॥३८॥
आर्षश्चैवाथ दैवश्च गान्धर्वश्चासुरस्तथा ।
राक्षसोऽनन्तरस्तस्मात्पैशाचस्त्वष्टमः स्मृतः ॥३९॥
सत्कृत्याहूय कन्यां तु ब्राह्मे दद्याद् त्वलंकृतां ।
सह धर्मं चरेत्युक्त्वा प्राजापत्यो विधीयते ॥४०॥
वस्त्रगोमिथुने दत्त्वा विवाहस्त्वार्ष उच्यते ।
अन्तर्वेद्यां तु दैवः स्यादृत्विजे कर्म कुर्वते ॥४१॥
इच्छन्तीमिच्छते प्राहुर्गान्धर्वो नाम पञ्चमम् ।
विवाहस्त्वासुरो ज्ञेयः शुल्कसंव्यवहारतः ॥४२॥
प्रसह्य हरणादुक्तो विवाहो राक्षसस्तथा ।
सुप्तमत्तोपगमनात्पैशाचस्त्वष्टमोऽधमः ॥४३॥
एषां तु धर्म्याश्चत्वारो ब्राह्माद्याः समुदाहृताः ।
साधारणः स्याद्गान्धर्वस्त्रयोऽधर्म्यास्त्वतः परे ॥४४॥
परपूर्वाः स्त्रियस्त्वन्याः सप्त प्रोक्ता यथाक्रमम् ।
पुनर्भूस्त्रिविधा तासां स्वैरिणी तु चतुर्विधा ॥४५॥

३४ c — Y सततं; d — N कन्या-.

३५ b — M2 अदृप्टां; D X नरः; c — D स विनेयस्त्व.

३६ b — NMS व्यङ्गाः; NMS संस्पृप्टमैथुनाः; M2 L L4 संस्पृप्टमैथुना; c — D दुप्टान्य-; B5 दृप्टान्य-

३७ d — Y add

पञ्चोन्मादाः समाख्याता वातपित्तकफोद्भवाः ।
चतुर्थो धननाशेन संनिपातेन पञ्चमः ॥ [?]

३८ d — D तथापरः; X ततः स्मृतः.

३९ a — D चैव हि; b — Y गन्धर्वश्चा; c — D B2 ऽनवरस्; d — NMS अप्टमोऽधमः.

४० b — D दद्याद् ब्राह्मे; NMS ब्राह्मीं दद्याद्; c — Y चरत्तेन; d — D विधिः स्मृतः.

४१ a — D वस्त्रगोमिथुनाभ्यां तु.

४२ a — D Y इच्छतः; b — D गान्धर्वं; Y पञ्चमः.

४३ c — D X सुप्तप्रमत्तोपगमात्.

४४ b — Y परिकीर्तिताः; d — D ततः.

४५ c — Jolly typo त्रितिधा.

कन्यैवाक्षतयोनिर्या पाणिग्रहणदूषिता ।
पुनर्भूः प्रथमा सोक्ता पुनः संस्कारमर्हति ॥४६॥
कौमारं पतिमुत्सृज्य यान्यं पुरुषमाश्रिता ।
पुनः पत्युर्गृहं यायात्सा द्वितीया प्रकीर्तिता ॥४७॥
असत्सु देवरेषु स्त्री बान्धवैर्या प्रदीयते ।
सवर्णायासपिण्डाय सा तृतीया प्रकीर्तिता ॥४८॥
स्त्री प्रसूताप्रसूता वा पत्यावेव तु जीवति ।
कामात्समाश्रयेदन्यं प्रथमा स्वैरिणी तु सा ॥४९॥
मृते भर्तरि या प्राप्तान्देवरानप्यपास्य तु ।
उपगच्छेत्परं कामात्सा द्वितीया प्रकीर्तिता ॥५०॥
प्राप्ता देशाद्धनक्रीता क्षुत्पिपासातुरा च या ।
तवाहमित्युपगता सा तृतीया प्रकीर्तिता ॥५१॥
देशधर्मानपेक्ष्य स्त्री गुरुभिर्या प्रदीयते ।
उत्पन्नसाहसान्यस्मै सान्त्या वै स्वैरिणी स्मृता ॥५२॥
पुनर्भुवां एष विधिः स्वैरिणीनां च कीर्तितः ।
पूर्वा पूर्वाजघन्यासां श्रेयसी तूत्तरोत्तरा ॥५३॥
अपत्यमुत्पादयितुस्तासां या शुल्कतो हृता ।
अशुल्कोपनतायां तु क्षेत्रिकस्यैव तत्फलम् ॥५४॥
क्षेत्रिकस्य यदज्ञातं क्षेत्रे बीजं प्रदीयते ।
न तत्र बीजिनो भागः क्षेत्रिकस्यैव तद्भवेत् ॥५५॥
ओघवाताहृतं बीजं क्षेत्रे यस्य प्ररोहति ।
फलभुग्यस्य तत्क्षेत्रं न बीजी फलभाग्भवेत् ॥५६॥
महोक्षो जनयेद्वत्सान्यस्य गोषु व्रजे चरन् ।

४६ c — X D प्रोक्ता.
४७ b — NMS या त्वन्यपुरुपाश्रिता; D या त्वन्यपुरुपं श्रिता; c — D इयात्;
४८ B5 om this verse. c — D सवर्णाय सपिण्डाय.
४९ a — NMS प्रसूता वाप्रसूता वा; c — D कामाद्या संश्रयेद् d — D स्वैरिणी प्रथमा तु सा.
५० b — D मृते भर्तरि संप्राप्तान्देवरादीनपास्य या; d — NMS तृतीया.
५१ b —Y क्षुत्तृण्णाव्यसनार्दिता; d — NMS चतुर्था.
५२ a —NMS अवेक्ष्य; d — D अन्या सा; Y चतुर्थी; Jolly अन्त्या सा;NMS सा द्वितीया प्रकीर्तिता; Y add
स्वैरिणीनां चतसृणां सा श्रष्ठा तूत्तरोत्तरा ।
विकल्प (स) तदपत्यानां रिक्थपिण्डोदकादिपु ॥ [Dhko 1978]
५३ a —X D विधिस्त्वेपां; Jolly विधिस्त्वेप; b -- X D प्रकीर्तितः; c —Jolly पूर्वा जघन्यासां.
५४ c —D अशुल्कोपहृतायां; d — NMS भवेत्.
५५ a — NMS अज्ञानात्; b -- Y प्रकीर्यते; d — X D फलम्.
५६ a — B2 दांपवाताहृतं; L L4 ओघवाताहतं; c — NMS फलभाग्; D Y फलभुक्तस्य; D क्षेत्री; B om this verse.

तस्य ते यस्य ता गावो मोघं स्यन्दितमार्षभम् ॥५७॥
क्षेत्रिकानुमतं बीजं यस्य क्षेत्रे प्रमुच्यते ।
तदपत्यं द्वयोरेव बीजिक्षेत्रिकयोर्मतम् ॥५८॥
नर्ते क्षेत्रं भवेत्सस्यं न च बीजं विनास्ति तत् ।
अतोऽपत्यं द्वयोरिष्टं पितुर्मातुश्च धर्मतः ॥५९॥
नाथवत्या परगृहे संयुक्तस्य स्त्रिया सह ।
दृष्टं संग्रहणं तज्ज्ञैर्नागतायाः स्वयं गृहे ॥६०॥
प्रदुष्टत्यक्तदारस्य क्लीबस्य क्षमकस्य च ।
स्वेच्छयोपेयुषो दारान्न दोषः साहसो भवेत् ॥६१॥
परस्त्रिया सहाकालेऽदेशे वा भवतो मिथः ।
स्थानसंभाषणामोदास्त्रयः संग्रहणक्रमाः ॥६२॥
नदीनां संगमे तीर्थेष्वारामेषु वनेषु च ।
स्त्री पुमांश्च समेयातां ग्राह्यं संग्रहणं भवेत् ॥६३॥
दूतीप्रस्थापनैश्चैव लेखासंप्रेषणैरपि ।
अन्यैरपि व्यभिचारैः सर्वं संग्रहणं स्मृतम् ॥६४॥
स्त्रियं स्पृशेददेशे यः स्पृष्टो वा मर्शयेत्तथा ।
परस्परस्यानुमते तच्च संग्रहणं भवेत् ॥६५॥
भक्षैर्वा यदि वा भोज्यैर्वस्त्रैर्माल्यैस्तथैव च ।
संप्रेष्यमानैर्गन्धैश्च सर्वं संग्रहणं स्मृतम् ॥६६॥
दर्पाद्वा यदि वा मोहाच्छ्लाघया वा स्वयं वदेत् ।
ममेयं भुक्तपूर्वेति सर्वं संग्रहणं स्मृतम् ॥६७॥
पाणौ यश्च निगृह्णीयद्वेण्यां वस्त्रान्तरेऽपि वा ।

५७ d — D स्कन्दितम्; NMS स्पन्दितम्.

५८ a — D क्षेत्रिकानुमते; b — D समर्प्यते; X प्रकीर्तिते; d — L L4 M2 M3 -क्षेत्रिकानुमतो.

५९ a — D न स्यात्क्षेत्रं विना; X न तत्क्षेत्रं भवेत्; Y ऋते क्षेत्राद्भवेत्; b — D वा; Y तं.

६० a — D नाप्यपत्यं; b — Jolly typo त्रिया; c — D च संग्रहं.

६१ a — D अदुष्टत्यक्तदारस्य; b — D क्षयिकस्य; Y पतितस्य; c — D सेच्छानुपेयुपो; NMS स्वेच्छैरुपेयुपो; Y स्वेच्छानुपेयुपो; NMS दारैर्; d — X D साहसे.

६२ d — Y संग्रहणः क्रमात्; X संग्रहणं क्रमात्.

६३ X om this verse. d —D स्त्रीपुंसौ यत्समीयातां तच्च संग्रहणं स्मृतम्.

६४ N om this verse. a — D वापि; b — D लेख-; c — D च विविधैर्दोपैर्; NMS अपि व्यतीचारैः; D ग्राह्यं; d — D वुद्धैः.

६५ B4 om this verse. b — L4 स्पृष्ट्वा; L M3 स्पृष्टा; c — D परस्परस्यानुमतं सर्वं; d — D X स्मृतम्; D Y add

उपकारक्रिया केलिः स्पर्शो भूपणवाससाम् ।
सहखट्वासनं चैव सर्वं संग्रहणं स्मृतम् ॥ [J. 12.66]

६६ B4 L L4 M3 om this verse. a — Y D वाभक्षैर्; ab — D वस्त्रैराभरणैर्माल्यैः पानैर्भक्ष्यैस्तथैव च; d — D वेद्यं; D वुद्धैः; N MS भवेत्.

६७ B4 om this verse. c — Y तच्च; d — BM भवेत्;

तिष्ठ तिष्ठेति वा ब्रुयात्सर्वं संग्रहणं स्मृतम् ॥६८॥
स्वजात्यतिक्रमे पुंसामुक्तमुत्तमसाहसम् ।
विपर्यये मध्यमस्तु प्रातिलोमे प्रमापणं ॥६९॥
कन्यायामसकामायां द्व्याङ्गुलस्यावकर्तनम् ।
उत्तमायां वधस्त्वेव सर्वस्वहरणं तथा ॥७०॥
सकामायां तु कन्यायां सवर्णे नास्त्यतिक्रमः ।
किंत्वलंकृत्य सत्कृत्य स एवैनां समुद्वहेत् ॥७१॥
माता मातृष्वसा श्वश्रूर्मातुलानी पितृष्वसा ।
पितृव्यसखिशिष्यस्त्री भगिनी तत्सखी स्नुषा ॥७२॥
दुहिताचार्यभार्या च सगोत्रा शरणागता ।
राज्ञी प्रव्रजिता धात्री साध्वी वर्णोत्तमा च या ॥७३॥
आसामन्यतमां गत्वा गुरुतल्पग उच्यते ।
शिश्नस्योत्कर्तनं दण्डो नान्यस्तत्र विधीयते ॥७४॥
पशुयोन्यामतिक्रामन्विनेयः स दमं शतम् ।
मध्यमं साहसं गोषु तदेवान्त्यावसायिषु ॥७५॥
अगम्यागामिनः शास्ति दण्डो राज्ञा प्रचोदितः ।
प्रायश्चित्तविधावत्र प्रायश्चित्तं विशोधनम् ॥७६॥
स्वैरिण्यब्राह्मणी वेश्या दासी निष्कासिनी च या ।
गम्याः स्युरानुलोम्येन स्त्रियो न प्रतिलोमतः ॥७७॥
आस्वेव तु भुजिष्यासु दोषः स्यात्परदारवत् ।
गम्या अपि हि नोपेयास्ताश्चेदन्यपरिग्रहाः ॥७८॥
अनुत्पन्नप्रजायास्तु पतिः प्रेयाद्यदि स्त्रियाः ।
नियुक्ता गुरुभिर्गच्छेद्देवरं पुत्रकाम्यया ॥७९॥
स च तां प्रतिपद्येत तथैवा पुत्रजन्मतः ।
पुत्रे जाते निवर्तेत विप्लवः स्यादतोऽन्यथा ॥८०॥

६८ B4 om this verse. a — D यच्; b — D वस्त्राञ्चले.

६९ B4 om this verse. a —D सजात्यतिशये; b — D दण्ड उत्तमसाहसः; c — D मध्यमस्त्वानुलोम्येन; d — D प्रातिलोम्ये;

७० ab —B4 om; d — D सर्वसंग्रहणं.

७१ b —D संगमे.

७४ b —N गुरुतल्पा उदाहृता; c — D तस्य; d — D दण्डो.

७५ b —D पशुयोनावतिक्रामन्प्रवृत्तः; NMS सदशं; B2 प्रथमसाहसम्; d — MNS एवान्तावसयिपु.

७६ a — D चास्ति; d — D प्रायश्चित्तविधानं तु पापानां स्याद्.

७७ b — L L4 M2 निस्वामिनी; M3 निस्वामिनां; d — NMS प्रातिलोम्यतः.

७८ d — D यत्ता परपरिग्रहाः; Y यदि ता सुपरिग्रहाः; L4 यतास्तास्यु परिग्रहो; M3 यतस्ताः स्यु परिग्रहाः, M2 यतस्ताः सपरिग्रहाः, L यतस्तास्य परिग्रहाः.

८० B4 om this verse. b — NMS पुत्रजन्मनः; d — D संकरः.

घृतेनाभ्यज्य गात्राणि तैलेनाविकृतेन वा ।
मुखान्मुखं परिहरन्गात्रैर्गात्राण्यसंस्पृशन् ॥८१॥
स्त्रियं पुत्रवतीं वन्ध्यां नीरजस्कामनिच्छन्तीम् ।
न गच्छेद्गर्भिणीं निन्द्यामनियुक्तां च बन्धुभिः ॥८२॥
अनियुक्ता तु या नारी देवराज्जनयेत्सुतम् ।
जारजातमरिक्थीयं तमाहुर्धर्मवादिनः ॥८३॥
तथानियुक्तो भार्यायां यवीयाञ्ज्यायसो व्रजेत् ।
यवीयसो वा यो ज्यायानुभौ तौ गुरुतल्पगौ ॥८४॥
कुले तदवशेषे तु संतानार्थं न कामतः ।
नियुक्तोगुरुभिर्गच्छेद् भ्रातृभार्यं यवीयसः ॥८५॥
अविद्यमाने तु गुरौ राज्ञो वाच्यः कुलक्षयः ।
ततस्तद्वचनाद्गच्छेदनुशिष्य स्त्रिया सह ॥८६॥
पूर्वोक्तेनैव विधिना स्नातां पुंसवने शुचिः ।
सकृदा गर्भाधानाद्वा कृते गर्भे स्नुषैव सा ॥८७॥
अतोऽन्यथा वर्तमानः पुमान्स्त्री वापि कामतः ।
विनेयौ सुभृशं राज्ञा किल्बिषी स्यादनिग्रहात् ॥८८॥
ईर्ष्यासूयसमुत्थे तु संरम्भे रागहेतुके ।
दम्पती विवदेयातां न ज्ञातिषु न राजनि ॥८९॥
अन्योन्यं त्यजतोर्नागः स्यादन्योन्यविरुद्धयोः ।
स्त्रीपुंसयोर्निगूढाया व्यभिचारादृते स्त्रियाः ॥९० ॥
व्यभिचारे स्त्रिया मौण्ड्यमधःशयनमेव च ।

८१ B4 om this verse. b — Y तैलानामविकृतेन; d — Y M2 गात्राणि संस्पृशेत्;
D add कुले तदवशेपे हि संतानार्थं न कामतः ।

८२ B4 om this verse. a — Jolly वन्ध्यां; ab— NMS नीरजस्कामनिच्छन्तीं वन्ध्यां पुत्रवतीं स्त्रियं.

८३ B4 om this verse. d — D B B2 ब्रह्मवादिनः.

८४ a — D यां भार्यां; b — Y यवीनां; d — D add
नियुक्तो गुरुभिर्गच्छेदनुशिप्यास्त्रियं च सः ।
B2 add
भ्रातुर्ज्येप्ठस्य भार्या या गुरुपत्न्यनुजस्य सा ।
यवीयसस्तु या भार्या स्नुपा ज्येप्ठस्य सा स्मृता ।। [Manu 9.57]

८५ D om this verse. a — B तदेव शेपे. d — NMS add
ज्येप्ठभार्यां कनिप्ठां वा गच्छेद् गुरुनियोगतः ।
कुलसन्तानरक्षा तु फलं समधिगच्छतः ।। [NMS 13.87]

८६ D om this verse. b — BM B2 वास्य; Y कुलक्षये c — B4 स तस्य वचनाद्; d — B4 स हि; NMS च सः.

८७ a — D पुर्वोक्तेन विधानेन; b — Jolly स्नुपां; d — D तथैव.

८८ c — Jolly B2 C निनेयौ; d — D विप्लवः; X -सत्करः; D अतोऽन्यथा; NMS अनिग्रहे.

८९ b — D संवन्धे; M2 राजहेतुके; c — D विवदियतां.

९० a — D अतोऽन्यं;D आगः; c — NMS न तुढाया; d — Y स्त्रियः.

कदन्नं वा कुवासश्च कर्म चावस्करोज्झनम् ॥९१॥
स्त्रीधनभ्रष्टसर्वस्वां गर्भविस्रंसिनीं तथा ।
भर्तुश्च वधमिच्छन्तीं स्त्रियं निर्वासयेद्गृहात् ॥९२॥
अनर्थशीलां सततं तथैवाप्रियवादिनीम् ।
पूर्वाशिनीं च या भर्तुः स्त्रियं निर्वासयेद् बुधः ॥९३॥
वन्ध्यां स्त्रीजननीं निन्द्यां प्रतिकुलां च सर्वदा ।
कामतो नाभिनन्देत कुर्वन्नेवं स दोषभाक् ॥९४॥
अनुकूलामवाग्दुष्टां दक्षां साध्वीं प्रजावतीम् ।
त्यजन्भार्यामवस्थाप्यो राज्ञा दण्डेन भूयसा ॥९५॥
अज्ञातदोषेणोढा या निर्गता नान्यमाश्रिता ।
बन्धुभिः सा नियोक्तव्या निर्बन्धुः स्वयमाश्रयेत् ॥९६॥
नष्टे मृते प्रव्रजिते क्लीबे च पतिते पतौ ।
पञ्चस्वापत्सु नारीणां पतिरन्यो विधियते ॥९७॥
अष्टौ वर्षाण्युदीक्षेत ब्राह्मणी प्रोषितं पतिम् ।
अप्रसूता तु चत्वारि परतोऽन्यं समाश्रयेत् ॥९८॥
क्षत्रिया षट् समास्तिष्ठेदप्रसूता समात्रयम् ।
वैश्या प्रसूता चत्वारि द्वे समे त्वितरा वसेत् ॥९९॥
न शूद्रायाः स्मृतः कालो न च धर्मव्यतिक्रमः ।
विशेषतोऽप्रसूतायाः संवत्सरपरा स्थितिः ॥१००॥
अप्रवृत्तौ स्मृतः धर्म एष प्रोषितयोषिताम् ।
जीवति श्रूयमाणे तु स्यादेष द्विगुणो विधिः ॥१०१॥
प्रजाप्रवृत्तौ भूतानां सृष्टिरेषा प्रजापतेः ।
अतोऽन्यगमने स्त्रीणामेवं दोषो न विद्यते ॥१०२॥

९१ a — Y व्यभिचारा; c — Y कुवसं; d — NMS चावस्करोञ्छनम्.

९२ a — B C स्त्रीधर्म-; b — NMS गर्भविस्राविणीं; d — D पुरात्.

९३ d — D क्षिप्रं; D गृहात्; X नरः.

९४ c — NMS कामं तां; d — Y सर्वत्र; L L4 न; B2 add
अप्रजा न नवमे दशमे तु मृतप्रजां ।
एकादशे स्त्रीजननी सद्यस्त्वप्रियवादिनी ॥ [cf. Manu 9.81]

९५ a — NMS अनुरुपां.

९६ B4 om this verse; a — Y अज्ञातदोपामुढा; NMS अज्ञातदोपादुप्टा; Bhava अज्ञातदोपाद्रूढा; b — D Bhava निर्दोपा;

९७ b — NMS पत्यौ प्रव्रजिते नप्टे क्लीवेऽथ पतिते मृते.

९८ a — L L4 उपेक्षत; b — NMS ब्राह्मणं.

९९ b — Y समास्त्रयम्; d — D वर्पे; NMS अप्रजा.

१०० a — D काल, bcd and verse 101a — D om .

१०१ B4 om this verse and the remainder of Chapter 12.

१०२ a — D अप्रवृत्तौ तु; b — D दृप्टिर्; c — NMS ऽन्यथागमे; d — D एप.

आनुलोम्येन वर्णानां यज्जन्म स विधिः स्मृतः ।
प्रातिलोम्येन यज्जन्म स ज्ञेयो वर्णसंकरः ॥१०३॥
अनन्तरः स्मृतः पुत्रः पुत्र एकान्तरस्तथा ।
द्व्यन्तरश्चानुलोम्येन तथैव प्रतिलोमतः ॥१०४॥
उग्रः पारशवश्चैव निषादश्चानुलोमतः ।
उत्तमेभ्यस्त्रयस्त्रिभ्यः शूद्रापुत्राः प्रकीर्तिताः ॥१०५॥
ब्राह्मण्या अपि चाण्डालसूतवैदेहका अपि ।
अपरेभ्यस्त्रयस्त्रिभ्या विज्ञेयः प्रतिलोमतः ॥१०६॥
अम्बष्ठो मागधश्चैव क्षत्ता च क्षत्रियासुताः ।
आनुलोम्येन तत्रैको द्वौ ज्ञेयौ प्रतिलोमतः ॥१०७॥
वैश्यापुत्रास्तु दौष्यन्तयवनायोगवा अपि ।
प्रातिलोम्येन यत्रैको द्वौ ज्ञेयौ चानुलोमजौ ॥१०८॥
सूताद्याः प्रतिलोमास्तु ये जातिप्रतिलोमजाः ।
ते संकराः श्वपाकाद्यास्तेषां त्रिः सप्तको गणः ॥१०९॥
सवर्णो ब्राह्मणीपुत्रः क्षत्रियायामनन्तरः ।
अम्बष्ठोग्रौ तथा पुत्रावेवं क्षत्रियवैश्ययोः ॥११०॥
एकान्तरस्तु दौष्यन्तो वैश्यायां ब्राह्मणात्सुतः ।
शूद्रायां क्षत्रियात्तद्वन्निषादो नाम जायते ॥१११॥
शूद्रा पारशवं सूते ब्राह्मणादुत्तरं सुतम् ।
आनुलोम्येन वर्णानां पुत्रा ह्येते प्रकीर्तिताः ॥११२॥
सूतश्च मागधश्चैव पुत्रावायोगवस्तथा ।
प्रातिलोम्येन वर्णानां तद्वदेतेऽप्यनन्तराः ॥११३॥
अनन्तरः स्मृतः सूतो ब्राह्मण्यां क्षत्रियात्सुतः ।
मागधायोगवौ तद्वद् द्वी पुत्रौ वैश्यशूद्रयोः ॥११४॥
ब्राह्मण्येकान्तरं वैश्यात्सूते वैदेहकं सुतम् ।
क्षत्तारं क्षत्रिया शूद्रात्पुत्रमेकान्तरं तथा ॥११५॥

१०३ b — L पज्-; L4 सज्-; M3 स.

१०५ D om this verse; a — M2 L4 पाराशरश्च; L4 पारशरश्च

१०६ a — NMS ब्राह्मण्याम्; b — NMS चण्डाल-; c — NMS त्रिभ्यो.

१०७ c — Y यत्रैकां.

१०८ D om this verse. b — N तथाम्वष्ठो यवनायांगवा.

१०९ ab — D क्षत्राद्याः पतिलोमाः स्युरनुलोमास्त्विमे स्मृताः; b — NMS ज्ञेयावप्रतिलोमजौ; c — NMS ससंकराः; d — D संस्काराश्चरुपाकाद्यास्तेपां त्रिः सप्त कोप्ठतः; Jolly संस्काराश्चरुपाकाद्यास्तेपां त्रिः सप्त वै मताः; M2 ससंस्काराश्च पाकाद्यास्तेपां त्रिः सप्तकोणतः.

१११ a — D चम्वाप्ठो.

११२ a — NMS द्व्यन्तरं.

११३ a — B2 has this verse after 114. d — D क्षत्तृवैदेहकावपि.

ह्यन्तरः प्रातिलोम्येन पापिष्ठः सति संकरे ।
चाण्डालो जायते शूद्राद् ब्राह्मणी यत्र मुह्यति ॥११६॥
राज्ञा परीक्ष्यं न यथा जायते वर्णसंकरः ।
तस्माद्राज्ञा विशेषेण त्रयी रक्ष्या तु संकरात् ॥११७॥

११६ c — NMS B2 C चण्डालो; d — BM आहृति.

११७ ab — D om; c — X प्रतिदिने; d — N परीक्षा वर्णसंकरात्; D स्त्रियो रक्ष्यास्तु संकरात्; X संरक्षात्संकान्नृपः; D add इति श्री नारदीये धर्मशास्त्रे स्त्रीपुंसयोगो नाम द्वादशं विवादपदम्समाप्तम्; X add स्त्रीपुंसयोगं द्वादश भदभिन्नं समाप्तम्; NMS add इति स्त्रीपुंसयोगो द्वादशं विवादपदम्.

व्यवहारपदानि

१३ दायभागः

विभागोऽर्थस्य पित्रस्य पुत्रैर्यत्र प्रकल्प्यते ।
दायभाग इति प्रोक्तं तद्विवादपदं बुधैः ॥१॥
पितर्यूर्ध्वं मृते पुत्रा विभजेयुर्धनं पितुः ।
मातुर्दुहितरोऽभावे दुहितॄणां तदन्वयः ॥२॥
मातुर्निवृत्ते रजसि प्रत्तासु भगिनीषु च ।
निरष्टे वाप्यमरणे पितर्युपरतस्पृहे ॥३॥
पितैव वा स्वयं पुत्रान्विभजेद्वयसिस्थितः ।
ज्येष्ठं श्रेष्ठविभागेन यथा वास्य मतिर्भवेत् ॥४॥
बिभृयाद्वेच्छतः सर्वाञ्ज्येष्ठो भ्राता यथा पिता ।
भ्राता शक्तः कनिष्ठो वा शक्त्यपेक्षः कुले क्रिया ॥५॥
शौर्यभार्याधने हित्वा यच्च विद्याधनं भवेत् ।
त्रीण्येतान्यविभाज्यानि प्रसादो यश्च पैतृकः ॥६॥
मात्रा च स्वधनं दत्तं यस्मै स्यात् प्रीतिपूर्वकम् ।
तस्याप्येष विधिर्दृष्टो मातापीष्टे यथा पिता ॥७॥
अध्यग्न्यध्यावहनिकं भर्तृदायस्तथैव च ।
भ्रातृमातृपितृभ्यश्च षड्विधं स्त्रीधनं स्मृतम् ॥८॥
स्त्रीधनं तदपत्यानां भर्तृगाम्यप्रजासु च ।
ब्राह्मादिषु चतुःष्वाहुः पितृगामीतरेषु तु ॥९॥
कुटुम्बं बिभृयाद् भ्रातुर्यो विद्यामधिगच्छतः ।
भागं विद्याधनात्तस्मात्स लभेताश्रुतोऽपि सन् ॥१०॥

२ a — NMS उपरते; D ऊर्ध्वं गते; b — D विभजेरन्; D क्रमात्.

३ a — L निवृत्त-; c — D निवृत्ते; B4 निरक्षे; B2 विनष्टे; B B2 वापि मरणे; D वापि रमणे; L4 वापि रमणो d — NMS उपरतेऽस्पृहे; Y उपगते स्पृहे.

४ b — M2 L -स्थिते; L4 वयसंस्थिते; c — D वा श्रेष्ठभागेन; d — NMS यथा वा स्व-; Y यथैवास्य.

५ d — Y भक्त्यपेक्ष-; NMS शक्त्यपेक्षं; D श्रियः.

६ a — Y शौर्यविद्याधने; M3 L4 शौर्यभार्याधनं; D चांभे; c — L4 अविभार्यानि.

७ c — BM B4 भवेद्धर्मो; d — D मातापि हि.

८ a — NMS अध्यग्न्यध्याहवनिकं; c — NMS भ्रात्रा दत्तं पितृभ्यां च; D भ्रातृमातृपितृप्राप्तं; d — M2 add दत्तं च प्रीतिकर्मणि पितृमातृसुतप्राप्तमिति पाठान्तरम् [cf. Manu 9.194].

९ b — D Y तु; d — L4 इतरासु; D च.

१० a — D Y धातुर्; b — D Y या; NMS अधिगच्छति.

वैद्योऽवैद्याय नाकामो दद्यादंशं स्वतो धनात् ।
पितृद्रव्यं तदाश्रित्य न चेत्तेन तदाहृतम् ॥११॥
द्वावंशौ प्रतिपद्येत विभजन्नात्मनः पिता ।
समांशभागिनी माता पुत्राणां स्यान्मृते पतौ ॥१२॥
ज्येष्ठायांशोऽधिको देयः ज्येष्ठाय तु वरः स्मृतः ।
समांशभाजः शेषाः स्युरप्रत्ता भगिनी तथा ॥१३॥
क्षेत्रजेष्वपि पुत्रेषु तद्वज्जातेषु धर्मतः ।
वर्णावरेष्वंशहानिरूढाजातेष्वनुक्रमात् ॥१४॥
पित्रैव तु विभक्ता ये हीनाधिकसमैर्धनैः ।
तेषां स एव धर्मः स्यात्सर्वस्य हि पिता प्रभुः ॥१५॥
कानीनश्च सहोढश्च गूढायां यश्च जायते ।
तेषां वोढापिता ज्ञेयस्ते च भागहराः स्मृताः ॥१६॥
अज्ञातपितृको यश्च कानीनोऽनूढमातृकः ।
मातामहाय दद्यात्स पिण्डं रिक्थं हरेत च ॥१७॥
जाता ये त्वनियुक्तायामेकेन बहुभिस्तथा ।
अरिक्थभाजस्ते सर्वे बीजिनां एव ते सुताः ॥१८॥
दद्युस्ते बीजिने पिण्डं माता चेच्छुल्कतो हृता ।
अशुल्कोपगतायां तु पिण्डदा वोढुरेव ते ॥१९॥
पितृद्विट् पतितः पण्डो यश्च स्यादौपपातिकः ।
औरसा अपि नैतेंऽशं लभेरन्क्षेत्रजाः कुतः ॥२०॥
दीर्घतीव्रामयग्रस्ता जडोन्मत्तान्धपङ्गवः ।
भर्तव्याः स्युः कुले चैते तत्पुत्रास्त्वंशभागिनः ॥२१॥
द्विरामुष्यायणा दद्युर्द्वाभ्यां पिण्डोदके पृथक् ।

११ c — D पित्र्ये द्रव्यं; Y पित्र्यं द्रव्यं; D समाश्रित्य.
१२ a — BM om this verse;. d — NMS धावे; B2 add
अनुपघ्नन्पितृद्रव्यं श्रमेण यदुपार्जितम् ।
स्वयमीहितलब्धं तन्नाकामो दातुमर्हति ॥ [Manu 9.208]
१३ a — D X ज्ञेयः; b — D कनिष्ठायावरः; d — B4 BM C अप्राप्ता.
१५ c — NMS भागः; d — D add
व्याधितः कुपितश्चैव विपयासक्तमानसः ।
अन्यथाशास्त्रकारी च न विभागे पिता प्रभुः ॥ [J 13.16]
१६ c — Y वोधे पिता; BM B2 ज्ञेयास्; d — B4 नागराः.
१७ b — NMS M3 L L4 गूढमातृकः c — M2 पितामहाय; NMS च.
१८ c — D अरिक्थभाजः सर्वे स्यूर्.
१९ a — L4 M3 वीजिनो; b — L4 M3 हृताः; c — B4 अशुल्कोपहृतायां; NMS अशुल्कोपनतायां.
२० a — L L4 M3 घटितः; N पिण्डो; D पण्ढो; L L4 M3 पाण्डुर्.
२१ c — B4 कुलस्यैते; NMS कुटुम्ब्यास्ते; Y कुलमेते.

रिक्थादर्धांशमादद्युर्बीजिक्षेत्रिकयोस्तथा ॥२२॥
संसृष्टिनां तु यो भागस्तेषामेव स इष्यते ।
अतोऽन्यथांशभाजो हि निर्बीजिष्वितरानियात् ॥२३॥
भ्रातॄणामप्रजः प्रेयात्कश्चिच्चेत्प्रव्रजेत्तु वा ।
विभजेयुर्धनं तस्य शेषास्तु स्त्रीधनं विना ॥२४॥
भरणं चास्य कुर्वीरन्स्त्रीणामा जीवितक्षयात् ।
रक्षन्ति शय्यां भर्तुश्चेदाच्छिन्द्युरितरासु तु ॥२५॥
स्याद्यस्य दुहिता तस्याः पित्रंशो भरणे मतः ।
आ संस्काराद्भजेदेनां परतो बिभृयात्पतिः ॥२६॥
मृते भर्तर्यपुत्रायाः पतिपक्षः प्रभुः स्त्रियाः ।
विनियोगात्मरक्षासु भरणे च स ईश्वरः ॥२७॥
परिक्षीणे प्रतिकुले निर्मणुष्ये निराश्रये ।
तत्सपिण्डेषु वासत्सु पितृपक्षः प्रभुः स्त्रियाः ॥२८॥
पक्षद्वयावसाने तु राजा भर्ता स्मृतः स्त्रियाः ।
स तस्या भरणं कुर्यान्निगृह्णीयात्पथश्च्युताम् ॥२९॥
स्वातन्त्र्याद्विप्रणश्यन्ति कुले जाता अपि स्त्रियः ।
अस्वातन्त्र्यमतस्तासां प्रजापतिरकल्पयत् ॥३०॥
पिता रक्षति कौमारे भर्ता रक्षति यौवने ।
पुत्रा रक्षन्ति वैधव्ये न स्त्री स्वातन्त्र्यमर्हति ॥३१॥
यच्छिष्टं पितृदायेभ्यो दत्त्वार्णं पैतृकं च यत् ।
भ्रातृभिस्तद्विभक्तव्यमृणी न स्याद्यथा पिता ॥३२॥
येषां च न कृताः पित्रा संस्कारविधयः क्रमात् ।
कर्तव्या भ्रातृभिस्तेषां पैतृकादेव ते धनात् ॥३३॥
अविद्यमाने पित्र्येऽर्थे स्वांशादुद्धृत्य वा पुनः ।

२२ c — D X C अर्धं समादद्युर्, c — B om.

२३ a — D संसृष्टानां; c — B4 अनन्यतोंऽशभागेऽपि; D अनपत्योंऽशभाम्योऽपि; L4 अन्यपतोंऽसत्याम्यो; d — D X निर्वीजेष्व्.

२४ a — D अप्रजाः; b — L4 M3 प्रव्रजेत वा; NMS प्रव्रजेत्तथा; c — D विभजेरन्; d — NMS B2 स्त्रीधनात्.

२५ b — D च.

२६ a — D या तस्य; N स्याद्द्याद्; M3 L4 जातस्य; b — D पित्र्योंऽशो; c — D आ संस्कारं भजेरंस्तां.

२९ a — B4 पक्षद्वयावसादे; D om this verse. b — B BM C स्त्रियः स्मृतः; d — BM B2 पृथक्; BM च्युतम्.

३० ab — D om.

३१ a — D पुत्रास्तु स्थविरे भावे; NMS रक्षन्ति वार्द्धके पुत्रा.

३२ a — Y यदिष्टं दायभागेभ्यो; d — M3 मूली; NMS पिता यथा.

३३ a — D तु; d — NMS BM C तद्; L L4 तैर्.

अवश्यकार्याः संस्कारा भ्रातृणां पुर्वसंस्कृतैः ॥३४॥
कुटुम्बार्थेषु चोद्युक्तस्तत्कार्यं कुरुते च यः ।
स भ्रातृभिर्बृंहणीयो ग्रासाछादनवाहनैः ॥३५॥
विभागधर्मसंदेहे दायादानां विनिर्णये ।
ज्ञातिभिर्भागलेख्यैश्च पृथक्कार्यप्रवर्तनात् ॥३६॥
भ्रातृणामविभक्तानामेको धर्मः प्रवर्तते ।
विभागे सति धर्मोऽपि भवेदेषां पृथक्पृथक् ॥३७॥
दानग्रहणपश्वन्नगृहक्षेत्रपरिग्रहाः ।
विभक्तानां पृथग्ज्ञेयाः पाकधर्मागमव्ययाः ॥३८॥
साक्षित्वं प्रातिभाव्यं च दानं ग्रहणमेव च ।
विभक्ता भ्रातरः कुर्युर्नाविभक्ता परस्परम् ॥३९॥
येषामेताः क्रिया लोके प्रवर्तन्ते स्वरिक्थिनाम् ।
विभक्तानवगच्छेयुर्लेख्यमप्यन्तरेण तान् ॥४०॥
यद्येकजाता बहवः पृथग्धर्माः पृथक्क्रियाः ।
पृथक्कर्मगुणोपेता न ते कृत्येषु संमताः ॥४१॥
स्वान्भागान्यदि दद्युस्ते विक्रीणीरन्नथापि वा ।
कुयुर्यथेष्टं तत्सर्वमीशन्ते स्वधनस्य ते ॥४२॥
औरसः क्षेत्रजश्चैव पुत्रिकापुत्र एव च ।
कानीनश्च सहोढश्च गूढोत्पन्नस्तथैव च ॥४३॥
पौनर्भवोऽपविद्धश्च लब्धः क्रीतः कृतस्तथा ।
स्वयं चोपगतः पुत्रा द्वादशैत उदाहृताः ॥४४॥
तेषां शड् बन्धुदायादाः षडदायादबान्धवाः ।

३४ a — NMS पित्रर्थे; b — M3 पित्रर्थेप्वांशद्.

३५ a — D यश्चोक्तस्; c — D भ्रातृभिर्भरणीयोऽसौ; L4 भ्रातृभिर्भवनीयो सौ; d — NMS -भोजनैः; B BM -वादनैः.

३६ b — L4 दायादाने; D विनिर्णयः; c — B4 यः; NMS तु; d — Jolly -कायप्रवर्तनात्; NMS -कार्यं प्रक्ल्पना; L4 -कार्ये प्रवर्तनात्; M2 प्रवर्तते.

३७ ab — L4 om. c — D हि; d — D तेपां भवेत्.

३९ b — NMS नाविभक्ताः.

४० a — NMS द्विधा; L4 एता; L4 क्रियाः; b — L4 स ऋक्थनाम्; d — D add
वसेयुर्ये दशाव्दानि पृथग्धर्माः पृथक्क्रियाः ।
विभक्ता भ्रातरस्ते तु विज्ञेया इति निश्चयः ॥ [J 13.41]

४१ d — BM न कृत्वे तेपु संमताः; C न कृत्ये तेपु संमताः; B स तेपु कृतसामत (?).

४२ a — NMS अंशान्; b — NMS L4 M3 विक्रीणीयुर्; X Y तथापि; d — D ईशास्ते; NMS ईशते; D तु; D add
ऊर्ध्वं विभागाज्जातस्तु पित्र्यमेव हरेद्धनम् ।
संसृष्टास्तेन वा ये स्युर्विभजेरन्निति स्थितिः ॥ [J 13.44]

४३ a — Jolly ओरसः; Jolly typo चव; b — L4 M3 पुत्रिकापुत्रम्.

४४ b — NMS कृता; c — NMS पुत्रो.

पूर्वः पूर्वः स्मृतः श्रेयाज्जघन्यो यो य उत्तरः ॥४५॥
क्रमाद्ध्येते प्रपद्येरन्मृते पितरि तद्धनम् ।
ज्यायसो ज्यायसोऽभावे जघन्यस्तदवाप्नुयात् ॥४६॥
पुत्राभावे तु दुहिता तुल्यसंतानदर्शनात् ।
पुत्रश्च दुहिता चोक्तौ पितुः संतानकारकौ ॥४७॥
अभावे तु दुहितॄणां सकुल्या बान्धवास्ततः ।
ततः सजात्याः सर्वेषामभावे राजगामि तत् ॥४८॥
अन्यत्र ब्राह्मणात्किंतु राजा धर्मपरायणः ।
स स्त्रीणां जीवनं दद्यादेष दायविधिः स्मृतः ॥४९॥

४५ a — D एषां; NMS तेषु; d — D add
छिन्नभोगे गृहे क्षेत्रे संदेहो यत्र जायते ।
लेख्येन भोगविद्भिर्वा साक्षिभिर्वा समाहरेत् ॥ [J 13.48]

४६ a — B NMS om. b — D वा धनम्; c — L4 ज्यायसोर्लाभे; D ज्यायसोऽलाभे; d — D कनीयान्रिक्थमर्हति.

४७ b — D -कारणात्; c — D चोभौ.

४८ c — D सजातिः.

४९ a — NMS अन्यात्तु ब्राह्मणात्ततु; D अन्यत्र ब्राह्मणेभ्यः स्याद्; c — D तत्स्त्रीभ्यां; NMS तत्स्त्रीणां; d — D add इति नारदीये धर्मशास्त्रे दायभागे नाम त्रयोदशं व्यवहारपदम्; N add इति दायभागनाम विवादपदं समाप्तम्.

व्यवहारपदानि

१४ साहसम्

सहसा क्रियते कर्म यत्किंचिद्बलदर्पितैः ।
तत्साहसमिति प्रोक्तं सहो बलमिहोच्यते ॥१॥
तत्पुनस्त्रिविधं ज्ञेयं प्रथमं मध्यमं तथा ।
उत्तमं चेति शास्त्रेषु तस्योक्तं लक्षणं पृथक् ॥२॥
फलमूलोदकादीनां क्षेत्रोपकरणस्य च ।
भङ्गाक्षेपोपमर्दाद्यैः प्रथमं साहसं स्मृतम् ॥३॥
वासःपश्वन्नपानानां गृहोपकरणस्य च ।
एतेनैव प्रकारेण मध्यमं साहसं स्मृतम् ॥४॥
व्यापादो विषशस्त्राद्यैः परदारप्रधर्षणं ।
प्राणोपरोधि यच्चान्यदुक्तमुत्तमसाहसम् ॥५॥
तस्य दण्डः क्रियापेक्षः प्रथमस्य शतावरः ।
मध्यमस्य तु शास्त्रज्ञैर्ज्ञेयः पञ्चशतावरः ॥६॥
वधः सर्वस्वहरणं पुरान्निर्वासनाङ्कने ।
तदङ्गच्छेद इत्युक्तो दण्ड उत्तमसाहसे ॥७॥
अविशेषेण सर्वेषां एष दण्डविधिः स्मृतः ।
वधादृते ब्राह्मणस्य न वधं ब्राह्मणोऽर्हति ॥८॥
शिरसो मुण्डनं दण्डस्तस्य निर्वासनं पुरात् ।

१ d — D add

मनुष्यमारणं स्तेयं परदाराभिमर्शनम् ।
पारुष्यं द्विविधं ज्ञेयं साहसं च चतुर्विधम् ॥ [J. 14.2]

२ a — B B2 प्रोक्तं.

३ c — B B2 भङ्गाक्षेपावमर्दाद्यैः.

४ b — M2 गृहोपक्षरणस्य; d — B B2 विदुः.

५ b — D परदाराभिमर्शनम्.

६ b — Y प्रथमः स्याच्छतावरः; d — NMS दृष्टः; D (except L L4 M3) add उत्तमे साहसे दण्डः सहस्रावर इष्यते ।

७ b — B निर्वासनाकले; Y निर्वासनाकरे; d — B2 add

मासकं (sic) तु बुधाः प्राहुः काकिनीना चतुष्टयम् ।
विंशतिर्यत्पुनस्तेषां स मुख्यः पण उच्यते ॥ [Bhāradvāja Dhko 534]
पणानां द्वे शते सार्धे प्रथमः साहसः स्मृतः ।
मधयमः पञ्च विज्ञयः सहस्रं त्वेव चोत्तमः ॥ [Manu 8.138]

८ c — B विपाद्.

ललाटे चाभिशस्ताङ्कः प्रयाणं गर्दभेन च ॥९॥
स्यातां संव्यवहार्यौ तौ धृतदण्डौ तु पूर्वयोः ।
धृतदण्डोऽप्यसंभोज्यो ज्ञेय उत्तमसाहसे ॥१०॥
तस्यैव भेदः स्तेयं स्याद्विशेषस्तत्र चोच्यते ।
अतिसाहसमाक्रम्य स्तेयमाहुश्छलेन तु ॥११॥
तदपि त्रिविधं प्रोक्तं द्रव्यापेक्षं मणीषिभिः ।
क्षुद्रमध्योत्तमानां तु द्रव्याणामपकर्षणात् ॥१२॥
मृद्भाण्डासनखट्वास्थिदारुचर्मतृणादि यत् ।
शमीधान्यमुद्रादीनि क्षुद्रद्रव्यमुदाहृतम् ॥१३॥
वासः कौशेयवर्जं च गोवर्जं पशवस्तथा ।
हिरण्यवर्जं लोहं च मध्यं व्रीहियवा अपि ॥१४॥
हिरण्यरत्नकौशेयस्त्रीपुंगोगजवाजिनः ।
देवब्राह्मणराज्ञां च द्रव्यं विज्ञेयमुत्तमम् ॥१५॥
उपायैर्विविधैरेषां छलयित्वापकर्षणम् ।
सुप्तप्रमत्तमत्तेभ्यः स्तेयमाहुर्मनीषिणः ॥१६॥
सहोढग्रहणात्स्तेयं होढेऽसत्युपभोगतः ।
शङ्का त्वसज्जनैकार्थ्यादनायव्ययतस्तथा ॥१७॥
भक्तावकाशदातारः स्तेनानां ये प्रसर्पताम् ।
शक्ताश्च य उपेक्षन्ते तेऽपि तद्दोषभागिनः ॥१८॥
उत्क्रोशतां जनानां च ह्रियमाणे धनेऽपि च ।
श्रुत्वा ये नाभिधावन्ति तेऽपि तद्दोषभागिनः ॥१९॥
साहसेषु य एवोक्तस्त्रिषु दण्डो मनीषिभिः ।

९ b — B दण्डवहिर्; d — B -आङ्कपर्याणं; B2 add
गुरुतल्पे भगः कार्यः सुरापाने सुराध्वजः ।
स्तेये च श्वपदं कार्यं ब्रह्महण्यशिराः पुमान् ॥ [Manu 9.237]
१० a — BMC द्वौ; c — B असंभोज्ये; D असंभाप्यो; d — M2 उत्तमसाहसः.
११ a — NMS तु; b — B C तूच्यते; C दृश्यते; c — BM C अपि-; NMS आधेः; D आधिः; d — D आधिश्; M3 L4 NMS आधि-.
१२ b — NMS महर्पिभिः; d — M2 M3 L4 -कर्पणं.
१३ b — Y -तृणानि; c — D शमी धान्यं कृतान्नं च; NMS फलं चान्यकृतान्नं च.
१४ a — NMS यद्.
१५ d — D विज्ञेयं द्रव्यम्.
१६ a — D सर्वैः; b — B C कलयित्वापकर्पणम्; D कल्पयित्वापकर्पणम्; M2 कालयित्वापकर्पणम्.
१७ a — B सहांढग्रहणास्यनां; b — L4 हांढमप्युपभांगतः; D हांढमत्युपभांगतः; NMS हांढऽसत्यतिभांगतः; c — D असज्जनैकत्वाद्; d — D अन्यायव्ययतस्.
१८ b — Y च सर्पतां; c — NMS L L4 M3 शक्तौ; Y च यं; L L4 M3 वधस्.
१९ Y om this verse. b — D तथा.

स एव दण्डः स्तेयेऽपि द्रव्येषु त्रिष्वनुक्रमात् ॥२०॥
गवादिषु प्रणष्टेषु द्रव्येष्वपहृतेषु वा ।
पदेनान्वेषणं कुर्युरा मूलात्तद्विदो जनाः ॥२१॥
ग्रामे व्रजे विवीते वा यत्र संनिपतेत्पदम् ।
वोढव्यं तद्भवेत्तेन न चेत्सोऽन्यत्र तन्नयेत् ॥२२॥
पदे प्रमूढे भग्ने वा विषमत्वाज्जनान्तिके ।
यस्त्वासन्नतरो ग्रामो व्रजो वा तत्र पातयेत् ॥२३॥
समेऽध्वनि द्वयोर्यत्र तेन प्रायोऽशुचिर्जनः ।
पूर्वापदानैर्दृष्टो वा संसृष्टो वा दुरात्मभिः ॥२४॥
ग्रामेष्वन्वेषणं कुर्युश्चण्डालवधकादयः ।
रात्रिसंचारिणो ये च बहिः कुर्युर्बहिश्चराः ॥२५॥
स्तेनेष्वलभ्यमानेषु राजा दद्यात्स्वकाद्धनात् ।
उपेक्षमाणो ह्येनस्वी धर्मादर्थाच्च हीयते ॥२६॥

२० a — B य एपोक्तंस्; L4 यत्र वोक्तस्
२१ a — NMS BM B4 प्रनप्टेपु; c — D पदस्यान्वेपणं; d — Y विपदां.
२२ a — Y विविक्ते; b — N संनिहितं; M3 L4 संनियते.
२३ c — Y यत्रासन्नतरो; d — BM C ग्रामे व्रजे.
२४ a —B वातस्; b — NMS स्तेय-; L प्रयो; c — D पूर्वापवादैर्; B B2 D दुप्टो.
२५ d — BM C पालाव्रजेपु च.
२६ b —Y मनो; D Y गृहात्; c — Y एतस्मिन्. d — D add इति नारदीये धर्मशास्त्रे साहसं नाम चतुर्दशं व्यवहारपदम्; NMS add इति साहसं चतुर्दशम् विवादपदम्; N add इति साहसं नाम विवादपदं समाप्तम्.

व्यवहारपदानि

१५-१६ वाग्दण्डपारुष्ये

देशजातिकुलादीनामाक्रोशन्यङ्गसंहितम् ।
यद्वचः प्रतिकूलार्थं वाक्पारुष्यं तदुच्यते ॥१॥
निष्ठुराश्लीलतीव्रत्वात्तदपि त्रिविधं स्मृतम् ।
गौरवानुक्रमादस्य दण्डोऽप्यत्र क्रमाद्गुरुः ॥२॥
साक्षेपं निष्ठुरं ज्ञेयमश्लीलं न्यङ्गसंयुतम् ।
पातनीयैरुपक्रोशैस्तीव्रमाहुर्मनीषिणः ॥३॥
परगात्रेष्वभिद्रोहो हस्तपादायुधादिभिः ।
भस्मादिभिश्चोपघातो दण्डपारुष्यमुच्यते ॥४॥
तस्यापि दृष्टं त्रैविध्यं मृदुमध्योत्तमं क्रमात् ।
अवगूरणनिःसङ्गपातनक्षतदर्शनैः ॥५॥
हीनमध्योत्तमानां तु द्रव्याणां समतिक्रमात् ।
त्रीण्येव साहसान्याहुरतत्र कण्टकशोधनम् ॥६॥
विधिः पञ्चविधस्तूक्त एतयोरुभयोरपि ।
विशुद्धिर्दण्डभाक्त्वं च तत्र संबध्यते यथा ॥७॥
पारुष्ये सति संरम्भादुत्पन्ने क्षुब्धयोर्द्वयो ।
स मन्यते यः क्षमते दण्डभाग्योऽतिवर्तते ॥८॥
पारुष्यदोषावृतयोर्युगपत्संप्रवृत्तयोः ।
विशेषश्चेन्न दृश्येत विनयः स्यात्समस्तयोः ॥९॥
पूर्वमाक्षारयेद्यस्तु नियतं स्यात्स दोषभाक् ।
पश्चाद्यः सोऽप्यसत्कारी पूर्वे तु विनयो गुरुः ॥१०॥

१ b— D -संयुतम्.

२ c — D तस्य; d — B दश्धां; NMS दण्डोऽपि त्रिविधः स्मृतः.

३ b — D अश्नील ह्यजसंहितं; c — B पतनीय उपक्रोशस्.

४ a — BM om this verse. c— D भस्मादीनाम्; D उपक्षेपैर्. N चोपघातं.

५ a — NMS तत्रापि; d — Jolly अवगोरणनिःशङ्क-; B -दर्शनात्.

६ b — Y त्रयाणाम्; D अपकर्पणात्; d — NMS प्रोक्तं.

७ c — D विशुद्धि-.

८ D om this verse. b — BM C पारुष्यं संभवोत्पन्न सहासा क्रुद्धयोर्द्वयोः; c — BM C संहन्यते; d — BM C दण्डर्द्धादि निवर्त्तते.

९ a — NMS पारुष्यदोपधुतयांर्.

१० a — B B2 आकारयेद्; d — M2 पूर्वं तु विनयेद्गुरुं.

द्वयोरापन्नयोस्तुल्यमनुबध्नाति यः पुनः ।
स तयोर्दण्डमाप्नोति पूर्वो वा यदि वेतरः ॥११॥
श्वपाकपण्डचण्डालव्यङ्गेषु वधवृत्तिषु ।
हस्तिपव्रात्यदारेषु गुर्वाचार्याङ्गनासु च ॥१२॥
मर्यादातिक्रमे सद्यो घात एवानुशासनम् ।
न च तद्दण्डपारुष्ये दोषमाहुर्मनीषिणः ॥१३॥
यमेव ह्यतिवर्तेरन्नेते सन्तं जनं नृषु ।
स एव विनयं कुर्यान्न तद्विनयभाङ्नृपः ॥१४॥
मला ह्येते मनुष्येषु धनमेषां मलात्मकम् ।
अपि तान्घातयेद्राजा नार्थदण्डेन दण्डयेत् ॥१५॥
शतं ब्राह्मणमाक्रुश्य क्षत्रियो दण्डमर्हति ।
वैश्योऽध्यर्धं शतं द्वे वा शूद्रस्तु वधमर्हति ॥१६॥
विप्रः पञ्चाशतं दण्ड्यः क्षत्रियस्याभिशंसने ।
वैश्ये स्यादर्धपञ्चाशच्छूद्रे द्वादशको दमः ॥१७॥
समवर्णद्विजातीनां द्वादशैव व्यतिक्रमे ।
वादेष्ववचनीयेषु तदेव द्विगुणं भवेत् ॥१८॥
काणमप्यथवा खञ्जमन्यं वापि तथाविधम् ।
तथ्येनापि ब्रुवन्दाप्यो राज्ञा कार्षापणावरम् ॥१९॥
न किल्बिषेणापवदेच्छास्त्रतः कृतपावनम् ।
न राज्ञा धृतदण्डं च दण्डभाक्तद्व्यतिक्रमात् ॥२०॥
लोकेऽस्मिन्द्वाववक्तव्यावदण्ड्यौ च प्रकीर्तितौ ।
ब्राह्मणश्चैव राजा च तौ हीदं बिभृतो जगत् ॥२१॥
पतितं पतितेत्युक्त्वा चौरं चौरेति वा पुनः ।
वचनात्तुल्यदोषः स्यान्मिथ्या द्विर्दोषतां व्रजेत् ॥२२॥

११ d — D वोत्तरः.

१२ b — D श्वपाकमेद-; M3 L -शवेपु; N श्वपाकमेदचण्डालवेश्यावधकवृत्तिपु; d — D हस्तिपव्रात्यदासेपु गुर्वाचार्यातिगेपु. NMS om this verse.

१३ a — B रक्ष्यो; d — D स्तेयम्.

१४ b — D अतिवर्तेत नीचः; B सक्तं जनी (?); D त्रिपु.

१५ a — L मलाखेते; BM C मनुप्याणां; c — NMS अतस्.

१७ a — Y D पञ्चाशद्ब्राह्मणो दण्ड्यः.

१८ b — D BM समवर्णैर्दिजानां; B B2 समवर्णपु सर्वेपु.

१९ a — B C वाप्य्; NMS वा यदि वा; d — D दण्ड्यो दण्ड-; NMS कार्पापणात्परम्.

२० d — B C दण्डभाग्यो व्यतिक्रमेत्; NMS दण्डयेत्तद्व्यतिक्रमे.

२१ b — D X अवध्यौ; d — D X विभ्रतो.

२२ b — NMS चोरं; d — NMS द्विर्दोपभाग्; NMS भवेत्; D add
एकजातिर्द्विजातींस्तु वाचा दारुणयाक्षिपन् ।
जिह्वायाः प्राप्नुयाच्छेदं जघन्यप्रभवो हि सः ॥ [Manu 8.270, J 15-16.22]

नामजातिग्रहं तेषामभिद्रोहेण कुर्वतः ।
निखेयोऽयोमयः शङ्कुः शूद्रस्याष्टादशाङ्गुलः ॥२३॥
धर्मापदेशं दर्पेण द्विजानामस्य कुर्वतः ।
तप्तमासेचयेत्तैलं वक्त्रे श्रोत्रे च पार्थिवः ॥ २४
येनाङ्गेनावरो वर्णो ब्राह्मणस्यापराध्नुयात् ।
तदङ्गं तस्य छेत्तव्यमेवं शुद्धिमवाप्नुयात् ॥२५॥
सहासनमभिप्रेप्सुरुत्कृष्टस्यावकृष्टजः ।
कट्यां कृताङ्को निर्वास्यः स्फिग्देशं वास्य कर्तयेत् ॥२६॥
अवनिष्ठीवतो दर्पाद्द्वावोष्ठौ छेदयेन्नृपः ।
अवमूत्रयतः शिश्नमवशर्धयतो गुदम् ॥२७॥
केशेषु गृह्णतो हस्तौ छेदयेदविचारयन् ।
पादयोर्नासिकायां च ग्रीवायां वृषणेषु च ॥२८॥
उपक्रुश्य तु राजानं वर्त्मनि स्वे व्यवस्थितम् ।
जिह्वाछेदाद्भवेच्छुद्धिः सर्वस्वहरणेन वा ॥२९॥
राजनि प्रहरेद्यस्तु कृतागस्यपि दुर्मतिः ।
शूले तमग्नौ विपचेद् ब्रह्महत्याशताधिकम् ॥३०॥
पुत्रापराधे न पिता न श्ववाञ्छुनि दण्डभाक् ।
न मर्कटे च तत्स्वामी तैरेव प्रहितो न चेत् ॥३१॥

२३ a — D नामजातिग्रहांस्त्वेषाम्; b — D अतिद्रोहेण; d — D शङ्कुज्वलन्नास्ये दशाङ्गुलः; cd — B लौहं निखानयेच्छक्तं शूद्रस्याष्टादशाङ्गुलं.

२४ a — M2 धर्मेण; b — B B2 विप्राणाम्.

२५ a — D येनाङ्गेनावर-; c — NMS एव; d — B शुद्धिर्नोपेति सोऽन्यथा (sic).

२६ a — Y समासनम्; M2 महासनम्; b — NMS उत्कृष्टस्यापकृष्टजः; Y उत्कृष्टावरवर्णजः; c — NMS कटिदेशेऽङ्क्य; B कटिदेशेऽस्था-; d — D स्फिचौ वास्यावकर्तयेत्.

२७ d — BM C अपशर्धयतां.

२८ b — M2 अवधारयन्; c — D दाढिकायां तु; d — Y D add
त्वक्छेदकः शतं दण्ड्यो लोहितस्य च दर्शकः ।
मांसभेत्ता तु पङ्निष्कान्प्रवास्यस्त्वस्थिभेदकः ॥ [J 15.29]

२९ a — M2 M3 L4 उपाक्रुश्य तु; NMS उपाक्रुश्य च; b — D कर्मणि; c — D छुद्धः.

३० c — B शूलान्; C शूल्यं.

३१ b — D नाश्वे न; N न शुनि; D तेनैव; d — D add इति नारदीये धर्मशास्त्रे वाक्पारुष्यं दण्डपारुष्यं च पञ्चदशं व्यवहारपदम्; X add इति वाग्दण्डपारुष्य नाम विवादपदं समाप्तम्; NMS add इति वाग्दण्डपारुष्यं पञ्चदशं (पांदशं) च विवादपदम्.

व्यवहारपदानि

१७ द्यूतसमाह्वयम्

अक्षवर्ध्रशलाकाद्यैर्देवनं जिह्मकारितम् ।
पणक्रीडा वयोभिश्च पदं द्यूतसमाह्वयम् ॥१॥
सभिकः कारयेद्द्यूतं देयं दद्याच्च तत्कृतम् ।
दशकं तु शतं वृद्धिस्तस्य स्याद्द्यूतकारिता ॥२॥
द्विरभ्यस्ताः पतन्त्यक्षा ग्लहे यस्याक्षदेविनः ।
जयं तस्यापरस्याहुः कितवस्य पराजयम् ॥३॥
कितवेष्वेव तिष्ठेयुः कितवाः संशयं प्रति ।
त एव तस्य द्रष्टारः स्युस्त एव च साक्षिणः ॥४॥
अशुद्धः कितवो नान्यदाश्रयेद्द्यूतमण्डलम् ।
प्रतिहन्यात्र सभिकं दापयेत्तत्स्वमिष्टतः ॥५॥
कूटाक्षदेविनः पापान्निर्भजेद्द्यूतमण्डलात् ।
कण्ठेऽक्षमालामासज्य स ह्येषां विनयः स्मृतः ॥६॥

१ a — B अक्षवन्धशद्यकाद्यैर् (?); D अक्षब्रध्रशलाकाद्यैर्; Y अक्षतप्रशलाकाद्यैर् (?); b — D देवेन; c — B B2
पणः क्रीडा; B पयांभिश्; d — B2 add
द्यूतं समाह्वयं चैव राजा राष्ट्रान्निवारयेत् ।
राज्यान्तकरणावेतौ द्वौ दोषौ पृथ्वीक्षिताम् ॥ [Manu 9.211]

२ c — D च; d — Y तत्र; D द्यूतकारिणः.

३ a — L M2 M3 L4 द्विरभ्यस्ता; b — NMS गेहे; Y ग्रहेयुरक्षवेदिनः; D ग्लहे
यद्यक्षवेदिनः; c — M3 तस्यापरस्याह; d — B कितवस्यापराजयम्.

४ a — D तिष्ठेरन्; c — N तेषां; d — D त एव स्युस्तु.

५ a — NMS अशुद्धं; NMS नान्यं c — Y सविकं [?]; d — B NMS दापयन्तं.

६ b — D निहरेद्; Jolly निर्हरेद्; d — Y एषु; D add
अनिर्दिष्टतया राज्ञा द्यूतं कुर्वीत मानवः ।
न स तं प्राप्नुयात्कामं विनयं चैव सोऽर्हति ॥ [J 17.7]
अथवा कितवा राज्ञे दत्त्वा भागं यथोदितम् ।
प्रकाशं देवनं कुर्युरेवं दोषो न विद्यते ॥ [J 17.8]
इति नारदीये धर्मशास्त्रे द्यूतसमाह्वयो नाम षोदशं व्यवहारपदम्; X add इति द्यूतसमाह्वयं समाप्तं;
Y add इति द्यूतसमाह्वयं नाम विवादपदं समाप्तं; NMS add इति द्यूतसमाह्वयाख्यं सप्तदशं
विवादपदम्.

व्यवहारपदानि

१८ प्रकीर्णकम्

प्रकीर्णके पुनर्ज्ञेया व्यवहारा नृपाश्रयाः ।
राज्ञामाज्ञाप्रतीघातस्तत्कर्मकरणं तथा ॥१॥
पुरप्रदानं संभेदः प्रकृतीनां तथैव च ।
पाषण्डनैगमश्रेणीगणधर्मविपर्ययाः ॥२॥
पितृपुत्रविवादश्च प्रायश्चित्तव्यतिक्रमः ।
प्रतिग्रहविलोपश्च कोप आश्रमिणामपि ॥३॥
वर्णसंकरदोषाश्च तद्वृत्तिनियमस्तथा ।
न दृष्टं यच्च पूर्वेषु तत्सर्वं स्यात्प्रकीर्णके ॥४॥
राजा त्ववहितः सर्वानाश्रमान्परिपालयेत् ।
उपायैः शास्त्रविहितैश्चतुर्भिः प्रकृतैस्तथा ॥५॥
यो यो वर्णोऽवहीयेत यो वोद्रेकमनुव्रजेत् ।
तं तं दृष्ट्वा स्वतो मार्गात्प्रच्युतं स्थापयेत्पथि ॥६॥
अशास्त्रोक्तेषु चान्येषु पापयुक्तेषु कर्मसु ।
प्रसमीक्ष्यात्मनो राजा दण्डं दण्ड्येषु पातयेत् ॥७॥
श्रुतिस्मृतिविरुद्धं च जनानामहितं च यत् ।
न तत्प्रवर्तयेद्राजा प्रवृत्तं च निवर्तयेत् ॥८॥
न्यायापेतं यदन्येन राज्ञाज्ञानकृतं च यत् ।
तदप्यन्यायविहितं पुनर्न्याये निवेशयेत् ॥९॥
राज्ञा प्रवर्तितान्धर्मान्यो नरो नानुपालयेत् ।
दण्ड्यः स पापो वध्यश्च लोपयन्राजशासनम् ॥१०॥
आयुधान्यायुधीयानां वाह्यादीन्वाह्यजीविनाम् ।

१ a — Y प्रकीर्णकं पुनर्ज्ञेयं; D प्रकीर्णकः पुनर्ज्ञेयां; b — D व्यवहारो नृपाश्रयः; B नृपाश्रयात्. c — B राज्येन्-.
२ a — B B3 NMS पुरप्रदान-; D संभेदं; d — M2 पाखण्ड-; D विपर्ययः.
३ a — D पितापुत्रविवादश्; c — B व्रतिग्रहलोमश्; BM C प्रतिग्राहलोमश्.
४ d — B C सर्वं तस्मात्प्रकीर्णके; BM सर्वं ताभ्यां प्रकीर्णके; M3 L4 प्रकीर्णकैः.
५ d — D प्रकृतीस्; N प्रकृतस्; Y has the following order of verses: 5, 9-11, 6-8, 12.
६ a — D ऽपहियेत; b — D यो य उद्रेकमाप्नुयात्; d — Y यागात्.
७ c — NMS प्रसमीक्ष्यात्मना; d — BM B दुष्टेपु; B जातयेत्.
८ b --- D X यद् भूतानाम्.
९ a — Y न्यायाप्तेनं तद्; Y राज्ञाज्ञानेन यत्कृतम्; D राज्ञादानं कृतं भवेत्; c — Y अन्यायविहित.
१० Y om this verse. D च वर्जितान्; c — NMS नह्यः.

वेश्यास्त्रीणामलंकारं वाद्यातोद्यानि तद्विदाम् ॥११॥
यच्च यस्योपकरणं येन जीवन्ति कारुकाः ।
सर्वस्वहरणेऽप्येतान्न राजा हर्तुमर्हति ॥१२॥
अनादिश्चाप्यनन्तश्च द्विपदां पृथिवीपतिः ।
दीप्तिमत्वाच्छुचित्वाच्च यदि नस्यात्पथश्च्युतः ॥१३॥
यदि राजा न सर्वेषां वर्णानां दण्डधारणम् ।
कुर्यात्पथो व्यपेतानां विनश्येयुरिमाः प्रजाः ॥१४॥
ब्राह्मण्यं ब्राह्मणो जह्यात्क्षत्रियः क्षात्रमुत्सृजेत् ।
स्वकर्म जह्याद्वैश्यस्तु शूद्रः सर्वान्विशेषयेत् ॥१५॥
राजानश्चेन्नाभविष्यन्पृथिव्यां दण्डधारणम् ।
शूले मत्स्यानिवापक्ष्यन्दुर्बलान्बलवत्तराः ॥१६॥
सतामनुग्रहो नित्यमसतां निग्रहस्तथा ।
एष धर्मः स्मृतो राज्ञामर्थश्चामित्रपीडनात् ॥१७॥
न लिप्यते यथा वह्निर्दहञ्छ्श्वदिमाः प्रजाः ।
न लिप्यते तथा राजा दण्डं दण्ड्येषु पातयन् ॥१८॥
आज्ञा तेजः पार्थिवानां सा च वाचि प्रतिष्ठिता ।
ते यद् ब्रूयुरसत्सद्वा स धर्मो व्यवहारिणाम् ॥१९॥
राजा नाम चरत्येष भूमौ साक्षात्सहस्रदृक् ।
न तस्याज्ञामतिक्रम्य संतिष्ठेरन्प्रजाः क्वचित् ॥२०॥
रक्षाधिकारादीशत्वाद्भूतानुग्रहदर्शनात् ।
यदेव राजा कुरुते तत्प्रमाणमितिस्थितिः ॥२१॥
निर्गुणोऽपि यथा स्त्रीणां पूज्य एव पतिः सदा ।
प्रजानां विगुणोऽप्येवं पूज्य एव नराधिपः ॥२२॥

११ b — D B2 शिल्पद्रव्याणि शिल्पिनाम्; c — M2 वैश्यस्त्रीणाम्; NMS अलंकारान्; BM C अलंकारां;
d — D वाद्यातांद्यादि.
१२ a — B2 om this verse. b — N कारकः; D कारवः.
१३ a — Y अभावादिर्; ab — D अनिर्देश्यावनिन्द्यौ च राजा ब्राह्मण एव च; c — B अशुचित्वाच्.
१४ b — NMS नियतं; M2 -धारणाम्.
१५ a — NMS हन्याट्; cd — D शूले मत्स्यानिवाश्नीयुर्दुर्वलान्वलवत्तराः.
१६ ab — D स्वकर्म जंह्याद्वैस्यस्तु शूद्रः सर्वं विशेपयेत्; b — NMS दण्डधारणे; B दण्डधारिणः; c — M2 जले; B
इवापक्ष्याड्; cd — D राजानश्चेन्नाकरिप्यन्प्रजानां दण्डधारणम्.
१७ d — NMS चापीडयन्प्रजाः; M2 त्वामित्रपीडनात्.
१८ b — D अपि; c — NMS तथा न लिप्यते राज; d — B दुप्टेपु.
१९ a — D प्रज्ञा; d — L व्यवहारिणा.
२० a — D राजेति संचरत्य्.
२१ c — B यदेन राजा क्रीयते (?); Y यदेव राजा क्रियते; D यदेव कुरुते राजा.
२२ a — D निर्वलां; d — D प्रजापतिः; D add
राज्ञामाज्ञाभयाद्यस्मान्न च्यवेरन्पथः प्रजाः ।

तप:क्रीता: प्रजा राज्ञा प्रभुरासां ततो नृप: ।
ततस्तद्वचसि स्थेयं वार्ता चासां तदाश्रया ॥२३॥
पञ्च रूपाणि राजानो धारयन्त्यमितौजस: ।
अग्नेरिन्द्रस्य सोमस्य यमस्य धनदस्य च ॥२४॥
कारणादनिमित्तं वा यदा क्रोधवशं गत: ।
प्रजा दहति भूपालस्तदाग्निरभिधीयते ॥२५॥
यदा तेज: समालम्ब्य विजिगीषुरुदायुध: ।
अभियाति परान्राजा तदेन्द्र: स उदाहृत: ॥२६॥
विगतक्रोधसंतापो हृष्टरूपो यदा नृप: ।
प्रजानां दर्शनं याति सोम इत्युच्यते तदा ॥२७॥
धर्मासनगत: श्रीमान्दण्डं धत्ते यदा नृप: ।
सम: सर्वेषु भूतेषु तदा वैवस्वत: यम: ॥२८॥
यदा त्वर्थिगुरुप्राज्ञभृत्यादीनवनीपति: ।
अनुगृह्णाति दानेन तदा स धनद: स्मृत: ॥२९॥
तस्मात्तं नावजानीयान्नाक्रोशेन्न विशेषयेत् ।
आज्ञायां चास्य तिष्ठेत मृत्यु: स्यात्तद्व्युतिक्रमात् ॥३०॥
तस्य वृत्ति: प्रजारक्षा वृद्धप्राज्ञोपसेवनम् ।
दर्शनं व्यवहाराणमात्मनश्चाभिरक्षणम् ॥३१॥
ब्राह्मणानुपसेवेत नित्यं राजा समाहित: ।
संयुक्तं ब्राह्मणै: क्षत्रं मूलं लोकाभिरक्षणे ॥३२॥
ब्राह्मणस्यापरीहारो राजन्यासनमग्रत: ।
प्रथमं दर्शनं प्रात: सर्वेभ्यश्चाभिवादनम् ॥३३॥
अग्रं नवेभ्य: सस्येभ्यो मार्गदानं च गच्छत: ।
भैक्षहेतो: परागारे प्रवेशस्त्वनिवारित: ॥३४॥

व्यवहारादतो ज्ञेयं संवृत्तं राजशासनम् ॥ [J 18.23]
स्थित्यर्थं पृथिवीपालैश्चरित्रविपया: कृता: ।
चरित्रेभ्यांऽस्य तत्प्राहुर्गरीयां राजशासनम् ॥[J 18.24]

२३ b — NMS आसीत्; Y तस्मात्; d — B C राज्ञा; Y चैपां तदाश्रयात्; M2 चापां तदाश्रयात्.

२४ a— L4 राजानां.

२५ a — N कारणम वनिमित्तम्.

२६ c — B C परं; d — Y समुदाहृत:.

२८ d — D स्मृत:.

२९ b — B अर्थिगुरु: प्रा-; b — D पृथिवीपति:; ab — NMS यदातिथिगुरुप्राज्ञान्भृत्यादीनवनीपति:.

३० b — D च विशेपत:; d — NMS -व्यतिक्रमे; BC -अरिक्रमात्.

३१ a — D धर्म:; d — BM चैव लक्षणम्; D उत्थानं च स्वकर्मसु.

३२ cd — L M3 om. c — D क्षेत्रं; d — D लोकाभिवृद्धये.

३३ ab — L M3 om. b — NMS ऽजघन्यासनम्; d — NMS सर्वेपां.

३४ a — BM B X अग्रान्नेवेभ्य:; D संमेभ्यां.

समित्पुष्पोदकादानेष्वस्तेयं सपरिग्रहात् ।
अनाक्षेपः परेभ्यश्च संभाषश्च परस्त्रिया ॥३५॥
नदीष्ववेतनस्तारः पूर्वमुत्तारणं तथा ।
तरेष्वशुल्कदानं च न चेद्वाणिज्यमस्य तत् ॥३६॥
वर्तमानोऽध्वनि श्रान्तो गृह्णन्ननिवसन्स्वयम् ।
ब्राह्मणो नापराध्नोति द्वाविक्षू पञ्च मूलकान् ॥३७॥
नाभिशस्तान्न पतितान्न द्विषो न च नास्तिकात् ।
न सोपधान्नानिमित्तं न दातारं प्रपीड्य च ॥३८॥
अर्थानां भूरिभावाच्च देयत्वाच्च महात्मनाम् ।
श्रेयान्प्रतिग्रहो राज्ञामन्येषां ब्राह्मणादृते ॥३९॥
ब्राह्मणश्चैव राजा च द्वावप्येतौ धृतव्रतौ ।
नैतयोरन्तरं किंचित्प्रजाधर्माभिरक्षणात् ॥४०॥
धर्मज्ञस्य कृतज्ञस्य रक्षार्थं शासतोऽशुचीन् ।
मेध्यमेव धनं प्राहुस्तीक्ष्णस्यापि महीपतेः ॥४१॥
शुचीनामशुचीनां च संनिपातो यथाम्भसाम् ।
समुद्रे समतां याति तद्वद्राज्ञो धनागमः ॥४२॥
यथा चाग्नौ स्थितं दीप्ते शुद्धिमायाति काञ्चनम् ।
एवमेवागमा सर्वे शुद्धिमायान्ति राजसु ॥४३॥
य एव कश्चित्स्वद्रव्यं ब्राह्मणेभ्यः प्रयच्छति ।
तद्राज्ञाप्यनुमन्तव्यमेष धर्मः सनातनः ॥४४॥
अन्यप्रकारादुचिताद् भूमेः षड्भागसंज्ञितात् ।
बलिः स तस्य विहितः प्रजापालनवेतनम् ॥४५॥

३५ a — D समित्पुष्पोदकादीनां ह्य. B B2 समित्पुष्पोदकादाने; BM समित्पुष्पोदकाद्येव; b — BM स्तेयश्च; D सपरिग्रहम्; B2 अपरिग्रहात्; c — D अनपेक्षः.
३६ c — M2 भवेष्व्; NMS करेष्व्; d — D वणिज्यायां भवेत्स्थितिः.
३७ b — D अनशनः; NMS एकासनः; c — D नापराधी स्याद्; d — NMS मूलिकान्, d — D द्वाविक्षू द्वे च मूल्के.
३८ b — D नापि; c — M3 लोपसन्नान्; M2 गोपसन्नान्; D — नोपसन्नान्; D — निर्निमित्तं.
३९ a — D अर्थिनां; c — D परिग्रहो; d — D सर्वेषां; NMS अन्येभ्यो.
४० a — L4 ब्राह्मणाश्; b — D X दृढव्रतौ; c — D X नानयोर्; d — D प्रजा धर्मेण रक्षताः.
४१ a — N गुणज्ञस्य; c — B C भध्यमेन; d — D add
यो राज्ञः प्रतिगृह्णाति लुब्धस्योच्छास्त्रवर्तिनः ।
स पर्यायेण यातीमान्नरकानेकविंशतिम् ॥ [J 18. 44, Manu 8.47]
४२ c — NMS स तत्र; c — B B2 तथा; d — B राज्ञा; NMS राज्ञां.
४३ a — NMS यदा; D ह्यग्नौ; M2 स्थिते; b — Y शुचित्वं याति; NMS शुद्धिमाप्नोति, c — D एवं धनागमा; d — Y शुचिं.
४४ a — NMS यदा च; c — M3 L4 तत्राज्ञाप्य्.
४५ a — B अन्यत्र कायाद्; C NMS अन्यत्र काराद्; b — M2 M3 L4 भूम्या यद्भागसंक्षितम्; d — NMS -वेतनः.

शक्यं तत्पुनरादातुं यदब्राह्मणसात्कृतम् ।
ब्राह्मणाय तु यद्दत्तं न तस्य हरणं पुनः ॥४६॥
दानमध्ययनं यज्ञस्तस्य कर्म त्रिलक्षणम् ।
याजनाध्यापने वृत्तिस्तृतीयस्तु प्रतिग्रहः ॥४७॥
स्वकर्मणि द्विजस्तिष्ठेद्वृत्तिमाहारयेत्कृताम् ।
नासद्भ्यः प्रतिगृह्णीयाद्वर्णेभ्यो नियमेऽसति ॥४८॥
अशुचिर्वचनाद्यस्य शुचिर्भवति पुरुषः ।
शुचिश्चैवाशुचिः सद्यः कथं राजा न दैवतम् ॥४९॥
विदुर्य एव देवत्वं राज्ञो ह्यमिततेजसः ।
तस्य ते प्रतिगृह्णन्तो न लिप्यन्ते द्विजातयः ॥५०॥
लोकेऽस्मिन्मङ्गलान्यष्टौ ब्राह्मणो गौर्हुताशनः ।
हिरण्यं सर्पिरादित्य आपो राजा तथाष्टमः ॥५१॥
एतानि सततं पश्येन्नमस्येदर्चयेच्च तान् ।
प्रदक्षिणं च कुर्वीत तथा ह्यायुर्न हीयते ॥५२॥

४६ a — B शकुन (?); BM शकृत्; D आहर्तुं; b — Y यदःब्राह्मणसात्कृतम्; D यत्र ब्राह्मणसात्कृतम्; c — D ब्राह्मणेभ्यस्; Y ब्राह्मणस्य; d — NMS तस्याहरणम्; N तस्यापि हरेत्.

४७ b — D कर्मास्यांक्तं; d — D च; L4 परिग्रहः.

४८ a — D स्वधर्मे ब्राह्मणस्; b — D नृपात्; c — D परिगृह्णीयाद्; d — All mss सति.

४९ a — M3 L4 यस्तु; b — D मानवः; c — D सम्यक्.

५० a — NMS विदुर्यस्यैव; c — NMS हि, ' — D कथंचन; NMS कदाचन.

५१ d — N राजन एव च.

५२ a — M2 वसतं; b — Y स्तुयात्; D स्वयम्; d — D यथास्यायुः प्रवर्धते; B2 add

मन्त्रब्राह्मणशिपय [?] तं स्मृत्वा तु महर्पयः ।
स्मृतिं व्यारचयन्तस्मादभिन्ना श्रुतितः स्मृतिः ॥ [?]
वेदाः सहाङ्गाश्चत्वारो मीमांसा न्यायविस्तरः ।
धर्मशास्त्रं पुराणं च विद्या ह्येताश्चतुर्दश ॥ [Dhko 4.886, 889, Bhā 12. App 13.7]
आयुर्वेदो धनुर्वेदो गान्धर्वश्चेति ते त्रयः ।
अर्थशास्त्रं चतुर्थं च विद्या ह्यष्टादश स्मृताः ॥ [Bhā 12, App 13.9]
आसां तु धारणं पुण्यं लोकद्वयहितं तथा ।
विद्यास्तस्मादिमा एव विज्ञेया मनुरब्रवीत् ॥ [?]

D add इति श्रीनारदीये धर्मशास्त्रे प्रकीर्णकं नाम व्यवहारपदं सप्तदशम् (M3 L4 अष्टदशं) समाप्तं चेदं नारदीय धर्मशास्त्रम्; X add इति प्रकीर्णकं नामाष्टादशमं विवादपदं समाप्तम्; Y add इति प्रकीर्णकं नाम विवादपदं समाप्तम्; NMS add एतेषाम् अत्र प्रकीर्णकं समाप्तम्.

परिशिष्टम्

१९ स्तेयम्

द्विविधास्तस्करा ज्ञेयाः परद्रव्यापहारिणः ।
प्रकाशाश्चाप्रकाशाश्च तान्विद्यादात्मवान्नृपः ॥१॥
प्रकाशवञ्चकास्तत्र कूटमानतुलाश्रिताः ।
उत्कोटकाः साहसिकाः कितवाः पण्ययोषितः ॥२॥
प्रतिरूपकराश्चैव मङ्गलोद्देशवृत्तयः ।
इत्येवमादयो ज्ञेयाः प्रकाशलोकवञ्चकाः ॥३॥
अप्रकाशाश्च विज्ञेया बहिरभ्यन्तराश्रिताः ।
सुप्तान्प्रमत्तांश्च नरा मुष्णन्त्याक्रम्य चैव ते ॥४॥
देशग्रामगृहघ्नाश्च पथिघ्ना ग्रन्थिमोचकाः ।
इत्येवमादयो ज्ञेया अप्रकाशाश्च तस्कराः ॥५॥
तान्विदित्वा सुकुशलैश्चारैस्तत्कर्मकारिभिः ।
अनुसृत्य गृहीतव्या गूढप्रणिहितैर्नरैः ॥६॥
सभाप्रपापूपशालावेशमद्यान्नविक्रयाः ।
चतुष्पथाश्चैत्यवृक्षाः समाजाः प्रेक्षणानि च ॥७॥
शून्यागाराण्यरण्यानि देवतायतनानि च ।
चारैर्विनेयान्येतानि चौरग्रहणतत्परैः ॥८॥
तथैवान्ये प्रणिहिताः श्रद्धेयाश्चित्रवादिनः ।
चरा ह्युत्साहयेयुस्तांस्तस्करान्पूर्वतस्कराः ॥९॥
अन्नपानसमादानैः समाजोत्सवदर्शनैः ।

१ c — BM प्रकाशश्; BM B4 K3 अप्रकाशश्; d — Y विन्द्याद्; K5 सत्यवान्.

२ a — D तु ते; X प्रोक्तः c — NMS BM उत्कोडकाः; Jolly उत्कोचकाः; C4 उत्केडकाः; C उत्काटकाः; NMS सोपधिकाः; d — N पुण्ययोपितः.

३ b — Y मङ्गलादेव वृत्तयः; NMS मङ्गलादेशवृत्तयः; B मङ्गलादैववृत्तयः; d — Jolly -तस्कराः.

४ a — NMS तु; b — B B2 अन्यत्र चाश्रिताः c — B B2 C मुप्टां; D मुप्यां प्रसक्ताश्च नरा; NMS सुप्तान्मत्तान्प्रमत्तंश्च; d — BM B8 K3 K7 मुखन्त्य्; B B2 C4 K मुपन्त्य्; Y आक्रम.

५ b — B B2 C K C4 पन्थघ्ना; Jolly यज्ञघ्ना; K2 om.; B3 B4 K5 पथघ्ना; b — BM B8 K3 K7 पथि गच्छन्ति याचकाः; d — NMS तु.

६ a — MT om this verse; verses 6-12 are missing in Jolly's ms (C); a — NMS सुनिपुणैश्; B3 स्वकृशलैश्; b — NMS चोरैस्; B तस्कर-; c — NMS ग्रहीतव्या; d — NMS गूढैः प्रणिहितैर्; X गूढाश्रेणिहितैर्.

७ b — X सभाप्रपाः पूप-; Y -सालावेशमद्यानुविक्रयाः; d — B3 समाजः; NMS समाज-.

८ c — B3 चोरैर्; B4 K2 K5 चरैर्; c — Y विचेयान्य्; d — NMS चोर-; X चौरसंग्रह-.

९ c — NMS चोरा; B वर; c — B4 K5 उत्सादयेयुस्; d — NMS तस्करा; d — B X -तस्करैः.

तथा चौर्यापदेशैश्च कुर्युस्तेषां समागमम् ॥१०॥
ये तत्र नोपसर्पन्ति सृताः प्रणिहिता अपि ।
तेऽभिसार्य गृहीतव्याः सपुत्रपशुबान्धवाः ॥११॥
यांस्तत्र चौरान्गृह्णीयात्तान्विताड्य विडम्ब्य च ।
अवघुष्य च सर्वत्र वध्याश्चित्रवधेन ते ॥१२॥
न त्वहोढान्विताश्चौरा राज्ञा वध्या ह्यनागमाः ।
सहोढान्सोपकरणान्क्षिप्रं चौरान्प्रशासयेत् ॥१३॥
स्वदेशघातिनो ये स्युस्तथा पन्थावरोधिनः ।
तेषां सर्वस्वमादाय भूयो निन्दां प्रकल्पयेत् ॥१४॥
अहोढान्विमृशेच्चौरान्गृहीतान्परिशङ्कया ।
भयोपधाभिश्चित्राभिर्ब्रूयुस्तथा यथाकृतम् ॥१५॥
देशं कालं दिशं जातिं नाम वा संप्रतिश्रयम् ।
कृत्यं कर्मकरा वा स्युः प्रष्टव्यास्ते विनिग्रहे ॥१६॥
वर्णस्वराकारभेदात्ससंदिग्धनिवेदनात् ।
अदेशकालदृष्टत्वाद्वासस्याप्यविशोधनात् ॥१७॥
असद्व्ययात्पूर्वचौर्यादसत्संसर्गकारणात् ।
लेशैरप्यवगन्तव्या न होढेनैव केवलम् ॥१८॥
दस्युवृत्ते यदि नरे शङ्का स्यात्तस्करेऽपि वा ।
यदि स्पृश्येत लेशेन कार्यः स्याच्छपथः ततः ॥१९॥

१० a — X -महादानैस्(महादानैस् ?); NMS महादानैः; d — NMS प्रससर्पणम्.

११ a — Y तन्त्र; a — Y नोपसर्पन्ते; B नोपसर्पयन्ति; c — NMSऽभिसृत्य ग्रहीतव्यः; d — NMS add
अचोरा अपि दृश्यन्ते चोरैः सह समागताः ।
यादृच्छिकान्नैव तु तान्राजा दण्डेन शासयेत् ॥ [NMS 18.64]

१२ a — NMS चोरान्; b — K3 K7 विडंविनः; NMS तानाताड्य निवध्य च; B2 तान्विताड्य निवध्य च; c — BM अवघ्नन्ति.

१३ a — B न स्वहोधान्विताश्चिरा; NMS लोप्त्रादिरहिताश्चोरा; b — Y (except B) वध्या राज्ञा अनागसः; B वध्या राज्ञा अनागमः; NMS X अनागमम्; c — Y स्तेयकारणात्; d -- B8 C4 K K3 K7 चोरान्; d — X प्रकाशयेत्; NMS चोरान्क्षिप्रं विवासयेत्.

१४ b — NMS मार्गोपरोधिनः; Y यज्ञावरोधिनः; B पन्थावरोधनः; B4 K2 पन्थापरोधिनः; d — NMS प्रवर्तयेत्.

१५ a — NMS सहोढान्; BM K3 K7 चारान्; b — NMS गृहीत्वा; C B3 यदि शङ्कया; c — Y चिन्ताभिर्; B चित्र्याभिर्; d — NMS ब्रूयुः सत्यं यथा हि ते.

१६ a — NMS तथा; b — NMS रूपं प्रतिश्रयम्; BM वा तं प्रश्रियम्; c — NMS कर्म सहायांश्च; d — NMS स्युर्निगृह्य ते.

१७ a — BM वर्णस्वराकर-; b — C4 B3 K7 संसदि त्वनिवेदनात्; c — X अवेश-; B अदेशकाले दृष्टत्वाद्; cd — BM B8 K3 K7 om.

१८ ab — BM B8 K3 K7 om; b — K5 लेखैर्; all other mss. (except NMS) लेख्यैर्; d — B4 K2 K5 होढो नैव; B वधेनैव.

१९ a — K5 C4 have verses 19-26 after 29; b — NMS तस्करो न; c — N D स्पृशेत; B4 K2 K5 लेखेन; K5 चिह्नेन fh mn; d — K K2 B C शपथं; d — NMS नरः.

चौराणां भक्तदा ये स्युस्तथाग्न्युदकदायका: ।
आवासदा देशिकदास्तथैवोत्तरदायका: ॥२०॥
क्रेतारश्चैव भाण्डानां प्रतिग्राहिण एव च ।
समदण्डा: स्मृता ह्येते ये च प्रच्छादयन्ति तान् ॥२१॥
राष्ट्रेषु राष्ट्राधिकृता: सामन्ताश्चैव चोदिता: ।
अभ्याघातेषु मध्यस्था यथा चौरास्तथैव ते ॥२२॥
गोचरे यस्य मुष्येत तेन चौरा: प्रयत्नत: ।
मृग्या दाप्योऽन्यथा मोषं पदं यदि न निर्गतम् ॥२३॥
निर्गते तु पदे तस्मिन्नष्टेऽन्यत्र निपातिते ।
सामन्तान्मार्गपालांश्च दिक्पालांश्चैव दापयेत् ॥२४॥
गृहे वै मुषिते राजा चौरग्राहांस्तु दापयेत् ।
आरक्षकान्राद्रिकांश्च यदि चौरो न लभ्यते ॥२५॥
यदि वा दाप्यमानानां तस्मिन्मोषे तु संशय: ।
मुषित: शपथं शाप्यो मोषे वैशोध्यकारणात् ॥२६॥
अचौरे दापिते मोषं चौर्यवैशोध्यकारणात् ।
चौरे लब्धे लभेयुस्ते द्विगुणं प्रतिपादिता: ॥२७॥
चौरहृतं प्रयत्नेन सरूपं प्रतिपादयेत् ।
तदभावे तु मूल्यं स्याद्दण्डं दाप्यश्च तत्समम् ॥२८॥
काष्ठकाण्डतृणादीनां मृन्मयानां तथैव च ।
वेणुवैणवभाण्डानां वेत्रस्नाय्वस्थिचर्मणाम् ॥२९॥

२० a — NMS चांराणां; b — NMS तथाप्युदक-; BM तथा स्युर्जलदायका; c — BM C B8 K K3 देशिकाश्च; d — NMS BM K2 K5 तथैवान्तरदायका:.

२१ b — B C4 प्रतिग्राहण; c — NMS सर्वे; Jolly तु ते.

२२ a — BM राष्ट्रे राष्ट्रेऽधिपकृता:; B8 K3 K7 राष्ट्रे राष्ट्रेऽधिपकृतात्; c — Y अभ्याघाते तु; NMS विज्ञेया; Y वध्यस्था; d — NMS चांरास्.

२३ a — B सां चरे; NMS मुपितं; b — NMS चोर:; c — NMS गृह्य; d — B2 यदि देशान्; B B2 निर्गत:.

२४ a — Jolly यदा; NMS तस्मान्; Y यस्मिन्; b — Y निपातयेत्; Jolly न पातयेत्; c — BM C -पालाश्; d — B C C4 K दिपालाश्.

२५ a — NMS तु; b — BM चौराण्याह्या: प्रयत्नत:; K3 चौर ग्रामा च तिप्ठति; NMS दापयेद्दण्डवासिकान्; c — NMS आरक्षिकान्वाहिकांश्; d — NMS चोरो.

२६ a — Jolly दांपकर्तैप; Y दाप्यकं तेपां; X दाप्यतां तेपां; b — NMS ससंशये; c — NMS कार्यो; X B B2 दाप्यो; d — B मोपवैशुद्धि-; C वैशुद्धिकारणात्; BM B8 K7 काययेत्.

२७ a — NMS अचोरे; X अचौरो; B K3 अचौर; BM B B2 C K7 K3 B8 चापि ते; B4 K2 K5 चौरितें; Jolly वोधितो; a — BM K3 B8 मोक्षं; NMS मांपे; b — NMS चोरान्वेपणकारणात्; K2 K5 चौरे; C चौरो; d — NMS उपलव्धे लभेरंस्ते द्विगुणं तत्र दापितात्.

२८ a — B K K2 C चौरे(रैर्) हृतं; BM चौरै(र्) हृतं; अचोरे; NMS चौरैर् हृतं; Jolly प्रपद्यैव; C BM प्रपन्नैव.

२९ a — B -भण्डानां; Jolly वेत्रसस्यास्थिचर्मनो:; BM वेत्रसास्वस्थिचर्मणा:; cd — NMS om. From here to 19.40 NMS verses are composed of the second half of one verse as pādas ab and

शाकहरितमूलानां हरणे फलपुष्पयोः ।
गोरसेक्षुविकाराणां तथा लवणतैलयोः ॥३०॥
पक्वान्नानां कृतान्नानां मद्यानामामिषस्य च ।
सर्वेषामल्पमूल्यानां मूल्यात्पञ्चगुणो दमः ॥३१॥
तुलाधरिममेयानां गणिमानां च सर्वशः ।
एभ्यस्तूत्कृष्टमूल्यानां मूल्याद्दशगुणो दमः ॥३२॥
धान्यं दशभ्यः कुम्भेभ्यो हरतोऽभ्यधिकं वधः ।
न्यूनं त्वेकादशगुणं दण्डं दाप्योऽब्रवीन्मनुः ॥३३
सुवर्णरजतादीनामुत्तमानां च वाससाम् ।
रत्नानां चैव मुख्यानां शतादभ्यधिकं वधः ॥३४॥
पुरुषं हरतः पात्यो दण्ड उत्तमसाहसः ।
सर्वस्वं स्त्रीं तु हरतः कन्यां तु हरतो वधः ॥३५॥
महापशून्स्तेनयतो दण्ड उत्तमसाहसः ।
मध्यमो मध्यमपशुं पूर्वः क्षुद्रपशुं हरन् ॥३६॥
चतुर्विंशावरः पूर्वः परः षण्णवतिर्भवेत् ।
शतानि पञ्च तु परो मध्यमो द्विशतावरः ॥३७॥
सहस्रं तूत्तमो ज्ञेयः परः पञ्चशतावरः ।
त्रिविधः साहसेष्वेव दण्डः प्रोक्तः स्वयंभुवा ॥३८॥
प्रथमे ग्रन्थिभेदानामङ्गुल्यङ्गुष्ठयोर्वधः ।
द्वितीये चैव तच्छेषं दण्डः पूर्वश्च साहसः ॥३९॥

the first half of the following verse as pādas cd (NMS 18.82 = NāSmṛ 19.29 cd and 30ab, and so on.

३० a — B हरितशाकमूलानां; B4 C4 K2 K3 शाकं हरित-; bcd — BM om; b — Jolly तृणपुष्पयोः, X फलमूलयोः.

३१ abc — BM om; d — Y B3 दयः (देयः?).

३२ a — B तुलाधममेयानां; b — Y सर्वतः; d — Jolly अष्टगुणो; B दयः (देयः?).

३३ b — B वाधिकं; BM ऽप्यधिकं; C B8 K K3 व्यधिकं; c — BM B B3 C K2 K5 न्यूनं; NMS घृतं, X वेकादशगुणं.

३४ a — NMS हिरण्य-; c — BM B8 K3 मुक्तानां; d — Jolly अभ्यधिके.

३५ a — B4 K2 K5 पुरुपान्तरतः; BM पादाद्; NMS वासो; X पत्यां; b — B3 B4 K2 दण्डा; BM C B8 C4 K दण्डं; B3 B4 K2 दण्डस्तूत्तमसाहसः; c — B स्त्रिय हरतः सर्वस्वं; B हन्यां; BM B C हन्यं, B8 C4 K K3 K7 हन्यात्; d — NMS सर्वस्वं स्त्रीं तु कन्यां तु हरतो वध एव च.

३६ NMS om this verse; a — C B3 K3 महापशूंस्तु नयतो; c — B -पशूं; BM B8 K3 BM - पशुः.

३७ b — C परे; Jolly चर्णवति; B आ नवति; c — Jolly चतुःशतपरो यश्च; BM शतानि पञ्च चत्वारो; B8 K3 शतानि पञ्च चतुरो; K शतानि पञ्च तु वरो.

३८ ab — B4 om; K2 adds as fh mn.; c — B2 त्रिभेदः; B4 K5 एपु; d — NMS उक्तः; B C C4 K स्वयंभुवाक्.

३९ b — BM B2 B8 C4 K3 अङ्गुल्याङ्गुष्ठयोर्; c — B3 K C4 K3 तज्ज्ञेयं; NMS यच्छेपं; d — K C4 B8 K3 K7 तु; B स्व; BM C B8 K3 साहसं.

गोषु ब्राह्मणसंस्थासु स्थूरायाश्छेदनं भवेत् ।
दासीं तु हरतो नित्यमर्धपादविकर्तनम् ॥४०॥
येन येन विशेषेण स्तेनाङ्गेन विचेष्टते ।
तत्तदेवास्य छेत्तव्यं तन्मनोरनुशासनम् ॥४१॥
गरीयसि गरीयांसमगरीयसि वा पुनः ।
स्तेने निपातयेद्दण्डं न यथा प्रथमे तथा ॥४२॥
दश स्थानानि दण्डस्य मनुः स्वयंभुवोऽब्रवीत् ।
त्रिषु वर्णेषु यानि स्युर्ब्राह्मणो रक्षितः सदा ॥४३॥
उपस्थमुदरं जिह्वा हस्तौ पादौ च पञ्चमम् ।
चक्षुर्नासा च कर्णौ च धनं देहस्तथैव च ॥४४॥
अपराधं परिज्ञाय देशकालौ च तत्त्वतः ।
सारानुबन्धावालोक्य दण्डानेतान्प्रकल्पयेत् ॥४५॥
न मित्रकारणाद्राज्ञा विपुलाद्वा धनागमात् ।
उत्स्रष्टव्यः साहसिकस्त्यक्तामा मनुरब्रवीत् ॥४६॥
यावानवध्यस्य वधे तावान्वध्यस्य मोक्षणे ।
भवत्यधर्मो नृपतेर्धर्मस्तु विनियच्छतः ॥४७॥
न जातु ब्राह्मणं हन्यात्सर्वपापेष्वपि स्थितम् ।
निर्वासं कारयेत्काममिति धर्मो व्यवस्थितः ॥४८॥
सर्वस्वं वा हरेद्राजा चतुर्थं वावशेषयेत् ।
भृत्येभ्योऽनुस्मरन्धर्मं प्राजापत्यमिति स्थितिः ॥४९॥
ब्राह्मणस्यापराधे तु चतुःस्वङ्को विधीयते ।
गुरुतल्पे सुरापाने स्तेये ब्राह्मणहिंसने ॥५०॥
गुरुतल्पे भगः कार्यः सुरापाने ध्वजः स्मृतः ।
स्तेये तु श्वपदं कृत्वा शिखिपित्तेन कूटयेत् ॥५१॥

४० b — B BM B2 B8 K3 K7 स्थूलायाश्; X स्थूनायाश्; B2 छिन्नं भवेतः (?); d — X अर्धपादस्य छेदनम्.

४१ a —NMS Jolly यथाङ्गेन; b —Y स्तेनोंऽशेन; C तेनांशेन; NMS Jolly स्तेनो नृपु; c —B B8 तद्देवास्य; NMS छेत्तव्यम्तत्तदेवास्य.

४३ c — NMS तानि; d —Y ब्राह्मणं; C अक्षतः; N रक्षतः; NMS अक्षतो ब्राह्मणो व्रजेत्.

४४ a — B8 K3 K7 उपस्थाम्; b —X हस्त-; X पञ्चमः; d — NMS स्तनौ.

४५ c — NMS आलोच्य; d — NMS दण्डं दण्ड्येषु पातयेत्.

४६ a — BM B2 X -करणाद्; NMS राज्ञां; d — NMS उत्स्रष्टव्याः साहसिकास्तस्करा लोकवञ्चकाः.

४७ a — BM B8 K3 यावन्निवध्यस्य; C C4 K यावन्निवधस्य; b — BM B8 K3 तावद्; c — B नृपत्य.

४८ b — BM B8 K3 K7 सपापेष्वपि संस्थितम्; c — Y निर्वास्यं; NMS समग्रधनमक्षतम्; d — K2 om.

४९ a — B8 K3 K7 om this verse; NMS सर्वं वापि; c — NMS विप्रेभ्यो; BM B B2 C C4 K न तेभ्यो; Jolly एतेभ्यो; d — B स्थितः.

५० a — NMS Jolly अपराधेषु; c — BM B गुरुतल्प-.

५१ a — BM भगाः; B8 K3 K7 भगा-; K C4 C B भग-; BM कार्याः; b — NMS सुराध्वजः; d — B -वित्तेन; NMS पूरयेत्; C4 K K2 कुडयेत्; B कुटुम्वयेत्.

विशिराः पुरुषः कार्यो ललाटे भ्रूणघातिनः ।
असंभाष्यश्च कर्तव्यस्तन्मनोरनुशासनम् ॥५२॥
राजा स्तेनेन गन्तव्यो मुक्तकेशेन धावता ।
आचक्षाणेन तत्स्तेयमेवं कर्तास्मि शाधि माम् ॥५३॥
अनेना भवति स्तेनः स्वकर्मप्रतिपादनात् ।
राजानं तत्स्पृशेदेन उत्सृजन्तं सकिल्बिषं ॥५४॥
राजभिर्धृतदण्डास्तु कृत्वा पापानि मानवाः ।
निर्मलाः स्वर्गमायान्ति सन्तः सुकृतिनो यथा ॥५५॥
शासनाद्वा विमोक्षाद्वा स्तेनो मुच्यते किल्बिषात् ।
अशासनात्तु तद्राजा स्तेनस्याप्नोति किल्बिषम् ॥५६॥
गुरुरात्मवतां शास्ता शास्ता राजा दुरात्मनाम् ।
अथ प्रच्छन्नपापानां शास्ता वैवस्वतो यमः ॥५७॥
अष्टापाद्यं तु शूद्रस्य स्तेये भवति किल्बिषम् ।
द्विरष्टापाद्यं वैश्यस्य द्वात्रिंशत्क्षत्रियस्य तु ॥५८॥
ब्राह्मणस्य चतुःषष्टीत्येवं स्वायंभुवोऽब्रवीत् ।
तत्रापि च विशेषेण विद्वत्स्वभ्यधिकं भवेत् ॥५९॥
शारीरश्चार्थदण्डश्च दण्डस्तु द्विविधः स्मृतः ।
शारीरा दशधा प्रोक्ता अर्थदण्डास्त्वनेकधा ॥६०॥
काकण्यादिस्त्वर्थदण्डः सर्वस्वान्तस्तथैव च ।
शारीरस्त्ववरोधादिर्जीवितान्तस्तथैव च ॥६१॥

५२ a — Jolly अशिराः; Y शिशिराः; b — Jolly NMS C4 K ब्रह्म-

५३ a — B8 K3 K7 राज-; b — B B2 -केशिनि; NMS धीमता; c — Y अचक्षणेन; d — Y कर्मास्मि; B कर्मोऽस्मि.

५४ a — C C4 B8 K K3 तेन; b —NMS प्रतिवेदनात्; c —Jolly राजा तथा; BM B B2 C B8 K3 एनम्. d — BM B2 C उत्सृजेत्तु; B8 K K3 उत्सृज्यं तु; N स्वकिल्विपम्; K C4 ह्यकिल्विपम्.

५५ a — B K C4 राजभि-; b — B पापा मानवा.

५६ a — B3 NMS वापि मोक्षाद्; b — NMS मुच्येत; B किल्विपम्; c — NMS अशासत्तमसौ; d — BM प्राप्नोति; B3 K2 K5 om -प्नोति; BM reverses ab and cd.

५७ b — BM राजा चैव; X दुरा सदा (?); BM दुरात्मनः; c — Jolly अतः; B B2 C C4 K अत्र; d — B वैदस्वतो.

५८ a — X अप्टापाद्यस्य; BM B K अप्टापद्यं तु; b —B स्तेयं; c — BM B B8 K K7 C4 अप्टापद्यं; B4 K5 अप्टापादं; B3 अप्टापाद्यो; K2 अप्टापादे; NMS द्व्यप्टापाद्यं तु; X वैशस्य.

५९ b — NMS चतुःपप्टिं मनुः c —Jolly विद्यापि; BM B B8 C4 K K7 K3 वृत्रापि (?); B2 C वृतापि; d — BM अप्यधिकं; cd — NMS om.

६० a — B शरीरश्च; a —Y B2 -दण्डस्य; b — B2 द्विविधाः; c — Y शारीरं; B शारीर; NMS शारीरां; X दशधाः; NMS द्विविधः; Y प्रोक्तम्; NMS प्रोक्तो; d — B -दण्डं; Y -दण्डस्; NMS ह्यर्थदण्डस्.

६१ a — C C4 X K काकिण्यादिप्व्; B काकिण्यापिप्व्; BM B8 K3 K7 काकिण्यास्वर्थदण्डः स्यात्; b — B सर्वास्वान्तस्; K2 K5 स्वरस्वान्तम्; c — NMS त्ववरोधादि-; B B2 संनिरोधादिर्; B8 C C4 K K3 K7 संनिधाधादिर्.

काकण्यादिस्तु यो दण्डः स तु माषापरः स्मृतः ।
माषावराद्यो यः प्रोक्तः कार्षापणपरस्तु सः ॥६२॥
कार्षापणापराद्यस्तु चतुःकार्षापणः परः ।
द्व्यवरोऽष्टापरश्चान्यस्त्र्यवरो द्वादशोत्तरः ॥६३॥
कार्षापणाद्या ये प्रोक्ताः सर्वे ते स्युश्चतुर्गुणाः ।
एवमन्ये तु विज्ञेयाः प्राक्च ते पूर्वसाहसात् ॥६४॥
कार्षापणो दक्षिणस्यां दिशि रौप्यः प्रवर्तते ।
पणैर्निबद्धः पूर्वस्यां षोडशैव पणाः स तु ॥६५॥
माषो विंशतिभागस्तु ज्ञेयः कार्षापणस्य तु ।
काकणी तु चतुर्भागो माषस्य च पणस्य च ॥६६॥
पाञ्चनद्याः प्रदेशे तु संज्ञा या व्यावहारिकी ।
कार्षापणप्रमाणं तु निबद्धमिह वै तया ॥६७॥
कार्षापणोऽण्डिका ज्ञेयाश्चतस्रस्तास्तु धानकः ।
तद्द्वादश सुवर्णस्य दीनारश्चित्रकः स्मृतः ॥६८॥
वार्त्तां त्रयीं चाप्यथ दण्डनीतिम्
राजानुवर्तेत्संततताप्रमत्तः ।
हन्यादुपायैर्निपुणैर्गृहीतान्
पुरे च राष्ट्रे निगृह्णीयात्पापान् ॥६९॥

६२ b — BM अर्थावरः; all other mss. मापावरः; c —BM BM C C4 K K3 K7 पापावराद्यो; N पापावराजां; NMS कार्पापरार्धो corrected to मापापरार्धो; Jolly ऽयं; d — N यः.

६३ a — Y कार्पापणावरद्यस्; NMS कार्पापणापरार्धस्; b —Y चतुःकार्पापणावरः; NMS चतुःकार्पापणोत्तरः; c — B3 K5 द्विपरो; B B3 C ऽप्टपरश्.

६४ C Jolly om this verse; c — B8 C4ऽपि; NMS वोद्धव्याः; d — B8 C4 साहसाः.

६५ b —BM B B8 K3 K7 रूपाः; B3 रूपा; B4 K2 K5 रूपी; NMS रूढः; c — B विवद्धः; d — N विंशतिस्तु; B B8 C4 K7 पणः.

६६ NMS om this verse; a —BM K2 मापा; b —B4 K5 ज्ञेयाः; C4 K2 ज्ञेया c — BM K3 काकिनी, B4 C K C4 काकनी; B4 K5 काकिनन्; d — BM पनस्य; Jolly पलस्य.

६७ a — NMS B4 पञ्चनद्यः; B3 K2 K5 पाञ्चनद्य; a —B8 प्रवेशे; b —BM B8 C C4 K K3 संज्ञ; b — B B8 K3 व्यवहारिकी; Jolly व्यावहरिको; d — B निवद्धाम्; B4 K5 निवन्धम्; d — BM B B2 B8 C C4 K K3 K7 नैतया.

६८ a —B2 दण्डिका; NMS ऽव्धिका; C गेया; b —K3 C ताश्चतस्रस्; B2 चतस्रितास्; B चतत्रिभास् (?); b — B3 K2 BM धानका; B C B8 C4 धानकाः; c — Jolly सुवर्णस्तु; NMS सुवर्णं स्याद्; d —B B2 दीनाराश्; BM C B8 C4 K K3 K7 चित्रकस्य च; Jolly दीनाराख्यः स एव च.

६९ a —C B3 K3 तु यां; c —Y मतताप्रमत्तः; K 2 सततं प्रमत्तः; NMS राजानुवर्तेत सदाप्रमत्तः; d —NMS विविधैर्; NMS BM गृहीत्वा; e — Jolly तयैव; f —C C4 K शास्त्रेव निगृह्य; Y शास्त्रे च निगृह्य, NMS राप्ट्रे च विघुप्य; f —NMS चारान्; B4 K2 K5 om.

D add इति नारदप्रोक्तायां संहितायां चौरप्रतिपेधो नाम प्रकरणं समाप्तम् । समाप्तं चेदं नारदीयं धर्मशास्त्रम्, X add चौरप्रतिपेधं नाम समाप्तम्. Y add चौरप्रतिपेधं नाम प्रकरणं समाप्तम्; B3 add समाप्तं नारदप्रोक्तञ्च धर्ममानवमिति.

परिशिष्टम्

२० दिव्यानि

यदा साक्षी न विद्यते विवादे वदतां नृणाम् ।
तदा दिव्यैः परीक्षेत शपथैश्च पृथग्विधैः ॥१॥
सत्यं वाहनशस्त्राणि गोबीजरजतानि च ।
देवतापितृपादाश्च दत्तानि सुकृतानि च ॥२॥
महापराधे दिव्यानि दापयेत्तु महीपतिः ।
अल्पेषु च नरः श्रेष्ठः शपथैः शापयेन्नरम् ॥३॥
एते हि शपथाः प्रोक्ताः सुकरास्स्वल्पसंशये ।
साहसेष्वभिशापे च विधिर्दिव्यः प्रकीर्तितः ॥४॥
संदिग्धेऽर्थेऽभियुक्तानां प्रच्छन्नेषु विशेषतः ।
दिव्यः पञ्चविधो ज्ञेय इत्याह भगवान्मनुः ॥५॥
धटोऽग्निरुदकं चैव विषं कोशश्च पञ्चमः ।
उक्तान्येतानि दिव्यानि दूषितानां विशोधने ॥६॥
संदिग्धेष्वभियुक्तानां विशुद्ध्यर्थं महात्मना ।
नारदेन पुनः प्रोक्ताः सत्यानृतविभावनाः ।
वादिनोऽनुमतेनैनं कारयेन्नान्यथा बुधः ॥७॥

१ a — Y (except B2) add before this श्लोक:
ब्रह्महा पितृहा गांघ्नो मातृहा गुरुहा तथा ।
वालहा भ्रूणहा चैव तथैव गुरुतल्पगः ॥ [?]
B2 add instead
संशयस्थास्तु ये केचिन्महापतकिनश्च ये । [NMS 20.1]
तांश्च दिव्यैः परीक्षेत समयश्च पृथग्विधः ॥ [?]
Y (includig B2) continues
मर्यादाभेदकः स्त्रीघ्नो यान्यांल्लोकानि् ह गच्छति ।
तांल्लांकान्प्राप्नुयान्मिथ्या यः प्रश्नमनृतं वदेत् ॥ [?]
सत्येन पूयते साक्षी धर्मः सत्येन वर्धते ।
तस्मात्सत्येन वक्तव्यं सर्ववर्णपु साक्षीणा ॥ [Manu 8.83];
३ b — C K5 K2 C4 B3 चरतां.
४ d — B2 अन्यः; B2 प्रकल्पितः.
७ b — C K5 K2 महात्मनाम्.

धटः

चतुर्हस्तौ तुलापादावुच्छ्रयेण प्रकीर्तितौ ।
षड्ढस्तं तु तयोर्दृष्टं प्रमाणं परिमाणतः ॥८॥
पादयोरन्तरं हस्तं भवेदध्यर्धमेव च ।
शिक्यद्वयं समासज्य धटे कर्कटके दृढे ॥९॥
तुलयित्वा नरं पूर्वं चिह्नं कुर्याद्धटस्य तु ।
कक्षास्थानेन तं तुल्यमवतार्य ततो धटात् ॥१०॥
समयैः परिगृह्यैनं पुनरारोपयेन्नरः ।
तस्मिन्नेवं कृते सा चेत्कक्षेस्थाप्य सुनिश्चला ॥११॥
तुलितो यदि वर्धेत शुद्धः स्यान्नात्रे संशयः ।
समो वा हीयमानो वा न विशुद्धो भवेन्नरः ॥१२॥

८ b — Y उच्छ्रयेणा; B add

अन्यथा ह्यक्रमेणैषां (...) सर्वत्र धटधारणम् ॥ [?]
वर्षासु समयां वह्नेः शिशिरे च धटः स्मृतः ।
ग्रीष्मे सलिलमेवोक्तं विषं काले सुशीतले ॥ [J 1.254]
नार्तानां शुद्धिरेव स्यान्न विषं पित्तरोगिणाम् ।
श्वित्र्यन्धकुनखादीनां नाग्निः शुद्धिर्विधीयते ॥ [J 1.255]
सव्रतानां भृशार्तानां व्याधितानां तपस्विनाम् ।
स्त्रीणां च न भवेद्दिव्यं यदि धर्मस्त्ववेक्ष्यते ॥ [J 1.256]
शिरोवर्ती यदा न स्यात्तदा दिव्यं न दीयते ।
कारणैः सहितं प्राप्तं न दिव्यं चार्थिनां नृणाम् ॥ [J 1.257]
तत्प्रज्ञेन विनीतेन धार्मिकेन विजानता ।
उभयोरपि संयोगाद्दिव्यं देयं प्रयत्नतः ॥ [J 1.258]
न शीते तोयशुद्धिः स्यान्नोष्णकालेऽग्निशोधनम् ।
न प्रावृषि विषं दद्यात्प्रवाते न तुलां नृणाम् ॥ [J 1.259]

९ d — X तु कटके; Y B2 add

तत्रैकपार्श्वे पुरुषमन्यत्र तुलयेच्छिलाम् ॥ [?]
सुवर्णकारा वणिजः कुशलाः कर्मकारकाः ।
अवेक्षेरन्धटतुलां तुलानां धारणे विदः ॥ [J1.274]

११ b — B ends here.

१२ a — N हीयते; d — Y B2 sub

ऋज्वी धटतुला कार्या खादिरी तैन्दुकी तथा । [J 1.263 ab]
शिंशपा तदभावे तु शालं वा कोटरैर्विना ॥ [J 1.264 cd]
चतुरस्रा त्रिभिः स्थानैर्धटकर्कटकादिभिः ॥ [J 1.263 cd]
खादिरं कारयेत्तत्र निर्व्रणं शुक्लवर्जितम् ॥ [J 1.264 ab]
एवंविधानि काष्ठानि धटार्थं परिकल्पयेत् ।
सभाराजकुलद्वारे सरायतनचत्वरे ॥ [J 1.265]
निखेयो निश्चलः पूज्यो धूपगन्धानुलेपनैः ।
दध्यक्षतहविर्दुग्धकृतपावनमङ्गलैः ॥ [J 1.266]
धर्मरक्षार्थम् आहुतैर्लोकपालैरधिष्ठितः ॥ [J 1.267 ab]
रात्र्यह्नोपोषिते स्नाते आर्द्रवाससि मानवे ।
पूर्वाह्णे सर्वदिव्यानां प्रदानमनुकीर्त्यते ॥ [J 1.268]

धर्मपर्यायवचनैर्धट इत्यभिधीयसे ।
त्वं वेत्सि सर्वभूतानां पापानि सुकृतानि च ।
त्वमेव धट जानीषे न विदुर्यानि मानुषाः ॥१३॥
व्यवहाराभिशस्तोऽयं मानुषस्तुल्यते तथा ।
तदेव संशयापन्नं धर्मतस्त्रातुमर्हसि ॥१४॥

अग्निः

अत ऊर्ध्वं प्रवक्ष्यामि लोहस्य विधिमुत्तमम् ।
द्वात्रिंशदङ्गुलानि तु मण्डलान्मण्डलान्तरम् ॥१५॥
अष्टाभिर्मण्डलैरेवमङ्गुलानां शतद्वयम् ।
चतुर्विंशत्समाख्यातं संख्यातत्त्वार्थदर्शिभिः ॥१६॥
कल्पितैर्मण्डलैरेवमुषितस्य शुचेरपि ।
सप्ताश्वत्थस्य पत्त्राणि सूत्रेणावेष्ट्य हस्तयोः ॥१७॥
विदध्यात्तप्तलोहस्य पञ्चाशत्पलसंमितम् ।
हस्ताभ्यां पिण्डमादाय शनैः सप्तपदं व्रजेत् ॥१८॥

शिरोपस्थापनं कृत्वा अभियोक्त्युपस्थिते ॥
दिव्यप्रदानमुद्दिष्टमन्यत्र नृपशासनात् । [J 1.269]
निर्वाते वृष्टिरहिते शिरारोपितपत्त्रकम् । [J 1.276 cd]
तुलाशिरोभ्यामुत्सृष्टं विचलं न्यस्तलक्षणम् ॥ [± J 1.273 cd]

१३ a — Y -शब्देन, b — X अभिधीयते; c — X देव सर्वसत्त्वानां; e — X यथावदेव.

१४ a — Y एष पापाभिशस्तो; b — Y पुरुषः शुद्धिमिच्छति; c — Y एनं संशयारूढं, d — Y add
तुलितो यदि वर्धेत स विशुद्धो हि धर्मतः ।
समो वा हीयमानस्तु न विशुद्धो भवेन्नरः ॥ [J 1.283]
समेन समतामेति हीयमानस्तु हीयते ॥ [?]
अधोगतिर्न शुध्येत शुधेतोर्ध्वगतिस्तथा ।
समोऽपि हि विशुद्धः स्यादित्येषा त्रिविधा तुला ॥ [Dhko 484]
एषां हितस्तु लोकस्य शुद्धिरव्यभिचारिणी ॥ [?]

१६ a — Y B3 B4 सप्तभिर्.

१७ d — Y add सचैलं स्नातमाहूय [YāSmṛ 2.97a] <...> आर्द्रवासा समाहिताः । [?]
ॐ धर्माय नमः ।

१८ d — Y sub
ज्योतिरन्तश्चरो देहे देहिनामपि पावकः ।
प्रवृत्तिनिवृत्तानां तु कर्मणां च प्रवर्तकः ॥ [?]
अभियुक्तानामेतेन यथा मिथ्या न पावकः ।
अनेन धर्मशीलेन सत्यशीलो भविष्यति ॥ [?]
अभितप्तस्य लोहस्य पञ्चाशत्पलिकं भवेत् ।
हस्ताभ्यां पिण्डमादाय सोपवासः शुचिर्नरः ॥ [?]
स्थित्वैकस्मिन्ततोऽन्यानि व्रजेत्सप्तपदं शनैः ॥ [J 1.296cd]
ततः सुतप्तं संदंशैः संग्रहितमनातुरैः ॥ [?]
दद्युक्तलोहकारैश्च तप्तं शपथमन्त्रितम् ।
महादीप्ताशनिस्पर्शविद्युत्संपातसंनिभम् ॥ [?]
न वालैर्न च वृद्धैश्च लोहकारैः सुयन्त्रितम् ।

न मण्डलमतिक्रामेन्नाप्यर्वाक पादयेत्पदम् ।
न च पातयेताप्राप्तः यावद्भूमिर्प्रकल्पिता ॥१९॥
तीर्त्वानेन विधानेन मण्डलानि समाहितः ।
अदग्धः सर्वतो यस्तु स विशुद्धो भवेन्नरः ॥२०॥
भयाद्वा पातयते यस्त्वदग्धो यो विभाव्यते ।
पुनस्तं हारयेल्लोहं स्थितिरेषा पुरातनी ।
अनेन विधिना कार्यो हुताशसमयः स्मृतः ॥२१॥
त्वमग्ने सर्वभूतानामन्तश्चरसि साक्षिवत् ।
सुकृतं दुःकृतं लोकेनाज्ञातं विद्यते त्वया ॥२२॥
प्रच्छन्नानि मनुष्याणां पापानि सुकृतानि च ।
यथावदेव जानीषे न विदुर्यानि मानुषाः ॥२३॥
व्यवहाराभिशस्तोऽयं पुरुषः शुद्धिमिच्छति ।
तदेनं संशयापन्नं धर्मतस्त्रातुमर्हसि ॥२४॥

जलम्

अतः परं प्रवक्ष्यामि तोयस्य विधिमुत्तमम् ।
नातिक्रूरेण धनुषा प्रेरयेत्सायकत्रयम् ॥२५॥
मध्यमस्तु शरो ग्राह्यः पुरुषेण यवीयसा ।
प्रत्यानीतस्य तस्याथ स विशुद्धो भवेन्नरः ॥२६॥

वलवद्भिर्दृढैर्नित्यं देयमेवंविधैर्नरैः ॥ [?]

१९ b — Y पातयेत्. c — X प्रापयेताप्राप्तः; Y पापयतां प्राप्तां; d — Y -भूमिप्रकल्पितां.

२० c — Y सर्वथा.

२१ a — Y पातयते वा; X वा पातयेद्वा; b — N तु दग्धे; d — Y add
आसन्नपदं मर्यादानिष्क्रान्तो योऽनिना सह ।
तस्यायाममतिक्रम्य कर्यात्करनिरीक्षणम् ॥ [?]
पूर्वरूपेपु चिह्नेपु लक्षणैर्लक्षितेपु च ।
यस्य हस्तौ जयस्तस्य विपरीते पराजयः ॥ [?];
f — X हतासससमयः स्मृतः; Y जयाजयविधिक्रमः.

२२ a — Y om verses 22-24; b — X अन्तर्वससि.

२५ d — Y add
क्रूरं धनुः सप्तशतं नातिक्रूरं तु पट्शतम् ।
मन्दं पञ्चशतं ज्ञेयमेप प्रोक्तो धनुर्विधिः ॥ [J 1.307]
धनुर्वाह्वोः समं क्षेप्तुः कृत्वा तोरणकं परम् । [?]
तस्याधः प्रेरयेद् वाणानेप वाणविधिः स्मृतः ॥ [?]

२६ c — Y om this verse; cd — Y sub.
मध्यमस्य शरस्यार्थे पुरुपस्तु जवान्वितः । [?]
तमेव स शरं गृह्य पररुपस्तत्समोऽपरः । [?]
तलाहतः (?) समागच्छेद्यथाप्राणेण वेगवान् । [?]
पञ्चाशतो धावकानां यस्तेपामजितो जवे । [±Dhoko 501]
तं नियोज्य स तस्यार्थे धर्म एव न हीयते ॥ [?]

अन्यथा न विशुद्धः स्यादेकाङ्गमपि दर्शयेत् ।
स्थानादन्यत्र वा गच्छेद्यस्मिन्पूर्वं निवेशितः ॥२७॥
स्त्रियस्तु न बलात्कार्या न पुमानपि दुर्बलः ।
भीरुत्वाद्योषितो मृत्युः कृशस्यापि बलात्कुर्यात् ।
सहसा प्राप्नुयात्सर्वांस्तस्मादेताश्च मज्जयेत् ॥२८॥
तोयमध्ये मनुष्यस्य गृहीत्वोरू सुसंयतः ॥२९॥
सत्यानृतविभागस्य तोयाग्नी स्पष्टकृत्तमौ ।
यतश्चाग्निरभूदस्मात्ततस्तोयं विशिष्यते ॥३०॥
क्रियते धर्मतत्त्वज्ञैर्दूषितानां विशोधनम् ।
तस्मात्सत्येन भगवञ्जलेश त्रातुमर्हसि ॥३१॥

विषम्

अतः परं प्रवक्ष्यामि विषस्य विधिमुत्तमम् ।
तुलयित्वा विषं पूर्वं देयमेतद्धिमागमे ॥३२ ॥
न पूर्वाह्णे न मध्याह्ने न संध्यायां तु धर्मवित् ।
शरद्ग्रीष्मवसन्तेषु वर्षासु च न दापयेत् ॥३३॥
भग्नं च दारितं चैव धूपितं मिश्रितं तथा ।
कालकुटमलंबुं च विषं यत्नेन वर्जयेत् ॥३४॥
शार्ङ्गहैमवतं शस्तं गन्धवर्णरसान्वितं ।
महादोषवते देयं राज्ञा तत्त्वबुभुत्सया ॥३५॥

२७ d — N निवेपितात्.
२८ e — K3 B8 सहसा; f — K3 B8 वर्जयेत्.
२९ b — Y add

तावत्तिष्ठेत नियतो यावत्प्राप्तः स सायकः । [?]
अवतीर्य जले विद्वान् स्नातः प्रयत्तमानसः । [?]
श्रावयेत यथान्यायमेभिर्मन्त्रपदैः शुभैः । [?]
ॐ नमो धर्माय ।
यतस्त्वमसि भूतानां जलेश सुखशीतलः । [?]
त्रायस्वैनं नरं पापात्पश्यसि त्वं शुभाशुभम् । [?]
आदिदेवोऽसि भूतानां लोकस्याप्यायनं महत् । [?]

३० c — N ततश्.
३१ d — Y add

ततो निमज्जेत्सलिले सर्वाण्यङ्गान्यदर्शनात् । [?]
प्राप्तं तु सायकं दृष्ट्वा जलादुत्तीर्य बुद्धिमान् । [NMS 20.28cd]
प्रणिपत्य नृपं गच्छेत्सर्वांश्चैव सभासदः । [NMS 20.28gh]

३२ b — Y add

यस्मिन्काले यथा प्राप्तं यादृपं च प्रकल्पितम् । [J 1.318cd]
यावन्मात्रं समुद्दिष्टं संख्यातत्त्वार्थदर्शिभिः ॥ [J 1.319ab]

३५ b — N add 12.38ab here.

न बालातुरवृद्धेषु नैव स्वल्पापराधिषु ।
विषस्य तु यवान्सप्त दद्याच्छोद्ये घृतप्लुतान् ॥३६॥
विषस्य पलषड्भागाद्भागो विंशतिमस्तु यः ।
तमष्टभागहीनं तु शोद्ये दद्याद् घृतप्लुतम् ॥३७॥
यथोक्तेन विधानेन विप्रान्स्पृष्ट्वानुमोदितः ।
सोपवासश्च खादेत देवब्राह्मणसंनिधौ ॥३८॥
विषं वेगक्रमापेतं सुखेन यदि जीर्यते ।
विशुद्धमिति तं ज्ञात्वा राजा सत्कृत्य मोक्षयेत् ॥३९॥
त्वं विष ब्रह्मणः पुत्रः सत्यधर्मरतौ स्थितः ।
शोधयैनं नरं पापात्सत्येनास्यामृतीभव ॥४०॥

कोशः

अतः परं प्रवक्ष्यामि कोशस्य विधिमुत्तमम् ॥४१॥
पूर्वाह्णे सोपवासस्य स्नातस्यार्द्रपटस्य च ।
सशुकस्याव्यसनिनः कोशपानं विधीयते ॥४२॥
यद्भक्तः सोऽभियुक्तः स्यात्तद्दैवत्यं तु पाययेत् ।
सप्ताहाद्यस्य दृश्यते द्विसप्ताहेन वा पुनः ।
प्रत्यात्मिकं तु यत्किंचित्सैव तस्य विभावना ॥४३॥
द्विसप्ताहात्परं यस्य महद्वा वैकृतं भवेत् ।
नाभियोज्यः स विदुषां कृतकालव्यतिक्रमात् ॥४४॥

३६ b — Y add
नोन्मत्तार्ते तथा व्यङ्गे न च दद्यात्तपस्विपु । (?);
c — N यवाः; d — N घृतप्लुताः.
३७ cd — X om.
३८ a — This half verse is found in the mss. after 20.35 ab.
३९ c — K3 K5 B8 विशुद्धिं विदितं; d — K K3 C4 add ॐ नमो धर्माय.
४० c — K5 शापात्; d — Y add इति मन्त्रं पठेत्तत्र विधिना विभक्षणे.
४२ d — Y add
मुहूर्ते समतिक्रान्ते जिह्वानिर्लेखना कृता । [?]
सभारांमन्त्रिणश्च (?) जिह्वा दग्धैव धर्मतः ॥ [?]
दग्धे तु दण्डयेद्राजा मारासारं परीक्ष्य च । [?]
निरुजं निर्व्रणं कृत्वा सभास्थाने विशांधितः । [?]
समित्पावकपुष्पैश्च राजा सत्कृत्य मांक्षयेत् । [?]
४३ b — N add
यद्भक्तः सोऽभियुक्तः स्यात्तद्देवतं तु पाययेत् ।
प्रत्युच्चार्य तु संदिग्धं प्राण्मुखं समुपस्थितम् ॥ [?]
B2 add
अ(न्य?)भक्तिविहीनः स्यादादित्यं प्रति पाययेत् । [?]
अर्चयित्वा च तं देवं प्रक्षाल्य च पुनः पुनः ।
एवं संश्रावयित्वा तु पाययेत्प्रसृतित्रयम् ॥ [Dhko 513]

महापराधे निर्धर्मे कृतघ्ने क्लीबकुत्सिते ।
नास्तिकव्रात्यदासेषु कोशपानं विवर्जयेत् ॥४५॥
यथोक्तेन प्रकारेण पञ्च दिव्यानि धर्मवित् ।
दद्याद्राजाभियुक्तानां प्रेत्य चेह च नन्दति ॥४५॥
न विषं ब्राह्मणे दद्यान्न लोहं क्षत्रियो हरेत् ।
न निमज्ज्याप्सु वैश्यश्च शूद्रः कोशं न पाययेत् ॥४७॥
वर्षासु न विषं दद्यात्हेमन्ते नाप्सु मज्जयेत् ।
न लोहं हारयेद्ग्रीष्मे न कोशं पाययेन्निशि ॥४८॥

नारदीयधर्मशास्त्रः समाप्तः

४५ c — N नास्तिकप्राभ्यदासेपु; d — X add शरद्ग्रीष्मवसन्तेपु क्षितियाप्सु निमज्जयेत् (?) । [?].
४७ d — B2 दापयेत्.
४८ d — X add
तुलनीयौ तु राज्ञा वै पारदारिकतस्करौ ।
ध्रुवानां च प्रमाणं स्यात्तुलायाश्च तदन्तरं ।। [?]
स यादाकः शुश्रु <..........> ।
चतुर्यागेन <..........> पेणवश्चतुङ्गुलाः ।।
वैपुला न द्विहस्तात्तु पष्ठिस्तत्रापि दापयेत् [?] ।
तुलावर्णश्च कर्तव्या निर्व्रणं शुप्कवर्जितम् ।
शिंशपा तदभावे तु शालं वा कप्टकैर्विना । [±J 1.264ab]
एवंविधानि काप्टानि धटार्थे कल्पिता इति । [±J 1.265ab]
Y add
स्त्रीणां तु न विपं प्रोक्तं न चापि सलिलं तथा ।
धटकोपादिभिस्तासामतस्तत्त्वं विचारयेत् । [Dhko 452]
न कश्चिदभियोक्तारं दिव्येपु विनियोजयेत् ।
अभिशस्ताय दातव्यं दिव्यं दिव्यमिति स्मृतः । [KāSmṛ 244]
अतः परं तप्तमापप्रकरणम् [निर्?]उच्यते ।
सौवर्णे राजते ताम्र आयसे मृण्मयेऽपि वा ।
गव्यं घृतमुपादाय तदग्नौ स्थापयेच्छुचिः । [J 1.344]
भ्रमद्वीचितरङ्गाढ्यं मानसस्यातिभीपणम् ।
घृतं चानेन मन्त्रेण सकृत्तदभिमन्त्रयेत् ।। [±J 1.346]
ॐ नमो धर्माय ।
परं पवित्रममृतं घृत त्वं यज्ञकर्मसु ।
दह पावक पाप्मानं हिमशीतं शुचौ भव ।। [+J 1.347]
सौवर्णीं राजतीं ताम्रीमायसीं वा सुशोभिताम् ।
सलिलैरसकृद्धौतां प्रक्षिपेत्तत्र मुद्रिकाम् ।। [±J 1.345]
उपोपितं स्नानमात्रमार्द्रवाससमागतम् ।
ग्राहयेन्मुद्रिकां तां तु घृतमध्यगतां तथा ।। [PiSmṛ 179]
आयसं कारयेत्पात्रं ताम्रं वा पोडशाङ्गुलं ।
चतुरङ्गुलखातं तुमृन्मयं वापि मण्डलम् ।। [PiSmṛ 170]
पूरयेद् घृततैलाभ्यां पलैर्विंशतिभिस्तु तत् । [PiSmṛ 171]
सुतप्ते निक्षिपेत्तत्र सुवर्णस्य तु मापकम् ।
अङ्गुप्ठाङ्गुलियोगेन उद्धरन्तप्तमापकम् ।। [PiSmṛ 172]

करा्ग्रं न धुनुयात्तु विस्फोटश्च न जायते ।
शुद्धो भवति धर्मेण पितामहवचो यथा ।। [PiSmṛ 173]
प्रदेशिनीं ततश्चास्य परीक्षेयुः परीक्षकाः ।
यदि विस्फोटिका न स्याच्छुद्धोऽसावन्यथाशुचिर् ।। [PiSmṛ 180]
इति पि<अ>तामहम्तप्तमापप्रकरणं समाप्तम् ।
इदमल्पधीयां नृणां दुर्विज्ञेयं यथोदितं ।।
नारदीयं यदस्तीह न्यायाशास्त्रं महार्थवत् ।
तस्येयं लिख्यते टीका स्पस्टा नेपालभापया ।
इमां विज्ञाय भूपाद्याश्चरन्तु न्यायवर्त्मना ।।
इति मानवन्यायशास्त्रे नारदप्रोक्तायां संहितायां न्यायधर्मपदानि समाप्तानि.

END NOTES

[1] L2 पदौर्; P पदार्.

[2] P हि.

[3] P om.

[4] P प्रथमं.

[5] P यत्र.

[6] M M2 J J2 A V3 R सदेश-; C2 C3 K4 L L3 L4 G तद्देश-; V5 सुदेश-.

[7] P पर्पल्लक्षणं.

[8] P वर्णाश्रमविभागौ.

[9] P दायानुक्रमः.

[10] C3 K4 G L3 L4 श्राद्धावशौचकल्पां.

[11] P शौचाचारविकल्पां; C3 K4 G L3 L4 om.

[12] P भगवान्मनुर्.

[13] P रहस्यस्थानान्येवं चतुर्विंशति प्रकरणानि । एतदत्र श्लोकशतसहस्रेण साशीतिनाध्यायसहस्रेण च भगवान्मनुरुपनिबध्य देवर्षये नारदाय प्रायच्छत् ।

[14] P गणुणैरेत.

[15] P add तं च महर्षये मार्कण्डेयाय प्रायच्छत् । स च तस्मादधीत्य तथैवायुःशक्तिमपेक्ष्य मनुष्याणागाढभिः सहस्रैः संचिक्षेप तं च सुमतये भार्गवाय प्रायच्छत् ।

[16] P सुमतैर्.

[17] P om.

[18] P om.

[19] M2 V3 V6-8 -नाशाद्; G L3 L4 -ह्रस्वाद्.

[20] P om.

[21] Jolly अधीयवे.

[22] This verse is found in N followed by इत्येवमारभ्य कर्मप्रकारव्याख्यातव्यम् । तत्र नवमं प्रकरणं व्यवहारो नाम यत्रेमामादौ देवर्षिनारदः सूत्रीयां मातृकां चकार । अस्या मुखः ।

[23] B 5 add

आदित्यचन्द्रावनिलानलौ च द्यौर्भूमिरापो हृदयं यमश्च ।
अहश्च रात्रिश्च उभे च संध्ये धर्मश्च जानाति नरस्य वृत्तम् ।। [Bhā 1.68.29]

[24] P om.

[25] P यत्रेमाम्.

[26] P सूत्रीयां.

[27] D अस्याभिमुखं; D add

लोकसंरक्षणार्थाय धर्मसंस्थापनाय च ।
राज्ञां दोपहरश्चैव व्यवहारः प्रकीर्तितः ।। [?]

[28] NMS add मनुः प्रजापतिर्यस्मिन्काले राज्यमवूभुजत् । [?]

[29] M4 वहु-.

[30] M4 समुपवेपितयोर्विनीतवेपयोस्.

[31] P L2 निर्लोतित्वात्.

[32] P यत्या.

[33] P add या वाह्यार्थीम् (?) वा.

[34] P भारह् (?).

[35] P रतरीक्षतम् (?).

[36] P प्रार्थतां.

[37] P त.

[38] P add the numeral 2.

[39] P सप्रतिपत्यं.

[40] P तदा रसेव.

[41] P कुलैदयस् (?).

[42] P एनैते (?).

[43] P -प्रवर्त्तधर्मानो.

[44] Jolly राज्ञा नियुक्तः.

[45] P आधिकर्मकृद्वत्तं.

[46] P योगः परस्य दीयते सत्त्वाभियोग.

[47] P व्यवहारे.

[48] M4 वट्पद्रमे.

[49] P अवावदुग्रामस्थितस्य; M4 अभाववदुग्राम-.

[50] M4 यथा; M4 अवावदुग्राम-.

[51] P om.

[52] P L2 त्यक्षमाणम्.

[53] P य; L2 या.

[54] P विभूत्वाद्.

[55] D add

अर्थानर्थावुभौ वुद्ध्वा धर्माधर्मौ च तावुभौ ।
वर्णक्रमेण सर्वेषां पश्येत्कार्याणि कर्मिणां ।। [Manu 8.24]

[56] L2 राजा-.

[57] P अन्तां.

[58] P add न.

[59] P add न.

[60] P चार्त्तं.

[61] P सन्नांऽभिनन्दति.

[62] P व्यवहारेणं (?).

[63] P द्रष्ट-.

[64] P साधुन् (sic) उदासिन-.

[65] M4 -चक्रिया-; P L2 -चक्रिका-.

[66] Mātṛkā 2 is found only in ms P.

[67] D after Mā 1.23 -कार्यं.

[68] D after Mā 1.23 -विनिर्णयः.

[69] Jolly धन्यर्थी.

[70] P वादि.
[71] P sh mn; Jolly विनिवेशयेत्.
[72] P अन्योन्य.
[73] P ऽनया-.
[74] P प्रमाणवर्जित.
[75] Jolly पुलाकाश्रय-.
[76] P नामा.
[77] P आगमे वर्जितं.
[78] Jolly वादे.
[79] Jolly विन्दुमात्रविहीना वा पदवर्णविदुष्टा वा; P sh mc -वर्णपूनाधिका तु या.
[80] Jolly राजकुला-.
[81] P add न.
[82] P ऽभिमानस्तप्स्यताम्.
[83] P प्रत्याकर्णितपादाभ्याम्.
[84] P प्राप्तावसायान्.
[85] P आहूतव्यपलायी.
[86] There is a gap in the text. It reads क्रियाद्वे -ति.
[87] P यदि.
[88] P पड्(M4 खड्)वासनं पापुपेति राज्ञोक्तोऽगं वधमर्हति ।
[89] P आत्रमति.
[90] P क्रियाणक-.
[91] P न्यासस्थपनिकम्.
[92] P बरणमाणकादिनां
[93] P om.
[94] P साक्षिकं दूपणं.
[95] Jolly पक्षानुत्सार्य तु सभ्यैः कार्यो विनिश्चयः सदा.
[96] P नेह.
[97] P एवाकृतप्रतिभूनिवद्ध एव किंचित्तरं तम्.
[98] P दमः.
[99] P जयपत्रवत्.
[100] Jolly om.
[101] P add न.
[102] R add this verse after 3.1.
[103] D धर्मज्ञो.
[104] Jolly अनुजीवति.
[105] P -क्षुणात् (?).
[106] P अतोऽतो.
[107] P प्रधानाप्रधाने
[108] M4 -मोक्षः.
[109] P sh mc for प्रवर्तितुं तं जयतामुपेक्षताम्.
[110] P sh mc न तु
[111] P add कायात् घन्ते (?).

[112] P अर्थिनां.

[113] P -आंत्तमाधमर्णयोर्.

[114] P -अकृतर्णो.

[115] P न पुत्र-; P sh mc add -पौत्र-.

[116] P मुन्द, P अथ; L2 अथ प्य् [sic].

[117] P श्लोकांत्तरार्ध.

[118] P M4 ऋणादान-.

[119] P -दुःखवोधाः.

[120] P असंप्राप्ता-.

[121] P देवाधारण.

[122] P add वैव हा.

[123] P न भवतिर्.

[124] P श्रीधरः.

[125] P प्रयच्छतः.

[126] P संविधिः.

[127] P अपम्यं; P fh mc उपम्यं.

[128] P विस्तराः.

[129] P अक्षुण्णत्वम्.

[130] P प्रवर्तनः.

[131] P शव्दार्था-.

[132] P पौत्रात्.

[133] P अर्थ-.

[134] P न्यर्थार्थ-.

[135] P add केन दद्याद्.

[136] Jolly उत्क्षिप्तं.

[137] P उद्यमाकं.

[138] L2 व्यथितं.

[139] P वैयावृत्यंकारः.

[140] P भाण्डमायांगस्थिताः.

[141] P dittography from 1.14 प्रतिपत्रं तु दद्यादित्यर्थः । यतो रिक्थमृणं ततः । [NāSmṛ 1.14d] अत्र या स्त्री विधवीभूतापुत्रा च । तत्र सैव यदि भर्त्रा म्रियमाणेन निरूपिता ततः पतिकृतमृणं दद्यात् । अथवा सैव रिक्थग्राहिणिर्णं दद्यात् ।

[142] P तत्रामेव (?).

[143] P सा.

[144] P कुटुम्वं स्वं प्रार्थ.

[145] P -रहिता.

[146] P ऋणकस्य.

[147] P om.

[148] P दायाद्यैर्.

[149] P unclear; L2 कस्त्व कस्य (?).

[150] P स्त्रियां.

[151] P तदा असमाः.

[152] P पितृनाम्.
[153] P -विद्यमानम्.
[154] P पुत्रः हारी.
[155] P पुत्रहारी.
[156] P पुत्रहारी.
[157] P तस्य तदा.
[158] P धनं.
[159] P ग्रन्थकारगुरुतश्.
[160] P वा.
[161] P मता.
[162] P स्वैरिणीर्दिष्टा.
[163] M4 om.
[164] P गृहनायका.
[165] P प्रभावाऽप्रौढः.
[166] P om.
[167] P प्राप्त-.
[168] P अधरपरिवग्रपेक्षया (?).
[169] K2 K5 B3 add भूमेर्गुरुतरी माता न तावत्.
[170] Jolly अप्टग्यात्.
[171] P व्यवहारस्य त्वक्षमः; L M4 व्यवहारत्वक्षमः.
[172] P M4 चाधर्यस्याधरस्यास्वतन्त्रत्वं.
[173] P add एतेपु परतन्त्रेपु.
[174] P ताहने (?).
[175] P -कृतकृताकृत्यांपसंहार.
[176] P अधिकस्याकाले.
[177] P काण्डस्पृष्ट.
[178] D पतिताका स्त्रीवत्.
[179] P स्वर्गावततो.
[180] P L2 तुछकं मदनं; M4 कं मदनं.
[181] P आसवा.
[182] P अभ्वसभाः.
[183] P माप्येन.
[184] P -पलक्षिते.
[185] P परिच्छिन्नं.
[186] P निःसंदिग्धी-.
[187] P L2 ततो ह्यं यस्य (?); M4 ततां ह्यन्धस्य.
[188] M4 असाक्षिप्रशंसा.
[189] P L2 पगे (?); M4 गे (?); Jolly स्थले.
[190] P आधार-.
[191] P L2 यात्रो-; M4 यात्रो-.
[192] P om.
[193] Jolly यदि.

[194] P स्वार्थमुत्तुं (?).
[195] P प्रतिमासीं.
[196] P चापोगण्ड.
[197] P पुज्यते.
[198] P लभते.
[199] P L2 ऽन्यास; M4 ऽन्धास.
[200] P निक्षेपमध्य.
[201] P L2 अनुपरवंस्याः; M4 अनुपवंस्याः.
[202] P एकं.
[203] P न भवति.
[204] Jolly अपाहर्तुं.
[205] P वृद्धपितामहेनाहृतं.
[206] P L2 अमारं.
[207] P M4 अप्रमाणेत्य्.
[208] P om इति.
[209] P धर्मदत्तादि-.
[210] P प्रमाणः.
[211] P L2 -शब्द-; M4 -शब्दः.
[212] P कुशीदम्.
[213] P कुशीदेन.
[214] P कुशीदिनां.
[215] Jolly ता.
[216] P L2 यदि तं.
[217] P L2 मुनिमक्तम्.
[218] P L2 करावृद्धिर्; M4 कारावृद्धिर्.
[219] P -परिणाम-.
[220] P मास.
[221] P पण-.
[222] P मलिक-.
[223] P L2 मास.
[224] P add 20.
[225] M4 वर्धतो.
[226] P जल्पितावृद्ध्या.
[227] P प्रीतिदत्तस्य.
[228] P -पादका एव.
[229] P -प्रयोगेन तत्.
[230] P L2 -धने न.
[231] P add श्लोकः.
[232] P L2 -मुस्थहेतू; M4 -मुख्यहेतू.
[233] P L2 प्रणशने.
[234] P -स्थानं प्रतिभुवं.
[235] L2 न च.

[236] M4 व-.
[237] P सतौ.
[238] P L2 ह्यसी.
[239] M4 जीवसञ्ज्ञकां (?). This verse is defective.
[240] P यत्.
[241] P गृह्णाति.
[242] P समस्थापक-.
[243] P धनकि-.
[244] P पुरस्तदा.
[245] P द्विगुणां.
[246] P L2 वलेना-.
[247] P L2 पञ्चकेन.
[248] P om.
[249] M4 रूपप्रधान-; P ह्य (?)अपप्रधान-.
[250] P क्षुणकं (?).
[251] M4 भाग्यस्य; P L2 भोग्यस्था.
[252] P L2 add आधिना धनिना संभवितेन (?).
[253] P dittography यावच्च विचारितकालावभोग्य एव तस्मिन्सोपकारे कौसीदीवृद्धिं न कश्चिदाप्नुयात्.
[254] P L2 ऋणे-.
[255] P L2 अप्रतिपाराति (?)
[256] P संज्ञैव.
[257] P -कृते.
[258] P चिन्था.
[259] P एव.
[260] P L2 अप्रमाणम्.
[261] M4 -संवन्धः.
[262] P L2 प्रास्थः; M4 प्राप्तः.
[263] P येन विद्यमानः.
[264] P तदानापेक्षया.
[265] P वादीदं.
[266] P L2 त इप्टदर्शितम्; M4 तस्य द्रप्ट्दर्शनम्; P L2 अधि.
[267] P प्रश्नवागताः.
[268] P L2 तस्यागतः.
[269] P L2 साक्षिलेखक उदास्यादयां; M4 साक्षिलेखक दास्यदयां.
[270] P L2 इप्टारः.
[271] P L2 -धर्मपत्रेण.
[272] P -निरापाच्; L2 -निरायाच्.
[273] P L2 कालकान्तान्तरे.
[274] P only -विशुद्धपत्रं.
[275] P L2 अमुकयत्नने M4 अमुकपत्तनेव.
[276] M4 सता.
[277] P युज्यमानतार्थता.

278 P L2 कथनम्.

279 P कीदृशास्य.

280 P L2 आधिप्रत्यय-.

281 M4 आरूढं

282 P अभिलिखितं.

283 P -पदकानां.

284 Jolly अन्वयजाति-.

285 M4 द्रव्यसंवन्धां निःसंवन्धां न युज्यते.

286 P व्याख्याय.

287 P L2 -नाम्नः; M4 -नाम्ने.

288 P -वशत्वातिदांपात्.

289 P and its copies have the end of the commentary on this verse under verse 126.

290 P दीक्षिव्यवस्थितं,

291 M4 निर्हरेद्.

292 P L2 क्रियापादन-.

293 P L2 लिखितहृत-.

294 P उपन्यसति.

295 P and its copies have here a portion of the commentary on verse 126, probably due to a folio being out of place in the exemplar.

296 P L2 भ्रंसितातिं; P L2 om अथवा; M4 अत.

297 P L2 विन्दुरूपम्.

298 P and its copies have the portion of the commentary beginning here and ending under verse 125.

299 P om.

300 P जनाधिक-.

301 P अवसुभूतेपु,

302 P यत्

303 M4 चायं.

304 See note 189.

305 P and its copies have here the end of the commentary on verse 124.

306 P -उक्ति-.

307 P वणिक्य-.

308 P L2 ईदृशी.

309 P add स्लोकः.

310 P L2 सप्टान्धक.

311 P शंगण. (?)

312 P L2 मदीयं तृतीयं.

313 P L2 निपित्तिः; M4 निपिंत्तिः.

314 P प्रतिवादिना.

315 P L2 गृहीतकं.

316 P L2 दत्तकम्.

317 L2 om.

[318] L2 om.
[319] P छंत्तुं.
[320] P विपक्रेता,
[321] P परोक्षे च न कर्तव्यः.
[322] P चान्यं.
[323] P विज्ञाताचारम्.
[324] P add सः.
[325] P साक्षिम्.
[326] P एकम्.
[327] P साक्षिणम्.
[328] P वसतां कारं.
[329] P add तं.
[330] M4 निविक्षाक्षर-.
[331] Jolly विश्रांसेद् (?).
[332] Jolly विश्रांसो.
[333] Jolly विश्रमार्थं.
[334] P तत्राक्षसमम्; P अर्थज्ञातम्.
[335] P कांत (?).
[336] P अक्षरसत्यम्.
[337] P तर्द्रप् (?).
[338] M4 -सम्यमानो; L2 P -सभ्यमाना.
[339] P पर्याय.
[340] M4 तत्र गदितं.
[341] P om.
[342] P प्रपद्यते; Jolly स दापयेत्.
[343] P -वलापेक्ष्यं.
[344] Jolly ये
[345] L2 शायत्य्; P शययति; Jolly शाययत्य्.
[346] Jolly शिले चारित्रेऽभियांगो; P -पण्डनाभियोगो..
[347] P अत्र युक्तं;
[348] P add यस्य
[349] P L2 अपरदेश-.
[350] P विकरोति.
[351] Manu धनिन्यार्ये.
[352] Scil. यो यथा निक्षिपेद्धस्ते यमर्थं यस्य मानवः ।
स तथैव ग्रहीतव्यो यथा दायस्तथा ग्रहः ॥ [Manu 8.180, J 2.3]
[353] P कृत्वा.
[354] P -मुद्रिता.
[355] P L2 तथा-.
[356] P द्विविधस्य.
[357] P असंमितेन.
[358] Gap in the text marked with a dash in P and L2, not marked in M4.

[359] P -रचितं.

[360] P L2 इत्याधिकारी; M4 इत्यधिकारी.

[361] P अज्ञानो.

[362] P धुर्यकवृशवृभोगः.

[363] P om.

[364] P उक्ते.

[365] P यस्य.

[366] P om.

[367] P om.

[368] P वद्भिर् (?).

[369] P एक.

[370] P नुद्रिरिति ते देवदातवयम् (?).

[371] P इव ज्ञेयम्.

[372] P ददाति.

[373] P संहित

[374] P कृत्वाग्रतः.

[375] Jolly शासनीयः.

[376] a — P क्षत्रियस्य; b — M4 ब्राह्मणाः क्षत्रिया विशः.

[377] b — P निक्षते.

[378] a — P वंश्यस्य.

[379] d — P स्यात्.

[380] P अष्टौ चान्द्रायण मताः.

[381] a — P ध?अश्रवणाद्.

[382] P असंतेवासि.

[383] P गुरुपाथये जल्पतः.

[384] P तं.

[385] P प्रयोद्.

[386] P ends at this point, adding श्रीसंवत् १९२६ समै (समये?) मीती भाद्रे शुदि १० वार बुधवार.

TRANSLATION

MĀTRKĀ (Prolegomena)

1. LEGAL PROCEDURE

[The vulgate begins with a prose introduction after *maṅgala* (introductory) verses which are almost certainly the handiwork of Kalyāṇabhaṭṭa, because of the repetition of the word *kalyāṇa*:]

Here, Lord Manu Prajāpati composed the first treatise which was for the welfare of all beings and which became the means of maintaining proper conduct. These were its twenty-four chapters:

1. **The creation of the world.**
2. **The classification of beings.**
3. **The extent of the land of the virtuous.**
4. **The constitution of the assembly.**
5. **The prescription of sacrifice according to the Vedas and the limbs of the Vedas.**
6. **Proper conduct.**
7. **Legal procedure.**
8. **The banishment of offensive persons.**
9. **The conduct of the king.**
10. **The distinctions between the castes.**
11. **The distinctions between the stages of life.**
12. **The law of marriage.**
13. **Arrangements between men and women.**
14. **The order of succession.**
15. **The prescription of funerary rites.**
16. **The arrangements for acts of purification.**
17. **Indication of what may and may not be eaten.**
18. **Discussion of what may be sold.**
19. **Discussion of what may not be sold.**
20. **The kinds of sin.**
21. **Description of heavens and hells.**
22. **Penances.**
23. **Upaniṣads.**
24. **Secret teachings.**

Manu Prajāpati composed it in 100,000 verses and 1,000 chapters and entrusted it to the divine sage Nārada. He learned it from him and said, "Because of its size, men

> **cannot easily use this book," and he abridged it to 12,000 verses and bestowed it upon the great sage Mārkaṇḍeya. Mārkaṇḍeya learned it from him, considered the capabilities of human lives, and abridged it to 8,000 verses and bestowed it upon Sumati Bhārgava. Sumati Bhārgava thus learned it from him in turn, and said, "The capabilities of men are greatly lessened because of the shortening of their lives," and he condensed it to 4,000 verses. It is this one which men and their recently departed fathers read, and gods and gandharvas read the one which is 100,000 verses long.**
> **This is its first verse:**
> **"This was all darkness. Nothing whatever was discerned.**
> **There the four-faced, self-existent Lord became manifest."** [Manu 1.5ab, 6ad]
> **After having been so introduced, chapter follows chapter seriatim. The ninth of these chapters is called Legal Procedure and the divine sage Nārada wrote this introduction to it in the manner of the sūtras.**

The list of 24 chapters given here corresponds generally to the contents of the extant Manu. Medhātithi, in his commentary on Manu 1.58, discusses the reference to a text as *mānava* even though it may not have been written by Manu; he says, "Nārada recounts, 'This book of 100,000 verses composed by Prajāpati was successively abridged by Manu and others.'" At the time of Medhātithi (9th c. A.D.), then, the tradition of redactions of the Nāradasmṛti was known. It is possible to speculate that Medhātithi knew this introduction to the vulgate text of NāSmṛ, yet this is not necessarily so, since the claim of successive abridgements of an ur-text is a common one in Sanskrit literature. It is found in various Sanskrit textual traditions (see the Introduction to Bṛhas, pp. 81-82 for a list of such 100,000-verse ur-texts) and, significantly, it is alluded to in the first chapter of Manu (1.58). The reason given for these successive abridgements—the diminishing capacity of men—is based on the theory of the four ages in which men become successively worse in comportment, righteousness, health, etc. This theory is found in many places, but it is succinctly set forth in Manu 1.81-86. It is the subject of Mā 1.1-2.

1-2. When men had dharma as their sole purpose and were speakers of the truth, then there was no legal procedure, no enmity, and no selfishness. Legal procedure came into being at the time when dharma was lost among men. The overseer of legal procedures is the king; he has been made the rod-bearer.

NMS 1.1-2. J Mā 1.1-2. The lengthy commentary on Mā 1.2 is probably the handiwork of Kalyāṇa. It is verbose and tends to stray from the point: this is characteristic of those passages in which Kalyāṇa refers to himself (see 1.102,

1.106, 1.107, and 1.114). The comment is interesting for its mention of two matters. It says that the parties to the dispute should sit together, humbly or properly attired. It also claims that there are eight specific faults to the plea. This number is not given elsewhere, and discussions of the faults of a statement in court give varying numbers (see, for example, KāSmṛ 136-140 and 173-174 and VyaMā 292).

3. There are two methods for clarifying a matter in dispute between two people: a document and witnesses.

NMS 1.3. J Mā 1.3. This verse is remarkable for its omission of the third type of human evidence, possession (*bhukti*). Neither Bhava nor A note this in their comments, although A does say that human evidence *relies* on witnesses and documents. Later writers were troubled by this verse, which is only cited five times altogether (Dhko 217)—an indication that it was never of currency? Viśvarūpa on YāSmṛ 2.70 states that this verse only mentions two forms of evidence because they were the most commonly used. SaVi 111 states that these two forms of evidence are the weightier ones.

4. There are two types of legal procedure: with a guaranty and without a guaranty. The one with a guaranty has, in writing, a stake of an additional amount.

NMS 1.4. J Mā 1.4. This verse and the commentary on it are discussed in detail in my article, "The Judicial Wager in Hindu Law," ABORI 62 (1981), 135-145. The lengthy comment with its example of the impoverished son of an official again sounds like Kalyāṇa.

5. When a dispute includes a guaranty, the losing party must pay both the fine and the guaranty he had made.

NMS 1.5. J Mā 1.5. The term *sākoṭana* in the commentary is troublesome. It must be derived from the root *kuṭ*, "bend, break," but it is unattested in any other text (for other occurrences see Mā 1.33 commentary and notes, also the commentary on Mā 1.59, 1.11, and 1.34). In the commentary on 1.34 the term *ākoṭana* is glossed *tāḍana*, "striking, chastising." Prakrit *ākoḍana*, "pierce, penetrate," Hindī "*ghuseṛnā* " is attested in PSM (Paṇha 1.3). We may understand *ākoṭanadravya* as "a punishing amount of money"—i.e. the *paṇa* is to include a "punishing" amount as a slap at the opponent—which, in the context, is just what the person who was certain of his case (*avaṣṭaṃbhaniścaya*) and angry (*svāmarṣa*) would want to introduce into the case. The means for doing this is the *paṇa*. The *cvi* compound *kharīkaraṇa* means "to make harsh," as in *svasatyāvaṣṭambha-kharīkaraṇārtham paṇam upanyasya* "having placed a stake in order to make it harsh (for his opponent) because of his certitude about the truth."

6. The plaint is called the essence of lawsuits. If there is something wrong with it, the speaker loses, but if he carries it off, he wins.

NMS 1.6. J Mā 1.6. The commentary seems to be incomplete or corrupt. The hypothetical example of the reply given in the commentary is unclear. The verse cited at the end of the commentary is unknown elsewhere.

7. Local groups, guilds, assemblies, an appointed judge, and the king: these are the venues for legal proceedings. They are mentioned in ascending order of importance.

NMS 1.7. J Mā 1.7. The definitions of these courts are found in several places in the legal literature (compare text and commentaries on Manu 8.2, YāSmṛ 2.3, and Bṛhas 1.58; also Kane, HDh 3.280-281). A says that a *kula* consists of a few men; a *śreṇi* consists of citizens along with leading merchants; a *gaṇa* is an assembly from the ranks of brāhmaṇas, etc.; and the appointed judge is the chief judge. A seems to be saying that the first three of these are courts of initial jurisdiction (*trayaḥ padārthā vyavahārapratiṣṭhāhetavaḥ*).

8. It has four feet, four bases, four means, four beneficiaries, extends to four, and produces four.

NMS 1.8. J Mā 1.8. Identical with AgPur 253.1cd and 2ab. The subject here and through Mā 1.24 is legal procedure (*vyavahāra*). The several groups of four are enumerated in the following verses: the four feet, in 10; the four bases, in 11; the four beneficiaries, in 12; the four to whom it is extended, in 13; and the four that are produced, in 14.

9. It has eight limbs, eighteen titles, one hundred branches, three sources, two accusations, two gates, and two pathways.

NMS 1.9. J Mā 1.9. These groups are enumerated in Mā 1.15-24; the eighteen titles in 16-19; the 100 branches in J Mā 1.20-25 (see note to Mā 1.20); the three sources in 21; the two accusations in 22; the two gates in 23; and the two pathways in 24. Even though ms P omits this verse, the commentary indicates that the verse was originally part of the text.

10. The four feet of legal procedure are dharma, legal procedure, custom, and the king's decree; each latter one overrules the former.

NMS 1.10. J Mā 1.10. The two occurrences of the term *vyavahāra* must be translated slightly differently. The first one is the technical term for legal procedure, and the second is the more general usage, i.e. a dispute at law. See Kane, HDh 3.259-261 and Robert Lingat, "Les quatre pieds du procès," JA (1962), 489-503, for further discussion of this verse. Bṛhas 1.8 makes it clear that these are the four feet of the decision (*vinirṇaya*) rather than of *vyavahāra*. On the relative strength of these four feet see also Kane's notes to KāSmṛ 1.36-43.

11. Dharma is based on truth; legal procedure on witnesses; custom on what is recorded; the decree on the edict of the king.

NMS 1.11. J Mā 1.11. A and Bhava agree that these four "bases" are listed in ascending order. If a case is resolved simply by both parties telling the truth, that is a proceeding based on dharma. If the dispute is settled only by the testimony of witnesses, this is a situation where the legal proceeding (*vyavahāra*) "overrules" a proceeding based on dharma. A understands the term *caritraṃ pustakaraṇe* to mean that the witnesses have clearly recorded their statements on birch bark, or a register (? *saṃpuṭika*), and that these statements overrule earlier ones made in a legal proceeding. Bhava indicates that it may mean that a case is decided on written evidence, but he is not certain of this and offers a variant reading: *caritraṃ saṅgrahaḥ puṃsām* "custom is the assemblage of men" (this reading is found in Kau 3.1.40), and suggests that this means that the rules are those traditional rules peculiar to particular places, regions, or groups. When all of these first three options fail, the appeal to the king is binding, hence it "overrules" the others, i.e., it alone is applicable when the others are not applicable. See Ludo Rocher's article, "*caritraṃ pustakaraṇe*," *Indologica Taurinensia* 7 (1979), pp. 345-350, where a full discussion of this verse and its variant readings may be found. See also KāSmṛ 35-36 and Kane's translation and notes to those verses. The Pitamaha verse quoted at the end of the commentary is an explicit statement of the sequence of appellate jurisdiction.

12. It is said to have four means because it is effected by the four expedients—conciliation, etc. It has four beneficiaries because it protects the four stages of life.

NMS 1.12. J Mā 1.12. The four means are conciliation, division, gift-giving, and punishment according to both A and Bhava (see also Kau 1.13.12). Bhava explains that conciliation is a sort of flattery: "Speak the truth. You are born of a noble family of scholars. Your people will be blessed." According to Bhava, gift-giving is forgiving a portion of the debt; division consists of threats, etc., while punishment means chastisement, exacting tribute, and the like.

13. It extends to four because it involves in equal parts the perpetrators, the witnesses, the judges, and the king.

NMS 1.13. J Mā 1.13. A and Bhava explain this verse to mean that each of these four share equally in the merit or the sin depending on whether a dispute is heard correctly or incorrectly.

14. It is known to produce four, because it is the cause of these four: dharma, wealth, fame, and the people's respect.

NMS 1.14. J Mā 1.14. Bhava comments that dharma comes from protection of the upright, both noble and ignoble, and that this is done by hearing disputes correctly. Wealth comes from accepting fines from the defeated. Fame comes from behaving correctly and without greed.

15. It has eight limbs: the king and his men, the judges, the texts, the accountant, the scribe, gold, fire, and water.

NMS 1.15. J Mā 1.15. The king and his men are one "limb." The men serve in the king's stead whenever the king is not able to attend to the matter personally. According to A, texts such as those of Manu, Nārada and Viśvarūpa are repositories of the truth. This is an odd list. The two *mūlasmṛtis* of Manu and Nārada are expected, but the inclusion of Viśvarūpa, a commentator on YāSmṛ, is not. Kane gives the time when Viśvarūpa flourished as 750-1000 A.D. and the date of Asahāya between the sixth c. and the mid-eighth c. A.D. This would make a reference by A to Viśvarūpa most unlikely. There is reference to other works by a Viśvarūpa and quotations both in prose and in verse attributed to him found in later *nibandhas* (see HDh 1.564-565). It is possible that the Viśvarūpa mentioned here is not the commentator on YāSmṛ, but the author of a "lost" *mūlasmṛti*. The accountant should be a local, respected merchant, and the scribe is to record the proceedings. The elements of gold, fire, and water are said by A to be three visible forms of the deity Dharma who, through ordeals that use these elements, points out truth and falsehood.

16-20. These are its eighteen titles: Non-payment of Debts, Deposits, Partnership, Resumption of Gifts, Breach of Contract for Service, Non-payment of Wages, Sale without Ownership, Non-delivery of What Has Been Sold, Reneging on a Purchase, Non-observance of Conventions, Land Disputes, Relations between Men and Women, Partition of Inheritance, Violent Acts, Verbal and Physical Assault, Gambling, and Miscellaneous; these are further divided into 108. It is said to have one hundred branches because of the variety of men's deeds.

NMS 1.16-20. J Mā 1.16-20. Jolly took the verses given in the commentary to be part of the text of NāSmṛ, but this is unlikely. For a translation and discussion of these verses see my article, "A Bogus Passage in Jolly's Nārada-smṛti," IIJ 27 (1984), 201-205. The variant reading found in ms P for Mā 1.20 and the lengthy enumeration of the various subdivisions of the eighteen titles of law sound like the addition of Kalyāṇa, although whether it is his work or A's cannot be said with certainty. The 132 subdivisions of the eighteen *vyavahārapadas* are referred to again in the commentary on NāSmṛ 1.64. The precise number 132 is cast in doubt by the actual enumeration of the subdivisions in the commentary: in some cases the actual list of the subdivisions does not match the number given at the end of the enumeration; see, for example, the *dāyabhāga* list. It is interesting that the commentator mentions only five ordeals here: the balance, the fire, the water, the poison, and the holy water (items 21-25 in the *ṛṇādāna* list; compare the chapter on ordeals below).

21. It is said to have three sources because it arises from passion, anger, or greed. These three create disputes.

NMS 1.21. J Mā 1.26. Identical with AgPur 252.9cd-10ab.

22. It has two kinds of accusations: those based on suspicion and those based on fact. Suspicion arises from association with bad characters; fact is when stolen goods and the like are found.

NMS 1.22. J Mā 1.27. The distinction between accusations based on suspicion and those based on fact is an important one for the administration of ordeals (see my article, "A Note on the *kośadivya*," ALB 40 (1976), 152-165). A says that the locus for deciding these two types of cases is: before the deity for accusations based on suspicion (i.e., ordeals are to be used because of the absence of hard evidence), and before the king for accusations based on fact.

23. It has two gates because it involves two sides of an argument: one side is the claim of the plaintiff, and the opposite side is the reply to it.

NMS 1.23. J Mā 1.28.

24-25. It is said to have two pathways because it proceeds according to fact or error. Fact means it is based on concern for the truth, error means it is based on disregard for the truth. Since the king is responsible for implementing dharma, he should not put up with error however subtle it may be. The king should resort to fact alone since dharma is the root of his prosperity.

NMS 1.24-25. J Mā 1.29, 31. The word *chala* has two meanings, a mistake and a deliberate error. As an example of a proceeding involving a mistake, A gives the case of a man who loaned 500 *drammas* to Devadatta in Vaṭapadraka (Baroda?), but who misremembers the name of the place and in the court says that the loan was made to Devadatta in Saṃvāduka village. Even though Devadatta owed him the money, the decision went against the plaintiff because of this error in his plaint. A—or, judging by the style, Kalyāṇa—further quotes a verse which Jolly took to be part of the text of Nārada, but which is unknown in any other Nārada ms. and is not quoted in any other text:

Even ordeals are rendered invalid by frauds in the statements. Thus there must be no mistake with regard to the place, the time, the amount, etc. [JMā1.30]

This understanding of *chala* is the common one. The technical meaning is sophistry, or "the giving of false interpretations to the words of an adversary in discussion" (A.B. Keith, *Indian Logic and Atomism*, Oxford, 1921, p.154). A gives the standard example of this technical meaning: *navakambala* (as a *bahuvrīhi* compound) can mean either "the one who has a new blanket" or "the one who has nine blankets." Sophistry is a deliberate misunderstanding of such a term by an adversary: when the plaintiff says that he has a witness and points him out by saying he is the man with the new blanket, and the respondent replies that there is no one present who has nine blankets. Nārada's view of this is given in Mā 1.25. *Chala* is also discussed in J Mā 2.25 (see Appendix). See also J.D.M. Derrett's discussion of *chala* in "Some Features of Public Law in Smṛti Sources," ALB 42 (1978), 1-31. SmṛSā attributes Mā 1.25 to Yājñavalkya (compare YāSmṛ 2.19).

26-27. Just as a fire has seven flames, the self-disciplined king who conducts trials according to dharma has seven rewards: dharma, wealth, fame, the people's respect, support, great esteem from his subjects, and an eternal place in heaven.

NMS 1.26-27. J Mā 1.32-33. Bhava explains that the seven flames are the seven tongues of the fire which are identified in MU 1.2.4 (see also RV 1.146.1). The exact meaning of *upagraha* is hard to render in a single word. It means support, favor, alliance, conciliation, assistance, even refuge (see Kau 7.7.1, 5.1.11, 12.1.16, 2.23.11, 2.10.34, etc.; also VaSmṛ 19.30).

28. Therefore, when the king takes the judgment seat, he should abandon selfishness, be neutral to all beings, and take on the vow of Vaivasvata.

NMS 1.28. J Mā 1.34. Vaivasvata is Yama, the god of death who sits in judgment of mortals, and his vow, according to A, is to mete out punishment to them.

29. With a calm mind, abiding by the opinion of the chief judge, placing the dharma texts above all, he should hear the legal proceedings in the correct order.

NMS 1.29. J Mā 1.35. A adds that the king should not be distracted by music, dancing, or commercial transactions while he is hearing cases. The correct order is given at Mā 1.30.

30. The hearing should be fourfold: first, the appearance should be made, then the title of the legal proceeding, the inquiry, and the decision.

NMS 1.30. J Mā 1.36. A explains *āgama*, here translated as "appearance," as the relationship (*sambandha*), i.e., the facts of the case. Bhava says that *āgama* means the hearing of the statement of the plaintiff. After this, the title of law under which the plaint falls is to be determined.

31. The one who hears the case should conduct the legal proceedings skillfully, so that there be no contradiction between the texts on dharma or the texts on polity.

NMS 1.31. J Mā 1.37. In his interpretation, A anticipates the issue of occasional contradictions between texts on dharma and texts on polity, taken up in Mā 1.33, and suggests that both types of texts should be considered in varying degrees. In agreement with Mā 1.34, he adds that nothing should be done that contradicts common practice.

32. Just as a hunter would pursue the tracks of a wounded deer by traces of blood in the forest, so he (the judge) should pursue the tracks of dharma.

NMS 1.32. J Mā 1.38. Samu attributes this verse to Kātyāyana; it is also very similar to Manu 8.44. See also Bhā 12.132.21.

33. When there is a disagreement between a text on dharma and a text on polity, the text on polity should be ignored and the text on dharma should be followed.

NMS 1.33. J Mā 1.39. See also YāSmṛ 2.21 and Kau 3.1.43. The rare word in A's commentary, *ākoṭanā*, must mean "severe" in this context (see note to Mā 1.5). As Bhava makes clear, dharma texts are superior to artha texts because the latter have a visible purpose, a fact that renders them less compelling than the dharma texts which have an indiscernible purpose and are therefore inviolable according to the mīmāṃsā rules of interpretation.

34. When there is a contradiction between a dharma text and custom, it is right to apply common sense, for custom prevails over dharma.

NMS 1.34. J Mā 1.40. A cites two verses from well-known *smṛtis* (YāSmṛ 1.68 and NāSmṛ 12.97) which advocate remarriage for women, and he says frankly that such statements are disregarded by the people in common practice. He further notes that the texts prohibit marriage between maternal relatives, but that this is the practice in "the south." The third verse he cites is unknown elsewhere, but it is the strongest statement of the superiority of tradition over texts: "Wherever a practice has been affirmed by tradition, it should never be overturned by what the texts say."

35. Lord Dharma is indeed subtle, beyond the ken of the senses, and difficult to contemplate; therefore he (the king) should conduct legal proceedings by way of what is directly perceived.

NMS 1.35. J Mā 1.41. A explains that "by way of what is directly perceived" (*pratyakṣamārga*) means either by inference based on indications, or by the "way" (*mārga*) of the ancient teachings of the wise, the virtuous, and the learned.

36. Even an innocent man may be convicted of theft, and a thief may go free; after all, the innocent Māṇḍavya was found guilty of theft in a trial.

NMS 1.36. J Mā 1.42. The story of Aṇīmāṇḍavya is found in Bhā 1.101. Thieves hid stolen goods in the hermitage of the sage Māṇḍavya. When the king and his men pursued the thieves to the hermitage, Māṇḍavya, who had undertaken a vow of silence, refused to tell them which way they had gone. The stolen goods were found in his possession. He was accused of being a thief, judged guilty and impaled on a stake (*aṇī*). Because of his miraculous powers he did not die, but retained a portion of the stake in his body as a penance. See Kau 4.8.12 for another reference to the Māṇḍavya story, but with the difference that Māṇḍavya confessed—wrongly—to being a thief out of fear of torture (impalement). In the accounts of Māṇḍavya, Dharma is always personified, hence the designation in Mā 1.35 *bhagavān dharma* "Lord Dharma."

37. Transactions between women, at night, outside the village, inside a house, or between enemies should be done again even when completed.

NMS 1.37. J Mā 1.43. A gives two different interpretations of "between women:" transactions done by women, and transactions witnessed by women only. The night is for sleeping, not for transactions, hence a transaction could not be verifiable even if it were done in one's own—sleeping—presence. Bhava makes it clear that the remaining situations are not allowed because of the absence of witnesses and, in the case of enemies, because the witnesses could be expected to lie. He also points out that such transactions are not prohibited altogether, but that they ought to be redone, properly.

38. In cases about debt and the like, because of the complexity of disputes and because of the limited capacity of memory, he may, if he chooses, grant a delay in order to ascertain the truth.

NMS 1.38. J Mā 1.44. A points out that the delay spoken of here is a delay in requiring the reply of the respondent to a charge involving a transaction that took place in the distant past.

39. He should hear the dispute at once in cases dealing with cattle, land, gold, women, theft, abuse, urgent matters, assault, and accusations of grave sins.

NMS 1.39. J Mā 1.45.

40. He who pursues a doubtful case without informing the king will be liable to harsh punishment, and his case will not be successful.

NMS 1.40. J Mā 1.46. Bhava's commentary makes it clear that the subject of this verse is self-help. It is wrong for a man to resolve a doubtful dispute by force without informing the king. Presumably the king would be able to see to it that the doubtful matter would be settled justly without regard to which party could wield the most force. Bhava says that a doubtful case is one that has not been decided.

41. When a complaint is about to be lodged and the respondent absconds and ignores the order, the plaintiff should arrest him until he is summoned for the hearing.

NMS 1.41. J Ma 1.47. Bhava says that absconding means not acting in a way conducive to a resolution of the dispute. Subodhinī and Bālambhaṭṭī on YāSmṛ 2.5 both agree with A's explanation. See my article, "*āsedha* and *ākrośa* —Arrest in the Sarasvatīvilāsa," *Indology and Law: Studies in Honour of Professor J. Duncan M. Derrett*, pp. 205-222.

42. Arrest is of four kinds: (a) confinement to a place, (b) for a certain period of time, (c) prohibition of travel, and (d) restriction of activity. Should there be such an arrest, the one arrested must not violate it.

NMS 1.42. J Mā 1.48. A gives examples of the four kinds of arrest: (1) confinement to a place—"If you go from this place now, there will be a royal order against you." (2) arrest for a certain period of time—"If you leave this town within such-and-such a period, etc." (3) prohibition of travel—"If you go to the place from which you came ..." (4) restriction of activity—"If you persist in this activity, etc."

43. One arrested by his foe while crossing a river, in a wilderness, in a dangerous place, or during a calamity, or any such circumstance, would not be guilty if he violates that arrest.

NMS 1.43. J Mā 1.49. The translation of the verse in the commentary is:

> **He should take up again those cases which have been heard in the presence of the king by friends, associates and relatives and which involve twice the normal fine.** [J Mā 1.50]

Jolly included this verse with reservations, just as A did. A says that it is not relevant to the subject under discussion, but that he has included it because it is found in his exemplar. This verse is not found in any other ms and it is unknown to any other writers on *dharmaśāstra*, hence it must have been a marginal note which had found its way into the exemplar of A. The fact that it was included in spite of its obvious irrelevance and doubtful authenticity is indicative of the conservatism of commentators such as A.

44. If one who is arrested at the proper moment violates that arrest, he should be subpoenaed. The one who wrongly makes an arrest must be punished.

NMS 1.44. J Mā 1.51.

45-47. One about to marry, one affected by disease, one about to offer a sacrifice, one in calamitous circumstances, one who is already accused by another, one engaged in business for the king, cowherds in the cow pasture, farmers harvesting crops, artisans while working, warriors in battle, a minor, a messenger, one about to give a gift, one observing a vow, and one in a trying situation should not be arrested, nor should the king summon them.

NMS 1.45-47. J Mā 1.52-54. These are mostly self-explanatory, but A restricts the explanation of one about to give a gift to one doing so on a *parvan* day. According to ViPu 3.11.118 these days are *amāvasyā, paurṇimā, caturdaśī, aṣṭamī,* and *ravisaṃkrānti*. Bhava gives reasons for each of these exceptions to arrest, most of which are obvious, but he does add that farmers are exempt from arrest right up to the end of the harvest because their work is important to the populace and to the king.

48. One who has been accused should not make an accusation against the one who accused him as long as he has not disposed of the matter brought against him. Nor should one accuse someone who has been accused by someone else, for one does not strike a stricken animal.

NMS 1.48. J Mā 1.55. This is one of the few Nārada verses which are not quoted by any subsequent writer on *dharmaśāstra*. This may be due to the greater currency of YāSmṛ 2.9 which says basically the same thing. Both A and Bhava say that the intent of the first half of the verse is to prevent the accused from launching a counteraccusation before settling the original dispute. The metaphor refers to the rule found in Manu 9.42 which says that a hunter who shoots a wounded animal loses his arrow because the prey belongs to the one who shot it first.

49. Once one lodges a plaint, he should not introduce any changes to it, nor should he adopt another position altogether. If he does so, he loses his first claim.

NMS 1.49. J Mā 1.56. A gives the following examples: (1) changes in the plaint—first claiming the amount due is ten gold *gadyāṇakas*, and then later, seeing an opportunity for greater profit, claiming that the amount due was really two hundred; and (2) adopting another position—first claiming for himself twenty *gadyāṇakas*, and then later claiming that fifty *drammas* should be paid to his son. VyaMā 292, VyaCi 94, and VīMi on YāSmṛ 2.6 all attribute this verse to Bṛhaspati.

50. One must not make a false accusation. A false accuser incurs sin and the punishment prescribed for it.

NMS 1.50. J Mā 1.57. Bhava says that the punishment prescribed for the alleged crime is the punishment which should be visited upon the false accuser.

51. The marks of one who is losing his case are: delaying under some pretext, not speaking in court, or denying what he had said.

NMS 1.51. J Mā 1.58. A gives examples of the pretexts under which a man might seek a delay: "I am not clever enough, I am not pure enough, so I am not giving an answer."

52. One who absconds after he has been summoned and one who would not contest the case after he has been apprehended should be subpoenaed by the king. He loses the case.

NMS 1.52. J Mā 1.59. The two verses in the commentary elaborate on other ways a person may lose a suit:

> **One who is questioned about something which has been correctly reported and does not acknowledge it as true, or one who denies a statement and then later agrees with it.** [J Mā 1.60]
>
> **In virtue of all the (aforementioned) causes, he (the king) should declare duly defeated those who say, 'There are witnesses,' but who do not produce them when ordered to do so.** [J Mā 1.61]

These two verses are found in no other mss and are quoted in this form in only one place (Apa on YāSmṛ 2.16). In fact, these are two Manu verses (8.54 and 57 with minor variations) which have found their way into a branch of the Nārada ms tradition. This supposition may be supported by the fact that Manu 8.54 and 57 are given in SmṛCi 561 but attributed to Nārada.

53-54. When lawsuits have been resolved, evidence becomes useless except for a document or witnesses that were not previously announced. As

the benefits of rain are useless for ripe grain, so evidence is useless for resolved lawsuits.

NMS 1.53-54. J Mā 1.62-63. Verse 53 is an exception to J Mā 1.61 found in the commentary on Mā 1.52. The point of this verse is that evidence that exists but has been overlooked for a legitimate reason should be admitted into the trial even if it is not introduced as evidence at the proper time. A gives the following examples: an accident or being intimidated in the presence of the king and the court, or mental confusion. For the king to exclude this evidence on procedural grounds would be tantamount to sophistry. A explains the stipulation "not previously announced" to mean evidence mentioned before the beginning of the trial, but not previously mentioned in the trial proper; i.e., the existence of this evidence was publicly known, though not officially introduced. Presumably, the common knowledge of the existence of evidence before the trial would serve as a check against the manufacturing of evidence at the time of the trial. The VyaCi cites these verses (at 201 and 438) and attributes them once to Kātyāyana and once to Nārada. The VyaNir of Mayārāma Misra and the Setu (both at Dhko 222b) also attribute these verses to Kātyāyana.

55. Even an untrue statement made at the proper time is admitted as evidence, but a true statement which, out of carelessness, was not mentioned at the proper time is not admitted.

NMS 1.55. J Mā 1.64. Bhava offers an example: If a man who claims that he is owed ten *suvarṇas* and who has mentioned this amount in the plaint remembers later in the trial that the correct amount was twelve *suvarṇas* and claims that amount in the course of the trial, he will lose two *suvarṇas* because of his failure to mention "twelve" at the correct time (the time of the written plaint). A says that this is the fault of the party to the suit, not the fault of the court.

56. One who feels that a case has been adjudged and settled in a manner inconsistent with dharma may have the case tried again after agreeing to pay twice the penalty if he loses.

NMS 1.56. J Mā 1.65. A says that *tīrita* and *anuśiṣṭa* are technical terms used in legal texts (see Manu 9.233). He defines *tīrita* as the judgment (*nirṇaya*) reached by the judges after hearing the arguments of the parties, while *anuśiṣṭa* is the pronounced punishment (*nigaditadaṇḍa*) arrived at after considering the magnitude of the crime. Aparārka on YāSmṛ 2.80 attributes this verse to *smṛtyantara* "some other text."

57. If a legal proceeding is improperly heard, the judges should incur that penalty, for no one keeps to the straight and narrow without the threat of punishment.

NMS 1.57. J Mā 1.66. Bhava states that the penalty incurred by the judges is twice that which would apply in the case about which they were wrong.

58. A judge who would give an incorrect verdict out of passion, ignorance, or greed is not worthy of the office, and the king should punish him harshly.

NMS 1.58. J Mā 1.67. A says that the singular "judge" should not be misunderstood. If one judge is guilty of bias and the other judges go along with his wrong judgment because they have no clear opinion of their own, the king should find out the biased judge and punish him. If there are several guilty judges, then they must be punished.

59. However, the king especially, if he wants to fulfill his obligations, must examine what is right and what is wrong, for men's motives are diverse.

NMS 1.59. J Mā 1.68. A says that the circle of acquaintances in a person's life may influence him. Since the king's circle is larger than anyone's, he must be even more careful to avoid their influence. The compound *sabhyākoṭana* means something like a warning thrust or slap at the judges (see note to Mā 1.5).

60-61. There are men who give false testimony out of greed, and there are other evil people who forge documents. Therefore the king must vigorously test both of these: documents according to the norms for documents, and witnesses according to the norms for witnesses.

NMS 1.60-61. J Mā 1.69-70.

62-64. There are many types: some who lie may seem to be truthful, and some who are honest may seem to be untruthful. Therefore scrutiny is in order. The sky looks like a flat surface and the firefly seems to be aflame, but there is no surface in the sky and no fire in the firefly. Therefore one has to examine things even though they happened in plain sight. One who pronounces judgment on these things after investigating them does not fail in his duty.

NMS 1.62-64. J Mā 1.71-73.

65. If a diligent king always hears lawsuits in this way he will spread his brilliant fame widely in this world, and reach the pinnacle of the abode of the sun.

NMS 1.65. J Mā 1.74. For the meaning of *bradhna* "sun," see Louis Renou, JA 1939, p. 333. The pinnacle of the abode of the sun is the highest heaven, the king's reward after death.

MĀTṚKĀ

3. THE COURT

1. One should never speak in a trial unless he has been appointed to do so; one who has been appointed must speak without favoring either side.

NMS 1.66. J Mā 3.1. The verse in the commentary means:

> **One who knows the *śāstra* ought to speak whether or not he has been appointed. One who lives according to the *śāstra* speaks with divine authority.** [J Mā 3.2]

For the meaning of *sākoṭana*, here "strictly, or vigorously," used in the commentary, see note to Mā 1.5.

2. If a judge speaks appropriately he incurs neither hatred nor sin; but if he speaks otherwise he incurs both.

NMS 1.67. J Mā 3.3. A defines appropriate speech as speech that contradicts neither the texts nor good conduct. Inappropiate speech is an impediment in this world (it produces hatred) and in the next (sin), according to A.

3. The king should appoint righteous judges who have been carefully investigated. Like good bulls, they must be able to bear the burden of legal proceedings.

NMS 1.68. J Mā 3.4. Bhava stipulates that the task of appointing judges is one the king must bear alone, without reliance on others.

4-6. The members of the king's court should be experts on the science of dharma; they should be of good family, truthful, and unbiased. They support dharma, but the king is its root. Therefore, the king should settle legal matters along with these virtuous ones. When legal disputes are faultless, the judges are faultless. Since their faultlessness comes from dharma, dharma should be the only thing they pronounce.

NMS 1.69-71. J Mā 3.5-7. A makes it clear that the king is responsible for the correct settlement of a lawsuit.

7. When righteousness and truth are sullied by unrighteousness and falsehood under the very eyes of these judges, then they, too, are sullied.

NMS 1.72. J Mā 3.8. This verse is the same as in Manu 8.14.

8. When righteousness is wounded by unrighteousness in the court, then the members of the court are also wounded unless they remove those thorns.

NMS omits. J Mā 3.9. Compare Manu 8.12. Removing thorns is a simile for law enforcement (see Mā 3.15). According to A, overlooking such assults on righteousness is one of those offences which results in being reborn as a dung-beetle.

9. One should only enter the court prepared to speak the truth. The man who does not speak or who speaks falsely is a sinner.

NMS 1.73. J Mā 3.10.

10. Those judges who go to the court and sit in silent thought and then do not speak when the time comes, are no better than liars.

NMS omits. J Mā 3.11.

11-12. One fourth of the guilt goes to the perpetrator; one fourth to the witnesses; one fourth jointly to the members of the court; and one fourth to the king. When punishment is meted out to those who deserve it, the king and the members of the court are sinless; blame is given where blame is due.

NMS 1.74-5. J Mā 3.12-13. Compare Manu 8.18-19.

13. One who goes to the court and gives a nonsensical verdict without paying attention to the facts is like a blind man who eats fish without attending to the bones.

NMS 1.76. J Mā 3.14. A says that this verse is intended to point out the distinction between those who have studied the texts on legal procedure and those who have not. Those who have not are like the blind person who eats fish, bones and all, and is injured as a result.

14-15. Therefore a judge should attend court without passion or hatred, and he should speak in such a way that he does not suffer damnation. Just as a wise doctor would remove a thorn with his instruments, so the Chief Judge should remove a thorn through legal proceedings.

NMS 1.77-78. J Mā 3.15-16. A says that the Chief Judge is able to eliminate even undiscerned problems (thorns) through legal proceedings just as a doctor can remove a thorn that is invisible to the eye.

16. When all the members of the court think, "This is correct," then all the thorns have been removed from the case, but if there is no such unanimity, then the case remains a thorny one.

NMS 1.79. J Mā 3.17.

17. A court is not a court if there are not elders. Elders are not elders unless they pronounce dharma. Dharma is not dharma unless there is truth. Truth is not truth if it is mixed with sophistry.

NMS 1.80. J Mā 3.18.

TITLES OF LAW

CHAPTER 1

NON-PAYMENT OF DEBTS

1. The subject of Non-payment of Debts covers: which debts are to be paid and which are not to be paid, and by whom, when, and how, according to the rules for giving and taking.

NMS 2.1. J 1.1. A uses the words *adhamarṇa* and *uttamarṇa* (usually debtor and creditor), but with an unusual explanation of them. The second he takes to mean the debt to the ancestors which is paid by *śrāddha* offerings. The first is the sort of debt one normally encounters in this world—interest on loans of gold, grain, or garments. This understanding of these words is found later in the text as well—see 1.5, for example.

2. When the father is dead and the sons are divided, they must pay his debts in proportion to their shares. If they have not divided the inheritance, he who heads the family must pay the debt.

NMS 2.2. J 1.2. Bhava states that there are three possibilities: (1) if the sons have divided the inheritance, they divide the debt according to their shares of the estate; (2) if they have not divided, but intend to do so, they pay off the debt from the estate prior to dividing the remaining property; and (3) if the sons remain undivided, the son—or other heir—who assumes the responsibility for the family also assumes responsibility for the debt.

3. If an undivided paternal uncle, or a brother, or the mother incurs a debt for the sake of the family, then it must be paid in full by the heirs.

NMS 2.3. J 1.3. A is careful to point out that this verse applies to both divided and undivided heirs. Divided heirs pay according to their shares; undivided heirs pay in common.

4-5. When his sons have inherited a debt which they did not dispute but also did not pay off, his grandsons are responsible for the debt of their grandfather. Liability for a debt ceases with the fourth generation. Fathers wish for sons for their own sakes, thinking, "He will release me from both sacred and worldly debt."

NMS 2.4-5. J 1.4-5. Here we encounter Nārada's view on how long a debt continues in a family. This is far from a clear-cut issue. The problem in this verse comes with the ablative *caturthāt*. It can mean either that the obligation stops with or after the fourth generation. The unanimous view is that it stops with the fourth generation, i.e., that the fourth generation does not have to pay the debt. The next problem is, how are the generations counted? Is the first generation the debtor or the debtor's son? The method of calculating the generations in this case is probably consistent with that of calculating other degrees of relationships in Hindu law—the *propositus* is always counted. This would mean that Nārada is saying that only the debtor, his son and his grandson are liable for the debt—not the debtor's great-grandson. This contradicts the general rule that inheritance and the performance of the funerary rites (*śrāddha*) are co-extensive (see 1.5, for example). The resolution of this problem, which receives considerable attention from later writers, is that the great-grandson is liable for the debt if he inherits ancestral property, but not otherwise (see, for example, Mitā on YāSmṛ 2.51). This matter is thoroughly discussed by Kane, HDh 3.442 ff., Heramba Chatterjee, *The Law of Debt in Ancient India*, pp. 99-103, and Raj Kumar Sarvadhikari, *The Principles of the Hindu Law of Inheritance*, pp. 103 ff.

The intent of the remarkably long, difficult, and occasionally corrupt commentary on these verses is to prove that the fourth descendant (counting the *propositus*) is liable for the debts (see note to 1.78). In order to force the verses to agree with the general rule that inheritance and *śrāddha* are co-extensive, A (or Kalyāṇa) first resorts to a system of counting generations which does not include the *propositus*: *caturthāt mūlikasya pañcamatvāt*, "because the *propositus* is the fifth". He further supports his view by quoting a verse that is not known in any other source:

> **Three ancestors must be worshiped and three descendants must afford sustenance. This lineage of a man relies on the fourth generation for repayment of the two debts (i.e., sacred and secular).**[1] [J 1.6]

It is ironic that the author of this verse is stated explicitly by A to be "Great-Great-Grandfather" (*vṛddhaprapitāmaho 'py etad āha*), an otherwise unknown sage. The way the verse is introduced in the commentary indicates that it was not understood by A to be a Nārada verse. It is obvious that much of this commentary is the work of Kalyāṇa, since he mentions himself by name and the rambling prose is the same as in those other places where he mentions himself. As a further argument, he introduces an episode supposed to have occurred in Pāṭaliputra that has been often cited and summarized in the literature (see, for example, Kane, HDh 3.288-290; Lallanji Gopal, *The Śukranīti: a Nineteenth Century Text*, p. 27; K.P. Jayaswal, *Calcutta Law Journal* 1913, XVII, p. 59.). The historicity of this anecdote is suspect, both for its unique account of an instance of champerty in classical India

1 Jolly's translation of *upajīvya* as "must be reverenced" is incorrect; it means "must be existed upon", i.e., "must be a support." The word *agrataḥ*, literally "from the first" here means "from the propositus."

and for its too perfect congruence with the view the commentator is attempting to support. The rambling style and the contents—a profusion of extraneous matters and an emphasis on typology of statements—point to Kalyāṇa as its author. Even though the commentary is corrupt in places, it is possible to follow the general narrative—the portion in square brackets is a concise paraphrase:

> **In the glorious city of Pāṭaliputra there was a brāhmaṇa merchant named Śrīdhara. For the sake of his own and his family's prosperity he lent his hard-earned wealth, 10,000 *drammas*, at 2 interest per month. Thus, at the end of one month, he received 200 *drammas* in interest from Devadhara. By the end of the second month, Devadhara had died from the effects of an accident; his son had died of cholera. His great-grandson, the young Mahidhara, survived. He was addicted to gambling, liquor, and prostitutes. His sons and maternal uncles took over for him.**
>
> **A brāhmaṇa referred to as Learned Durdhara approached them and told them that the merchant Śrīdhara should not be paid even a *rūpaka*. "I will protect you, even in court, with the rules of law." They replied, "If you can do that, we will pay you 1,000 *drammas* as a fee. We are delighted with you, Sir." The feeling was mutual. After the second month had come and gone, the merchant Śrīdhara demanded his 200 *drammas* in periodic interest from the maternal uncles who took care of Mahidhara's family. They replied, "Even the principal is not yours; how can you talk of interest?" The brāhmaṇa, Learned Durdhara, quoted the rule, "debt ceases with the fourth generation."** [NāSmṛ 1.4d]
>
> **Upon hearing this, Śrīdhara swooned as if he had been hit by a blow from an invisible hammer. When he regained his senses, he went to the court accompanied by his relatives, family, and friends with loud grumbling about the law. Upon hearing the news of Śrīdhara's blow from an invisible hammer, the court summoned Devadhara's great-grandson, Mahidhara, along with his maternal uncles, and having accepted sureties from both sides in accordance with the law, addressed the maternal uncles of Mahidhara, "Why are you not paying the periodic interest to Śrīdhara?"**
>
> **They appointed the brāhmaṇa Durdhara to the task of their own victory or defeat and to speak for them. This is what he said: "These merchants have been friends of my family for generations. I speak for them. Have you gentlemen not heard this statement of Nārada,**

'... his grandsons are responsible for the debt of their grand-father. Liability for a debt ceases with the fourth generation.'

[NāSmṛ 1.4cd] ?

According to this, Devadhara's great-grandson Mahidhara is the fourth generation and does not pay. Moreover, Yājñavalkya has stated,

'A debt recorded in a document should be paid by three generations only.' [YāSmṛ 2.90ab]

Here, too, only three generations repay the debt."

This statement of Learned Durdhara was beyond the pale of legal rules. The headman, Learned Śekhara Bhaṭṭa, who knew the truth of all the sciences and was guided by the consensus granted by the assembled great men, laughed at it and made this timelessly correct statement in order to instruct Learned Durdhara, "O Durdhara, Sir, you are not well-versed in the different meanings of statements in the legal texts, nor in the explanation of the meanings of words. Let me instruct you in both straightaway. In the entire legal corpus, as elsewhere, the meaning of a sentence may be one of 26 types:

1. vidhi	14. liṅgadarśana
2. niyama	15. artha
3. parisaṃkhyā	16. prakaraṇa
4. utsarga	17. liṅga
5. apavāda	18. saṃnidhi
6. niṣedha	19. anupapatti
7. prasava	20. arthāpatti
8. samuccaya	21. bhūtārthavāda
9. vikalpa	22. aupamya
10. aṅgāṅgitva	23. gauṇārthadarśana
11. arthavāda	24. mukhyārthadarśana
12. anuvāda	25. nirāsa
13. vyavasthā	26. nirbījārthavādatā

These and other ways to interpret sentences are well-known in legal science; they must be diligently studied by those who wish to know the meaning of the law. [?]

For, if one does not correctly understand these various meanings of sentences, if he arrogates to himself the truth, he would be like one expecting to swim the ocean. [?]

Therefore, Durdhara, you miss the point because you are not well-versed in these statements of the law. Similarly, you are not well-versed in explaining the meanings of words.

[Nārada 1.4abc says that grandsons have to pay the debts that were not paid by the sons. It is a sentence of the *vidhi* type. It therefore can only be meaningful if it establishes something that had not been established already; otherwise it suffers from the fault of rehashing old material (*carvitacarvaṇadoṣa*).

In this case the debtor himself does not count in the number of generations referred to. Since he made the debts, it is obvious that he would be liable for their payment. So, in the statement, "his sons have inherited a debt which they did not dispute but also did not pay off," in NāSmṛ 1.4 the word "his" refers not to the original debtor, but to the original debtor's son.

NāSmṛ 1.4 really means: "Whatever debts the grandsons did not pay the great-grandson shall pay."

Durdhara is also inept at interpreting the meaning of words in the texts and the following five points are made:

(1) NāSmṛ 1.4d says, "ceases with the fourth generation." This means "after the fourth," i.e. it establishes the duty of the great-grandson and says that only the great-great-grandson does not have to pay.

(2) YāSmṛ 2.90ab says, "it has to be paid by three generations." This is a *vidhi* and it means the next three generations must pay, even though they did not make the debt themselves.

(3) NāSmṛ 1.5 refers to the higher debt and the lower debt together. If two items are mentioned together, it means that they apply or do not apply in the same way. We know that the higher debt must be paid by three generations below the *propositus*. The lower debt, therefore, also must be paid by three generations below him.

(4) J 1.6 says explicitly that "the fourth" shall pay both kinds of debts.

(5) Since the creditor does not return the deposit as long as the debt is not paid, even if it took one hundred generations, no generation is debtless during that time.]

Thus, stupid 'Learned' Durdhara, you did not explain the meaning of the law. On account of wrong meanings, they (Mahidhara, et al.) committed a sin born of ignorance. And one other thing, Not-So-Learned Durdhara, have you not heard this?

> **'He who takes the inheritance must pay the debt, the same goes for the one who takes the woman.'** [YāSmṛ 2.51ab]

Further,

> **'Debt comes with inheritance.'** [NāSmṛ 1.14d]

and further,

> **'Of these three—(1) the one who takes the property, (2) the one who takes the wife, and (3) the son — the**

> **one who takes the property takes the debt.'** [NāSmṛ 1.20ab]
>
> **This is a rule stated for paternal property in general.**
>
> **The money, 10,000 in total, belongs to Śrīdhara alone, and continues to do so; including the monthly interest. Out of greed in taking a fee you wanted to bankrupt Śrīdhara. You have no shame."**
>
> **Having said this, the end of the Not-So-Learned Durdhara ...**

I believe that the exemplar of ms P had a missing folio and that the section of the commentary that follows is actually the introduction to the next verse (NāSmṛ 1.6).

A series of decisions in the courts of modern India have changed the traditional interpretation of the liabilities of the son, grandson, and great-grandson. The traditional distinction was that the son was liable to pay the principal and the interest, the grandson was liable to pay only the principal but no interest, and the great-grandson was liable only to the extent that the paternal estate came into his hands. The son and the grandson were personally liable (See Kane, HDh 3.442 ff.). The effect of *Masit v. Damodar* (1926) 53 I.A. 204, *Peda v. Sreenivasa* (1918) 41 Mad. 136 (F.B.), and *Jamboo Rao v. Annappa* (1941) Bom. 177 (F.B.) is that the son, grandson, and the great-grandson are liable equally for ancestral debts, but not personally liable, and that their liability is co-extensive and confined to the extent that they have joint property in their possession (see also Derrett, "Pious Obligation of a Hindu Son," 1970 KLT (J) 59, and R.K. Ranade, "Pious Obligation at Hindu Law," 52 Bom. L.R. (J) 1.)

6. Thus, once a son is born, he should assiduously forsake his own interests in order to release his father from debt, lest he would fall into hell.

NMS 2.6. J omits. The adjective *jātena* "born" may be an allusion to the *śruti* passage on which this doctrine is based: TaiSaṃ 6.3.10.4 *jāyamāno vai brāhmaṇas tribhir ṛṇavā jāyate*, "A brāhmaṇa at birth is born with a three-fold debt." This Nārada verse is well known to the commentaries and *nibandhas*, although Apa on YāSmṛ 2.50 seems to indicate that it is a verse of Bṛhaspati. Immediately following this verse, recension D has the following three verses. They appear to have been marginal notes in its exemplar:

> **Therefore he who receives more and yet does not pay the owner will be born in the house of his creditor as his slave, servant, wife, or beast.** [?]
>
> **If a man does not pay on demand a debt or a promise, that amount increases until it becomes one billion.** [J 1.7]
>
> **If it reaches one billion he is born again and again as a slave in his house in order to repay his debt.** [J 1.8]

No subsequent writer knows the first verse in quite the same way, nor does any writer attribute this idea to Nārada. KāSmṛ 591 expresses the same idea, also Bṛhas 10.123 (See Renou, *Etudes Védiques*, vol. 11, page 58, verse 44). Although the latter two verses are not found in ms P, Jolly included them in his edition. The fact that they violate the normal rule of accrued interest, the rule of *dāmdupaṭ*, further enhances the likelihood that they were originally marginal glosses that found their way into the text of recension D. Nārada subscribes to the view of *dāmdupaṭ* although he recognizes that there may be regional variations (see 1.90-92 and Kane, HDh 3.419-427).

7. If an ascetic or an agnihotrin dies in debt, all of the merit from his austerities and sacrifices belongs to his creditors.

NMS 2.7. J 1.9. Several writers attribute this verse to Vyāsa (see Dhko 714). A says that, even though the merit acquired by the debtor is considerable, it all slips through his fingers like water if he dies in debt.

8. The father need not pay his son's debt, but the son must pay his father's except for those made out of lust or anger, or for liquor, gambling, or suretyship.

NMS 2.8. J 1.10. See NāSmṛ 1.12 and note. The pious obligation is discussed in J.D.M. Derrett, "Indica pietas; a current rule derived from remote antiquity," *Zeitschrift der Savigny-Stiftung für Rechtsgeschichte*, Romanistische Abteilung 86 (1969), 37-66, reprinted in Derrett, ECMHL vol. 4, pp.142-172. See also the commentary on *Onkar v. Babu Ram*, A.I.R. 1981 All. 128, in my article, "More Avenues for Delay in the Pious Obligation," JILI 26.3 (1984), pp. 355-359.

9. If a father himself orders his son to contract a debt for the support of the family, or in time of peril, he should repay his son.

NMS 2.9. J 1.11. Bhava stresses that, under normal circumstances, only the father can direct the son to enter into a debt for which he, the father, is liable. No other member of the family can do so. The son (or even the mother, etc.) is empowered to enter into a debt which binds the father in order to support the family and in times of peril, which Bhava explains as illness, legal matters, and ransom. This verse is omitted in ms P but, since P preserves the comment, there can be no doubt that it was originally part of the text as commented on by A.

10. If a student, an apprentice, a slave, a woman, or an agent spends money for the sake of the family, that expense must be borne by the head of the household.

NMS 2.10. J 1.12. A explains that "an agent" is a business agent. An apprentice is a student who lives with his master for a stipulated period of time in order to learn a craft. For the distinction between a student and an apprentice, see 5.8-19; for slaves, see 5.24 ff. In all of these cases the debt must be incurred for the sake of the family.

After this verse recensions X and P include a verse which is nearly identical to Manu 8.166 (Jolly accepted it as Nārada's):

> **If the debtor is dead and the debt was an expenditure made for the family, the relatives must pay it back out of their money even if they are separated.** [J 1.13]

The fact that this verse is similar to Manu 8.166 and that recension X has it immediately followed by Manu 8.195,

> **He who gives or takes something privately must repay it privately; the return is like the delivery.**

makes it likely that these were marginal notes which have worked their way into the text. No subsequent authority attributes these verses to Nārada (see Dhko 696 and 680). The likelihood of these being marginal notes is further enhanced by the fact that the precise role of the head of the household mentioned in this verse has not been explained at this point—it is explained by implication in 1.11. A perspicacious scribe or reader might have included one or both of these verses of Manu as an explanation.

11. If the father or the paternal uncle or even the eldest brother goes abroad, the son (or other heir) does not have to repay the debt until after the twentieth year.

NMS 2.11. J 1.14. A limits the amount of interest that can be collected in this case to an amount appropriate to the material loaned (see 1.90-92) and not to an unlimited accruing of interest. Debts made for emergencies (see 1.9) by those left behind must be paid even by divided coparceners (see note to 1.10). Bhava makes it clear that the son must pay only after the completion of twenty years, not in the twentieth year.

Recension D includes the following verse after 1.11:

> **The son has to pay the debt of those who are sick, insane, old, or living abroad for a long time even though they are alive.**

This verse is probably a marginal gloss. It is never cited by any other writer as a Nārada verse, although it is quoted four times as a verse of Kātyāyana, and twice it is attributed to both Kātyāyana and Bṛhaspati (Dhko 712).

12. As long as they are alive, even a single one must pay the debt made by others who have been authorized to do so, but if they are dead then a man's son is not liable to pay the debt of others.

NMS 2.12. J 1.15. The subject matter under discussion in this section is the liability of a son for his father's debts. The point made in this verse is a very specific one: "joint and several" surety. When two or more parties provide a surety and agree to be held liable either all together (jointly) for the whole amount, or individually (severally) for the whole amount, one man may have to pay the entire amount. As Bhava makes clear, if only one of the parties to the surety is alive he must pay the entire amount, but if he dies as well, then the debt falls (jointly) to the sons of the parties to this surety. In this case, each son is liable only for his father's portion of the surety, since the sons of the original parties did not enter into the joint and several suretyship. See 1.106 and A's comment where the types of sureties are discussed and this verse is mentioned again.

The verse quoted in the commentary is unknown elsewhere:

> **The creditor may, as he wishes, bring his claim to any survivor, even to the best survivors, i.e. to the best of the surviving partners.**

It is cited again in the commentary on 1.106 where it is attributed to Kalyāṇa.

Ms L2 is defective here. It omits the verse and the first portion of the commentary up to *dāpyaḥ pararṇam eko 'pīty asya ślokasya*. Jolly notes that this verse is omitted, yet both P and M4 have it. It is possible that Jolly used Bīhler's personal copy (L2) and later acquired a new copy (M4) made directly from P.

13-14. A wife does not have to pay a debt made by her husband or by her son unless she agreed to do so or unless she had made the debt jointly with her husband. A sonless widow who has been appointed by her dying husband should pay his debts; or else his debts must be paid by his heir. Debt comes with inheritance.

NMS 2.13-14. J 1.16-17. As A makes clear, in order to be liable for her husband's debts, the widow must be his heir. If she is unfit to inherit, the debts are the responsibility of whoever inherits the estate. Bhava points out that these provisions of appointment apply only if the husband is about to die, not if he is in good health or if he is enamored of another woman such as a female slave. Bhava further says that if there are no heirs, the king takes the property and is liable for the debts.

15. A debt entered into by the wife never becomes her husband's debt, unless it was made when the men of the family were in distress, for family expenses never cease.

NMS 2.15. J 1.18. Bhava notes that this verse is the concomitant of 1.13: the wife does not have to pay his debts and he does not have to pay her debts (with some exceptions). A points out that a debt contracted by the wife for the sake of the family's relief must be repaid by the head of the family (not just by the husband). The last sentence of A's commentary is corrupt. VyaPra 274 attributes this verse to Kātyāyana.

16. This is not so for the wives of washermen, hunters, cowherds, and purveyors of liquor. The incomes of those men and their families are dependent on their wives.

NMS 2.16. J 1.19. It is only in these low castes that one finds the "aberration" of the husband being dependent on the wife. For more on these castes see Kane, HDh 2.69 ff. and Horst Brinkhaus, *Die Altindischen Mischkastensysteme,* passim. A makes it clear that the husband has no choice in these cases—he is liable for the debts of his wife. Since the family relies on her for its living, anything she does is for their sakes—including entering into debt.

17. If a mother abandons her son and goes to live with another man, the son alone takes the inheritance and she loses everything.

NMS 2.17. J 1.20. This verse cannot be correct as it is found in ms P and printed by Jolly (as Jolly himself noted in his translation). The Newārī mss and NMS have the word *ṛktham* or *riktham* "inheritance." This must be the correct reading, not either of the variants, *dhanam* or *dravyam*, nor, as some *nibandhas* have it, *ṛṇam* (see Dhko 699). This verse refers to the situation mentioned in13.12, in which the wife takes a share equal to a son's at partition. If a woman is so wanton as to take up with another man after the death of her husband, she forfeits that inheritance and it reverts to her abandoned son (see Manu 5.148-149, 158). A says that if a widow who has a son and *strīdhana* of her own, abandons her son and takes up with another husband, the other husband alone gets the *strīdhana*. But if she has nothing of her own and takes her husband's property to the other man, he does not get it; it goes to the son. Bhava is troubled by this verse and offers alternative interpretations. He first interprets it to refer to a case where a woman leaves her son against the son's wishes, and the man to whom she goes becomes the owner of her *strīdhana*. Then he shifts to an emphasis on debt and pays no attention to the word *riktham*. He says that if a woman is destitute, she has lost what was given to her (namely her *strīdhana*), and therefore she cannot be held liable for her husband's debts. Or, he says, she has given all of her wealth to her son before going to the other man, and hence he has only her person and does not obtain her wealth. In this case, any debts contracted by her are the liability of the man to whom she has gone and not the liability of the son. This interpretation is no doubt colored by the following verse (1.19). Neither interpretation is likely.

The most plausible explanation of this verse is the one I have given above. The question remains, why is this verse found here and not in the chapter on inheritance? What does it have to do with debt? If our understanding is correct—that we are talking about a woman who has inherited under the rules of 13.12—then along with this portion of the estate she would inherit that proportion of the debt as well (see 1.14) which her new man would share in insofar as he takes her wealth. In this verse (1.17), however, the son takes all the wealth (inheritance) of the woman and is therefore solely responsible for the debts of the family. See H. Chatterjee, *The Law of Debt*, pp. 119-122, and Kane, HDh 3.452-

454. There is plenty of support for this interpretation to be found in modern court decisions. See, for example, *Moniram v. Kerry* L.R. 7 I.A. 115; *Sellam v. Chinnamal* 24 Mad. 441; and *Nehalo v. Kishen* 2 All. 150 (full bench) all of which speak of the investiture of the husband's estate in the widow regardless of her chastity after its investiture. However, *Vithu v. Govind* 22 Bom. 321 (full bench) and *Murugayi c. Viramakali* 1 Mad. 226 state that subsequent remarriage of a widow, even if legalized under the provisions of the Hindu Widows' Remarriage Act (XV of 1856), will result in her forfeiting her husband's estate, which will pass to her heirs as if she were dead. The apparent irrationality of these two views—an unchaste woman may keep the estate, but a legally married woman forfeits—has been eliminated by the Supreme Court in *Punithavalli v. Ramlingam* 1970 S.C.1730, where it held that the pertinent section of the Hindu Widows' Remarriage Act (i.e., section 2) is in conflict with the Hindu Succession Act (Act 30 of 1956), section 14(1) which allows full ownership of her property to a woman. This decision eliminates the possibility that a woman would forfeit her share of her deceased husband's estate upon her remarriage, which is the claim of this verse.

18. If a woman takes her valuables and her offspring and joins another man, he must either pay the debts of her late husband or give her up.

NMS 2.18. J 1.21. A stipulates that the offspring mentioned here are minors. He states that the other man may not see any advantage in taking on the woman if her deceased husband had a lot of debts; in that case he is blameless if he abandons her with her estate intact. Only a creditor gets it. Although A seems to understand that the other man in this verse and the preceding verse is a second husband, the SmṛCa (vol. 3.2 pp. 405 and 407) explains the "other" as "maternal uncles, etc."

Recension D adds the following verses after NāSmṛ 1.18:

A wife, a son's wife, a grandson's wife, and the gifts to the wife: one who takes these must pay the debts; the same goes for one who lives off the (inherited) land. [J 1.25]

All activity of the *varṇas* originates in the wife. The one who takes a man's wife takes his property. [?]

The first of these two verses occurs only in sub-recension R.[2] Since it is not found anywhere else, it seems likely that it is a marginal gloss which was wrongly included in an exemplar of R. The second verse, too, is little known. Only the second half is ever quoted—in Mitā on YāSmṛ 2.51 (where the attribution to Nārada is unclear) and in ViTā 520 where it is only identified as "*smṛti*."

19. A man who marries the wife of one who died without any property or sons takes on her deceased husband's debts; that is all the property he had.

2 In ms P this verse is found in A's comment on 1.21.

NMS 2.19. J 1.22. According to A and Bhava the verb *upaiti* refers to marriage, with all its attendant responsibilities. Jolly follows the reading of ms P: *saiva tasya dhanam* (which is also found in Mitā on YāSmṛ 2.51, PaMā 275, and the VyaPra 271, but see 268) and translates, "she is considered as his property." All other manuscripts have the neuter pronoun *tat*. Whether a wife is considered property or not is a very important and controversial matter. See Derrett, "The Development of the Concept of Property in India c. A.D. 800-1800," in ZVR 64.2 (1965), 99 note 334, also in ECMHL vol. 2, p. 92 note 334. But see especially VyaMa 92 and VyaCi 501.25 (quoting Bhavadeva), where the "propertyness" of a wife is explicitly denied. The Mitā on YāSmṛ 2.175 contradicts this, but this same verse of YāSmṛ prohibits the usual rights of alienation with regard to a wife or son. See also Medhātithi on Manu 8.164, where the sale of a wife or offspring is said to be unrighteous (*bahir dharmāt*), although it must be admitted, as Derrett points out, that there were instances of such sales. There can be no doubt that a man had certain rights (*adhikāra*) over his wife, and it is likely that what this verse means to say is that the man who marries such a woman assumes these rights. These limited rights were all the "wealth" that the deceased had.

A further question is whether these provisions for debt in remarriage are intended for all. It would seem so, even though widow remarriage is prohibited elsewhere (Manu 5.162). KāSmṛ 567 restricts these provisions to those castes—some of which are listed in NāSmṛ 1.16—in which it is traditional for a woman to remarry: "The debt which is contracted by purveyors of liquor, etc. who are without property or sons should be paid by the one who enjoys their wives." This is precisely the view of ViRa page 65, which gives this comment on NāSmṛ 1.19: *idam api nāradīyavacanaṃ kātyāyanoktaśauṇḍikādiviṣayaṃ netavyam*. This may be the view of these writers, but 1.17-20 seem clearly to allow for widow remarriage.

20. Of these three—(1) the one who takes the property, (2) the one who takes the wife, and (3) the son—the one who takes on the property also takes on the debt. The son is liable for the debt if no one takes either the wife or the property, the taker of the wife if no one takes the property or if there is no son.

NMS 2.20. J 1.23. The basic rule is that whoever takes the property is responsible for the debt. But if there is no property, then who pays the debt? It could either be the one who takes the wife or it could be the son. If there is no wife to be taken, the son must pay the debt, and if there is no son, the one who takes the wife must pay the debt. A points out that the verse does not discuss certain permutations. If there is a son but the property goes to someone else, or if one person takes the property and another the wife, in both cases the person who takes the property pays the debt. If there is no property, but both a widow and a son, A says that it depends on what sort of wife the deceased debtor has left behind. If she is young, beautiful, lusty, and desirable, then the man who takes her is liable for the debts, because she is the deceased's only wealth (see 1.19). If the wife is not like that and is taken in by a man who only gives her food for her work, then the son must pay. In all these cases, the assumption must be that, when there is an heir who supercedes the son, it is because the son is unqualified to inherit (see 13.20-21). The general rule is that such a disqualified son only assumes liability for the debts as a last resort (see H. Chatterjee, *Law of Debt*, pp. 122-126).

21. One who marries the last type of *svairiṇī* or the last type of *punarbhū* must pay her husband's debt.

NMS 2.21. J 1.24. The list of *svairiṇīs* (wanton women) and *punarbhūs* (remarried women) is given at 12.45-53. Jolly has misunderstood this verse. Since he followed the reading of ms P "*antimā...uttamā* " in the first half of the verse, he apparently felt that the two words were meant to be opposites. He therefore read the verse as referring to the last *svairiṇī* and the first *punarbhū*. Bhava's commentary gives a detailed explanation of why this cannot be correct. This is the rank order (from lowest to highest) given in the text:

Punarbhū

1. a virgin who has only joined hands in the wedding ceremony;
2. a woman who left the husband of her youth, went to another and returned to her original husband;
3. a widow who has no brothers-in-law who can give her offspring (via the levirate marriage), and is instead given to a man of the same caste who is not a *sapiṇḍa*.

Svairiṇī

1. a woman who leaves her husband, whether or not she has children, and lives with another man;
2. a widow who rejects her brothers-in-law and out of love goes to live with another man;
3. a foreigner, one purchased, or one in desperate straits who offers herself to a man as a slave;
4. a raped woman who is later given to another man.

Concerning the *svairiṇī*, Bhava says that for (1) the husband is still alive, so the new man should not be liable for his debts. In the case of (2) the brother-in-law would inherit the husband's estate and also the husband's debts; therefore the new man is not liable for those debts. According to Bhava, taking up with *svairiṇī* (3) entails no debt since she is herself "property" (*dhana*) offered in a transaction. Only in (4) is the new man liable for the debts, since this man accepts the woman who is given to him by her relatives. In this last case, the presumption must be that the woman is a widow and she is forced against her will to take up with another man in order to produce offspring (but see 12.52 and note).

In the case of the *punarbhū*, (1) can be married again because the first ceremony was not completed. In (2) the husband is still alive and pays his own debts. Only in (3), where a widow is given to a man by her relatives, is that man liable for the debts of the first husband. In this last case the new man takes the widow and the estate according to the preceding verses.

The verse *bhāryā snuṣa* ... in A's commentary seems out of place here, and would be better after 1.18, which is where recension D has it (see the note to 1.18 for a translation of this verse). The subsequent verse quoted in A's commentary is probably a marginal gloss, since it is unknown elsewhere and is suspicious in light of 13.24 and 13.46-48 which do not allow a widow to inherit under any circumstances:

> **If brothers are divided and separate with regard to wives, activities, and wealth, and one of them should die sonless, his wife inherits his wealth.**
> [following J 1.25]

22. Except in distress, transactions undertaken by women are invalid, especially the giving, pledging, or selling of a house or field.

NMS 2.22. J 1.26. A says that any transaction undertaken by women is as if it had not been undertaken. Bhava adds that the word *viseṣataḥ* "especially" means that even in times of distress a woman cannot give, pledge, or sell a house or a field. She can only do that with slaves, jewelry, gold. and cattle in times of distress.

Recension D adds a verse which is unknown elsewhere:

> **Women have no authority to give away or sell. During her lifetime, a woman has power regarding food.**

23. Even these transactions are valid if the husband assents; or in the absence of a husband, the son; or in the absence of either a husband or a son, the king.

NMS 2.23. J 1.27. See Manu 5.148.

24. Even after her husband's death, a woman is free to use or give away what he has given her out of affection, with the exception of immovables.

NMS 2.24. J 1.28. Bhava says that the wife's absolute estate in such gifts also applies to things given to her for the sake of ritual acts and gifts intended for her security. He further states that while she does not have absolute estate in immovables, she is entitled to enjoy them for the duration of her life. "Immovables," according to A, are houses, fields, etc. Bhava adds gardens to the list. See 8.2.

25. Business conducted by a slave is regarded in the same way: it is invalid unless it is done at his owner's command. A slave is not his own master.

NMS 2.25. J 1.29. Bhava points out that this verse is a continuation of the preceding rule; the transactions of slaves are invalid unless they are done in an emergency. Slaves are able to dispose of property given to them out of affection, but, just as in the case of women, they cannot do so with immovables.

26-27. Business conducted by a son against the wishes of his father is also invalid. A son and a slave are the same in this respect. For even though he may be independent, if he is a minor, he cannot enter into debt. Only the most senior son is independent, seniority being determined by character and age.

NMS 2.26-27. J 1.30-31. Both A and Bhava state that a son whose father is still living and who is undivided is in the same situation as a slave and a wife concerning the disposal of property. Bhava states the usual rule that the age of majority is sixteen. He also says that seniority for brāhmaṇas, etc. is determined by character, while for śūdras the determiner is age. A points out that the independence of a son on the death of his father and his concomitant ability to enter into debt are prohibited unless the son has achieved his majority. See 13.5.

28. In this world there are three who are independent: the king, the teacher, and every householder of every caste in his own home.

NMS 2.28. J 1.32. A says that independence is a relative concept. An individual may be independent with regard to one person but dependent with regard to someone else. For example, a teacher is independent with regard to his students, and a householder of any class is independent with regard to his household, but both are dependent with regard to the king.

29-30. All subjects are dependent; the king is independent. The student is dependent; the teacher is independent. Women, sons, slaves, and other retainers are dependent; the householder is independent with regard to that which he has inherited.

NMS 2.29-30. J 1.33-34. 1.30 is attributed to Kauṇḍinya at VyaMā 288 and ViVya folio 4a.

31-32. Until his eighth year a child is considered the same as an embryo, and until the sixteenth year he is a youth, also called a *pogaṇḍa*. After that, he is competent in commerce and independent, provided his parents are dead. If they are alive, however, he is dependent, no matter how old he is.

NMS 2.31-32. J 1.35-36. A explains that a child is incompetent with regard to matters such as purity, etc. until his eighth year. He is then competent with regard to matters of purity, study, etc., but not until his sixteenth year is he competent in matters of commerce. VyaMā 316 says that according to some the age of a *poganḍa* ends with his twentieth year.

These two verses have been the basis for determining the age of majority for Hindus in modern Indian courts; see *inter alia*, *Mothoormohun v. Sourendro*, 1 Cal. 108, *Shivaji v. Dattu*, 12 Bom. H.C.R. 281, *Reade v. Krishna* 9 Mad. 391, 397. These rulings have been set aside by the Hindu Minority and Guardianship Act (Act No. 32 of 1956), which defines a minor as one who has not completed the age of eighteen years. With regard to marriage the ages of the parties were first limited by statute in the Child Marriage Restraint Act of 1929, which fixed the minimum ages at 15 for girls and 18 for boys. The Child Marriage Restraint (Amendment Act) of 1978 raised these ages to 18 for girls and 21 for boys, although marriages performed in violation of this provision are neither void nor voidable. The writers on dharma themselves were not in agreement about the age of majority. In contradiction with Nārada's view that majority is reached at the beginning of the sixteenth year, there are those who hold that majority begins at the end of the sixteenth year, e.g. Haradatta on GauDha 10.48, ViRa 599, and Vya Pra 263. VyaMā 316 argues that the twentieth year is the year of majority.

1.32 is omitted in ms P, but the commentary is found there.

33. The father is the more important of the parents, because of the obvious superiority of the seed. In the absence of the possessor of the seed, the mother is superior, and in her absence, the first-born son.

NMS 2.33. J 1.37. Bhava explains the superiority of the seed to the field with the analogy of placing gold into a pot (the father having the seed and the mother being the field into which it is sown; see Manu 9.33 ff.). The gold will always be of greater value than the pot which contains it. This verse appears to contradict the famous provisions of Manu 9.3 concerning the perpetual dependence of a woman.

34. To say that someone is independent means that he has persons dependent on him, and that he is empowered to discipline, expend, and sell them.

NMS 2.34. J 1.38. The independent ones being spoken of here are the king, the teacher, and the householder mentioned above (1.28). A says that *anuśiṣṭi*, literally, "instruction" means chastising and discipline. Bhava says that it means dictating what to do and what not to do. The three activities described here are applied to the persons who are dependent on the independent masters—for example, disciplining a son, relinquishing a daughter, and selling a slave.

35. Those who know the teachings of the śāstra say that anything done by a minor or by one who is not independent is invalid.

NMS 2.35. J 1.39. Bhava reiterates that the minor is less than sixteen years of age, and A repeats the fact that even an independent child is legally incompetent (see 1.27). Slaves are always incompetent regardless of their age. Both A and Bhava state that the *śāstra* in question is the *dharmaśāstra*. This verse is attributed to Kauṇḍinya at VyaMā 288 and ViVya folio 4a.

36-37. They say that even if an independent man transacts something, but he does so after becoming abnormal, it is invalid. He becomes dependent for this reason. To be abnormal means to be affected by lust or anger, or afflicted with disease, fear or addiction, or to be consumed by love or hatred.

NMS 2.36-37. J 1.40-41. Because of this abnormal behavior one cannot be independent and is therefore legally incompetent. The question is, how many characteristics of abnormal behavior are listed here? A says that there are seven, as indicated in the translation. Bhava, however, argues that there are eight: the seven listed above, plus *abhiyukta* "the state of being formally accused by another in the king's court." This latter view is not found elsewhere and seems unlikely. If a man who is accused is declared to be abnormal, and this condition carries with it the status of dependence and, therefore, legal incompetence (1.36), this would place an intolerable burden on anyone accused in the king's court. Since there can be a considerable lapse of time between the accusation and the resolution of a suit, the accused would be at a personal loss in the meantime. There could even be some question about the accused's ability to enter a plea in response to an accusation in court if he were to have been declared incompetent. Bhava recognizes his interpretation to be an alternative to that given in the translation above. The first verse is attributed to Kauṇḍinya at VyaMā 288 and ViVya folio 4a.

38. A transaction which is done by the head of a family, whether he is the eldest or not, as long as he is normal, is valid. A transaction done by one who is not independent is invalid.

NMS 2.38. J 1.42. This is the summary verse of the section on valid and invalid transactions. The text refers to the head of the family since being the head of the family is determined as much by ability as by age (see 1.27 and 13.5).

39. Wealth is the basis of all transactions; effort is needed to acquire it. Its preservation, increase, and enjoyment are ordained in that order.

NMS 2.39. J 1.43. A states that preservation means protection from two- and four-legged creatures, etc. Growth involves agriculture, interest on loans, commerce, etc. Following these comes the enjoyment of worldly and divine happiness. This verse is cited at CaVarCint 1.41.

40. There are three kinds of wealth: white, spotted, and black, each of which is sevenfold.

NMS 2.40. J 1.44. The scheme of "white," "spotted," and "black" wealth is found also in ViSmṛ 58.1-12, where the explanation of the terms is more explicit than what follows in Nārada. This verse is cited in CaVarCint 1.41. Viśvarūpa on YāSmṛ 3.252 attributes a similar verse to Nārada:

śuklaṃ ca śabalaṃ caiva kṛṣṇaṃ ca trividhaṃ dhanam |
śuklaṃ nyāyārjitaṃ dharmyam itarad vyāvahārikam ||

1.40 is unknown elsewhere.

41. There are seven kinds of white wealth depending on whether it was acquired through: (1) knowledge, (2) prowess, (3) austerities, (4) a maiden, (5) a student, (6) a sacrificer, or (7) inheritance. Whatever is acquired with it is also white wealth.

NMS 2.41. J 1.45. Medhātithi on Manu 4.226 cites this and the following two verses in the context of explaining the phrase *svāgatair dhanair* "by means of properly procured wealth." This seems to be the only place where these verses are cited. A explains that the maiden is a source of wealth because of marriage, presumably referring to dowry or bride price. Bhava is clearer on this point and explicitly refers to bride price (*śulka*). Bhava says that a student is a source of wealth because of his fee to the teacher.

This description of the means of acquiring "white" wealth is different than that of Manu 10.115, which describes the seven lawful modes of acquiring property:

Manu	**Nārada**
1. inheritance (*dāya*)	1. knowledge (*śruta*)
2. finding, or friend's gift (*lābha*)	2. prowess (*śaurya*)
3. purchase (*kraya*)	3. austerities (*tapas*)
4. conquest (*jaya*)	4. a maiden (*kanyā*)
5. investment (*prayoga*)	5. a student (*śiṣya*)
6. work (*karmayoga*)	6. a sacrificer (*yājya*)
7. acceptance of gifts from good people (*satpratigraha*)	7. inheritance (*anvaya*)

42. Spotted wealth is obtained by (1) lending at interest, (2) agriculture, (3) commerce, (4) tribute, (5) artistry, (6) service, and (7) doing favors.

NMS 2.42. J 1.46. A explains tribute (*śulka*) as dowry, which can be righteous or unrighteous; Bhava says that it is military tribute, etc. Medhātithi on Manu 4.226 reads *sevā* for *śulka* (see Medhātithi's commentary and ViSmṛ 58.1-12). A stipulates that the wealth acquired by brāhmaṇas in these seven ways is called spotted. Presumably, the wealth acquired in this way would not be spotted for a vaiśya or a śūdra (see VaSmṛ 2.13-20).

43. Black wealth is acquired by (1) deceit, (2) gambling, (3) acting as a messenger, (4) affliction, (5) forgery, (6) violence, and (7) treachery.

NMS 2.43. J 1.47. See Medhātithi on Manu 4.226. For a discussion of the typology of thieves, see NāSmṛ 19.2. The category of deceit includes such things as bribery (which is explicitly mentioned in ms P and commented on by A). The illegality of a bribe under Hindu law was confirmed by the High Court of Bombay in *Shri Sitaram Pandit v. Shri Harihar Pandit* (1910) 35 Bom 169.

44. It is by means of wealth that sale and purchase, giving and receiving, enjoyment, and all sorts of transactions take place.

NMS 2.44. J 1.48. This verse is cited in no other *dharmaśāstra*, commentary or digest.

45. Whatever a man does, the results he obtains in this world and in the next are of the same quality as the type of wealth he used.

NMS 2.45. J 1.49. According to Bhava, this verse means that a man whose wealth is "white" will have "pure" results; "spotted" wealth yields "mixed" results; and "black" wealth yields sorrow.

46. It is also said that there are twelve kinds of wealth: three of these are common to all castes and the rest differ according to one's caste.

NMS 2.46. J 1.50. This verse is cited only at CaVarCint 1.43. The following verses contain an analysis of the means of acquiring wealth which differs from other sources, for example Manu 10.115.

47. Three sorts of wealth are common to all classes: inheritance, a gift out of affection, and what is acquired along with a wife.

NMS 2.47. J 1.51. Bhava says that inherited wealth means such things as villages, fields, and houses. Verses 1.47-62 are cited by no writer on *dharmaśāstra*. While this is slightly surprising, it may be explained by the fact that Manu 10.74-131 provide more detail and are more likely to be cited than Nārada.

48-50. There are three kinds of wealth particular to a brāhmaṇa: that which is obtained by acceptance of gifts, from sacrificers, and from students. There are three kinds of wealth particular to a kṣatriya: that acquired in wars, royal revenues, and fines from court cases. There are three kinds of wealth particular to a vaiśya: agriculture, animal husbandry, and commerce. A śūdra's wealth comes from whatever the three higher classes are willing to give him.

NMS 2.48-50. J 1.52-54. According to verse 1.46 there are twelve ways of acquiring wealth: three general and nine particular (in the latter case, three for each of the three twice-born castes). The mode of acquisition for the śūdra appears to be the thirteenth, but Bhava explains that his mode of acquisition is actually a gift out of affection—one of the three common modes of acquisition. For a concise discussion of the principles involved in these verses, see L. Rocher's article, "Caste and Occupation in Classical India: the Normative Texts," in *Contributions to Indian Sociology* (NS) 9.1 (1975),139-151.

51. These are the righteous ways in which the several castes may acquire wealth; it would be unrighteous to do so in any other way, except if there is a serious calamity.

NMS 2.51. J 1.55.

52. In times of calamity the occupation of the next lower caste is prescribed for a brāhmaṇa, and failing that, the occupation of a vaiśya, but never the occupation of the lowest caste.

NMS 2.52. J 1.56. A states that calamity refers to difficulty in supporting one's family, but Bhava points out that the word for "calamity" in the text is expressed in the plural, therefore it cannot be limited to any one situation, but refers to any life-threatening circumstance.

53. In no way should a brāhmaṇa do the work of a śūdra, nor a śūdra that of a brāhmaṇa, for in both cases this would lead to their becoming outcastes.

NMS 2.53. J 1.57. Kane, HDh 2.118-132 discusses alternatives to the prescribed livelihoods for the four *varṇas*.

54. A brāhmaṇa and a śūdra may not do each other's work, but the work of a kṣatriya or a vaiśya is permissible because these are common to all.

NMS 2.54. J 1.58. This verse means that a brāhmaṇa can stoop as low as the kṣatriya and the vaiśya livelihoods in times of distress. A says that these options are also open to a śūdra in times of extreme distress. This latter view is not a common one. YāSmṛ 1.120 and Manu 10.99-100 seem to limit the śūdra's options to the livelihood of a vaiśya. See L. Rocher, "Caste ...," pp. 145-146. For the consequences of a śūdra performing a penance reserved for brāhmaṇas, see Raghuvaṃśa 15.50-51 and Rām 7.64-67.

55. A brāhmaṇa who has survived a calamity by means of the livelihood of a kṣatriya should purify himself and abandon that kṣatriya livelihood.

NMS 2.55. J 1.59. Bhava draws a parallel between a brāhmaṇa who ceases to work at a kṣatriya's occupation after the passing of the calamity with a man who ceases to take medicine after he is well. See YāSmṛ 3.35 ff. for a similar discussion. The penance prescribed for resorting to these occupations is the same as that for a twice-born who has never learned the Sāvitrī or the Vedas, namely three *kṛcchras* (Manu 11.192-193). The *kṛcchra* penance is one in which the man eats only once in the morning for three days, and once in the evening for the next three days. During the next three days he should eat only food which is given to him unsolicited, and in the next three days he should fast.

56. However, a brāhmaṇa who continues in that livelihood because he enjoys it, has strayed from the correct path, is unfit to be associated with, and is called an "arrow-back."

NMS 2.56. J 1.60. The ms of A's commentary is quite corrupt here. Bhava explains that a *kāṇḍapṛṣṭha* "arrow-back" is a professional soldier, and that the brāhmaṇa becomes a kṣatriya.

57-59. Even if a brāhmaṇa should have to do the work of a vaiśya, he must not sell milk, curds, ghee, honey, beeswax, lac, molasses, spices, liquor, meat, porridge, sesame, linen, soma, flowers, fruit, jewels, men, poison, weapons, water, salt, cakes, herbs, indigo, silk, hides, bones, goat-hair blankets, animals with uncloven hoofs, earthenwares, buttermilk mixed with water, hair, oil-cakes, vegetables, and medicinal herbs.

NMS 2.57-59. J 1.61-63. See 1.168. For similar lists see also Manu 10.85-90; YāSmṛ 3.36-39; GauDha 7.8-22; VaSmṛ 2.24-31; ĀDha 1.7.20.11 ff.

60. A brāhmaṇa may sell dry wood and grasses with the exception of fragrant materials, *rakā* grass, reeds, thorn apple, roots, and chaff.

NMS 2.60. J 1.64. The reading of ms P (*kuśād*) for *tuśād* is supported by Manu 10.88, which explicitly forbids the sale of *kuśa* grass by a brāhmaṇa.

61. He may sell what has fallen by itself, bamboo, the *badara* and *iṅguda* fruits, rope, and cotton thread as long as it is still natural.

NMS 2.61. J 1.65. Both A and Bhava explain *avikṛta* "natural" to mean that it has not been dyed any other color.

62. He may trade sesame for the same amount of grain if it is necessary for the sake of medicine when there is illness or for the purpose of sacrificing.

NMS 2.62. J 1.66. See Manu 10.94 for other exceptions.

63. When a brāhmaṇa has strayed from the right path by selling what should not be sold, the king should set him back on the proper path by means of strict punishment.

NMS 2.63. J 1.67. Bhava says that the king should reestablish the brāhmaṇa in his own dharma. He also specifies that strict punishment means the kind of punishment that would deter him from selling it again.

64. Those in authority must rigorously protect the modes of proof, because modes of proof are ruined if they are not expertly handled.

NMS 2.64. J 1.68. This verse has been troublesome to the commentators. A (whose reading *prameyāni* for *pramāṇāni* is unique among the mss) comments as follows:

> **A *prameya* (object of cognition) is anything that needs to be known exactly and truthfully. All of these become clear when they are determined by *pramāṇas* (means of cognition). For example, something that is countable, by its number; something that is weighable, by the scale; something that is measurable, by its dimensions. Logical/philosophical arguments are also *prameyas*; their *pramāṇas* are perception, etc. In the same way, in the case at hand the 18 *vyavahārapadas* are *prameyas* ; they become clear when determined by *pramāṇas*, in this case documents, witnesses, possession, and ordeals ... Even though these *pramāṇas* are traditionally accepted, they should not be admitted if they are flawed by a plethora of challenges from persons with scores to settle. For, if one tries to clarify *prameyas* by means of *pramāṇas* which are not clear, it will not work.**

SmṛCa 123 states that this verse refers to that portion of a legal proceeding (the *pratyākalitavicāra*, see Apa p. 616 on YāSmṛ 2.8) in which the burden of proof is assigned by judges to one of the two contending parties. In this interpretation, *pramāṇāni* in *pāda* c is understood to mean the *pramāṇakartṛs* "presenters of evidence," i.e., those upon whom the judges have placed the burden of proof. The judges must take care to see that the evidence is properly protected and presented because uncertainty about the evidence will lead to the loss of the suit by the person upon whom the burden of proof has been placed.

VyaPra 78 disagrees with this interpretation and says that this verse means that evidence must be protected because inexactly determined evidence, i.e., evidence which has become corrupt due to such things as fluctuation from original testimony, etc., causes that evidence to be lost and renders it useless for reaching a verdict. This view is supported by two verses of Bṛhas (Dhko 413) which caution that all three modes of human proof may become lost unless care is taken to preserve them. VyaKa 97 and VyaSau (Dhko 221) attribute this verse to both Nārada and Kātyāyana.

65. If someone else has appropriated his property, the owner gets it back by means of three kinds of evidence: a document, witnesses, and possession.

NMS 2.65. J 1.69. A comments as follows:

> **There is this praise for documents:**
> **If the Creator had not made documents—the best of eyes—this world would not function as well as it does.** [J 1.70]
> **A document—the best of eyes—cuts through all doubts in the ascertainment of the place, time, result, material, amount, or limit.** [J 1.71]
> **Next, praise for witnesses:**
> **One who has taken something on a road and wishes to deny it is identified by witnesses as having been on that road and, though hard to convict, is convicted.** [J 1.72]
> **Next, praise for possession:**
> **A document may have many flaws, and witnesses are not immune to old age and death, but continuous possession settles the matter—it is not dependent on material things.** [J 1.73]
> **These are the three things that serve as evidence. By means of them an owner recovers property that was not returned to him, even though his ownership is called into question.** [J 1.74]

The verses which constitute A's commentary here are certainly not Nārada verses as Jolly concluded. They are found in no other ms than P, and they may be discounted on stylistic grounds. Nārada is too sober and juridical to suddenly extol the document in such a fanciful way, and it is also unlike him to invoke the Creator in this way. This passage is likely the work of Kalyāṇabhaṭṭa.

Bhava comments on 1.65 that evidence is the means by which wealth is preserved, because a simple statement that one has earned the property is useless; one must be able to prove one's status as the owner of the property. See also VaSmṛ 16.7 and KāSmṛ 214ab. The second half of this verse is quoted only by SmṛSā folio 118 (Dhko 235); the first half is attributed to Vyāsa by SmṛCa 23, Prakā (Dhko 235), Samu (Dhko 235), VyaKa 258, VyaCi 697 (at 218 to Kātyāyana), etc.

66. A document is always strong evidence; witnesses only as long as they are alive; possession after a passage of time. This is the consensus in the śāstras.

NMS 2.66. J 1.75. A makes clear the comparative strengths of the three types of evidence. A carefully preserved document will settle a matter even after the parties have died; their descendants will be able to settle the dispute for generations. Thus a document is stronger than witnesses. The validity of continuous possession (by a man and his heirs) is not limited by time.

67. This threefold natural proof is listed in descending order of strength. Possession is the strongest of these.

NMS 2.67. J 1.76. This verse appears contradictory. The first part ranks the three modes of proof in descending order: document, witnesses, and possession. The second half says that possession is strongest. A recognizes this problem and explains away the contradiction in the following manner. In the case of immovables, possession without a title (i.e., a document) is inadequate—he cites 1.76 in support of this. Thus possession is weak evidence in this case. However, if possession is reinforced by witnesses or by a title (document), then possession is the strongest evidence. Possession reinforced by witnesses would not overcome possession supported by a title, however; thus in this case a document would be the strongest evidence, hence the rank order of documents over witnesses.

The adjective "natural" (*dṛṣṭa*) restricts the modes of proof to human means and does not include ordeals and oaths, the "super-natural" (*adṛṣṭa* or *daiva*) modes of proof. According to A, these superhuman proofs are included in the last *pāda* of this verse. This portion of the verse says: *bhuktir ebhyo garīyasī* "possession is strongest of these." The plural pronoun must refer to three or more things. Since only three modes of proof have been mentioned—possession being only one of them—only two remain and one might expect that the dual pronoun (*ābhyāṃ*) would be used instead of the plural. This is the reading of recension D. A explains that possession is superior to three modes—witnesses, documents, and ordeals. This is correct because of the general rule that ordeals are not admissible if there is natural evidence available. Obviously, if possession can be shown, it eliminates the possibility of resorting to an ordeal; also, ordeals are, in general, prohibited for disputes about immovables (see Dit 47 ff.). This is a far better explanation of the plural pronoun *ebhyo* than the far-fetched explanation of Vācaspati Miśra (VyaCi 452-456.6 and 501-501.4).

68. It is especially the case for immovables that, even if there is a document and even if there are witnesses who are still alive, the matter is not certain if there is no possession.

NMS 2.68. J 1.77. This verse is a clear statement of the weakness of a document and witnesses without possession. A states that possession and a title are mutually dependent. Any single means of proof is no proof. The matter is really certain when there are two types of proof. This is especially so for immovables (see 1.76 ff.). Bhava agrees that uninterrupted possession is the strongest mode of proof, but he stops short of requiring two modes of proof to prove one's case. On this point, see Manu 8.200 and YāSmṛ 2.27. Bhava specifies the immovables: a field, a house, a garden, a tank, a boundary (see 1.73).

69. If a man, during his lifetime and under his very eyes, foolishly allows his own things to be used by others, that possession places them under the control of the one who is using them.

NMS 2.69. J 1.78. A stipulates that the things in question are bipeds, quadrupeds, immovables, etc., and says that it makes no difference how the user first acquired them (by gift, by force, or by finding them). GauDha 12.37-38 includes an exception on this subject: property is not lost to the owner if it has been used by learned brāhmaṇas or royal officials. On the exemption of learned brāhmaṇas, see Patrick Olivelle, "Renouncer and Renunciation in the Dharmaśāstra," in *Studies in Dharmaśāstra,* R.W. Lariviere, ed., Calcutta 1983, pp.148-9. A adds that if a man stands to lose his ownership while he is alive, then it is all the more the case if he dies.

70. A property owner who watches in silence when something of his is being used by others nearby for ten years, has no right to take it back.

NMS 2.70. J 1.79. A states that this verse is not meant to create deception, but to protect the permanence of transactions. He suggests that an owner should speak up daily, monthly, or annually, in which case he does not forfeit his ownership. This verse is identical to Manu 8.147. VyaKa 187 and numerous other writers (see Dhko 383) explicitly attribute it to both Manu and Nārada. Prakā (Dhko 404) attributes it to Uśanas.

71. A lawsuit by one who looks on and remains silent is not successful if the above-mentioned time has passed.

NMS 2.71. J 1.79 note. This verse is omitted by recensions P and Y. It is found in X following 1.73. In D it follows 1.70. This is also its position in NMS and seems most appropriate. This verse is important for its claim that lack of vigilance will forfeit one's right of ownership. The alternate reading for *sidhyati*, i.e., *vidyate*, would make this point more forcefully, since it would say that the lawsuit "does not exist."

72. As long as the owner is not mentally incompetent or a minor, and his property is being used legitimately in his presence, the possessor is entitled to that property.

NMS 2.72. J 1.80. A explains that someone is "mentally incompetent" if he is afflicted with a long-term and very serious disease, or is without the faculties of speech, sight, or hearing. A minor is someone who is less than sixteen years old (see 1.31). Bhava says that the minor in this case refers to an orphan. This verse is nearly identical to Manu 8.148 and GauDha 2.3.34.

73. A pledge, a boundary, the property of children, unsealed and sealed deposits, women, the king's property, and a learned brāhmaṇa's property are not lost through possession.

NMS 2.73. J 1.81. A says that a boundary is to be restored even if it has been violated for a long time. Bhava states that the women mentioned here are servants or slaves. A stipulates that the property of the king spoken of here means land, and the property of a well-versed brāhmaṇa means cows. This verse is identical to Manu 8.149 and Vasmṛ 16.16. Yāsmṛ 2.25 adds to this list the property of a mental incompetent (*jaḍa*).

74. Even these pledges, etc., are lost due to adverse possession in the presence of the owner for twenty years, but not women or the king's property.

NMS 2.74. J 1.82. Samu attributes this verse to Bṛhaspati. A's view differs from the translation and from 1.73. He reads this with 1.75 and says that what is exempted is women's property. He also says that the only property of the king that is exempted is land. As MaBhā on GauDha 12.34 observes, this verse means that after twenty years the property of a child (see 1.72) is lost by adverse possession.

75. The property of women and kings is never lost, even if it is possessed without title for hundreds of years.

NMS 2.75. J 1.83. A makes clear that, because of this rule, even uninterrupted possession does not affect property rights in these cases.

76. If there is possession but no title, in that case the absence of a title, not the possession, is conclusive.

NMS 2.76. J 1.84. Similar to Manu 8.200. Verses 1.70-72 and 1.74 establish that it is possible to acquire ownership of property by means of possession which meets certain criteria. Verse 1.76 implies that a man who has in hand some property, but not under the circumstances prescribed at 1.70 and 1.74, does not legally "possess" that property, and only a valid title will prove ownership. If "A" occupies a plot of land without title for eight years and "B" who has the title attempts to claim the land from him, then "B" will be determined to be the owner, because the title overrules mere possession. Verses 1.70 and 1.74 add the crucial qualifications which make possession valid evidence. Verse 1.76 attempts to make clear that squatters cannot take property merely by occupying or using it.

At this point Jolly includes the following three verses from recension D:

> **Possession acquires validity by means of a clear title. Possession without a clear title is not valid.** [J 1.85]
> **One who claims mere possession without title is considered a thief, because of his deceptive pretense of possession.** [J 1.86]
> **The king should punish that sinner who has possession—even for hundreds of years—without title, as if he were a thief.** [J 1.87]

These verses are not found in P, nor in NMS, nor in the Newārī mss. Jolly makes no note of the fact that they are omitted in P and does not state in his edition why he suddenly follows D instead of his usual pattern of accepting the readings of P. These verses are well attested in a wide range of commentaries and digests, but they are also attributed variously to Yājñavalkya, Manu, Kātyāyana, Bṛhaspati, Vyāsa, and even Pulaha (see Dhko 401, 406, 407), as well as to Nārada. This is an example of the inflation of the original text of Nārada by the integration of extraneous verses from other sources.

77. Possession without a title does not supercede ownership, but when the user dies the property may be used by his heirs.

NMS 2.77. J 1.88. A stipulates that the heirs to a squatter have a right to the use of the property only if that squatter had not been challenged by the owner of the property. Therefore the owner must not look on quietly while such usage is taking place. Bhava concurs in this interpretation. One must understand by this that unchallenged usage either for ten years (1.70) or until the user's death creates an estate in tail for the heirs.

The following verse is given by Jolly immediately after this verse, but it is found only in recension D:

> **In a case within memory, possession as well as a title for the land leads to ownership; in a case beyond memory and where there is no title, possession for three generations.** [J 1.89]

78. When the individual who initiated the possession himself is brought to court, the burden of proof is on him. Mere possession settles a matter only for those things obtained by inheritance from the father.

NMS 2.78. J 1.90. A's view is that the burden of proof is on the user when he is challenged. He must show how he came to possess the property. Even though inheritance from the father is a condition for proof by possession, if the possession has been challenged, and if the user dies before the dispute is settled, then inheritance by his heirs does not give them a clear claim to the property. As Bhava says on this verse, they must settle the matter in court (see 1.80).

The following verse is found after 1.78 only in recensions P and D:

> **Something which has been in the possession of three previous generations from the father cannot be taken away, even though wrongfully acquired, because of uninterrupted possession for three generations.** [J 1.91]

The commentary makes clear that this rule of adverse possession for three generations applies to movable and immovable property. The last sentence of the commentary looks like an addition of Kalyāṇa. This verse reinforces the "four-generation" theory of A as formulated in his commentary on 1.5. For a full discussion of the verse [J 1.91] and its variants see R.C. Hazra, "Dharma—Its Early Meaning and Scope," *Our Heritage* 7 (1959), 29 ff.

79. There are six things without title: a deposit entrusted to an intermediary, something stolen, a deposit, something seized by force, something loaned for a particular purpose, and something used in the owner's absence.

NMS 2.79. J 1.92. A gives an unusual explanation of the term *anvāhita*, taking something valuable in exchange for something worthless. The usual meaning of this term is a deposit entrusted to an intermediary, as I have translated it. See Niranjan Roy, "The Ancient Hindu Law of Pledges and Bailments," *Journal of the Department of Letters* (University of Calcutta), 32 (1939),1-120; and Susan Oleksiw, "The Definition and Treatment of Nyāsa in Dharmaśāstra Literature," JAOS 102 (1982), 119-124. The term *yācita*, literally, "requested," is explained by A as something requested for some particular business or activity. A and Bhava agree that possession in these instances does not constitute valid evidence.

80. If a litigant dies after a case has been duly initiated, his son must settle the matter; possession does not extend to the son.

NMS 2.80. J 1.93. This is an elaboration on 1.78.

81. If something has been possessed for three generations and is then passed on, even without a title, it cannot be taken away, because the possessor now has the "entitlement" of three consecutive generations.

NMS 2.81. J omits. This verse is omitted in ms P. The second half is identical to the second half of J 1.91 (see note to 1.78), but this verse treats a more general circumstance. Whereas J 1.91 discusses wrongful acquisition, this verse states that possession for three generations constitutes ownership regardless of the manner in which it was originally acquired. This verse has been attributed to different authors: Harīta (Dhko 420), Vyāsa (Dhko 422), and even Manu (Dhko 389).

82-83. Even if there are witnesses, they cannot be accepted after the death of the property owner, except for statements the owner personally made to them on his deathbed. For the statement of witnesses is not valid evidence

if the respondent in a case has died. In order to determine such a case, a document which has been attested would be valid evidence.

NMS 2.82-83. J 1.94-95. Examples of unacceptable statements given by A are: "My creditor has given me such and such cow, buffalo, bull, or field on such and such occasion or period, and 'so and so,' who are good witnesses, know this," or "Your father owed me one hundred *drammas*, and 'so and so' are witnesses to this." See 1.144. The reading (*tasya jīvitaḥ*) given by Jolly and found only in ms P seems unlikely. It would mean that a document was valid only during the lifetime of the party to the document. This is clearly not the case if we consider such things as copper-plate grants, and if we consider the admonitions of Vyāsa (cited in Apa p. 690 on YāSmṛ 2.91) to the effect that a document executed by one man and in the possession of another must be carefully scrutinized for authenticity. Such a situation would arise when a distant heir produces an old title to some disputed property. The required number of witnesses to a document was ordinarily two or more (see also 1.121 and YāSmṛ 2.87).

84. If a man, though sick, has announced some righteous matter, then, even after his death, a witness constitutes valid evidence. This rule also applies to the six things, a deposit entrusted to an intermediary, etc.

NMS 2.84. J 1.96. A gives as an example of a righteous matter a promise to make a righteous gift. The six things are those mentioned at 1.79. If any of these are done, but not in the presence of his sons, then the witnesses can attest to his wishes. This is as close as the classical Hindu Law comes to testamentary disposition. KāSmṛ 566 is explicit on this subject and declares that the intent to make a righteous gift is binding upon the heirs even after the death of the promisor. Bṛhas 14.14 explicitly prohibits testamentary disposition, however, so that the view of Nārada and Kātyāyana must represent an exception to this. The stipulation concerning the absence of the sons is important because the will of the testator must be upheld against the claim of the heirs and, presumably, if the heirs were not in the testator's presence when he made this disposition, they might refuse to believe it, hence the necessity of witnesses.

85. In all matters such as debt, etc. the last action is more binding than any preceding one. In the case of gifts, deposits, or purchases, the first action is more binding than any later one.

NMS 2.85. J 1.97. The point of this verse is that the status of transactions which fall under the eighteen titles of law is determined by the last event in the sequence of the transaction. That is, the repayment of a loan (which, obviously, comes after the making of the loan in the first place) is the binding act since it eliminates the original debt. Exceptions to this are matters such as gifts, deposits, or purchases, where the first person to have accepted a gift, or to have accepted a deposit, or to have made a purchase is the one who has the claim to that item. Should an unscrupulous man attempt to sell something twice, for example, the first person to have purchased it would be the one with the valid claim to it, and not the second "buyer." This verse of Nārada is apparently unknown to subsequent writers on *dharmaśāstra*, but YāSmṛ 2.23 which has an identical meaning is cited numerous times.

86. Increasing one's property without losing the principal is a desirable source of profit through investment; this is called money-lending and those who live by it are called money-lenders.

NMS 2.86. J 1.98. This verse is unusual for its application of the word *sthāna*. The translation "investment" follows the interpretation of Bhava. A gives a very different interpretation for the term *sthāna*. He says that the interest derived is dependent on three things: the material, one's own condition, and the rules about interest in the other party's country.

The next three verses in Jolly's edition (J 1.99-100) are from Manu (8.140-142) and are not found in any Nārada mss except the corrupt P. They must be interpolations, probably to be attributed to either A or Kalyāṇa:

> **A money lender may take 1.25% of the principal as interest every month as prescribed by Vasiṣṭha.** [J 1.99]
> **Two, three, four, or five per cent is fair. He may take this as interest per month from the four castes respectively.** [J 1.100]
> **Or he may take two per cent, remembering the practice of the righteous, for taking two percent does not make him a sinner in the matter.** [J 1.101]

87-89. According to the śāstras there are four kinds of interest on a loan: corporal, periodical, stipulated, and cyclical. Corporal interest is one quarter *paṇa* per day with no diminution of the capital. Periodical interest is that interest which is paid every month. Stipulated interest is interest to which the debtor has agreed. Cyclical interest is interest on interest.

NMS 2.87-89. J 1.102-104. These verses are translated according to the explanation of the commentators, A and Bhava. "Corporal" interest is explained by A as interest which is paid daily on the capital at an agreed upon rate such as one *paṇa* or one quarter-*paṇa*, etc., but without any diminution of the principal. A question which is not clearly addressed in A's commentary is the relationship which this form of interest has with the practice of "selling" oneself into slavery to work off a debt (see 5.25-26). This matter and the various interpretations of this verse by other writers are discussed by H.N. Chatterjee, *Debt*, pp. 37-41. One point which Chatterjee does mention is the fact that A says that the daily payments may be made by the practice of taking interest from daily wages.

"Stipulated" interest is, according to A, interest agreed upon by the borrower which is in excess of the interest rates allowed by the legal texts. Thus, if a man is unworthy and hence a bad risk, or if he is otherwise a good man, but in severe straits and therefore a bad risk at the time of the loan, the lender may extract a promise of ten percent of the loan to be paid in addition to the normal repayment schedule. The point here is that additional risk (not, as Chatterjee, *Debt*, p. 35 claims, potential profit) warrants the additional interest.

Jolly and Chatterjee both translate *cakravṛddhi* as "compound interest," which is misleading to a modern reader. Actually it is what we know as simple interest. "Cyclical" interest is explained by A with the example of a loan made at five per cent interest per month. Such a loan would double the principal in 20 months, double again in 40 months, double again in 60 months, etc. (which seems to violate the general rule of *dāmdupaṭ* that total interest on a loan is limited to an amount equal to the principal, see Chatterjee, *Debt*, pp. 48-54). Moreover, the amount of time the money is used determines the amount of money to be paid: under the five per cent example, if 33 *drammas* are borrowed for 4 months, then the borrower would pay back a total of 40 *drammas* (in round numbers the principal plus the simple interest for four months). Apparently the difference between this "cyclical" interest and "periodical" interest is that the latter must be paid at the end of each period, whereas "cyclical" interest is paid only once—at the time of the repayment of the entire loan plus accrued interest. Bhava concurs with A's explanations of these terms, except that for him "cyclical" interest only accrues until the principal is doubled, but then if that total is not repaid the interest begins to accrue on the original principal again—a bit of panditry which preserves the rule of *dāmdupaṭ*. A also seeks to preserve the rule which says that interest can only accrue until it equals the amount of the principal (*dāmdupaṭ*), and states at the end of his comment that when a man has loaned an amount to the king and that amount has increased by five per cent twenty times (i.e., when the interest equals the principal), then the principal should be repaid. This still leaves the "interest" outstanding, and this then begins to accrue interest. Once it doubles, then another payment must be made (which would be equal to the original principal), etc. Hence the definition of "cyclical" interest as "interest on interest." The commentary on this verse was probably supplemented by Kalyāṇa. The examples, among other things, sound like his style. All of these methods of charging interest are forbidden by Manu. See Manu 8.151-153 and commentators.

90-91. The rule that debts yield interest applies everywhere, but the rules differ according to local custom, depending on where the debt is made. Depending on the country the interest may grow to two, three, four or even eight times the principal.

NMS 2.90-91. J 1.105-106.

92. Interest on gold, grain, and clothing may grow to two, three, and four times the principal respectively; interest on clarified butter, eight times; on women and cattle the interest is their offspring.

NMS 2.92. J 1.107. A makes clear that the amounts of interest are double for gold, three times for grain, four times for clothes, and eight times for liquids. These amounts are in direct proportion to the possibility of the adulteration of the material loaned or, in the case of clothes, the diminution of their value by use. Bhava adds that an alternative form of interest on women and cattle would be the products of the cattle, milk, etc., and the labor of the woman. This verse is quoted by A under verse 1.1.

93-95. For thread, cotton, fermented seeds, tin, lead, all weapons, skin, copper, and iron, as well as for all other (such) materials including bricks, Manu Prajāpati has declared continuous interest. For all oils, liquor, honey, and ghee, as well as molasses and salt the rate of interest is eight times.

NMS and Jolly omit these verses. *Akṣayya*, literally "imperishable" is not a common term used for interest. Taken literally, it might mean that the amount of money in accrued interest would be unlimited, since under any of the other formulas, once the maximum amount has been reached the interest rate declines to nothing. NāSmṛ 1.95 has a close parallel in KāSmṛ 511. The subject of the interest on such commodities is a common one; see ViSmṛ 6.16 and Bṛhas 10.23, as well as Kane, HDh 3.420-422, and Chatterjee, *Debt*, pp. 55-60.

96. One should never make loans out of friendship without stipulating the interest. Even without a previous stipulation, interest accrues after half a year.

NMS 2.93. J 1.108. Bhava adds that the rate of interest in such cases is that which is normal for the region. Jolly includes the following verse which is found only in ms P:

> **A loan made out of friendship can never yield interest if repayment is not requested. If repayment is requested but the loan is not repaid, then the interest rate is five per cent.**
> [J 1.109]

This is a gloss on verse 1.96 which had found its way into the manuscript tradition from which A worked when he wrote his commentary. A says that the interest begins to accrue six months from the day the request was made. J 1.109 is found only in ms P. The verse is found elsewhere, but in only one place, Apa on YāSmṛ 2.37, is it attributed to Nārada, and even here the attribution is ambiguous. Dhko 627a is incorrect in its listing of sources for this as a Nārada verse: the NṛPra does not quote the verse, and the ViTā quotes "Aparārka." Most texts attribute this verse to Kātyāyana (see Dhko 633a).

97. Thus the rule concerning interest—the legal return on a loan—has been proclaimed. However, the interest set for grains is called usury.

NMS 2.94. J 1.110. This verse marks the change in subject from proper rates of interest to usury. It seems odd that grain should be singled out as an example for usurious practices. Judging from the difficulties which the commentators have with this verse, it must also have struck them as odd. A gives a preposterous explanation for the nonsensical reading *karmaṇaḥ* which he has in his text: he says that it is sometimes used to mean "gold."

98. A vaiśya, to be sure, might survive a catastrophe by engaging in usury, but usury is not for a brāhmaṇa even in times of great catastrophe.

NMS 2.95. J 1.111. A says that the normal occupation of a vaiśya is agriculture etc.; yet doing it to collect interest on grain is ordinarily forbidden to him, but in a catastrophe he may choose to survive by such usury. This option is strictly forbidden for a brāhmaṇa. Bhava adds that because of the explicit prohibition for brāhmaṇas, this option is possible for kṣatriyas, but because of the explicit mention of the possibility for vaiśyas, it is to be understood that it is not desirable for kṣatriyas. He also cites, however, another interpretation which says that usury is also strictly forbidden to kṣatriyas.

99-100. If one is in debt to a brāhmaṇa and his heirs, but that brāhmaṇa is no more, then it should be paid to his family; failing them, to his relatives. When there are no members of his family and no relatives then the debt should be paid to his fellow caste members; if there are none, it should be cast on the waters.

NMS 2.96-97. J 1.112-113. If the brāhmaṇa to whom the money is owed is no longer, then it should be paid to his descendants. If that is not possible, it should be paid to his father, paternal uncle, or their sons (*kulya*), and failing that alternative, to his mother, sister, or her sons (*bandhu*). Bhava's commentary is corrupt here, but his reading *sapiṇḍebhyo* for *svakulyasya* means, he tells us, that the creditor's *sapiṇḍas* for seven generations are eligible for the debt repayment before any cognate has a legitimate claim to the property. Bhava also points out that in each of these options, the original brāhmaṇa is the propositus, i.e., it is his father, mother, uncle, sister, etc. who are intended. A explains that the last option might be fulfilled by spending the money for some meritorious deed like excavating a tank. Bhava does not mention this option, but explains that casting the money onto the waters in the case of brāhmaṇas is the correct final option. He cites in support some rather obscure passages from the *Nāradaparivrājakopaniṣat*, "The waters are all the *devatās*," and "A brāhmaṇa is all the *devatās*," hence the appropriateness of casting on the waters the money owed to a brāhmaṇa. He further says that in the case of kṣatriyas and vaiśyas the last option is for the money to be given to other kṣatriyas and vaiśyas, respectively. In all of these cases, according to Bhava, the king is to be the distributor of the money which has been repaid.

101. The creditor should give a receipt to the debtor upon receiving a payment. If he is asked for a receipt and does not give one, he loses the remainder.

NMS 2.98. J 1.114. This verse represents an advance over YāSmṛ which merely requires (at 2.93) that the creditor, if asked, provide a receipt in his own hand, but does not provide for a punishment for failure to do so. Bhava says that this punishment includes the loss of the outstanding principal as well as the remaining interest due.

102. When the debt has been cleared he must give back the bond, and if there is no bond then he should give a receipt. Thus the creditor and the debtor become free of obligation to one another.

NMS 2.99. J 1.116. A implies that the only time that there would not be a bond to be returned to the debtor is if it had been stolen, destroyed, or lost. The commentary here shows indisputable evidence of Kalyāṇa's tampering since he cites himself, although the exact place from where this is quoted is not clear—"*triṣaṣṭipatraprakaraṇe*". The reading given here is that found in M4. See the commentary on verse 1.114 below where this text (?) is mentioned again—*yathoktaṃ triṣaṣṭilekhyaprakaraṇakārakakalyāṇabhaṭṭena*. See also 1.106, 1.107, 1.144. This seems to be a separate (and otherwise unknown) treatise on documents written by Kalyāṇa.

103. There are two means of assurance, a surety and a pledge. A document and witnesses are the two modes of proof which clarify matters.

NMS 2.100. J 1.117. A says that the two modes of proof, a document and witnesses, clarify the four components in a debt—the amount of the principal, the amount of interest, the surety, and the pledge.

104. The sages observe that the surety is of three types and for three purposes: for appearance, for payment, and for honesty.

NMS 2.101. J 1.118. A says that: (1) a surety for appearance is required when an alleged debtor denies that he owes money, and he is required by the creditor to appear at a trial. The surety proclaims to the creditor that he is the guarantor of the debtor's appearance; (2) a surety for payment is when a man, in an effort to secure a loan, offers a second or third man as sureties, either jointly or severally; (3) a surety for honesty is to be provided when the debtor denies that he owes the creditor money. The creditor requires a surety to guarantee the reliability of the debtor until the creditor can have the matter resolved by some means such as the rice ordeal.

105. If the debtors do not repay, or if one's honesty has been disputed, then the surety must pay the debt. The same is true if he fails to make the debtor appear.

NMS 2.102. J 1.119. The commentary attributed to A has the sound of Kalyāṇa about it at this point. It is uncharacteristically lengthy and homiletic in tone when compared to the rest of A's commentary. The verses of Vṛddhavasiṣtha in the—in places, obviously corrupt—commentary are not found elsewhere. The enumeration of nine types of sureties is also unknown elswhere and represents a number larger than any other source. The nine kinds of sureties are:

1. *sāmānyagrāhaka*—for a joint debt;
2. *svāṃśadāyaka*—for only one's portion of a debt;
3. *darśana*—for appearance;
4. *upasthāna*—for attendance;
5. *pratyaya*—for reliability;
6. *dharmajalpita*—for veracity;
7. *pālana*—for protection;
8. *sāti*—for delivery (?);
9. *śīla*—for character.

The exact meaning of these terms in this context and the character of each surety are unknown. See VyaPra 248 where Hārīta claims there are five and Vyāsa seven types of sureties. See Heramba Nath Chatterjee, "Studies in the Verses Relating to Nirṇaya in the Vyāsasmṛti," in *Indology and Law Studies in Honour of Professor J. Duncan M. Derrett*, pp. 124-5.

106. If there are several sureties, they must pay the respective amounts for which they are liable. If they are jointly liable, then they must pay as the creditor wishes.

NMS 2.103. J 1.120. Much of A's commentary is a discussion of the matter of joint or several liability which he has already discussed in the comment on 1.12. The explicit attribution of the verse (*ye jīvanti* ...) to Kalyāṇa is again clear evidence of his tampering with the text of A. Kalyāṇa's verse was cited in 1.12, but without attribution. It is unknown elsewhere. Verse 1.106 is ignored by all subsequent writers on dharma. This may be due to the greater currency of YāSmṛ 2.55 which says essentially the same thing and is cited very often by subsequent writers. 1.106 is identical with ViSmṛ 6.42, but that verse is also uncited by any subsequent writer.

107. If the surety is harassed by the creditor into paying him, the debtor must pay the surety twice that amount.

NMS 2.104. J 1.121. A adds that if the surety voluntarily pays the amount to the creditor without even being told to do so or without being harassed into doing so, but merely so that he might be entitled to collect from the debtor twice the amount paid, then the debtor need only pay him the original amount. The test for the application of the doubling rule is whether or not anyone has been troubled by some fault of the debtor. If so, then the amount is doubled. The verse (*ṛṇidvayaṃ* etc.) quoted by *prakaraṇakāra* Kalyāṇa is one of the Vṛddhavasiṣṭha verses quoted in the commentary on 1.105.

Jolly's edition includes as Nārada verses (J 1.122-123) the two Manu verses (8.49-50) quoted in the commentary. This passage is an addition to A's commentary by Kalyāṇa who mentions himself explicitly. These verses are not found in any manuscript other than P, and they are never attributed to Nārada by any other writers. According to the commentary, the four modes of obtaining success (*sāman* "conciliation," *bheda* "division," *upapradāna* "gifts," and *daṇḍa* "violence") as enumerated by Cāṇakya (see Kau 2.10.47 ff.) are the same as four of the five modes of recovering a debt. Here these same modes are given different names: *sāman* = *dharma*, an appeal to righteousness; *bheda* = *vyavahāra*, a trial at law; *upapradhāna* = *chala*, fraud or temptation; and *daṇḍa*, a sort of self-help in which the debtor is seized and bound. The fifth means, *ācārita*, is the practice of fasting until the debtor fulfills his obligation.

108. A pledge is that over which authority is given, and it is of two kinds: that held for a limited period of time, and that held until the obligation has been discharged.

NMS 2.105. J 1.124. According to A the division of pledges is between those which are movable or immovable, and of each of these two types there are (1) pledges held for a limited time and (2) pledges held indefinitely until the debt is paid. A pledge held for a limited time is also of two types according to A: one collected from a third party who has held the pledge, and one held by the creditor himself for a specified length of time. When a pledge is held indefinitely, the profits or benefits from holding the pledge continue to accrue to the creditor as long as the debt is unpaid. On this subject in general see Niranjan Roy, "The Ancient Hindu Law of Pledges and Bailments," *Journal of the Department of Letters* (University of Calcutta), 32 (1939), 1-120.

109. It is also said to be of two types in a different sense: one to be kept, and one to be used. The pledge must be returned as it was; if it is not, then the creditor's profit is lost.

NMS 2.106. J 1.125. A says that if a pledge is merely to be kept and the holder of the pledge uses it, then he loses the profit to which he would have been entitled at the time the debt is repaid. On the other hand, if a creditor has a pledge which he is supposed to use, grain, a dwelling, etc., but he does not use it, then he loses the profit in that case as well, because the usufruct was to be his profit.

110. The same is true if there is any change in the pledge due to the negligence of the creditor. If he loses the pledge, the profit is lost, unless it was lost through fate or the king.

NMS 2.107. J 1.126. A gives as examples of negligence in the case of a pledge to be used the unseasonable or excessive use of a bull, or the loss of an eye or the breaking of a horn, etc. In the case of a pledge to be kept, an example of negligence would be leaving it out in the open. Loss due to the king would be the confiscation of a man's entire estate because of some serious offense, and loss due to fate might be such a thing as having it taken by a thief. The length of this commentary, which includes three verses from Manu (8.143, 144, and 150), points to Kályāṇa as the author. Jolly was incorrect to read these verses as part of the Nārada text. They are not found in any manuscript except P (and its copies), and they are not attributed to Nārada by any writer. Jolly indicates in his edition that his J 1.127 (Manu 8.144) is attributed to Nārada by some commentary or digest writer, but I have been unable to find such an attribution.

111. When a pledge becomes worthless with time, even though it was protected, another pledge should be designated or the money should be repaid to the creditor.

NMS 2.108. J 1.130. This verse seems to be attributed to Vyāsa by SmṛCi 120, but the attribution is unclear.

112. If it happens that the debtor becomes unable to pay due to some reversal of fortune, he should be made to repay the debt gradually as he becomes able to do so.

NMS 2.110. J 1.131.

113. If he is able to repay the money to the creditor but does not do so out of mean-spiritedness, the king should make him pay and take five per cent for himself.

NMS 2.109. J 1.132. This solution to the problem of what to do in the event that the debt is not paid is evidence that Nārada did not allow for the pledge to become the property of the creditor in case of default by the debtor. This agrees with the view of Manu (8.143, quoted in the commentary on 1.110) but is different from that of YāSmṛ 2.63 and Bṛhas 10.51 and 55, which hold that the pledge can, in the event of default, be sold in the presence of witnesses in order to recover the debt. The commentary on this verse shows evidence of having been supplemented by Kalyāṇa. The verse which Jolly includes in his text of Nārada (J 1.133) but which is unknown outside of this commentary, must be taken to be the creation of Kalyāṇa and not a Nārada verse. J 1.133 is a paraphrase of Manu 8.139 and is intended to be an impediment to unnecessary litigation before the king, since it provides for a stiff penalty for a debtor who admits his debt before the court:

If the defendant confesses, the king should make him pay 10%
as a penalty, twice that if he does not confess. [J 1.133]

The point is that the matter should have been settled before the case came to the court. The commentary on this supplementary verse says that if the debtor has lied and been found by the court to owe the money, then the creditor should, by means of the proceedings, firmly establish what is due to him.

114. If the debtor accidentally loses the entire amount of the debt, a document is required recording his caste, name, and place of origin.

NMS 2.111. J 1.134. This verse addresses the situation in which the debtor is unable to make the repayment on time for reasons beyond his control. The commentary on this verse once more refers to Kalyāṇa's expertise in the matter of documents. The commentary makes it clear that the document is to be executed by the debtor. Bhava explains the need for a document by the fact that the loss of the entire amount may occasion disagreement between the parties. The term *saṃjñā* is explained slightly differently by the two commentaries. A says that it means that "the property is established" by means of the name (*saṃjñayā*), and Bhava says that it means a proper name such as Vajrendra, Nīlamarataka, etc.

115. There are two kinds of documents: those written in one's own hand or in another's hand. Some are witnessed, and some are not. Their validity depends on local convention.

NMS 2.112. J 1.135. The interpretation of this verse by A and by Bhava is slightly different. A says that a document in one's own hand does not require a witness, but a document in another's hand does. He also says that the reference to local convention is only meant to affirm the importance of local custom. Bhava states that in some places witnesses are required for the validity of any document and in other places they are not. PaMā 130 seems to attribute this verse to Kātyāyana.

116. A valid document is one which does not contradict local practices, is clear, contains the appropriate characteristics, and is neither out of order nor incomplete.

NMS 2.113. J 1.136. A's examples of the contradiction of local practices are: giving what should not be given, and entering into a contract with a dependent person. See A. Thakur, *Hindu Law of Evidence*, pp. 166-167. The commentary again shows explicit evidence of the work of Kalyāṇa. His verse (*likhitaṃ lakṣaṇajñena* etc.) is not known in any other work. It is, however, very close to ViSmṛ 7.11. Bhava explains that appropriate characteristics mean the statement of the time of the loan, the amount, the time it is due, the penalty for non-payment, etc. According to the editors of the Dhko (357), Prakā (folio 36) attributes this verse to Kātyāyana. I have been unable to verify this.

117. A document which has been executed by one who is intoxicated, by one who has been charged, by a woman, by a minor, by force, by intimidation, or by deception is not valid.

NMS 2.114. J 1.137. This verse is similar to ViSmṛ 7.10. A is careful to point out that the force spoken of in this verse is force which is extraneous to the matter in dispute. Bhava says being charged means having been charged by another party (in another dispute). Ms P omits this verse, but, since it contains the commentary on it, the omission is obviously due to scribal error.

118. A document is also invalid if the witnesses, the creditor, the debtor, or the scribe are dead, unless a pledge continues in effect.

NMS 2.115. J 1.138. Bhava interprets the expression "a pledge continues in effect" differently than A. Bhava takes the expression to mean that it requires a pledge of an immovable such as land, as opposed to the pledge of a cow or the like, because the latter sort of pledge is non-enduring and can be forgotten. Thus, under the circumstances discussed in this verse, only the pledge of an immovable renders the document valid. A says that the death of the parties tends to render a document invalid because of the possibility of forgery.

119. There are two kinds of pledges: movable and immovable. Both are valid as long as they are in one's possession, not otherwise.

NMS 2.116. J 1.139. A states that a deposit without possession is invalid even if it is recorded. Bhava says that deposits are valid only if there is possession, and that deposits that are in one's possession are valid even if there is no document accompanying the deposit. Bhava conceives one other possible permutation, but he says it is one that is hard to imagine: the possibility of a deposit which is neither in the possession of the creditor nor recorded in a document.

120. A document which has been shown time and again and which has been mentioned repeatedly continues to be valid even if the witnesses are dead.

NMS 2.117. J 1.140. Both A and Bhava state that the document described in this verse is valid even if all the original parties are dead, including the debtor and the creditor. In that case the successors to the original parties become the principals in the document. A says that the document is to be shown every time payment is requested.

121. A document which has never been seen or heard of before is not valid for a lawsuit even if the witnesses are still alive.

NMS 2.118. J 1.141. A says that the reason that such a document is not valid is because of suspicion of forgery. Bhava has a different interpretation. He says that it is a hyperbole to say that such a document is invalid "even if the witnesses are alive," since the document is invalid due to its not having been properly presented before; the question of witnesses is moot.

122. When a document has been deposited in another country, or burned, or badly written, or stolen, a delay is granted if the document is still extant, but the testimony of one who had seen the document serves in the place of a document which is no longer extant.

NMS 2.119. J 1.142. The unusual length of the comment, the anecdotal quality of the examples given, and the fact that Kalyāṇa refers to himself on several occasions as the author of a treatise on documents (see, e.g. 1.102, 1.106, 1.107, and 1.114) all point to him as the author. The commentary says that the provisions of this verse apply equally to the plaintiff and the respondent in a lawsuit. For example, if a debtor, when brought to court as a respondent, asks to see the document proving his debt and the creditor does not have it in hand, the judge is authorized to grant a delay so that the creditor can find the document. If that document no longer exists, then the witnesses, scribe, or other reliable person who saw the document can give evidence. The same is true if the numbers, letters, or words of a document have been obliterated. The other example which is given in the commentary is that of a debtor who, when asked to pay his debt, claims to have a document which proves that he does not owe the money. If that document is not in his possession, he may be granted a delay to find it. Bhava says that in the case of a lost document a new document can be drawn up if the parties are agreed.

123. If there should be any doubt about the authenticity of a document, the doubt should be removed by consideration of the handwriting, the transaction, peculiar marks, and reasonable inference.

NMS 2.120. J 1.143. This verse has been a troublesome one for commentators. The terms *kriyā, cihna, prāpti,* and *yukti* have been interpreted in various ways. A and Bhava say that *kriyā* refers to the witnesses who are named in the document. Viśvarūpa on YāSmṛ 2.92 (which lists many of the same means for removing doubt about a document) says that *kriyā* means the character of the scribe. Mitā on YāSmṛ 2.92 agrees with A and Bhava. Apa on the same YāSmṛ verse says that it refers to the likelihood of a transaction between the parties; if it is not possible that they had a common transaction (as in the unlikely case of a transaction between an Āryan and a Dravidian), then the document is invalid.

A explains the term *cihna* as distinctive characteristics of the writing of the scribe. Bhava, obscurely, says it means an agreement about the completion of the transaction at the time. Viśvarūpa and Apa agree that the word means a seal, and this may be what Bhava intends as well: some sort of mark made by the parties to indicate their approval of the document at the time of its composition. The Mitā says that it may mean the appearance of certain distinctive marks in the text such as the word *Śrī*. According to A the term *prāpti* may refer to one of two things: (1) how the document was obtained, and (2) the demeanor of the speaker, i.e., whether he is nervous or not (while speaking of the document). Bhava says that it means a document produced at the wrong time (before or after the transaction was alleged to have taken place), or, it may be a document which has been assented to in the presence of someone. Viśvarūpa and Apa again agree and say that the term means consideration of whether or not the two parties were residing in the same area at the same time (and would thus have been unable to conduct such business). A explains the term *yukti* as meaning a sort of common-sense deliberation on whether a claim is reasonably possible. He cites the example of a claim that a pauper from a family of paupers is the lender of 100,000 *drammas*. This is, generally, also the understanding of Bhava, Viśvarūpa, and Apa. Some writers have taken the terms as a compound rather than as separate means as I have done (*prāptiyukti* = reasonable inference). Mitā on YāSmṛ 2.92, VyaMā 339, and VyaPra 149 understand the text in this way and take it to refer to essentially the same sort of circumstantial evidence spoken of above. On the problem of *yukti*, etc. see L. Rocher, "The Theory of Proof in Ancient Hindu Law", pp. 359-362, and A. Thakur, *Hindu Law of Evidence*, pp. 192-194.

124. A document which contains the name of another person or which was made for another purpose, if it is suspect, should be examined for its relevance, title, and reasonableness.

NMS 2.121. J 1.144. The long comment on this verse is not solely the work of A; it is yet another instance of Kalyāṇa's expanding the commentary with anecdotal explanations of the verse. The anecdotes are two examples of when it is necessary to examine a document. In the first case, a man loaned money, the right to recover the debt was alleged to have been transferred to another man who entered his name on the document to that effect, and the son of the original lender claimed that the document was not valid. This is an example of the necessity for careful scrutiny of a document which contains the name of another person. In the second case, a brāhmaṇa from Broach (Bhārukaccha), Ādityabhaṭṭa, loaned a brāhmaṇa from Kaira (Kheṭaka), Somabhaṭṭa, 2000 *drammas*. Ādityabhaṭṭa had no children, so he gave the right to recover the debt to one Dīkṣitamaṅgalabhaṭṭa of Narmadātīrtha, but he did not execute a document to that effect; he simply gave the original document to Dīkṣita, and had four people witness the act. This claim was later challenged by Ādityabhaṭṭa's brother, Buddhabhaṭṭa. The document said that the money was due to Āditya and not to Dīkṣita, therefore Buddha, the heir to Āditya, would have a claim on the money. This is an instance in which a document for another purpose would need to be carefully examined. As Kalyāṇa points out, these cases are not clear-cut, and their doubtful nature especially requires that the decision of the court be properly recorded. Kalyāṇa has composed three verses that define the terms *saṃbandha*, *āgama*, and *hetu*. He says that *saṃbandha* may be based on lineage, family relationship, marriage, friendship, or common business interests. *Āgama* may be based on inheritance, purchase, pledge, seizure, affection, or acquisition. *Hetu* is based on reasoning and reasonable cause. These terms are also discussed in the places mentioned in the note to 1.123.

125. A document may only be overruled by another document. A case which relies on witnesses may be overruled by other witnesses. A document being superior to witnesses, however, witnesses may be overruled by a document.

NMS 2.122. J 1.145. A says that the debtor should get a document in the handwriting of the creditor releasing him from the debt. On the other hand, if the original document is lost, the creditor needs to get another document stating that fact. Bhava agrees that a document can only be set aside by another document. He also says that when one party relies on a document and the other on witnesses, the party relying on the document prevails, but the document which overrules witnesses must be one which has been attested to by witnesses. A document attested to by witnesses is the stronger evidence.

126. If a document is torn, broken, stolen, worn, lost, or badly written, another document should be made. These are the rules for documents.

NMS 2.123. J 1.146. There was apparently a folio out of place in the exemplar of ms P, since verse 1.126 occurs before 1.125 in P. In this case, again, Kalyāṇa explicitly contributes to the commentary by indicating how to cope with documents that have become defective.

127. When two parties are in dispute over doubtful transactions, things are clarified by witnesses because they saw, heard, or experienced first-hand what happened.

NMS 2.124. J 1.147. A stipulates that witnesses qualify because they are impartial, a point which Bhava also emphasizes in his commentary on the next verse.

128. A person is called a witness if he has heard something with his own ears or seen something with his own eyes, i.e., if he has heard what someone else has said or seen what he has physically done.

NMS 2.125. J 1.148. See Manu 8.74. This verse gives an etymology of the terms *sākṣin* "witness:" *samakṣadarśanāt* "seen something with his own eyes".

129. The wise distinguish eleven kinds of witnesses: five are appointed and six are not appointed.

NMS 2.126. J 1.149.

130. There are five kinds of appointed witnesses: a witness to a document, one who has been reminded, a casual witness, a secret witness, and an indirect witness.

NMS 2.127. J 1.150. This verse is translated here in accord with the commentary of A. A says that a secret witness is one who hears while concealed behind a wall. A witness to a document has his name entered on the document. An indirect witness gives testimony based on what he has heard from an actual witness. This is not to be confused with "hearsay" evidence, which is expressly forbidden according to Medhātithi on Manu 8.74, where he says that hearsay evidence is that which is third- or fourth-hand. The indirect witness is one who is told something by a first-hand witness who is about to depart for another country or who is about to die, according to Bṛhas 5.13 (see NāSmṛ 1.147). "One who has been reminded" is one who serves in place of a document to validate a transaction and who, in order to fulfill this function, must be periodically reminded by the parties to the transaction so that he might keep his memory fresh (see KāSmṛ 371-3 and NāSmṛ 1.150). Bhava says that a casual witness is one who happens to be in the vicinity when a transaction takes place and can relate what happened there. See Bṛhas 5.4 for a similar list of witnesses.

131-132. The sages proclaim that there are six types of witnesses who are not appointed: the community, the chief judge, the king of those involved in the transaction, one who is familiar with the matter, someone else who was involved by the plaintiff, and, in family disputes, the members of the family.

NMS 2.128-9. J 1.151-2. A explains that "the community" means the community where the matter took place. The chief judge, of course, is the chief judge of the court in which a case was heard. The king is a witness for an act which took place in his presence. The witness involved by the plaintiff is, apparently, one who was sent by the plaintiff to listen to the defendant (see SmṛSā cited in Dhko 298). The division of witnesses into appointed and unappointed is not unique to Nārada (see, for example, Manu 8.117 and ViSmṛ 8.41, as well as Bṛhas at VyaCi 246). The enumeration of eleven types of witnesses is unique. In the estimation of Viśvarūpa (on YāSmṛ 2.71) this division of types of witnesses by Nārada is for the benefit of the uninformed. It may have been that in the minds of some experts on legal procedure these distinctions are of little consequence in the actual prosecution of a matter before a court. See Kane, HDh 3.339-340, and A. Thakur, *Hindu Law of Evidence*, pp. 15-22. These verses are found in KāSmṛ 356-357 as well. VyaMā 320, VyaKa 99, and VyaSau (Dhko 297) explicitly attribute them to both Nārada and Kātyāyana.

133. Witnesses must come from good families, be upright, pure of birth, deed and purpose, no less than three in number, unimpeachable, unsullied, and intelligent.

NMS 2.130. J 1.153. A says that for these witnesses to be "unsullied" they must be free from avarice and have pure minds, which means that they must be steeped in the *śāstras*. "Unimpeachable" means well-known. Although they should be three in number, A says that they may be two or only one if that is acceptable to both parties. Bhava adds that to be unimpeachable is also to be free from physical afflictions and that to be unsullied means to be ritually pure and intent on worshiping the gods and brāhmaṇas. For Bhava the witnesses are required to be intelligent in that they should be able to adapt and to accumulate facts, as well as be able to deliberate on what is proper and improper. Concerning the number of witnesses, see Kane, HDh 3.331-2.

134. Brāhmaṇas, kṣatriyas, vaiśyas, and even śūdras, if they are free from reproach, may be witnesses for their respective castes, or else they may all serve as witnesses for every caste.

NMS 2.131. J 1.154. Bhava is careful to point out that the preferred pattern is that witnesses testify in matters concerning their own castes and that the presence of the words *vā punaḥ* "or else" indicates that this second option is not an equal option. This is the accepted view (see, for example, Manu 8.68-69, GauDha 2.4.1-4, YāSmṛ 2.69).

135. Members of guilds should be witnesses for fellow guild members; members of a specific group for fellow group members; outcastes for other outcastes; women for other women.

NMS 2.132. J 1.155. A says that there are eighteen kinds of guilds. This is no doubt another instance of this popular number being used to mean "several." R.C. Majumdar states that the traditional number of guilds given in *Jātakas* was eighteen (*Corporate Life in Ancient India*, pp. 3 ff.). This is also the number given in VyaPra p. 9. The number of guilds named in various *Jātakas* and inscriptions is far more than that, however (see the partial list given by Majumdar, *loc. cit.*, where 28 are named). For "groups" A refers to *bhāṭas* who were, according to Vedavyā 1.12 (p. 357 where they are called *bhaṭa*), a śūdra group who performed a certain (unspecified) task. They were a subgroup of *antyajas* according to the same text, verse 1.13. The word *bāhya* mentioned in this verse is also a designation for a low-caste group (see ĀDha 1.3.18 where it is said that Veda study is to cease for the day when a *bāhya* enters the village). The commentary of Haradatta Miśra on this Āpastamba text says that a *bāhya* is a person like an *ugra*, *niṣāda*, etc.

136. If anyone should come to be hated amongst his guild or other group, then he may not serve as a witness for them, because they all hate him.

NMS 2.133. J 1.156. A says a member of a guild, etc. might come to be hated for reporting to the king or for slander or assault. This verse is attributed to Kātyāyana at Prakā (Dhko 310).

137. The wise have also indicated in the texts five ways in which witnesses are disqualified: because of explicit rules to that effect, because of faults, because of contradiction, because of voluntary testimony, and because of intervening death.

NMS 2.134. J 1.157. These disqualified witnesses are discussed in the following verses.

138-139. Learned brāhmaṇas, etc. are disqualified because of explicit rules to that effect; thieves, etc. because of obvious faults; and when witnesses disagree in a dispute, they are disqualified because of contradiction; one who has not been summoned, but who comes and gives testimony of his own will is disqualified because his testimony is voluntary; disqualification because of intervening death occurs when a party to the dispute has died, except if he mentioned the witness when he was about to die.

NMS 2.135-136. J 1.157a-b. These verses are omitted in the recension on which A commented. The rules disqualifying brāhmaṇas are given in 1.140. VyaCi 281 and SmṛSā 101-102 explain the exception to the last disqualification in this way: when a man is about to die he may summon his son or other heir and say, "That one owes me so much money, and so-and-so knows all about it." In this case, the latter would be a qualified witness.

140. Learned brāhmaṇas, ascetics, the elderly, and men who have renounced the world—these are the ones who are disqualified as witnesses because there are explicit rules to that effect. No other reason is called for in these cases.

NMS 2.137. J 1.158. Bhava explains that a learned brāhmaṇa should not be called as a witness because of his attachment to study and recitation of the Veda. An ascetic may be dwelling in a forest or engaged in austerities. Bhava defines "elderly" as more than eighty years old. He further says that the reason for the disqualification of all of these men, which is not given here, is that they are constantly engaged in virtuous acts. For the legal disabilities of world renouncers, see Patrick Olivelle, "Renouncer and Renunciation...," pp. 146-147. PaMā 101 and VyaU folio 48a explicitly attribute this verse to Yājñavalkya.

141. Thieves, violent criminals, mercenaries, gamblers, and killers are disqualified as witnesses because they are evil; the truth is not found in them.

NMS 1.138. J 1.159. There is a gap in ms P which indicates that a portion of the text is missing. Unfortunately, we do not know what, if any, commentary is missing. Bhava says that a *caṇḍa* "mercenary" is someone who kills for money and does so at the behest of others. He explains *vadhaka* with the term *saunaka* "hunter, butcher." For the use of this verse in an actual *vyavasthā*, see J.D.M. Derrett, "An Original Vyavasthā in the Field of Vyavahāra: Scholars at Work about the Beginning of the Last Century," ALB 39 (1975), pp. 43-64; reprinted in *Essays*, vol. 2, pp. 277-298.

142. Where the king has admitted testimony of witnesses in order to decide a particular matter and their testimony is contradictory, the witnesses are disqualified because of that contradiction.

NMS 2.139. J 1.160. Bhava says that when witnesses are individually questioned on the same matter by the king and they contradict one another out of passion, hatred, or greed, and lie, then they are disqualified as witnesses. This verse is omitted in mss P and L2 (see note to 1.141).

143. One who has not been summoned as a witness but comes of his own free will and testifies is called an informer in the śāstras. He is not worthy to be a witness.

NMS 2.140. J 1.161. The word *sūcin* used to mean "informer" is unique to this verse (Bhava glosses it with *sūcaka*). VyaKa 114 and VyaMa 37 read *svayam* in place of *sūcīti*.

144. Since one cannot serve as a witness or give testimony on a viable claim when there is no claimant, such a witness is disqualified by intervening death.

NMS 2.141. J 1.162. See NāSmṛ 1.82-83. The commentary on this verse is incomplete, although this is not indicated in the mss. The suspected missing passages are marked by asterisks in the text.

145. If two parties are in dispute over a matter and both have witnesses, the plaintiff's witnesses should be heard first.

NMS 2.142. J 1.163. The lengthy commentary is partially if not completely the work of Kalyāṇa, as stated in its final sentence. The long example of a dispute over the ownership of cattle in which the rule of this verse is applied is not really germane and is clearly the work of Kalyāṇa. The example says that a plaintiff describes his missing cattle which he alleges to be in the possession of the respondent, and says that he has four witnesses who will support his claim. The respondent says that the description is so vague and general that it would apply to any cattle, and he, the respondent, can bring four witnesses of his own who will testify that the cattle are rightfully his. The commentator says that in this case the witnesses of the plaintiff prevail. What is not made clear in the commentaries of A or Bhava on this verse is that this rule applies to the question of the burden of proof. In general, the burden of proof falls on the party who claims something positive (such as "The cattle are stolen") and not on the party who claims something negative (such as "I did not loan him the money"). See DiTa pp. 21-22. The presumption of this verse and the next one is that the original claim is some positive assertion, which means that the burden of proof falls on the plaintiff. This understanding of the verse is made clear in the commentary on 1.146 and at VyaCi 181.8-186.1 and Candra 125.

146. If the case is such that the plaint is less powerful than the response, then the witnesses of the respondent should be questioned.

NMS 2.143. J 1.164. A indicates a situation in which the witnesses of the respondent are to be questioned. He gives the example of a plaintiff who claims that he loaned the respondent money but that the respondent has not repaid the money. The respondent replies that he did borrow the money, but that he also repaid it. In this case, the positive assertion—that the money was repaid—is the assertion which must be proved. Since this assertion is that of the respondent, his witnesses must be examined in the trial. The weakness of the plaint is that it asserts a negative point—"the money was not repaid." This example involves the reply known as *pratyavaskandana* (see Bṛhas 3.19 and the discussion of this concept at VyaCi 141.29-147.2).

147. One should not secretly approach a witness designated by an opponent, nor should one try to alienate him from the other party. One who does this loses his case.

NMS 2.144. J 1.165. A mentions other means of alienating a witness, such as threatening, abusing, bribing, etc. VyaKa 81 and VyaSau (Dhko 314) both attribute this verse to Nārada and to Kātyāyana.

148. If a designated witness should die or leave the area, the testimony of those who report what he told them is valid evidence, because a judicial inquiry by indirect means is valid.

NMS 2.145. J 1.166. The validity of indirect testimony has already been discussed in 1.130. A says that the indirect witnesses may come to know of the testimony of the witness from statements on his deathbed or just before he departs on a journey and that this testimony may be elicited by the plaintiff or volunteered by the witness. Bhava points out that indirect witnesses must be three or more so that dishonesty can be detected. This verse seems to have been ignored by all subsequent writers on dharma (see Dhko 299b).

149. A document retains its validity even after a very long time. If he is literate, he should write it himself; if not, he should have it written by someone else.

NMS 2.146. J 1.167. A says that the document is one in which a witness subscribes his name, identifying himself as a witness. If he cannot write or is not familiar with the conventions of writing documents, then he may have his name written by someone else.

150. The testimony of a witness who has been reminded remains valid for eight years, that of a casual witness for five years.

NMS 2.147. J 1.168. Ms P is defective. If there was any commentary on this verse it has been lost. Bhava states that these periods of validity are determined by the likelihood that the witnesses will remember what transpired, hence the shorter time for the casual witness who would not try as hard to remember.

151-153. The testimony of a secret witness lasts for three years. Indirect witnesses give valid evidence for up to one year. Alternatively, these restrictions of time concerning witnesses may be disregarded, since those persons who know the texts say that the validity of a witness depends on his memory. A man whose memory and hearing remain unafflicted may serve as a witness giving valid testimony even after a very long time.

NMS 2.148-150. J 1.169-171. Bhava notes that some witnesses may forget sooner than the time allowed for them to be valid witnesses, and some may remember longer than the time allowed; therefore one should allow memory to determine the status of a witness as valid evidence, and not just the limitation of time. A says the last two verses lift the restrictions of the first (*niyamapratiṣedha*). VyaMā 323 considers them to be exceptions (*apavāda*) to the first. According to Bhava, the word *ca* "and" in 1.153 indicates that all the senses are intended, not just hearing. These verses are explicitly attributed to Hārīta by SmṛCa 185, as well as by Prakā 52 and Samu 30 (see Dhko 343).

154. Six other types of disputes may be settled without witnesses. The wise say that mere indications constitute valid evidence for these.

NMS 2.151. J 1.172. Bhava says that the disputes spoken of here are disputes for which there may well be witnesses, but they are decided because of the circumstances of the case, and their resolution is based on those circumstances and not on what witnesses directly saw or heard.

155-156. A man who has a firebrand in his hand may be an arsonist. A man who has a weapon in his hand may be an assassin. A man

who is caught tête-à-tête may be an adulterer. A man who is caught near a dike with a spade in his hand may be a destroyer of dikes. A man who has an axe in his hand is obviously a forest cutter.

NMS 2.152-153. J 1.173-174. Bhava makes clear that these verses apply to those instances where a crime was recently committed. The kind of inference to be made is based on the fact that an arsonist is likely to be seen near the house which has been set afire. The assassin may be seen at the murder scene with a drawn sword, or a strung bow, or some other bloody weapon, or it may be noticed that he came upon the scene of the crime but did not sound the alarm. The destruction of a dike refers to the destruction of boundaries between irrigated fields. In rice-cultivating areas this practice has devastating consequences for crops and is still a common way of exacting revenge see M.N. Srinivas, *The Remembered Village,* Berkeley, 1976, pp. 122-129.

157-158. A man who has these outward signs may be the one who committed the crime. These are the cases that may be settled without witnesses, but in a case of assault there must be an investigation. Someone might, out of hatred, make marks on himself and assault another. That is why in this case the investigation is to be conducted according to the indications, motives, condition, and capability.

NMS 2.154-155. J 1.175-176. Bhava says that the outward signs are such things as torn clothes, bruised ears, etc., i.e., signs which indicate that a man has been in a fight. He further states that in these six cases it is not necessary to have statements from the plaintiff and the defendant, but in a case of assault, outward signs are not sufficient; there must be further investigation. According to Bhava, "indications" are stammering, sweating, dryness of mouth, and the like (see 1.175-178); "motives" are things like the degree of injury; "condition" is determined by factors such as the presence of swelling due to an injury and whether it is likely that the nature of the injury is self-inflicted; "capability" refers to whether or not the parties involved would be able to do what has been alleged in light of their respective strengths. The second verse is explicitly attributed to Hārīta by SaVi 160. PraKā attributes it to Prajāpati.

159-169. None of the following should be questioned: those who have an interest in the matter, friends, companions, enemies, notorious offenders, those afflicted with a disease, those who are contaminated, a slave, a vile person, one who is faithless or aged, a woman, a child, an oil presser, one who is drunk, insane, negligent, afflicted, a gambler, an indiscriminate sacrificer, one who travels long distances, a sailing merchant, an anchorite, a sick man, a greedy man, a learned brāhmaṇa, one who violates his dharma, a eunuch, an actor, a heretic, one who was not initiated, one who abandons his wife and homefires, one who offers illicit sacrifices, one who shares meals, a friend, an enemy, a spy, relatives, maternal relatives, a known criminal, a

dancer, one who sells poison, a snake catcher, a poisoner, an arsonist, a share-cropper, the son of a śūdra woman, a minor sinner, one who is depressed, rash, fatigued, impoverished, or of low caste, a heretic, a student who has not completed his studies, one who is stupid, a dealer in oils or roots, one possessed by spirits, one who is hated by the king, a weather forecaster, an astrologer, a wicked person, one who sells himself, one who is missing a limb, a pimp, one with bad nails, or dark teeth, or leprosy, one who betrays his friends, one who is totally selfish, a seller of liquor, a magician, one who is greedy or cruel, one who is quarreling with a guild or other group, a butcher, or a painter, or a beggar, an outcaste, a forger or a juggler, one who has given up mendicancy, a robber, a servant of the king, a brāhmaṇa who sells men, poison, weapons, water, salt, cakes, or herbs, a twice-born who is a usurer, one who has strayed from his own dharma, a headman, a bard, one who serves the lowly, one who has a dispute with his father, one who is divisive. All these are disqualified as witnesses.

NMS 2.156-166. J 1.177-187. After a digression on the subject of cases that do not require witnesses, the text returns to the general subject of witnesses. A says that these rules apply to all instances where witnesses are called, not just in cases of slander (*vākpāruṣya*, see 1.157). Verse 1.159 is nearly identical with Manu 8.64. Compare Manu 8.64-67 with NāSmṛ 1.159-172. A stipulates that the slave is one who was born in one's house. Bhava states that the vile person is one whose character is such that he constantly exploits others' weaknesses whereas A says it is a person who is deceitful. Bhava explains "one who is faithless" (*aśraddha*) as a person who does not have faith in the afterlife, gods, brāhmaṇas, dharma, etc. The reading of ms P is *aśrāddha*, which A explains as being someone unworthy of confidence. Bhava says that the *grāmayājaka*, the "indiscriminate sacrificer," is one who has no concern with which of the scriptural passages has a visible purpose and which does not. A explains this to mean the village priest (*grāmartvij*). See Manu 4.205 for another disparaging reference to the promiscuous sacrificer. Bhava explains the exclusion of sailing merchants: they must urinate and defecate in the water, which is strictly forbidden (see Manu 4.46-48). He says that a eunuch is excluded from being a witness because his present state is due to some previous misdeed. A holds that eunuchs are excluded because they are unable to have children, and thus, presumably, are unable to fulfill their debts to the gods, the *ṛṣis*, and the ancestors. According to Bhava, actors are not to be witnesses because they do not hold the truth in high esteem. A says that a heretic is one with false views. Whereas A interprets the compound *aricara* to mean an enemy and a spy, Bhava says that it means one who consorts with the enemy and hence is a friend of one's enemy. On the exact range of relatives included in the term *sanābhi*, see KāSmṛ 362. Bhava says that the term "śūdra woman" may also include a woman of the twice-born castes who has strayed. Thus we may assume that the offspring of any illegitimate union is excluded from serving as a witness. A holds that the earlier crimes of a "known criminal" include the evil deeds committed in previous lives. Bhava understands *varṣanakṣatra-sūcaka* as weather forecaster, but A says that the term means simply "astrologer." Bhava observes that these men are excluded from serving as a witnesses because they are unreliable. "One who sells himself" is a special and uncommonly lowly class of slave. Bhava points out that one who is missing a limb is, like the eunuch in 1.161, someone who is presumably being punished for a previous sin. The word for "pimp" (*bhagavṛtti*) is subject to two interpretations according to A. It may mean one who lives by the earnings of a woman, or one who commits fellatio. A gives two interpretations for *ugra* : (1) cruel, and (2) the son of a kṣatriya man and a śūdra woman. Bhava says that the sale of the things listed disqualifies a brāhmaṇa as a witness because selling them is explicitly forbidden to brāhmaṇas (see Manu 10.86-93). Usury is not forbidden to vaiśyas, but it is forbidden to a brāhmaṇa (see 1.58 and 1.98). A's explanation of "one who is divisive" is unclear. Bhava glosses the term with the word *piśuna* "backbiting." VyaPra 119 says that it is one who causes a rift between friends. This long list of disqualified witnesses is attributed to Prajāpati by Prakā and Samu (Dhko 343). Compare this list with the list of those who are excluded from the *śrāddha* (see Manu 3.151-166).

170. All those who have been described as disqualified witnesses, starting with slaves and vile persons, may nevertheless be witnesses when the case is sufficiently serious.

NMS 2.167. J 1.188. VyaCi 304 quotes the second half of this verse and attributes it to Kātyāyana.

171. In all cases of violence, theft, adultery, and both kinds of assault he should not investigate the qualifications of the witnesses.

NMS 2.168. J 1.189. A says that in these cases the mere fact that a witness has been mentioned in the plaint or reply means that his testimony must be heard. This verse is nearly identical with Manu 8.72, and VyaMā 327, VyaKa 117, VyaPra 120 explicitly attribute it to both Manu and Nārada.

172-174. Yet, even in these cases, no child, single person, woman, forger, relative, nor enemy qualifies as a witness since they may give false testimony. A child might prevaricate because of his ignorance, a woman because of her lack of veracity, a forger because of his tendency to lie, relatives out of affection, an enemy to take revenge. On the other hand, if both parties to a lawsuit agree, a single person, even though ordinarily disqualified, may be questioned in the court as a witness.

NMS 2.169-171. J 1.190-192. A points out that the reasons listed in 1.173 disqualify these persons from serving as witnesses even in serious cases. This verse is attributed to Kātyāyana by VyaTa 216 and Setu124-125 (Dhko 312). Concerning the single witness see Derrett's article, "An Original Vyavasthā ...," for the use of verses 172 and 174 in a *vyavasthā*.

175-178. If a witness betrays himself by his own faults, i.e., if he acts as if he were sick, if he shifts about and looks to this one and that one for assistance, if he coughs uncertainly and without reason, sighs repeatedly, scratches in the dirt with his feet, and tugs at his arms and clothes, if his face changes color, his forehead sweats, and his lips become dry, and if he stares upwards or to the side, if he speaks a great deal, hurriedly, without control, and without being questioned, he should be considered a false witness, and the king should punish him for that sin.

NMS 2.172-175. J 1.193-196. There is a break in the text of ms P just after *pāda* a of 1.175. Bhava explains that these verses list the indications by which one can identify false witnesses. The number of variant readings for 1.176 found in the digests is considerable. All of these variants are different ways to identify a false witness—laughing for no reason, whining, etc. (see Dhko 313a notes). Bhava says that the falsehood of a witness is worse than the falsehood of the respondent in a case because in the latter instance the party is lying for his own sake, or possibly out of ignorance, but in the case of a witness, he is lying for someone else, and with full knowledge; therefore he should be punished vigorously.

179. He who tells his testimony to others and later denies it should be punished more harshly than a false witness.

NMS 2.176. J 1.197.

180. After summoning together the witnesses who are of established character and familiar with the case he should place them firmly under oath and question them separately.

NMS 2.177. J 1.198. Bhava seems to say that there are two ways for the king to ensure that witnesses tell the truth. He may either order them to tell the truth, which he says is "firmly placing them under oath," or he may make them swear oaths on the gods, fire, gold, seeds, etc., the standard oaths, see DiTa pp. 51ff. VyaU 49a explicitly attributes this verse to Kātyāyana.

181. A brāhmaṇa should be required to swear by the truth. A kṣatriya should be required to swear by his weapons and vehicles. A vaiśya should be required to swear by his cattle, seeds, and gold. A śūdra should be required to swear by all sins.

NMS 2.178. J 1.199. This verse is identical with Manu 8.113. The various commentators explain the last provision in several ways: the śūdra should be threatened with the sins committed against cattle, seeds, gold, etc., or with the guilt of the theft of these things, or with the loss of these things. Bhava says that he should be threatened with the (consequences) of the five grave sins (killing a brāhmaṇa, drinking, theft, incest, and association with those who commit these crimes).

182. He should instill great fear in the witness by means of ancient dharma texts extolling the truth and reviling untruth.

NMS 2.179. J 1.200. Bhava cites Manu 8.81-82 as examples of such verses.

183-185. He who gives false testimony will go begging with a cup at the house of his enemy, naked, shorn, wretched, hungry, and thirsty. He who gives false testimony will often see his enemies while begging at the outer gate of the city which is prohibited to him. He who fails to speak the truth will spend his nights like a superseded wife, like one who has lost at dice, and like one whose limbs are oppressed by a heavy burden.

NMS 2.180-182. J 1.201-203. Bhava explains that the cup with which he begs is such that he cannot receive very much. Verse 1.183 is nearly identical with VaSmṛ 16.33 and Manu 8.93. Compare 1.184-185 with Bhā 5.35.24-25. On the superseded wife see Manu 9.46, 77-85, and 95 and Kau 3.2.41.

186-187. A witness who, like a cow's ear, flops back and forth in his testimony binds one thousand of Varuṇa's fetters on himself. After one hundred years one of his fetters is undone. Thus he is released from the entire bondage after one hundred thousand years.

NMS 2.183-184. J 1.204-206. Varuṇa is depicted iconographically as bearing a noose with which he entraps sinners. This characteristic is well attested in the Veda (RV 1.24.13; 1.25.2; 1.28.5; 5.85.8; 7.86.5). The Aitareya Brāhmaṇa 4.16.6 mentions the fetters of Varuṇa as the punishment for liars. See also Bhā 2.61.67-68 and Manu 8.82 (cited by Bhava in his commentary on 1.200), which states that one who gives false evidence is bound by Varuṇa's fetters for one hundred existences. The commentators Medhātithi and Kullūka say that these fetters are the "serpentine rope of dropsy." On Varuṇa as *dharmapati* see Terence P. Day, *The Conception of Punishment in Early Indian Literature*, pp. 30-32. The additions of ms P given in the footnotes to the text and printed by Jolly are unique:

> **After a man has been freed from the fetters he is born as a woman.** [J 1.205cd]
> **[If he speaks falsely] concerning livestock, cows, horses, humans, gold, or land respectively ...** [J 1.206cd]

188. Hear, gentle one, how many relatives are killed by one who speaks falsely in various matters respectively.

NMS 2.185. J 1.207. This verse is identical with Manu 8.97. The commentators on Manu give various explanations of what it means to "kill" in this case.

Medhātithi, Govindarāja, Kullūka, and Sarvajñanārāyaṇa agree that it means to cause them to fall into hell. Rāghavānanda says that it means causing them to fall from heaven and to be reborn as animals.

189. One who lies about livestock kills five; one who lies about cattle kills ten; one who lies about horses kills one hundred; one who lies about men kills one thousand.

NMS 2.186. J 1.208. Bhava explains that the numbers refer to generations before and after the witness. This verse is similar to Manu 8.98, BauDha 1.10.35cd and 36ab, and Bhā 5.35.26. The word *paśu* means simply "livestock," not as Jolly (following Bühler on Manu 8.97) has it, "(small) cattle." Bhava says that it means goats, sheep, donkeys, camels, etc. See the commentary of Sāyaṇa on AV 3.10.6 and 11.2.9 for a similar list of glosses for *paśu*.

190. One who speaks falsely about gold kills the born and the unborn. One who lies about land kills everything. Do not speak falsely about land.

NMS 2.187. J 1.209. This verse is identical with Manu 8.99 and Bhā 5.35.27. It is explicitly attributed to both Manu and Nārada by VyaKa 133. Medhātithi and Kullūka on Manu 8.99 stipulate that to "kill" here means to incur guilt equal to that he would incur for actually killing them. Rāmacandra says that to "kill" means to send to hell. "Everything" is explained in various ways by the commentators on Manu: Sarvajñanārāyaṇa and Rāghavānanda explain it as meaning more than 1000; Nandana and Kullūka take it to mean all animated beings.

191. They say Truth is the one thing which is unequaled; it purifies the soul. It is the stairway to heaven, the boat which carries one to the opposite bank of the river.

NMS 2.188. J 1.210. With this verse the text changes from warnings about the effects of false testimony to praising Truth. Some Manu mss include this verse (see V.N. Mandlik, *Mānavadharmaśāstra*, p. 924).

192. One thousand horse sacrifices and Truth have been weighed in the balance, and Truth has been found to be superior.

NMS 2.189. J 1.211. The horse sacrifice is a common penance for various crimes, usually murder (see Manu 11. 75 and 83). For a description of this elaborate sacrifice, see A.B. Keith, *The Religion and the Philosophy of the Veda and the Upanishads*, pp. 343-347, and Kane, HDh 2.1228-1239. One may get an idea of the superlative nature of this praise of Truth by noting that a single horse sacrifice is adequate penance for the worst of crimes—killing a brāhmaṇa (see TaiSaṃ 5.3.1-2). This verse is identical to ViSmṛ 8.36 and Bhā 12.156.26. VyaKa 126 and

VyaCi 337.1 attribute it to both Viṣṇu and Nārada. VyaMā 331 seems to attribute 1.193-197 to both Nārada and Viṣṇu, but the text as edited is unclear.

193. A reservoir is superior to one hundred wells. A sacrifice is superior to one hundred reservoirs. A son is superior to one hundred sacrifices. Truth is superior to one hundred sons.

NMS 2.190. J 1.212. Identical to Bhā 1.69.21.

194. It is through Truth that the earth supports everything; Truth makes the sun rise; through Truth the wind purifies; Truth makes the water flow.

NMS 2.191. J 1.213.

195. Thus it is revealed to us: "Truth alone is the supreme gift. Truth alone is the supreme austerity. Truth alone is the supreme dharma of everyone."

NMS 2.192. J 1.214.

196. The gods virtually are Truth. Mankind is untruth. He whose mind is fixed on Truth becomes divine even in this world.

NMS 2.193. J 1.215. Bhava says that the gods are the result of Truth and men are the result of falsehood. VyaKa 34 attributes this verse to Bṛhaspati, although at 133 the same text attributes it to Nārada. VyaNi attributes this verse to Bṛhas twice (at 8 and 10), as do VyaSau and Prakā (Dhko 98).

197-199. Abandon falsehood; speak the Truth. Truth will lead you to heaven. Speak untruth and you will hurtle to the most terrible hell. In hell the pitiless, powerful attendants of Yama will cut out your tongue and ceaselessly cut you with their swords. Unprovoked, they will pierce you with spears while you cry out helplessly; they will raise you up and throw you headlong into the pools of fire.

NMS 2.194-196. J 1.216-218. See Manu 8.94.

200. You will endure these terrible tortures of hell for a long time, and escape only to be reborn in the foul wombs of vultures, crows, and the like.

NMS 2.197. J 1.219. Bhava glosses *abhavyāsu* "foul" with *pāpāsu* "evil".

201. Learn the sins inherent in falsehood and the virtues in Truth, speak the Truth and save yourself. Do not condemn yourself.

NMS 2.198. J 1.220. VyaPra 128 and SaVi 159 attribute the first half of this verse to Vasiṣṭha

202-204. Neither relatives, nor friends, nor wealth, however great, have the power to rescue those who have plunged into the terrible darkness. Remember, the *pitṛs* rely on you when you undertake to be a witness: "Will he save us, or will he condemn himself?" Truth is the very soul of a man. On Truth everything depends. In every single instance, you will improve your circumstances.

NMS 2.199-201. J 1.221-223.

205. Everything between the night you were born and the night you die will become pointless if you distort the truth.

NMS 2.202. J 1.224. This verse is a troublesome one in each of the manuscript traditions. It apparently means that one's life is rendered futile by false testimony. Following this verse ms P adds:

> **Those worlds which are reserved for killers of brāhmaṇas, women, and children, and for ingrates are also for those who speak falsely.** [J 1.225]

This is omitted in every other ms at this point. X and B2, however, add it between 1.182 and 1.183. D adds it between 1.183 and 1.184. Y and NMS omit it altogether. It is very similar to Manu 8.89, and VyaCi 362 attributes a variant of this verse to both Manu and Nārada.

206. There is no greater righteousness than Truth and no greater sin than falsehood; therefore one should speak only the Truth, especially when serving as a witness.

NMS 2.203. J 1.226. Similar to Manu 8.82. VyaMā 331 seems to attribute this verse to Viṣṇu, but that text as edited is unclear.

207. If a scoundrel with no fear of hell casts aside his word for the benefit of someone else, what would that sinner not do for himself?

NMS 2.204. J 1.227.

208. All things depend on Speech, Speech is their root: they arise out of Speech. A man who perjures himself would steal anything.

NMS 2.205. J 1.228.

209-210. If the witnesses disagree, the majority rules. If there is no majority, the testimony of those who are virtuous should be accepted; if these are equal, the testimony of those who have the better memories. When the witnesses for each side have equally good memories, their testimony is excluded because the rules about witnesses are subtle.

NMS 2.206-207. J 1.229-230. These verses speak of the common situation in which the witnesses for one party disagree with the witnesses for the other party. In that case the judge must rely on the criteria of majority, reliability, and strength of memory. A says that some interpret these verses to pertain only to testimony about things that were not witnessed first-hand, while others have these provisions apply only to witnesses named in the plea. A holds that they apply to whatever witnesses there are for both sides. Bhava says that such cases may be settled either by other witnesses or by ordeals. In those cases where the witnesses for a party disagree among themselves, 1.142 and KāSmṛ 359 indicate that all the witnesses for that party are rendered incompetent by virtue of that disagreement.

D adds a verse which is not found in any other ms:

The wise ones do not wish to absolve, even by an ordeal, the plaintiff who has somehow been abandoned by his own witnesses through an act of fate.

[J 1.231]

211. When a witness appears in person to give testimony, but does not speak consistently with the written statement on the relevant matters, it is as if his testimony were not given.

NMS 2.208. J 1.232. The commentary of A is corrupt. The point of this verse is that the witness should not vary in his testimony from what was recorded earlier in the plaint. The nature of such variance may be seen in the following verses.

212. If witnesses disagree concerning place, time, age, material, amount, condition, or birth, that testimony is said to be untrue.

NMS 2.209. J 1.233. This verse is omitted in ms P, and it is possible that part of the commentary on 1.211 is a portion of the commentary on this verse.

213. When witnesses state either less or more than the amount, that, too, is considered inadmissible. This concludes the rules about witnesses.

NMS 2.210. J 1.234. A's commentary is corrupt. It seems to refer to some passage other than the verses immediately preceding. Bhava says that the witnesses in a case involving "ten" may testify that "seven" or "twelve" were involved. Since the amount, "ten," was recorded in the original plaint, this testimony of the witnesses is inadmissible. PaMā 114 explicitly attributes this verse to Bṛhas.

Immediately following this verse X and B2 add the following verse:
The witness who experiences illness, fire, or the death of a relative within seven days of his testimony is exposed. [Manu 8.108 and Dhko 323]

This verse is very similar to Manu 8.108 and is explicitly attributed to both Manu and Nārada by VyaKa 143, SmrSā folio 103, DaVi 347, and SmṛCi 124, while Apa on YāSmṛ 2.81, VyaCi 408, and VīMi on YāSmṛ 2.79 give it as a Nārada verse. It was probably a marginal notation which found its way into the text.

214-215. When a creditor, out of carelessness, has neither a document nor witnesses, and the plaintiff denies the matter, there are three ways to deal with it. A timely reminder, indirect proof, and thirdly an oath: by these means and in this order should the king reach a decision.

NMS 2.211-212. J 1.235-236. According to both A and Bhava, the timely reminders should be given in the presence of witnesses. "Indirect proof" is inferring the existence of a debt from the fact that something had been previously accepted by the debtor or previously agreed to. According to both A and Bhava, an oath means both oaths and ordeals (see DiTa 348.2-4). PaMā 91 seems to attribute this verse to Kātyāyana.

216. If a man is reminded repeatedly, three, four, five times, and does not refute the claim, he eventually has to pay.

NMS 2.213. J 1.237. The specific mention of "three, four, five times" may be a provision for the different treatment accorded vaiśyas, kṣatriyas, and brāhmaṇas respectively. This verse, too, appears to be attributed to Kātyāyana in PaMā 91.

217. But if he denies the reminders, then he should pursue the matter by means of indirect proof concerning the place, the time, the matter, the relationship, the amount, the act, etc.

NMS 2.214. J 1.238. A claims that the means of indirect proof enumerated here must be resorted to seriatim. This seems unlikely. This verse, as well as the preceding two, appears to be attributed to Kātyāyana in PaMā 91.

218. If even indirect proof is ineffective, he should press him by means of ordeals such as the fire, water, good deeds, etc., in accordance with the matter in question, the time, and his strength.

NMS 2.215. J 1.239. This verse refers to various types of ordeals and oaths which may be resorted to in the event that other methods fail. The ordeals and oaths are to be administered in accordance with the seriousness of the matter (see DiTa p.22 ff.), the time of the year (see DiTa p.19 ff.), and the strength of the person who must undergo the ordeal (see DiTa p.24 ff.). These factors will help to determine which oath or ordeal is to be administered in each case. The three verses quoted in A's commentary are unknown elsewhere (Kalyāṇa's work?). This verse also appears to be attributed to Kāṭyāyana at PaMā 91.

219. If the shining fire does not burn him, or water holds him under, then he escapes that grave accusation. If the reverse happens, then he must be considered a sinner.

NMS 2.216. J 1.240. After this verse the D family of mss inserts:

> **An ordeal is the mode of proof for a transaction in a forest, in a deserted place, at night, inside a house, or for violence, or denial of deposit.** [J 1.241]

This passage is not found in any other manuscripts, with the exception of P which gives it in a very different place (Jolly's Mā 2.30).

220. In accusations concerning the character of women, in cases of theft, violence, and all cases of denial this is the only way to proceed.

NMS 2.217. J 1.242. A says that ordeals are prescribed in these cases, but for an ordeal to be used in the case of a denial it must involve a serious charge (see my article, "A Note on the *kośadivya,*" ALB 40 (1976), 152-164; also DiTa pp. 7 and 24).

221-222. For oaths are said to be for the gods and the sages as well. Vasiṣṭha swore an oath when he was suspected of being an evil spirit. Similarly, when the seven sages assembled for the sake of Indra, they calmly swore an oath in order to clear one another in the matter of the lotuses.

NMS 2.218-219. J 1.243-244. The story of Vasiṣṭha is narrated by Medhātithi, Kullūka, and Sarvajñanārāyaṇa on Manu 8.110. Vasiṣṭha was accused by Viśvāmitra of having become a demon and of eating Viśvāmitra's one hundred sons. Vasiṣṭha swore an oath in front of Paijavana in order to prove his innocence. The episode of the lotuses is recounted at Bhā 13.94-96. This story is the subject of a study by Rosa Klein-Terrada, *Der Diebstahl der Lotusfasern*.

223-224. If one who has committed a transgression or a crime does not deny the accusation, or if he confesses in court of his own free will, then his punishment should be half of what is normal for that offense. But if, because of his wicked nature, he conceals the fault and is later defeated, in that case, the members of the court resent it and a severe punishment is handed down.

NMS 2.220-221. J 1.245-246. According to Bhava, the penalty applies to criminal and civil matters as well as to religious matters. Fines, punishments, and penances are to be required in only half the normal amounts if the offender confesses voluntarily. A says that a false denial will result in a punishment twice as severe if he is later found guilty. These last two verses serve to encourage confession in an effort to avoid lengthy trials.

CHAPTER 2

DEPOSITS

1. When one deposits his own property out of confidence, and without apprehension, this, according to the wise, is the title of law called Deposits.

NMS 3.1. J 2.1. A says that confidence in the person who accepts the deposit is crucial. If the depositor does not have confidence in him, he would not give him so much as a single cowrie shell without witnesses and documents attesting to the deposit, but if he has confidence in him, the depositor would give him a thousand gold coins without requiring a witness or document.

Jolly took the verses quoted in A's commentary to be Nārada's even though they are found in no ms other than P. This is all the more improbable since the second (M 8.180) is not quoted in full, but is cited by the *pratīka* only. The third verse (*na ced dadyāt*. ...) is unknown except for a lone citation in NṛPra 144, where it is not explicitly attributed to any author and where it follows M 8.180. These are most likely expansions of the commentary (by Kalyāṇa?):

> **A wise man should leave a deposit with one who is from a good family, who is virtuous, knows his duty, is honest, influential, and wealthy.**
>
> [M 8.179, J2.2]
>
> **A man should get back exactly what he handed over: it should come back just as it was given.** [M 8.180, J 2.3]
> **If someone refuses to give back what has legally been deposited with him, he should be apprehended, and once he has been convicted by means of ordeals, etc., he must be made to pay.** [J 2.4]

2. An *aupanidhika* deposit is something which is put in a container, without its contents disclosed, and put in another man's house.

NMS 3.2. J 2.5. A gives the examples of twenty *gadyāṇakas* wrapped in red cloth tied in a knot, and a pearl necklace wrapped in a cloth sealed with a knot. The contents of the cloth are not disclosed, and when the deposit is returned the knot/seal must be in the same condition. If it is not, the holder of the deposit is liable.

3. There are two kinds of deposit: with and without a witness. It must be returned under the same circumstances. If it is not, there must be an ordeal.

NMS 3.3. J 2.6. A deposit which was given over in the presence of witnesses must be returned in the presence of witnesses. If there were no witnesses at the time of the deposit, they are not necessary at the time of its return. If the deposit is returned under different circumstances, or if it has been lost and the holder denies responsibility, then he must undergo an ordeal or an oath.

4. If the holder of the deposit is asked by the depositor to return it and he does not, the king should punish him and make him give it. If the deposit is lost, he must pay its equivalent value.

NMS 3.4. J 2.7. A says that if the deposit has been asked for by the depositor, yet has not been returned, and in the mean time there has been some unavoidable calamity brought about by the king or by fate, then the loss is suffered by the one who has been holding the deposit, not the depositor. The depositary's normal exemption from liability in calamity (set forth in 2.6) ceases immediately upon the depositor's request for return of the deposit.

5. If the holder of the deposit makes a profit from it without the permission of the depositor, he must be punished and return the deposit plus a penalty.

NMS 3.5. J 2.8.

6. If the deposit is lost along with the property of the holder of the deposit, it is the depositor's loss. The same is true if the loss is caused by the king or fate. This is not so, however, if there has been some chicanery.

NMS 3.6. J 2. 9. Jolly took the Manu verses cited in the commentary to be Nārada verses, but they are not found in any ms other than P. M 8.186-187 (J 2.10-11) are attributed to Nārada in only one other place (at PaMā 287). However, M 8.186 is not found in the often more reliable BI edition of PaMā (Vyavahāra-kāṇḍa page 209). The BI edition explicitly attributes M 8.187 to Manu and not to Nārada. Manu 8.189 and 8.191 are nowhere attributed to Nārada. The translations of these verses are as follows:

> **One who voluntarily returns the deposit to the close relatives of a deceased depositor should not be charged by the king or by the depositor's relatives.**
>
> [Manu 8.186, J 2.10]
>
> **One should try to obtain the deposit tactfully rather than by deceit. He should take into consideration the character of the holder of the deposit and settle the matter by conciliation.**
> [Manu 8.187, J 2.11]

> **The depositary does not have to return a deposit that was stolen by thieves, lost in water, or burned by fire, unless he kept part of it.** [Manu 8.189, J 2.12]
> **One who does not return a deposit and one who demands the return of a deposit he did not make should both be punished as thieves and be made to pay an equivalent amount.** [Manu 8.191, J 2.13]

7. These same rules apply to deposits for particular purposes and to deposits entrusted to an intermediary, etc., as well as to a deposit with an artisan, a deposit for protection, and a mutual deposit.

NMS 3.7. J 2. 14. This verse lists the other types of deposit known to Nārada (six in all; see the commentary on 2.1). The first type has already been mentioned, the (1) *aupanidhika*, a deposit hidden inside another item (2.2). The (2) *yācita* is defined by A as what has been borrowed for a particular purpose. Bhava specifies that the *yācita* might be such things as clothes, jewels, etc. deposited for use during a wedding. He gives a slightly unusual definition of (3) *anvāhita*, which normally means the deposit of something with an intermediary who will then deliver it to the primary depositary. Here, however, A gives the example of a certain kind of bull which is deposited solely for a particular task. Since the task is one to which another animal is better suited, then that better-suited animal is the one which is passed on. Thus, if the task is bearing a burden, a *duryakavṛṣabha* bull is better suited, and that is the one that is delivered. Bhava gives the more usual explanation of a man from Mathurā who is in Kanyākubja where he owns property, and who asks someone else to deliver it to his house in Mathurā. The definition of (4) *nyāsa* and (5) *upanidhi* are corrupt in A's text. Bhava gives as an example of the deposit left with an artisan the giving of gold to a goldsmith on condition that it be returned after a certain period of time. The notion of mutual deposit, (6) *pratinyāsa*, is explained by A as giving something to one person who holds it for a given period of time, or for a specific purpose, and then hands it on to another person. Bhava says that it is a deposit in which one party claims, "I protected your property; now you protect mine." See Niranjan Roy, "Law of Pledges and Bailments," *Journal of the Department of Letters* (Calcutta University), 32 (1939), 1-120. One must exercise a certain amount of caution with regard to the textual citations in this article. See also Susan Oleksiw, " The Definition and Treatment of Nyāsa in Dharmaśāstra Literature," JAOS 102 (1982), 119-124.

8. The man who accepts a wealthy minor is subject to the same rules. All six deposits are subject to the same rules.

NMS 3.8. J 2.15. A enumerates the six types of deposits differently than in the preceding verse. He says that they are (1) *yācita*, (2) *anvāhita*, (3) *śilpahasta*, [(4) *nyāsa*, (5) *pratinyāsa* (presumably, both are omitted in ms P)], and (6) *pauganḍa*. This leaves out the *aupanidhika*. Bhava recognizes that there are other enumerations of the different types of deposits. Here, again, we have the explicit mention of Kalyāṇa in the commentary.

CHAPTER 3

PARTNERSHIP

1. When merchants and the like undertake a joint venture, that is referred to under the title of law called Partnership.

NMS 4.1. J 3.1. Bhava mentions others who are subject to the rules of partnership: priests, laborers, and farmers.

2. They undertake a joint venture to make a profit, and their contributions are the basis of this venture; thus it is on this basis that they share proportionately in the proceeds.

NMS 4.2. J 3.2. A gives an example of a venture which requires 1000 drammas: one partner contributes 500 drammas (50%), two partners each contribute 200 drammas (20%), and one contributes 100 drammas (10%). They each bear the profits and losses of the venture in these proportions.

3-4. The proportion of loss, expenditure, or profit which each partner should bear is directly related to his investment. The proportion contracted for strictly determines his responsibility with regard to merchandise, sustenance, expenditures, payments, freight, and looking after valuables.

NMS 4.3-4. J 3.3.

5. If any one partner is negligent, or does something which is prohibited, or without the consent of all the other partners, he must pay for the resulting loss.

NMS 4.5. J 3.5.

6. One who, through his own efforts, saves the property of the partnership from a predicament brought about by fate, robbers, or the king, is entitled to a share of one tenth.

NMS 4.6 J 3.6. Bhava says fate means such things as flood or fire, and the king's threat comes about when the king violates the normal rules of commerce. A states that the partner who protects the common property must receive his reward of one tenth if he did it alone, and at the risk of his life.

7. If one partner should meet with a calamity, his heir should take over his share. If there is no heir, then one of the others, or, if they are all able, all the other partners.

NMS 4.7. J 3.7. The nature of a partnership is clearly one in which the partners must be expected to contribute proportionately even after the initial investment. This means that whoever takes over for a partner who has died or is incapacitated must be able to do so. He must accept the responsibility (*adhikāra*) of the former partner. After the original partner's heirs, according to A, one of the remaining partners may take over the share, or all the partners may take over the share, but in every case the assumption of the share is contingent on a person's capacity to do so.

8. In the same way, when a priest meets with a calamity, another priest should complete the sacrifice and should take from him a proportion of the negotiated fee.

NMS 4.8. J 3.8. The term "another" here is to be understood to mean a priest who is suitably qualified for the task. The distribution of the *dakṣiṇā* is a complicated matter and the subject of provisions in the smṛti literature. The "negotiated fee" means the portion of the entire *dakṣiṇā* which is due to the priest for completion of his share of the ritual. The portion of this which the substitute priest gets is pro-rated against the amount of the original priest's task he performs. If he did all of the work for the original priest, then he gets the entire share of the original priest, but if he only did a portion of the original priest's work, then he is entitled only to an appropriate portion of the original priest's share (see the discussion at SmṛCa 436-439).

9. If a priest abandons a faultless sacrificer who has committed no offence, he should be punished, and so should a sacrificer who abandons a faultless priest.

NMS 4.9. J 3.9. A gives as examples of motives for abandoning a sacrificer in mid-sacrifice: anger, greed, etc.

10. There are three types of priests: one who is beloved by one's ancestors, one who is hired by the sacrificer, and one who does his priestly duties of his own free will out of affection.

NMS 4.10. J 3.10. A priest who is "beloved by one's ancestors" is a family retainer.

11. The rule above applies to hereditary priests and priests one chose oneself, but there is no fault in abandoning one who sacrifices of his own free will.

NMS 4.11. J 3.11. A sacrificer may choose to dismiss a priest who sacrifices for him voluntarily, and according to A the reasons are that the sacrificer may have found another priest who is better or who appeals to him more. As long as the sacrificer pays the appropriate portion of the fee to the dismissed voluntary sacrificer, he incurs no fault for the dismissal.

12. When a merchant comes to a toll booth, he must pay the appropriate tax; he should not avoid it: it is considered the king's tax.

NMS 4.12. J 3.12. See Kau 2.21 for the details of tolls and tariffs.

13. One should be fined eight times the amount he evaded if he avoids a toll booth, does not buy and sell at the appointed time, or lies about the amount.

NMS 4.13. J 3.13. Bhava says that lying about the amount means underestimating the value of the commodity. He adds that overestimating its value is not a crime, however, since the king still gets his due.

Jolly took the two verses given in the commentary to be Nārada's, but they are found in no ms other than P, and they are cited in no other source:

> **They say that a wise man should avoid taxing that portion of a learned brāhmaṇa's property which is used for his household, but not that which is used for business.** [J 3.14]
> **He should not tax the gifts received by brāhmaṇas, the property of stage actors, and what can be carried on one's back.** [J 3.15]

14-16. If a traveling merchant should come from another country and die, the king must protect his merchandise until his heirs appear. If there are no heirs, then he should send it to his family or relatives; if there are none, then he should hold it for a decade. Once the merchandise which has no owner and no heir has been held for ten years, the king may keep it for himself without being unrighteous.

NMS 4.14-16. J 3.16-18. Bhava adds that if the goods are such that they will not endure for that period of time, then the king should sell them and keep the money for ten years. Bhava says that if someone should come after the ten year holding period and make a claim for the merchandise, then the king has the option of giving it to him or not as he likes.

CHAPTER 4

RESUMPTION OF GIFTS

1. When one has improperly given something and then wishes to take it back again, that comes under the title of law called Resumption of Gifts.

NMS 5.1. J 4.1. Bhava says that "improperly" means that the gift was given to an unworthy recipient.

2. In legal proceedings gifts are considered to be of four kinds: what should and should not be given, and legitimate and illegitimate gifts.

NMS 5.2. J 4.2. The difference between illegitimate gifts (*adatta*) and what should not be given (*adeya*) is that the former are null and void, i.e., no gift ever took place, whereas *adeya* means that the gift took place but that it is voidable. Yet, under normal circumstances, neither *datta* nor *deya* gifts are voidable once the gift has been accepted.

3. There are eight kinds of things which should not be given, one kind of thing which may be given, seven kinds of legitimate gifts, and sixteen kinds of illegitimate gifts.

NMS 5.3. J 4.3.

4-5. The teachers say that the following should not be given away even by one who is suffering a very serious calamity: a deposit entrusted to an intermediary, a deposit for a particular purpose, a pledge, property held in common, a deposit, a son, a wife, all of one's property if there are heirs, and what has been promised to someone else.

NMS 5.4-5. J 4.4-5. Bhava explains the *anvāhita* deposit "a deposit entrusted to an intermediary" in the same manner as he did at 2.7 and "commonly held property" as the property of undivided brothers, etc. He states that if there are no heirs, there is no fault in giving away all one's property. Verses 4.4-5 list nine things which should not be given, not eight as announced in 4.3. Verse 4.5 is attributed to both Nārada and Bṛhaspati at SaVi 280.

6. He may give away whatever property is left over after he has provided for his family; if he gives away anything more, he is at fault.

NMS 5.6. J 4.6. Jolly took the verse quoted in the commentary to be a Nārada verse, but it is not germane, nor does it occur in any ms other than P:

> **One who has enough wealth to support the family for three years or more should drink *soma*.** [J 4.7]

7. Those who know about gifts say that the following are legitimate gifts: proceeds of commerce, wages, something given out of gratification or out of affection or gratitude, bride price, and a gift given for a favor.

NMS 5.7. J 4.8. Bhava says that a gift given in consideration for a favor may be something which benefits one in a future life.

8-10. An illegitimate gift is one which is given by someone out of fear, anger, sorrow, impulse, or infatuation, as a bribe, as a joke, through a switch or deceit; one which is given by a child or an idiot, one who is not independent, one who is distressed, one who is intoxicated or insane, or who wishes to get something in return thinking, "He will do such and such for me." So, too, is a gift illegitimate when it is given out of ignorance thinking that an unworthy recipient is worthy, or that it will be used for a worthy purpose and it turns out not to be the case.

NMS 5.8-10. J 4.9-11. A gives examples for these several illegitimate gifts. A gift out of fear is when a man is robbed in a forest under threat of death. A gift given out of anger is when a man suddenly returns to his house, finds that his wife has given a seat to a brāhmaṇa and, in a fit of anger at this situation, says to the brāhmaṇa, "Anything found in my house, whatever you see—chairs, beds, etc.—is yours." A gift given out of sorrow is when someone, afflicted with sorrow to the point that he wishes to die, says, "I am going to the forest right now; I am giving my house to brāhmaṇas." A gift out of impulse is when someone suddenly gives 100 *suvarṇas* to a brāhmaṇa. A gift meant to be a bribe is when a litigant says to a judge, "If you grant me a victory, I will give you a bribe of 100." As an example of a gift given through a switch or deceit, A relates the story of a man enamored of a prostitute named Cūtamañjarī (literally, "mango blossom"), who had been taken away by an influential man who lived a distance of thirty *yojanas* away (200-300 miles). Someone approached him with an offer to "show him" Cūtamañjarī in return for a reward. He immediately agreed. Thereupon he was shown a flower plucked from a mango tree. A gift given in distress is when a man is being swept away by a river torrent and says, "I am about to die! Save me and I will give you 100 *suvarṇas*." A gift given to an unworthy recipient is when a man gives a gift to a śūdra under the misapprehension that he is a brāhmaṇa because the śūdra was wearing a sacred thread. The last type of illegitimate gift is a gift intended for the worship of a deity which is eventually used for gambling, prostitutes, and other unrighteous deeds. SaVi 284 attributes the first half of 4.8 to Bharadvāja. ViVya folio 37 attributes 4.9-10 to Bṛhaspati.

11. One who, out of greed, accepts an illegitimate gift, and one who offers something that should not be given, should be punished as the recipient of an illegitimate gift and as the giver of what should not be given. NMS 5.11. J 4.12.

CHAPTER 5

BREACH OF CONTRACT FOR SERVICES

1. If someone who had agreed to render a service does not do so, that comes under the title of law called Breach of Contract for Service.

NMS 6.1. J 5.1. SaVi 289 attributes this verse to Bṛhaspati.

2. The wise have shown in the texts that there are five kinds of people who do service: four are laborers, and the fifth consists of the fifteen kinds of slaves.

NMS 6.2. J 5.2.

3. The laborers are: a student, an apprentice, a hired man, and an overseer. The slaves are those born in the house, and the like.

NMS 6.3. J 5.3. Bhava says that an an overseer is someone who is charged with looking after the family's business (see verse 22). The work of a student is described at 8-14, an apprentice's at 15-19, a hired man's at 20-21, an overseer's at 22, and the slaves' at 24-26.

4. The wise say that all of these have in common the fact that they are dependents, but their particular merit and livelihood are determined by caste and occupation.

NMS 6.4. J 5.4. Bhava explains their particular merit as their purity or impurity depending on the purity or impurity of their work, whereas A says that it is determined by their birth. Bhava explains their livelihood as meaning that they do such things as eat leftover food, or wear cast-off clothing, while A says that it depends on the type of work they do.

5. There are two types of work: pure and impure. Impure work is done by slaves. Pure work is done by laborers.

NMS 6.5. J 5.5. ViCa 144 attributes this verse to Bṛhaspati.

6-7. Cleaning the doorway, the bath area, the road, or the toilet, touching private parts, gathering or disposing of waste, urine, or feces, and, last of all, attending to the master's limbs when he so desires, this is what is known as impure work. Work other than this is pure.

NMS 6.6-7. J 5.6-7. Cleaning the doorway may refer to the service provided by certain lower castes of collecting refuse from in front of individual households. Each day the courtyard of a house is swept, and the sweepings are then simply deposited in the lane in front of the door (see William and Charlotte Wiser, *Behind Mud Walls*, Berkeley, 1971, p. 171). Bhava explains touching private parts as massaging or anointing. He explains tending to the master's limbs as shampooing, massaging the feet, etc. ViCa 144-145 attributes these verses to Bṛhaspati.

8. Until he has completed his studies, a pious student should be servile to his teacher and behave in the same way toward his teacher's wife and son.

NMS 6.8. J 5.8.

9-11. He should be abstinent, beg for food, sleep on the ground, be unadorned, and be the last to bed and the first to rise in his teacher's house. He should never approach the teacher or remain in his presence without permission. As long as he is able, he should, without question, do any work asked of him. He should study at the appropriate time, as long as his teacher is not averse to it, he should be attentive and take a seat or bench lower than his teacher's.

NMS 6.9-11, J 5.9-11. Bhava says that being unadorned means not wearing such things as garlands, carrying an umbrella, wearing sandals, etc. These verses are not cited by any subsequent writer on *dharmaśāstra*. For a discussion of the rules of conduct for a student, see Kane, HDh 2.305-312 and 3.483. Jolly attributes to Nārada a verse found in the commentary, yet it is unknown in any other place than ms P, and it is likely that it was a marginal notation which found its way into the text or was added by Kalyāṇa:

> **Knowledge is like a river which always flows to the lowest spot; therefore let one who seeks knowledge always behave humbly towards his teacher.** [J 5.12]

12-14. If he does not obey, the teacher may punish him; he may beat him with a rope or a split bamboo cane as long as he does not hurt him. He must not beat him harshly, nor on the head or chest; but after chastising him, he must encourage him; otherwise the king must punish the teacher. When the student has finished he should give an honorarium to his teacher and return to his own house. Thus the livelihood of the student has been declared.

NMS 6.12-14. J 5.13-15.

15. One who wishes to learn his own craft should, with the permission of his relatives, reside with a master for a well-defined period of time.

NMS 6.15. J 5.16. The permission of relatives and the definite period of time are required because the family loses the labor of the apprentice while he is living with his master. Such a loss must be carefully planned for and delimited. ViCi 64-65 and ViVya folio 38 attribute this verse to Bṛhaspati.

16. The master should instruct him and feed him from his own household; he should not make him do any other work, and he should treat him like a son.

NMS 6.16. J 5.17. The second half of this verse is found at ViVya folio 28 where it is attributed to Bṛhaspati.

17. If an apprentice abandons a righteous master who is instructing him, he may be forced to stay and is liable to be punished and confined.
NMS 6.17. J 5.18. The second half of this verse is found at ViVya folio 28 where it is attributed to Bṛhaspati.

The verses in the commentary are unknown from any other source. They interrupt A's commentary in mid-sentence, and must be a later insert.

18. Even if he has been fully instructed, the apprentice must stay for the entire duration, and the profit from the work he does during this time belongs to his master.

NMS 6.18. J 5.19. SaVi 290 and ViVya folio 38 attribute this verse to Bṛhaspati.

19. When the time comes, the apprentice who has learned his craft should pay every respect to his master, take his leave, and go home.

NMS 6.19. J 5.20. SaVi 290 attributes this verse to Hārīta. Jolly took the verse in the commentary to be Nārada's, but it is not found in any ms other than P, and is most likely an addition by Kalyāṇa:

> **"Or if he has fixed a salary, realizing the student's skill, the student may take it, but he must not live in someone else's house."** [J 5.21]

The commentary says that after the teacher has seen that the student has expertise in the knowledge (of the craft) and some salary has been mentioned, then the student may take it, but he may not live in the house of his master.

Here ms P ends, and thus the only surviving fragment of A's commentary.

20. There are three kinds of hired men: highest, middle, and lowest. Their wages depend on what they do, how well they do it, and their loyalty.

NMS 6.20. J 5.22. Bhava says that if a servant is capable, but not loyal, then he is paid little for his work. If he is loyal but not very able, he is paid according to what he does, but if he is both loyal and able, then he is paid a great deal.

21. This is the threefold division of hired men: soldiers are the highest, farmers are the middle, and bearers are the lowest.

NMS 6.21. J 5.23. Bhava explains that bearers are those who carry wood, water, fodder, or grain on a daily basis as the opportunity presents itself; in other words, they are not contract laborers, but hired as needed. ViVya folio 38 attributes this verse to Bṛhaspati.

22. One who has been charged with responsibilities pertaining to family matters is known as an overseer, and he is also called a *kauṭumbika*.

NMS 6.22. J 5.24. Bhava says that such a servant is in charge of the family's movable assets. SmṛCa 117 states that he is the overseer of fields, gold, etc. ViTā 631 seems to attribute this verse to Bṛhaspati.

23. The aforementioned four are called pure laborers; the rest—fifteen kinds of slaves—do menial work.

NMS 6.23. J 5.25.

24-26. One born into a household, one who was purchased, one who was acquired, one who was inherited, one who was supported in time of famine, one who was pledged by his master, one freed from a large debt, one who was obtained by battle, one who was won in a wager, one who came forward and said, "I am yours," one who gave up world renunciation, a bonded laborer, one who becomes a slave for maintenance, one who takes up with a female slave, and one who sells himself—these are the fifteen slaves mentioned in the texts.

NMS 6.24-26. J 5.26-28. The term *kṛta* is translated "bonded laborer" in accord with Bhava's explanation of this term: one who agrees to work for his "owner" for a fixed period of time. This is also the explanation given by other commentators (see, e.g., Mitā on YāSmṛ 2.182). Bhava says that a slave who was purchased is a slave purchased from a previous owner. ViCa 144 attributes 5.24 to Bṛhaspati.

27. Among these, the first four cannot be freed from slavery except by the grace of their owner; their slavery is hereditary.

NMS 6.27. J 5.29. The slave born into a household, one who has been purchased, one who was acquired, and one who was inherited must be slaves forever, unless their owner chooses to free them. Candra 47 attributes this verse to Vyāsa.

28. If any one of these rescues his master from a life-threatening situation, he should be freed from slavery and inherit like a son.

NMS 6.28. J 5.30. Bhava says that this provision for freedom applies to all fifteen kinds of slaves, not just to the four kinds mentioned in the preceding verse. This is also the view, for example, at SmṛCa 199, but there one who is a slave because he has has given up world renunciation is excluded (see 5.33). VyaU folio 102 attributes this verse to Manu.

29. One who was supported in time of famine is freed from that slavery by giving a pair of cows; labor alone cannot repay what is consumed in time of famine.

NMS 6.29. J 5.31. Bhava says that this gift should result in freedom even if the owner does not want to free the slave. The first half of this verse is cited at SaVi 293, where it is attributed to Kātyāyana.

30. A slave who was pledged as security for a loan is freed from slavery after his owner pays the money, but if the owner leaves him instead of paying the debt, it is as if he had been sold.

NMS 6.30. J 5.32. If the owner of the slave exceeds the time which he had fixed to pay his debt and free the slave, then it is as if the slave had been bought.

31. One who became a slave for a debt is freed from slavery after he has paid the debt plus the interest. The bonded laborer is freed after his time has been served.

NMS 6.31. J 5.33. The first half of this verse is attributed to Bṛhaspati at ViVya folio 39.

32. One who came forward and said, "I am yours," one obtained in war, and one won in a wager, each of these is freed if he produces another person to perform the same work.

NMS 6.32. J 5.34. This verse is attributed to Bṛhaspati at ViVya folio 39.

33. One who gives up world renunciation becomes a slave of the king: he can never be freed, nor can he be purified.

NMS 6.33. J 5.35. Bhava says that the king is the owner of what otherwise has no owner. See the note to 5.37.

34. One who became a slave in order to receive maintenance is freed when he ceases to receive that maintenance. One who became a slave for taking up with a female slave is freed by giving up that female slave.

NMS 6.34. J 5.36. The apparent difference between the slave who sought sustenance in time of famine (5.29) and the slave who sought sustenance in another time is that the support given to the slave in time of famine is more dear than that which is given in more plentiful times. Therefore the slave who sought support in time of famine must do more to gain release than simply give up the maintenance.

35. The wretch who gives up his freedom and sells himself is the lowest of them all; he is never to be freed from slavery.

NMS 6.35. J 5.37. Bhava says that the one who sells himself is the most evil of all the fifteen kinds of slaves.

36. Those who were abducted by robbers and then sold, or who were enslaved by force, must be freed by the king. The fact that they were made slaves is unacceptable.

NMS 6.36. J 5.38. Bhava states that the status of being a slave was imposed on these through no fault of their own, and therefore the king must release them. He further explains that the ones who were enslaved by force were the victims of those who were dear to them.

37. Slavery in the inverse order of the castes is not allowed, except for one who has abandoned his specific duties; slavery is considered to be like wifehood.

NMS 6.37. J 5.39. This verse means that a brāhmaṇa can have a member of any of the three lower castes as a slave, a kṣatriya can have a member of the two castes lower than himself as a slave, etc., but a kṣatriya cannot have a brāhmaṇa for a slave, for example, since this would be the inverse order of castes. Bhava stresses that even members of higher castes can become slaves of members of higher castes, if they abandon the duties of their respective castes. They can then be forced to perform duties on request, like a wife. For a discussion of this verse and the debate on the question of whether a brāhmaṇa who gave up being a world renouncer could be made a slave, see Patrick Olivelle, "Renouncer and Renunciation in the Dharmaśāstras."

38. If one who is already a slave offers himself, saying, "I am yours," he should not be accepted; the original owner would be able to take him back whenever he likes.

NMS 6.38. J 5.40. Bhava says that the previous mention of the slave who offers himself in this way (5.25) referred to a person who was independent. SaVi 294 attributes this verse to Kātyāyana.

39. Three persons are said to have no property: a wife, a slave, and a son. Whatever they get belongs to the one to whom they belong.

NMS 6.39. J 5.41. Presumably this stricture would not include *strīdhana*, the property of the wife given to her at the time of her wedding by her family, and throughout her marriage by her husband out of affection. This protected property usually excluded immovables (see HDh 3.770-802). Compare this verse with Manu 8.416 and Śabara on Mīmāṃsāsūtra 6.1.12-13.

40-41. When one is favorably disposed, and wishes to free his slave, he should take a jar of water from the shoulder of the slave and break it. He should anoint his forehead with unhusked grain and flowers, say three times, "You are not a slave," turn him to the east, and let him go.

NMS 6.40-41. J 5.42-43. This act of taking the pot filled with water and breaking it seems to be a symbolic ending of the labor of the slave. Bhava says that the following is to be stated (by the owner) when both of them are holding the pot: "I am going to do myself what you had to do. I no longer have use for your work."

42. From this time forth his status is reaffirmed by the treatment of his former owner, food and gifts may be accepted from him; he has become a respectable person.

NMS 6.42. J omits. The act of emancipation grants a man access to normal social and ritual intercourse just like other independent members of society. SaVi 295 attributes this verse to Bṛhaspati.

CHAPTER 6

NON-PAYMENT OF WAGES

1. There is a series of rules about payment and non-payment of wages for hired men. This title of law is called Non-payment of Wages.

NMS 7.1. J 6.1.

2. The employer should regularly pay the wages to the hired man as agreed: in advance of the work, during the work, or at the end.

NMS 7.2. J 6.2. Bhava says that the time of payment is agreed upon between employer and employee. ViRa 156 states that both the time and the rate may be settled in such an agreement: one-fourth in advance, one-third when the job is half done, and the rest when the job is done.

3. Unless there has been a special agreement with the hired man, a merchant, herdsman, or farm worker should receive one-tenth of the profit, cows, or produce respectively.

NMS 7.3. J 6.3. SaVi 298 attributes this verse to Kātyāyana.

4. When they take up an implement for a task, they should use it responsibly and without dishonesty.

NMS 7.4. J 6.4. Bhava makes it clear that the *upakaraṇa* here is an implement owned by the employer and appropriate for the task at hand—a scale, a rope, or a plow. If the employee uses these implements dishonestly, he is to be punished with the loss of his wages.

5. If someone has promised to do a job but does not, he should be paid and then forced to do it. If he takes the pay and does not do the job, then he must give back twice the amount of his pay.

NMS 7.5. J 6.5. Bhava says that the employer may force the employee to do the job he had promised by such means as forcibly detaining him. He also states that the amount which the employee must pay—twice his pay—is a refund of the amount he was paid, plus an equal amount as a fine.

6. If he abandons the job before the agreed time has expired, then he is liable to lose his pay. If it is the employer's fault that he left, then he should be paid for as much work as he has done.

NMS 7.7. J omits.

7. When a cart is loaded and ready to go and the one who has hired it dismisses it on the road, he must pay one-sixth of the wages he had promised. One who does not pay after he has had a job done should be made to pay the wages plus interest.

NMS 7.8. J 6.6. Bhava explains that this verse refers to the hiring of a conveyance. According to the first half the owner must pay one-sixth of the promised wages if he changes his mind after the vehicle is loaded.

8. A merchant who reserves a conveyance must pay one fourth of the wages if he does not use it and all the wages if he abandons it once it is halfway to its destination.

NMS 7.6. J 6.7.

9. A carrier who does not do his job forfeits his wages. If he becomes obstinate at the start, he must pay twice his wages.

NMS 7.9 J 6.8. The second half of this verse is intended to protect a merchant from the possibility of a carrier loading the shipment and then attempting to bargain for a higher price. Bhava says that the carrier would have to pay twice his wages if he has accepted payment in advance and then refuses to do what he had contracted to do.

10. If goods are lost and it is the carrier's fault, he must pay for what was lost, unless it was due to circumstances beyond his control.

NMS 7.10. J 6.9. The phrase "circumstances beyond his control" translates the compound *daivarājakṛta*, literally, something done by a divine force or by the king. Bhava says that the negligence or irresponsibility of the carrier makes him liable for payment for lost goods, but if a fateful occurrence such as a fire causes the loss then he is not liable.

11. In addition to all the milk once a week, the wages for tending one hundred cows for one year is a yearling cow; for tending two hundred cows, a milch cow.

NMS 7.11. J 6.10. Instead of "in addition to" Bhava reads "or all the milk from the cows once a week."

12. The owner should deliver the cows to the cowherd every morning. He must bring them back in the evening after they have grazed and drunk.

NMS 7.12. J 6.11. SmṛCa 207 says that this applies to those who are charged with the protection of all domestic animals (*paśu;* see 6.16 and 6.19).

13. If danger should befall the cows the cowherd should deal with it to the best of his ability. If there is nothing he can do, he must promptly run and tell the owner.

NMS 7.13. J 6.12. Bhava lists some of the dangers to cattle: wolves, injury due to rough ground or in a water crossing, insects, etc. (see, however, 6.15). The cowherd should minister to the injured animals with medicines, etc. as best he can, and then if he is unable to save them he must quickly inform the owner. If he does this, he is not at fault.

14. If he does not struggle, or if he raises an inadequate cry, and does not inform the owner, the cowherd is liable for the cow and for a fine to the king.

NMS 7.14. J 6.13.

15. If there is any loss due to insects, or if dogs kill it, or if it dies on rough ground, or from any other preventable cause, then the loss falls to the cowherd alone.

NMS 7.15. J 6.14. The phrase "any other preventable cause," literally, "by the agency of man" (*puruṣakāreṇa*) is the opposite of "circumstances beyond his control" in 6.10. This verse is identical with Manu 8.232. VyaKa 416, ViRa 173, and Setu (Dhko 917) attribute it to both Manu and Nārada.

Recension N adds a verse which is similar to Manu 8.234. This is not found in any of the other recensions; compare 6.19. It means:

> **If animals die, he must give to their owner the tails, the entire hide, the female organs, the innards, the sinew, and the bile, and point out the brands.**

16. If sheep or goats are stalked by wolves and the herdsman does not rescue them, he is liable for whatever the wolves carry off and kill.

NMS 7.16. J 6.15. VyaKa 416, ViRa 173, and Setu (Dhko 917) attribute this verse to both Manu and Nārada.

17. If the animals are in herds freely grazing in the forest and a wolf attacks them and kills one of them, the herdsman is not culpable.

NMS 7.17. J omits. This verse is nearly identical with Manu 8.236.

18. If an animal is stolen by thieves, the herdsman is not culpable as long as he raises an alarm and informs his master when and where the incident happened.

NMS 7.18. J 6.16. Bhava says that the herdsman may also report to an agent of the owner. This verse is nearly identical with Manu 8.233. VyaKa 415, ViRa 172, ViCi 81, VīMi on YāSmṛ 2.165, and Setu (cited in Dhko 916) all attribute it to both Manu and Nārada.

19. This is how disputes concerning all herdsmen are settled. If animals die, the herdsman should be cleared if he shows the brands, etc.

NMS 7.19. J 6.17. The second half of this verse refers to the admonition that the cowherd should bring the horns, hooves, etc. to prove to the owner that an animal has died (see Manu 8.234). Presumably, this evidence would insure that the animal had not been sold or stolen by the cowherd and then reported dead. A brand is needed so that the owner would be certain that it was the hide, horn, etc. of his own animal that was being shown to him (see the note to 6.15). VyaPra and VyaU cite only the second half of this verse, and attribute it to Vyāsa.

20. If a prostitute takes her fee and then does not assent, she must repay twice that amount. The same goes for a man who does not pay the fee after he has been with her.

NMS 7.20. J 6.18.

21. If a man approaches a prostitute unnaturally or arranges for her to be taken by several men, he should be made to pay her eight times her fee plus that much as a fine.

NMS 7.21. J 6.19. Bhava says that if a man pays a prostitute and she does not assent to his taking her in an unnatural way (literally, in a place other than the vagina), he must pay her eight times her price and in addition he must pay a fine of an equal amount to the king. According to Bhava the reason for the first penalty is that these acts were not agreed to, and the reason for the penalty to the king is that these acts are prohibited. ViCi 77, Setu (Dhko 851), and ViVya folio 42 attribute this verse to the Matsyapurāṇa. ViTā 654 seems to attribute at least the second half to Bṛhaspati.

22. If someone builds a house on another person's land and pays him rent while living there, he may, when he leaves, take the thatch, wood, and bricks along.

NMS 7.22. J 6.20. SaVi 301 attributes this verse to Hārīta. Jolly accepts as Nārada's a verse which follows in recension D only:

> **He who lives on someone else's land without paying rent and without permission may never take the grass and timber when he leaves.** [J 6.21]

23. Rented merchandise must be returned when the rental period is completed. The renter is responsible if there is any damage or loss, unless it was due to an accident.

NMS 7.23. J 6.22.

CHAPTER 7

SALE WITHOUT OWNERSHIP

1. When someone secretly sells a deposit or property another person lost, and he either received it or took it away, this is known as Sale without Ownership.

NMS 8.1. J 7.1.

2. If the owner identifies property of his that was sold by someone else, he may resume possession of it. If the purchase was made openly, the buyer is innocent; if it was done in secret, he is a thief.

NMS 8.2. J 7.2. Bhava says that if a man discovers that his cattle have been sold in this way and he proves his ownership, then he may recover them. If such a sale was conducted in full view of the elders of the community, no guilt attaches to the buyer; all he loses is the purchase price. PaMā 292-293 attributes this verse to Manu.

3. If a man buys from a slave who does not have his owner's permission to sell, or in secret from a cheat for less than the item is worth, or when the time is wrong, he shares in the guilt.

NMS 8.3. J 7.3. Bhava says that the guilt spoken of here is that of thievery, and both the buyer and the seller share in it.

4. The buyer must not conceal his title; his innocence depends on that title. If he does not have a title, he is as guilty as the seller and deserves to be punished like a thief.

NMS 8.4. J 7.4. Recension N adds a verse which is similar to Manu 8.199:

> **Thus, a gift or even a sale which is not made by the owner is considered invalid in legal proceedings. This is the rule.**
> [Dhko 762]

This verse is often attributed to Nārada in later *nibandhas*, but it is also attributed to Yama at VyaPra 291.

5. The rule in a case of sale without ownership is the following: the seller should return the property to the owner, return the purchase price to the buyer, and pay a fine to the king.

NMS 8.5. J 7.5.

6. If a man finds a treasure that was buried by another, he should take it to the king; all treasure trove goes to the king, except in the case of brāhmaṇas.

NMS 8.6. J 7.6. Bhava says that the king is the owner of everything which has no other owner. Whatever a brāhmaṇa finds is his to keep, but others get only whatever the king might give them from the treasure trove.

7. Even a brāhmaṇa who finds treasure should immediately inform the king; he may have it after the king gives it to him. If he does not inform the king, he is a thief.

NMS 8.7. J 7.7. This verse allows the king to reap the spiritual merit of giving a gift to a brāhmaṇa.

8. One should inform the king even about finding one's own lost property. Then he may keep it legitimately; otherwise it would be illegal.

NMS 8.8. J 7.8.

CHAPTER 8

NON-DELIVERY OF WHAT HAS BEEN SOLD

1. When something has been sold, but not delivered to the purchaser, that comes under the title of law called Non-delivery of What Has Been Sold.

NMS 9.1. J 8.1.

2. In this world there are two kinds of things: movable and immovable. Under the rules for purchase and sale, both of these are called commodities.

NMS 9.2. J 8.2. Bhava says that movables are such things as elephants, horses, and men; while immovables are such things as fields, gold, and houses. All are salable.

3. According to the wise, there are six types of commodity transactions: by number, weight, measure, labor, beauty, or splendor.

NMS 9.3. J 8.3. Bhava gives examples for these six categories: by number: cows, horses, and garments; by weight: molasses, cotton, resin, sandal, and saffron; by measure: rice, etc.; by labor: the decorative products of particular crafts; by beauty: garments, female slaves, swords, etc.; by splendor: jewels, etc. For another reference to this rule see 18.23 and Bhava's commentary on NMS 19.84-85.

4. One who sells something for a certain price and fails to deliver it to the purchaser must be made to compensate him for any loss pertaining to immovables and for the lost profits from movables.

NMS 9.4. J 8.4. Bhava explains this verse in the following way. When a seller does not deliver what he has sold, he must compensate for whatever loss the purchaser sustains as a result of the item being used (wear and tear) during the period of non-delivery. Even if the item is not used, there is loss to the purchaser since he could not use it during the period of non-delivery. He must be compensated for that as well. In the case of movables, the profit obtained by the seller from their use in the interim must be paid to the purchaser as well. This means that there is a sort of dual penalty for non-delivery: the purchaser must be compensated for any depreciation his property might suffer during the period of non-delivery, but he must also receive compensation for not being able to benefit from the actual possession of it. The means of determining the amounts in these cases is not specified. Presumably this would be one of the matters taken up by the court in such a dispute. There is mention elsewhere of experts who determine amounts of compensation in financial disputes (see Kau 3.13.35). The general rule here is that in the case of non-delivery the seller is liable for any and all losses.

5. If there should be a loss in value, the seller should deliver the commodity and make up the difference. This rule applies to local transactions. In the case of foreign transactions, he must deliver the commodity plus the profit that would have been made abroad.

NMS 9.5. J 8.5. Bhava gives the example of five a *palas'* weight of saffron which was sold for one *dīnāra*. The cost of saffron dropped by half between the time of the sale and the delivery; hence the seller had to give the original five *palas* of saffron plus the increase, namely five more *palas* of saffron. The rules set forth in this and the previous verse would effectively eliminate any profits to the seller from a delay in the delivery of commodities and place the burden of loss from delay in delivery of commodities on the seller. In the case of those who travel abroad Bhava gives the following example: a man buys saffron in Kashmir at the price of ten *palas* for one *dīnāra;* if the purchaser can expect to sell it elsewhere for twice that price, and if the seller does not deliver it, then he must compensate the purchaser for the profits he would have made as well as for the cost of the original transaction.

6. If the commodity which has been sold is damaged, burned, or stolen, the loss is the seller's alone, because he did not deliver it after the sale.

NMS 9.6. J 8.6.

7. If the seller has shown a faultless item and then delivered a flawed one, he must pay the purchaser twice the price and the same amount as a fine.

NMS 9.7. J 8.7.

8. If a man sells something to one person and delivers it to another, then he, too, must be made to pay twice the price and the same amount as a fine.

NMS 9.8. J 8.8.

9. If the purchaser buys something but does not accept delivery of it, then the seller commits no wrong by selling it to someone else.

NMS 9.9. J 8.9.

10. This is the law for a commodity which has been paid for. If it is has not been delivered due to some other agreement, the seller does not violate these laws.

NMS 9.10. J 8.10. This rule means that 8.4-9 apply to circumstances in which a purchaser is entitled to and desires immediate possession of what he has purchased. If he has agreed with the seller to take delivery at a later date, then the remedies for loss set forth in these verses are not available to him.

11-12. Merchants deal in all commodities in order to make a profit, but their profit varies depending on the price. Therefore a merchant should vigorously fix the price at the proper time and place, and he should not be dishonest. This brings honor to the merchant's trade.

NMS 9.11-12. J 8.11-12. SaVi 312 attributes these verses to Vyāsa, and Samu (Dhko 888) to Bṛhaspati.

CHAPTER 9

RENEGING ON A PURCHASE

1. When one has purchased something and then does not want it, that comes under the title of law called Reneging on a Purchase.

NMS 10.1. J 9.1. Bhava says that the purchaser may be concerned that the purchase was not proper and so may renege on it.

2. When someone has purchased something and paid for it, and then decides that it was wrong to have done so, he may return it, undamaged, to the seller on the same day.

NMS 10.2. J 9.2. Bhava seems to comment on the word *avikṛtam* "unchanged" instead of the word *avikṣatam* which is found in all manuscripts.

3. If the purchaser returns it on the second day he must pay one-thirtieth of the purchase price, on the third day twice that; after that he can no longer return it.

NMS 10.3. J 9.3. SaVi 317 attributes this verse to Kātyāyana.

4. The purchaser should personally examine the commodity for quality and defects before purchasing it. Once he has examined and approved the thing he has purchased, it may not be returned to the seller.

NMS 10.4. J 9.4. The examination has to take place before the purchase. Bhava further states that the seller is not obliged to take it back even on the first day under these circumstances.

5-6. The trial period for milch cows is three days; five days for beasts of burden; one week for pearls, diamonds, and coral; two weeks for men; one month for women; ten days for all types of grain; and for metals and garments, one day.

NMS 10.5-6. J 9.5-6. Bhava notes that one can come to know the character of a man in a period of two weeks, and hidden traits will come out in a woman within one month. SaVi 316 attributes these verses to Kātyāyana, PaMā 361 seems to attribute them to Vyāsa, and ViCi 90 and Setu (Dhko 894) explicitly attribute them to both Vyāsa and Nārada.

7. A garment which is used, ragged, or dirty cannot be returned to the seller even if it was in that condition when it was purchased.

NMS 10.7. J 9.7. Bhava says that "used" means more than just used; it means worn out, and "dirty" means having holes in it, etc. SaVi 316 attributes this verse to Kātyāyana.

8-9. A garment loses one-eighth of its value when it is washed once; one-fourth when washed twice; three-eighths when washed three times; and half when washed four times. After it has lost half its value, each time it is washed it loses one-fourth of its current value until it is in tatters and worn out. When a garment is worn out, there is no rule about loss of value.

NMS 10.8-9. J 9.8-9. Each of the first four washings reduces the original value by one-eighth. Bhava explains that each washing reduces the value of the garment by one-eighth of its original value. Thus, after eight washings it is worthless. This is slightly different from what the text says: on the fifth washing a garment loses one-eighth of its original value, i.e., one quarter of its current value which had been reduced to half of its original value by the previous four washings. The next washing reduces it by another one quarter of its current value to 3/32 of its original value.

10-12. All metals must be forged. They incur a loss due to the contact with fire while they are being worked. Gold loses nothing; silver loses 2% tin and lead lose 8%. Copper and things made of it lose 5%. There is no specific rule for iron because it is composed of different elements.

NMS 10.10-12. J 9.10-12.

13-15. When cloth is prepared there is either loss or gain. For spun cotton and wool cloth there is a gain of 10% if the thread is coarse, of 5% if it is medium, of 3% if it is fine. Now for cases of loss. For fabrics containing hair or embroidery, there is a loss of one-thirtieth. There is neither gain nor loss for fabrics made of silk or bark.

NMS 10.13-15. J 9.13-15. Bhava says that the increase is an increase in weight. He explains "embroidery" (*karmakṛta*) as special features produced by artisans and understands it as an adjective modifying "fabrics made of silk or bark." This is quite forced. It is clear from the commentaries and the variant readings that this technical passage on cloth was an unfamiliar subject.

16. A merchant who is familiar with the commodities in which he trades should not renege on a purchase. He should know their potential gain and loss and their provenance as well.

NMS 10.16. J 9.16. Concerning the matter of provenance, Bhava seems to allude to a sort of connoisseurship which a merchant should have for his material. According to him there are particular traits due to the place of origin even for items that do not have obvious distinguishing features. He further states that there is profit in following all these instructions, yet punishment if they are not followed. Samu (Dhko 895) attributes this verse to Kaśyapa. SaVi 316 cites the second half and attributes it to Hārīta.

CHAPTER 10

NON-OBSERVANCE OF CONVENTIONS

1. The rules that govern heretics, corporate bodies, and the like are called their conventions; the Non-observance of Conventions is a title of law.

NMS 11.1. J 10.1.

2. The king must protect the conventions of heretics, corporate bodies, guilds, councils, troops, groups, and the like in towns and in the countryside.

NMS 11.2. J 10.2. Bhava glosses "heretics" with the terms for Buddhists (*śākya*) and naked ones (*nagna*). He explains "corporate bodies" (*naigama*) as merchants, yet mentions that others say that it means the citizenry. He explains the other terms as follows: guilds (*śreṇi*) are weavers, gardeners, etc.; councils (*pūga*) are various associations of elephant keepers, innkeepers, herdsmen, and wrestlers; troops (*vrāta*) are groups of soldiers.

3. Whatever their laws, duties, rules for worship, or mode of livelihood are, he must permit them.

NMS 11.3. J 10.3.

4. He must prohibit them from doing anything that is inimical to the king, offensive to his subjects, or an impediment to his purposes.

NMS 11.4. J 10.4. This is an exception to the previous verses. Bhava gives examples: for something inimical to the king, bringing something from another country against the king's wishes; for something offensive to his subjects, exalting a low individual such as one who deals in oils; and something which is an impediment to his purposes a huge, costly festival.

5. If they secretly form confederacies, carry arms in a hostile manner, or fight amongst one another, the king must not tolerate it.

NMS 11.5. J 10.5.

6. Those who sow disharmony among groups should be severely punished, because if such persons are ignored they spread an epidemic of fear and terror.

NMS 11.6. J 10.6. Bhava says that to be severely punished means to undergo physical punishment. According to him, the way disharmony is sown among groups, is by such means as speaking against the king and at the same time praising his enemy.

7. If an act which is not prescribed in the scriptures has been committed, a king who desires the ultimate good should nullify it.

NMS 11.7. J 10.7. Bhava adds that if an act which is prescribed in the scriptures, such as the expenditure of money for sacrifices, temples, and the like, has been done incorrectly, then the king should not nullify it. The ninth-century commentator Viśvarūpa (on YāSmṛ 2.190) confirms that this verse is Nārada's concluding summation of the law on this subject.

CHAPTER 11

LAND DISPUTES

1. If determinations have to be made about dikes, paddies, boundaries, tilling or non-tilling, all of which pertain to land, that is a Land Dispute.

NMS 12.1. J 11.1. The usual title for this section is *sīmāvivāda* "Boundary Disputes." According to Bhava, dikes are levies that retain the water which has been channeled to the crops; paddies are where the crops grow; boundaries divide villages, etc.; a tilled field is one where agriculture takes place, and a non-tilled field is fallow land.

2. In conflicts over land boundaries the determination is made on the evidence of neighbors who are also the elders of the city, village, or group.

NMS 12.2. J 11.2. Bhava says that the dispute is to be settled by those who are important in the city or town, who have the authority, and who are senior by their pre-eminence.

3-5. In the case of the village boundaries, those who make their living by farming outside it, cowherds, bird catchers, hunters and others who inhabit the forest should delineate the boundary which is marked by such things as pots—of chaff, charcoal, or crockery—shrines, trees, and by familiar markers such as ant hills, mounds, depressions, elevations, etc., and paddies, groves, roads, or old dikes.

NMS 12.3-5. J 11.3-5. Bhava says that the materials—grain, charcoal, crockery—are to be placed in pots and the pots are placed in various spots, and it is by knowing where these landmarks are that the senior members of a group can determine the boundaries.

6. In the case of fields whose markers have been carried off by rivers, removed, or lost, the determination should be based on conjecture about that place and by evidence of possession.

NMS 12.6. J 11.6. Bhava explains "conjecture about that place" as inferring that there was a village in a place from the evidence of lumps of earth, trees, wells, etc.

and by that means determining the boundary between two villages. Samu (Dhko 945) attributes this verse to Bṛhaspati.

7. If the neighbors should testify falsely in this determination, then the king should punish each and every one with the middle fine.

NMS 12.7. J 11.7. Bhava says that the middle fine is 500. Although he does not specify the unit, he probably means 500 *paṇas* (see Manu 8.138).

8. If others, such as the elders of a group, are dishonest, they should be punished and each made to pay the lowest fine.

NMS 12.8. J 11.8. The lowest fine is 250 *paṇas*. SaVi 491 attributes this verse to Yājñavalkya, RāKau 463 attributes it to Manu.

9. One man, however trustworthy, should not delineate the boundary; because of the importance of this duty, it should be done by several people.

NMS 12.9. J 11.9. To show that several people ought to be involved in settling boundaries, Bhava refers back to Nārada 1.190.

10. If one man were to delineate the boundary he must fast, have a collected mind, wear a red garland and garment, and place some soil on his forehead.

NMS 12.10. J 11.10. Bhava observes that the settlement of the boundary by only one man is to be done only if there are no other qualified men available. He says that the reason that the single man should be dressed in a red garland and garment is that this is the way dead people are dressed, and he should consider himself dead if he performs his task wrongly. Bhava once more refers to Nārada 1.190.

11. When there are no knowledgeable persons and no markers, the king himself should set the boundary between both, as he sees fit.

NMS 12.11. J 11.11.

12. These rules also apply to disputes about houses, gardens, reservoirs, shrines, etc. and fallow land between villages.

NMS 12.12. J 11.12. Recension D adds two verses which are unknown anywhere else as Nārada verses. J 11.13 is often quoted (in 16 different texts), but always as a Kātyāyana verse. The translation of these verses is:

> **The fruits and flowers of trees which have grown up right on the boundary between two fields should be assigned commonly to the owners of the fields.** [J 11.13]
> **When trees growing in one man's field sprout branches in his neighbor's field those branches are considered the neighbor's because they are not growing in the owner's field.** [J 11.14]

13. Crossroads, a holy place, a road and a path must not be obstructed by refuse, a mound, a pit, a watercourse, or a drain and the like.

NMS 12.13. J 11.15. Bhava glosses the term *syandanikā* "a drain," as a place where urine and bath water flow. Recension D adds a verse which is unknown in any other source:

> **The king should punish with the highest fine those who, either by carelessness or deliberately, cause such obstructions.** [J 11.16]

14. A dike through another man's field is not prohibited. Even though there may be some loss, the gain is considerable. When one loses something, one wants to gain by it.

NMS 12.14. J 11.17. This is an apparent reference to an irrigation device which would require one man to sacrifice a portion of his field for the common good. The benefit is great enough for him and for the others that the loss is insignificant.

15. There are two types of dikes: one which is dug out and one which is built up. The one which is dug out is for bringing in water, and the one which is built up is for holding water.

NMS 12.15. J 11.18. The two types of "dikes" are irrigation channels and dams.

16. Grain does not grow without adequate water, but it is ruined by too much water. It is as bad to have too much water as it is to have too little.

NMS 12.16. J 11.19.

17. If anyone, without asking the owner, uses a dike which had been used previously but had fallen into disuse, he should not reap the profits from its use.

NMS 12.17. J 11.20. If a man repairs someone elses's old and neglected dike, but he does not ask the owner's permission, then he may not receive the benefits of the repaired dike, but Bhava adds that there will be benefit for him (presumably of an other-worldly sort) if he did it for the sake of righteousness and not for profit.

Derrett, RLS, p.190 note 5 has suggested that this and the next verse refer to damage done to dikes during warfare.

18. However, if the owner and his descendants are dead, he may undertake the work on that dike with the permission of the king.

NMS 12.18. J 11.21. Bhava says that, since the death of the owner and his descendants means that there is no owner of the dike from whom one could ask permission, it is necessary to ask the king. This situation cannot have occurred often in classical India; the list of heirs and potential heirs is too long.

19. Otherwise he would make the same mistake as the deer hunter who wastes his arrows by shooting at an animal that has already been shot by someone else.

NMS 12.19. J 11.22. The example of the hunter is given in Manu 9.73 as well and is illustrative of wasted effort since he has shot at an animal that someone else has already shot, and hence owns. The situation is the same with regard to unauthorized repair of dikes. The verse found in the variants is:

> **Those who know the past call the earth (*pṛthivī*) the wife of Pṛthu, and say that the field belongs to the one who cleared it and the deer to the one who owns the arrow.** [Manu 9.44]

20. If the owners of a field are incapacitated, dead, or have disappeared, and someone cultivates the field unchallenged, the crop is his.

NMS 12.20. J 11.23. SaVi 340 attributes this verse to Kātyāyana.

21. If the owner of the field returns while the field is being cultivated, he may reclaim it after paying completely for the work done in that otherwise fallow field.

NMS 12.21. J 11.24. Bhava indicates that the amount to be paid for the work of cultivation is one-eighth of the crop. SaVi 340 attributes this verse to Kātyāyana.

22. For a period of seven years he takes one-eighth of the crop, in the eighth year he resumes possession of the field.

NMS 12.22. J 11.25. The land which is spoken of in this verse is "waste" land (11.21, *khila*), i.e. land defined in the next verse as having been fallow for three to five years. The cultivation of this land is different from the cultivation of land which has been left fallow for a lesser period. When the owner returns he is not allowed to resume possession from the cultivator immediately. It is a gradual process that requires eight years. In each of these eight years the owner resumes a portion. Bhava seems to say the portion which the owner takes is one-eighth for each of seven years, and by the eighth he resumes full possession. SaVi 340 attributes this verse to Kātyāyana.

23. A field which has been fallow for one year is called half-waste, for three years, waste, and after five years it has the (legal) status of jungle.

NMS 12.23. J 11.26. Bhava elaborates on this verse by saying that if a field which has been fallow for one year, is cultivated by a stranger and the owner comes back, then the owner may take one-fourth of the crop, and he resumes possession after only four years. Thus the provisions found in 11.22 apply only to land which has lain fallow for three to five years. Land that remains fallow for a longer period becomes the king's (see note to 7.6).

24. A field which has been used for three generations or a house that was inherited cannot be lost through adverse possession, unless the king interferes.

NMS 12.24. J 11.27. The point of this verse is that possession for three generations or inheritance of property normally result in the possessor or inheritor becoming the owner (or at the very least having permanent tenure rights, see the discussion at VyaCi 452 ff.). This verse allows for the possibility of the king's interference on behalf of the original owner. It is possible for the king, if he is so inclined (*prasādāt*), to preserve the rights of the original owner even though others have used the property for three generations. This verse says that land must be held for three generations before adverse possession is effective, while improvements to land such as a house only require that it be inherited (i.e., possessed for fewer generations). Bhava does not make this distinction; he mentions only possession for three generations for both a field and a house. He says that if the king interferes and gives the property in question back to the original owner, the possessors have no recourse (*tatra na vaktavyam*), but without this interference the possessors are not obliged to return the property to the original owner. The comment contains a strange reading (*upacitadānena*) which seems unlikely.

25. When a fence has been broken through and grain destroyed by cows or other animals, the herdsman should be punished unless he tried to prevent it, to the best of his ability.

NMS 12.25. J 11.28. Bhava adds that if people failed to erect a fence, then the herdsman is not liable, nor is he liable if he was not able to prevent it.

26. If grain has been destroyed right down to the ground, then the owner may claim an equal amount, the herdsman may be let off after a beating, but the owner of the cows should be punished.

NMS 12.26. J 11.29.

27. One must take special care in warding off a cow within ten days of giving birth, a large bull, goats, sheep, or an elephant, but their owner should not be punished.

NMS 12.27. J 11.30. Bhava says that the owner of the field is responsible for its protection. Presumably these animals are either to be treated delicately because of their condition, or because they are notoriously hard to handle.

28. For a cow he should make him pay one *māṣa*; for a female buffalo, two *māṣas*; for a goat and sheep with their young, the fine would be one-half *māṣa*.

NMS 12.28. J 11.31.

29. There is no fine for elephants and horses because they are considered protectors of the people, nor for a pregnant cow, a cow that has just given birth, or one that is in heat.

NMS 12.29. J 11.32. This verse is cited numerous times as a verse of Uśanas (see Dhko 920).

30. The fine is said to be twice as much if the animal lies down in the field and four times as much if it stays in the field. The herdsman should be punished like a thief if his animals wander in a field while he looks on.

NMS 12.30. J 11.33cd and 34ab. Bhava says that "staying" in the field means to spend a night in the field, hence to do much more damage. If the animals are allowed to do their damage while the herdsman looks on he should be punished as a thief in addition to being fined for the damage.

The half-verses found in the variants occur only in recension D. One of the variants, which Jolly gives in his text (but over which he expresses doubt—see his translation of this verse and the notes thereon), *chinnanāsāyāṃ*, means cows with pierced noses. Jolly expressed puzzlement over why a cow with a pierced nose should incur a greater fine than any other. The answer is that the cow's nose is pierced in order to insert a device in the septum by which the animal can be controlled. If the animal has this sort of control available and still it is allowed into a field to do damage, then the fine should be greater because the negligence is greater.

31-33. If a herdsman allows cattle to escape into a field, there is no punishment for their owner; the herdsman deserves to be punished. If a herdsmen has been detained by the king, struck by lightning, bitten by a snake, has fallen from a precipice, has been attacked by a lion or tiger, or falls sick, then he is not at fault, and neither is the owner of the cows.

NMS 12.31-33. J 11.35-37.

34. A man who seeks to repay grain eaten by cows must give an amount of produce to his neighbor equivalent to that which was eaten. The owner of the cows gets the fodder, the farmer gets the grain.

NMS 12.34. J 11.38. According to Bhava, the fodder is the chaff and stalks, i.e. the remains of the damaged crop. Since the owner of the cows fully compensates the farmer for the grain lost, he may keep what he has paid for. This portion of the text is awkward; hence the many additions and variants in the mss.

35. If a field is located next to a village, a paddock, or a main road, and it is not fenced off, the herdsman is not responsible for damage done to it.

NMS 12.35. J 11.40. Bhava says that in these cases the loss is entirely the field owner's.

36. On the side of a field near a road a fence should be built large enough so that a camel cannot see over it, horses and cows cannot jump over it, and a pig cannot break through it.

NMS 12.36. J 11.41. ViTā 670 attributes this verse to Kātyāyana. NMS adds verses which are not found in this place in any other ms (see the variants for 11.34).

37-38. The house and the field are what the family lives on; therefore the king should not disturb them since they are the foundation of the family. When the populace prospers the wealth and righteousness of the king prosper, and they decline when the populace declines. Therefore a king should attend to this cause of his prosperity.

NMS 12.39cd-40. J 11.42-43.

CHAPTER 12

RELATIONS BETWEEN MEN AND WOMEN

1. The chapter which gives the rules for marriage, etc. for women and men is called Relations Between Men and Women. It is a title of law.

NMS 13.1. J 12.1. See A.A. Vigasin, "Notes to Nāradasmṛti XII," in *Summaries*, pp. 172-176 for general remarks and specific comments on this chapter.

2. Before a woman and a man are joined in marriage, a selection must be made. The selection is followed by the taking of the hand; thus the sacrament is twofold.

NMS 13.2. J 12.2. Bhava mentions a variant reading for *saṃbandhād*: *saṃyogād*.

3. Of these, the selection is not binding when a fault is discovered in one of the partners, whereas the taking of the hand accompanied by the recitation of *mantras* is a binding indication of marital status.

NMS 13.3. J 12.3. Bhava mentions the variant reading *pāṇigrāhaṇikā mantrā niyatāh*. He says that, if the two partners come to dislike one another at the stage of selection, then the marriage is stopped. After the recitation of the mantras and the taking of the girl's hand, however, the sacrament is complete and is binding for life.

4. When a brāhmaṇa, kṣatriya, vaiśya, or śūdra gets married, it is better to have a wife of the same caste. Likewise for the woman, it is better to have a husband of the same caste.

NMS 13.4. J 12.4. Bhava says that, because of the use of the comparative "better," the preferable alternative for a member of each of these four classes is to marry someone of his own caste. But it also indicates that other marriages exist.

5. A brāhmaṇa may marry women of the other three lower castes, a śūdra woman may marry men of the other three higher castes. A kṣatriya may take a wife of the two lower castes; a vaiśya may take a wife of the next lower caste; a vaiśya woman may have a husband of the two higher castes; a kṣatriya woman, a husband of the next higher caste.

NMS 13.5-6. J 12.5-6. The terms translated "lower castes" and "higher castes" are *ānulomyena* and *prātilomyena*. The term *anuloma* means, literally, "with the hair"; in English the idiom is "with the grain." *Pratiloma* means the opposite. These two terms are used to describe marriages. The principle involved is that the male must be of equal or higher caste than his wife according to the ranking of castes in 12.4. Such a marriage is described as *anuloma*, and it is valid and approved. If the woman is of a higher caste than her husband, the marriage is described as *pratiloma*, and it is not valid or approved. The offspring of such a marriage are of a lower caste than either of their parents (see 12.103 ff).

7. One should not marry a relative within seven degrees of relationship of one's father or five degrees of one's mother, nor someone from the same *gotra* or the same *pravara*.

NMS 13.7. J 12.7. The matter of who is eligible to marry whom has been one of much controversy and confusion. The general rule is the one given here. The degrees of prohibited relationship for marriage are seven degrees in the paternal line and five degrees in the maternal line. The manner of counting those degrees is not agreed upon in all texts, and there are numerous exceptions. For a summary of these matters see Kane, HDh 2.452-478. A person's *gotra* is basically his lineage traced through his family name. His *pravara* is his lineage traced through descent from a vedic sage. See J.Brough, *The Early Brahmanical System of Gotra and Pravara: A Translation of the Gotra-Pravara-Mañjarī of Puruṣottama-Paṇḍita*; Kane, HDh 2.478-500; and G.S. Ghurye, *Two Brahmanical Institutions: gotra and charana*.

8-10. One should examine a man's virility by his congenital physical characteristics. If his virility is certain, then he is eligible to take a girl. His vertebrae, knees, bones, shoulders, and neck should be well-built. The nape of his neck should be tough, as well as his torso, thighs, and skin. He should have a smooth gait and voice. His feces should sink in water, his urine should be noisy and foamy. If he has these characteristics he is virile; if not, he is impotent.

NMS 13.810. J 12.8-10. Bhava says that the word "bones" refers to the bones below the knee, the shin, as well as other bones. He glosses the term *ghāṭā*, "nape of the neck," with "hair." I translate the term *paṇḍaka* as "impotent" rather than the conventional term "eunuch." A eunuch would be easily identifiable by a simple physical examination. The term must be taken to mean, broadly, a male who is unable to impregnate a woman. These characteristics are listed here to aid in determining if the man will be able to impregnate a woman; therefore the term impotent must be understood to include sterility, inability to have an erection, etc. as indicated by the following verses. The variant *retas* for *viṭ* found in recension D would indicate that his semen rather than his feces is to be found to sink. The reading *viṭ* is reinforced by Kau 3.18.6 where it is mentioned among tests for impotence. The Dīka on YāSmṛ 1.55 attributes this verse to Devala.

11. Impotent men are known by the experts in the science to be of fourteen different kinds, some curable, some not. The rules about them are as follows.

NMS 13.11. J 12.11.

12-13. They are: one impotent from birth, one who has been castrated, one capable of sexual intercourse only fortnightly, one whose impotence is the result of the curse of his teacher, or illness, or the anger of the gods, one who is impotent except when jealous, a homosexual, one who ejaculates prematurely, one who engages in oral intercourse, one who cannot ejaculate, one who is sterile, one who is shy, and one who is virile with others than his wife.

NMS 13.12-13. J 12.12-13. The one who is impotent except when jealous, according to Bhava, is one who is aroused only by watching his wife with another man. Bhava interprets a *sevya* "homosexual" as a man who is only aroused by other men. He explains the term *vātaretas*, literally, "wind semen," as semen which is carried off by the wind instead of being deposited in the vagina. The term *mukhebhaga* is subject to several different interpretations according to Bhava. One explanation is that the man is only potent when engaging in non-vaginal intercourse (*bhagād anyatra bhagakāryaṃ bhavati. puṃstvaṃ na bhaga iti kecit*). Another possible explanation is that such a man is potent only when another male performs fellatio with him (*anye pareṇa svamukhe kriyamāṇe puṃstvam upajāyate sa mukhebhaga iti*). Another explanation which he mentions, but rejects as unlikely, is that *mukha* means "first" and so refers to a man only impotent in the presence of virgins. The "one who is shy" is one who is bashful and fails to be aroused by his wife. The Smṛtisārasamuccaya (Dhko 3.606, 1094) attributes these verses to a purāṇa.

14. The first two cannot be cured. For the one referred to by the term "fortnightly" the waiting period is a month; for the next three, a year.

NMS 13.14. J 12.14. Bhava explains that, since the first two are incurable, their wives should leave them. This is an exception to the rule that the sacrament of marriage is permanent. For the next two, one should wait a month. If their condition is established within that period, they may be abandoned. The same is true for the next three for whom the waiting period is one year. Leaving them after the waiting period involves no fault. This waiting period must be observed. Anyone who marries off one of these impotents without revealing the flaw is to be punished.

15. Even though they are no longer virgins, the wives of the next four, beginning with "one who is impotent except when jealous," should leave their husbands as if they were outcastes.

NMS 13.15. J 12.15. The four spoken of here are "one who is impotent except when jealous, a homosexual, one who ejaculates prematurely, one who engages in oral intercourse." If this is true for women who are no longer virgins, Bhava says, then it is all the more true for women who have been married but are still virgins.

16. If a husband who cannot ejaculate or who is sterile, cannot be cured, his wife may take another husband after a period of one year.

NMS 13.16. J 12.16. There can be little doubt that this passage supports the remarriage of women who have been denied the right to have a husband who can to impregnate them.

17. If one who is shy loses his erection during intercourse with his wife and she is not bashful, she should tend to this weakling with other men's wives, women, young girls, etc.

NMS 13.17. J 12.17. The readings of this verse are varied. The purpose of this admonition, clearly, is to attempt to arouse the husband.

18. If he is virile with another woman, but not with his wife, then the wife may take another husband. This is what is to be done according to Prajāpati.

NMS 13.18. J 12.18. Bhava understands the phrase *etat kāryaṃ prajāpateḥ*, to mean "this is to be done by the king." Can it be that the commentator, uneasy with the notion of a wife being able to leave her husband, attempts to reduce this apparently sacred rule to a positive legal command of the king?

19. Women were created for the sake of offspring. The woman is the field, the offspring belong to the possessor of the seed. A field should be given to one who has seed; one without seed is not entitled to a field.

NMS 13.19. J 12.19. SmṛCa Saṃskārakāṇḍa 210 attributes this verse to Kātyāyana, as does the Smṛtimuktāphala (Dhko 3.607).

20. A girl should be given by her father personally, or by her brother with her father's consent, or by her maternal grandfather, maternal uncle, or by her paternal relatives or maternal relatives.

NMS 13.20. J 12.20. The terms "paternal relatives" (*sakulya*) and "maternal relatives" (*bandhu*) are used in different ways in different texts (see Kane, HDh

3.731 ff. for a précis of the treatment of these terms). Bhava glosses them respectively with the terms *sapiṇḍa* "an heir, usually a blood relative" and *sambandhin* "a relative by marriage." In one sense, the terms, as Jolly translates them, may be used to refer to agnates and cognates. Bhava says that after the father, the mother has the responsibility to arrange the girl's marriage. This seems to contradict the rest of the verse and the following verse. It is interesting to note that after the girl's brother, the responsibility falls to her maternal relatives.

21. If none of these is available, her mother does it, if her status has not changed. If her status has changed, then her fellow caste members should do it.

NMS 13.21. J 12.21. Bhava says that the mother's status has not changed if she is virtuous and that she has remained faithful to her husband.

22. If there is no one else, the girl should resort to the king, and, with his approval of her selection, she should arrange the marriage herself.

NMS 13.22. J 12.22. PaMā 100, MaRa (Dhko 3.664), Sindhu 1075 (the first half of the verse), and SaṃRa 498 (the first half of the verse) all attribute this verse to Manu.

23. He should be of the same caste and suitable from the standpoint of family, appearance, age, and learning. She should live with him in righteousness and in due time give birth to sons.

NMS 13.23. J 12.23. These are the guidelines for the woman who makes her own choice.

24. If a man accepts a girl and then leaves the country, she should wait for three menstrual periods and then select another bridegroom.

NMS 13.24. J 12.24. Bhava says that this provision applies only when a young woman is abandoned by her fiancé, not to a little girl who has been betrothed. Further, this only applies when she has been betrothed, but the marriage has not taken place. If the one who gave her away is absent or unwilling to do it again, so long as the girl waits for three menstrual periods and selects another, she incurs no censure.

25. A girl should not ignore her puberty; she should inform her relatives of it. If they do not give her to a husband, they are just like embryo killers.

NMS 13.25. J 12.25. Bhava says that a girl is at fault if she does not inform her relatives of the onset of puberty. If the relatives have been informed, and fail to act, they should be punished like embryo killers. A similar verse is attributed to Yama in SaṃPra 770.

26-27. Every time she has a menstrual period without a husband, the one who has failed to give her in marriage is guilty of the sin of killing an embryo. Therefore a father must give his daughter in marriage—once—before the onset of puberty. If he does not, he incurs great sin. This is the rule for the virtuous.

NMS 13.26-27. J 12.26-27. Bhava states that the girl's father should arrange her marriage while she is still a little girl (*nagnikā*).

28. One receives one's inheritance—once. One gives away one's daughter—once. One says, "I must give this gift"—once. These are three things which are done only once.

NMS 13.28. J 12.28. The partition of inheritance is done only once. Since marriage is a lifetime sacrament, one can only give one's daughter in marriage once (although Nārada is remarkable for his provision for remarriage of women, see12.12 ff.). Once a person has given something, he has relinquished his ownership of it and he cannot give it again. This verse is identical with Manu 9.47. It is remarkable because it is attributed to many authors by the *nibandhakāras*: DāTa 182 and ViCa 95 attribute this verse to Manu, Nārada, Kātyāyana, and Bṛhaspati; Candra 90 attributes it to Manu, Nārada, and Kātyāyana.

The verses found in N and Y (and given in the variants to this verse) are found in no other mss. The translations of these verses is as follows:

> **Soma would possess a woman once her special characteristics have made their appearance, a *gandharva* would possess her once she develops breasts; Agni is said to be present in her menstruation.** [GṛSaṃPa 2.19]
> **Therefore a father should give away his daughter before she has these characteristics, before she menstruates or has breasts, and before Soma and the others possess her.** [GṛSaṃPa 2.20]

29. These rules are for the first five forms of marriage, beginning with the *brāhma* form. The other three forms, beginning with the *āsura* form, also involve a gift, but it depends on the bridegroom's character.

NMS 13.29. J 12.29. The eight forms of marriage are enumerated in 12.38-44. Bhava explains that in the first five forms of marriage the father gives his daughter away once, but in the last three he may give her to another bridegroom if a more suitable one is found. The girl may also be given to a another man if there is a larger bride-price offered, or in case of distress. Bhava also gives a variant reading *na* for *ca*, and says that in this reading the giving would depend on the character of the bridegroom in the first five, but not in the other three. Here it would depend on the payment, and other circumstances that attend each of these three forms of marriage.

30. If the girl has already fetched a bride-price and a better bridegroom should happen to come along, then one might stretch the truth about righteousness, wealth, or desire in whatever way is necessary.

NMS 13.30. J 12.30. This interesting verse condones prevarication in order to strike a better matrimonial deal. Bhava says that there is no fault in telling a lie to get out of the first arrangement and entice a second, more desirable suitor into a marriage agreement. One may tell a lie connected with righteousness etc., about the girl's character, her family, her beauty, etc.

31. One must not defame an innocent girl, nor an innocent suitor. If there is some fault, then there is no sin if they give up on one another.

NMS 13.31. J 12.31. This verse seems to apply either to the father of the girl or to another suitor. The father might be tempted to slander a suitor if he were hoping to get out of a commitment to give his daughter, and another suitor might try to eliminate competition by slandering other suitors, or, if disgruntled, he might be tempted to slander the girl. GṛhaKa 63 and GṛhaRa 53 attribute this verse to both Kātyāyana and Nārada.

32. When a man has legally committed a girl to a suitor, but fails to give her away, and the suitor is not at fault, the king should punish him like a thief.

NMS 13.32. J 12.32. Bhava says that legally committing a girl means accepting the bride price in the presence of witnesses. This would apply, then, to the Āsura form of marriage (see 12.42).

33. If one gives away a girl who has some fault but does not make that fault known he should be punished by the king with the lower fine.

NMS 13.33. J 12.33. Bhava says that one giving the girl away should say, for example, "She is afflicted with a serious and vile disease" (see 12.36). If he warns the suitor and then gives the girl away, he commits no fault. This verse is identical with Manu 8.224.

34. A man who, out of malice, says that a virgin girl is not a virgin and cannot prove his claim should incur a fine of one hundred.

NMS 13.34. J 12.34. Bhava says that if the man can prove his allegation, then there is no punishment. The unit of measure for the fine is not specified, but is usually *paṇas*. However, the type of *paṇa* is a source of controversy; there were copper, silver and gold *paṇas*. VyaMa 255 says that when there is only a number mentioned for a fine, but no mention of the type of coin, then one is to understand that copper *paṇas* are intended. This verse is identical with Manu 8.225.

35. If a man accepts a girl who is faultless and then abandons her, he, too, should be fined, and, even if he does not want to, he must marry her.

NMS 13.35. J 12.35. Bhava says that even though this verse does not explicitly state the amount of the fine in this case, the word "too" indicates that the fine is the same as in the previous verse, i.e., one hundred (*paṇas*).

36. These are flaws in a girl: affliction with a serious and vile disease, deformity, lack of virginity, brazenness, love for someone else.

NMS 13.36. J 12.36. Bhava explains brazenness as shamelessness. He also says that these flaws are merely examples.

37. These are flaws in a suitor: being insane, an outcaste, a eunuch, unlucky, abandoned by his family, and the first two flaws of a girl.

NMS 13.37. J 12.37. The verse which recension X adds after 12.37 is also quoted by Bhava in his commentary.

> **There are five kinds of insanity: those which arise in the wind-humor, bile, or phlegm, that which comes from losing one's wealth, and that caused by a complicated disorder of the body's humors.**

According to Bhava, an outcaste is one who has committed a serious sin such as theft of gold and has been thrown out of his caste as a result. One who is unlucky is one who is to be reviled by everyone. The first two faults of the girl are disease and deformity (see 12.36).

38-39. There are eight forms of marriage sacraments for the caste members. The *brāhma* is first, then comes the *prājāpatya*, next are the *ārṣa*, *daiva*, *gāndharva*, and *āsura* , followed by the *rākṣasa*, the *paiśāca*, is the eighth.

NMS 13.38-39. J 12.38-39. On the subject of the forms of marriage see Heramba Chatterjee, *The Social Background of the Forms of Marriage in Ancient India*.

40-43. In the *brāhma* form he should invite the suitor, receive him honorably, and give him the girl covered with ornaments. The *prājāpatya* form is when he says to the suitor, "Perform your duties together." Marriage is of the *ārṣa* form when garments and a pair of cattle are given; it is of the *daiva* form when the girl is given in a sacrificial enclosure to a priest who is

sacrificing. When the girl and the suitor mutually seek out one another, that is the fifth, the *gāndharva* form. It is of the *āsura* form when a bride-price changes hands. The next form is called *rākṣasa* because of the forcible abduction involved. The *paiśāca* form is last and lowest because the girl is violated while she is asleep or unconscious.

NMS 13.40-43. J 12.40-43. These verses are quoted nowhere else. The reason is undoubtedly that the verses of Manu (3. 20-35) are better known and clearer. We know from Manu that the gifts of cows and garments spoken of in this verse are given by the bridegroom to the father of the bride. This is not clear from the present Nārada verse, nor does Bhava clarify it. No doubt this is because this form of marriage (like the others) was well-known to any reader of this text. In his comment on Manu 3.29, Kullūkabhaṭṭa states emphatically that this gift is not to be understood as a bride-price. Otherwise it would be hard to distinguish the *ārṣa* form of marriage from the *āsura* form. Bhava notes that in the *daiva* form of marriage, if the father receives any payment, it must go exclusively to the daughter because of the prohibition against selling one's children, whereas in the *āsura* form of marriage, all that is happening is the sale of one's child. This is an indication of the extent to which such a marriage is disapproved.

44. The first four, beginning with the *brāhma* form, are proclaimed to be righteous. The *gāndharva* form is neutral. The next three forms are unrighteous.

NMS 13.44. J 12.44. Bhava states that "neutral" means that the *gāndharva* form of marriage is neither righteous nor unrighteous.

45-48. There are seven other types of wives. They have previously been with another man and are listed in order. Three of them are *punarbhūs*, four are *svairiṇīs*. The first type of *punarbhū* is a girl who is still a virgin and who is only sullied to the extent that she has joined hands in the wedding ceremony. She may undergo the sacrament of marriage again. The second type is a woman who abandons her childhood husband to take up with another man and then returns to the house of her husband. When a woman has no brothers-in-law and is given by her relatives to a man of the same caste who is not a *sapiṇḍa*, that is the third type.

NMS 13.45-48. J 12.45-48. For a discussion of some of the implications of being a *punarbhū* (remarried woman) or a *svairiṇī* (a loose woman), and the importance of the order in which they are listed, see 1.21. The first *punarbhū* is a girl who has joined hands with the bridegroom in the ritual of marriage, but whose marriage was not consummated. She must undergo the sacrament again in her second marriage. The new husband of the third *punarbhū* must be of the same caste as the wife (and, ideally, therefore, the same caste as the dead first husband), but he may not be a *sapiṇḍa* of the wife. Presumably, this would be an instance of levirate marriage in which the new husband serves as a substitute in the absence of brothers-in-law.

49-52. The first type of *svairiṇī* is a woman whose husband is still alive, and who, whether or not she has children, takes up with another man. When a widow rejects her brothers-in-law, even though they are suitable, and takes up with someone else out of passion, this is the second type. A foreigner, one who was purchased as a slave, or one suffering from hunger and thirst and who comes forward, saying, "I am yours"—this is the third type. A woman who has been raped and then given to another man by her elders in accord with local custom is the last type of *svairiṇī*.

NMS 13.49, 51, 52, 47. J 12.49-52. Bhava says that the person with whom the second *svairiṇī* takes up is someone who is inferior to her brothers-in-law, who are the suitable men for her. The statement which the third *svairiṇī* makes, "I am yours," is precisely the formula used by one type of slave (see 5.25). Bhava's comment indicates that he was aware of differing opinions about the descriptions of the woman who is listed here as the last type of *svairiṇī*. He says that it refers to a woman who has been with a man either because she was raped before she had a husband, or because she was abandoned by her husband. This is a situation in which the woman though not guilty in any moral sense, has been sullied and hence is not eligible for a normal marriage. Where local practice allows it, she could still be given in marriage to some other man. Thus such a woman would be the most innocent of the *svairiṇīs*, in keeping with the reverse order of culpability given in the next verse. See Kane, HDh 2.608-609, for yet another interpretation. The difficulties involved in ranking these women may have caused the reordering attested in NMS. The list of *punarbhūs* and *svairiṇīs* in NMS differs from that of all other recensions. They compare in the following way:

NāSmṛ

Punarbhū

1. a virgin who has only joined hands in the wedding ceremony;
2. a woman who left the husband of her youth, went to another man, and returned to her original husband;
3. a widow who has no brothers-in-law who can give her offspring (via the levirate marriage), and is given to a man of the same caste who is not a *sapiṇḍa*.

Svairiṇī

1. a woman who leaves her husband, whether or not she has children and lives with another man;
2. a widow who rejects her brothers-in-law and out of love goes to live with another man;
3. a foreigner, one purchased with money, or one in desperate straits who offers herself to a man as a slave;
4. a raped woman who later is given to another man.

NMS

Punarbhū

1. a virgin who has only joined hands in the wedding ceremony;
2. a raped woman who later is given to another man. (= NāSmṛ *svairiṇī* 4)
3. a widow who has no brothers-in law who can give her offspring (via the levirate marriage), but is instead given to a man of the same caste who is not a *sapiṇḍa*.

Svairiṇī

1. a woman who leaves her husband whether or not she has children and lives with another man;
2. a woman who left the husband of her youth, went to another man, and returned to her original husband (= NāSmṛ *punarbhū* 2);
3. a widow who rejects her brothers-in-law and out of love goes to live with another man (= NāSmṛ *svairiṇī* 2);
4. a foreigner, one purchased with money, or one in desperate straits who offers herself to a man as a slave (= NāSmṛ *svairiṇī* 3).

Although he follows NMS in his commentary on 12.45-48, Bhava's commentary on 1.21 indicates without any doubt that he had before him a list of *punarbhūs* and *svairiṇīs* which agrees with the list found in NāSmṛ and not with the list found in NMS.

Recension Y adds a verse not known in any other source:
Of the four *svairiṇīs* each successive one is better than the previous one. Their offspring fare differently in matters of inheritance, funerary offerings, and the like. [Dhko 1978]

53. These are the rules for those who are called *punarbhūs* and *svairiṇīs*. They are listed in rank order highest to lowest and lowest to highest, respectively.

NMS 13.53. J 12.53. Bhava notes that some would read this verse differently and have the rank order of the lowest to highest apply to both the *punarbhūs* and the *svairiṇīs*. Since, however, a ranking from lowest to highest for the *punarbhūs* would result in a virgin being ranked lower than a non-virgin, the rank order must necessarily be from the highest to lowest. For the *svairiṇīs* the rank order is clearly from lowest to highest.

54. If any of these women was acquired by a bride-price her children belong to the one who impregnated her. The children of a woman who was not acquired by a bride-price belong to her husband.

NMS 13.54. J 12.54. Bhava states that this verse applies to the seven *punarbhūs* and *svairiṇīs*. Samu (Dhko 1101) appears to attribute this verse to Kātyāyana.

55-57. When seed is sown in a field without the knowledge of the owner of the field, the owner of the seed has no share in the crop; it belongs to the owner of the field alone. When one man's seed is carried out of his field by water or wind, and grows in another's field, the crop belongs to the owner of the field, not to the owner of the seed. When a mature bull wanders into someone's cowpen and breeds calves on the cows there, the calves belong to the owner of the cows. The bull's seed flowed uselessly.

NMS 13.55-57. J 12.55-57. Bhava says that some view these verses as metaphors for the woman who was not acquired by a bride-price, while others say that they apply to all the women under discussion. The offspring belong to the husband alone. The other man does not receive funerary offerings from them, nor do they mourn after his death. According to Bhava the first verse applies to a case where the woman is motivated by lust. The second to an event not actuated by lust, but happening by fate, and the third to a case where the man is motivated by lust.

58. When seed is cast on a field with the owner's consent, the crop is considered to belong to both the owner of the seed and the owner of the field.

NMS 13.58. J 12.58. Bhava observes that, when a husband allows another man to have a child with his wife, the child belongs to both men. The child has an interest in the wealth, funerary offerings, etc., of both men.

59. Without a field there would be no crop. Without seed there would be no crop. Therefore, the offspring they desire rightly belongs to both the mother and the father.

NMS 13.59. J 12.59. Bhava notes that if one of the parents does not want to do so, the joint ownership described in this verse prevents the other parent from giving away, selling, or abandoning the child. Samu (Dhko 1103) appears to attribute this verse to Kātyāyana.

60-61. If a man has intercourse with an attached woman somewhere other than his own house, it is known as adultery by the experts, but not if she came to his house on her own. It is not a punishable crime when someone has intercourse with the wife of a man who has abandoned her because she is wicked, or with the wife of a eunuch or of a man who does not care, provided the wife has initiated it, of her own volition.

NMS 13.60-61. J 12.60-61. Bhava takes the second verse to be an exception to the first; that is, even if the intercourse takes place in such a woman's house, there is no crime of adultery. The important point to note in these verses is that a woman who is "attached" is one who is under the protection of another man. This includes wives, daughters, other relatives, and even servants (see 12.77-78); hence the term is broader in scope than the western concept of adultery which is generally confined to sexual intercourse with someone other than one's marriage partner. DaVi attributes 12.60 to Kātyāyana. VyaKa 582 and DaVi 158 attribute 12.61 to both Nārada and Kātyāyana. ViRa 386, ViCi 175, and Setu (Dhko 1882) attribute 12.61 to Viṣṇu.

62. When a man meets another man's wife in secret, at an improper time, or in an inappropriate place, staying, conversing, and joking with her, constitute three successive steps to adultery.

NMS 13.62. J 12.62. Bhava explains that, as long as these things are done in the open and in the presence of respectable people, there is nothing wrong, but if they are done at night or even during the day but in an inner room they constitute stages of adultery.

63-64. When a man and a woman meet at the confluence of rivers, at river crossings, in parks, or in forests, that, too, would have to be viewed as adultery. Dispatching women messengers, sending letters, and other irregular behavior, all this constitutes adultery.

NMS 13.63-64. J 12.63-64.

65-66. It is adultery when a man touches a woman in an improper place, or when he allows himself to be touched, and they do this with mutual consent. Sending food and drink, garments, garlands, or fragrances, all of this constitutes adultery.

NMS 13.65-66. J 12.65, 68. Bhava lists the improper places as the breasts, lips, etc. He indicates that there is mutual consent as soon as they fail to express any anger; it is not necessary that they enjoy it. Apa on YāSmṛ 2.284 attributes these verses to Vyāsa. They are identical with Manu 8.358. Jolly accepts as Nārada's a verse found only in recensions D and Y:

> **Doing favors, sporting, touching ornaments or clothes, sitting on a bed together: all of this indicates adultery.** [J 12.66]

67. When, out of vanity, or inadvertently, or as a boast a man declares that he has had a certain woman, all this constitutes adultery

NMS 13.68. J 12.69. The mere claim that a woman has commited an indiscretion constitutes adultery since it amounts to sullying a protected woman (see the note to 12.60). This is true even though no sexual contact took place.

68. When a man takes a woman by the hand, by the braid, or by the upper garment, or if he pleads with her to stay, all of this constitutes adultery.

NMS 13.69. J 12.67. See 1.155.

69. If a man has illicit intercourse with a woman of his own caste, he must pay the highest fine; if a woman of a lower caste, the middle fine; but if a woman of a higher caste, he must be put to death.

NMS 13.70. J 12.70. VyaPra 398 attributes this verse to both Manu and Nārada; it is attributed to Manu alone by Mitā on YāSmṛ 2.284, PaMā 464, SaVi 468, NṛPra 207, VyaU folio 136, and ViTā 799.

70. If a man has illicit intercourse with a virgin who does not consent, he must have two fingers cut off. If she is of a higher caste, he must be beaten to death and have all his property confiscated.

NMS 13.71. J 12.71. Bhava notes that there are different opinions about the punishment for this crime. Some say that the term *vadha* means "beating," while others say that it means "death." No fewer than eight texts attribute this verse to Sankha or Śaṅkha and Likhita (see Dhko 1848).

71. If he does so with a willing virgin of his own caste there is no crime, but he must give her ornaments, treat her honorably, and marry her.

NMS 13.72. J 12.72.

72-74. It is incest to have any one of these women: one's mother, mother's sister, mother-in-law, maternal uncle's wife, father's sister, the wife of a paternal uncle, or of a friend, or of a student, one's sister, sister's friend, daughter-in-law, one's daughter, teacher's wife, a cousin, a woman who has come for protection, a queen, a female renouncer, a wet nurse, a nun, and a woman of a higher caste. The punishment prescribed in these cases is the cutting off of the penis, nothing less.

NMS 13.73-75. J 12.73-75. Bhava explains that the term "nothing less" in verse 74 precludes the substitution of a fine for the corporal punishment prescribed. See Manu 8.363 and YāSmṛ 2.293.

75. If a man has sexual intercourse with a domestic animal he should be punished with a fine of one hundred; the middle fine is prescribed for intercourse with cows or with very low caste women.

NMS 13.76. J 12.76. "Very low caste women" means, according to Bhava, *cāṇḍālās*, etc. See the note to 12.34.

76. When a man has sex with a woman with whom it is forbidden, the king imposes a fine to punish him. This penance purifies him according to the rules about penance.

NMS 13.77. J 12.77. According to Bhava, the punishment prescribed by the king is the penance, no other penance is required. The relationship between punishment and penance is a controversial one within the tradition and among scholars, see Kane, HDh 4.72 ff., and Lingat, *The Classical Law of India*, pp. 232 ff.

77-78. Intercourse is permitted with a *svairiṇī*, a non-brāhmaṇa woman, with a prostitute, a slave, or a woman who has no master, as long as she is of a lower caste; if she is of a higher caste it is not permitted. If, however, any of these are maidservants, then the crime would be the same as if they were other men's wives, for, even though it is permitted to have sex with these, they are not to be approached if they belong to someone else.

NMS 13.78-79. J 12.78-79. The second verse qualifies the first.

79-80. If a woman who has no children loses her husband, she should be appointed by her elders to go to her brother-in-law in order to have a son. He should continue to receive her until a son is born, but this must cease as soon as a son is born. To do otherwise would be evil.

NMS 13.80-81. J 12.80-81. These verses discuss the institution of levirate marriage. According to Bhava, the woman is appointed to this sort of union by such persons as her father-in-law, and her sole desire in doing this must be to have a son, not pleasure. The first half of 12.79 is not cited elsewhere.

81. Their limbs should be anointed with ghee or unprocessed oil, their faces averted, and they should not embrace each other's limbs.

NMS 13.82. J 12.82. The reason for the use of unprocessed oil is not explained; perhaps it is considered ritually purer. The point of this verse is to ensure that levirate union involve no physical pleasure.

82. He should not have intercourse with a woman who has a son, is barren, or beyond menopause, or one who does not consent, who is pregnant, of ill-repute, or who has not been appointed by her relatives.

NMS 13.83. J 12.83-84. Intercourse with any of these women would be wrong if the intercourse was done by *niyoga* (levirate union). The woman who already has a son would obviously not need to enter into a levirate union. A woman who is barren or beyond menopause cannot produce children, so the intercourse would be only for pleasure. The woman's consent is necessary for *niyoga*, and if she is already pregnant, there is no necessity for further sexual intercourse. The disqualification on the grounds of ill-repute is less clear: even if she had been an unfaithful wife, the children conceived would still "belong" to her husband (see 12.55-57). Both the woman's consent and the approval of her elders are required for a levirate marriage.

83. If a woman should give birth to a son by her brother-in-law without having been appointed, the experts in the law say that the son is a bastard and not entitled to inherit.

NMS 13.84. J 12.84-85. A child born of such a union without the sanction of the relatives is outside the pale of the family. One born of a union between a widow and someone other than her brother-in-law would be even further outside the pale.

84-85. If without being appointed a younger brother has intercourse with the wife of his elder brother, or if an elder brother has intercourse with the wife of his younger brother, both are guilty of incest. If he is the only male left in a family, an elder brother may be appointed by his elders to go to his younger brother's wife for the sake of offspring, not out of lust.

NMS 13.85-86. J 12.83, 85cd-86ab, 86cd. The levirate union is a last resort, and under these extraordinary circumstances, according to Nārada, an elder brother may be appointed to go to a younger brother's widow, or a younger brother may be appointed to go to the widow of an elder brother.

NMS has an additional verse:
Or, a younger brother may go to his elder brother's wife if he is appointed by his elders. The result of this intercourse is the preservation of the family lineage. [NMS 13.87]

86. If there are no elders, the king should take cognizance of the decline of the family, and order the brother-in-law to have sexual intercourse with the woman.

NMS 13.88. J omits. The king should make the necessary arrangements for the perpetuation of the family's lineage when there are no relatives to make the decision. In such a situation he must designate the brother-in-law to do the task so that the family may have offspring.

87. In accord with the rules previously stated: (a) she must have ritually bathed after her monthly menstruation; (b) he becomes pure once the *puṃsavana* ritual has been performed; (c) he must copulate with her only once or until she becomes pregnant; and (d) once she becomes pregnant she becomes like a daughter-in-law to him.

NMS 13.89. J 12.87. Bhava makes it clear that "the rules previously stated" means things like smearing the limbs with ghee or avoiding contact with the other person's limbs. In order to be prepared for sexual intercourse, the woman must have performed a ritual bath at the end of her period (see Kane, HDh 2.802-805). The male is apparently considered impure during the levirate. However, he recovers his ritual purity once the woman has conceived and the ritual to insure that the fetus is a male child has been performed (see R.B. Pandey, *Hindu Saṃskāras*, pp. 60-63). Once the woman becomes pregnant their relationship changes, and she becomes like his daughter-in-law. This is true even if the male is younger.

88. If the man or the woman should conduct themselves otherwise, because they are motivated by passion, they both should be severely punished by the king. He sins if he fails to restrain them.

NMS 13.90. J 12.88.

89. A husband and wife should not bring a quarrel to their relatives or to the king if their anger is caused by their love for one another and arises from jealousy or envy.

NMS 13.91. J 12.89. The point of this verse is that parties to such disputes have no *locus standi* in courts presided over by kinsmen or by the king.

90. There is no sin if a man and a woman who cannot get along separate, except if the woman was kept in seclusion and was unfaithful.

NMS 13.92. J 12.90. The fate of an unfaithful wife is spelled out in the next verse. Bhava who has the variant reading *tūḍhaya* for *nigūḍhāyā* in NMS, understands the verse to mean that a separation is allowed only in the case of women who are not married (presumably concubines), and that a man should never part with his wife, except if she is unfaithful.

91. If a woman is unfaithful she should be shaved, made to sleep on the ground, and be given bad food and worn out garments, and assigned the task of removing waste.

NMS 13.93. J 12.91. Bhava says the food which she should be given is coarsely ground grain (*saktu*), and "removing waste" means cleaning out the latrine.

92. A woman who squanders away the family's wealth as if it were her own, who has an abortion, or who wishes death for her husband should be banished from the house.

NMS 13.94. J 12.92. Bhava says that this means that such a woman should be abandoned. Recension D has the variant *purāt* "from the city" for *gṛhāt* "from the house."[3] All *nibandhakāras* read *gṛhāt* here, including the PaMā 476—the evidence of the mss of PaMā supports the reading *gṛhāt*, but Islāmpurkar, the editor, has "corrected" the text to read *purāt* (the BI edition, *vyavahārakāṇḍa* p. 325, reads *gṛhāt*).

93. A wise husband should banish a wife who is dissolute, or who always speaks harshly, or who eats before he does.

NMS 13.95. J 12.93. Bhava defines a dissolute woman as one who drinks, attends fairs, or consorts with low-caste women.

94. One should not take pleasure in a wife who is barren, gives birth to female children, is of ill-repute, or is always unpleasant. A man who does shares in her faults.

NMS 13.96. J 12.94. NMS reads *kāmaṃ tāṃ* for *kāmato*; Bhava however records the latter as a variant. He says that a man who refuses to make love to such a wife commits no offence and should not be punished.

95. If a man deserts a wife who is agreeable, irreproachable in her speech, skillful, virtuous, and has given birth to sons, the king should use severe punishment to force him to resume his responsibilities.

---

3 Bhava has *gṛhāt* here, but *grāmāt* in the gloss for the same verb *nirvāsayed* in the next verse.

NMS 13.97. J 12.95.

96. If a woman who was married to a man who has a previously unknown fault leaves him, but does not go to another man, she should be appointed to do so by her relatives; if she has no relatives she should do so on her own.

NMS 13.98. J 12.96.

97. There are five catastrophes in which women are required to take another husband: if the husband disappears, dies, becomes a world-renouncer, becomes a eunuch, or an outcaste.

NMS 13.99. J 12.97. Bhava states that this rule applies only to women who are still virgins when these catastrophes befall them. Such women must go to another husband out of a desire for children, not out of a desire for a husband. MaBhā on GauDha 18.4 attributes this verse to Bṛhaspati.

98-102. A brāhmana woman should wait eight years for a husband who has gone away; but if she has no children, she should wait only four years before going to another man. A kṣatriya woman should wait six years, three years if she has no children. A vaiśya woman should wait four years if she has children, two years if she does not. There is no waiting period for a śūdra woman. She commits no breach of righteousness, especially if she has no children. The normal thing, however, is to wait a year. These rules apply to women whose husbands have gone away and not been seen. If the husband is still alive and has been heard of, these waiting periods should be doubled. Prajāpati created creatures so that they might have offspring; therefore if a woman goes to another man under these circumstances there is no sin entailed.

NMS 13.100-104. J 12.98-102 (omits NāSmṛ 12.100). Bhava points out that these rules apply to the first catastrophe mentioned at 12.97, i.e, when the husband disappears. In this situation the husband may or may not be dead. If he is dead the situation changes to the second sort of catastrophe listed at 12.97. If the man is still alive, his wife may or may not hear from him. These rules apply to the situation where the wife does not hear from her husband. Bhava says that the longer period of time is to eliminate sexual desire as a motive for remarriage. The shorter period is to enable the woman to have children while she is still young. Bhava understands the rule for the śūdra woman to require that she wait a year if she has a child, but to allow her to marry another man without delay if she does not. It is better if she waits a while, but early remarriage is not forbidden. The last verse states that the "Lord (*pati*) of Creatures (*prajā*)" created things so that they might have offspring (*prajā*). ViRa 447-448 and ViBha (Dhko 1112) attribute these verses to Devala.

103. This is the set of rules for births from approved marriages. Births from unapproved marriages are known as "mixing of the castes."

NMS 13.105. J 12.102. I have translated the terms *ānulomya* and *prātilomya* with the phrases "approved marriages" and "unapproved marriages" respectively; see 12.5 and note.

104. Sons born from approved and unapproved marriages are described as "first degree," "second degree," and "third degree."

NMS 13.106. J 12.103. This refers to the degrees of separation between the marriage partners. In an *anuloma* marriage a brāhmaṇa male can have a son with a brāhmaṇa female (a *savarṇa* son), with a kṣatriya female (an *anantara* or "first degree" son), with a vaiśya female (an *ekāntara* or "second degree" son), and a śūdra female (a *dvyantara* or "third degree" son). A kṣatriya male cannot have a *dvyantara* or "third degree" son since there are only three castes from which he may choose to marry in an *anuloma* marriage—kṣatriya, vaiśya, and śūdra. The reverse is true for sons from *pratiloma* marriages. See 12.110-116 for a further discussion of this topic.

105. Sons born to a śūdra woman from approved marriages, i.e. with men of the three highest castes are called *ugra*, *pāraśava*, and *niṣāda*.

NMS 13.107. J 12.104. According to Bhava the son of a śūdra woman by a brāhmaṇa is a *pāraśava*; by a kṣatriya, a *niṣāda*; and by a vaiśya, an *ugra*. This is not the usual view. The *niṣāda* is usually considered the offspring of a brāhmaṇa male and a śūdra female, and the *ugra* that of a kṣatriya male and a śūdra female. See Kane, HDh 2.73-74 and 86-88. The "system" of naming mixed castes is chaotic. See Horst Brinkhaus, *Die altindischen Mischkastensysteme*, especially pp. 188 ff.

106. Sons born to brāhmaṇa women from unapproved marriages, i.e. with men of the three other castes, are called *cāṇḍāla*, *sūta*, and *vaidehaka*.

NMS 13.108. J omits. The offspring of a brāhmaṇa female by a śūdra male is a *cāṇḍāla;* by a kṣatriya male, a *sūta;* by a vaiśya, a *vaidehaka*.

107. A son born to a kṣatriya woman from an approved marriage is known as an *ambaṣṭha;* from unapproved marriages, a *māgadha* and a *kṣattṛ*.

NMS 13.109-110. J 12,105. The *māgadha* is fathered by a vaiśya, the *kṣattṛ* by a śūdra.

108. A son born to a vaiśya woman from an unapproved marriage is known as an *āyogava;* from approved marriages, a *dauṣṣanta* and a *yavana.*

NMS 13.110. J omits. The *dauṣṣanta* is fathered by a brāhmaṇa, the *yavana* by a kṣatriya, and both are *anuloma* offspring; the *āyogava* is fathered by a śūdra.

109. Those born of unapproved marriages between such castes as *sūtas*, etc., are the mixed castes such as *śvapākas*, etc., and they form three groups of seven.

NMS 13.111. J omits. Among the mixed castes there can also be *anuloma* and *pratiloma* marriages. According to Bhava there are seven which are the lowest ranking: marriages between two *cāṇḍālas* , between a male *cāṇḍāla* and a female *vaidehaka*, *sūta*, brāhmaṇa, kṣatriya, vaiśya, or śūdra. Then Bhava simply says that the same is true for a *vaidehaka* and a *sūta*. Jolly's suggestion is that the number twenty-one is arrived at by adding the six original mixed castes enumerated here (*cāṇḍāla*, *vaidehaka*, *sūta*, *kṣattṛ*, *māgadha*, and *āyogava*) to the fifteen mixed castes mentioned by Manu 10.31 and Bhā 12.48.18 ff. (see Bühler's notes to his translation of Manu 10.31. That the commentators struggle to come up with the number fifteen in this instance is indicative of the artificial nature of the enumeration of mixed castes. See Brinkhaus, *Mischkastensysteme*, p. 192.) It is difficult to see how such combinations can be limited to twenty-one. Bhava himself says that the divisions of such mixed castes as the *śvapāka*, etc. are endless. It may be that enumeration in sets of seven came to be the idiom for speaking of *antyajas* or mixed castes. For example, in the *Smṛtīnāṃ Samuccayaḥ* p. 113, Yamasmṛti 33 says that there are seven *antyajas*. (The same verse may be found attributed to Angiras in *Dharmaśāstrasaṃgraha*, edited by Jīvānanda Vidyāsāgara, pp. 554.) Mitā on YāSmṛ 3.260 notes this enumeration of seven *antyajas* and says that there are seven more *antyajas* which are not as low as the seven *antyajas* mentioned by Yama.

110-112. The son of a brāhmaṇa with a brāhmaṇa female is of the same caste. The son of a brāhmaṇa male with a kṣatriya female is a son of the first degree. The *ambaṣṭha* and the *ugra* are the same sort of son to the kṣatriya and the vaiśya, respectively. Sons of the second degree are: the son of a brāhmaṇa male and a vaiśya female, or a *dauṣṣanta*, and the son of a kṣatriya male and a śūdra female, or a *niṣāda*. The son farthest removed is the son born to a śūdra female by a brāhmaṇa male, or a *pāraśava*. All of these are the sons born from approved marriages between the castes.

NMS 13.112-114. J 12.106-109. Bhava names the son of a brāhmaṇa male and a kṣatriya female a *mūrdhābhiṣikta*. He points out that only a brāhmaṇa can have a son of the "third degree" (see the note to 12.104).

113-116. The *sūta*, *māgadha*, and *āyogava* are the first degree sons born of unapproved marriages between the castes. The first degree son born to a brāhmaṇa female by a kṣatriya male is a *sūta;* sons born in the same degree by a vaiśya and a śūdra male are a *māgadha* and *āyogava*, respectively. A second degree son born to a brāhmaṇa female by a vaiśya male is a *vaidehaka;* and a second degree son born to a kṣatriya female and a śūdra male is a *kṣattṛ*. In the mixing of castes, the worst of all is the *cāṇḍāla* who is born when a brāhmaṇa female goes astray with a śūdra male; this is the third degree son of an unapproved marriage.

NMS 13.115-117 (omits NāSmṛ 12.114). J 12.109-113. The *māgadha* is the offspring of a kṣatriya female by a vaiśya male; the *āyogava* is the offspring of a vaiśya female by a śūdra male. Just as the brāhmaṇa is the only one who can have a third degree son from an *anuloma* marriage, so the brāhmaṇa female is the only one who can have a third degree son from a *pratiloma* marriage.

117. The king must watch that there be no mixture of castes; therefore, he should carefully protect all three against mixture.

NMS 13.118. J omits. Bhava says that the three which the king is to protect are the three-fold science, i.e. the three vedas [see the discussion at Kau 1.2 where the sciences for the king are variously given as two (economics and politics [*vārttā* and *daṇḍanīti*]), three (economics, politics, and the three vedas), and four (this is the view of Kauṭilya; economics, politics, the three vedas, and logic [*anvīkṣikī*])]. It is more probable that the three are the women of the three superior castes and their marriages. The reading of D confirms this (*striyo rakṣyās tu saṃkarāt*) "he should carefully protect the women against mixture."

CHAPTER 13

PARTITION OF INHERITANCE

1. When sons proceed to partition the paternal estate, that is the title of law the wise call Partition of Inheritance.

NMS 14.1. J 13.1. This verse is pivotal in the discussion of partition by both the Mitākṣarā and Dāyabhāga schools. For a concise presentation of the comments on this verse by Jīmūtavāhana and Vijñāneśvara, see I.S. Pawate, *Dāya-vibhāga: or the Individualization of Communal Property and the Communalization of Individual Property in the Mitakshara Law*, pp. 25 ff.

2. After their father's death the sons may divide his property. Daughters divide the property of their mother; if there are no daughters, their offspring.

NMS 14.2. J 13.2. Bhava does not offer much explanation of "their offspring;" he simply glosses it "the daughter's sons, etc." This would mean that the *strīdhana* is inherited by a woman's grandsons, although the term "etc." affords great scope for the inclusion of others. The variety of interpretations by various texts concerning the devolution of *strīdhana* is too great to be summarized here (see Kane, HDh 3.788-802).

3. Partition may take place when the mother has ceased to menstruate, when the sisters are married, and when the father is still alive but impotent or no longer aroused by desire.

NMS 14.3. J 13.3. The preceding verse states that partition generally takes place after the parents' death. The present verse describes other special circumstances when partition may take place. The circumstances are probably cumulative; that is, they would all be required for the recommended partition to take place. The mother's menopause and the father's impotence or lack of desire would eliminate the possibility of conception of new coparceners, the marriage of the sisters would have been effected by the use of the joint paternal property so that the burden would not fall on any one share of the divided estate, and once married they would not be eligible for a share of the estate (13.13).

4. Or, the father may, of his own volition, partition his estate among his sons while he is still vigorous. He may give the best portion to the eldest or in any other way that suits him.

NMS 14.4. J 13.4. Bhava says that the word *svayam* "of his own volition" here indicates that there is no coercion involved in the partition.

5. Or, if they so desire, the eldest brother may act as the father and maintain the others, or even the youngest brother if he is able, for when it comes to administering family affairs, it is competence that matters.

NMS 14.5. J 13.5. This verse indicates that partition is not mandatory after the death of the father.

6. In addition to gifts from the father, there are three types of property not subject to partition: property acquired by valor, through a wife, or from learning.

NMS 14.6. J 13.6. The types of property mentioned here are not joint family property, and, therefore, they can be alienated as the owner wishes. For property other than that mentioned in this verse, the head of the family does not have absolute freedom to dispose of it; he can alienate it only for specific purposes having to do with the welfare of the family. Concerning property acquired by learning, see 13.10-11.

7. This rule also applies if a mother gives her property to someone out of affection; the mother is master of her property just as the father is of his.

NMS 14.7. J 13.7. Bhava says the mother's gift to her son must have been made out of affection; if it was given in any other way, it is subject to partition. This is not a unanimous view (see Kane's discussion of succession to *strīdhana*, HDh 3.788-802).

8. A woman's property is of six kinds: what she receives in front of the wedding fire, during the wedding procession, from her husband, brother, mother, or father.

NMS 14.8. J 13.8. This verse is identical with Manu 9.194. It is attributed to Kātyāyana and Manu at ViRa 522, ViCi 215, and Setu (Dhko1452). VyaKa 693 attributes it to Manu, Kātyāyana, and Nārada with slight variations.

9. A woman's property goes to her children. If she has no children, it goes to her husband—provided she was married to him in one of the first four forms of marriage, the *brāhma*, etc. If she was married in one of the other types of marriage, then her property goes to her parents.

NMS 14.9. J 13.9. If the woman has no offspring and was married by means of the *brāhma*, *prājāpatya*, *ārṣa*, or *daiva* form, her property goes to her husband. If she was married by means of the *gāndharva*, *āsura*, *rākṣasa*, or *paiśāca* form, her property goes to her parents. These forms of marriage are described at 12.38-44.

10. If a man supports his family while a brother pursues an education, he deserves a share of the gains of that education even though he might be uneducated himself.

NMS 14.10. J 13.10. This traditional rule was obviated in modern India by the *Hindu Gains of Learning Act* (No. XXX of 1930), wherein section 3a specifically addresses this situation and provides that property acquired as a result of education is the acquirer's separate property and is not subject to any claim by a member of his family as a result of "himself or his family having, while he was acquiring his learning, been maintained or supported, wholly or in part, by the joint funds of his family, or by the funds of any member thereof." ViCi 213 and VīMi on YāSmṛ 2.119 attribute this verse to Kātyāyana, VyaNi 445 attributes it to Manu and Viṣṇu.

11. An educated man need not give a share of his own property to a man who is uneducated if he does not want to, provided he did not rely on paternal property to acquire it.

NMS 14.11. J 13.11. The uneducated man spoken of here is obviously a coparcener (see the note to the preceding verse).

12. If a father partitions his estate, he should keep two shares for himself. After her husband's death, the mother should get an equal share with the sons.

NMS 14.12. J 13.12.

13. The eldest son should receive an extra share; he is entitled to the best share. The other sons and their unmarried sisters should get equal shares.

NMS 14.13. J 13.13. The eldest son gets two shares. He also may choose first and take whatever he prefers as his first share. The rest of the shares must be equal. The provision for the unmarried sisters is remarkable, but see 13.47.

14. The same applies to sons born of a levirate union, if they were born according to dharma. If they are of lower caste, provided they are legitimate, their share is diminished proportionately.

NMS 14.14. J 13.14. A *kṣetraja* son is one who is born from a levirate marriage (see 12.79-88). If the rules of the levirate marriage are not followed, however, a son born of such a union is not entitled to inherit (see 12.83). The proportions for the various classes of sons are given by Bhava: having divided the property into ten parts, the son of a brāhmaṇa by a brāhmaṇa wife would take four parts, the son of a kṣatriya wife, three parts; the son of a vaiśya wife, two parts; and the son of a śūdra wife, one part. In the case of a kṣatriya the estate should be divided into six parts and the son of a kṣatriya wife would take three parts; of a vaiśya wife, two parts; and the son of a śūdra wife, one part. In the case of a vaiśya, the estate would be divided into three parts, and the son of a vaiśya wife would take two parts, and of a śūdra wife, one part. Another way to describe this is that the son of the kṣatriya wife takes one fourth less than the share of the son of the brāhmaṇa wife, the son of the vaiśya wife takes one third less, and the son of the śūdra wife takes one half. According to Bhava, when there is only one son born from a brāhmaṇa wife but many from the other classes, then they take shares in accordance with their mother's share. Bhava further says that a son born of an appointed daughter (*putrikāsuta*, a son born of a man's daughter who is appointed to act as a son for his grandfather) has a share equal to his maternal grandfather's. There are three further situations which Bhava mentions: (a) a son born out of wedlock, (b) a son born of a woman pregnant at the time of her marriage, and (c) a son born of an unfaithful woman (see 13.16). The shares respectively allotted to these are one-half, one-fourth, and one-eighth of the share of a regular son.

15. The partition done by the father is legally binding on the co-parceners whether the shares are equal or not, because the father is the master of everything.

NMS 14.15. J 13.15. I translate the term *dharma* as "legally binding." Bhava seems to say that the partition spoken of here is similar to a will. He says that, fair or not, the partition done by the father is binding and should be respected after his death. It is binding whether it is fair or not.

Jolly accepts as Nārada's a verse which is unique to recension D:

A father who is ill, raging, engrossed in affairs, or who conducts himself in an unrighteous manner, is not the master when it comes to partition.

[J 13.16]

16. A son born out of wedlock, or of a woman pregnant at the time of her marriage, or of an unfaithful wife is considered to be the son of the man his mother marries and receives a share of that man's estate.

NMS 14.16. J 13.17. The term *gūḍhā* here must mean a woman who has conceived the child in secret, i.e., was unfaithful. The first half of this verse is similar to Manu 9.160ab. It is attributed to Bṛhaspati at VyaKa 717, ViRa 552, VyaPra 486, ViTā 365, and VyaU (folio 149).

17. A son born out of wedlock, whose father is unknown, and whose mother does not marry should offer the funerary offering to his maternal grandfather and receive a share of his estate.

NMS 14.17. J 13.18. Bhava points out that this refers to the son of a woman who was not yet engaged, otherwise the father would be known. Since, in this case, the son cannot offer the funerary rite to his father, he must do so to his mother's father.

18. Sons born to a woman who was not appointed to bear a child, whether she was with one man or many, do not have a share in their mother's husband's estate. They are the sons of those who begat them.

NMS 14.18. J 13.19. This verse refers to the situation in which a son is born to a widow, but that son is not the product of a properly sanctioned levirate marriage. Bhava says that the rule of the bull applies in this case (see 12.57). Since her elders did not appoint her to give birth to a son for the benefit of her deceased husband, the offspring in this case belong to the one who impregnated the woman. The sons must offer the funerary rites to the impregnator, and they share in his estate.

19. If their mother was paid for her favors, they must offer the funerary rite to their begetters. If she was not paid, they must offer the funerary rite to her husband.

NMS 14.19. J 13.20. See 12.54. In Bhava's view this verse is directed to all widows, appointed or not. As long as a woman was not paid for the sexual contact of the levirate union, her son is her husband's heir and offers the funerary rites to him. He cites the opinion of others to the effect that such sons offer the funerary rites to the deceased father, but they are not heirs. Bhava rejects this interpretation in light of the rule that the one who offers the funerary rites is also an heir. This verse and Bhava's interpretation seem to contradict the rule about *niyoga* (12.83) requiring that the widow be appointed. Perhaps this rule would apply to a situation in which a widow could find no one, not even the king (see 12.86), to appoint her. Under such circumstances a woman could still fulfill her responsibility to her deceased husband. The only stricture is that she must not be paid.

20. Sons who hate their father, are outcastes, impotent, or guilty of a minor sin do not share in the estate even if they are natural-born sons, all the more so for the sons of an appointed widow.

NMS 14.20. J 13.21.

21. Those who are afflicted with chronic or serious illness or who are idiots, insane, blind, or crippled, must be given maintenance within the family, but their sons receive a share.

NMS 14.21. J 13.22. These sons cannot inherit; yet their sons are eligible for their shares. Apa on YāSmṛ 2.140 attributes the first half of this verse to Manu.

22. Sons of two fathers should make the funerary offerings to each one separately, and they should receive half a share from their natural father and their adoptive father.

NMS 14.22. J 13.23. Bhava explains that these are sons born either in a levirate marriage or to an appointed daughter. In either case, the sons are born under an agreement that they will belong to both their progenitor and their mothers' husbands. If there are other sons, they receive half a share; but if there are no other sons, they are sole heirs.

23. The shares of reunited coparceners devolve to them alone; failing them, the shares revert to the original coparceners. If they, too, are without issue the shares go to other heirs.

NMS 14.23. J 13.24. This is an important verse judging from the number of times it is cited and commented upon in *nibandhas* (Dhko 1552-3). Bhava says that when coparceners have reunited and one of them dies without children, then his share goes to the other reunited coparceners, it does not go to other still separated brothers. If a reunited coparcener dies without issue and there are no reunited brothers to inherit his share, then the original, separated brothers take the inheritance. If there are no eligible heirs among the original coparceners and they have no sons, then other heirs inherit. ViRa 602-603 makes clear that the inheritors in this last instance are those who would not otherwise receive a share of the estate (*sapratibandha* heirs). See the notes to the next verse, and compare the comments of SmṛCa 305, ViCi 249, and especially VyaPra 513.

24. If one of the brothers has no children and dies or renounces the world, the rest of the brothers should divide his share, except for the *strīdhana*.

NMS 14.24. J 13.25. Bhava says that the subject here is the disposition of the property of brothers who have separated and not reunited. If one of them dies or becomes an ascetic, and he is without children, then the rest of the brothers divide his estate. The only exception to this is the *strīdhana*, but even here there is a special case. Bhava says that the word *strīdhana* should not be taken in its normal sense of "woman's property," but it should be understood to mean the money necessary to support a deceased brother's widows. Once they die, then that money, too, is to be divided among the separated brothers. VyaKa 756, ViRa 603, and ViCi 249-250 attribute this verse to Śaṅkha.

25. They should provide maintenance for his wives as long as they live, if they remain faithful to him; if not, they should cut them off.

NMS 14.25. J 13.26. Bhava says that the condition for this support is a vow of chastity. VyaKa 749 and 756, ViRa 593, ViCi 250, DīKa 45, and VyaPra 541 attribute this verse to Śaṅkha; ViTā 425 to both Śaṅkha and Nārada.

26. If he has a daughter, her father's share is considered to be for her maintenance. It should be used to support her up to the time of her marriage; after that her husband should provide for her maintenance.

NMS 14.26. J 13.27. Bhava interprets this to refer to two different circumstances. The first statement applies to separated brothers. If one among separated brothers has no sons, but dies, leaving a daughter, his daughter inherits his share for her maintenance. If the brothers were not separated at the time of his death, but later proceed to partition, the second statement applies: the dead man's share is used by one of his brothers to maintain the daughter until her marriage; after that, she has no further claim to it, and it reverts to the brother who assumed the responsibility. VyaKa 756, ViRa 603, ViCi 250, Candra 98, VyaPra 541, VyaMa 68, and ViTā 425 all attribute this verse to both Nārada and Śaṅkha.

27. If a woman has no sons, and her husband dies, her husband's family is her master. They have the authority to appoint, protect, and maintain her.

NMS 14.27. J 13.28. Bhava explains *viniyoga* as *niyoga*, appointing her to give birth to a son via a levirate marriage.

28. If the husband's family is extinct, has no males, is destitute, and if there is no extended family, then her father's family is her master.

NMS 14.28. J 13.29. Thus, the woman should resort to her own family only if the entire family of her husband (including the most distant *sapiṇḍas*) is unable to support her.

29. If neither family can, then it is for the king to maintain her. He should provide for her maintenance and prevent her from going astray.

NMS 14.29. J omits.

30. Independence ruins women, even those born into a good family; therefore Prajāpati ordained that they should not be independent.

NMS 14.30. J 13.30.

31. While she is a child, her father protects her; while she is a young woman, her husband; when she is a widow, her son: a woman is not fit to be independent.

NMS 14.31. J 13.31. This is a common notion in *smṛti* literature. No one quotes this verse from Nārada, but that is no doubt because it is found in Manu at 9.3, Bhā 13.47.13, 13.21.19, and 1.605*, Rām 2.29.15 and 673*, BauDha 2.2.53, and VaSmṛ 5.3.

32. The brothers should first pay off their father's debts to insure that he is not a debtor, only then do they divide the rest of his estate.

NMS 14.32. J 13.32.

33. If the father did not perform the prescribed sacraments for some of the brothers, the other brothers should pay for their performance out of the paternal estate.

NMS 14.33. J 13.33. The money required for the performance of the various sacraments must be taken out of the common paternal estate before it is divided into coparceners' shares.

34. If there is no paternal property, those who have previously undergone the sacraments are required to pay for their brothers' sacraments out of their own shares.

NMS 14.34. J 13.34. Here, the phrase "out of their own shares" may indicate that the brothers who are required to pay in this instance are brothers who have previously separated from the family and taken their shares. If the father dies leaving uninitiated sons but no money to pay for the sacraments, their separated brothers would have to pay for the sacraments out of their own funds which would include a portion of their father's estate. Presumably, the wording of this verse would limit the liability of the separated brothers to the amount of that portion of the paternal estate which they took when they separated.

35. If one brother is designated to look after the family's affairs and he undertakes to do so, then the other brothers should sustain him with food, clothing, and transportation.

NMS 14.35. J 13.35. Bhava says this rule applies to families in which the brothers are separated as well as those in which they are not separated.

36. If there is doubt about the legality of a partition, any needed determination concerning the heirs will be done on the basis of the evidence of

relatives, documents pertaining to the partition, and whether or not they conduct their affairs separately.

NMS 14.36. J.13.36. According to Bhava the question is "What portion belongs to whom?" "Conducting their affairs separately" is elucidated at 13.38-42.

37. There is only one common set of righteous observances for brothers who are not separated. If they are separated each one is responsible for his own righteous observances.

NMS 14.37. J 13.37. Bhava says that for brothers who are not separated, duties such as the *vaiśvadeva* ritual, feeding mendicants, and looking after guests are carried on in common, whereas if they are separated, then each one will do this separately. This increase in religious observance is the reason why Manu (9.111) says that partition is better than living jointly.

38. Giving, receiving, possessing animals, food, houses, and fields, cooking, religious observances, earning and expenditure are done individually by those who are separated.

NMS 14.38. J 13.38. Samu (folio 145) attributes this verse to Bṛhaspati.

39-40. Separated brothers may act as witnesses or sureties for one another, give to and receive from one another, but brothers living jointly may not. Coparceners who publicly engage in these acts should be understood to be separated even if there is no document to that effect.

NMS 14.39-40. J 13.39-40. If coparceners mutually do the things mentioned, then that constitutes evidence of their having separated (see 13.36 and SaVi 441).

Jolly accepts as Nārada's a verse which is found only in recension D, and which is never cited as a Nārada verse. Aparārka on YāSmṛ 2.149, SmṛCa 311, SaVi 443, and Samu 145 all attribute it to Kātyāyana:

> **Brothers who live separately for ten years and perform religious observances separately must be known to have separated. That is certain.** [J 13.41]

41-42. When several people who are descended from one ancestor perform religious observances individually, do their work individually, individually reap the benefits of their work, and do not consult about their affairs, if they give or sell their own shares, they may do all that as they like; they are masters of their own property.

NMS 14.41-2. J 13.42-3. Recension D adds a verse which is nearly identical with Manu 9.216:

> **If a son is born after partition, he is an heir only to his father's estate. If the coparceners have reunited, then they should share in the partition with him. That is the rule.** [J 13.44]

43-44. There are twelve kinds of sons: a natural-born son, a son born of an appointed widow, the son of a daughter, a son born out of wedlock, the son of a woman pregnant at the time of her marriage, the son of an unfaithful woman, the son of a remarried woman, a foundling, a son given up by his parents, a son who was purchased, an adopted son, and a son who offered himself.

NMS 14.43-44. J 13.45-46. Several of these kinds of sons have been described at 13.16-17. The son of a daughter (*putrikāputra*) is the son born of an appointed daughter who promises that her first son will serve as a son to her father. The legitimacy of this institution is still being debated in modern Indian courts (see *Shyam Sunder* v. *State of Bihar* A.I.R. 1981 S.C. 178). Bhava gives as an example of a foundling, Kṛpa, the son of the sage Śaradvat Gautama who was abandoned, and found and adopted out of pity (*kṛpā*) by Śaṃtanu who pronounced him and his sister his children, proceeded to raise them and to see to it that they were administered the sacraments (see Bhā 1.120). As an example of a son who was purchased Bhava cites the legend of Śunaḥśepa, the middle son of a sage, who was purchased to serve as a subsitute for a stolen sacrificial victim in a king's sacrifice (see one account of this legend in Rām 1.60-61). NāSmṛ 13.44 is identical with Manu 9.216.

45-46. Of these, six are inheriting relatives, six are non-inheriting relatives. They are listed in descending rank order. When the father dies, these sons, in order, acquire his estate; in the absence of each superior type, the next lower inherits.

NMS 14.45-46. J 13.47, 49. The first six, beginning with the natural-born son and ending with the son of an unfaithful wife, inherit from other members of the family as well as from their father. The remaining six inherit from their father, but not from his relatives. Bhava says that each category prevails in the absence of the preceding one, but this seems simplistic. 13.46 likely applies to the inheritance of the father's estate by a joint family in which there is more than one type of son. This latter situation is a thorny question with several suggested answers; see Manu 9. 134 and 163, KāSmṛ 857 (and especially the note to the translation), and DaCa pp. 64 ff., especially 67. Verse 13.45 is similar to Manu 9.159 and to a verse in the Kālikāpurāṇa (Dhko 1376). It is attributed variously to Saṅkha (Dhko 1282) and Parāśara 4.19 (Dhko 1352).

Recension D inserts between 45 and 46 a verse which is unknown elsewhere:

> **When there is some doubt about a house or a field whose possession has been interrupted, one should settle it by means of a document, by consulting experts on possession, or by witnesses.** [J 13.48]

47. If a man has no sons, his daughters inherit since they are just as much part of his lineage; both a son and a daughter continue the lineage of their father.

NMS 14.47. J 13.50. Bhava explains that the way in which a daughter continues a father's lineage is through the institution of the *putrikāputra*, the son born of an appointed daughter. This does not mean, according to Bhava's view, that the daughter inherits in her own right. SmṛSā (Dhko 1511) attributes this verse to Manu; ViCa 115 attributes the first half to Devala.

48. If he has no daughters, his close relatives inherit, next his distant relatives, then his fellow caste members, and failing all of these, the king.

NMS 14.48. J 13.51. Bhava explains "close relatives" (*sakulya*) as *sapiṇḍas* (see the note to 12.20).

49. This last provision does not apply to brahmaṇas. A righteous king should provide sustenance to the man's widows. This is the law of inheritance.

NMS 14.49. J 13.52. If a brāhmaṇa dies without heirs his property should be given to other brāhmaṇas. The king is entitled to the remainder of the estate of members of other castes, after he has duly provided for the maintenance of the widows. GauMi on 28.19 attributes this verse to Bṛhaspati.

CHAPTER 14

VIOLENT ACTS

1. An act which is performed with violence (*sahasā*) by those who are insolent in their strength is called a Violent Act (*sāhasa*). In this world violence (*sahas*) is called strength.

NMS 15.1. J 14.1. Jolly accepts as Nārada's a verse which is unique to recension D. It is attributed to Bṛhaspati by a host of texts (Dhko 1645), while Apa on 2.72 attributes it to Manu, and VyaNi 76 to Kātyāyana:

> **These are the four types of violent acts: murder, theft, assaulting another man's wife, and the two kinds of assault.**
> [J 14.2]

2-5. In the texts, violent acts are said to be of three degrees, the lowest, the middle, and the highest. The descriptions of each of these are as follows: violent acts of the lowest degree consist of breaking, stealing, destroying, or otherwise ruining such things as fruits, roots, water, or agricultural implements and the like. Violent acts of the middle degree consist of doing the same sorts of things to clothes, domestic animals, food, drink, or household utensils. Violent acts of the highest degree consist of killing through the use of poison, weapons, etc., molesting another man's wife, or doing anything that might cause his death.

NMS 15.2-5. J 14.3-6. Bhava observes that such texts as the Manusaṃhitā rank acts of violence on the basis of the relative seriousness of the act. The agricultural implements mentioned by Bhava are the plow, yoke, and the traces of a team. The household utensils he mentions are pots, chairs, mortars, pestles, and winnowing baskets. He explains that a way one might cause a person's death is to tell him falsely that his son has been killed.

6. The punishment fits the deed: the experts in the *śāstra* set the fine for violent acts of the lowest degree at a minimum of 100, for the middle degree, a minimum of 500.

NMS 15.6. J 14.7. According to Bhava, the fines are 100-500 for the lowest degree, and 500-1000 for the middle degree. The unit of fines here is probably copper *paṇas* (see the note to 12.34). The half verse in the variants is found only in recension D of the Nārada mss, although it is quoted very often (fifteen times,

Dhko 1643). It states that the minimum fine for the highest degree of violence is 1000. This is the figure given by Bhava as the maximum for the middle degree of violence.

7. Corporal punishment, confiscation of a person's entire property, banishment from town, branding, and the chopping off of a limb are the punishments for violent acts of the highest degree.

NMS 15.7. J 14.8. The term *vadha* "corporal punishment" can also mean "killing," but such a rendering would be inappropriate in this context. Bhava glosses it "beating, etc." Bhava says that the limb to be cut off is the one with which the crime was committed. In Bhava's view, these punishments are cumulative. As the offense gets more serious, additional punishment is inflicted.

Ms B2 has two additional verses:

The wise ones say that one *māṣaka* equals four *kākinīs* and twenty of them equals one *paṇa*. [Bharadvāja Dhko 534]

250 *paṇas* is the fine of the lowest degree, 500 is the middle degree, and 1000 is the highest. [Manu 8.138]

8. These punishments apply uniformly to everyone, except that no corporal punishment should be inflicted on a brāhmaṇa. A brāhmaṇa ought not to be corporally punished.

NMS 15.8. J 14.9. Bhava says that the five types of punishment for crimes of the highest degree of violence apply uniformly to kṣatriyas, vaiśyas, and śūdras. The same thing applies to the punishments for the other two degrees of violence. The only exception is that brāhmaṇas are not to be corporally punished even if they commit a crime which deserves such punishment. The reason for their exemption, according to Bhava, is that this caste is to be revered.

9. For him the punishment is shaving his head, banishing him from town, branding his forehead with a symbol of his crime, and parading him on an ass.

NMS 15.9. J 14.10. These punishments are listed in order as punishments for increasingly serious crimes, according to Bhava. He says that the sign of a dog, for example, might be placed on the man's forehead.

Ms B2 inserts a Manu verse that specifies symbols to be branded on the forehead:

For incest, a vagina; for drinking liquor, the symbol for liquor; for theft, a dog's paw; for killing a brāhmaṇa, a headless man. [Manu 9.237]

10. Those who have committed a violent act of either of the first two degrees may still be accepted into society after they have been punished, but

one who has committed a violent act of the highest degree, cannot eat with others even after he has been punished.

NMS 15.10. J 14.11.

11. Theft is a special category of violent acts. The difference is that what the rest achieve by extreme violence, theft achieves by deceit.

NMS 15.11. J 14.12.

12-15. This, too, say the wise, is of three degrees, depending on the value of the object, for items are ranked according to their value as petty, medium, or highest. Petty items are such things as earthenware, seats, cots, bone, wood, leather, grass, pulses, and beans. Medium items are clothes, except for silk; domestic animals, except for cows; metals, except for gold; rice and barley. The highest items are gold, gems, silk, women, men, cattle, elephants, horses, and items belonging to gods, brāhmaṇas, or kings.

NMS 15.12-15. J 14.13-16. Bhava gives examples: for earthenware—pots, etc.; for seats—stools; for bones—combs, etc. His examples of middle items are clothes made of leaves, fine cloth, wool, copper, iron, lead, etc. He says that such things as jewels are excluded from this category.

16. The wise say that using a variety of means to deceive people who are asleep, insane, or intoxicated, and rob them of such things constitutes theft.

NMS 15.16. J 14.17. Bhava enumerates some of these means: messages, forged documents, breaking and entering, picking pockets, etc.

17. Theft may be inferred from the possession of stolen goods; even if there are no stolen goods, from high living. Suspicion of theft may be based on association with bad characters or on spending without income.

NMS 15.17. J 14.18.

18-19. Those who provide food or shelter to thieves who are on the run, or who do not stop them even though they could, share in their guilt. Those who do not come running when people are crying out for help or when they see property being taken, also share in the guilt.

NMS 15.18-19. J 14.19-20. The liability set forth in 14.19 applies especially to officers of the realm (see 19.22).

20. The punishments the wise have pronounced for the three degrees of violent acts apply in the same way to thefts depending on the three kinds of items stolen.

NMS 15.20. J 14.21. The punishments for the lowest, middle, and highest degrees of violence apply to the three degrees of theft, based on the value of the items stolen, always keeping in mind the circumstances and the people involved, says Bhava.

21-24. When cattle, etc. have vanished or when items have been stolen, people who know how should follow the trail from the start. Wherever the trail leads, whether to a village, farm, or pasture, the responsibility lies with the local residents unless they can show that it goes elsewhere. If the trail is obscured or lost because of rough ground and there are settlements nearby, then the nearest village or farm should be held responsible; if there are two the same distance away, then that one where the residents are known to be mostly of bad conduct, criminals, or keepers of bad company.

NMS 15.21-24. J 14.22-25. Bhava says that the fear of being held responsible should motivate people to be vigilant and guard against thieves. He explains bad company as outcastes, those who consort with slave women, gamblers, or liquor vendors, etc.

25. In villages *caṇḍālas*, executioners, and the like, and people accustomed to going about at night should conduct the search; outside villages, those who live outside should.

NMS 15.25. J 14.26. Those familiar with the territory where the trail leads should conduct the search.

26. If the thieves are not caught, the king should compensate for it out of his own treasury; for a king who fails in this is a sinner whose righteousness and fortunes are lost.

NMS 15.26. J 14.27. Bhava says that the reason why the king must compensate for the theft is that he is responsible for protecting his subjects against theft; if a theft occurs, then he has not properly discharged his duties. GauDha 2.1.41 (10.47), Manu 8.40, YāSmṛ 2.36, Bhā 12.76 all state that the king must provide compensation for all unrecovered stolen goods.

CHAPTERS 15 AND 16

VERBAL AND PHYSICAL ASSAULT

1. An abusive or coarse statement which is intended to be contemptuous of a region, caste, family, and the like is called Verbal Assault.

NMS 16-17.1. J 15-16.1. Bhava names as other possible subjects for verbal abuse a man's learning, craft, and relatives. For an overview of the title of law discussed in this chapter, see Ludo Rocher, "The Definition of Vākpāruṣya," *P.K. Gode Commemoration Volume*, pp. 1-12.

2. It is of three kinds: harsh, vulgar, and violent. As they increase in severity, so do the respective punishments.

NMS 16-17.2. J 15-16.2. The three kinds of verbal abuse are listed in ascending order of severity; the punishment for each increases proportionately. VyaNi 484 and Apa on YāSmṛ 2.204 attribute the first half of this verse to Kātyāyana (the latter quotes only the first half).

3. The wise say that harsh abuse includes reviling, vulgar abuse includes coarseness, and violent abuse consists of accusations resulting in outcasting.

NMS 16-17.3. J 15-16.3. Bhava gives as an example of harsh abuse "Such a mother and father you have, and yet you don't know anything!" An accusation which would cause outcasting might be an accusation of theft or incest. Apa on YāSmṛ 2.204 attributes this verse to Kātyāyana.

4. Injuring others physically with one's hand, foot, or weapon, or throwing ashes and the like on them, is called Physical Assault.
NMS 16-17.4. J 15-16.4. Bhava explains "throwing ashes and the like on them" as sprinkling or smearing them with impure substances.

5-6. It, too, is of three kinds, slight, medium, and highest, depending on whether there is a threat, a random blow, or a wound. There are three kinds of violence, small, medium or great, depending on the value of the items involved in the transgressions. These thorns must be removed.

NMS 16-17.5-6. J 15-16.5-6. Bhava says that in the highest degree of assault blood is drawn. He understands the second verse to refer to items that were stolen, and observes that the punishment for theft was discussed in the preceding chapter. He says this in spite of the use of the term *sāhasa* "violent acts," which is the subject of the preceding chapter, the topic here may not be theft, but damage to another person, an extension of physical assault (see Kau 3.19, Manu 8.288 and 296-8, or YāSmṛ 2.225-229 and 233). The statement "These thorns must be removed" refers to the king's duty to apprehend wrongdoers. This is an expression which is commonly used when discussing the duties of a king (see Manu 9.252-3). SaVi 480 attributes these verses to Manu.

7. For both of these there are five different situations when it comes to assigning innocence and guilt:

NMS 16-17.7. J 15-16.7. In keeping with his interpretation of the preceding verse, Bhava takes the situations described in the following verses to apply to cases of theft as well as of assault.

8. If an assault arose out of rage and both parties are agitated, the one who calms down is to be admired and the one who carries on is to be punished.

NMS 16-17.8. J omits.

9. If two persons are engaged in an assault on one another and no difference in their behavior is obvious, they should both receive the same punishment.

NMS 16-17.9. J 15-16.8. Bhava spells out that they are subject to equal punishment when it is not apparent who is being assaulted and who is not. SaVi 476 attributes this verse to Sumantu. DaVi 232 attributes it to Kātyāyana. ViTā 725 seems to attribute it to Yājñavalkya.

10. The one who starts the fracas is certainly at fault, and the one who responds is also wrong, but the former receives the heavier penalty.

NMS 16-17.10. J 15-16.9. Bhava makes clear that both parties in this case are to be punished. PaMā 86 attributes this verse to Kātyāyana.

11. When both are equally involved, the one who keeps at it is the one who is punished, whether he started it or not.

NMS 16-17.11. J 15-16.10. Presumably one of the embattled parties has relinquished his attacks; that one, Bhava tells us, is not to be punished, but the one who continues with his attacks is the one who bears the punishment, whether he started it or not.

12-13. If a *śvapāka*, a man who is impotent, a *caṇḍāla*, a cripple, a butcher, an elephant driver, a man who is uninitiated, their wives, or the wives of an elder or a preceptor should violate customary rules, an immediate beating is their punishment; the wise say that physical assault on these is not a crime.

NMS omits. J 15-16.11-12. Bhava comments on these two verses even though they are not found in NMS. He says that, even though beating or even killing these persons for violation of customary rules does not involve a crime and the ones who do the beating are not punishable, it is not something the king should encourage. Bhava further says that if any of those listed here should offend elders or preceptors they should be killed. If they commit verbal or physical assault against others, then the punishment is corporal punishment (*vadha*). A *śvapāka* is a particularly low caste, see Kane, HDh 2.97.

14-15. The virtuous man whom they offend is the very one who should punish them; the king has no role in their punishment. Because they are the impure of mankind, their property is naturally impure; thus, the king may have them beaten, but he should not fine them.

NMS 16-17.12-13. J 15-16.13-14. This is a remarkable view which exempts a considerable portion of the populace from the imposition of fines by the king. It is possible that this was seen as a significant disability, since it meant that physical punishment is the only way for these people to atone for transgressions (see 15-16.25 and 29, and Lingat, *Classical Law of India*, pp. 63-65 and 232 ff.). These verses constitute an important verification for the history of Nārada's text. The early commentator Apa, on YāSmṛ 2.212, confirms that they followed one another in his text of the Nāradasmṛti.

16-18. A kṣatriya who insults a brāhmaṇa should be fined 100, a vaiśya who does so, 150-200, and a śūdra who does so should receive corporal punishment. If a brāhmaṇa insults a kṣatriya, he should be fined fifty, twenty-five if he insults a vaiśya, and the fine is twelve in the case of a śūdra. When twice-born men are insulted by members of their own castes the fine is twelve. If the insult is something which should never be uttered, the fine is double.

NMS 16-17.14-16. J 15-16.15-17. These punishments apply to the crime of verbal assault (see the note to 12.34). These verses are identical with Manu 8.267-269. Numerous *nibandhas* attribute them to Manu and Nārada (VyaKa 478 and VyaNi 486 for the first, VyaNi 487 for the second, VyaKa 478, ViRa 249, DaVi 204, and VyaPra 380 for the third).

19. If someone calls another person one-eyed or crippled or whatever, even if he really is, the king should make him pay a minimum of one *kārṣāpaṇa*.

NMS 16-17.17. J 15-16.18. This verse is identical with Manu 8.274. ViRa 247-248 attributes it to Manu, Nārada, and Viṣṇu.

20. One should not abuse someone for a sin after he has purified himself in accordance with the sacred texts or after he has been punished for it by the king. One who commits this offense should be punished.

NMS 16-17.18. J 15-16.19.

21. In this world there are only two persons who are exempt from accusation and punishment—the brāhmaṇa and the king—, for these two support the world.

NMS 16-17.19. J 15-16.20.

22. One who calls an outcaste an outcaste or a thief a thief is as guilty as the thief or the outcaste; if he is wrong, then his sin is double.

NMS 16-17.20. J 15-16.21. Bhava gives a lengthy comment on this verse, and notes that it constitues a continuation of 15-16.20. The person being called thief or outcaste is one who has undergone the punishment or penance for his crime, and therefore is not to be harassed. In the case of an outcaste, presumably, the person would have been fined or otherwise punished by his caste and then readmitted to the caste. To remind one that he was previously a thief or an outcaste is wrong, and results in the guilt incurred by the former thief or outcaste being visited on the one who brings up the old charge. The sin is doubled if the person accused of being a thief never was a thief. In the same way, if the person accused never was a thief, outcaste, etc. the accuser incurs twice the sin for his accusation. This verse is identical to Vasiṣṭha 20.40. SaVi 479 attributes it to Bṛhaspati, but only quotes the first three *pādas*.

23. If a śūdra maliciously assails their name or caste he should be pierced with an iron spike eighteen *aṅgulas* long.

NMS 16-17.21. J 15-16.23. This verse is similar to Manu 8.271. All commentators who cite it attribute it to both Manu and Nārada. Recension D inserts before it the verse that immediately precedes in Manu (8.270). VyaKa 480, ViRa 253, PaMā 434, VyaNi 487, DaVi 206, and Setu (Dhko 1788) all attribute it to both Manu and Nārada:

> **A once-born who reviles a twice-born with harsh words should have his tongue cut out, for he is of lower origin.** [J 15-16.22].

The reason for this addition must have been to provide an antecedent for *teṣām* "their" in 15-16.22. As Bhava makes clear, "their" refers to the twice-born. As examples of names he mentions *sautilaka* and *dattilaka*, which are diminutives (cf. Louis Renou, *Grammaire Sanscrite*, Paris, 1961, p. 236 for references). The use of these familiar forms by a śūdra would be most insulting (see Manu 2.120-137, especially 2.126). Bhava specifies that the iron spike should be thrust in the offender's mouth. An *aṅgula* is approximately three quarters of an inch (see DiTa Introduction p. 29).

24. If he has the arrogance to instruct the twice-born in righteousness, the king should have hot oil poured into his mouth and ears.

NMS 16-17.22. J 15-16.24. Bhava points out that, since the purpose is to punish the śūdra, the oil should be very hot, not merely warm. This verse is similar to Manu 8.272. All commentators attribute it to both Manu and Nārada, except PaMā 434 and VyaNi 488, which attribute it to Bṛhaspati.

25-28. If a person of low caste offends a brāhmaṇa with a certain limb, that very limb must be cut off; this is how he atones for it. If a person of low caste tries to sit on the same seat as one of a higher caste he should be branded on the hip and banished, or he should have his buttocks cut. If he has the arrogance to spit, the king should order his lips cut off; to urinate, his penis; to break wind, his anus. If he grabs the hair, feet, nose, throat, or genitals, the king should, without hesitation, order both his hands cut off.

NMS 16-17.23-26. J 15-16.25-28. Bhava notes that mutilation constitutes the entire punishment; there is no monetary fine. These verses are very similar to Manu 8.279 and almost identical with Manu 8.281-283. All commentators know the last as both a Manu and a Nārada verse.

Recensions Y and D add a verse which is identical to Manu 8.284, and which no *nibandha* attributes to Nārada:

> **If he breaks the skin or draws blood, he should be fined 100; if he damages muscle, six *niṣkas;* if he breaks a bone, he should be banished.**
> [J 15-16.29].

29-30. If a man insults a king who is engaged in his duties, his atonement is to have his tongue cut out or all his property confiscated. If an evil-minded man assails a king, even a sinful king, it is worse than murdering one hundred brāhmaṇas. He should be skewered and roasted in a fire.

NMS 16-17.27-28. J 15-16.30-31.

31. A father is not responsible for the misdeeds of a son, nor are the owners of a dog or a monkey for theirs, unless they instigated them.

NMS 16-17.29. J 15-16.32.

CHAPTER 17

GAMBLING AND CONTESTS

1. Crooked games of dice, leather bits, ivory pieces, and the like, and wagers on strength, make up the title of law called Gambling and Contests.

NMS 18.1. J 17.1. There are two types of gambling mentioned here. Gambling with dice, etc. and contests of strength. Bhava says the contests of strength may take the form of cock fights, fights between young rams, races of young bulls, etc. He counts this as the sixteenth *vivādapada* (but see the variants for 17.6).

Ms B2 adds the following verse:

The king should eliminate gambling and contests from his kingdom. The king must take care, since these vices will destroy a kingdom. [Manu 9.221]

2. The *sabhika* conducts the gambling; he must pay out the winnings that must be paid. His share of the gambling proceeds is ten per cent.

NMS 18.2. J 17.2. The percentage that goes to the person in charge of the gambling, the *sabhika*, is different in various texts. YāSmṛ 2.199 mentions two figures: 5% and 10%. PaMā 574 and the VyaPra 565 interpret this to mean that his share was 10% for a wager under 100 *paṇas* and 5% for a wager over 100 *paṇas*. Apa understands it to mean that he is to receive 5% from the victorious gambler and 10% from the loser. Bhava understands the verse to mean that the person whose share of the proceeds is 10% is the winner, while the *sabhika* pays the remainder to the king's court.

3. When a player rolls the same number twice, he is declared the winner, and his opponent is the loser.

NMS 18.3. J 17.3. This verse appears to give a rule which determines the winner and loser in a game of dice. The term *dvirabhyasta* is a problem. It might mean that the dice give the same number in two rolls, or it could have several other meanings. Bhava's commentary is not very helpful here: *dvirabhyastāḥ ekarupāḥ tṛtīyo 'nyaḥ sattvasya* (?) "two rolls are the same and the third is different." This verse is not discussed in Heinrich Lüders' *Das Würfelspiel im alten Indien*. Compare KāSmṛ 938, which Kane translates tentatively: "Where (the throw) of a man playing with dice in gambling is the same or double (of the previous throw) there the (former) gambler is the winner and his protection (from the other gamblers) is to be arranged for."

4. If a dispute arises among gamblers, gamblers should serve as judges and witnesses for it.

NMS 18.4. J 17.4. Bhava adds that this is the only circumstance in which gamblers can serve as judges; they could not serve in this capacity in the king's court. Gamblers also constitute the only witnesses in such a case; it is not necessary to test them as to their suitability.

5. A gambler who has not cleared his debts may not frequent another gaming place, he should not impede the *sabhika*, and he should pay him what he wants.

NMS 18.5. J 17.5. Bhava says that, even if there is a disagreement about payment the gambler may not resort to another establishment.

6. Cheats who play with crooked dice should have a necklace of dice hung around their necks and be thrown out of the gaming place. That is their punishment.

NMS 18.6. J 17.6. Jolly accepts as Nārada's two verses which are found only in recension D:

> **If a man gambles without the king's permission he should not get his stake, and he ought to be punished.** [J 17.7]
> **On the other hand, if gamblers pay the king the portion due to him, they may play in public; they would not be at fault.** [J 17.8]

CHAPTER 18

MISCELLANEOUS

1-4. The title of Miscellaneous includes disputes connected with the king, violations of his edicts, the performance of his work, granting villages, the disposition of the constituents of the kingdom, deviations from their duties by heretics, adherents of the Veda, guilds, and corporations, disputes between father and son, violations of penances, the suspension of donations, the anger of monks, the sin of mixing castes, restrictions on their livelihoods, and whatever has not been covered thus far. All this is to be found under Miscellaneous.

NMS 19.1-4. J 18.1-4. The first four verses of this chapter constitute a table of contents for this title of law, although not exactly of the contents of this chapter. Bhava's commentary is extremely brief, and so are the comments of most other authors who cite these verses, with the exception of the SaVi 496-499. The king and his role are the subjects of verses 5-32 in this chapter. The constituents of the kingdom (*prakṛti*) are enumerated at Kau 6.1: they are the king (*svāmin*), his minister (*amātya*), the subjects (*janapada*), the fortress (*durga*), the treasury (*kośa*), the army (*daṇḍa*), and allies (*mitra*). The term *āśraminaḥ* in 18.3 which I translate as "monks," i.e. those who dwell in *āśramas*, could also mean those who are in one of the four stages of life as mentioned in the following verse. The verses in this chapter are rarely cited by subsequent writers.

5. An attentive king should protect all the stages of life with all the means prescribed by the texts and by the four techniques.

NMS 19.5. J 18.5. The "stages of life" are student, householder, forest dweller, and renouncer. The "four techniques" are conciliation (*sāma*), gifts (*upapradāna*), dissension (*bheda*), and force (*daṇḍa*) (see Kau 2.10.47 ff.).

6-9. When any caste is superseded or when a caste affects undue superiority the king should note that they have strayed and he should return them to their rightful place. When other evil deeds are committed that contravene the dictates of the texts, the king, himself, should look into the matter and visit punishment on those who deserve it. The king must not do anything opposed to *śruti* or *smṛti* nor anything which is inimical to his people; if such things do take place, he must put a stop to them. If an edict

which is unjust has been enacted by some other king out of ignorance, he should rectify that injustice as well.

NMS 19.6-9. J 18.6-9. Bhava gives the example of a king who has "caused the royal revenue to decline" as a type of error a subsequent king should rectify. DaVi 18-19 attributes 19.8-9 to Nārada, Kātyāyana, and Yama. VyaMā 279 and VyaKa 11 attribute 19.8 to Nārada, Kātyāyana, and Yama, and 19.9 to Nārada and Kātyāyana.

10. If a man does not uphold the righteous laws promulgated by the king, he is evil; he should be punished and beaten for violating the king's edict.

NMS 19.10. J 18.13. The way in which righteous laws are promulgated is set forth in 18.19.

11-12. The weapons of soldiers, the vehicles of carriers, the ornaments of public women, the instruments of musicians, and any tools by which artisans make their livings are not to be taken by the king even when he confiscates a man's entire property.

NMS 19.11-12. J 18.10-11. Bhava says that the vehicles in question are such things as elephant or horse drawn chariots, oxen, etc. The musical instruments which he mentions are the *vīṇā*, and the *murava* (*muraja*? a kind of percussion instrument ?).

13. The king is the only man who has neither beginning nor end, for he is illustrious and sacred, as long as he does not swerve from his path.

NMS 19.13. J 18.12. Bhava explains that the king's duties are without beginning or end for what he does is *dharma*, which has no beginning or end. It remains authoritative in all times. He also points out that the king's illustriousness has no beginning, and his sanctity has no end. NāSmṛ 18.13-23 are completely ignored by subsequent writers in the field of *dharmaśāstra*.

14-16. If the king did not punish every caste when they stray from their paths, his subjects would perish. The brāhmaṇa would neglect his priestly office, the kṣatriya would relinquish his power, the vaiśya would neglect his work, and the śūdra would be more distinguished than all of them. If there were no kings on earth to wield the staff, the strong would cook the weak like fish on a skewer.

NMS 18.14-16. J 18.14-16.

17. Always to show favor to the virtuous and to restrain the wicked, such is the duty of kings; material gain comes from oppressing their enemies.

NMS 19.17. J 18.17.

18. Just as fire is not tainted even though it is forever burning the creatures of this world, so a king is not tainted when he punishes those who deserve it.

NMS 19.18. J 18.18.

19. The power of kings is the edict. It is based on their word: whatever they say, right or wrong, is the *dharma* for litigants.

NMS 19.19. J 18.19. Bhava says that the *tejas* of the king is so great that whatever he decrees, good or bad, is *dharma* for the people.

20. The Thousand-Eyed One roams the earth embodied as the king. There is nowhere for people to go if they violate his edict.

NMS 19.20. J 18.20. In classical India the usual identity of the god Dharma is with Yama, the god of death. Here we have an epithet, "thousand-eyed," used for Dharma, which is ordinarily applied to Indra. Indra is identified with Dharma early in the tradition (see *Śatapathabrāhmaṇa* 13.4.3.14).

21. Whatever a king does is authoritative, because of his responsibility for protection, his authority, and his vigilance for the welfare of creatures.

NMS 19.21. J 18.21.

22. Just as wives must always worship their husband even if he has no redeeming qualities, so, too, a king must be revered by his subjects, even if he has no redeeming qualities.

NMS 19.22. J 18.22. Recension D adds two verses which are unknown elsewhere:

> **Since it is respect for the king's edicts that keeps his subjects from straying from their paths, the king's decrees must be known to be based on legal proceedings.** [J 18.23]
> **In order to ensure stability kings support the traditional norms of behavior, but a king's decree overrules those norms.** [J 18.24]

23. The king has purchased his subjects through austerities, therefore he is their master; thus whatever he says must be obeyed, their livelihood depends on him.

NMS 19.23. J 18.25. Bhava says that a king's subjects must look upon his pronouncements as they would upon their own fathers', otherwise the law of the jungle would prevail.

24-31. Kings of immeasurable power take on five forms: those of Agni, Indra, Soma, Yama, and Kubera. A king is called Agni when, for good reason or not, he becomes consumed with anger and burns his subjects. A king is called Indra when he relies on his power, seeks victory, raises his weapon, and attacks the enemy. A king is called Soma when he appears before his subjects devoid of anger or agitation and in a cheerful mood. A king is Vaivasvata Yama when he takes the *dharma* seat in full majesty, and metes out punishment equitably to all creatures. A king is called Kubera when he obliges with gifts those who beseech him: elders, the wise, servants, and others. Therefore one must not underestimate him, nor insult him, nor exceed him. One must obey his edict; to violate it would result in death. His function is to protect his subjects, honor the elderly and the wise, adjudicate disputes, and protect himself.

NMS 19.24-31. J 18.26-33. Compare Manu 9.303 ff. Verses 18.24-32 are cited only in PraKā (Dhko 588).

32. A steadfast king should always honor brāhmaṇas; royal power and brāhmaṇas are the basis for the protection of the worlds.

NMS 19.32. J 18.34. Bhava adds that if the brāhmaṇas were treated in any other way they would become angry and destroy the royal power.

33-36. The privileges of a brāhmaṇa are: immunity from punishment; the seat of honor vis-à-vis kṣatriyas; being the first one seen in the morning; respectful salutation from everyone; the best share of the new crops; the right of way when he travels; unrestricted entry into others' houses to beg; no charge of theft when he gathers firewood, flowers, or water even if they belong to someone else; protection from insults; freedom to converse with other men's wives; the right to cross rivers without paying the toll; the right to cross first; and exemption from duty on these crossings as long as he is not engaged in commerce.

NMS 19.33-36. J 18.35-38. The term *parihāra* usually means "shunning," its negative *aparihāra* has the technical meaning "immunity from punishment" when applied to brāhmaṇas (DaVi 43 glosses it *daṇḍābhāva* "absence of punishment"), yet Bhava says that the sight of a brāhmaṇa should not be avoided under any circumstance. He also notes that seeing a brāhmaṇa first in the morning confers religious merit on the person who sees him. The term *saparigrahāt* is translated "even if they belong to others" in accordance with the explanations of DaVi 43 and Bhava, both of whom gloss it *paraparigrahāt*. Conversing with another man's wife is generally viewed as adulterous (see 12.62-68).

37. If a brāhmaṇa becomes tired while traveling, he commits no sin by helping himself to two stalks of sugar cane or five tubers, as long as he does not dwell there.

NMS 19.37. J 18.39. Bhava adds that he incurs no sin even if he takes these without the permission of the owner.

38. He should not accept anything from a man accused of a crime, or from an outcaste, or from an enemy, or from an atheist, or from one in distress, and not without cause or by extortion.

NMS 19.38. J 18.40. There is no verb in this verse. Bhava understands it to limit the persons from whom a brāhmaṇa may receive gifts (*gṛhṇan* in 18.37). Verses 18.38-52 are not quoted by any other writer on *dharmaśāstra*.

39. Except for a brāhmaṇa, of all the rest, it is best to accept gifts from kings, since they have plenty of wealth, and since this is to be given to the high-minded.

NMS 19.39. J 18.41. The syntax of this verse is a bit fractured. Bhava, who has the easier reading *anyebhyo* for *anyeṣām*, clearly states that a gift from a brāhmaṇa is best (see 18.47), better even than from the king.

40. There is no difference between a brāhmaṇa and a king: both are sworn to protect the people's *dharma*.

NMS 19.40. J 18.42. Bhava explains that both protect the people, the king by defending them, the brāhmaṇa by teaching the *dharma*.

41. Even if a king is harsh, it is said that his wealth is pure if he knows the *dharma* and the correct modes of conduct, and if he punishes those who are impure in order to protect his people.

NMS 19.41. J 18.43. Bhava says that Nārada's intention is to dispel the mistaken notion that a harsh king's wealth is necessarily impure and therefore unacceptable to a brāhmana.

Recension D adds a verse of Manu which Bhava quotes in his commentary on 18.41:

One who accepts a gift from a king who is greedy and acts counter to the sacred texts will go to the twenty-one hells one after another.

[J 18.44, Manu 8.47]

The twenty-one hells are enumerated in Manu 4.88-90.

42-43. Just as waters, pure and impure, become indistinguishable once they merge in the ocean, so does wealth once it comes into the possession of the king. Just as gold becomes pure when it is placed in a blazing fire, so everything becomes pure when it comes into the possession of kings.

NMS 19.42-43. J 18.45-46. Bhava insists that even wealth acquired from wicked people becomes pure when it comes to the king. Since the king is the supporter of brāhmaṇas, it is important to establish that his possession of even tainted wealth (see 1.41-44 for the description of the kinds and degrees of purity in wealth) purifies it, so that brāhmaṇas can accept gifts from him without concern for the question of its purity. Manu 4.84-87 gives a list of kings from whom gifts are not to be accepted.

44. If any man gives his property to brāhmaṇas the king must agree to it; that is the eternal rule.

NMS 19.44. J 18.47. Since much of a brāhmaṇa's property could be exempt from taxation and was certainly exempt from escheat to the king, the gift of one's property to brāhmaṇas could be a way of evading taxation. This verse is intended to overrule any objection the king might have to such a transaction.

45. The king's revenue comes from another source called "one-sixth of the earth." This levy constitues his wages for protecting his subjects.

NMS 19.45. J 18.48. Bhava comments on the reading *anyatra kārād* for *anyaprakārād*, and ties this verse to the preceding one. The point is that the king cannot prohibit gifts to brāhmaṇas, even though these gifts could then be exempt from his taxation, but must be content to take only his normal one-sixth of all other revenue sources. One-sixth is the king's normal cess on agricultural products, and the figure came to be a formulaic statement of the king's share (see Dwijendra Nath Jha, *Revenue System in Post-Maurya and Gupta Times*, pp. 61-62). According to Manu 8.304-305, the king takes one-sixth of the merit or demerit of his subjects. Though this verse is reported in Dhko 1940 as being cited in VyaNi, it is not found in the critical edition of that text.

46. One may take back what he has given to non-brāhmaṇas, but what has been given to a brāhmaṇa may not be resumed.

NMS 19.46. J 18.49.

47-48. He has three duties: to make gifts, study, and perform sacrifices. Performing sacrifices for others, teaching, and accepting gifts are how he earns his livelihood. A twice-born should be steadfast in his own duties, and sustain himself by his own livelihood. Under normal circumstances he should not accept gifts from low castes.

NMS 19.47-48. J 18.50-51. Bhava glosses *niyame 'sati* "under normal circumstances" with *anāpadi* "non-emergency", i.e. this rule applies under normal circumstances, but when there is a calamity then other means of livelihood are available (see Ludo Rocher, "Caste and Occupation in Classical India: the normative texts," *Contributions to Indian Sociology* (NS) 9 (1975), 139-151). "Twice-born" in this text means a brāhmaṇa, and not the three upper castes which, in theory, are eligible for initiation and hence to become "twice born."

49-50. How could one say that the king is not divine when, with a word, he can make the guilty innocent and the innocent guilty? Twice-born who realize that an infinitely powerful king is divine are not sullied when they accept his gifts.

NMS 19.49-50. J 18.52-53.

51-52. There are eight auspicious things in this world: a brāhmaṇa, a cow, fire, gold, clarified butter, the sun, water, and, finally, the king. One should always look up to them, honor, worship, and be reverential to them, for in this way life is not shortened.

NMS 19.51-52. J 18.54-55. The phrase *pradakṣiṇaṃ kurvīta*, which I translate "be reverential," refers to the practice of circumambulating with one's right side to the object of reverence.

ADDENDA

CHAPTER 19

THEFT

1. There are two kinds of thieves who steal other people's goods: cheats and sneak thieves. The self-respecting king must discover them.

NMS 18.53. J Pariśiṣṭa 1. Very similar to Manu 9.256. This verse of Nārada's is never cited subsequently, but the Manu verse is cited several times.

2-3. Of these, the cheats are those who use dishonest weights and measures, those who are corrupt, violent robbers, gamblers, prostitutes, forgers, and those who live by telling fortunes. These and the like are known to be cheats.

NMS 18.54-55. J Pariśiṣṭa 2-3. Bhava says that those who use dishonest weights and measures are thieves who are merchants. The term *utkoṭaka* "those who are corrupt" is read variously, as can be seen in the variant readings. The word commented upon by Bhava is *utkodaka*, and he glosses it *utkocabhakṣa* "one who takes bribes." The term *utkoṭaka* is not attested elsewhere, but the ms evidence indicates that this was most likely the reading here, and it is etymologically appropriate: it is derived from the root *kuṭ* "to be bent, crooked, to be dishonest, to cheat." Bhava lists forgers of documents and counterfeiters among forgers, and astrologers, interpreters of omens and clairvoyants among fortune tellers. He says that the king should make the effort to check such things as weights every month. See Kau 4.1 and 4.2 for the suggested supervision of artisans and traders.

4-5. Sneak thieves work both indoors and outdoors. These men attack and rob those who are asleep or intoxicated. Those who attack whole regions, villages, houses, or travelers on roads, pickpockets, and the like are also sneak thieves.

NMS 18.56-57. J Pariśiṣṭa 4-5. Bhava explains "indoors and outdoors" to mean populated areas and the forest. Compare with Manu 9.257-259.

6. He should find them out by means of very clever spies who work with them. Secretly placed men should follow and apprehend them.

NMS 18.58. J omits. Bhava, who has the variant reading *corais* "thieves" for *cārais* "spies", explains that the king should find them out through clever thieves, have them traced by former thieves who pose as thieves and have them arrested on the spot. Alternatively, those who pose as thieves may announce that there is a particularly appealing opportunity for theft in such and such a place, and lead them to an ambush. On the use of spies see KāNī12.28, ViDhPu 2.24.63, and Bhā 5.34.32.

7-8. Assembly halls, watering places, bakers' shops, brothels, places where liquor or food is sold, crossroads, sacred trees, gatherings, theaters, vacant houses, forests, and shrines: these should be patrolled by spies whose job it is to catch thieves.

NMS 18.59-60. J omits. See Manu 9.264 ff. Apa on YāSmṛ 2.268 attributes this verse to both Manu and Nārada.

9. Others, namely trustworthy former thieves who are convincing talkers, should likewise be employed as spies, and should urge on the thieves.

NMS 18.61. J omits. Bhava suggests that a spy might say, "This is the *mantra* which makes one invisible. With this *mantra* you will not be seen," and then, arrange for the thieves to enter a house in broad daylight, where the king can apprehend them. I take the term *citravādin* to mean one who can convincingly carry off a story about a "*mantra* which makes one invisible." It could also mean someone who is able to speak the particular dialect of thieves. See Kau 4.5 for a more extensive discussion of the use of spies to catch thieves. The use of former thieves to catch other thieves makes sense, in that these men would be easily turned to the task of spying for the king since the alternative would be the king's punishment. See Kau 1.11.4-8, where ascetics who have given up their vows are similarly to be recruited to spy for the king.

10-11. They should make the acquaintance of the thieves by offering them food or drink, inviting them to a party or festival, or by pretending to organize a robbery. Those who do not come to the meeting but go away, even though they had agreed to come, should be pursued and arrested, along with their sons, animals, and relatives.

NMS 18.62-63. J omits. Bhava says explicitly that the ones who are to engage in this activity are former thieves. Compare with Manu 9.268.

NMS adds a verse which is not found in the other recensions, but which is well attested in other *nibandhas:*

> **Even non-thieves are seen in the company of thieves, but the king should not punish them if (their association) is accidental.** [NMS 18.64]

12. Those thieves whom he apprehends should be beaten, paraded, humiliated, and then tortured.

NMS 18.65. J omits. The word *vadha* can mean severe beating or death; it means the former in this case. Bhava says that the king should beat the thieves with a club, then parade them around on an ass, and having announced them at crossroads, etc., he should chop them up, beat them, or burn them to death as an example. For punishment by torture (here, *citravadha*) see DaVi 20-21 and Kau 4.11.1.

13. But the king should not corporally punish as thieves persons who are not in possession of stolen goods, for it may be that they simply do not have a title to property they own; however, if they are in possession of stolen goods or own burglary tools, he should promptly punish them.

NMS 18.66. J Pariśiṣṭa 6. See also Mā 1.36 and 19.15. Compare Manu 9.270. See Burrow, "Two Śaka Loanwords in *Manusmṛti,* " *Ural-Altaische Jahrbücher* 47 (1975), 30-34 for his theory of the Śaka origin of the term *hoḍha.*

14. He should confiscate all the property of those who maraud in their own regions and obstruct roads, and impose severe sanctions on them.

NMS 18.67. J Pariśiṣṭa 7. Bhava states that these criminals should not be put to death, but punished by such means as cutting off their hands or feet. This verse is attributed to Nārada and Kātyāyana by ViRa 317, VyaNi 508, DaVi 125, and Setu (Dhko 1748). Apa on YāSmṛ 2.273 attributes it solely to Kātyāyana.

15. Those who were arrested on suspicion of theft, even though they did not possess stolen goods, should be tested by various means of intimidation; they might then tell exactly what happened.

NMS 18.68. J Pariśiṣṭa 8. Bhava comments on the reading *sahoḍhān.* He says that one should keep in mind the episode of Māṇḍavya (see Mā 1.36) and not come to too hasty a conclusion. If there is no evidence of wrongdoing, the king should resort to means which instill fear. This consists of threats against the thief and his family. Through the use of torture, threats, etc. a confession might be extracted (see 19.19).

16. While being detained they should be interrogated about place, time, direction, caste, name, hideout, occupation, and accomplices.

NMS 18.69. J Pariśiṣṭa 9. Bhava, whose text shows a number of variant readings, lists the questions, "Where did you come from?," When did you come here?," "From what direction or region did you enter?," What is your caste?," "What is your name?," "By what entrance did you come in?," "Where was your hideout?," "Who helped you?."

17-18. They can be found out, not only by the stolen goods, but also by circumstantial evidence, for example by changes in complexion, voice, or appearance, a hesitant explanation, being seen at the wrong place or time, evasiveness about their residence, immoral expenditures, previous thefts, and association with bad characters.

NMS 18.70-71. J Pariśiṣṭa 10-11. Bhava says that the indicators of a thief mentioned here are turning pale when questioned, stammering, giving a clear answer, but with fear or despair apparent, being seen in a deserted place or at night, not speaking clearly about where they live, etc., immoral expenditures such as gambling, liquor, slave girls, etc. Kau 4.6 contains an extensive list of the ways by which one might discover criminal activity through knowledge of suspicious activity. Compare 1.174-179 and KāSmṛ 385-386.

19. If a man has a reputation for being a scoundrel and a suspicion should arise that he is also a thief, then if there is any circumstantial evidence against him, he should swear an oath.

NMS 18.72. J Pariśiṣṭa 12. Bhava notes that the oath which should be administered is the usual one in which the man swears by his cows, seeds, gold, the head of his son, etc. It is interesting that he should mention this oath which is more or less specific to vaiśyas (see Manu 8.113-114). The procedure for the administration of oaths may be found in DiTa Introduction pp. 51 ff.

20-21. Those who give thieves sustenance, fire and water, shelter, directions, or an alibi, or who buy or even accept goods from them are considered equally liable, and so are those who conceal them.

NMS 18.73-74. J Pariśiṣṭa 13-14. I translate *uttaradāyaka* as "giving an alibi" taking *uttara* in the technical sense of "reply to a charge." The second half of 19.21 is frequently attributed to Kātyāyana (Dhko 1762). Compare Manu 9.271 and 278.

22. If governors and feudatories are asked for help against thieves in their territories, and they fail to respond, they are themselves just like thieves.

NMS 18.75. J Pariśiṣṭa 15. See 14.19. The term *sāmanta* can mean either "neighbor" (which is what all commentators on this verse and on Manu 9.272 understand) or it can mean a "neighboring prince, feudatory chief" (cf. Kau 7.18.29 and HDh 3.1007), especially in juxtaposition with *rāṣṭrādhikṛta* (see also 19.24 with *mārgapāla* and *dikpāla*). Similar to Manu 9.272.

23. He in whose region something is stolen must diligently pursue the thieves or else pay back the stolen goods if the tracks do not lead elsewhere.

NMS 18.76. J Pariśiṣṭa 16. Compare 14.23 and Manu 8.40. This verse continues to discuss the responsibility of government officers. ĀDha 2.10.26.2-8 states that the area of one *yojana* around a city and one *krośa* around a village must be protected by the appointed officers; if something is stolen within that area these men must repay it. GauDha 2.1.41 (10.47), Manu 8.40, YāSmṛ 2.36, Bhā 12.76 and NāSmṛ 14.26 all state that the king must give compensation for all unrecovered stolen goods.

24. If the tracks lead elsewhere, or are lost there but found again in another place, the king should make the feudatories, the guardians of the frontiers, or the governors of the borders make restitution.

NMS 18.77. J Pariśiṣṭa 17. A *mārgapāla* may have been the same as a *mārgapati* "the guardian of a frontier or pass" mentioned in inscriptions (see D.C. Sircar, *Indian Epigraphical Glossary*, p. 200 for references). A *dikpāla* is less certain. Kane (HDh 3.987) speculates that it was an officer in charge of the borders of a kingdom. ViCi 145 explains that a *dikpāla* is a *deśapati*, which he glosses as "one responsible for the protection of a particular region." This list of governmental officers supports the translation of *sāmanta* in its technical meaning of "feudatory" (see KāSmṛ 813). According to Bhava the ones to be punished are the feudatories, etc. of the place where the trail was lost. Presumably, they are to be punished for their negligence in letting the thieves get away in the area under their jurisdiction.

25. If a house is burgled and the thief is not caught, the king should make the thief-catchers, the watchmen, and the provincial officers pay.

NMS 18.78. J Pariśiṣṭa 18. The office of *rāṣṭrika* is attested in Prakrit inscriptions (see D.C. Sircar, *Indian Epigraphical Glossary*, p. 278, see also Paṇha 1.5 p. 94, Prakrit *raṭṭhia* glossed by Hindī *sūbedār*). Bhava makes no comment on this verse other than to say that its meaning is obvious. ViRa 341 explains *cauragrāha* as one who has been specially appointed to search after thieves, *ārakṣaka* as one appointed to protect the village. ViCi 145 glosses *ārakṣaka* with *koṭavāra* (Hindī *kotwāl*) "police." There were a number of other designations for those officers responsible for catching thieves: YāSmṛ 2.271 mentions a *cauroddhartṛ* and Kau 4.13 speaks of a *corarajjuka*. With some variations this verse is attributed to Kātyāyana by Apa on YāSmṛ 2.271, ViRa 343, ViCi 147, DaVi 86, and Setu (Dhko 1752-3). VyaKa 552 attributes it to both Kātyāyana and Nārada.

26. If, however, those who are made to pay are in doubt about the theft, then the victim should swear an oath to remove the doubt.

NMS 18.79. J Pariśiṣṭa 19. This provision is designed to discourage anyone from faking a robbery or exaggerating a claim. Since watchmen, district officers, etc. must make good a stolen item according to19.23-25, there must have been the temptation to lodge a false complaint or to exaggerate the value of things stolen in order to do the classical Indian equivalent of "collecting on the insurance." If those who are liable are suspicious about the existence or the amount of the theft, they can require that the victim swear an oath. This verse is attributed to Vṛddhamanu at Mitā on YāSmṛ 2.272, Apa on YāSmṛ 2.271, VyaKa 554, ViRa 345, PaMā 449, DaVi 88, and ViTā 792.

27. If others than the thief have been made to pay for stolen goods in order to clear the theft, and the thief is later caught, they are vindicated and should receive twice the amount.

NMS 18.80. J Pariśiṣṭa 20.

28. In so far as possible one should return anything stolen by a thief in its original condition; if not, he should be made to pay its value and a fine in the same amount.

NMS 18.81. J Pariśiṣṭa 21. Apparently the person who must return the goods or pay the fine, etc. is the thief or any person who somehow comes into possession of stolen goods, or any of the above mentioned officers who are responsible for recovering stolen goods. The verse cannot refer to the king because of the mention of a fine. Bhava does not make this clear, and since there is only one other place in which this verse is cited (ViVya folio 53) we have no other commentators to help us.

29-31. For stealing inexpensive items such as wood, cane, grass, and the like, utensils made of clay, bamboo, things made of bamboo, reeds, sinew, bone, or leather, vegetables, greens, tubers, fruits, flowers, milk products, sugar cane products, salt, oil, cooked food, prepared food, liquor, meat, the fine is five times the value.

NMS 18.82-84ab. J Pariśiṣṭa 22-24. Manu 8.324-331 has a similar but more detailed list. Kölver (ZDMG 123 (1973), 340) is understandably troubled by the presence of *vetra* "reed" in a compound the other elements of which are animal products. The emendation *keśa* "hair" which he suggests seems an unlikely word to have been misread as *vetra*. The citations of this verse have *tathā* for *vetra* (Dhko 1749). Bhava glosses "cooked food" with "sweetmeats;" "prepared foods" with "grits, pressed rice, parched grain, etc." (see14.13).

32. The same goes for all things sold by weight, measure, or lot. For more valuable items than these the fine is ten times the value.

NMS 18.84cd-18.85ab. J Pariśiṣṭa 25. Bhava says that, when something with a value of one *dīnāra* is stolen, the fine is ten *dīnāras*, out of which one *dīnāra* goes to the victim and the rest is kept by the king. Similar to Manu 8.321.

33. For stealing more than ten *kumbhas* of grain the penalty is corporal punishment. For stealing less than that, the thief should be made to pay eleven times the amount as a fine, so says Manu.

NMS 18.85cd-18.86ab. J Pariśiṣṭa 26. See Manu 8.320. Whether Manusmṛti is actually being quoted here or whether this is simply an invocation of the mythical Manu is not possible to say. Govindarāja, Kullūka, and Raghavānanda in commenting on Manu 8.320 explain that the corporal punishment is beating, amputation, or death depending on the nature of the thief and of the owner. See also Śaṅkha quoted at DaVi 130, which prescribes corporal punishment and amputation for theft of gold and silver. ViCi 137 attributes this verse to Bṛhaspati. No one quotes it as a Nārada verse.

34. For stealing more than one hundred worth of gold, silver, etc., or of the finest clothes or gems, the penalty is death.

NMS 18.86cd-18.87ab. J Pariśiṣṭa 27. Similar to Manu 8.321. The unit of measure is unclear. The commentators on Manu 8.321 suggest several alternatives, *pala, karṣa, kārṣāpaṇa, niṣka*, etc. with, according to some, the added possibility that the units are to be determined by the items stolen or the units of measurement current in a particular locality (see particularly Medhātithi, also ViSmṛ 5.79-82).

35. For stealing a man the punishment is the highest fine; for stealing a woman, all his property; for stealing a maiden, corporal punishment.

NMS 18.87cd-18.88ab. J Pariśiṣṭa 28. The amount of the fines are given in 19.37-38. Manu 8.323 stipulates the theft of men "of good family." Bāla on YāSmṛ 2.275 attributes the second half of this verse to Kātyāyana.

36. For stealing large domestic animals the punishment is the highest fine; for the theft of medium domestic animals, the middle fine; for stealing small domestic animals, the lowest fine.

NMS omits. J Pariśiṣṭa 29.

37-38. The lowest fine is between twenty-four and ninety-six. The middle fine is between two hundred and five hundred. The highest fine is between five hundred and one thousand. This is the threefold punishment proclaimed by the Self-Existent One with regard to fines.

NMS 18.88cd-18.90ab. J Pariśiṣṭa 30-31. According to Bhava the exact fine levied will be proportionate to the crime. These amercements vary among authors on *dharmaśāstra*. Manu 8.138 gives the numbers 250, 500, and 1000. Śaṅkha-Likhita (Dhko 571b) gives 24 to 91, 250 to 500, and 600 to 1000. YāSmṛ 1.366 gives 270, 540, and 1080. The amercements given are for theft. For crimes of violence (*sāhasa*; for the distinction between theft, *steya*, and violence *sāhasa* see NāSmṛ 14.11) the amercements are, according to NāSmṛ 14.6, a minimum of 100, 500, and, as Bhava makes clear, 1000. The units of measurement are a problem and the source of much discussion and dispute (see HDh 3.393n and D.C. Sircar, *Studies in Indian Coins*, pp. 86-91). The Self-Existent One here is, of course, Manu Svayambhuva (see Manu 1.3 and 58). This scheme of amercements is not to be found in the extant Manusmṛti.

39. For the first offense a pickpocket should have his thumb and forefinger cut off; on the second offense the rest of his fingers, plus the lowest fine.

NMS 18.90cd-18.91ab. J Pariśiṣṭa 32. Bhava specifies that the fingers to be cut are those of the right hand. The last *pāda* of this verse is a bit incongruous in that a small fine is added to chopping off the rest of the fingers. This verse is cited in full in three places (ViRa 320, PaMā 441, and VyaU folio 127a) and in every instance *pāda* d reads: *tṛtīye vadham arhati* "on the third offense he should be killed." This is also the reading of *pāda* d of Manu 9.277. It should be noted that Kau 4.10 makes amputation an optional punishment for the first three offenses (the severity of the amputation increases with each offense: two fingers, five fingers, the right hand), while the alternative is a fine of the first, second, or third amercement. On the fourth offense the man should be killed.

40. For stealing cows which belong to brāhmaṇas the penalty is cutting the thief's achilles tendon. For stealing a female slave, the mandatory punishment is cutting off half of a foot.

NMS 18.91cd and 18.92ab. J Pariśiṣṭa 33. The translation of this verse given in my article, "More Equine Lexicography: the Hamstring is Not Connected to the Nose," JAOS 103 (1983), 421-422 was based on the reading *chedane* (parallel to *bhedane* in Manu 8.325). The cutting of the achilles tendon is therefore the penalty imposed on the thief, not an injury inflicted on the cow. The explanation of *sthūrā* "hock," or its correspondent in humans, "achilles tendon," remains valid, as does that of the crippling effect of its cutting. Compare Manu 8.325.

41. With whatever particular limb a thief commits his crime, that very limb should be cut off. This is the directive of Manu.

NMS 18.92 cdef. J Pariśiṣṭa 34. Compare Manu 8.334.

42. He should inflict a heavy penalty for a serious theft and a light penalty for a minor one, but not the same as for the first offense.

NMS 18.93. J Pariśiṣṭa 35. Bhava says that no matter the magnitude of the crime, the second offense requires a heavier penalty. This verse is ignored by all commentators and digest writers (Dhko 1749). See ViSmṛ 3.93 where the king is forbidden from pardoning a man guilty of a second offense.

43-44. Manu, the son of the Self-Existent One, has said that there are ten places for punishment, which apply for the three lower castes, a brāhmaṇa always being exempt. They are the genitals, the belly, the tongue, the hands, the feet, the eyes, the nose, the ears, property, and the body.

NMS 18.94-95. J Pariśiṣṭa 36-37. Bhava makes no comment on these verses, but they correspond to Manu 8.124-125, about which Kullūka comments that corporal punishment is for serious crimes, financial punishment for less serious crimes. Kullūka notes that when corporal punishment affects the body it means death.

45. He should inflict these punishments on the basis of an accurate determination of the offenses, their time and place, and a consideration of status and inclinations.

NMS 18.96. J Pariśiṣṭa 38. Bhava lists as relevant: the magnitude of the crime, the scene of the crime, whether the accused was behaving normally or not, whether there was a famine or not, and whether it was life-threatening, whether or not the thief and his victim were brāhmaṇas, kṣatriyas, etc., and the persons for which the thief commited his crime. Which of the punishments listed in 19.43-44 is appropriate will be decided on that basis. Compare with Manu 8.126.

46-47. Neither to make friends, nor to gain even great wealth should the king send forth a violent criminal as a free man, so Manu has stated. A king incurs as much unrighteousness in releasing a guilty man as in hurting an innocent one. There is righteousness in exacting punishment.

NMS 18.97-98. J Pariśiṣṭa 39-40. These verses are never cited as Nārada's, and the similar verses of Manu (8.347 and 9.249, see also 8.310-311, 317) are cited only once (SmṛCi 345) and three times (Dhko 582) respectively.

48. On no account should he strike a brāhmaṇa even if he has committed every possible sin. The righteous course is that he may, if he wishes, have him exiled.

NMS 18.99. J Pariśiṣṭa 41. See Manu 8.380, 9.241, and KāSmṛ 483. ViTā 85 attributes the reading of Manu 8.380 to Nārada. Manu 8.381 states that to kill a brāhmaṇa is the greatest crime on earth and therefore a king should not even think about it (see NāSmṛ 14.8). RāTa 4.96 ff. mentions an episode in which a brāhmaṇa guilty of murder is exempted from the death penalty. However, KāSmṛ 806 does allow the death penalty for a brāhmaṇa for crimes such as abortion, attacking women, and stealing gold.

49. Or the king may take all his property or leave him one fourth, invoking the law of the Creator for his dependents. That is the rule.

NMS 18.100. J Pariśiṣṭa 42. The reading *bhṛtyebhyo* "dependents" refers to the status of brāhmaṇas as worthy of and requiring the support of the king. Part of the king's responsibility is to see to it that *dharma* is adhered to by all the factions of his kingdom. If they stray he must punish them, so in this way he is the patron of brāhmaṇas. He is also their supporter in that he gives them gifts, tax exemptions, etc.; vis-à-vis the king, then, they are dependent on them.

The usual division of three degrees of punishment would work here if the amercements were one-fourth, one-half, or all of the brāhmaṇa's property. The extraordinary nature of the punishment may be seen from the fact that the property of a brāhmaṇa may never escheat to the king (see Manu 9.188-189).

50. However, when a brāhmaṇa commits one of four crimes, incest, drinking liquor, theft, and assault on another brāhmaṇa, branding is prescribed.

NMS 18.101. J Pariśiṣṭa 43. The term *gurutalpa*, literally the "guru's bed," stands for sexual intercourse with all prohibited females, one's mother, sister, aunt, guru's wife, etc. (see 12.72-74). Bhava stipulates that the theft spoken of here is the theft of another brāhmaṇa's gold. This interpretation is necessary, he reasons, because there is 1) no qualification of the word "theft" in the verse, and 2) it is listed together with other *mahāpātakas* "grave sins" in accordance with the ViDhaSū 5.1-2. which prohibits corporal punishment for brāhmaṇas. Only theft of gold from a brāhmaṇa is a *mahāpātaka*. This is the unanimous opinion of the commentators on Manu as well. Such a qualification is made necessary by other provisions and allowances for theft by brāhmaṇas, for example, the theft or appropriation of materials required for a sacrifice (Manu 11.11-21), which is not to be punished by a righteous king.

This verse is also attributed to Uśanas (see Dhko 596).

51-52. For incest, the brand should be a vagina; a flag for drinking liquor; a dog's paw for theft, and he should cauterize it with "peacock bile." A headless man should be branded on the forehead of a killer of a brāhmaṇa, and he is not to be spoken to. This is the directive of Manu.

NMS 18.102-103. J Pariśiṣṭa 44-45. The term "peacock bile" cannot be meant literally. It must refer to some sort of bluish material which could serve both to cauterize the wound of a brand and would enhance the visibility of the wound by adding color to it like a tattoo. Such a substance would likely be something like the salt copper sulfate (blue vitriol). The idea of a tattoo is also implied by the variant reading of NMS *pūrayet*, where the wound would be "filled" with the substance. DaNī 6 claims that the branding should be done with the juice of the *bhallātaka* tree for brāhmaṇas and with a hot iron hook for all others. Compare

Manu 9.237. The word *bhrūṇa* has two meanings: an embryo and a brāhmaṇa. GauDha uses the word in both ways: for a woman who has an abortion at 3.3.9 (21.9) and for the slayer of a brāhmaṇa at 2.8.11 (17.11). BauDha 4.1.29 also uses it to mean the slayer of a brāhmaṇa. The Vaikhā 1.1 (p. 2) explains that a *bhrūṇa* is one of the eight kinds of brāhmaṇas. Caland (Vaikhā translation, p. 2) says that the commentator Veṅkaṭeśa explains a *bhrūṇa* as equal to a *ghorācārika* (see Vaikhā 8.5, p. 115), a householder who studies the Veda but does not teach it, lives by gleaning, etc. (see Manu 4.5). Vaikhā 6.16 (p.100) states that a brāhmaṇa who abandons his fire is a brāhmaṇa slayer (*bhrūṇahan*). Note that NMS and two other mss have the variant reading *brahmaghātinaḥ*. The commission of a violent crime of the highest degree results in an ostracization similar to that mentioned here (see 14.10).

53. The thief should approach the king with his hair loosened, running, confessing his theft, "Yes, I did it. Punish me."

NMS 18.104. J Pariśiṣṭa 46. Compare Manu 8.314-315. The commentators on Manu claim that this is the procedure for someone who stole gold from a brāhmaṇa. Loosened hair is a sign of abjection (common in Bhā, e.g. 3.62.19, 4.62.3, 10.8.101, etc.) in this case, and not the violation of etiquette listed in PiSmṛ 17 (Dhko 131-132). Concerning the latter, see J.D.M. Derrett "Some Features of Public Law in Smrti Sources," ALB 42 (1978), 1-31.

54-56. The thief becomes free of sin by confessing his deed. That sin befalls the king who releases him while he is still tainted by it. Men who received punishment from the king for the sins they committed are cleansed and go to heaven just like doers of good deeds. A thief is freed from guilt by punishment or by exoneration, but the king who does not punish a thief incurs his guilt.

NMS 18.105-107. J Pariśiṣṭa 47-49. The second verse is identical with Manu 8.318 and VaSmṛ 19.30, the third with Manu 8.316.

57. Self-respecting men are punished by their gurus, evil men by their king, secret sinners by Yama Vaivasvata.

NMS 18.108. J Pariśiṣṭa 50. Yama is the god of the dead and regent of the realm of the dead. He is the son of Vivasvat (the Sun) and as such is one of the siblings of Manu. See Wendy O'Flaherty, *Hindu Myths*, 1975, pp. 60-70, 318-319. ViRa 626 attributes this verse to Hārīta.

58-59. Guilt for a theft is eightfold for a śūdra, sixteenfold for a vaiśya, thirty-twofold for a kṣatriya, and sixty-fourfold for a brāhmaṇa, thus said the son of Svayambhu. Moreover, guilt is especially great for the learned among them.

NMS 18.109-110. J Pariśiṣṭa 51-52. Bhava records a difference of opinion about just what 18.59 should mean. Some say that it means that eight times, sixteen times, etc. the amount stolen is to be paid as a fine. Others say that eight times, etc. the sin is incurred. These verses are similar to Manu 8.337-338. Kölver (*op.cit.*) in 19.59 reads the variant *vṛtrāpi* as *dvātrāpi* and suggests—on the basis of Manu 8.338—*dvidhāpi*. The manuscript evidence does not support this.

60-61. Punishment is said to be twofold: corporal and pecuniary. There are ten kinds of corporal punishments, and many kinds of pecuniary punishments. Pecuniary punishment ranges from one *kākiṇī* up to one's entire property, corporal punishment from arrest up to execution.

NMS 18.111-112. J Pariśiṣṭa 53-54. Compare this view with Manu 8.129. See 19.43-44 for the ten places for corporal punishment

62-64. The punishment which begins with one *kākiṇī* has a maximum of one *māṣa*. That which begins with a minimum of one *māṣa* has a maximum of one *kārṣāpaṇa*. That which begins with a minimum of one *kārṣāpaṇa* has a maximum of four *kārśāpaṇas;* that with a minimum of two has a maximum of eight; another has a minimum of three and a maximum of twelve. The ranges of fines which begin with one *kārṣāpaṇa* all have four gradations. The same is true for others, provided that the maximum is lower than the amount of the first amercement.

NMS 18.113-115. J Pariśiṣṭa 55-56; omits 19.64. Bhava spells out that the fines listed in 19.63 are graded in four levels. In the first example, the judge has the option of exacting a fine of one, two, three, or four *kārṣāpaṇas* depending on the circumstances. This gradation in four levels applies to every range of fines measured in *karṣāpaṇas*, irrespective of the minimum amounts, as long as the minimum is less than 250 *kārṣāpaṇas*, which is the lowest amercement (see Manu 8.136-138). He also notes that if the gradation in four levels were to be applied to the fine in which one *karṣāpaṇa* is the maximum, the minimum would be four *māṣas*. This is evidently based on a computation according to which sixteen *māṣas* (or *māṣakas)* equal one *kārṣāpaṇa* (see for example Kau 2.19.1-3 and Manu 8.136). This is in contradiction with 19.66 (a verse not found in NMS) which states that there are twenty *māṣas* in one *kārṣāpaṇa*. This section on coins is treated in my article "Coins in the Nāradasmṛti's Chapter on Theft," *Journal of the Numismatic Society of India* 44 (1982), 108-113. DaVi 56 attributes the second half of 19.62 to Kātyāyana.

65. In the south the *kārṣāpaṇa* is made of silver. In the east it is composed of *paṇas*, sixteen of them.

NMS 18.116. J Pariśiṣṭa 57. The reading *rūḍhaḥ* "common" for *raupyaḥ* "made of silver" is unique to NMS. See my article cited in the note to 19.62-64.

66. A *māṣa* is one twentieth of a *kārṣāpaṇa,* and a *kākiṇī* is one fourth of a *māṣa* or of a *paṇa.*

NMS omits. J Pariśiṣṭa 58. Jolly's reading of *pala* for *paṇa* is also found at ViRa 8. DaVi 28 attributes this reading of the ViRa to an error in writing. SmṛCa 231 DaVi 27, VyaPra 177, ViTā 274, RāKau 410,and Prakā 63 attribute this verse to Kātyāyana. MaBhā on GauDha 12.19, GauMi on the same verse, and SaVi 181 attribute it to Uśanas.

67-68. The designation which is common in the region of the Panjab for the value of a *kārṣāpaṇa* is applicable here. A *kārṣāpaṇa* is known as an *aṇḍikā*; four of these make a *dhānaka*; twelve of these make a stamped *dināra* of gold.

NMS 18.117-118. J Pariśiṣṭa 59-60. Bhava does not elaborate on these verses except to say that they establish the value of fines. On the subject of the *dīnāra*, see the note to Mā 2.24. SmṛCa 231 attributes these verses to Kātyāyana, Prakā 63 to Bṛhaspati.

69. The king should always diligently attend to business, the Vedas, and the administration of justice; he should use skillful means to capture and punish the guilty in the city and the countryside.

NMS 18.119. J Pariśiṣṭa 61. Bhava explains that *vārttā* "business" includes agriculture, husbandry, and trade, and lists the three Vedas as *ṛc*, *yajus*, and *sāman* (see Kau 1.2-4). He adds that the king should heed the *arthaśāstra* in the conduct of his duties.

ADDENDA

CHAPTER 20

ORDEALS

[Concerning this entire section, see the Introduction and the introduction to my edition of Raghunandana Bhaṭṭācārya's Divyatattva (DiTa). Subtitles have been introduced so that the reader may compare the various sections on ordeals. It is important to note that the "NMS" and "Jolly" numbers given in the notes to this chapter do not indicate that identical or even nearly identical verses are found in NMS or Jolly, but only that similar statements are made there.]

1-2. When parties to a lawsuit have no witnesses, the king should examine the parties by means of ordeals or one of the following oaths: the truth; vehicles and weapons; cattle, seeds, and silver; the feet of gods and ancestors, gifts, and good works.

NMS omits. J 1.247-248. Verse 2 lists the materials by which a party must swear an oath. According to Manu 8.113-114, the first oath applies to brāhmaṇas, who are only asked to speak, with the presumption that they will speak the truth. Thus brāhmaṇas wager their veracity in swearing by the truth. Kṣatriyas should wager their vehicles and weapons, vaiśyas their cattle, seeds, and silver. The last items would reasonably be thought to apply to śūdras, but there is some uncertainty about what śūdras should swear by (see DiTa p. 51). It may be that these oaths are common to all classes. SmṛCa 223 states that these last items are representative of oaths which are commonly used.

3-4. The king should administer ordeals in matters involving serious offenses; in minor matters, that best of men should make the accused swear an oath. These oaths indeed have been prescribed as effective in minor disputes, but when violent crimes are involved, the rules for ordeals apply.

NMS omits. J 1.249-250.

5-6. Lord Manu has said that there are five ordeals for those accused in doubtful matters, especially if the events took place in secret: the balance, fire, water, poison, and, finally, holy water. These are the ordeals prescribed for the exoneration of the falsely accused.

NMS 20.2. J 1.251-252. The term *dūṣita* may mean "defiled" or "corrupted;" here it means one who has been sullied by a false accusation.

7. Nārada, the great-souled one, has prescribed ordeals, which reveal what is true and false, for the exoneration of those accused in doubtful matters. A wise man should administer an ordeal with the consent of the plaintiff, not otherwise.

NMS 20.3 and 7. J 1.253 and 258cd.

The Balance

8-9. To support the balance, two posts, each six *hastas* long, should be set two *hastas* deep. The distance between the two posts should be one and one-half *hastas*. Rope supports should be fixed to the solid hooks at the ends of the balance beam.

NMS 20.4-6. J 1.262-263. For a scale drawing of the balance with the parts labeled, see Appendix E of DiTa.

10-11. The accused should be weighed a first time and the balance marked against the counterweight; the man should be taken off it. After he has given his sworn testimony the accused should again be made to get onto the balance and be weighed in the same manner until the balance comes to a stop.

NMS 20.7. J 1.275 and 277. The man is made to get into the balance and weighed against the counterbalance. The position of the balance beam at this time is marked, and it is this mark which is used as the standard to see whether he has gained or lost weight as a result of his statement in the ordeal.

12. If the accused weighs more when he is weighed, he is definitely innocent; but if he weighs the same or less, he is guilty.

NMS 20.8. J 1.283. The question of the man's guilt or innocence is determined by whether he weighs more, less, or the same on the second weighing. The interpretation of the various readings has been problematic. Some texts claim that a man is innocent if he weighs more, others that a man is innocent if he weighs less. For a discussion of some of these problems see J.D.M. Derrett, "Ancient Indian 'Nonsense' Vindicated," JAOS 98 (1978), 100-106, and my response to that article at DiTa pp. 28-33.

13-14. "You are called the Balance [*dhaṭa*] because that name is synonymous with righteousness [*dharma*]. You know the sins and virtues of all creatures. You alone, O Balance, know what men do not know. The man

who stands accused in this case is being weighed; therefore, please righteously deliver him from this suspicion."

NMS 20.9-10. J 1.277-278. 20.13 gives a folk etymology of the term for balance, *dhaṭa*.

The Fire

15-16. Next, I will explain the supreme law of the iron ordeal. It requires circles the diameters and intervals of which equal thirty-two *aṅgulas*. Eight circles encompass a total number of two hundred forty *aṅgulas* according to the experts in such matters.

NMS 20.11-13. J 1.285-286. The fire ordeal is sometimes called the iron ordeal because it involves carrying a fiery iron ball. An *aṅgula* is approximately three quarters of an inch (see DiTa p. 29). The number, 240 *aṅgulas*, is arrived at by adding the total distance of 16 *aṅgulas* for each of the eight circles (128 *aṅgulas*) plus the distance between the circles (112 *aṅgulas*). For a discussion of this ordeal see DiTa pp. 33-39.

17-21. After the accused has been ritually purified and entered the delineated circles, one should tie seven *aśvattha* leaves on his hands with strings and prepare a smooth, hot iron ball weighing fifty *palas*. The accused should take this in his hands, and slowly walk through the seven circles. He should not step over any circle nor in between them, nor should he drop the ball outside that portion of the earth which has been designated before he has covered the prescribed distance. If he calmly traverses the circles in the prescribed manner, and remains completely unburned, he is innocent. If he drops the iron ball out of fear, but appears to be unburned, he must carry it again; this is the ancient practice. The ordeal of fire should be conducted in accordance with these rules.

NMS 20.15-19. J 1.287, 296-299. A ball weighing fifty *palas* would weigh approximately five pounds. See DiTa pp. 35-39.

22-24. "You, O Fire, penetrate the hearts of all creatures; you are like a witness. You know the good and evil deeds which men do not know. You know precisely the secret sins and virtues of mankind—even those not known to men themselves. The man who stands accused in this case hopes to be vindicated; therefore, please righteously deliver him from this suspicion."

NMS 20.19-20. J 1.291.

The Water

25-27. Next, I will explain the supreme rule for the water ordeal. Three arrows should be shot from a bow that is not too strong. The middle arrow should be brought back by an extremely fast runner; when he brings it back, the accused is found innocent. He is, on the contrary, found guilty if he lets even a single limb show or moves from the spot where he went under.

NMS 20. 22-27. J 1. 304, 309, 312. This elliptical description of the water ordeal does not make clear that the accused must remain under water during the time that the runner is going and coming and that if the runner is able to see any part of the accused above the water level upon his return, the accused is guilty. If the accused remains under water, however, he is innocent.

28. Women should not be forced to undergo this ordeal, nor should a weak man; it might scare a woman to death, and to administer it forcibly to a weak man might kill him. If any of these have to be seized forcefully, they should not be made to go under water.

NMS 20.25. J 313-314.

29. He should remain calm and grasp the thighs of the man in the water.

NMS 20.27. J omits. It is in this position that the accused should remain while awaiting the runner to return with the arrow. The man whose thighs he should grasp is standing waist deep in the water (see DiTa pp. 38-40).

30. Water and fire are best for clearly distinguishing what is true and what is false; water is better than fire, since fire has its origin in it.

NMS omits. J 1.316. The myths according to which fire either hides in or emerges from water are many and ancient in India (see, for example Ṛg-veda 10.51 and Bṛhaddevatā 7.61-64 and 7.73-80).

31. "Those who know the essence of the law purify those who have been falsely accused; therefore, O Lord, King of Waters, please deliver him with the truth."

NMS 20.30. J 1.317.

The Poison

32-33. Next, I will explain the supreme rule for the poison ordeal. The poison should be given during the winter and in proper amounts. One

who knows the law would never administer this ordeal in the morning, or at noon, or at twilight, or in autumn, or summer, or spring.

NMS 20.32. J 1.318-320.

34. Poisons that are broken, crushed, scented, or mixed, *kālakūṭa*, and *alaṃbu* should be carefully avoided.

NMS 20.33. J 1.321. This verse presents a list of ways in which poison is not to be prepared. *Kālakūṭa* is the poison produced from the churning of the ocean and subsequently drunk by Śiva (for example, see Brahmāṇḍa 1.2.25). It is mentioned in the Aṣṭāṅgahṛdaya (Calcutta, 1890) *uttarasthāna* 35.4. According to Ṭoḍaramalla in his Āyurvedasaukhya, it is studded with innumerable black spots and was originally produced from the blood of a demon named Māli. It is available in mountains like Ahichatra, Malaya, Koṅkaṇa,and Śṛṅgavera (see Dash and Kashyap, *Materia Medica* pp. 98-99). The second type of poison, *alaṃbu*, is mentioned in Buddhist sources, however not as a poison; it is defined as a bottle gourd (see BHSD vol. 2, p. 68). The Sanskrit form, *alābu* (f.), is mentioned in Suśruta 1.46.211 where, along with other properties, this gourd is described as being a laxative and diuretic, and at 1.46.215 where it is said to be an emetic as well. Hans Losch (*Rājadharma*, p.194) identifies it as *Lagenaria vulgaris, Curcubita lagenaria*.

35-37. If a king wishes to know the truth, he should administer to those accused of a major crime the *śṛṅga* poison from the Himālayas, which has the proper aroma, color, and flavor, but not to children, the sick, or the elderly, nor to those accused of minor offenses. Seven grains of poison mixed with clarified butter should be administered to the accused. One twentieth of a sixth of a *pala* of poison minus one eighth, mixed with clarified butter, should be administered to the accused.

NMS 20.34-37. J 1.322-323. This poison is mentioned in the Aṣṭāṅgahṛdaya (Calcutta, 1890) *uttarasthāna* 35.4 as *śṛṅgī*, and identified by Losch, (*Rājadharma*, p. 220) as *Trapa bispinosa, Ficus infectoria, Ficus indica*. In the Āyurvedasaukhya it is called *śṛṅgaka* (see Dash and Kashyap, *Materia Medica*, pp. 98-99). As Jolly points out, there are 960 *yavas* in one *pala*. (960 x 1/20 x 1/6) - 1/8 = 7 *yavas*.

38. An accused who has been approved in accordance with the preceding rule should touch brāhmaṇas, fast, and then swallow the poison in the presence of the gods and brāhmaṇas.

NMS omits. J omits.

39. If the poison is peacefully digested without paroxysms or languor, the king, realizing that the accused is innocent, should treat him with respect and release him.

NMS 20.38. J 1.326.

40. "You, O Poison, are the son of Brahman, grounded in the joy of truth and righteousness, clear this man of sin and through truth become like ambrosia for him."

NMS omits. J 1.325.

The Holy Water

41. Next, I will explain the supreme rule for the Holy Water.

NMS 20.39. J 1.327.

42. The Holy Water must be administered in the morning to an accused who believes in god, is free from vice, has been fasting, and is still wearing the wet clothes from a ritual bath.

NMS omits. J 1.328.

43. He should drink water which has bathed the deity to whom he is devoted. If anything unusual happens to him within one or two weeks of taking the Holy Water this shows his guilt.

NMS 20.40. J 1.330.

44. Even if something major happens to him after two weeks, he is not to be charged because the period set by the wise has passed.

NMS 1.41. J 1.331.

45. The ordeal of the Holy Water should not be administered to those accused of grave offenses, to those who are devoid of righteousness, ungrateful, despised eunuchs, atheists, those who have not undergone initiation, and slaves.

NMS 20.43. J 1.332.

46. If one who knows the law administers these five ordeals in the aforementioned manner to those accused by the king, he will be praised in this world and the next.

NMS 20.46. J 1.333.

47. He should not administer the poison to a brāhmaṇa, nor should a kṣatriya carry the iron; a vaiśya should not be plunged into water, nor should a śūdra be allowed to drink the Holy Water.

NMS omits. J 1.335.

48. He should not administer the poison in the rainy season, nor plunge the accused in water in the cold season; no one should have to carry the iron in the hot season, or drink the Holy Water at night.

NMS omits. J 1.334.

Here ends the Nāradadharmaśāstra.

APPENDIX

2. THE PLAINT

The second chapter of the Mātṛkā included in Jolly's edition and translation occurs only in ms P. As indicated in the Introduction to the companion Text (pp. xxx-xxxi), it is not part of the original Nāradasmṛti. The translation given here is that of the text which Asahāya believed to be Nārada's. Verses quoted in his commentary which Jolly took to be Nārada verses are translated in the notes.

Once the plaintiff has determined that the strength of his case warrants it, he should have his plaint recorded. He should be motivated by his own interest and resolved to do all that needs to be done. [J Mā 2.1]

A says that the plaintiff should be motivated by his own interest, not by the urging of the king or of an opponent.

The respondent should enter his reply as soon as he knows the claim of the plaintiff. Or he may be allowed to record his reply on the next day, or three days, or even a week later. The plaintiff properly and immediately becomes the victor at the third stage of the trial.

[J Mā 2.2-3]

A explains that if the respondent has not given his reply by the third stage of the trial, the plaintiff automatically wins the case. Since the second stage of a trial is the reply, this implies that if the respondent delays so long that the court begins to hear the evidence (the third stage), the plaintiff automatically wins the case by default. VyaMā 299 and VyaKa 67 attribute the first verse to both Nārada and Kātyāyana, while Candra 114 and VyaSau (at Dhko 173) attribute it to Kātyāyana alone. The second verse is cited in its entirety only once, at VyaSau (Dhko 161b); the first half is often cited and attributed to Bṛhaspati (Dhko 153a).

There are four types of reply: denial, admission, exception, and prior judgment. [J Mā 2.4]

A reply by "exception" is when the respondent makes some admission, but when it is of such a nature that it amounts to an exception to the plaint. For example, if the plaint states that the respondent owes 100 gold pieces, a reply by way of exception might be, "Yes, I borrowed 100 gold pieces, but I repaid them." For a fuller discussion of *pratyava-skandana*, see VyaCi 141.28ff. A reply by a prior judgement is when the respondent can prove that the matter has already been adjudicated in his favor in another court. VyaNi 49, VyaSau (Dhko 173b), and VyaMa 14 attribute this verse to Kātyāyana. VyaMā at 300 attributes it to Nārada and at 305 to Vṛddhaśatātapa. VyaKa 68 attributes the first to Bṛhaspati. There are numerous variants in the *nibandhas*. All this points to the uncertain provenance of this verse.

Jolly gives as a Nārada verse a verse quoted in A's commentary:

There are four kinds of denial: "This is false," "I don't know anything about it," "I was not there," and "I was not born at that time." [J Mā 2.5]

Jolly's reason for giving it separate status as a Nārada verse may have been that it is cited in four places (SmṛCi 544, SmṛSā [Dhko 164b], VyaTa 207 and Setu [Dhko 164b]; the latter two also attribute the verse to Vyāsa). This verse is also variously attributed to Prajāpati (PaMā 73), Hārīta (VyaNi 50), and Kātyāyana (no less than one dozen citations are given at Dhko 176a). It is likely that A quoted this verse to explain the reply by way of denial, but he does not appear to have taken it to be a Nārada verse.

There are four types of reply, depending on its relation to the plea of the plaintiff: a denial, the opposite, an exception, and prior judgement. [J Mā 2.6]

A says that this verse which is someone else's was found in his exemplar and hence he includes it, even though it repeats the four kinds of reply and is difficult to interpret. It is unknown anywhere else. I translate it according to the explanation of A, yet the terms *punar* and *śabdasamāgamam* used in the technical senses of exception and prior judgement are unusual. Ordinarily one would expect *punar*, in a technical sense, to be related to an appeal to another court, not to an exception.

As long as the respondent has not entered his reply to the plaint, the plaintiff may have the record amended as he wishes.

[J Mā 2.7]

A plaint is faulty when it refers to the wrong things or parties, when it is nonsensical, when it omits the amount or title, when it is too brief or too long, or when it is incomplete. [J Mā 2.8]

Jolly took verses quoted in the commentary to be Nārada verses. With the exception of J Mā 2.15 (which is identical with Manu 8.164), none of these verses are known elsewhere, and they read like verses composed by the commentator (either A or Kalyāṇa) to elaborate on Mā 2.7:

When B wants a thing (X) from C, there are three kinds of reference to wrong things or parties: (1) B and no one else should be the receiver, (2) X and nothing else should be the

thing, and (3) he should have it from C and no one else. [J Mā 2.9]

"A friend of yours treats me as an enemy; I summoned you here lest it stretch my patience." [J Mā 2.10]

If the amount or the desired result of the suit is not mentioned, this is called "omission of the amount." A plea thus flawed is to be rejected. [J Mā 2.11]

[J Mā 2.12-13 are corrupt, and make no sense as they are found in the ms.]

He (the king) should reject a plaint that is tattered, blurred, or damaged by water, oil, etc., even if it is legible and intelligible. [J Mā 2.14]

Even if a plaint is well-founded, it is not a true plaint if it falls outside the normal practice of dharma. [J Mā 2.15]

The plea, "I gave this to him when he was residing on the edge of the earth," is outside the normal practice of dharma and does not succeed. [J Mā 2.16]

When one introduces new letters and changes the contents, the evidence becomes confused, and so does the investigation. [J Mā 2.17]

A gives the example of a plaintiff who first states a certain amount and later states a larger amount. The existence of two different statements confuses the judges and the investigation.

If a plaintiff makes a statement in court under the influence of one passion or other, one should first write down everything he says on a tablet or other writing material. [J Mā 2.18]

A explains "one passion or other" as desire, anger, and greed. He lists materials on which the statement might be written: a tablet, a leaf, birch bark, a register, or a wall. SaVi 78 attributes this verse to Gobhila, VyaKa 48 to Nārada and Kātyāyana, VyaNi 24 and VyaSau (Dhko 14) to Kātyāyana only.

After the judges have clearly determined what is necessary for a rational deliberation, everything else the plaintiff said should be deleted from the tablet. Whatever then remains on the tablet and is approved by the parties should be written down in the presence of witnesses, including the fact that both parties agreed to it. [J Mā 2.19-20]

These verses are not clear. Apparently, the judges edited the statement initially recorded by the plaintiff. The second verse may be a garbled version of a verse attributed to Pitāmaha at SmṛCa 140 and Pamā 130:

vādibhyām abhyanujñātaṃ lekhakena sasākṣikam |
likhitaṃ sarvakāryeṣu tat pramāṇaṃ smṛtaṃ budhaiḥ |

"A document which is approved by both litigants and by the writer, and which is witnessed, is recognized by the wise as evidence for all transactions." A's long comment is unclear in places. He seems to say that the verse is of a special type called "*spaṣṭāndhaka*" (clear-and-opaque), i.e., difficult to understand, but understandable with sufficient time.

Jolly took a verse quoted in the commentary to be a Nārada verse. It appears to be the work of Kalyāṇa and to have been composed for this comment:

> **When the plaintiff remembers something more than what was written by the two litigants, this is called reconsideration, and is written in his statement.** [J Mā 2.21]

The meaning "reconsideration" for the term *pratyākalita* is highly unusual. Nearly everywhere else this term has one of two meanings: the fourth stage of a trial, i.e., the announcement of the judgment (Bṛhaspati 2.1),or the determination by the judges of the burden of proof (Apa on YāSmṛ2.8). The only other meaning I know of for *pratyākalita* is the odd usage by Vācaspati Miśra at VyaCi 202.1, where he glosses it as "inference" (*anumāna*, see the editor's note on that passage). The commentator (A or Kalyāṇa) claims that either litigant can make additions to his statement later in the trial. This is odd since it is in direct contradiction with J Mā 2.33. RāKau 389 attributes the latter half of the first verse to Kātyāyana.

The plaintiff and the respondent may appoint people to speak on their behalf, but the defeat or victory is the plaintiff's or the respondent's. [J Mā 2.22]

According to A, the reason for appointing someone to speak before the court on behalf of one of the parties would be a physical ailment or lack of skill as a speaker. This verse is often attributed to Kātyāyana (see Dhko 130).

With the exception of a brother, father, son, or appointed representative, one who speaks on behalf of someone else should be punished. The same goes for one who contradicts himself in the proceedings. [J Mā 2.23]

If someone who is not a relative or the like volunteers to speak in a lawsuit out of self-interest, it is a misdemeanor which the king can prosecute on his own initiative. See Saṃvarta's list of misdemeanors which the king can prosecute (Dhko 134-135).

A man who abandons his previous statement and resorts to a different one is known as one who has made a losing statement, because the two statements are contradictory. [J Mā 2.24]

One does not fail in any dispute on account of a verbal error. Although in disputes about animals, women, land, or debt one should be chastised, still the cases are not lost. [J Mā 2.25]

Here the term *vākchala* means a verbal error rather than the sort of sophistry to which the term *chala* refers at Mā 1.25. The error spoken of here is not, apparently, a serious or intentional one, and hence it does not automatically cause the pleader to lose his case. Vijñāneśvara on YāSmṛ 2.9 confirms this interpretation when he says that such errors are not intentional, but the result of carelessness. See VyaMā 289 where the reading and the subsequent interpretation are different: one loses a case for *chala*, except if the case involves animals, women, land, or debt.

If the accused denies the charge, the accuser has to prove the case, except when the accused demurs. [J Mā 2.26]

The plea of *pratyavaskandana* "reply by way of an exception" is one in which the defendant demurs to the claim of the plaintiff, but adds some exception that renders the defendant free from liability. For example, if a man is charged with a debt of one hundred coins, he might reply that the debt did in fact exist, but that it was paid off completely. In such a case, the defendant must bear the burden of proof, since the general rule for burden of proof is that a positive statement must be proven (see Bṛhaspati 3.19 and VyaCi 141.36ff). The first half of this verse is well known as a Kātyāyana verse (see Dhko 174b). The second half is not quoted by any other commentator.

In the third stage of the trial, the plaintiff must present evidence to prove every single word recorded in the first stage. [J Mā 2.27]

PaMā 87 attributes this verse to Bṛhaspati.

There are two kinds of proof, human and divine: human proof is by means of documents and witnesses; divine proof is the balance and the like. [J Mā 2.28]

If a transaction was made by day, in a village, or town, or wherever it is possible to have witnesses, there is no call for divine proof. [J Mā 2.29]

VyaNi 74 and VyaSau (Dhko 218) attribute this verse to both Bṛhaspati and Nārada.

Divine proof is resorted to when a transaction was made in a forest, in a deserted place, at night, inside a house, or in a case of violence or denial of a deposit. [J Mā 2.30]

VyaMa 23 attributes this verse to Vyāsa.

When the plaint is opposed by a special plea, the accused must act as if he were the plaintiff. [J Mā 2.31]

The special plea spoken of here is the reply by way of an exception alluded to above (see the commentary and note to J Mā 2.26).

There are four types of defeated parties: one who absconds when he has been summoned, one who remains silent, one who is defeated by witnesses, and one who confesses. [J Mā 2.32]

A says that all of these four instances apply to those under trial.

There are five kinds of losers: one who changes his plea, one who shows contempt for the proceedings, one who does not appear, one who does not reply, and one who absconds when he has been summoned. [J Mā 2.33]

A states that two of the four circumstances enumerated in the preceding verse do not result in a final loss of the case. One who remains silent and one who absconds when he has been summoned can reenter their cases at a later trial. Both are liable for punishment, but they have not lost the cases under trial, whereas the other two—one who is defeated by witnesses, and one who confesses—lose their cases. According to him, the five circumstances enumerated in the present verse are also instances in which the pleader would be liable to punishment but would not necessarily lose his case. Each of them could resubmit it at a later time. See similar verses attributed to Kātyāyana (Dhko 207b) and Bṛhaspati (Dhko 205a). The juxtaposition of these two verses is odd. The comment of A serves to rationalize the apparent redundancy in these two verses, but they still have the ring of collected traditional verses placed side by side by the compiler of this chapter because they deal with the same topic.

Jewels such as rubies, gold objects such as *dīnāras*, pearls, coral, conch shells, etc., which are counterfeit are returned to the owner. [J Mā 2.34]

On the subject of the *dīnāra*, see A.B. Keith's refutation (at JRAS 1915, 504) of Jolly's view that the mention of the *dīnāra* indicates that the text cannot have been composed before the second century A.D. See also J.J. Meyer, *Über das Wesen der altindischen Rechtsschriften*, pp. 103 ff. This verse is unknown in any other source.

One who takes items that are the king's—garlands, ornaments, garments, or shoes—when they have not been given to him, should receive corporal punishment. [J Mā 2.35]

The reading given of the second half of the verse is a conjecture of Jolly based on the verb *ākrāmati* in the commentary of A. The reading in ms P is corrupt. This verse is unknown in any other source.

A purchase price, wages, a deposit, a fine, treasure trove, a frivolous gift, and gambling winnings do not accrue interest without stipulation to that effect. [J Mā 2.36]

A says that this is so even if the transaction is in arrears for a very long time. He explains a frivolous gift as something promised to a person such as a wandering actor.

If śūdras falsely accuse the twice-born, the king should have their tongues cut out, and have them impaled on a stake. [J Mā 2.37]

If the king does not do the prescribed cutting and impaling, he will incur the sin which he failed to punish.

With regard to an edict, a document, a title, a grant, a pledge, a letter, a purchase, a sale, the first to bring one of these matters to the attention of the king is known as the plaintiff, according to the experts in the rules. [J Mā 2.38]

A gives examples of plaints of these categories: an edict—"He does not heed the edict of the king;" a document—"This has been undertaken on the authority of this document;" a title—"That man has seized my female slave. Here is my title;" a grant—"He has seized this granted village and is taking the revenue from it. It is mine. Here is the grant;" a pledge— "The debtor first pledged this to me. Who else could have it, then?" a letter—"He does not deliver the goods even though I have claimed them in writing;" a purchase—"I purchased this tool from his own hand and paid the purchase price, but he does not deliver it to me." The sudden use of the *triṣṭubh* meter in this verse is unexpected.

When testimony has been impugned it is necessary to validate the witnesses first. Once the witnesses have been validated, he should clarify the testimony. [J Mā 3.39]

If there should be a groundless accusation, the one who made it should suffer the consequences that befall a man who shows contempt for the proceedings. This is so whether there was fraud or not. This verse is unknown elsewhere.

Those who are defeated because of some fault of the witnesses or judges should have their case heard again, but for those who are defeated because of their own actions there is no retrial. [J Mā 2.40]

A says that the litigant has a right to a retrial even if the cause of his defeat is his own testimony or at least the testimony of his own witnesses. As long as they are considered to have been wronged by the proceedings, they are eligible for a new trial. SaVi 54 and 501 attributes this verse to Bṛhaspati; VyaTa at 231 attributes it to Yājñavalkya.

Even one who confesses, one who is defeated by his own actions, and one defeated in the trial are entitled to have a verdict declared by the judges. [J Mā 2.41]

The three ways one might be defeated are: confession; one's own actions, such as fraudulent documents or false witnesses; and the testimony of witnesses. A says that the guilty may not be punished until the judges have pronounced the judgement.

The judges should reach a decision in a trial without bias. If a biased decision is reached, they will pay the price in this world and the next. [J Mā 2.42]

This verse is unknown in any other source.

The one whom the judges find guilty must be punished by the king in accordance with the texts; he must give the appropriate document of victory to the winner. [J Mā 2.43]

This has been declared by the Self-Existent One to be the beginning of legal procedure. If the beginning is in order, so will be the remainder of the proceedings, but not otherwise. [J Mā 2.44]

This verse is unknown in any other source.

BIBLIOGRAPHY

For editions of Sanskrit texts, see Abbreviations.

Bahadur, Kaisher
1971 *The Judicial Customs of Nepal.* 2nd ed. Kathmandu: Ratna Pustak Bhandar.

Banerjee, S[uresh] C[handra]
1978 "Vyavahāra Portion of the Agni-Purāṇa." *Purāṇam* 20.38-56.

Barth, Auguste
1914-27 *Quarante ans d'Indianisme: Oeuvres d'Auguste Barth.* 5 vols. Paris: E. Leroux.

Beal, Samuel
1963 *Si-yu-ki, Buddhist Records of the Western World: Chinese Accounts of India translated from the Chinese of Hiuen Tsiang.* Calcutta: Susil Gupta (reprint).

Bendall, Cecil
1902 *Catalogue of the Sanskrit Manuscripts in the British Museum.* London: Gilbert and Rivington.

Brinkhaus, Horst
1978 *Die altindischen Mischkastensysteme.* Alt- und Neu-Indische Studien 19, Wiesbaden: Franz Steiner.

Brough, John
1953 *The Early Brahmanical System of Gotra and Pravara: A Translation of the Gotra-Pravara-Mañjarī of Puruṣottama-Paṇḍita.* Cambridge: Cambridge University Press.

Bühler, Georg
1877 *Detailed Report of a Tour in Search of Sanskrit MSS made in Kāśmir, Rajputāna and Central India.* Extra number of *JBBRAS*: Bombay.
1885 Review of Jolly's TLL 1883, *Indian Antiquary,* 323-32
1962 *Indian Paleography.* Calcutta: Firma K.L. Mukhopadhyay.
1969 *The Laws of Manu.* SBE 25, New York: Dover (reprint).

Burrow, Thomas
1975 "Two Śaka Loanwords in Manusmṛti." *Ural-Altaische Jahrbücher* 47.30-34.

Caland, Willem
1927 *Vaikhānasasmārtasūtram. The Domestic Rules and Sacred Laws of the Vaikhānasa School Belonging to the Black Yajurveda.* Text: BI 242; translation: BI 251, 1929.

Cardona, George
1976 *Pāṇini: A Survey of Research.* In *Trends in Linguistics.* State of the Art Reports 6, edited by W. Winter. The Hague: Mouton.

Chatterjee [Śāstrī], Heramba [Nath],
1971 *The Law of Debt in Ancient India.* .Calcutta Sanskrit College Research Series 75, Calcutta: Calcutta Sanskrit College.
1972-74 *The Social Background of the Forms of Marriage in Ancient India.* 2 vols., Calcutta, 1972-74. Sanskrit Pustak Bhandar.
1982 "Studies in the Verses Relating to *nirṇaya* in the *Vyāsasmṛti.*" *Indology and Law: Studies in Honour of J. Duncan M. Derrett.* Edited by Günther-Dietz Sontheimer and Parameswara Kota Aithal, pp. 120-167. Beiträge zur Südasien-Forschung, Südasien-Institut, Universität Heidelberg, vol. 77, Wiesbaden.
1988 *Naradasmrtitattvaprakasika. Narada-smrti = The Institute of Narada: the text and a comparative study of the text with the texts of Manu, Yajnavalkya, Brhaspati, Katyayana,* the Sanskrit College, Calcutta.

Chintamani [Dikshit], T.R
1946 "Nārada Smṛti." *Dr. K.C. Kunhan Raja Presentation Volume,* pp. 153-196. Madras: Adyar Library.

Coedès, George
1968 *The Indianized States of Southeast Asia,* edited by Walter F. Vella and translated by Susan Brown Cowing, Honolulu: University of Hawaii.

Conrady, August
1891 *Fünfzehn Blätter einer nepalesischen Palmblatt-Handschrift des Nārada.* Leipzig: Gustav Fock.

Dareste, Rodolphe
1889 *Etudes d'histoire du droit.* Paris: L. Larose et Forcel.

Dash, Bhagwan and **Kashyap,** Lalitesh

1980 *Materia Medica of Āyurveda: Based on the Āyurveda Saukhyam of Toḍarānanda*. Delhi: Concept.

Day, Terence P.

1982 *The Conception of Punishment in Early India Literature*. Waterloo, Ontario, Canada: Wilfred Laurier University Press.

Derrett, J[ohn] D[uncan] M[artin]

1958 "*kuttā* : a Class of Land Tenures in South India." BSOAS 21.61-81; reprinted ECMHL vol. 1, pp. 280-302.

1964 "Law and the Social Order in India Before the Muhammadan Conquests." JESHO 7. 73-120.

1968 *Religion, Law and the State in India*. New York, 1968.

1969 "Indica Pietas: a Current Rule Derived from Remote Antiquity." *Zeitschrift der Savigny-Stiftung für Rechtsgeschichte. Romanistische Abteilung* 86.37-66; reprinted ECMHL vol. 4, pp. 142-172.

1973 *Dharmaśāstra and Juridical Literature*. A History of Indian Literature, edited by Jan Gonda, part of vol. 4, Wiesbaden: Harrassowitz.

1975 "An Original Vyavasthā in the Field of Vyavahāra: Scholars at Work about the Beginning of the Last Century." ALB 39.43-64; reprinted ECMHL vol. 2, pp. 277-298.

1978 "Some Features of Public Law in Smṛti Sources." ALB 42.1-31.

Fleet, J[ohn] F[aithfull]

1896 "The Dynasties of the Kanarese Districts of the Bombay Presidency." *Bombay Gazetteer*, volume 1, part 2, p. 465.

Gopal, Lallanji

1978 *The Śukranīti, A Nineteenth Century Text*. Varanasi: Bharati Prakashan.

Hasrat, Bikrama Jit

1970 *History of Nepal*. Hoshiarpur: VVRI.

Hazra, R[amesh] C[handra]

1959-60 "Dharma -- Its Early Meaning and Scope." *Our Heritage* 7.15-35 and 8.1-34.

Herbert, Jean

1949 *Nārada: Précédé d'une étude sur les Avatārs de Vishnou*. Lyon: Derain.

Hopkins, E[dward] Washburn

1885 "On the Professed Quotations from Manu Found in the Mahābhārata." JAOS 11.239-275.

1907 "Denarius and the Date of the Harivaṃśa." JRAS, 681-683.

1915 "The Denarius as a Proof of Date." JRAS, 504-505.

Jayaswal, K[ashi] P[rasad]
1911 "The Doctrine of Equity in Hindu Jurisprudence." *Calcutta Weekly Notes* 15. 38, 41, 42.
1913 "On the Origin of the Nārada-smṛti." *Indian Antiquary*, p. 306.
1913a "Advocates in Hindu India." *Calcutta Law Journal* 17.11, 59a-63a.
1920 "A Judgement of a Hindu Court in Sanskrit." *Calcutta Weekly Notes* 24.37, 149-151.
1930 *Manu and Yājñavalkya: A Comparison and a Contrast. A Treatise on the Basic Hindu Law*, Calcutta: Butterworth.

Jha, D[wijendra] N[arayan]
1967 *The Revenue System in Post Maurya and Gupta Times*. Calcutta: Punthi Pustak.

Jolly, Julius
1876 *Nāradīya Dharmaśāstra or The Institutes of Nārada. Translated for the First Time from the Unpublished Sanskrit Original*. London: Trübner.
1885 *Outlines of an History of the Hindu Law of Partition, Inheritance, and Adoption, as Contained in the Original Sanskrit Treatises*. TLL 1883, Calcutta: Thacker Spink.
1885-86 *The Institutes of Nārada together with copious extracts from the Nāradabhāṣya of Asahāya and other standard commentaries*. BI 102.
1969 *The Minor Law-Books*, SBE 33, reprint Delhi: Motilal Banarsidass.
1975 *Hindu Law and Custom* . Translated by Batakrishna Ghosh. Reprint Varanasi: Bharatiya Publishing House.

Kane, P[andurang] V[aman]
1925 "The Predecessors of Vijñāneśvara." JBBRAS n.s. 1.193-224.
1965-75 *History of Dharmaśāstra*. 5 vols. Pune: BORI (vols. 1-4, second revised edition).

Kölver, Bernhard
1973 "Zur Nāradasmṛti I. Varianten zu den Büchern XIV-XVIII und zum Pariśiṣṭa." ZDMG 123. 328-343.

Krader, Lawrence
1975 *The Asiatic Mode of Production: Sources, Development, and Critique in the Writings of Karl Marx*. Assen: van Gorcum.

Lariviere, Richard W[ilfred]
1976 "A Note on the *kośadivya*." ALB 40.152-164.
1981 "The Judicial Wager in Hindu Law." ABORI 62.135-145.

1981a *The Divyatattva of Raghunandana Bhaṭṭācārya: Ordeals in Classical Hindu Law.* New Delhi: Manohar.

1982 "*āsedha* and *ākrośa* -- Arrest in the *Sarasvatīvilāsa*." *Indology and Law: Studies in Honor of J. Duncan M. Derrett*, edited by Günther-Dietz Sontheimer and Parameswara Kota Aithal, pp. 205-222. Beiträge zur Südasien-Forschung, Südasien-Institut, Universität Heidelberg, vol. 77, Wiesbaden.

1982a "Coins in the Nāradasmṛti's Chapter on Theft." *Journal of the Numismatic Society of India* 44.108-113.

1983 "More Equine Lexicography: the Hamstring is Not Connected to the Nose." JAOS 103.421-22.

1984 "More Avenues for Delay in the Pious Obligation." JILI 26.355-359.

1984a "A Bogus Passage in Jolly's Nārada-Smṛti." IIJ 27.201-205.

1984b "An Institution Designed to Prevent Potential Abuses of Ordeals in Classical Hindu Law: the *śiraḥ*." JOIB 34.35-39.

1985 "A Compilation of Pitāmaha Verses Found in Two Manuscripts from Nepal." SII 10.103-132.

1989 *The Nārada-Smṛti. Text and Translation.* Two volumes. Department of South Asia Regional Studies, University of Pennsylvania, Philadelphia. "Novoe Izdanie 'Nārada-smṛti'." ["The New Edition of the 'Nārada-smṛti" translated into Russian by A.A. Vigasin] *Vestnik Drevnei Istorii* (Journal of Ancient History, Moscow) volume 1 (1989) 211-214.

1990 "Matrimonial Remedies for Women in Classical Hindu Law: Alternatives to Divorce" in Julia Leslie (ed.) *Rules and Remedies in Classical Indian Law*, E.J. Brill, 1991, pp. 37-45.

1991 The Last Resort for Dispute Settlement in Classical India," *Droit et Cultures* (Nanterre) Volume 22 (1992) pp. 25-32

1992 "Protestant, Orientalists, and Brāhmaṇas: Reconstructing Indian Social History" 1994 Gonda Lecture, Royal Netherlands Academy of Arts and Sciences, Amsterdam.

1997 "Dharmaśāstra, "Real" Law and "Apocryphal Smṛtis" in Bernhard Kölver (ed.) *Law, State, and Administration in Classical India,* R. Oldenbourg, Munich, (1997), pp. 97-109.
"Law and Religion in India," in *Law, Morality, and Religion: Global Perspectives,* edited by Alan Watson, University of California Press, (1997), pp. 75-94.

1998 "Textual Criticism vs. History: What can we know from the śāstra?" in Lienhard and Piovano (eds.) LEX ET LITTERAE: Studies in Honour of Oscar Botto, Edizioni dell'ORSO, Turin, (1998) 313-327.

Lingat, Robert

1978 *The Classical Law of India* (translation of *Les sources du droit dans le système traditionnel de l'Inde*). Translated with additions by J.D.M. Derrett, Berkeley: University of California.

Losch, Hans

1959 *Rājadharma*. Bonn: Orientalischen Seminars der Universität Bonn.

Lubockaja, Natalija Julianovna

1972 Drevneindijski trakat "Naradasmrti" (Avtoreferat dissertaciji [dissertation abstract]), *Akademija Nauk* SSSR Institut vostokovedenija, Moskva.

1973 SKR. "divya" I ego paralleli v indoevropejskoj terminologiji "Boz'ego suda" [Sanskrit "divya" and its parallels in the Indo-European Terminology of "God's Judgement") in *Oriental Studies* II, Tartu.

1974 "Kizuceniju pamjatnika drevneindijskogo prava 'Naradasmrti'" ["On the Study of Old Indian Law: Naradasmrti] in *pis'mennye pamjatniki Vostoka Istoriko—filologiceskie issledovanija* 1970 Moskva, Izdatel'stvo Nauka.

Zakony Narady (Naradasmrti), typescript, Academy of Sciences USSR, Moscow.

Lüders, Heinrich

1907 *Das Würfelspiel im alten Indien*. Berlin: Abhandlungen der Königlichen Gesellschaft der Wissenschaften zu Göttingen, Philologische-Historische Klasse, N.F. 9.2.

Majumdar, R[amesh] C[handra]

1918 *Corporate Life in Ancient India*. Calcutta: Surendra Nath Sen.

Mandlik, Vishvanath Naryan

1886 *Mānavadharmaśāstra* [and commentaries]. Bombay: Gaṇapata Kṛṣṇaji's Press.

Mazzarella, Giuseppe

1908 *Les types sociaux et le droit*. Paris: Octave Doin.

1913-38 *Etnologia analitica dello antico diritto indiano*. 3 vols. Catania: E. Coco.

Meyer, Johann Jacob

1927 *Über das Wesen der altindischen Rechtsschriften und ihr Verhältnis zu einander und zu Kauṭilya*. Leipzig: Harrassowitz.

Mishra, V.B.

1966 "The Date of Asahāya." *All-India Oriental Conference 22 (1965)*, Gauhati, pp. 177-179.

Nath, Sacin

1984 "Nārada-smṛti meṃ vidhivyavasāya." *Śodh* , 1.9-11.

O'Flaherty, Wendy D[oniger]

1975 *Hindu Myths* . Harmondsworth (England): Penguin Books.

Ojha, Garuishankar Hirachand
1959 *Prācīna Bhāratīya Lipimālā.* Delhi: Munshiram Manoharlal.

Oleksiw, Susan
1982 "The Definition and Treatment of Nyāsa in Dharmaśāstra Literature." *JAOS* 102.119-124.

Olivelle, Patrick
1983 "Renouncer and Renunciation in the Dharmaśāstras." in *Studies in Dharmaśāstra*, ed. R.W. Lariviere, pp. 81-152. Calcutta: Firma K.L. Mukhopadhyay.

Pandey, Raj Bali
1969 *Hindu Samskāras*. Delhi: Motilal Banarsidass.

Patil, D[evendrakumar] R[ajaram]
1963 *The Antiquarian Remains in Bihar*. Patna: Kashi Prasad Jayaswal Research Institute.

Pawate, I[sthalingappa] S[iddharamappa]
1975 *Dāyavibhāga: or The Individualization of Communal Property and the Communalization of Individual Property in the Mitakshara Law.* Dharwar: Karnatak University.

Raghavan, V[enkatarama]
1937 "Asahāya's Commentaries on the Smṛtis of Saṅkha and Likhita." *ABORI* 18. 205.

Ramachandra Dikshitar, V.R.
1951-55 *The Purāṇa Index.* 3 vols. Madras University Historical Series 19, Madras: Madras University.

Rangaswami Aiyangar, K[urichi] V[iraraghava]
1941 *Bṛhaspatismṛti (Reconstructed)*. GOS 85.

Regmi, D[illi] R[aman]
1965-66 *Medieval Nepal.* 4 vols. Calcutta and Patna: Firma K. L. Mukhopadhyay.

Renou, Louis
1961 *Grammaire sanscrite*. Paris: Adrienne Masonneuve.
1963 "Notes sur le Bṛhaspati-Smṛti." *Etudes Védiques et Paniniénnes* 11, Paris: E. de Boccard.

Ridding, Mary C.
1893 "A Manuscript of the Nārada Smṛti." JRAS 41-47.

Rocher, Ludo
1960 "The Definition of Vākpāruṣya." in *P.K. Gode Commemoration Volume*, pp.323-334. Pune: Oriental Book Agency.
1964 "The Theory of Proof in Ancient Hindu Law." *Recueils de la Société Jean Bodin* 18. 325-371.
1968-69 "'Lawyers' in Classical Hindu Law." *Law and Society Review* 3.383-402.
1975 "Caste and Occupation in Classical India: the normative texts." *Contributions to Indian Sociology* n.s. 9.139-151.
1979 "caritraṃ pustakaraṇe." *Indologica Taurinensia* 7. 345-350.
1986 *The Purāṇas*. A History of Indian Literature, edited by Jan Gonda, vol. 2.3, Wiesbaden, Harrassowitz.
1986 "Mixed Castes in the Brahmavaivartapurāṇa." *JAOS* 106.253-255.

Roy, Niranjan
1932 "The Ancient Hindu Law of Pledges and Bailments." *Journal of the Department of Letters* (University of Calcutta) 132.1-120.

Sahay, P. N. K.
1931 *A Short History of the Indian Bar*. Patna, 1931.

Sarkar, B[enoy] K[umar]
1937 *The Positive Background of Hindu Sociology. Book 1: Introduction to Hindu Positivism*. Sacred Books of the Hindus 32. Allahabad: Panini Office.

Sarma, Sreeramula Rajeswara
1985 *Writing Material in Ancient India*. Aligarh Oriental Series No. 5, Aligarh: Viveka.

Sarvadhikari, Rajkumar
1922 *The Principles of the Hindu Law of Inheritance*. 2nd ed. TLL 1880. Madras: The Law Book Depot.

Sen, Sukumar
1947 "The Story of Devadatta in the Mahābhāṣya." *Indian Linguistics* 12.189-196.

Sen-Gupta, N[aresh] C[handra]
1953 *The Evolution of Ancient Indian Law*. Calcutta: Eastern Law House.

Singh, Shivaji
1972 *Evolution of the Smṛti Law*. Varanasi: Bhāratīya Vidyā Prakāśana.

Sircar, D[inesh] C[handra]
1965 *Indian Epigraphy*. Delhi: Motilal Banarsidass.
1966 *Indian Epigraphical Glossary*. Delhi: Motilal Banarsidass.
1968 *Studies in Indian Coins*. Delhi: Motilal Banarsidass.

Śrīnivāsan, Śrīnivāsa Ayya
1980 *On the Composition of the Nāṭyaśāstra*. SII Monographie 1. Reinbek: Orientalistische Fachpublikationen.

Sukthankar, V[iṣṇu] S[itārāma]
1944 *Critical Studies in the Mahābhārata: V.S. Sukthankar Memorial Edition*. Pune: Karnatak Publishing House.

Thakur, Amareshwar
1933 *Hindu Law of Evidence*. Calcutta: University of Calcutta.

Tokunaga, Muneo
1981 "On the Recensions of the *Bṛhaddevatā*." *JAOS* 101. 275-286.

Trautmann, Thomas R[oger]
1971 *Kauṭilya and the Arthaśāstra: A Statistical Investigation of the Authorship and Evolution of the Text*. Leiden: E. J. Brill.

Vigasin, A.A.
1984 "Notes to Nārada-smṛti XII." in *Summaries of Papers presented by Soviet Scholars to the VIth World Sanskrit Conference October 13-20, 1984 Philadelphia, Pennsylvania, U.S.A.*, pp. 172-176. Moscow: Central Department of Oriental Literature, Nauka Publishers.

Vigasin, A.A. and **Samozvanceva**, A.M.
1998 *Dharmasastra Narady*, translation from Sanskrit to Russian and Commentary by Vigasin and Samozvanceva, Russian Academy of Sciences Institute of Oriental Studies, Moscow State University (named for Lomonosov), Institute of World Culture, Moscow.

CONCORDANCE

The letter "c" following a number indicates that the verse is found in the commentary.

The letter "n" indicates that the verse is found in the variant readings.

Jolly	Text	Jolly	Text	Jolly	Text
Mā 1.1	Mā 1.1	Mā 1.33	Mā 1.27	Mā 1.65	Mā 1.56
Mā 1.2	Mā 1.2	Mā 1.34	Mā 1.28	Mā 1.66	Mā 1.57
Mā 1.3	Mā 1.3	Mā 1.35	Mā 1.29	Mā 1.67	Mā 1.58
Mā 1.4	Mā 1.4	Mā 1.36	Mā 1.30	Mā 1.68	Mā 1.59
Mā 1.5	Mā 1.5	Mā 1.37	Mā 1.31	Mā 1.69	Mā 1.60
Mā 1.6	Mā 1.6	Mā 1.38	Mā 1.32	Mā 1.70	Mā 1.61
Mā 1.7	Mā 1.7	Mā 1.39	Mā 1.33	Mā 1.71	Mā 1.62
Mā 1.8	Mā 1.8	Mā 1.40	Mā 1.34	Mā 1.72	Mā 1.63
Mā 1.9	Mā 1.9	Mā 1.41	Mā 1.35	Mā 1.73	Mā 1.64
Mā 1.10	Mā 1.10	Mā 1.42	Mā 1.36	Mā 1.74	Mā 1.65
Mā 1.11	Mā 1.11	Mā 1.43	Mā 1.37		
Mā 1.12	Mā 1.12	Mā 1.44	Mā 1.38	Mā 2.1	Mā 2.1c
Mā 1.13	Mā 1.13	Mā 1.45	Mā 1.39	Mā 2.2	Mā 2.2c
Mā 1.14	Mā 1.14	Mā 1.46	Mā 1.40	Mā 2.3	Mā 2.3c
Mā 1.15	Mā 1.15	Mā 1.47	Mā 1.41	Mā 2.4	Mā 2.4c
Mā 1.16	Mā 1.16	Mā 1.48	Mā 1.42	Mā 2.5	Mā 2.4c
Mā 1.17	Mā 1.17	Mā 1.49	Mā 1.43	Mā 2.6	Mā 2.5c
Mā 1.18	Mā 1.18	Mā 1.50	Mā 1.43c	Mā 2.7	Mā 2.6c
Mā 1.19	Mā 1.19	Mā 1.51	Mā 1.44	Mā 2.8	Mā 2.7c
Mā 1.20	Mā 1.20	Mā 1.52	Mā 1.45	Mā 2.9	Mā 2.7c
Mā 1.21	Mā 1.20c	Mā 1.53	Mā 1.46	Mā 2.10	Mā 2.7c
Mā 1.22	Mā 1.20c	Mā 1.54	Mā 1.47	Mā 2.11	Mā 2.7c
Mā 1.23	Mā 1.20c	Mā 1.55	Mā 1.48	Mā 2.12	Mā 2.7c
Mā 1.24	Mā 1.20c	Mā 1.56	Mā 1.49	Mā 2.13	Mā 2.7c
Mā 1.25	Mā 1.20c	Mā 1.57	Mā 1.50	Mā 2.14	Mā 2.7c
Mā 1.26	Mā 1.21	Mā 1.58	Mā 1.51	Mā 2.15	Mā 2.7c
Mā 1.27	Mā 1.22	Mā 1.59	Mā 1.52	Mā 2.16	Mā 2.7c
Mā 1.28	Mā 1.23	Mā 1.60	Mā 1.52c	Mā 2.17	Mā 2.8c
Mā 1.29	Mā 1.24	Mā 1.61	Mā 1.52c	Mā 2.18	Mā 2.9c
Mā 1.30	Mā 1.24c	Mā 1.62	Mā 1.53	Mā 2.19	Mā 2.10c
Mā 1.31	Mā 1.25	Mā 1.63	Mā 1.54	Mā 2.20	Mā 2.11c
Mā 1.32	Mā 1.26	Mā 1.64	Mā 1.55	Mā 2.21	Mā 2.11c

Jolly	Text	Jolly	Text	Jolly	Text
Mā 2.22	Mā 2.12c	1.3	1.3	1.48	1.44
Mā 2.23	Mā 2.13c	1.4	1.4	1.49	1.45
Mā 2.24	Mā 2.14c	1.5	1.5	1.50	1.46
Mā 2.25	Mā 2.15c	1.6	1.5c	1.51	1.47
Mā 2.26	Mā 2.16c	1.7	1.5c	1.52	1.48
Mā 2.27	Mā 2.17c	1.8	1.5c	1.53	1.49
Mā 2.28	Mā 2.18c	1.9	1.7	1.54	1.50
Mā 2.29	Mā 2.19c	1.10	1.8	1.55	1.51
Mā 2.30	Mā 2.20c	1.11	1.9	1.56	1.52
Mā 2.31	Mā 2.21c	1.12	1.10	1.57	1.53
Mā 2.32	Mā 2.22c	1.13	1.10c	1.58	1.54
Mā 2.33	Mā 2.23c	1.14	1.11	1.59	1.55
Mā 2.34	Mā 2.24c	1.15	1.12	1.60	1.56
Mā 2.35	Mā 2.25c	1.16	1.13	1.61	1.57
Mā 2.36	Mā 2.26c	1.17	1.14	1.62	1.58
Mā 2.37	Mā 2.27c	1.18	1.15	1.63	1.59
Mā 2.38	Mā 2.28c	1.19	1.16	1.64	1.60
Mā 2.39	Mā 2.29c	1.20	1.17	1.65	1.61
Mā 2.40	Mā 2.30c	1.21	1.18	1.66	1.62
Mā 2.41	Mā 2.31c	1.22	1.19	1.67	1.63
Mā 2.42	Mā 2.32c	1.23	1.20	1.68	1.64
Mā 2.43	Mā 2.33c	1.24	1.21	1.69	1.65
Mā 2.44	Mā 2.34c	1.25	1.21c	1.70	1.65c
		1.26	1.22	1.71	1.65c
Mā 3.1	Mā 3.1	1.27	1.23	1.72	1.65c
Mā 3.2	Mā 3.1c	1.28	1.24	1.73	1.65c
Mā 3.3	Mā 3.2	1.29	1.25	1.74	1.65c
Mā 3.4	Mā 3.3	1.30	1.26	1.75	1.66
Mā 3.5	Mā 3.4	1.31	1.27	1.76	1.67
Mā 3.6	Mā 3.5	1.32	1.28	1.77	1.68
Mā 3.7	Mā 3.6	1.33	1.29	1.78	1.69
Mā 3.8	Mā 3.7	1.34	1.30	1.79	1.70
Mā 3.9	Mā 3.8	1.35	1.31	1.80	1.72
Mā 3.10	Mā 3.9	1.36	1.32	1.81	1.73
Mā 3.11	Mā 3.10	1.37	1.33	1.82	1.74
Mā 3.12	Mā 3.11	1.38	1.34	1.83	1.75
Mā 3.13	Mā 3.12	1.39	1.35	1.84	1.76
Mā 3.14	Mā 3.13	1.40	1.36	1.85	1.76c
Mā 3.15	Mā 3.14	1.41	1.37	1.86	1.76c
Mā 3.16	Mā 3.15	1.42	1.38	1.87	1.76c
Mā 3.17	Mā 3.16	1.43	1.39	1.88	1.77
Mā 3.18	Mā 3.17	1.44	1.40	1.89	1.77c
		1.45	1.41	1.90	1.78
1.1	1.1	1.46	1.42	1.91	1.78c
1.2	1.2	1.47	1.43	1.92	1.79

Jolly	Text	Jolly	Text	Jolly	Text
1.93	1.80	1.138	1.118	1.183	1.165
1.94	1.82	1.139	1.119	1.184	1.166
1.95	1.83	1.140	1.120	1.185	1.167
1.96	1.84	1.141	1.121	1.186	1.168
1.97	1.85	1.142	1.122	1.187	1.169
1.98	1.86	1.143	1.123	1.188	1.170
1.99	1.86c	1.144	1.124	1.189	1.171
1.100	1.86c	1.145	1.125	1.190	1.172
1.101	1.86c	1.146	1.126	1.191	1.173
1.102	1.87	1.147	1.127	1.192	1.174
1.103	1.88	1.148	1.128	1.193	1.175
1.104	1.89	1.149	1.129	1.194	1.176
1.105	1.90	1.150	1.130	1.195	1.177
1.106	1.91	1.151	1.131	1.196	1.178
1.107	1.92	1.152	1.132	1.197	1.179
1.108	1.96	1.153	1.133	1.198	1.180
1.109	1.96c	1.154	1.134	1.199	1.181
1.110	1.97	1.155	1.135	1.200	1.182
1.111	1.98	1.156	1.136	1.201	1.183
1.112	1.99	1.157	1.137	1.202	1.184
1.113	1.100	1.158	1.140	1.203	1.185
1.114	1.101	1.159	1.141	1.204	1.186
1.115	1.101c	1.160	1.142	1.205	1.187
1.116	1.102	1.161	1.143	1.206	1.187
1.117	1.103	1.162	1.144	1.207	1.188
1.118	1.104	1.163	1.145	1.208	1.189
1.119	1.105	1.164	1.146	1.209	1.190
1.120	1.106	1.165	1.147	1.210	1.191
1.121	1.107	1.166	1.148	1.211	1.192
1.122	1.107c	1.167	1.149	1.212	1.193
1.123	1.107c	1.168	1.150	1.213	1.194
1.124	1.108	1.169	1.151	1.214	1.195
1.125	1.109	1.170	1.152	1.215	1.196
1.126	1.110	1.171	1.153	1.216	1.197
1.127	1.110c	1.172	1.154	1.217	1.198
1.128	1.110c	1.173	1.155	1.218	1.199
1.129	1.110c	1.174	1.156	1.219	1.200
1.130	1.111	1.175	1.157	1.220	1.201
1.131	1.112	1.176	1.158	1.221	1.202
1.132	1.113	1.177	1.159	1.222	1.203
1.133	1.113c	1.178	1.160	1.223	1.204
1.134	1.114	1.179	1.161	1.224	1.205
1.135	1.115	1.180	1.162	1.225	1.205c
1.136	1.116	1.181	1.163	1.226	1.206
1.137	1.117	1.182	1.164	1.227	1.207

Jolly	Text	Jolly	Text	Jolly	Text
1.228	1.208	3.10	3.10	5.23	5.21
1.229	1.209	3.11	3.11	5.24	5.22
1.230	1.210	3.12	3.12	5.25	5.23
1.231	1.210c	3.13	3.13	5.26	5.24
1.232	1.211	3.14	3.13c	5.27	5.25
1.233	1.212	3.15	3.13c	5.28	5.26
1.234	1.213	3.16	3.14	5.29	5.27
1.235	1.214	3.17	3.15	5.30	5.28
1.236	1.215	3.18	3.16	5.31	5.29
1.237	1.216			5.32	5.30
1.238	1.217	4.1	4.1	5.33	5.31
1.239	1.218	4.2	4.2	5.34	5.32
1.240	1.219	4.3	4.3	5.35	5.33
1.241	1.219c	4.4	4.4	5.36	5.34
1.242	1.220	4.5	4.5	5.37	5.35
1.243	1.221	4.6	4.6	5.38	5.36
1.244	1.222	4.7	4.6c	5.39	5.37
1.245	1.223	4.8	4.7	5.40	5.38
1.246	1.224	4.9	4.8	5.41	5.39
		4.10	4.9	5.42	5.40
2.1	2.1	4.11	4.10	5.43	5.41
2.2	2.1c	4.12	4.11		
2.3	2.1c			6.1	6.1
2.4	2.1c	5.1	5.1	6.2	6.2
2.5	2.2	5.2	5.2	6.3	6.3
2.6	2.3	5.3	5.3	6.4	6.4
2.7	2.4	5.4	5.4	6.5	6.5
2.8	2.5	5.5	5.5	6.6	6.7
2.9	2.6	5.6	5.6	6.7	6.8
2.10	2.6c	5.7	5.7	6.8	6.9
2.11	2.6c	5.8	5.8	6.9	6.10
2.12	2.6c	5.9	5.9	6.10	6.11
2.13	2.6c	5.10	5.10	6.11	6.12
2.14	2.7	5.11	5.11	6.12	6.13
2.15	2.8	5.12	5.11c	6.13	6.14
		5.13	5.12	6.14	6.15
3.1	3.1	5.14	5.13	6.15	6.16
3.2	3.2	5.15	5.14	6.16	6.18
3.3	3.3	5.16	5.15	6.17	6.19
3.4	3.4	5.17	5.16	6.18	6.20
3.5	3.5	5.18	5.17	6.19	6.21
3.6	3.6	5.19	5.18	6.20	6.22
3.7	3.7	5.20	5.19	6.21	6.22n
3.8	3.8	5.21	5.19c	6.22	6.23
3.9	3.9	5.22	5.20		

Jolly	Text	Jolly	Text	Jolly	Text
7.1	7.1	10.7	10.7	12.1	12.1
7.2	7.2			12.2	12.2
7.3	7.3	11.1	11.1	12.3	12.3
7.4	7.4	11.2	11.2	12.4	12.4
7.5	7.5	11.3	11.3	12.5	12.5
7.6	7.6	11.4	11.4	12.6	12.6
7.7	7.7	11.5	11.5	12.7	12.7
7.8	7.8	11.6	11.6	12.8	12.8
		11.7	11.7	12.9	12.9
8.1	8.1	11.8	11.8	12.10	12.10
8.2	8.2	11.9	11.9	12.11	12.11
8.3	8.3	11.10	11.10	12.12	12.12
8.4	8.4	11.11	11.11	12.13	12.13
8.5	8.5	11.12	11.12	12.14	12.14
8.6	8.6	11.13	11.12n	12.15	12.15
8.7	8.7	11.14	11.12n	12.16	12.16
8.8	8.8	11.15	11.13	12.17	12.17
8.9	8.9	11.16	11.13n	12.18	12.18
8.10	8.10	11.17	11.14	12.19	12.19
8.11	8.11	11.18	11.15	12.20	12.20
8.12	8.12	11.19	11.16	12.21	12.21
		11.20	11.17	12.22	12.22
9.1	9.1	11.21	11.18	12.23	12.23
9.2	9.2	11.22	11.19	12.24	12.24
9.3	9.3	11.23	11.20	12.25	12.25
9.4	9.4	11.24	11.21	12.26	12.26
9.5	9.5	11.25	11.22	12.27	12.27
9.6	9.6	11.26	11.23	12.28	12.28
9.7	9.7	11.27	11.24	12.29	12.29
9.8	9.8	11.28	11.25	12.30	12.30
9.9	9.9	11.29	11.26	12.31	12.31
9.10	9.10	11.30	11.27	12.32	12.32
9.11	9.11	11.31	11.28	12.33	12.33
9.12	9.12	11.32	11.29	12.34	12.34
9.13	9.13	11.33	11.30	12.35	12.35
9.14	9.14	11.34	11.30n	12.36	12.36
9.15	9.15	11.35	11.31	12.37	12.37
9.16	9.16	11.36	11.32	12.38	12.38
		11.37	11.33	12.39	12.39
10.1	10.1	11.38	11.34	12.40	12.40
10.2	10.2	11.39	11.34n	12.41	12.41
10.3	10.3	11.40	11.35	12.42	12.42
10.4	10.4	11.41	11.36	12.43	12.43
10.5	10.5	11.42	11.37	12.44	12.44
10.6	10.6	11.43	11.38	12.45	12.45

Jolly	Text
12.46	12.46
12.47	12.47
12.48	12.48
12.49	12.49
12.50	12.50
12.51	12.51
12.52	12.52
12.53	12.53
12.54	12.54
12.55	12.55
12.56	12.56
12.57	12.57
12.58	12.58
12.59	12.59
12.60	12.60
12.61	12.61
12.62	12.62
12.63	12.63
12.64	12.64
12.65	12.65
12.66	12.65n
12.67	12.68
12.68	12.66
12.69	12.67
12.70	12.69
12.71	12.70
12.72	12.71
12.73	12.72
12.74	12.73
12.75	12.74
12.76	12.75
12.77	12.76
12.78	12.77
12.79	12.78
12.80	12.79
12.81	12.80
12.82	12.81
12.83	12.81n-82
12.84	12.82-83
12.85	12.83-84
12.86	12.84
12.87	12.87
12.88	12.88
12.89	12.89
12.90	12.90
12.91	12.91
12.92	12.92
12.93	12.93
12.94	12.94
12.95	12.95
12.96	12.96
12.97	12.97
12.98	12.98
12.99	12.99
12.100	12.100-101
12.101	12.102
12.102	12.103
12.103	12.104
12.104	12.105, 107
12.105	12.107
12.106	12.109n-110
12.107	12.110-111
12.108	12.111-112
12.109	12.112-113
12.110	12.113-114
12.111	12.114-115
12.112	12.115-116
12.113	12.116-117
13.1	13.1
13.2	13.2
13.3	13.3
13.4	13.4
13.5	13.5
13.6	13.6
13.7	13.7
13.8	13.8
13.9	13.9
13.10	13.10
13.11	13.11
13.12	13.12
13.13	13.13
13.14	13.14
13.15	13.15
13.16	13.15n
13.17	13.16
13.18	13.17
13.19	13.18
13.20	13.19
13.21	13.20
13.22	13.21
13.23	13.22
13.24	13.23
13.25	13.24
13.26	13.25
13.27	13.26
13.28	13.27
13.29	13.28
13.30	13.30
13.31	13.31
13.32	13.32
13.33	13.33
13.34	13.34
13.35	13.35
13.36	13.36
13.37	13.37
13.38	13.38
13.39	13.39
13.40	13.40
13.41	13.40n
13.42	13.41
13.43	13.42
13.44	13.42n
13.45	13.43
13.46	13.44
13.47	13.45
13.48	13.45n
13.49	13.46
13.50	13.47
13.51	13.48
13.52	13.49
14.1	14.1
14.2	14.1n

Jolly	Text
14.3	14.2
14.4	14.3
14.5	14.4
14.6	14.5
14.7	14.6
14.8	14.7
14.9	14.8
14.10	14.9
14.11	14.10
14.12	14.11
14.13	14.12
14.14	14.13
14.15	14.14
14.16	14.15
14.17	14.16
14.18	14.17
14.19	14.18
14.20	14.19
14.21	14.20
14.22	14.21
14.23	14.22
14.24	14.23
14.25	14.24
14.26	14.25
14.27	14.26
15-16.1	15-16.1
15-16.2	15-16.2
15-16.3	15-16.3
15-16.4	15-16.4
15-16.5	15-16.5
15-16.6	15-16.6
15-16.7	15-16.7
15-16.8	15-16.9
15-16.9	15-16.10
15-16.10	15-16.11
15-16.11	15-16.12
15-16.12	15-16.13
15-16.13	15-16.14
15-16.14	15-16.15
15-16.15	15-16.16
15-16.16	15-16.17
15-16.17	15-16.18
15-16.18	15-16.19
15-16.19	15-16.20
15-16.20	15-16.21
15-16.21	15-16.22
15-16.22	15-16.22n
15-16.23	15-16.23
15-16.24	15-16.24
15-16.25	15-16.25
15-16.26	15-16.26
15-16.27	15-16.27
15-16.28	15-16.28
15-16.29	15-16.28n
15-16.30	15-16.29
15-16.31	15-16.30
15-16.32	15-16.31
17.1	17.1
17.2	17.2
17.3	17.3
17.4	17.4
17.5	17.5
17.6	17.6
17.7	17.6n
17.8	17.6n
18.1	18.1
18.2	18.2
18.3	18.3
18.4	18.4
18.5	18.5
18.6	18.6
18.7	18.7
18.8	18.8
18.9	18.9
18.10	18.11
18.11	18.12
18.12	18.13
18.13	18.10
18.14	18.14
18.15	18.15-16
18.16	18.15-16
18.17	18.17
18.18	18.18
18.19	18.19
18.20	18.20
18.21	18.21
18.22	18.22
18.23	18.22n
18.24	18.22n
18.25	18.23
18.26	18.24
18.27	18.25
18.28	18.26
18.29	18.27
18.30	18.28
18.31	18.29
18.32	18.30
18.33	18.31
18.34	18.32
18.35	18.33
18.36	18.34
18.37	18.35
18.38	18.36
18.39	18.37
18.40	18.38
18.41	18.39
18.42	18.40
18.43	18.41
18.44	18.41n
18.45	18.42
18.46	18.43
18.47	18.44
18.48	18.45
18.49	18.46
18.50	18.47
18.51	18.48
18.52	18.49
18.53	18.50
18.54	18.51
18.55	18.52
P.1	19.1
P.2	19.2
P.3	19.3
P.4	19.4
P.5	19.5
P.6	19.13
P.7	19.14
P.8	19.15
P.9	19.16
P.10	19.17

Jolly	Text	Jolly	Text	Jolly	Text
P.11	19.18	P.28	19.35	P.45	19.52
P.12	19.19	P.29	19.36	P.46	19.53
P.13	19.20	P.30	19.37	P.47	19.54
P.14	19.21	P.31	19.38	P.48	19.55
P.15	19.22	P.32	19.39	P.49	19.56
P.16	19.23	P.33	19.40	P.50	19.57
P.17	19.24	P.34	19.41	P.51	19.58
P.18	19.25	P.35	19.42	P.52	19.59
P.19	19.26	P.36	19.43	P.53	19.60
P.20	19.27	P.37	19.44	P.54	19.61
P.21	19.28	P.38	19.45	P.55	19.62
P.22	19.29	P.39	19.46	P.56	19.63
P.23	19.30	P.40	19.47	P.57	19.65
P.24	19.31	P.41	19.48	P.58	19.66
P.25	19.32	P.42	19.49	P.59	19.67
P.26	19.33	P.43	19.50	P.60	19.68
P.27	19.34	P.44	19.51	P.61	19.69

पादानुक्रमणी

An asterisk (*) indicates that the पाद is found either in the commentary or in variant readings.

INDEX OF CASES

GENERAL INDEX